T0386676

AN ISLAND'S
ELEVEN

AN ISLAND'S ELEVEN

THE STORY OF
SRI LANKAN CRICKET

NICHOLAS BROOKES

FOR DAD, WHO PUT A BAT IN MY HAND, AND
MUM, WHO MADE SURE THERE WAS A PEN IN IT

First published 2022

The History Press
97 St George's Place, Cheltenham,
Gloucestershire, GL50 3QB
www.thehistorypress.co.uk

British Library Cataloguing in Publication Data.
A catalogue record for this book is available from the British Library.

ISBN 978 0 7509 9881 9

Typesetting and origination by The History Press
Printed and bound in Great Britain by TJ Books Limited, Padstow, Cornwall.

Trees for Life

CONTENTS

PREFACE

Considering the adulation that Sri Lankan cricket inspires, the subject has received strangely little attention from writers. Fans the world over consistently cite Sri Lanka as their 'second team' – and with good reason. No other cricketing nation has transitioned from whipping boys to world beaters so quickly. With the possible exception of Clive Lloyd's West Indies, no side has defied the odds so often. To my mind, no other team's cricket has carried such a strong national identity or rivalled Sri Lanka's freewheeling invention and ingenuity. Yet, of the established nations, only Bangladesh has received less coverage.

The 'canon' is tiny, and largely inaccessible. S.P. Foenander – affectionately known as 'The Wisden of the East' – was the first to seriously attempt to record cricket on the island; his *Sixty Years of Ceylon Cricket* (1924) gives much valuable insight into the early years. Likewise, S.S. 'Chandra' Perera's exhaustive *The Janashakthi Book of Sri Lankan Cricket* (1832–1996) does much to fill in the blanks that precede living memory; despite its occasional errors, it is a labour of love and a worthy resource for anyone looking to learn about cricket on the island.

That said, both Foenander and Perera were happy to remain as chroniclers – they report the facts in even-handed style, but forgo analysis and opinion, often overlooking the characters and colour that make Sri

Lankan cricket so special. More recently, Michael Roberts has cast an anthropological eye over the nineteenth century, zeroing in on cricket's relationship with fundamental issues like class and nationalism. These three writers have shaped my understanding of early Sri Lankan cricket; Roberts' discursive writing has provided measured insights into several subjects, not least the 'no-balling' of Muttiah Muralitharan by umpires Darrell Hair and Ross Emerson.

Equally, Sri Lanka's cast of writer-cricketers has been limited. Channa Gunasekara's two books offer a vivid snap-shot of mid-century cricket in Ceylon; his father Churchill, Bertie Wijesinha, Gamini Goonesena, Sunil Wettimuny and Anura Tennekoon have all produced enlightening works – but there is a striking paucity of literature focusing on the pre-Test era. All too often, Sri Lankan sports pages seemed more concerned with the County Championship than with Colombo's scene. Clearly Sri Lankan cricket writing was inhibited by colonial condescension, held back by the ugly imperial attitude that the island's game was somehow less worthy than cricket in England. Sadly, this paternalistic relationship stretched well beyond Test status: for a number of years, western writers' view of Sri Lankan cricket seemed coloured by the perception of the team as an insignificant newcomer.

Nor has recent success inspired a spate of autobiographies. Aravinda de Silva and Roshan Mahanama's efforts go a long way towards illuminating a seminal period in Sri Lanka's development, but most of the greats have eschewed the draw of the pen. It feels a shame that we have no memoirs from Ranatunga, Sangakkara, Muralitharan or Jayawardene. The dearth might partially reflect Sri Lanka's preference for oral rather than written history; still, it is impossible to imagine such influential cricketers from England or Australia – where the people love cricket far less – riding off into retirement without a book deal.

Sri Lankan cricket deserves far greater attention – a process which must, of course, start from within. There are promising signs: over the past two decades there has been a notable upsurge. Professor Ravindra Fernando has produced two exhaustive books on the great Mahadevan Sathasivam, Alston Mahadevan has lovingly chronicled the pre-Test era and Ranjan Mellawa has given the world an insider's account chocked full of wonderful stories.

Shehan Karunatilaka has scaled dizzying heights with *Chinaman*, a cricket novel that bears the soul of Sri Lanka and was ranked among *Wisden*'s greatest books of all time. And if the island can no longer lay claim to a world-class cricket team, it can at least boast ownership of a an outstanding cricket writer. Andrew Fidel Fernando covers past and present with a warmth, wit and wisdom which evades most scribes; Sri Lanka are lucky to have him.

All these writers have informed and inspired me; I hope that this work, in turn, will inspire others to cast their gaze over Sri Lankan cricket. For, as much as I've tried to 'tell the story of Sri Lankan cricket', this work is merely a starting point.

PROLOGUE

26.12.1995

'No-ball.'

Umpire Hair's cry cuts across the MCG Boxing Day chatter with all the shock and venom of a whipcrack.

The bowler – a 23-year-old Muttiah Muralitharan – looks perplexed. He walks back to his mark and continues bowling.

Soon, the penny drops. It falls to Bill Lawry to tell the world what's going on:

'I hope he's not calling him for throwing … He calls him very late, so I'm sure he's calling him for throwing.'[1]

★★★

On an island far away, hearts still warm with Christmas cheer turned to lumps of coal in a second. In Colombo and Kandy, Galle and Gampaha, Sri Lankans cursed at their TVs.

For this wasn't any ordinary cricket match. It was the biggest day in Australia's sporting calendar; a rare chance for a 13-year-old Test side to show the world what they could do. Hair's attack on Murali was an assault on all Sri Lanka – a disturbingly public humiliation.

As the spinner put it to me twenty-five years later, 'The only question I have is why didn't he do it before? Why did he wait for Boxing Day?'

★★★

Back in Melbourne, captain Ranatunga leaves the field for consultation.[2] Roshan Mahanama and Asanka Gurusinha appeal to the umpire; hand on hip, Murali politely asks what the problem is.

David Boon crashes an 'uncalled' delivery through the covers for 4. But the cricket has become incidental. A more vital game is being played out. It is murky, near inscrutable, but the stakes are high and the crowd transfixed. All 55,000 of them – in varying states of embarrassment and voyeurism – seem to fall quiet all at once. Tension whispers through the ground. There's something of the car crash about the scene, of eyes that should be averted but remain entranced.

Boon flicks a ball off middle stump to reach 50. The crowd cheer loudly, as much in relief as celebration. For a moment, the pressure eases. Not for Tony Greig. He finds no solace in the landmark:

'At the other end, Muralitharan is seeing his career float out of the window. He is being no-balled out of the game,' he tells the viewing audience, each syllable dripping with regret.[3]

★★★

With Murali no-balled seven times in the space of 3 overs, Ranatunga had little choice but to remove him from the attack.[4] But the Sri Lankan captain would not throw in the towel without a fight. At 3:30 pm, he re-inserted Murali from the Members' End. Hair, standing at square leg, left the young off-spinner alone. Murali was allowed to continue bowling, and even picked up Mark Waugh's wicket late in the day. But he was withdrawn from the attack permanently on day two, after Hair told Sri Lanka's management that he would call 'no ball' regardless of where he was standing.

14

The saga was just getting started. Nine days later, Ross Emerson – a former Sydney grade cricketer umpiring his first international match – called Murali four times, once for a leg-break where his arm appeared pencil straight. It was the last time he would bowl on the tour. Many questioned whether he would deliver another ball in international cricket.

Australia had tested Ranatunga's team to its very core.[5] Battered and bruised across three Tests, they'd been accused of ball tampering, branded cheats and brutally sledged. Now their star spinner's career lay in tatters. It was time to go home.

But they were heading back to a nation divided. The ethnic tensions that had barely bubbled beneath the surface of Sri Lankan society since independence had erupted into a merciless war in July 1983. Twelve and a half years later, the violence showed no signs of remission. While much of the conflict remained rooted in the north and east of the island, sporadic attacks had increasingly scarred and devastated Colombo – Sri Lanka's economic, political and cricketing capital. Across the length and breadth of the island Sri Lankans lived in unimaginable torment, trapped in the perpetual fear of being bombed, butchered or burnt.

Within days of the cricketers' homecoming, tragedy struck again – as LTTE rebels crashed a truck weighed down with explosive through the gates of Colombo's Central Bank.[6] The blast wreaked horrific destruction. Days after, police still unearthed mutilated bodies from the rubble. 91 lives were lost; of the 1,400 injured, 100 were left permanently blind.

With a nation in mourning, and a city in chaos, the last thing on anyone's mind was cricket. But in less than three weeks, Colombo's Premadasa Stadium was set to host Sri Lanka's opening World Cup match – the *biggest* game of cricket ever played on home soil. Their opponents were old friends turned arch-enemies: *Australia*.

There had been murmurs of an Australian boycott prior to the blast, so it was no surprise when the Australian Cricket Board (ACB) announced its cricketers would not travel to Sri Lanka.[7] West Indies quickly followed suit: this civil war had bloodied and blighted every aspect of island life, even a World Cup campaign couldn't escape its cruel grasp.

Rightly or wrongly, the Australian boycott was viewed through lenses muddied by *Murali-gate* and the preceding series' acrimony. When Shane

Warne asked how he could safely shop in Colombo, Sri Lanka's foreign minister replied by branding him a sissy. The saga dominated headlines. It seemed the island *needed* these games of cricket. With so much strife and division within, perhaps the people needed an enemy from without.

Sri Lanka bent over backwards to try to accommodate the wary cricketers.[8] Yet every suggestion – empty stadiums, sealed roads, the possibility of ferrying players straight from Madras – fell on deaf ears. Even a statement from the Tamil Tigers claiming the cricketers had 'nothing to fear' would not sway Australia or West Indies. Minds were made up.

Sri Lankan cricket was in the doldrums. The board was broke, with as little as $5,700 in its coffers.[9] Months before the World Cup, oddsmakers gave the team a one-in-sixty-six chance of lifting the trophy. Most felt the tournament would bring inevitable humiliation. Once it was done, it would be a struggle to attract sides to war-torn Sri Lanka.

There seemed little hope. None could have guessed what would happen next.

1

BEGINNINGS (1796–1956)

THE ROOTS OF CRICKET

I arrived at S. Thomas' on a hot, sleepy April afternoon. Drawn to the school by its rich cricket history, I'd agreed to teach English a couple of times a week in exchange for room and board. It sounded like a fair deal; and if I wanted to *really learn* about Sri Lankan cricket, there were few better places I could land.

My new home was in a solemn whitewashed building at the heart of the school's campus. It was impossible to ignore its history: there in the smooth stone floors dulled and patterned over time, in the splintering French doors and pockmarked, flaky wallpaper. There was no hot water. It smelled of dust and made my clothes grow mould; the fan clung onto the ceiling by little more than a thread.

But it wasn't all bad. Three creaky windows looked out onto an oval where some of the island's great captains – Tennekoon, Tissera, Duleep Mendis – had cut their teeth. I'd heard stories of an innings the mythic Mahadevan Sathasivam played in 1936. Straight away, the ground's history *inspired* me. And with a little bit of housekeeping, my desk and chair were installed right behind the bowler's arm.

I fell in love with that view. S. Thomas' is home to the most pictur-esque cricket ground I've ever laid eyes on: marked by a white-picket fence that could have fallen out of a Thomas Hardy novel, fringed on the south and west sides by tall coconut palms. From the stand above the pavilion you can catch a glimpse of the glistening ocean, the middle no more than 100 yards from the shore. Wind whips across the ground straight from the Laccadive sea, soothing spectators and bemusing visit-ing batsmen. Trains pass intermittently, a well-timed slog away. As dusk beckons and the sky gets splashed with shades from amber to violet, it is nothing short of magical.

This patch of paradise was lovingly cared for by eight groundsmen. They worked full time, seven days a week: typically languid, always barefoot, able to shift into overdrive out of nowhere on the eve of an important match. Their shed was next door to my flat: sometimes they would bring me lime water while I wrote; I'd often stop in and chat through the language barrier, watching a couple of overs of cricket.

It was rare for there to be none to watch. I arrived outside of the 1st XI season, but there were practices, junior matches, touring sides. On Sundays the grounds were rented out for corporate days or six-a-side tournaments. Between classes, slivers of concrete were swallowed by joyous games of softball. Once September and the cricket season rolled around, it was relentless – talk of the Big Match never far from lips.

During those first few months in Colombo, I understood that a deep love of cricket was one of the island's defining features – as Sri Lankan as rambutan or thambili. In a patchwork society oft-riven by differences of class and creed, cricket carries a rare pan-national appeal.

But, the game's history is arcane. Test status only arrived in 1981: the years prior are patchily recorded. Even first-class scorecards from the 1980s have largely been lost.[1] As historian Jane Russell told me when she first visited rural Sri Lanka in the 1970s, villages were awash with games of volleyball – but little cricket. So how did this game come to bury itself so deeply under the island's skin?

★★★

The first Brits arrived 222 years before me, when the East India Company moored in 1796.[2] Though I'd imagined a 'company man' wading into shore with bat in hand, ready to dispatch bowlers to all corners of the beach, it seems cricket wasn't the first thing on British minds. Perhaps they had their hands full with pilfer, pillage and plunder; or maybe they were left scratching their heads, trying to figure out the forces that drove this dizzying island.

Home to Sinhalese Buddhists, Hindu Tamils and Muslim Moors, Sri Lanka was a melting pot even before three colonial orders threw more ingredients into the mix.[3] Many Europeans found the island too lovely to leave behind – once settled, they became known as the Burghers. They straddled two worlds, forging a link between colonist and colonised and easing cricket's flow from British to Ceylonese. Sri Lanka's first great homegrown cricketers were almost exclusively Burgher: the Kelaarts and de Sarams, the Van Geyzels and de Kretsers, Allen Raffel and Cecil Horan. Right up to the 1970s, the Sri Lankan side was rarely without men of Burgher stock.

The game was slower to reach the island's other ethnic groups. Early British attempts to culturally influence the Sinhalese were inauspicious, their callous abuses of power filling an already suspicious people with mistrust. The ruthless response to 1817's Uva Rebellion soured British-Sinhalese relations, and the discord likely fed into local attitudes about cricket.[4] Prior to the British arrival, Lankan sport more or less consisted of wrestling and the occasional bullock race.[5] Bats and balls were foreign objects – confusing and concerning in equal measures. Sri Lanka's innate cricketing ability was slow to reveal itself, since for much of the nineteenth century, most rejected the sport.

Equally, cricket's growth was slowed by a colonial paradox. The British – who introduced, promoted and sought to spread the game – hindered its progress by wilfully excluding locals on the field, and by behaving in a superior and cruel manner off it. There are exceptions: Ashley Walker and George Vanderspar deserve to be lauded as two forebears of Sri Lankan cricket. Without their contributions, it may have followed a very different course.

★★★

With coffee planting taking hold in the hill country by the 1830s, Britons began flocking to the island in droves, eyes wide at the prospect of fortunes built on blood red berries.[6] In the early days it was frontier living, bereft of entertainment. Cricket offered a rare lifeline. S.S. Perera claims these rugged planters, who 'carved' grounds from 'leech infested hillsides' were the game's pioneers.[7] Foenander tells of sides travelling 50 miles on horseback for a day's play.[8] Clearly these men went to great lengths for cricket. Matches would begin at 7 am, allowing for a two-and-a-half-hour lunch when the sun was most punishing.[9] Play was followed by drinking sessions that ran deep into the night; bed was the hard ground of the host's coffee store.

Tea took over in the 1860s, bringing unimagined wealth to Sri Lanka – and drawing a flock of public-schooled planters: natural cricketing missionaries.[10] Two early planters' clubs, the Dimbula Athletic Cricket Club (DACC) and the Dickoya Maskeliya Cricket Club (DMCC) – their grounds perched 20 miles apart in the misty hills of Nuwara Eliya – soon developed a hearty rivalry.[11] The fixture provides us with Sri Lanka's first cricketing photograph – of the teams sprawled on the grass at Darawela.[12] Rows of bearded, white men peer distantly at the camera; jungle seems to sprout from the makeshift tent in the background. At first glance, they could be on a voyage of discovery. Only a pair of bats reveal their true purpose.

Hill-country cricket began to wane around 1900, as Colombo emerged as the game's indisputable centre. But the draw of the tea trade kept luring quality English cricketers well into the twentieth century; only once the British left the island did cricket and planting become incompatible. Darrell Lieversz, Ceylon's most accomplished swing bowler during the 1960s, briefly straddled both worlds. 'Very few planters had the opportunity of playing first-class cricket,' he wistfully told me. But Lieversz's boss Mike Ondaatje gave him total support. As his employee couldn't attend training sessions, he had a concrete pitch built at the Tebuwana Planters' Club. The pair would go down each evening after work: Lieversz bowling at one stump, while Ondaatje gathered the balls.

Still, a promotional transfer to the Duckwari Estate in Rangala took a sledgehammer to Lieversz's cricketing aspirations. His international career was over by the time he was 22. 'It was an extremely difficult decision,' he reflects. 'But I had to think of my future in planting.' Lieversz carried on playing for the DACC and the Kandy Sports Club, but his distance from Colombo made a serious career impossible.

The post-war decline of hill-country cricket is sad. Darawela was handsome enough to draw a visit from Tsar Nicholas II; while probably apocryphal, the story that Jack Hobbs named his cottage after the ground gives a sense of its impression.[13] Neighbouring Radella is equally lovely. Yet both have been left to languish, and are visibly withered by a lack of cricket. Today, the clubs are little more than crumbling remnants of a bygone era. As cricket in Sri Lanka developed, a cogent fact emerged: all roads lead to Colombo – and very few come back out.

★★★

Further west, a city was starting to emerge. In September 1832, an advert appeared in *The Colombo Journal*, inviting 'gentlemen who may feel inclined to lend assistance towards establishing A CRICKET CLUB' to meet at the library.[14] On 3 November, the paper reported on its inaugural match – a 10-wicket loss to the 97th Regiment.*

The city's cricket seems to have fallen dormant for some time – with little record of cricket, or the Colombo Cricket Club (CCC), during the 1840s or '50s. In 1860, CCC men took on a Ceylon Rifle Regiment team made up of Malay soldiers and British officers: for the first time, Europeans and Asians had met on the field in Sri Lanka.[15]

Twelve years later, a team of British soldiers took on an All-Malay side. The Malays were natural cricketers: often playing barefoot, they were dynamite in the field – quick to cover the ground and shy at the stumps, and usually blessed with safe pairs of hands.[16] Their interest in the game

---

* The wording of the advert, which states the CCC '*accepted* the challenge', and the fact they hosted the game at the Rifle Parade Grounds and won so comfortably suggests these soldiers were proficient and practised cricketers. Since the regiment arrived in Ceylon in 1825, when coffee planting was in its infancy, they may well have got to the game first – especially as facilitating cricket in the hills was no straightforward task. If so, Sri Lanka's first cricketers were likely Irish – the 97th was recruited from Ireland, and in 1826 acquired the title the 'Earl of Ulster's'.

was rewarded with a gift of land at the Rifle Parade Ground, and in 1872 the Malay Cricket Club was formed.[17]

With Burghers showing interest in the game too, by the 1860s cricket's reach was stretching beyond soldiers, sailors and planters. Several Burgher clubs coalesced to form the Colts in 1873: before long, they would emerge as the undisputed powerhouse of Ceylonese club cricket.[18] But while the game was flourishing in the city, it spread slowly to rural areas. Today you would be hard pressed to travel anywhere in Sri Lanka and not find kids playing softball, but it's a recent development – a consequence of Test status, TV broadcasts, and above all the 1996 World Cup.

For well over a century, cricket remained the plaything of the urbanised middle class. Colombo is the island's economic, political and administrative heartland; naturally, it emerged as its cricketing centre too. Unusually, Sri Lanka's first-class system is founded upon clubs rather than territorial teams: when the Ceylon Cricket Association (CCA) was formed in 1922, nine of thirteen were Colombo-based.[19] Likewise, the fourteen who competed in the 2018/19 Premier League tournament were all from Western Province – the farthest-flung being Badureliya Sports Club, whose ground is about 45 miles south of the city.

With so little money in the first-class game, even clubs like Galle and Kandy seem to be fighting a losing battle. A cricketer who wants to make it has no choice but to head to Colombo – despite the game's recent spread, just five of the fifteen members of the 2019 World Cup squad were born outside Western Province.[20] No national cricketer has emerged from the north since 1969. None has ever come from the east coast. Sri Lanka is still nowhere near tapping its full potential.

Logistics are clearly a factor,* but cricket's strong Colombo roots are also a reflection of the way the game reached local people. More than anywhere else in the world, cricket in Sri Lanka relies on schools as breeding ground, seminary and test site.

---

* While Western Province accounts for just 5.61 per cent of Sri Lanka's landmass, it is home to almost 30 per cent of the population. It follows naturally that the busiest area should become the country's sporting hub.

SCHOOL SPIRIT

The British arrival changed Sri Lanka forever. Before long, customs developed in a dreary corner of Europe began to weave their way into the fabric of this far-flung tropical island. During the early years of colonial rule, a new group of urbanised, Westernising elites sprung up – Sri Lanka's burgeoning middle class.*

Rather than amassing riches, middle-class status was achieved by adhering to British customs – especially language and dress.[21] In nineteenth-century Ceylon, Britishness became a commodity. Still today, many middle-class Sri Lankans harbour an offbeat affection for all things 'British'.

Colombo's anglicised schools were the first seminaries of Britishness. They taught the local elite the English language, but also helped develop a new class of man who identified England as the motherland and himself as citizen of Empire. Royal and S. Thomas' – Colombo's two pre-eminent schools – sprung up around the middle of the nineteenth century; before long, both were dabbling at cricket. As Michael Roberts has pointed out, the game was a 'conduit for Westernization' – a valuable tool, disseminating ideals like fair play and team spirit.[22]

College cricket really got going with the arrival of Ashley Walker, who came to Royal in 1876 as mathematics and boarding master.[23] A talented and experienced all-rounder,** Walker wasted no time developing cricket at Royal – soon writing to S. Thomas' sub-warden to suggest an inter-college clash. The Royal–Thomian rivalry, and the tradition of Big Match cricket, were born.

In an age where the island was still split between colonist and colonised, Walker showed a rare egalitarianism. Without his contributions, the spread of cricket would have been a much more protracted process. C.E. Corea, Royal cricketer from 1881 to 1885, wrote:

---

* In Sri Lanka, the term 'middle class' is a misnomer, referring to what anthropologist and cricket historian Michael Roberts describes as 'the top rungs of the social hierarchy below the British ruling strata'.

** The summer Walker sailed to Colombo, he had made 81 against the MCC at Lord's and been stumped off the bowling of W.G. Grace in Swansea.

Mr. Walker considered cricket an aristocratic game which only 'gentlemen' could appreciate. And when he saw that Ceylon boys took to cricket
keenly, he concluded that they were 'nature's aristocrats and gentlemen'.
He was absolutely colour blind, it was enough for him that he found in
the 'natives' of Ceylon in spite of their dark skin – perhaps because of it –
the instincts of men who 'play the game'. He would often tell us boys that
we had every reason to be proud of our country and nation. He made us
feel that in our aptitude for cricket we were the salt of the earth.[24]

Corea would go on to become President of the Ceylon National
Congress, Advocate of the Supreme Court and a tireless campaigner
for Ceylonese independence. Nor was his success an aberration. Royal
and S. Thomas' students quickly came to dominate Sri Lankan society;
the nexus of influence extending from Big Match cricketers soon grew
gargantuan. There is something stirring in the knowledge that Walker
was able to empower the boys through cricket, even as other aspects of
colonial life sought only to cut them down.

Corea claims the schools had matches in 1877 and 1878 – but the first
fully recorded fixture took place across three evenings in July 1879.[25] Play
began at 4 pm each day at the Galle Face Ground; the S. Thomas' team was
rowed across Beira Lake by ferry. The cricket itself was quite different from
what we know today. There were no whites or pads, and no boundaries
either – so each hit had to be run to the full. The scoring was 'slow and
low': one account claims Royal won due to good fielding, another that
S. Thomas' bowlers grew 'lax' when breakthroughs weren't forthcoming.
Walker's presence clearly had an impact too: his slow round-arm bowling
claimed 14 wickets, while his first-innings 33 was the game's top score.

Moving forward, the match was played over two days and featured only
students. The low scoring continued, mainly due to poor batsmanship
and treacherous, uncut wickets.* Despite the lack of runs, the spectacle of
Sri Lankan boys playing cricket caught the public's imagination. Locals
began to quietly gamble on games, hiding their coins in hollowed-out,

---

* In the series' first twenty years, there were only twelve team totals of more than
100, while sides were dismissed for less than 50 on twenty occasions. No batsman scored
a century during this time; nine bowlers claimed 10-wicket match hauls.

half coconut shells. The most popular bet was on the number of batsmen who would be dismissed without scoring.

Saint Peter's–Prince Alfred might be older (just), and Eton–Harrow more famous – but Royal vs S. Thomas' stands up as the greatest game in schoolboy cricket. In terms of standard, spectacle and significance, nothing else comes close. Between them, Eton and Harrow have produced fifteen England players; over 100 Royalists or Thomians have moved from schoolboy cricket to the national side.[26] And while Eton–Harrow is a one-day game that struggles to pull 5,000, the 'Battle of the Blues' tests (and likely exceeds) the SSC ground's 10,000 capacity for each of its three days of cricket.

As soon as I learnt about the Royal–Thomian, I felt drunk on its history. One of the first cricketers I met in Sri Lanka was Jehan Mubarak; when conversation turned to his Big Match debut, he smiled longingly – and then spoke and spoke.

'There was more pressure than on my Test debut, simply because there were more people there,' he explained. 'At the time no one was interested in watching Sri Lanka play Bangladesh. They were more interested in watching Royal vs S. Thomas'. For a Royalist or a Thomian, when you're 13, 14, 15 – all the other kids dream of playing for Sri Lanka – a Royalist dreams of playing for Royal.'

'The first one I watched was in '92 – when I was about eleven. That left a mark: I saw arguably the best innings ever played in a Royal–Thomian. It was by a guy called Gamini Perera, who scored 144 to save the match on the third day. We were 100-6 overnight, following on, and he *just* ... that was probably one of the best innings I've seen. And that made me want to be a cricketer.'

Mubarak's reverence for the match is not unusual. The great and the good of Sri Lankan cricket, from F.C. de Saram to Kusal Perera, cut their teeth on the Royal–Thomian. D.S. Senanayake – the mastermind of Sri Lankan independence whose name now adorns the Big Match trophy – made a pair in 1901.* Anura Tennekoon still remembers being

---

*   Demoted to bat at number ten the following year, D.S. managed a single run. His cricketing reputation was rescued by his sons Dudley and Robert: Dudley made 48* in 1927 and had F.C. de Saram trapped lbw two years later, Robert captained the side for three years up to 1932 and bowled Sargo Jayawickrema for a duck in 1930.

picked as a 15-year-old on the morning of the 1962 match; a decade later, Duleep Mendis announced himself by hammering a second Big Match hundred in as many years. Not all have found it so easy: though Ed Kelaart would emerge as a world-class all-rounder in the 1930s, his sole Royal–Thomian appearance passed without a run or wicket.

Everyone has their own Big Match tale to tell. Some still fight over a game in 1885 that was abandoned under suspicious circumstances. Others recall a topsy-turvy match in 1999, when each of the four innings was dominated by a different boy named Peiris. The Royal–Thomian had me hooked. The more I heard, the wider my eyes grew. I knew I had to experience it for myself.

★★★

While I was in Sri Lanka, S. Thomas' were the best schoolboy team in the country, a well-oiled machine driven by long-time coach Dinesh Kumarasinghe. Kalana Perera was the star of the side, but it didn't take long to realise that this was a team packed full of quality. They practised like pros – six times a week, on top of two physical training sessions – and played more cricket than you might have imagined possible. Rarely did I see any of the 1st XI wearing school uniform; some boys could end up playing north of 100 days cricket a year. They are for all intents and purposes at a cricket academy.

It makes sense. The Royal–Thomian is possibly the biggest event in Sri Lankan society: with its history and tradition, prestige and pageantry, plus the cash that comes from tickets and advertising, its draw is undeniable. Those in charge might not admit it, but cricket is just as important as anything that goes on in the classroom. Naturally, in the build-up to the game, its spectre becomes all consuming. For months, a huge poster hung outside the library at S. Thomas' counting down the days to the Big Match.

Each year, the school holds a cycle parade, where students ride the 6 miles from Galle Face back to Mount Lavinia, flanked by open-top buses and jeeps full of old boys and parents. They wave their black and blue flags and dance to papare, cheering their lungs out. I tagged along twice; both times, the procession was large enough to shut down traffic on Duplication Road. I couldn't help but imagine boys in boaters bringing Oxford Street to a standstill. They'd surely be pelted with rotten eggs; here the crowd just watched and waved.

The energy at the Big Match far transcends the atmosphere at an ordinary Test or ODI. I'd expected as much – but until you see it for yourself, it's difficult to square such an idea. There's an electricity on the first morning that's almost indescribable: the hawkers crammed onto Maitland Place, the thousands of ex-pat old boys back home, the giant pictures of the two schools' captains plastered across the papers' front page.

Then there's the noise. The Royal–Thomian is *loud*. Stands at the SSC – plus the large part of the ground that usually forms a grassy bank – are converted into 'tents', each one unique and impenetrable. There's the female-friendly Stables where DJ and dance floor replace cricket as main event, and the century-old Mustangs, with wood and rattan chairs for the politicians and moguls invited in. For one weekend each year, these venerable gents leave their solemnity at home and relive the heady days of their youth. Kids crane their necks to try to catch a glimpse of the fabled exotic dancers said to take up residence inside.

I was sitting in the genteel invitees box when the Prime Minister swaggered in, flanked by armed guards; in the OTSC Tent, uncles battle to be heard over competing rock and papare bands, spreading goodwill with shots of single malt and homemade short eats. At lunchtime, spectators are invited onto the ground for their own pitch inspection. Old friends linger on the boundary, reminiscing on far-off lives as flag-bearing schoolboys.

The 2019 match was worthy of every shred of revelry. It was high-quality cricket: Royal were always chasing the game – but they dug in, and until the final afternoon, looked like thwarting Thomian ambitions of a rare victory. Grown men went giddy when the final wickets fell; schoolboys flooded the field as Shalin de Mel heaved the winning runs through square leg. I spotted the usually stoic warden doing a little jig; he merrily declared a two-day holiday as reward for S. Thomas' first Big Match victory in twelve years. The party rolled on late into the night; when I wound my way home hours later, I could still hear victory cries of 'THORA', and whispers of the college song drifting across the air.

It's not just Royal and S. Thomas'. Late February to early April is 'Big Match' season in Sri Lanka – during this six-week period, the SSC grounds are barely used for anything else. Boys grow up understanding that cricket is serious business; that there's glory to be had by winning games for their college.

Shortly after Dinesh Chandimal was dropped as national captain, I watched him make a t20 century for NCC against Saracens. Though it was a public holiday, no one else bothered to turn up. Three-day matches carry the atmosphere of an exam hall; on the whole, club allegiances are non-existent.

It's perfectly plain why club cricket has failed to capture the public's imagination. On one hand, the physical proximity of the island's leading clubs negates local pride – the NCC, SSC and CCC are a stone's throw apart, on a leafy avenue in Cinnamon Gardens. On the other hand, you have homeless clubs – like Ragama and Chilaw Marians, who share a home in Katunayake, nowhere near Chilaw or Ragama.

The schedule is flimsy, and prone to be torn up at a moment's notice; SLC does nothing to promote matches and commercial interest is non-existent. Plus, with first-class status dangled in front of clubs in exchange for loyalty come board elections, the standard has sunk irredeemably. Seasoned viewers say club matches used to draw a crowd, but that the dilution of the domestic game, and the abundance of cricket now available on TV, has given rise to an unfortunate apathy. Sri Lanka's love of cricket considered, the ill health of the club game is a tragedy.

That said, schools cricket's prominence owes much to the island's quaint and unique brand of Anglophilia. The average middle-class Sri Lankan places a much greater formative impact on their schooling than a Westerner would. College songs are sung often and without irony, and there seems to be an all-pervasive, Victorian understanding that schools make men, rather than preparing boys for exams.

Like nowhere else in the world, Sri Lankan schooling is 'cradle to grave'. Watching your alma mater play invites a guttural response that club, and even country, cannot match. Cricketers in the 1960s played at least fifteen matches for their school in front of crowds of 6,000. The newspapers run polls where readers vote on the best schoolboy cricketers. Those who make a mark become celebrities and are expected to succeed at a higher level. Anura Tennekoon was picked for Ceylon at 17, having never played a club match. Half a century later, Niroshan Dickwella was fast-tracked to the Test side following a record-breaking season as Trinity captain.

By setting in motion the practice of inter-college cricket, Ashley Walker sowed the seeds for what would become the rich and fertile breeding ground of the Sri Lankan game. Before long, other English-style public schools took to cricket: Wesley, St Joseph's* and St Benedict's in Colombo, plus Trinity and St Anthony's in Kandy. These provided the bulk of Sri Lanka's international cricketers for the first half of the twentieth century. Post-independence, they were joined at the top table by Ananda and Nalanda, Colombo's leading Buddhist schools. When Sri Lanka played in its inaugural Test in 1982, only one player – D.S. de Silva from Galle – was not drawn from this pool.

There have long been accusations of bias, but Royal and S. Thomas' success seems to owe as much to good practice as nepotism. The schools have historically employed Sri Lanka's best coaches, and up to the 1960s were in possession of some of Colombo's only turf wickets. Then there are cricket's barriers to entry: bats and pads are expensive, less affluent parents unlikely to encourage their kids to pursue a sport that until recently offered no financial prospects. Elitism may have played a part, but there is a certain logic to Royal and S. Thomas' cricketing heritage.

The game has democratised in the past four decades, so much so that in recent years, the Sri Lankan side has often been without Royalists or Thomians. New powerhouses have emerged, like Richmond College in Galle and Prince of Wales, Moratuwa. The landscape may be changing, but there are comforting constants. Sri Lankans can be smug in the knowledge that their college cricket better prepares boys for the professional game than any other system in the world. And while support for the national side will continue to ebb and flow with the team's fortunes,

---

★   St Joseph's College south – later renamed St Peter's – was founded in 1922, and joined this elite group.

it is impossible to imagine that Sri Lanka could exist without its dizzying school spirit.

Play to the Whistle

Having brought cricket to the boys of Ceylon, Walker could have rested on his laurels. Instead, he went one step further – proposing a contest between the newly instructed locals and Ceylon's Brits.[27] Before long, the 'Europeans–Ceylonese' game was an annual fixture; for Colombo's crowds, it was unrivalled as spectacle. Many simply called it 'test' cricket.

But not all Brits were so encouraging. In 1926, Governor Clifford described Ceylon's anglicised elite as 'an essentially imitative people … proud of having imbibed such an exclusive British quality as the public school spirit'.[28] There is prickling cruelty in introducing a value system and then sneering at those who adopt it – an unkindness many English-speaking Ceylonese felt. No matter how fluently they adopted Western values and language, they remained subordinate, belittled by the British as 'natives'. Ultimately, Ceylonese society had a glass ceiling: its people were invariably treated as subjects rather than rulers.

Such denigration did not pass without backlash. In 1850, a group of Burghers from Royal College founded the journal *Young Ceylon*.[29] Taking its name from Mazzini's *Young Italy* movement, it was – in the words of Michael Roberts – 'a literary engine for … Ceylonese nationalism'. I found an old issue in the British Library: thumbing through its barely bound pages, I stumbled on a piece called 'The social improvement of the Ceylonese'.[30] It tackled colonial bigotry, highlighted the Burghers' role in assisting Sinhalese advancement and concluded with a striking extract from William Cowper's poem, *The Negro's Complaint*:

Black hair, black eyes, and dark complexion
Cannot forfeit Nature's claim:
Skins may differ, but Affection
Dwells in *white* and *black* the same.

The local team Walker assembled to play against his Europeans in 1881 was hardly representative of Sri Lankan society.[31] Ten had been to Royal or S. Thomas', and all eleven were Burghers. They might have styled themselves as 'Combined Colleges' or the 'Colombo Burghers'. In picking the moniker 'Young Ceylon' – and identifying themselves in *nationalist* terms – they added meat onto the bones of an already mouth-watering clash. It became more than a simple game of cricket: a contest between ruler and ruled.

Confrontations like these are especially important in the colonial con-text, where direct challenges to the ruling class were, if not impossible, certainly unwise. The historian Nira Wickramasinghe has highlighted instances where locals wore Sinhalese and European dress – say, sarong over trousers – in conjunction.[32] She calls these 'hybrid moments', 'a way of subverting the order of reason and progress instituted by colonialism'. By taking a game that was seen to epitomise Britishness and imbuing it with a nationalist drive, these cricketers created their own hybrid moment. They were, in a sense, voicing objections to the colonial order.

But in this case, Young Ceylon were no match for the experienced 'Europeans'. They lost by an innings and 92; in the second innings, Walker bagged nine, as six of the top seven registered ducks. Clearly, the Ceylonese were still learning. The next year, a match was proposed between the CCC and a past-and-present Royal XVIII. Lord Harris, visiting the island, accepted an invitation to captain the local side. He scored runs and took wickets, but could not lead the Royalists to victory. Nor could he lead them into the 'Europeans-only' pavilion, so he chose to stay outside and chat with his teammates – a gesture that struck a chord with all in attendance.[33]

After a six year break, the Europeans–Ceylonese series proper began in 1888, igniting fervid interest in Colombo.[34] Crowds thronged to Galle Face to see if their boys could beat the English at *their* game: the first match was drawn, but the following year George Vanderspar invited the Colts to play a repeat.* The European XI Vanderspar assembled was packed full of quality players: as Foenander bluntly put it, 'this galaxy of

---

*   Members of the Colts club made up the 'home' side from 1888 to 1902, but they always competed as 'Ceylonese', ensuring the contest maintained its nationalistic spark.

talent was generally expected to pulverise the Colts'. Yet the Europeans were shocked by the raw pace of young Colvin Kelaart. He took ten across the two innings, all clean bowled, as the Ceylonese completed victory by 5 wickets. Many a glass was raised to Kelaart that evening, but his performance proved no aberration. Much to their chagrin, the Europeans could not claim victory in the 'test' until 1899.

The first Ceylonese had taken to cricket with aplomb; and, before long, Colombo could lay claim to a bevy of homegrown stars. Twice in 1893, Colvin Kelaart's younger brother Tommy powered his country-men to victory over the Europeans. The second was a nail-biting nine-run win, which even inspired a poem:

> For well each active Colt maintain'd
> The fame of young Ceylon:
> Each point was finely lost or gain'd,
> The triumph finely won.
> But who from first to last was seen
> to play it steady through?—
> Who never falter'd on the green?
> Ah, Tommy! that was you!
>
> So here's to gallant Churchill then,
> An honest, manly heart!
> And here's to all his Englishmen,
> Who fitly bore their part!
> Here's to *our* Captain, and his band
> Of merry players too!
> And to our coolest heart and hand—
> Rare Tommy, —here's to you![35]

Whenever Tommy Kelaart sent wickets tumbling, he brought smiles to the faces of his countrymen. As fate would have it, the next decade offered him more opportunities to impress – not just against the island's finest, but against some of cricket's biggest names.

★★★

While Ashley Walker's enthusiasm clearly catalysed cricket's development, the island got an even bigger push thanks to geographical happenstance. Before the dawn of air travel, journeys between England and Australia required a stopover: once the Suez Canal opened in 1869, Colombo emerged as the natural point of transit.*

So when Ivo Bligh led his band of Englishmen Down Under in a bid to 'recover those Ashes' in 1882, the CCC sniffed an opportunity.[36] Why not invite them for a game of cricket? Since several of the club's members maintained connections with the MCC, it would be easy to organise. What's more, the cricketers who'd been cooped up on board for weeks on end were bound to be bursting for a game.

This first clash was a chastening experience for the Colombo Europeans, so used to dominating the local scene. In an 'odds' match, their 18 batsmen could only muster 92 in the first innings, and were 16-7 on second attempt when play mercifully drew to a close. It set in motion the practice of 'whistlestop' cricket, so-called because the ship's captain would supposedly sound his whistle when it was time for passengers – cricketers included – to reboard. Moving forward matches were played over a single day, and remained a regular feature right up to 1969. They gave cricket's best reason to play in Ceylon. From Don Bradman to Geoffrey Boycott, the game's elite visited – providing a yardstick for local cricketers, fuelling the imagination of Ceylon's sporting fans and heartily nourishing Colombo's scene. The whistlestops brought cricketing history to Sri Lanka.

Though tough going at first, there were signs of progress. By 1890, the local scene had advanced sufficiently for four homegrown cricketers, all Royalists, to be selected.[37] When W.G. Grace's All-England stopped the following year, Tommy Kelaart kept his place, joined by four more Ceylonese. The match burns bright in the imagination. Before play began, Governor Havelock ordered stands to be removed so Galle Face could 'accommodate the many'. A public holiday was

---

*   Initially, ships docked at Galle – en route to Australia in 1873, it was there that W.G. Grace disembarked. But soon after, a new artificial harbour was completed in Colombo. Moving forward, wayfaring cricketers would stretch their legs in Ceylon's fledgling new capital.

declared and 8,000 turned up to see Grace bat: while cricket as sport would long remain the plaything of the middle class, as spectacle, it was already spreading through urban society before the dawn of the twentieth century.

But if the crowds gathered in hope of runs, they were destined to be disappointed. Having made 19, the great W.G. Grace was dismissed by Tommy Kelaart. There is debate over how* – but whatever happened, Grace made no attempt to replace the bails. Instead, he gave Kelaart a congratulatory pat on the back before slowly shuffling back to the pavilion.

It is a compelling snapshot; perhaps the first truly *significant* moment in the history of Sri Lankan cricket. As one of the most famous men in Victorian England, Grace carried real mystique. When he came to the crease, crowds *expected* – certainly, few would have anticipated his early dismissal at the hands of a 20-year-old local lad. I can't help but picture Ashley Walker, beaming with pride at his prodigy's progress. The whole crowd must have swelled with patriotic zeal – one of their own had unseated the game's greatest batsman.**

Kelaart is forever connected to another medium slow left-armer, his great friend and clubmate, Dr Allen Raffel. Raffel's day in the sun came in October 1894.[38] Still just 19, he bowled remarkably against A.E. Stoddart's England XI, taking 14 for 70 during the course of the day. Four of his victims went without scoring; ten were bowled, including Stoddart – one of *Wisden*'s Five in 1893 – twice. He had two shots at a hat-trick, and is said to have 'shaved' the stumps more than he hit them. After the match, the England captain told George Vanderspar that Raffel and Kelaart were both good enough for county cricket.***

---

*   Foenander records him being bowled, while Grace remembers hitting his own wicket. Cricket writer Arunabha Sengupta claims that Grace was discomfited by the heat and chose to walk despite realising he was not out.

**   The crowd were equally excited by the appearance of the world-famous explorer H.M. Stanley, a shipmate of the cricketers. His arrival at the ground stole the spotlight away from Grace; annoyed at being 'eclipsed', W.G. hid sulking in the changing rooms.

***   Evidence does nothing to dispel this: the same English side who would go on to win a thrilling Ashes series 3-2 away from home had been dismissed for 76 and then left reeling at 88-8 during the course of a day at Galle Face.

Quite how seriously visiting sides took these games is another matter. Before 1900, they were 'odds' matches: with other passengers occasionally turning out and the ships' captains sometimes acting as umpires, there was a distinct air of amateurism. In truth, they were closer to spectacle than sporting contest: time constraints meant they inevitably ended in draws; sea-wearied stars likely saw them as little more than a runaround. Keith Miller once wrote that it was 'unfortunate of course, for those 12 players chosen for the match that they had to forego the pleasure and novelty of strolling down the tree-bordered lanes of Colombo'.[39]

Still, the whistlestops were important. As a far-flung cricketing colony, Ceylon was like an arid scrubland yearning for rainfall. These matches were short sharp bursts of water. They challenged and inspired. And as much as they were a source of inspiration, their value lay in what they taught Ceylon's cricketers about themselves. They helped temper an underdog complex; as Mano Ponniah put it to me, 'When you listen to commentaries, these guys are built up in your mind like superheroes. You create your own picture, then you see for yourself – and the reality could be quite different.'

Of course, the hosts entered each match well short of level footing – as a recipient of charity, grateful to be given a game. You'd think it would be a nationally binding experience, but Ceylon's cricketers could not always call on the support of the crowds. Decades after opening the batting for his country, Channa Gunasekara ruefully wrote:

> We had not yet stripped ourselves out of the colonial mind-set and had to battle it out before anti-local crowds, still worshipping the white sahibs. One dared not misfield, drop a catch, however difficult, or fumble a ball, or you would be the unfortunate recipient of an incessant barrage of hoots or even personal insults. It could be a very unnerving experience but true Sri Lankan courtesy would be extended to our visitors for a similar offence.[40]

It seems strange that the Ceylonese should not root for their own; but in a world without TV, crowds wanted to see cricket's stars at their best. They liked to watch visiting sides bat, and were usually obliged by their national captain. But could the hoots and howls also reflect the fact that Ceylon's cricket team – made up of those who trod the halls of Colombo's elite schools – did not entirely represent the man seated beyond the boundary?

Naturally, nine decades of cricket produced flashes that could not fail to spark nationalistic fervour. C.I. Gunasekara blasting Australian spinner Lindsay Kline for 24 in an over is probably the most famous – all who know of it zealously insist that Kline was never the same again. But the further back you dig, the more magic you unearth. In 1909, a Ceylon side – playing without Europeans for the first time – made two separate Australian XIs follow-on. Eleven years later, Bill Greswell ripped through the MCC to leave them reeling at 108-9, 14 short of Ceylon's total. And in 1961, a 21-year-old Michael Tissera stood up to Wes Hall en route to a famous century.

If the whistlestops did not keep Sri Lankan cricket well fed, they certainly stopped it from starving. Left to languish outside the ICC, the island needed visitors to test and develop their own cricketers. The journey from England to Australia gave the world's two best sides reason: whether they knew it or not, the casual games of cricket they played brought value. But, without George Vanderspar, the whistlestops – and Sri Lankan cricket – might have followed an entirely different course.

***

Walker aside, no Englishman gave more to Ceylonese cricket than Vanderspar.[41] His contributions reflect a genuine love of the game: after all, he was a dashing top-order batsman, useful under-arm bowler, tireless administrator and genuine innovator – all before his 30th birthday.

Born in Galle in 1851, his greatest legacy is the whistlestops: not just corresponding with foreign authorities or organising matches, but expanding their scope to include the Ceylonese.[42] In an openly discriminative society, few eyebrows would have been raised had the fixtures remained 'Europeans-only';* by inviting the best local

---

* The Colombo Cricket Club excluded local cricketers up to 1962; it would have been a travesty and a tragedy had the whistlestops advanced on a similar course.

cricketers to play in whistlestops, Vandespar gave them the experience they needed to flourish.

His fingerprints are all over the early days of Ceylon cricket. In 1884, he led a group to Calcutta – Ceylon's first touring side, and the first 'foreign' cricketers to visit India.[43] From then on, trips abroad became a regular feature. Initially they were for Europeans only – but having seen Kelaart and Edward Christoffelsz bowl brilliantly in their first whistlestop, Vanderspar invited them to join a tour to Singapore.* Cricket was helping to disrupt the segregation encouraged by colonial society.

As time wore on, the whistlestops were eclipsed by unofficial 'tests', three- or four-day games against international touring sides, usually en route somewhere else. This tradition can be traced back to Vanderspar too: he was waiting at Colombo harbour when George Vernon's team moored in 1889.[44] They travelled up to Kandy for the match; although Vanderspar dismissed Vernon and came close to completing a hat-trick, he could not prevent his men from being blown out by an innings inside three days. Ceylon was a way off matching the best that England or Australia could offer, but the scene was burgeoning. Lord Hawke's XI stopped en route to India in 1892, playing three two-day matches – against the CCC, Up Country and the Colts.

The Colts' inclusion was likely proposed by Vanderspar, who seems to have felt a genuine urge to grow the game. A year after the CCC moved to Maitland Place, Vanderspar bought the lease to the Galle Face ground at a cut price of Rs. 750.[45] There, he established the Colombo Sports Club to cater for lower-ranking Brits; straight away, he busied himself revamping Galle Face. Where the old pitch had been made of treacherous turf sloping down from the pavilion end, Vanderspar smoothed the ground, covering it with a new plumb matting wicket, the first of its kind in Ceylon.

The introduction of matting expedited cricket's spread across the island. Turf is costly and hard to maintain; and prior to the advent of

---

* Christoffelsz, blessed with raw pace, actually out-bowled Kelaart on the trip. He ripped through Hong Kong's Europeans, claiming match figures of 13 for 46. Destined for great things in the game, he found a lucrative job in Malaya and was seemingly lost to cricket altogether.

covers, Sri Lanka's climate was far from ideal for preserving pitches. Matting offered truer bounce, helping to redress the imbalance between batsman and bowler. Its introduction saw cricket grounds spring up across the island. The SSC installed a matting wicket in 1900; the Burgher Recreation Club (BRC) followed suit in 1901.[46] Still today, Sri Lankan cricket could not survive without matting. Vanderspar's modernising measures breathed new life into the game.

Walker and Vanderspar helped establish an infrastructure that allowed Ceylonese cricket to thrive; that it flourished so quickly was thanks to the extraordinary talent of the first locals who took to the game. During the 1890s, the Colts emerged as the undisputed powerhouse of the Colombo scene,* much of their success coming behind the bowling of Tommy Kelaart.[47] By 1902 he had taken 1,000 club wickets, each costing a miserly 5.1 runs. On Ceylon's duplicitous uncut pitches, his niggling accuracy was simply too much to handle.

★★★

During my first week at S. Thomas', I went to watch the boys play a one-day semi-final against Richmond College at St Peter's. As I perched on a plastic chair in the dusty pavilion, I spotted the warden (headmaster) surrounded by a group of old boys jockeying for attention. We hadn't really spoken: still dressed in his robes and carrying a stern expression, he had a gravitas that was a little intimidating – kind of like a mafia don, but a more pious version. We caught eyes. He beckoned me over.

It soon became clear he wasn't much of a cricket fan, nor was there much pride for him to claim that day. S. Thomas' lost badly, as a blue-eyed batter called Dhananjaya Lakshan swept, reversed and scooped his way to a glittering hundred. The warden and I chatted easily all the while – eventually, the talk turned to cricket. He told me his mother's name was Kelaart, and asked if I'd heard of her ancestor Tommy. Apparently Tommy was from a huge family; the warden wanted to know if I'd seen his *topee* (hat).

---

* Between 1886 and 1901, the Colts lost just 14 of their 169 games.

I had in fact seen Kelaart's topee – on show in the museum at Lord's. It is bulky, the kind of hat that would sit more comfortably on the head of an explorer. Strangely, he chose to keep it on while he bowled, lifting and replacing it as he entered his delivery stride. Maybe this was to unsettle batsmen – distraction aside, it is hard to imagine why anyone would want to bowl in such a thing.

Kelaart wasn't the Colts' only great bowler. Indeed, Foenander claims that Allen Raffel was even better in his prime: had injury not curtailed his bowling career in 1895, he surely would have matched Kelaart's vast haul of wickets.[48] In tandem, the duo were near unplayable.* Tragically, Raffel was done as a bowler by the age of 20. But for a fleeting moment, he and Kelaart set fire to cricket in Ceylon. Thanks to their exploits, the Colts earned the tag 'invincible'.

But the club existed on shaky ground. The 1893 Colombo–Colts match went a long way to undoing the amity which had characterised Ceylonese cricket in the nineteenth century.[49] When the CCC's captain began barracking Colts umpire W. Van Geyzel about a caught behind decision, Colvin Kelaart led his men from the field – foreshadowing Arjuna's actions in Adelaide 106 years later. The exasperated Bishop of Colombo managed to persuade them back inside the boundary – but the bickering wore on. The CCC's hon. secretary used his position as editor of *The Times of Ceylon* to deride Van Geyzel; when Van Geyzel responded with a lawsuit, the Colts were removed from the CCC's fixture list – frozen out for the next eleven years.

This pettiness hurt the Colts cricketers. While claims that they were excluded from Ceylon sides going forward are not entirely true, there was a clear cooling after the incident. Some Ceylonese played the whistlestop of 1896, but none from the Colts. At least, the lack of visitors in the first years of the twentieth century meant they did not miss too much.

But the club's players were ignored when Plum Warner's MCC planned a stopover in 1903: by now, this meant not only Kelaart's exclusion, but that of C.E. Perera, a recently emerged dashing right-hand

---

* The pair combined to take 15 for the Colts when Lorde Hawke's XI visited in 1892, 18 for Ceylon against the all-white Madras Cricket Club later in the year. Kelaart was 21, Raffel just 17.

batsman. It seemed a shame that two of the island's best should have to miss out because of bickering. So there was a certain poetic justice when Warner sent a telegram telling the CCC his men would be too tired to play.[50] Instead, they spent the day relaxing in Mount Lavinia. The Colts were welcomed back into the fold in 1904, but had learned a sobering lesson: the Europeans held all the power. Until Ceylon had a proper cricket body, they always would.

THE FIRST GREAT BATSMEN

For much of the nineteenth century, local cricket had been sustained by the Burghers, but a change began to take hold in the 1890s. While the Sinhalese on the whole resisted Westernisation, Ceylon's Tamils[*] proved more willing to learn English: from around 1870, their presence in the Civil Service swelled.[51] Exposed to English customs, they soon took to cricket. Two Tamil clubs sprung up in Colombo during the 1890s, merging to form the Tamil Union C&AC in 1899.[52] Its first home at Campbell Park was leased from the government for 50 cents a year.

Meanwhile, Buddhist revivalism was changing the face of Colombo.[53] Ananda College opened doors in 1886 – by teaching in English but retaining a Buddhist foundation, schools like Ananda gave those Sinhalese wary of Westernisation opportunities to rise through society. Nonetheless, these schools submitted to aspects of Britishness: by 1895, old-Thomian J.C. McHeyzer was coaching Ananda's boys at cricket.[54] Around the same time, some Sinhalese were warming to the idea of sending their sons to anglicised schools. By my estimation, around forty-five Sinhaelse boys played in the Royal–Thomian during the 1890s.

By 1898, schools cricket had advanced sufficiently for a Combined Colleges XI to take on the Colts.[55] In drawing the game, the schoolboys

---

[*]   In Sri Lanka, a distinction is drawn between 'Ceylon Tamils' – who have a long history on the island and descend from the Jaffna Kingdom – and the 'Hill Country Tamils', Indians brought to work on the plantations in the nineteenth and twentieth centuries. The latter group, naturally domiciled out of Colombo, remained removed from cricket until much later in the game's development.

gave an excellent account of themselves, and the fixture was rebooked for the following year. By chance, the 1899 team was made up exclusively of Sinhalese boys; remarkably, they led the invincible Colts by a single run after the first innings.[56] Seeing eleven of their own perform so admirably stirred a burning sense of pride in the watching Sinhalese. Suddenly, there were calls for a sports club of their own.

In fact, in D.L. de Saram, this 'all-Sinhalese' XI included at least one by with a heavy dose of Burgher blood. While still at S. Thomas', de Saram was establishing himself as one of the island's most destructive batsmen. He was not a tall man, but his shoulders seemed broad as the doors he walked through, his forearms the size of saplings. An inspiring leader and born entertainer on the field, beyond the boundary de Saram was shy, struggling badly with a stammer. He let his cricket do the talking – and was the kind of batsman uncowed by any bowler. When he came to the crease the field would spread; the crowd growing restless in anticipation of scything drives and dashing hooks.

In 1900 de Saram made history by scoring 105* for NCC, the first century by a schoolboy in club cricket.[57] But his allegiance would soon be tested. On 28 March 1899, H.J.V.I. Ekanayake called a meeting to discuss the founding of the Sinhalese Sports Club (SSC).[58] The next year, the club leased a plot of land in Victoria Park. Though cinnamon trees sprouted from the sandy soil, D.S. Senanayake and Danny Gunasekara worked tirelessly to get the ground ready for cricket.

Gunasekara and de Saram's names were on the teamsheet for the SSC's inaugural fixture in July 1901. No doubt the Colombo Sports Club fancied their chances against this fledgling local side, but by day's end they were humbled and sick of the sight of the teenaged de Saram. He dazzled with an unbeaten 132, 18 more than the Sports Club could manage.[59] It was a famous victory: the perfect start to life in cricket for the Sinhalese.

During the first years of the twentieth century, de Saram was the club's beating heart. He scored eleven of the first fifteen centuries – while no batsman scored a hundred against the SSC until 1906.[60] Alongside Kelaart, de Saram was invited to Bombay for India trials in December 1903; he was said to be a certainty for selection, until the tour collapsed due to lack of funding.[61]

The sense of opportunity lost was compounded by the lack of international visitors around the turn of the century: after 1896, No English or Australian side arrived for more than a decade. And when the whistlestops returned in 1908, the 'All-Ceylon XII' Vanderspar picked was without any truly Ceylonese men. T. W. Roberts* smashed 70 in an hour against the MCC amateurs. He should have walked out against a full-strength English side, but the professionals – a young Jack Hobbs included – requested their £5 match fee doubled. Vanderspar refused, filling their places with cricketers from the Garrison and Colombo Sports Club.[62]

The payment of professionals was becoming an increasingly thorny issue. When the homeward-bound Australians stopped in 1909, the CCC refused to cover their match fee.[63] Sniffing an opportunity, the SSC offered to sponsor the visit. They organised a gate, raising enough to offer the Australian pros £10 a man.[64] So for the first time, a team that truly represented Ceylon – rather than the colonists who presided over the island – would have the chance to play against cricketers of international calibre.

Danny Gunasekara captained a side including D.L. de Saram and his younger brother Fred, plus the 'Demon' Tommy Kelaart – by now fast approaching his 40th birthday. And since the Australians were travelling back from England in two separate parties, the island's budding cricketers would get two bites at the cherry.

The first to arrive were Monty Noble's XI: a scratch team including four Australians, J.M. Bryan of Kent and B.C.N. Knight, a planter who had previously turned out for Ceylon. The rest of the side was made up of fellow passengers, but still little was expected of the Ceylonese. They were skittled for 110, and the game seemed to be following a predictable course, until Kelaart and R.E.S. Mendis sparked a steepling Australian collapse. From 50-2, the visitors crashed to 68 all out – and now faced the indignity of following on against these small-island, part-time

---

*   Earlier in the year, Roberts had announced himself with a new island record, 241 for Kalutara Lawyers against their Galle counterparts. An Oxford-educated, brown-skinned Bajan, his case is an interesting one. Had he remained in his homeland, he would have been excluded from whites-only clubs – but in Ceylon, by virtue of not being local, he was allowed entry into places otherwise reserved for Europeans.

cricketers. Without doubt, this was the proudest day yet in the island's young cricket history.

Though the second group, led by Percy McAlister, were a tricker proposition,* the Ceylonese were unperturbed. After declaring at 183-5, they tore into the Australians – who crumbled to 78 and were asked to bat again. They were 59-4 on second attempt at day's end and were no doubt pleased to return to the comfort of their ship. Kelaart rolled back the years, taking 9 wickets; the Ceylonese were in dreamland. None of them had played a first-class match, but over the course of two weeks, they had shown they could mix it with some of the world's best cricketers. What's more, they had done it without the help of the Europeans who had taught them the game.

***

After a five-year hiatus, the Europeans–Ceylonese 'test' returned in 1910. The game belonged to the de Sarams. Captain D.L. put together a sturdy third-wicket partnership with his brother Fred, before the youngest – 19-year-old Eric Reginald de Saram – struck an unbeaten 59. D.L. took six as the Ceylonese cantered to victory; though it would have been a closer-run thing had the Europeans clung onto their catches.[65]

D.L. de Saram was in the thick of all things Ceylon cricket for the first quarter of the twentieth century. He took 5 for 61 in a whistlestop against the Australians in 1912, but joined the CCC's boycott when E.F. Waddy's New South Wales side visited two years later.**[66] It's a shame, as he would have been the unanimous choice to lead the unofficial 'test'; never before had a Ceylonese captained a European. As it was, the home side beat Waddy's Australians by 4 wickets on a crumbling NCC pitch.[67] For the first time, a touring team had been bested in Ceylon.

D.L. did lead a successful 'Ceylonese' tour to Bombay in 1919: with wins against the Europeans and Parsees, and a draw against the Hindus,

---

* In Warren Bardsley and Vernon Ransford, they possessed the two outstanding batsmen from the summer's Ashes.
** Some have suggested the de Sarams boycotted the game over the 'White Australia' policy. While this may be true, I can find no concrete evidence to support it.

the island's cricketers announced themselves overseas.[68] And at 29, E.R. de Saram finally seemed to be emerging from the long shadow cast by his brother. But visiting India brought perils: E.R. contracted typhoid on the tour, and died soon after returning home. Fred de Saram was so distraught that he fled to England with his family. Before long, they would be back; his son Frederick Cecil (F.C.) would leave an indelible mark on the game.

Though D.L. should have led Ceylon against Australia in 1921, the whistlestop was cancelled when the visitors' ship docked twelve hours late.[69] By now, he must have felt his day would never come – but he continued to give all he had to the country's cricket. His knowhow as a lawyer was vital in drafting the CCA's constitution, and later in 1922 he took his rightful place as national captain for the first time. Ceylon had its first homegrown leader.

Bill Gresswell, the island's best bowler during the first part of the twentieth century, spoke of de Saram in reverent tones. 'No better model cricketer or sportsman ever donned flannels in Ceylon,' he cooed.[70] 'Model' cricketer is a striking phrase, especially since there seems to be something prototypical about D.L. de Saram. He bowled fast off a short run, held local records for throwing a cricket ball and once launched Greswell for a 140-yard 6. When I picture him batting, I see a dizzying fusion of Duleep, Sanath and Aravinda. His star burned bright.

De Saram left serious cricket in 1924, just shy of his 42nd birthday. He passed a decade later – at 52, he was far too young. A man who had given so much to the island's cricket deserved to live long into his autumn, watching the fruits of his labour grow. At least he went knowing his family name would not be soon forgotten.

In 1931, D.L. umpired the Royal–Thomian.[71] It so happened that his nephew F.C. de Saram was captaining Royal. F.C. cracked a shimmering century – at 140, an lbw appeal went up against him. Uncle and nephew locked eyes; a broad grin broke across D.L.'s face. 'Young man, you've had enough,' he proclaimed. 'Yoooou're out!' It was less a finger of death than a passing of the torch. From that day on, D.L. de Saram must have known that his nephew was destined for greatness.

★★★

For all de Saram's achievements, in the early twentieth century the Colts were still king of club cricket. Tommy Kelaart terrified batsmen, and in C.E. Perera, the club found a batsman to hang its hat on.[72] If de Saram was Ceylon's best left-handed batter of the day, Perera was clearly the island's classiest right-hander. The pair form a neat contrast: de Saram, the muscular Christian, all crash, bang and wallop; Perera, the slender Buddhist, a picture of style and grace. It challenges logic that the former ended up playing most of his cricket for the Sinhalese club, the latter in a team largely composed of Burghers.

That Perera ended up at the Colts was surely down to J.C. McHeyzer, his coach at Ananda. McHeyzer spotted Perera's talent straight away, and likely helped him push through a move to Wesley College.[73] Even before his 20th birthday, Perera was a star. He made 71 for the Ceylonese against the Europeans in 1898; 64 and 32 for Combined Colleges against the Colts the following year.[74] He was a cricketer who rose to the big occasion, a fact he underlined in 1901 in one of the more remarkable matches in Sri Lanka's cricketing history.

With the Boer War raging on in South Africa, the British decided to send over 5,000 captured prisoners to Ceylon. Once the Stiffs Cricket Club sprung up at the prison camp in Diyatalawa, McHeyzer proposed a match against the Colts.* So on 4 July 1901, eleven prisoners of war boarded a train to Colombo. Since there was little prospect of their escape, the authorities allowed them small freedoms: they were lodged at the Mount Lavinia Hotel, essentially on parole under the supervision of their opening batsman Commandant Van Zyl.

The match itself was quite an event.[75] The Colts spent 600 Rs. constructing four stands: there was a public bar and a pavilion for the governor dressed by Ceylon's first florist. A marquee was put up for the players, who dined on lunches of soup, fish, dressed crabs, Irish stew, roast sirloin, mutton, ham, tongue, salads, Yorkshires and sultana puddings.

---

* This, and the match against Galle CC three months earlier, were the first instances of a South African side playing against non-white cricketers. Coincidentally, eighty-one years later Tony Opatha's Sri Lankan team became the first cricketers of colour to travel to Apartheid South Africa.

It was a far sight better than prison food, but haute cuisine was slim consolation for the suffering South Africans. Perera tucked into the Boer bowlers with relish, repeatedly carving them beyond the boundary rope. One hulking hit sailed into the Ladies' Stand, bringing shrieks of horror from those inside. Though his partners toppled regularly, Perera farmed the strike – and was eventually stranded on 90. Dismissed for 53 and 66, the Boers were beaten by 141 runs.

Perera was in the thick of things again when students and alumni from Elphinstone College visited in 1904.[*][76] The Elphinstone men had much in common with Ceylon's cricketers, and the tour was a great success – so much so that McHeyzer proposed a return two years later. So in February 1906, a sixteen-man party led by Dr Allen Raffel set off for Bombay.[77] The public picked up the bill of about £135 (Rs. 29,371.25) – a clear sign that cricket's popularity was growing among the affluent urban middle class.

At this stage, Bombay was India's leading cricketing city – and there seems to have been a general awareness that this was a worthy test for Colombo's cricketers. *The Times of Ceylon* sent a journalist along, and reports appeared regularly in the paper. On the whole, they were buoyant, and with good reason: the Ceylonese looked the part. They overcame an Elphinstone eleven that contained P.G. Wodehouse's brother Armine, and beat the Muslims and Parsis with an innings to spare.[**]

The Indians were full of compliments. The president of the Parsi Gymkhana promised to include at least three Ceylonese in the Indian side he hoped to take to England; the Parsi captain described Ceylon's batting as 'first class'.[78] Perera especially caught the eye: he passed 50 four times, including a mesmeric 80 in twenty-five minutes against the Bombay Gymkhana. D.E. Joseph was the best of the bowlers; had Kelaart been able to travel, the attack would have carried real threat. Only the fielding brought scorn. *The Times* reported:

---

[*]   This was the first truly Indian team to visit the island. They struck a thrilling victory over the Colts, who, 4 runs short, lost their last 3 wickets without adding a run. Perera was last out, caught on the fence trying to finish the match with a single brutal slog.

[**]   Their other three matches were drawn: only against a Hindu side featuring the great Palwankar Baloo did they struggle.

They strike one as being rather too casual and slack in the field …
Mr D Telang placed a ball beautifully to leg, but not a fielder stirred
after it, expecting a boundary and waiting for the spectators, who were
none of them within 20 yards of the spot, to return the ball. It failed to
reach the boundary and the batsmen ran six.[79]

The tour had been a happy one, but misery would soon befall Ceylon
cricket.[80] Within a year of getting back from Bombay, C.E. Perera was
dead. Like E.R. de Saram after him, he fell victim to typhoid. At first he
thought the illness was nothing serious,* but within a week his condition
had worsened. Obituaries poured in, hailing the 'lad, born and trained in
the humblest quarter of Colombo … who had somehow mastered the
secret which draws men in crowds and drives them frantic with delight
at the exhibition of good cricket'.[81]

Strangely, just before his death he was named captain of the SSC,
despite the fact he only turned out occasionally for the club. He never
got the chance to play for Ceylon; fate denied him the opportunity
to test his game against the stalwarts from England and Australia. His
untimely passing and a scarcity of records means he remains something
of an enigma, but all those who saw him were spellbound by his batting.

Despite his Buddhist faith, Perera was a sergeant in the Ceylon
Artillery Volunteers and was given a military funeral, his coffin draped in
the Union Jack. If inappropriate, it was nonetheless a heartfelt gesture; a
sign of the esteem in which he was held. Perera's time in the game was
all too fleeting. Still, he was the world's first great Buddhist batsman. Had
he stuck around longer, who knows what he might have achieved.

COMING AND GOING

Cricket was following a satisfying course. The British had set the game in
motion, and the Ceylonese were now starting to soar. At the turn of the
century, the island's best cricketers were all locals. But Ceylon remained

---

* Perera wrote a casual note to Dr Raffel asking him to visit, and was reluctant to
adhere to the dietary restrictions imposed by his club captain.

a jewel in Britain's imperial crown, continuing to lure men east. Among them were some serious cricketers. Vivian Crawford, once described as 'the most stylish hitter' by C.B. Fry, arrived in 1911 with fifteen years' first-class experience under his belt.[82] Percy May came the same year, taking up the assistant manager's post at the Golinda tea plantation.

But, the most important addition to Ceylon's cricket scene was a 19-year-old from Somerset. Bill Greswell moored in Colombo in the autumn of 1909 with a reputation.[83] Across two seasons in the County Championship, he had taken 94 wickets at 24.57 – and displayed an uncanny ability to move the ball in to the right-hander.* If batsmen could stop the ball cannoning into their stumps, they often found it ended up in the hands of the men sneakily posted around the corner.

The inswinger: this astonishing, till-now unknown, hooping delivery brought Greswell much success. Just before setting off for Colombo, he took 4 for 11 against the Australians; though still a teenager, his name was gaining traction in the Long Room at Lord's. Greswell wanted to stay and earn his Test cap, but his father had other ideas. He was to ship to Ceylon and join the family business, a decision he forever resented.

His loss was Sri Lanka's gain. From the day he arrived, right up until his departure in 1926, Greswell was the island's best bowler. Before he had time to unpack his bags, he was whisked away to Madras with the Europeans. Ceylon's colonists had often struggled on these trips, but with Greswell in their ranks, they won every game. He took 32 wickets at under 9 apiece – 22 of them bowled or lbw. Subcontinental batsmen were totally unprepared for his devious movement through the air and off the pitch.

The 1911 Europeans–Ceylonese 'test' made it clear that the island's cricketing landscape had shifted. The Europeans, without a victory since 1899, dominated the match. Crawford struck 140, before Greswell took 12 across the two innings – with these two in their ranks, the colonists were no longer the pushover the Ceylonese had grown accustomed to.

---

*   There has been some confusion over whether his primary weapon was the off-cutter or inswinger. A letter he wrote in 1965 suggests both deliveries were in his arsenal: 'the swerve, taking effect from about halfway was quite prodigious … When the ball pitched it followed the "in" direction at comparatively greater speed.'

Naturally, Greswell and Crawford quickly emerged as leaders for the local cricketers. They carried knowhow from the English game; under their tutelage, Ceylon's cricket took steady strides forward. Perera claims that 'Crawford taught the Ceylonese the art of batsmanship and Greswell the art of medium pace bowling'. This might be hyperbolic, but there's no arguing with his conclusion: 'With these two playing every week Ceylonese cricket improved tremendously.'

Crawford's first-class experience made him a natural choice to lead Ceylon. He captained whistlestops against the MCC in 1911 and Australia the following year, but his time on the island was fleeting. The outbreak of the First World War saw him head back to Europe – and put a stop to much of the cricket on the island. Colombo's cricket lovers had to endure eight barren years while they waited for the whistlestops to return. But 11 October 1920 was to be a famous day for Sri Lankan cricket. Greswell got Jack Hobbs, Harry Makepeace, Frank Woolley and Johnny Douglas for single-figure scores; where Ceylon had rapidly reached 122, the MCC staggered and stumbled for 72 overs. At day's end they were 108-9. In a letter home to his father, Greswell wrote:

> Their last man was in and they still had 15 or so to make … It would never have done for us to beat the All England side. They would have had their legs pulled for the rest of the tour … The weather was perfect and the wicket a real good one. There was an enormous crowd, fully 8,000 paying for admission … we had the match in our hands. Our fielding was simply miraculous. Douglas said he had never seen such fielding in his experience of cricket.[84]

You can understand Bill's disappointment – but this was a moral triumph for Ceylon, a giant-slaying if ever there was one. Those 9 or 10 wickets mattered little; things were moving in the right direction.

Greswell took 9 in the 1921 'test', but the locals had come on leaps and bounds in the past decade, and he couldn't stop them cruising to an innings victory. Indeed, when the MCC passed through three years later, he was one of just three Europeans selected. He made the inclusion count: Herbert Sutcliffe had averaged over 75 against South Africa during the summer, but was undone twice in a day by Greswell for a grand total of 17. Eleven days shy of his 35th birthday, Bill was at it again. He took 8 for 38 as the English slumped for 73; only calamitous Ceylonese batting prevented the day from ending an unqualified success.

Greswell's days in Ceylon were numbered. He picked up four Australian scalps in his final whistlestop, and soon after played one last game – a casual Europeans–Ceylonese match that featured some of the island's greatest cricketers. At 55, Tommy Kelaart wore whites for the final time; clearly, Ceylon was grateful for all Greswell had given.

But Greswell couldn't appreciate the good he had done. He boarded the boat back to England in 1926 with lingering hopes of playing Test cricket, but the call never came. The injustice of the missed opportunity left him bitter all his days.[*85] Part of his soul was stripped away when he was sent to Ceylon. Few could mistake Greswell for a happy man, but in his own words, he found 'heaven' when he bowled. There is no guarantee he would have been a success, but a bowler of his class deserved the chance to challenge himself against the best over five days.

Yet, in losing that opportunity, he became a crucial building block for another nation's cricket – and had more of an impact than he ever could have had in Somerset. With wily Bill Gresswell running in week after week, Ceylon's bowlers learned cunning and craft, and her batsmen to up their game. When he was around, foreign visitors were never assured of easy runs; above all, he left Ceylon cricket in a far better state than he found it. Were it not for Greswell's influence, would such a bevvy of brilliant cricketers have emerged from Colombo during the 1920s and '30s?

★★★

With cricket catching on at home, it wasn't long before a handful of wide-eyed wanderers looked to take the skills they'd acquired back to the game's cradle. Thanks to them, men from all corners of Britain got

---

★   Greswell struggled with life outside of the game. Trouble at work brought on a nervous breakdown in 1931; another after the war forced him to undergo electroshock therapy. Prior to the advent of proper anaesthetic it was a harrowing experience: on one occasion, he ran rather than facing the torment. Both of his marriages were unhappy; in later life he 'chopped logs and grew vegetables to sell at the greengrocers' for pennies' profit.

to know that cricket in Ceylon existed. Alfred Holsinger, a Thomian and probably the island's fastest nineteenth-century bowler, was the trailblazer, heading to the Isle of Wight in 1899 to start a new life as a professional cricketer.[86]

In exchange for 40 shillings a week, the 18-year-old Holsinger agreed to turn out for Ryde CC and keep the club's pitches in proper condition. As the first non-white professional to play cricket in England, he must have caused quite a stir. He took a wicket with his first ball for the club, and later in the season bagged all 11 in an innings, including 6 wickets in 6 balls. Before the year was out, local papers were dubbing him the 'Ryde Ranjitsinhji'.*

It is strange that he played no first-class cricket. Ryde was a feeder for Hampshire, and would no doubt have pushed Holsinger for a trial – but he never received the call. Instead, he lived a nomadic existence for the next two decades, plying his trade from Llanelli to Lincolnshire; enjoying stints in the Lancashire, Central Yorkshire and Durham leagues. He played good cricket wherever he went, but could not break into the upper echelons of the English game. Scorecards show he sometimes wasn't called upon to bowl; in all likelihood, he was a victim of discrimination. Cricket brought Holsinger neither fame nor fortune, but he was a pioneer – not just for Sri Lankans but for all minority cricketers.

The first Sri Lankan to truly make a mark in the UK was Churchill Hector Gunasekara.[87] The youngest of four cricketing brothers,** Gunasekara was a pianist and a dancer with slicked-back hair and piercing brown eyes – in many ways, the archetypal Sinhalese gent. Soon after captaining Royal in the 1912 Big Match, he packed his bags and followed his siblings to England. Within a week he'd scored a century for Acton, snapping his bat in half in the process. He started at Cambridge the following year: although he had come to study medicine, Gunasekara was

---

* In three seasons at the club, Holsinger took 249 wickets at an average of 9.58 and struck seven 50s.
** The eldest, Danny, was a founding member at the SSC and Ceylon captain in 1909, E.I. the first Sri Lankan to play for a London club. He and another brother, V.R. Gunasekara, played collegiate cricket at Cambridge – paving a path for their younger brother to follow.

about to embark on a cricketing journey that would stand the whole of Ceylon in good stead.

In his first months at Cambridge, Gunasekara struck up a friendship with K.S. Pratapsinhji, the nephew of Ranjitsinhji – the Indian prince, inventor of the leg glance and first Asian Test cricketer. The university's coach Albert Relf usually only coached blues, but was willing to make an exception for Pratapsinhji – and let Gunasekara tag along too. 'We had to go to the nets or [*sic*] cut the lectures,' he recalled. 'There was no alternative. We cut the lectures.'

Though Relf saw something in Gunasekara, not all at Cambridge were so welcoming. Despite the coach's request that he play in the Seniors' trial match – with an eye towards qualifying for Sussex – Gunasekara was passed over. 'Prejudice was one of the handicaps in Cambridge that we of the East had to get over,' he stoically wrote. 'That was our greatest obstacle.'

Relf helped dismantle it, publicly challenging Cambridge's captain over Gunasekara's omission. He was invited to the next trial, took 8 wickets and found himself in line for a Blue. But Europe was torn asunder with the outbreak of the First World War, and not a single ball was bowled at Fenner's for the next four summers.

In place of university cricket, Gunasekara found games for the recently formed Indian Gymkhana Club. They often played at Lord's – sometimes spotting the shadowy figure of Plum Warner sitting in the pavilion. Perhaps Warner was there the last Monday of August 1918, watching on as Gunasekara bowled two New South Wales players before cracking an unbeaten century opening the batting.

It seems no coincidence that he was invited back to Lord's that Saturday, for a charity match pitting Britain against the Rest of the Empire. This was a huge step up for Gunasekara. For the first time, he'd be mixing with the game's elite.* He made no real impression with bat or ball, but caught Lord Tennyson on the boundary with a gymnastic effort. Warner liked what he saw. He quietly asked if Gunasekara was qualified to play for Middlesex.

---

* The British XI, led by Warner, included eight once or future Test caps.

The young Ceylonese might have thought the proposition mere talk, but the next summer, when he turned up to Lord's to watch Middlesex resume action in the County Championship, the dressing room attendant handed him a note. It read, 'Sir, Mr. Warner would like to see you.'

Warner offered Gunasekara a three-game trial; so began his career as a first-class cricketer.* No Sri Lankan since has been part of a Championship-winning side; the medal he was awarded remained one of his proudest possessions until the day he passed away. During his first two seasons at Middlesex, he showed himself to be a nagging seamer and useful lower-order bat. In 1919 he claimed 36 scalps at a shade under 28 and added three 50s, including a battling, unbeaten 88 against Surrey at The Oval.

Yet it was his fielding that truly captured the imagination. Dubbed 'The India Rubber Man', one catch he took in the gully supposedly made Nottinghamshire batsman Garnet Lee too scared to play his favoured cut. *The Daily Telegraph* featured a cartoon of him snaffling a ball, elasticated limbs stretching in all directions.[88] And Warner, whose whole life was cricket, wrote 'one of the things I am least likely to forget is Gunasekara's beautiful fielding. He was a good companion and I am glad I had the opportunity of playing with him.'

Gunasekara went home a doctor, having received the best training a cricketer could hope for. He achieved so much back in Ceylon,** but memories made in England stayed with him all his days. In the autumn of his life, he wistfully recalled Hobbs correcting his cutting technique from the slips, and Warner cooking up plans for opposing batters on the eve of matches.

Above all, Gunasekara's English summers taught him that 'there is no greater freemasonry than the freemasonry … among cricketers'.[89] The skills he acquired were valuable – and his knowledge undoubtedly

---

* He played twelve times for Middlesex in 1919 and a further eighteen in 1920, when the club were crowned County Champions.
** Gunasekara captained his country at cricket, served as Colombo's Chief Medical Officer, and wrote several books and plays. Few realise he helped introduce crematoriums to Sri Lanka, reducing the need for costly, toxic pyres – or that he was nominated for an OBE in 1952. He rejected the honour, stating his desire to 'live … without ostentation and with the least possible ceremony'.

fed into Ceylon's cricket scene. But the contacts he made were equally important. Meeting Pratapsinhji showed Gunasekara that it helped to have friends in high places. In cricketing circles, it didn't get any loftier than the corridors at Lord's. Churchill Gunasekara's Middlesex stint would prove to be a blessing for all of Ceylon.

THE WINDS OF CHANGE

As the nineteenth century wore on, resistance towards colonialism grew.[90] With vernacular schools fostering a newly literate public, over 700 publications were launched between 1888 and 1927. Among them was Anagarika Dharmapala's* *Sinhala Bauddhaya*, an eight-page weekly that sought to rouse the Sinhalese masses. As *Nurti* plays challenged and mocked colonialism in Colombo, vendors began carrying books deep into the countryside, enlightening the rural poor. Slowly, literature was helping to construct a Ceylonese/Sinhalese identity. Since nationalism went hand in hand with a disapproval of colonial customs, it was one that left little space for cricket.

Clearly, Ceylonese nationalism was fuelled by British behaviour. While poorer labourers bore the brunt of British cruelty, richer Ceylonese still had to face the indignity of being kicked out of train carriages or excluded from clubs.** On the whole, the colonists' practices fell a long way short of what they preached.

When ethnic violence erupted between Sinhalese and Muslims in 1915, their inhumane response saw the British reputation plumb

---

*   Gloriously described by William McGowan as 'part messiah and part Malcolm X', Dharmapala was part of Colombo's 'middle class' – son of one of the island's wealthiest businessmen, student at both Royal and S. Thomas'. As a teenager when the Big Match was born, he would have come into contact with Ashley Walker and the game of cricket. But he rejected his English education and the trappings of wealth to become Ceylon's first modern-day anagarika, devoting his life to Buddhism. By the 1890s, he was known across the world.

**   McGowan claims the 'arrogance of the missionaries' – who in one pamphlet described Ceylon as a 'stronghold of Satan' – encouraged laymen who had 'attended Christian schools' to renew 'their interest in Buddhist roots' and financially support the Sangha.

new depths.[91] Police went on a shooting spree. Many were simply in the wrong place at the wrong time; some who couldn't speak English were assumed obstinate and gunned down. Worse still, white planters and businessmen drafted in as volunteers took the law into their own hands, shooting and flogging locals without reason or remorse. The scars from this untempered show of force would linger for years to come. Such brutality went a long way towards dismantling concepts of 'British justice' and shocked the independence movement into life. From this moment on, the need for self-governance was increasingly clear.

The few Sri Lankans involved in cricket were also pushing for greater autonomy. The Committee of Colombo Cricket Clubs was founded in 1914; its establishment the first step towards wresting power away from the Europeans.[92] Its treasurer, Dr John Rockwood, would prove especially influential.[93] In 1919, he organised a Ceylonese tour to Bombay; for the first time, the squad assembled came close to representing Sri Lanka as a whole. Alongside the usual cast of Burghers, Sinhalese – and the ever-present A.C. Ahamath of the Malays – were the Saravanamuttu brothers, Sri Lanka's first Tamil cricketers of note. And in M.K. Albert, the party included the island's first working-class cricketer.

Born in a small village outside Kalutara, Albert worked as a groundboy at his local club, laying matting wickets and bowling in the nets.[94] Luckily, O.G. de Alwis – the SSC's first captain, and a prominent local lawyer – spotted his talent, put a bat in his hand and had him promoted to the Kalutara Sports Club side. Once Albert left school, de Alwis found him work in the Railway Department. His unorthodox technique brought buckets of runs, not just for Kalutara and Railway CC, but for the SSC and Ceylon.

The railway played a vital role in Albert's story. Had he not been born close to the Colombo–Galle line, he would have had no access to cricket. It had not infiltrated the hinterland; for many, there was simply no route into the sport. As a working-class cricketer from outside Colombo, Albert was an aberration. He formed a brilliant if unlikely opening partnership with 'Chippy' Gunasekera: the duo pioneered calling 1s and 2s in Sinhala, much to the bemusement of the local Brits and their foreign opponents. Whether they knew it or not, it was a political act of self-identification. And in breaking the stranglehold of the Colombo middle class, Albert became more than a cricketer. For most of the 1920s he was Ceylon's most reliable run-getter, and a powerful symbol challenging the class boundaries which so rigidly segregated the island.

After the 1919 tour, Rockwood travelled to England to try to arrange a visit from the MCC.[95] When he was told the request should come through an official body, he set to work on forming the CCA, which finally came into being on 13 July 1922. Rockwood would serve as its president; Gunasekara made full use of his contacts at Lord's to ensure the body had the blessing of the MCC.

And when it came to planning the whistlestop in 1922, Rockwood resourcefully suggested that Ceylon might be tacked onto the MCC's tour of India in 1926/27. For the first time, the English would be stopping in Ceylon for more than a fleeting visit. A three-day match against the MCC was a mouth-watering prospect for Colombo's cricket lovers – yet there could be no escaping the fact it would be a markedly different ball game to the whistlestops. While those fleeting encounters encouraged happy-go-lucky cricket, it would take dogged determination to survive three days against England. The visitors would have time, and three warm-up matches, to prepare. And they were only coming from India: for once, there would be no wobbly sea legs for Ceylon's cricketers to exploit.

There were promising signs in the lead-up to the match. Rockwood paid for W.E. Lucas to bring a side from Bombay in February 1926[*] – despite their clear strength, they were no match for Ceylon.[96] Francis Brooke made 53 and 77*, and was invited to keep wicket for India against the MCC over New Year 1926. He had another solid outing, scoring 43 and 72; though India battled bravely for three days, they fell to a 4-wicket defeat.

Still, with the English nowhere near full strength, there were flickers of hope when Ceylon's cricketers welcomed the MCC. Sadly, they proved obliging hosts. The English piled on 431-8; M.K. Albert's 51 offered little

---

[*]   Lucas, the sole white, was the team's least accomplished player: all his teammates had featured in the Bombay Quadrangular, while seven – including the great C.K. Nayadu – turned out for India at some stage.

solace as Ceylon crumbled for 105. Though they fared better second time around, the crushing innings defeat went a long way to undoing strong showings in the previous years' whistlestops. Ceylon were a long way off competing with the best over three days' hard cricket.

That said, they were growing. Dr Gunasekara was now installed as captain, bringing a clear professionalism to the role.[97] Whereas de Saram preferred to lead by example, the doctor made sure to tell his men exactly what he expected of them. Ceylon had some great days under his leadership. He, Kelaart and Albert made 40s to steer the islanders to 211 against New Zealand in a whistlestop in October 1927; in response, the Kiwis were rocking at 9-3, though recovered somewhat to reach 197-9 by the close. Two years later, Albert cracked 72 and Kelaart took 3-35 to ensure it was honours even against the MCC.

The whistlestops came thick and fast, and 1930's match was a momentous occasion. None present could have realised the history they were witnessing. On 3 April at Colombo Cricket Club, Donald Bradman played his first game of cricket outside Australia. He treated the crowd to plenty of shots, and had reached 40 when something remarkable happened. With his very first ball in international cricket, debutant Neil Joseph had Bradman hit wicket.* *Don Bradman's Book*, published the same year, gives a glimpse of the game:

> Breakfast over, we went ashore at once to buy a topee each …
> The cricket enclosure was a pleasant surprise; it was an excellent ground, and a big crowd turned out to paint a picture of many colours. The people were most enthusiastic, and they had infinitely more than a nodding acquaintance with the game. Unfortunately there was rain, but there was not the slightest disposition to grumble. Folk just sat in silence to wait for a resumption of the game. The standard of play was appreciably higher than I expected … The local bowlers were quite good, especially one, Ed Kelaart, who did not a little destruction.[98]

---

* Bradman was only out once more in this manner, to the bowling of Lala Amarnath in 1947.

The praise Bradman heaped on Kelaart was well deserved. His off-breaks accounted for six of Australia's batsmen, and before the year was out he would make a real impression on one of the game's more eccentric figures. In December 1930, Rockwood managed to persuade the Maharajkumar of Vizianagram to bring his star-studded side to Ceylon.[99] With cricketers like Jack Hobbs, Herbert Sutcliffe, C.K. Nayadu and a 16-year-old Mushtaq Ali in the mix, Vizzy's mercenaries were a tricky proposition – perhaps stronger than the MCC team that so ruthlessly thrashed Ceylon four years earlier.

They stayed nearly a month, allowing for a comprehensive tour. For the first time a Ceylon Schools XI was assembled – exceeding all expectations by drawing a two-day match against the visitors. D.S. Jayasundera showed himself to be the rarest of gems – a Sri Lankan bowler with real pace – and rapped Sutcliffe hard on the thumb in the first over of the match. Danny Gunasekara's son Barney bowled well too, while Sargo Jayawickrema and F.C. de Saram showed real application with the bat.

De Saram and Gunasekara were rewarded with places in Rockwood's Ceylonese XI, and none could have been disappointed with their performances. Batting at three, de Saram cracked an unbeaten second-innings 77; his schoolmate Gunasekara took the new ball and claimed the prize scalp of Hobbs. Though Ceylon couldn't strike victory in the 'test', Vizzy was impressed by the islanders, and invited Ed Kelaart to come back to India and join his team.

So, four days after the Colombo match ended, Kelaart found himself playing first-class cricket in Madras. It could not have gone much better. He made 101 of his side's first-innings 216 and took 7 across the match to help Vizzy's XI record victory by 199.* Vizzy was so impressed he lobbied the Indian selectors to take Kelaart to England as part of the Test squad – but they opted to forgo a spinner.[100] Still, Kelaart's brief stint in India was a wonderful advert for Ceylonese cricket. He put his island in the shop window: Indians would have been more

---

* Kelaart stayed with the team for two more matches, and returned home averaging 33.75 with the bat and just 13.46 with the ball. Over the same period, Hobbs' runs came at 11.33.

familiar with their neighbours' cricketing abilities than the English, but seeing a Ceylonese perform brilliantly against some of their best struck a more far resonant chord than the occasional murmur drifting across the Palk Strait.

★★★

Just over a year after Kelaart's Indian audition, the island's cricketers got another chance to make an impression on their neighbours. Ceylon's first official tour was quite an event: over forty days, the team would play ten matches in cities flung far and wide.* Only in the last game of the tour – wearied by twenty full days of cricket and thousands of miles of train travel – were they undone. It was a real achievement.

A nasty outbreak of smallpox back home meant that Gunasekara missed much of the trip,** so Ed Kelaart captained both 'tests'.[101] In Lahore, his brother Mervyn stood up bravely to the pace of Nissar, scoring a century that gave Ceylon a 59-run first innings lead. When the game drew to a close, India were 64 short of their target with just 3 wickets in hand. Another session could well have brought a famous victory for the visitors.

Although Gunasekara was partially absent, his fingerprints are all over the tour. He was by this stage 38, but was still an asset on the field. Yet, his biggest contribution came before the party set off. Some of the selectors scoffed when he proposed Sargo Jayawickrema be included in the squad.[102] A lesser man might have yielded, but Gunasekara was insistent: Jayawickrema must travel.

The doubts were understandable. Still just 21, Jayawickrema had never featured for Ceylon. His only century of note had come in 1930, when he struck 128 for Royal against the SSC. None expected him to be one of the team's main run-getters: on tour he batted at seven, eight and eventually as high as six, but never in the top five.

---

*   From Bombay, they travelled north to Rajkot, Karachi and Lahore, before snaking back down India – through Patalia, Delhi, Nagpur and finally to Madras.
★★   As Colombo's Chief Medical Officer, he was expected home.

Yet he announced himself in extraordinary fashion – with scores of 24, 31*, 15*, 31*, 54, 4*, 26, 56, 79, 130, 0, 63, 41 (run out), 0 and 47.* Boosted by the pride of representing his nation – and the challenge of quality bowling – Jayawickrema raised his game beyond measure. He claimed not to have seen the first two balls sent down by Mohammed Nissar, but quickly adjusted to the pace and crashed the next three to the boundary. Channa Gunasekara insists that Nissar eventually refused to bowl to the hulking Jayawickrema.

Without his first-innings hundred in Delhi, Ceylon would have lost the second 'test'. From 75-4, Jayawickrema carried his team to 305; 9 wickets down at the end of the match, they clung on for the narrowest of draws. Across the tour, he shouldered a burden which would have withered many well beyond his years. It's disappointing that it was probably the zenith of career – but perhaps inevitable, given the lack of cricket. Over the next seventeen years, he played just twenty-three first-class matches. Given more chances, he'd have made a great mark on the game.

The same might be said for other members of the squad. Laddie Bakelman, a 30-year-old left-arm spinner said to be able to move the ball both ways, emerged from obscurity to take 41 wickets at 17.05. Bakelman had never played a whistlestop, and though he ended the trip in sensational form, didn't play another first-class match. Likewise, Hilton Poulier picked up 22 wickets on the trip but found opportunities limited going forward. His chances of turning out for Ceylon effectively ended after he lost his middle finger in a work accident in 1937.[103]

Questions may linger over the fairness and competence of the selectors, but the island's stocks were deeper than at any time in the past. Kelaart bowled brilliantly in India, and eleven batsmen scored a 50 during the trip. Ceylon itself seemed to be finally moving forward too.[104] Up-Country cricket had traditionally been a whites-only affair, but in 1930 A.L. Gibson agreed to be patron of the newly formed Dimbula Ceylonese Cricket Club. Two years later, the first match for

---

* Jayawickrema ended the tour with an average of 54.64, his medium pace bringing 21 wickets too.

'professionals' was organised.* They usually worked in sarong but wore trousers for the game – although they did take the field barefoot. In earlier times, the thought of them playing on the hallowed turf they looked after would have been met with derision. But thinking was beginning to shift. Cricket was opening up.

No single event encapsulated this progress more than M.K. Albert captaining Ceylon against Central Provinces during the India tour. Though just for a single game – Gunasekara was back home and Kelaart rested – it was still a triumph for egalitarianism. The men who came before him – and most of those who followed for the next half-century – were handpicked from Royal or S. Thomas'. Sathasivam, from Wesley, was an exception – but still very much entrenched in the local elite. Sri Lanka would have to wait until 1999 and Sanath Jayasuriya for another captain so far removed from the establishment.

Albert's life has always fascinated me. As a poor boy from the sticks, he was an oddity in a Ceylon team filled with Colombo gentlemen. Yet he thrived. It is a shame we don't know more about him. Like so many Sri Lankan cricketers, Albert deserves a full biography – but now, very few remember his name. I managed to find a man who knew his son, M.K. Quintus, apparently an apothecary at Colombo's General Hospital. He'd been to school at St Peter's and owned a house down Federica Road; if still alive, he'd be fast approaching 90. I couldn't track Quintus down, but was pleased to learn he existed, and to know that Albert's story had a happy ending. His career must be the first case of genuine social advancement being achieved through cricket in Sri Lanka.

The MCC's arrival in February 1934 should have been cause for cele-bration, but proved a visit marred by acrimony – most of which centred around the behaviour and attitude of England's captain, Douglas Jardine. Though he had shocked the world with the brutality of his bodyline tactics, Jardine did not arrive in Colombo on a charm offensive. Seeds of discontent had sprouted in India, where England played seventy-three days of cricket in the space of four months. Much to Jardine's displeasure, at least two of his men turned to the bottle.[105]

---

* The tag is misleading: they were in reality groundboys, whose daily lives consisted of preparing wickets and bowling in the nets.

Equally, he and tour manager E.W.C. Ricketts were riled by their correspondence with the CCA, who showed none of the deference the MCC had come to expect. The new president, E.M. Karunaratne, wanted a match played at Galle: if the English declined, they would have to leave a week early. Though the CCA asked the visitors not to bring their own scorer – nor their 'servants' or assistant manager – the MCC's request to make use of S.P. Foenander was denied. The whole exchange gave Ricketts the impression 'that the CCA was not particularly concerned with the comfort of the MCC team'.

The stance flies in the face of traditional Sri Lankan hospitality – and seems to reflect the anti-colonial feelings brewing at the time. Despite two previous visits to the island, Jardine had little sense that mindsets were shifting. If Terrence N. de Zylva's account of events can be believed, he was 'corrected' by the governor when he chastised a porter on arrival.[106] Jardine's sole response was that, 'A nigger must be treated as a nigger.'

According to de Zylva, there was more ugly racism before the tour was out. He claims that when the English were poured drinks, Jardine warned them to empty their glasses or they'd be served the dregs in fresh vessels. As a prominent nationalist, it may have been in de Zylva's interest to denigrate Jardine and tarnish England's reputation. But that alone should not condemn him as a liar. After all, there were other incidents too, which paint the England captain in a less than flattering light.

On the opening day of the 'test' against Ceylon, he flew into a rage when students in the one-rupee stand taunted Charles Marriott's action.[107] Jardine insisted on play being paused, and was jeered and heckled; at the interval, he made sure the ringleaders were removed. The police ejected eight, seemingly reluctantly as all had their rupees refunded.* Far fewer turned up to watch the second day's play. They did not miss much. Ceylon capitulated, and lost by 10 wickets: only Neil Joseph, who made a gutsy 78, and William Brindley – a senior police officer who took 5, and was probably Jardine's liaison with the local force – enjoyed any success.

---

* Jardine cabled back to Lord's with a pithy explanation. 'Simply, these fools had allowed lunatics from the asylum to witness proceedings.'

When it came to the drive to Galle, the car carrying Jardine broke down 10 miles short of the ground.[108] Furious, he refused lifts. Some reckon it was to prove a point; others have claimed he took exception to the colour of the drivers' skin. Whatever the truth, his stubbornness left the cricket-starved southern crowd with a pitiful excuse for a game. With well over two hours lost, the hosts had to declare after 29 overs so they could at least watch the English bat. Hedley Verity and Charlie Barnett were involved in a car crash on the way back to Colombo the next day, and ruled out of the following match. It can't have done much to lift already fractious spirits.

That said, they were heading back for what should have been the crown jewel of the tour: a game against a combined India–Ceylon XI at the CCC. The island's fans had never witnessed such a contest – an enthralling battle that pitted Asia's best against the colonial men who had brought and taught them the game. Sadly, it turned into a squalid affair that lit a fire under the Ceylonese and took another hammer blow to the English reputation on the island.

The match drew a mammoth crowd. Five of the Indians who'd recently taken on the MCC in a Test at Chepauk* made their way to Colombo – joining Brindley, Schokman, Jayawickrema, Joseph, Kelaart and Churchill Gunasekara to form what looked a formidable side. The ageing Gunasekara played as a captain in the truest sense: he batted at eleven and no longer saw fit for himself to bowl. Jardine decided not to play at all. If he was ill or injured it has never been mentioned** – you have to wonder if he omitted himself out of spite.

The game suffered little from his absence, with the cricket enthralling from the off. Amar Singh, who had bowled beautifully in Madras, was at it again. He took 6 for 62 as the visitors were blown away for 155. But the MCC were not about to roll over. With the chips down, 'Nobby' Clark turned to his old bodyline tactic. He was fast, and for the Asian batsmen of the era – unused to ducking or swaying – it was a fearsome onslaught. Vernon Schokman had his jaw broken and collapsed on his stumps.[109]

---

*   They were Dilawar Hussain, C.S. Nayadu, Amar Singh, Lala Amarnath and Syed Wazir Ali.

**   He returned for the final two games of the tour.

A local paper claimed that when an appeal for bad light was rejected, stand-in captain Bryan Valentine turned to his quicks. The bowlers are said to have appealed excessively and cursed when the umpires turned them down. Faced with the prospect of defeat, the English cast aside any shred of decorum. In true Jardine style, the spirit of cricket was replaced by a ruthless will to win.

Things descended further during the MCC's second innings. With the English in trouble at 71-9, Clark wandered down the wicket and began to attack the turf with boot and bat. Some say he dug a hole in the pitch; all on the field were stunned into silence. Eventually one of the umpires gathered his senses, and asked Clark what exactly he was doing.

At the changeover, Valentine told Clark to go and apologise. He refused, so a shamed Marriott and the stand-in captain went in his place. You might ask where Jardine was in all this. (Quite possibly, he was off shooting. According to his diary, he notched a dozen shoots during his months away.[110] His glory kills were meticulously recorded: an elephant, plus 'personally, one lion, one panther, one tiger, one bear, three crocodiles and numerous stags. PS plus countless snakes and innumerable smaller creatures.')

Despite the divot, the Asian batsmen showed few signs of distress. Set 130 to win, they reached 81 for 2 by nightfall – but the final day's play did not go according to plan. India and Ceylon lost their remaining 8 wickets for 40 runs. Agonisingly, they were 9 runs short of a landmark victory.

We'll never know what impact Clark's roadworks had on the result. Ricketts claimed that 'the roller had eliminated any trace of what may have occurred', and though he didn't see the incident, insisted that the divot wasn't in line with the wickets. Most in the crowd disagreed, claiming it was on a good length and in line with leg stump – a near perfect spot for a left-armer bowling over the wicket to exploit.*[111]

The response in Colombo was vitriolic. Column inches were crammed with bitter criticisms of the MCC. In one paper, Jardine was

---

* Of the last 8 wickets, 7 fell to Clark or Verity, England's two left-armers; 3 of Clark's 4 were bowled or lbw. Though he often went around the wicket, there's reason to suspect he bowled over on that fateful morning.

branded a 'dirty dog'.[112] He showed no contrition, declining an invitation to a CCA dinner. Unlike previous visits, few turned up to the harbour to bid the MCC farewell. Shortly before setting off, Jardine wrote to club secretary William Findlay:

> I am very glad in every way that we are cutting short our stay in Colombo [in order to play a charity match in Bombay] – the CCA has just fallen into the hands of the Ceylonese and the treatment generally accorded to us has annoyed the Europeans very much. A great contrast to India![113]

He wrote again from Delhi ten days later, on paper letter-headed 'Taj Mahal Hotel Bombay':

> I'm sorry Ceylon was so hostile – Page Croft was pretty right about them! The Clark incident was unfortunate, but they were not friendly before that and too much was made of the incident, inevitable in these days.

The reference to Henry Page Croft – the Conservative politician and staunch opponent of Indian self-governance – reveals plenty about Jardine. Narrow-minded and outworn, with his turned-up nose and harlequin cap, he failed to grasp that the world was changing. He belonged to a different age; it seems he simply couldn't understand the Ceylonese desire to be treated as equals.

The local reaction spoke volumes. S.S. Perera wrote that Jardine's 'snobbism and arrogance' led to him being 'cut out' of the island's history.[114] A letter printed in one of the papers reflected, 'Ceylon has paid very dearly to learn the game of cricket, because perhaps she blindly believed in British sportsmanship and fairplay [sic] at least on the field. The delusion, thanks to the MCC visit, has been once and for all dispelled.' One of the Australian dailies drew a similar conclusion: 'Jardine is one of the worst ambassadors … He is also England's champion snob. He has aroused more antagonism to Britain than anyone else in recent years, and all over a game of cricket, where it should be simple to play the game in the finest spirit of camaraderie.'[115]

Clearly, Jardine's actions became bigger than cricket. As captain of the MCC, he represented England, the British Empire and the colonial yoke which had suppressed the Ceylonese spirit for over a century. His boorish behaviour was another reminder to the people that the British ideals they'd had shoved down their throats were little more than a sham. He became a symbol of a corrupt colonial system.

Time and again during the first half of the twentieth century, the British had been laid bare. By now, their notions of justice and gentlemanly spirit – the very things the elite schools and cricket sought to spread – were folding in on themselves. Having been subjugated for so long, a nation was stirring against its oppressors. They would not have to wait long to be free. By the end of the next decade, Sri Lanka would have its independence.

THE EXTRAORDINARY DERRICK DE SARAM

As soon as D.L.'s nephew – F.C. de Saram, Derrick to all of Ceylon – was done with school, he boarded a boat for England.[116] He had a place at Oxford to study law, but it was in the Parks that he really set himself apart. At first, the move looked like it would hold his cricket back: as John Woodcock wrote in *Wisden* half a century later, 'Strange things happened in the world of cricket at Oxford in the '30s, few stranger than that de Saram, one of the finest bats at either University between the wars, should have only one trial in The Park in his first two years.'

That trial was the Freshmen's Match in April 1932; thereafter, de Saram played no cricket at Oxford for two full years. As far as we know, he did not pick up a bat again for sixteen months. What Woodcock implies, we can outright state: de Saram's race counted against him. Headstrong, he turned to tennis, easily earning his Blue. But he was stung when he was overlooked for the club captaincy. The willow came calling.

This is one of those moments on which a life can turn. Had there been no prejudice at Oxford – and de Saram been made tennis captain as he thought he deserved – he might not have found time for cricket at all. It's perfectly possible to imagine a world where his bat stayed at the back of a cupboard gathering dust.

But the Oxford Tennis Club's loss would benefit de Saram, Ceylon and cricket no end. In August 1933, he grabbed the chance to play for Hertfordshire in the Minor Counties. Though almost entirely unaccustomed to English conditions, there was none of the rustiness you might expect. Scores of 5, 101, 38, 106*, 40 (run out), 92, 61 and 36 reflected wonderfully on de Saram and Ceylon.* Oxford could look away no longer.

Debuting for the university the following May, he hammered a quality Gloucestershire attack for 176 in three hours. Perhaps because of his personality, there is a tendency to misremember de Saram's batting as dour and stodgy. No doubt, he was correct – but was equally capable of taking an attack apart at will. His maiden first-class knock in England included twenty 4s and a 6. Apparently, he wasn't the slightest bit daunted by the bowling he came up against.

In fact, while de Saram was catching his breath at the non-striker's end, the standing umpire noticed him chuckling. 'What's so funny?' he asked. Derrick turned to him, and simply said, 'If my friend was here, he would have these bowlers for breakfast.' He was talking about Sargo Jayawickrema. A natural leader, de Saram was not one to dish out compliments lightly. His reverence for Jayawickrema shows that he did not think himself leaps and bounds ahead of the batsmen back home. In fact, he once told an interviewer 'I'm just an ordinary batsman compared to my club mate.'[117]

Given the same opportunities, Jayawickrema might have achieved as much as de Saram. He was probably a more natural and inventive batsman – strong through the covers, equally capable of commanding pulls and open-faced glides through the slips.[118] De Saram had shots through the off side, but it was his on-side play that really stood out. He would pull with an almost straight bat, and drove exquisitely between mid-on and mid-wicket. Still, his greatest strength lay between his ears. He was dogged: as Bertie Wijesinha put it, 'de Saram had to be beaten. He would not yield willingly.'

---

* De Saram finished the season with an average of 68.42; a young Len Hutton averaged 69.90, but was far less prolific. His 699 runs came in 15 trips to the crease, compared to de Saram's 479 in 8. De Saram, a reluctant bowler, also took 4 wickets at 20.5 with his seamers.

The Australians stopped at Oxford in mid-May. For most, the game was over in four sessions – though the students' second innings was futile, de Saram still managed to exhilarate. He made 128 of the university's 216, including four sweetly struck 6s. Clarrie Grimmet was too good for the rest, but had to be withdrawn after de Saram's assault. Down Under, papers cooed over 'one of the best innings yet seen against the Australians', lauding de Saram for 'realising there is nothing to lose by taking risks'.[119] He only grew 'reckless' as he ran out of partners; if he had support from the other end, how long could he have gone on batting?

With a double hundred against Leevson-Gower's XI before the season was out, de Saram ended the year with a first-class average of 50.86 – becoming Ceylon's first Blue in the process.* His feats did not go unnoticed: that winter, he was invited to tour the West Indies with the MCC.[120] It might have been the start of a long Test career, but he told the men at Lord's he'd rather play for his own country. Perhaps he didn't realise Sri Lanka were still nearly half a century away from Test status.

Over the course of his last three years at Oxford, de Saram's run-scoring was relentless. He achieved more than any Sri Lankan cricketer before him – but while his feats are well remembered, it is fair to say he is revered rather than loved. He certainly doesn't inspire the same hysteric exultation as his great rival Sathasivam.

Maybe de Saram was born too late. He would have been adored had his heyday come earlier, but in an age when Ceylonese spirit started to soar, he represented the old, fusty English way. He was light-skinned, with a loud voice, an English accent and a haughty manner. In an unfortunate echo of Jardine, he often took the field in his worn harlequin cap. Some mistook his manner as contrived, not realising he spent much of his childhood away from Sri Lanka. Many still cling to the gripe that he perpetuated the Royal–Thomian bias – a salient feature of Sri Lankan cricket long past independence.

---

* In the season-ending list, he sits above players the calibre of Suttcliffe, Hendren and Hutton. Including the two games de Saram played against Vizzy's XI as an 18-year-old, his average through fourteen first-class matches was 51.13. Hutton, the best comparison due to the fact he played his first fourteen games in England in 1934, averaged 30.31 in this period. For Wally Hammond, the figure was 18.78. Statistics make a strong case for de Saram sitting pretty alongside the elite players of his day.

When I first moved to Colombo, I made an effort to get in touch with Derrick's son Dijen. He seemed intrigued that I was teaching at his alma mater and writing about the early days of Lankan cricket – and invited me into the family's legal firm for a meeting. Tucked away in the heart of Cinnamon Gardens, there's more than a touch of old Ceylon about the offices of D.L. and F. de Saram. It certainly seemed the sort of place Derrick would have been comfortable.

Dijen reminded me of the pictures I had seen of his father – he had the same kind, knowing eyes, and that unique Burgher complexion which seems to sit somewhere between Europe and Asia. Straight away I could tell he was proud of his father, who still casts an eye over the office from the vantage of several framed photographs. And with good reason. Dijen was in no doubt that it was de Saram's relentless drive that allowed him to achieve so much. Between sport, the army and the family firm, he had little time for hobbies – and would chastise his son for idling on the bus instead of using the spare hour to polish his Latin. Yet he wasn't a pushy parent. He never put pressure on Dijen's cricket – in fact when they were on opposite sides of the Big Match in 1967, he deviously exploited his son's tendency to pull at loose deliveries and had him caught in a trap at mid-wicket.[*]

There were aspects of de Saram's character which I thought might be awkward to discuss with his son, but Dijen was forthright.[121] 'My father had a fairly caustic sense of humour,' he explained. No doubt, there was a little cruelty in his comedy. He once needlessly declared with his good friend C.I. Gunasekara stranded on 99; and supposedly teased spinner Anura Polonowita about bringing a sarong to the SSC. But, most who knew him maintain he meant no harm; that, from his position of privilege, he had little sense that his words could wound. And that as much as he dished it out, he was perfectly happy being the butt of the joke.

Equally, he wasn't necessarily the snob he is often made out to be. Despite his noted Royal–Thomian bias, players have told me they

---

[*]   Derrick was coaching Royal, Dijen playing for S. Thomas'. It seems no coincidence that de Saram only switched to coaching S. Thomas' in 1969 – once Dijen had left school. This image of de Saram as unassuming parent doesn't chime with his regular perception as Sri Lankan cricket's autocrat.

remember seeing him in the changing room washing a young Bandula Warnapura's feet. Though he was controversial, I have met so many cricketers who praise his influence and very few with a bad word to say about him. Left to languish in jail in 1962, he spent time learning Sinhala, studying Buddhism and making household products. After his release, he and his wife were shopping, when she picked up a broom that she needed. De Saram inspected it closely. 'This is not perfect,' he said with a wry smile. 'I've done better'.

Other aspects of his character are often overlooked too. De Saram was brave: when Trincomalee was attacked in 1942, he was in the thick of things, commanding an air defence battery. During the 1958 riots, he single-handedly held off a baying mob despite only having rubber bullets in his gun. He worked tirelessly to better the SSC, and would often pay fees for those who couldn't afford them. He captained the club till he was almost 50, and wasn't too proud to carry the drinks as twelfth man or turn out for the 3rd XI once his best days were long gone.[122]

In later life, de Saram was a spirited administrator – while coaching at Royal, and then S. Thomas' right up to the year of his death. He became like a father to the boys, dropping them home in his mini-moke. And he started the tradition of moving the team into the hostel for a pre-Big Match camp. They would spend the week cooking up plans and building team spirit: Dijen remembers his father packing his bag, which always contained a chessboard and the complete works of Shakespeare.

Above all, Derrick de Saram was a man who truly loved cricket. He left England late in 1936: at 24, he should have been entering his prime. But he would play just three more first-class matches before the outbreak of war ruptured his career. Proper cricket did not come back to Colombo until March 1945. Many might have thought about hanging up bat and gloves for good. But not de Saram. He would soldier on for many years to come.

THE SELECTORS BLUNDER

Six weeks after Jardine was jeered out of Colombo, the Australians arrived for a whistlestop. Bradman sat out, but the rest still smashed

284 in 63 overs. Despite the assault, it was a day to remember – for the first time, the game could be followed across the island thanks to F.L. Goonewardene's radio commentary.[123] Cricket was creeping into the modern age.

That said, the match marked the sudden end of an era. With Gunasekara withdrawing due to a family bereavement, Ed Kelaart should have been an automatic choice as captain.[124] But the selectors plucked W.T. Brindley's name out of the hat. Kelaart was snubbed in a decision that had nothing to do with cricket and everything with race and status. Brindley, the high-ranking English police officer, was seen as a more suitable leader than Kelaart, a Burgher and a clerk in a tea firm.

So prejudice still reared its ugly head. For Kelaart, it was too much to bear. He withdrew from the match and never played for Ceylon again. Although 33, he had much more to give:* his abrupt departure leaves a very bitter taste. Stalwarts seemed to be vanishing all at once. Now nearly 40, M.K. Albert left the side; Dr Gunasekara stepped aside too. When John Rockwood died in 1935, there could be no denying that the landscape of Sri Lankan cricket had dramatically shifted.

Moving forward, 'Chippy' Gunasekera** would captain Ceylon. He was a sensible choice: since 1928, Chippy had combined his cricketing and legal careers with the coaching post at Royal – so had seen many of his charges come through the ranks.*** His first test as captain was a three-day game against the Indian University Occasionals. With four Test players in the team, they were trickier opposition than they sounded – and it proved to be a chastening start to life in charge for Chippy. Phiroze Palia cracked a century, and Dr Gunasekara – co-opted

---

*   He played twice for Vizzy in India during 1935, averaging 56 with the bat and 26.33 with the ball.

**   Chippy Gunasekera does not belong to the famous Gunasekara clan, who we encounter so often across these pages.

***   Much like de Saram, Gunasekera continued coaching until shortly before his death in 1975. David Heyn remembers him as the head coach at the NCC in the late 1960s and early 1970s, trying in vain to convert him into a more orthodox left-hander. A remarkable number of players would have come under Gunasekera's tutelage, from de Saram and Jayawickrema right the way through to the likes of Heyn, Ranjit Fernando and Michael Tissera.

to play against Ceylon – added 73*. Forced to follow on, Ceylon narrowly escaped with a draw.

Things soon got worse for Chippy.[125] He was strangely excluded from the squad for a whistlestop a fortnight later – despite the fact his 41* had helped stave off defeat against the Indian University Occasionals. Charles Allen, once captain of Haileybury and fresh off the boat from Britain, was picked in his place. Thankfully Allen was unavailable – so the selectors could at least redress the wrong inflicted on Gunasekera.

Still, the incident exposes some pretty muddled thinking. Two openers who had never played for Ceylon, G.S. Chalk and E.W. Buultjens, were selected. Vernon Shockman, in contention for the captaincy in the previous match, was dropped too. Jaysundera was in the twelve but could not make the team; Poulier was excluded altogether – leaving the side without a recognised seamer. It was a shambles, one that didn't escape the attention of the public. A poem published in one of the papers included the following lines:

> It'll do if we have two match winners
> (Say a couple of lads from school)
> Let the rest be just crocks or beginners,
> It's our duty to play the fool.
> …
> Great Heaven shed tears when it heard of the team,
> So it rained and it poured and thundered.
> The selectors stayed at home and had strawberries and cream,
> Did they care, if we knew they had blundered?

Clearly the public felt nepotism was impinging upon selection. The selectors' motives remain somewhat inscrutable, but there is no arguing that they had made two major missteps in the space of a year. In Kelaart and Gunasekera, they wronged two seniors who should have been valued – showing not just pro-British bias, but genuine incompetence.

Visits from abroad crowded the calendar in 1935: before October was out, the Australians arrived for an unofficial 'test' to kick off their tour of India. Ceylon handed out three more debuts: now in a state of flux, they struggled badly, losing by an innings and 127. In all likelihood, they could have batted a third time and not reached Australia's score. Amidst Jayasundera and Poulier's continued exclusion, the bowling lacked bite. The past eighteen months had certainly been testing. After improving for so long, cricket on the island suddenly hit a steepling downturn. The loss of key players, selectional malaise and a lack of clear thinking was undeniably damaging the side.

Though the batsmen found form when the MCC stopped in October 1936, an attack composed purely of part-timers carried little threat. At least when Julien Cahn's XI came to Colombo six months later, George Pereira emerged as a promising off-spinner. Cahn's team was full of quality players – on paper they looked a decent match for one of the weaker Test nations – but over the course of two weeks, Ceylon's cricketers more than held their own. Pereira took 8 as they dominated the first two-day match; de Saram cracked a breezy 102 to ensure a share of the spoils in the second. Only in the three-day 'test' did the wheels come off: dismissed for 207 on the opening day, Ceylon were always chasing the game.

Strikingly, the players chose Douglas Wright, a tea planter from Middlesex, as their captain for the match. He made 0 and 3, and didn't bowl; his selection ahead of Jayawickrema or de Saram shows how tight the colonial shackles held. Thankfully, Wright was the last European to captain Ceylon. The British presence was already waning, and white flight was further expedited by the outbreak of war, independence and the language laws of the 1950s. So Ceylon had control of their cricket from 1940. It could have been worse; the West Indies had to wade through twenty more years of subjection before they achieved the same.

While the bowling remained an issue, Ceylon's cricket was moving in the right direction again. Against Cahn's XI, the team only failed to post 300 once in four attempts. Almost in acknowledgment, de Saram and Jayawickrema were invited to play for The Rest against The Muslims in the semi-finals of the Bombay Pentangular. They shone in defeat: both made 50s in the first innings, before de Saram struck a classic 122* in the second. None of his teammates managed 30; come finals day, the same Muslim attack blew out the Europeans for 64 and 81. The duo's success was yet another reminder of the talent brewing in Ceylon.

At home, the game took a major stride forward in 1938 with the establishment of Ceylon's first club tournament.[126] From January to

June, the island's best teams would compete for the Daily News Trophy.*
Games had to last seven hours, so cricket now spilled over from Saturday
afternoon into Sunday. Surprisingly, Kalutara Town – one of the three
clubs from outside Colombo – lifted the trophy, largely thanks to the
bowling of Frank Porritt and H. Scharenguivel.

Curiously, neither was picked when Australia stopped over in March
1938 – in their absence, Ceylon's attack was hammered for 367 in
69 overs. Throughout the 1930s, the team's biggest weakness was an
inability to take wickets – a problem clearly aggravated by a consistent
failure to pick the best bowlers.

Most confounding is the case of D.S. Jayasundera, the fastest bowler on
the island, who roughed up Herbert Sutcliffe while still a schoolboy.[127]
Overlooked for the India tour in 1932/33, he was ignored by his country completely from October 1935 to December 1940. Though these
were his prime years, he was left waiting at the gates: only brought back
into the fold when Dr Gunasekara organised his own tour to Malaya.
Jayasundera was undoubtedly the star of the trip. His 22 wickets cost less
than 6 runs apiece, and guided the Ceylonese to victory in all four of
their matches.

If selectors doubted the quality of the opposition, there was further
proof of Jayasundera's prowess at home. In the second edition of the
Daily News, he claimed 70 wickets at 5.68 as the SSC sauntered to the
title. His prolonged omission remains inexplicable. It's hard to dismiss
the suspicion that his career would have followed a different course had
he been schooled at Royal or S. Thomas'. When he finally returned to
the Ceylon side for a tour of India in 1940/41, he led the attack with
17 wickets at 18.12.

Even without de Saram – mobilised in the war effort – the trip was
a huge success. Jayasundera took 6 wickets to help bring victory over
a strong Madras side; in the drawn first 'test', captain Jayawickrema's
138 guided Ceylon to a big first-innings lead. They led on first innings
against Baroda too; only in the second 'test' against India at Bombay were

---

* Sri Lanka's main first-class competition has held various names, including the
P. Sara Trophy, the Robert Senanayake Trophy and the Lakspray Trophy. Since the
1998/99 season, it has been styled as the Premier Trophy.

they outdone. Having clearly impressed, Jayasundera was invited to hang around until after Christmas and play for the Madras Governor's XI. But his recall came too late – there was no more cricket for Ceylon until 1945, and by then his best bowling days were behind him.

THE RISE AND FALL OF SATHA

There aren't many left who remember watching Satha bat, but all who can get a glint in their eye when they recall the magic he brought to cricket. The stories, unknown to most of the world, are well-worn legends for a generation of Sri Lankans. How he would strut to the middle in silk shirt and cravat, cap perched on his head, bat tucked in the crook of his arm.[128] How he would look to mid-on and hit through the covers, or walk across his stumps and whip the ball through square leg. How he would cut so late that the keeper swore the ball was in his gloves, or otherwise turn around and ask him to pick the shot. If Derrick de Saram was born too late, Mahadevan 'Satha' Sathasivam came too early. He would have been right at home in the moneyed t20 leagues of the twenty-first century.

Cricket was in his blood. His father Tiru laid concrete in the back garden so Satha could practise, and promised the boy a rupee for every run he scored.[129] From the age of 10, he was making a nuisance of himself at the Tamil Union, badgering bowlers to send him down a few balls after practice. 'Whenever the Tamil Union played a match I was at the ground an hour before play,' he recalled. 'I would wait there hoping a member of the team would be absent or get late. Invariably I got a chance of fielding and was a permanent substitute.'

He might well have been picked to play against the MCC in 1936, but lesser players of a similar age were chosen ahead of him. Still, opportunities came his way. Turning out for the Raja of Ramnad's XI in Tamil Nadu, Sathasivam struck centuries against South India and Pudukottai S.C. Wherever he went, runs flowed easily from his bat. Back home, he scored 285 at an average of 57 in the first year of the Daily News Trophy; the following season, he was the tournament's best batsman in the tournament by a distance, notching 569 runs at 43.77.

So, on cricketing grounds alone, Sathasivam's exclusion from Ceylon's tour to India in 1940/41 was unfathomable.* In all likelihood, his reputation counted against him. Cricketers of the day were expected to hold down jobs, but Satha was loath to work. When he was at his nadir thirteen years later, standing trial in court, the judge told ogling onlookers:

> He seems to have unfortunately – perhaps because he was a spoilt child, a particularly idle fellow – had very few short and rare periods of employment … he seems to have joined a band of people belonging to the 'idle rich', whose philosophy was well described by a sage who said that 'work is the curse of the drinking class'.[130]

There's more than a little truth to the allegation that Satha treated merry-making as a full-time role.[131] He credited his fleet footwork at the crease to nights ballroom dancing; often he'd drink until dawn, catch a few winks in his car and change into his flannels. After he retired, he was asked about the rumour that de Saram once brought him a gin and tonic at the water break. 'Derrick, always,' he blithely replied. 'Even Sargo [Jayawickrema] and Sathi [Coomaraswamy] right down the line. They knew that the occasional shot brought out the cavalier within me.'

Some would say drinking spilled over to the detriment of his cricket. He preferred to amble between the wickets and showed little interest in fielding. There are rumours of drunken dropped catches, of chases to the boundary left to his neighbours. But he was serious about batting. His strokeplay may have struck as effortless artistry, but it was rooted on a sound technique developed over hours of practice. Each morning he would stand in front of the mirror, bat in hand, and watch himself go through the motions.**

Four hundreds at home in 1943, including an unbeaten double, saw him invited to India with Jayawickrema to play for The Rest in

---

*   Especially so, since five couldn't make the trip. This meant nineteen men were picked ahead of Satha.

**   Sathasivam is often perceived as aloof or uncaring, yet his daughter Yajna told me that the conversation at home rarely strayed beyond cricket. By contrast, the 'obsessive' Derrick de Saram did not discuss the sport much at home.

the 1944 Bombay Pentangular.[132] This was Sathasivam's first-class debut, and the Muslims were fearsome opponents. Yet by the day's end he had 101 to his name, having put on 171 with Vijay Hazare. Though he batted within himself, striking just seven boundaries, there was a clear contrast between the stylish Satha and his stodgier partner. Both fell the following morning without adding a run.*

When international cricket returned to Colombo in 1945, Sathasivam could no longer be passed over. Ceylon's side had a real look of strength about it – but after a washed out first day, Vinoo Mankad spun webs around the hosts on a devilish drying track. No one could get to grips with the tacky wicket: India faltered for 179; second time around, Ceylon were sliding to defeat at 75-5.[133] But Sathasivam was playing a different game. He put on 69 with Pat McCarthy and 88 with Russell Heyn: only in the final over of the match did he allow himself a loose shot, holing out for 111. Across the match, no one else made 50.

Satha had saved the game for Ceylon, and shown an expectant crowd what he was capable of. With the island starved of quality cricket during the war years, 15,000 flooded into the newly built Oval for the final day's play. They might have got the wrong impression of Sathasivam: for once, he ran like the wind – his century including 66 singles.

Unusually, he failed twice when an Australian Services XI visited just before Christmas. Keith Miller made a powerful hundred, but Ceylon's batting broke down badly – it was a let-down to slip to an innings defeat against a side recently beaten in India. Only Heyn – so impressive in the field against the Indians – made a mark, his 2 for 42 and battling, second-innings fifty offering a slender ray of sunshine.

Since the MCC opted against playing a whistlestop en route to Australia in 1946, Ceylon once again faced a cricketing chasm. There were no international visits in 1946 or 1947: clearly, life outside the ICC meant constantly struggling for scraps. At least they could rely on India

---

* Sathasivam and Jayawickrema stuck around in India for the next couple of months. On the first day of 1945, Satha struck 80 in under an hour against C.K. Nayadu's XII. Jayawickrema made an equally explosive 123. A few days later, both made runs in a game overshadowed by Dennis Compton's run-a-minute century. Remarkably, they then caught the train all the way from Calcutta to Colombo to play on opposite sides of the Tamil Union-SSC clash. Both made centuries.

for support. The BCCI endorsed Ceylon's first official approach to the ICC: though it went no further, the help was encouraging.[134]

Nor did it stop there. The SSC had a good time of things in India over New Year 1946* – and the success of the tour paved the way for a CCA XI to head to Madras for a three-day game against South India in February 1947. For Ceylon, it was a momentous occasion. Though runs were shared around nicely, Sathasivam stole the show with a sublime 215 – a new record at Chepauk and, according to many, the finest innings ever played at the ground. Bertie Wijesinha, who made his first-class debut in the match, wrote 'Sathasivam wafted his magic blade and carved out a work of art'.[135] Sport is so often described as performance, but rarely has it been so apt. Satha played for the crowd, elevating batsmanship beyond the mere making of runs.

He'd arrived in Madras without a bat, so had to rush into town to pick up a 'Lindsay Hassett Autograph' before the match. On his way to the middle, a fan offered a bottle of scotch in exchange for a hundred. Satha simply nodded. The scotch was duly handed over when he returned to the pavilion at nightfall; its donor now offered a week's trip to Bombay if Satha could complete his double the following day. 'Taken,' he announced, as he swaggered into the night, bottle in hand.

Ben Navaratne woke early the next morning. Perturbed to find his roommate's bed empty, his shock grew when Sathasivam crashed through the door.[136] Navaratne shoved him under the shower, got him dressed and made sure he was downstairs in time for breakfast. Satha did the rest, adding 81 with minimal fuss. Neither of South India's totals matched his score: the hosts lost by an innings, with Robert de Kretser picking up 9 wickets.

Still, what endures from that game is Satha's brilliant batting. Years later, Rajan Bala asked Ghulam Ahmed who was the best batsman he'd bowled at.[137] 'You would not have heard about him,' replied the former Indian captain. 'M. Sathasivam of Ceylon. He did not allow me to land

---

* The players were entertained at the Maharaja of Baroda's summer palace; on the field, de Saram cracked two majestic centuries. In Bombay, Jayasundera rose from his sickbed just so he could bowl at Vijay Merchant – and had him trapped in front for 1 in the very first over of the match.

the ball most of the time during his double century against South India. The attack comprised other than me, Gopalan, Rangachari and Ram Singh* all of international standard, and Satha with wonderful footwork treated every bowler with disdain. Pace and spin came alike to him and he put all of us under terrific pressure. I have never seen a better innings all my life to this day, and it is unlikely I shall.' Even the finest cricketers spoke lovingly of Satha's batting. And he'd have more chances to impress. It just so happened that the following March, Satha would collide head-on with one of cricket's greatest teams. Bradman's Invincibles were coming to Colombo.

★★★

In 1948, Colombo was awash with talk of the deeds of another Don. It is easy to lose sight of the close connection between cricket and the country's political elite, but scratch beneath the surface and the reminders are everywhere – none clearer than Don Stephen Senanayake's appointment as president of the SSC in 1931.[138]

Senanayake was Sri Lanka's most influential politician during the first half of the twentieth century – but by no means the only powerful man with a serious interest in cricket. As Minister of Agriculture, he worked closely with Pakiasothy Saravanamuttu, the tea and rubber commissioner – probably the first in Sri Lanka to make a point of offering cricketers jobs.**[139] A proud clubman, 'Sara' had long felt the Tamil Union needed a proper home, and managed to persuade Senanayake to gift some marshland in Wanathamulla.

Saravanamuttu's project became more than a new home for his club; this was a stadium to carry the hopes of an aspiring nation. Unwilling to settle for anything but the best, he had bluegrass imported from Australia and produced a track unlike anything Colombo had seen.

---

*   Ram Singh did not actually play in the match – but still, the attack was clearly no straightforward proposition.

**   Saravanamuttu made a point of sending scouts to schools matches, and supposedly found Cadiravel Dharmalingham a role in his department after hearing about his double hat-trick for Trinity.

Channa Gunasekara claimed it the 'greenest, fastest and bounciest' in the world; Keith Miller supposedly wished he could roll it up and take it around in his pocket.[140] The Colombo Oval – renamed in P. Sara's honour in 1977 – was *the ground* in Sri Lanka for the next four decades. It hosted athletic meets, greyhound racing and even a Duke Ellington concert.[141] Yet were it not for the passion and drive of powerful men, Sri Lanka's cricket might have stayed in makeshift parks a good while longer.

Named leader of the house in 1942, Senanayake threw his full weight behind the Allied effort, realising wartime cooperation offered the shortest path towards political sovereignty.[142] Once war was over, he drafted a constitution, travelled to London and pressed the Colonial Office for full dominion status. And when India was granted independence in February 1947, Ceylon could no longer be denied. The country's first elections were held in August and September, D.S. was installed as the first Prime Minister – and on 4 February 1948, the Dominion of Ceylon gained independence from Britain.

So, the arrival of Australia's much-lauded cricketers a month later was bound to be a celebratory affair. Though Bill Brown, Sid Barnes, Keith Miller and Neil Harvey were stars in their own right, it was the prospect of one last glimpse of the great Don Bradman that set hearts fluttering across Colombo.* First though, the hosts had to pick a team.

Just over a year had passed since Satha's heroics in Madras, but tellingly he'd already fallen foul of the selectors. His happy-go-lucky nature never chimed well with those in power, and he now risked losing his place in the side altogether. So he approached the trial match with real restraint – notching a century over the course of three hours, before adding another in forty-five minutes.[143] The shackles were shrugged off, replaced by the usual tricks. Behind the stumps, Navaratne was asked to pick the shots: one ended up where the National Archives stand today, well over 100 yards from the middle of the CCC.

---

* Ceylon was certainly blessed. Bradman's baggy green was already hung up by the time he set foot in India, nor did crowds in the West Indies, South Africa or even neighbouring New Zealand get to watch him bat. Remarkably, England and Australia aside, Bradman only played cricket in Ceylon, the USA and Canada.

The selectors couldn't omit a man who'd just cracked a double-hundred – and since Jayawickrema decided he'd had enough of leading the side, the captaincy was up for grabs too. De Saram was the natural successor, but when the clubs came to vote Sathasivam secured nine of sixteen nominations.[*144] He would stand next to Bradman as captain of Ceylon.

For Uncle Percy, Sri Lanka's most enduring fan, it was his first experience of live cricket. 'My two brothers took me by train from Galle,' he told me seventy years later. 'We were on the grassy bank, *the Gandhi Stand*. All the poor people go there. The ticket was 25 cents. That was just after we got independence and there were flags here, there and everywhere. I think my brothers gave me a small flag to hold.'

In the wake of independence, Bradman and co. found a far more raucous city than the one they encountered eighteen years prior. Some 25,000 turned up for the match; traffic in Colombo was so bad police cursed Bradman's name.[145] So many squeezed into the Oval that it became a struggle to keep them outside the boundary ropes.[146] Cadjan roofs collapsed under the weight of backsides; with the ground packed to the rafters, many took to the trees. It was a proper day out, a chance for Colombo folk to see the greatest batter alive and celebrate their independence all at once.

Though The Invincibles would soon make history going thirty-one first-class games unbeaten in England, on a cloudy Colombo morning they were humbled by Ceylon's part-timers. Coomaraswamy bagged 3 wickets; Russell Heyn had Bradman caught at cover for a scratchy 20. During his hour at the crease, an 'eerie silence' enveloped the ground. 'This was a ghost of the Bradman we had read about,' complained schoolboy Neville Jayaweera. 'A legend drained of all credibility'. Only at the innings break did a mitigating factor come to light.

The Oval is unique in employing female groundskeepers:[**] since its inception, local Tamil ladies have tended the turf, drawing on an almost

---

[*] T.B. Marambe felt that de Saram 'clearly had not sufficient contact with the common man'; certainly, this was a telling snub.

[**] The first, Mariamma, was in fact the wife of the club's ground secretary Rasiah – since she was much younger than her husband, she would often perform duties on his behalf.

mystical connection to the land to produce first-rate pitches. But the club only had one frayed tape measure, and it seems the groundskeeper's assistant got himself in a muddle. The pitch was 20, not 22 yards. After the lunchtime discovery, Australia bowled from behind the crease and no more was said on the matter.* Sadly, rain stopped Ceylon building a head of steam: they could only bat 19.2 overs, and the match ended with Sathasivam and de Saram unbeaten on 6 and 7 respectively.

With the captaincy snub still raw, de Saram may have been reluctant to spend too much time in the middle with Sathasivam.[147] He declined an invitation to captain the CCA against Holkar two weeks later, and managed to persuade his clubmates at the SSC to boycott the tour altogether.** He must have done some arm-twisting: C.I. Gunasekara had only made his debut against Australia, and was yet to bowl or receive a ball in international cricket. Wijesinha was young in his career too – for these two especially, rejecting the call from their country must have stung. The CCA took a dim view of the decision. In June, the 'SSC six' were suspended for a year. Thankfully, by October the two sides reached an agreement and the ban was rescinded.

With controversy raging, the Holkar series faded into the background. A weakened CCA XI managed two draws before capitulating in the final game. Only Makin Salih passed 100; Satha – seemingly affected by questions over his captaincy – endured a run of lean scores. At least the boycott opened the door to players who otherwise would have languished on the sidelines: 17-year-old Gamini Goonesena was handed a first-class debut, offering a glimpse of his future potential with controlled and potent leg-spin.

Two months after Holkar headed home, The Board of Control for Cricket in Ceylon (BCCC) was formed to work alongside the CCA.[148]

---

* Many in Sri Lanka question this version of events, stating that a cricketer of Bradman's experience would surely have noticed the pitch was 2 yards short while he was at the crease. There have been reports that de Saram and Jayawickrema noticed the mistake before the match, but that authorities – eager to avoid embarrassment – dismissed their concerns. There are also those theorists who reckon a short pitch was put forth as an explanation, to comfort a crowd visibly upset by Bradman's sketchy innings.
** That meant Ceylon would have to do without Jayawickrema, Navaratne, Lucien de Zoysa, Bertie Wijesinha and C.I. Gunasekara.

P. Sara assumed leadership of the new body – the thinking seems to have been that a newly independent nation needed a new cricket body to represent it. But this grand gesture brought about little change. Wijesinha wrote:

> In 1948 Ceylon attained self-determination, but the cricket and its administration failed to keep pace with this political advance. Things went on much as usual … Dr Gunasekara … continued to voice his displeasure at the stagnant state of cricket. He was crying out for more and wider experience for our cricketers ultimately to aspire to inter-national recognition. [149]

Gunasekara realised that the casual nature of Ceylon's club game was holding its cricketers back. The island was not short of talent, but it lacked the infrastructure to bring out the best of players. A handful of matches, played over a day or a day and a half, was scant preparation for three-day cricket against Test-playing nations. But with most of the players working five-and-a-half-day weeks, there was little scope for expansion.

Equally, there were concerns over whether the club scene was provid-ing competitive enough cricket. Since the Premier Trophy began, the SSC had been champions eight times in eleven attempts. By 1947, they were strong enough to field two equal sides and still win the competi-tion. The 1950 final pitted SSC A vs SSC B, not exactly a rivalry for all time.

Properly prepared or not, there were international challenges aplenty for Ceylon's cricketers. The West Indies arrived for the first time in February 1949: thankfully the SSC rebels were back in the mix. Without their presence, the tour could have descended into humiliation. The 'tests' got off to the worst possible start. Ceylon toiled for 118 overs on the first day without a shred of joy: were it not for a run–out and a sharp stumping by Ben Navaratne, they might not have taken a wicket at all. At nightfall the West Indies declared on 462-2.

Though duly forced to follow on, the hosts carried hope into the final day thanks to the batting of new boys Mahes Rodrigo and C.I. Gunasekara. A flurry of wickets stopped them dead in their tracks, but Rodrigo* impressed all in attendance – carrying his bat and frustrating the West Indian bowlers for close to seven hours. Still short of his 21st birthday, he showed rock-solid technique and a true opener's temperament: each of his 135 runs was well earned.

Gunasekara was a different kind of player: his first instinct to smite rather than survive. When he arrived at the crease in the second 'test', de Saram greeted him with a stern warning: 'No funny stuff.'[150] But he could not control his impulses. A juicy full toss was served up, the captain's words forgotten. 'Sorry,' Gunasekara cried out, with the ball hurtling high in the air. Thankfully, it went sailing over the rope. He cracked and fizzed en route to 71, helping Ceylon hang on for a share of the spoils. They couldn't stop the West Indies gorging on runs, but the series at least spoke of an increasingly reliable batting unit.

But when Pakistan arrived in Colombo less than a month later, the islanders faltered badly. Blown away by high-quality seam bowling in the first 'test', even when Gunasekara and de Saram stood up with centuries in the second, they lost by 10 wickets. These were damaging defeats – especially since Pakistan were also on the outside of the ICC. By winning, they positioned themselves as next in line, and were awarded Tests status twenty-nine years ahead of Sri Lanka.

Ceylon's threadbare attack was put to the sword again when a star-studded Commonwealth XI arrived in February 1950.[151] The visiting seamers looked a more menacing prospect – and the challenge facing Ceylon grew overnight as rain lashed down on the uncovered Oval wicket. Given its state, 153 was a good effort: it would have been far fewer were it not for Sathasivam's transcendent 96. On the cusp of his century, he tried to heave Fred Freer to the boundary and was bowled – but his failure to reach three figures made little difference.

The innings made a mark on all who saw it. Stanley Jayasinghe – second top scorer that day with 17 – said all his runs came off the edge, while all Satha's were out of the middle of the bat. Channa Gunasekara, who skipped school to watch the game, claimed it was the best innings

---

* Sadly Rodrigo, also a useful wicketkeeper and Sargo Jayawickrema's nephew, was lost to rugby in 1952. He was just 25. Though he went on to captain Ceylon in his second sport, you feel he might have achieved a good deal more in whites.

he ever saw. There's no reason to doubt him: the great Frank Worrell was blown away too, and said if he had to pick a World XI, the first name on the team sheet would be M. Sathasivam of Ceylon.[152]

Though Satha was nearing 35, few realised it would be the last truly great turn he would play for his country. Ceylon headed to Pakistan in March 1950 – their first trip overseas in three years – but Sathasivam's father passed just before the tour began, and he came back to Colombo after two games.[153] Though his first three innings yielded just 13 runs, he reminded everyone of his class with his last knock for his country. On a duplicitous, drying track, Satha handled Fazal Mahmood and Khan Mohammad with aplomb, making 56 of the team's 151.

That innings aside, the less said about the tour the better. Ceylon crumbled to an innings defeat in the first 'test', and were embarrassingly thrashed by Karachi and Sindh: with de Saram and Gunasekara missing, the batting looked as frail as the bowling. The sole glimmers of hope were the leg-spin of Lucien de Zoysa and the batting of the schoolboy Jayasinghe. He followed an excellent 125 down the order with 80 against the 'test' team – looking remarkably assured for one so young.

Still, these scraps were slim consolation for Ceylon's dejected fans. In the past couple of years, they had seen their side hammered time and again. It was draining; for S.P. Foenander, almost too much to bear. He wrote in the *Ceylon Observer*, 'Let us give up this idea of Test cricket. Let us have a sense of proportion and not imagine our geese are swans … I hope it will be a long time before we send a Ceylon team to play Test matches.'[154] Ceylon were down in the dumps – the likes of Foenander thought it couldn't get much worse. Little did they know what lay around the corner.

★★★

9 October 1951 was a day like any other.[155] The blistering sun bore down on Colombo; like countless others in the city, a laundryman named Austin cursed the heat as he went about his business. As ever, he was glad for the sea breeze that washed over him as he turned onto St Alban's Place.

Nothing seemed out of the ordinary as he approached 'Jayamangalam'. The Sathasivams' two young daughters frolicked on the lawn; when Austin found no one in the house, he asked the girls where their parents were. One of them mumbled something about the garage; he decided to have a look.

There, he stood stunned and silent, as still as if his feet were stuck to the cool concrete floor. Mrs Sathasivam lay flat on her back, facing up towards the sky. Light crept in and streaked across her. There were little black smudges on the soles of her feet, a heavy wooden mortar resting upon her bruised and bloody neck. Her eyes were still open, but life had drained from her body.

Her husband had left the house at 10:30 am. He took a cab to the Galle Face Hotel, where he drank a glass of orange squash and several whisky sodas. He had planned to spend the evening with friends at the Tamil Union, but by then was confined to a cell, accused of murdering his wife. The news spread like wildfire. All across town, aunties and uncles stood in their gardens and whispered, 'Have you heard about Satha?' Most had him guilty as charged.

★★★

Since their wedding in 1940, the Sathasivams' marriage had not been without bumps.[156] Most hoped a wife would tame Satha, but he carried on with the life of a playboy cricketer. By 1949, he and Anandan had four daughters. But Satha was restless. Around 1950, he began seeing a British lady called Yvonne Stevenson. These were unhappy months for his wife, and when Satha arrived back from London in September 1950, he was told he wasn't welcome at home. With cash in short supply, he decided to stay with a friend called Haniffa.

Though Satha was served a summons relating to the divorce on 8 October, he still visited his wife. That very evening, he headed straight from the Tamil Union to Jayamangalam. The couple shared their marriage bed: the next afternoon, Anandan was found murdered. It isn't hard to figure why the finger was pointed at Satha, whose extramarital affairs and financial difficulties only heightened suspicions. He certainly had motive. The problem was that the facts did not add up.

Those who knew Sathasivam all agree he wasn't capable of murder. I was nervous about meeting his daughter Yajna – unsure how to dance around the horror that must have upended her childhood. But Yajna was open and unreserved. She told me that despite Satha's lifestyle, he was a spiritual man – and gentle, too. Once, he was driving when a butterfly flew into the windscreen and was killed. Distraught, Satha insisted on stopping the car and laying it to rest on the side of the road.

I didn't need Yajna's testimony to absolve her father. The more I read, the more I was convinced of Satha's innocence. He and his wife weren't alone on the morning of their murder. After Anandan was killed, William – a house servant who had been in the family's employ for eleven days – wandered out onto St Alban's Place, his pockets stuffed full of stolen jewellery.[157]

Having flogged the gems, he got a haircut, ditched his clothes and hot-footed it home to Tangalle, over 100 miles away. Police found William after a week-long manhunt: his body was covered in scratches and he admitted murdering Mrs Sathasivam. But when he was dragged in front of IGP Richard Aluvihare, he claimed he had been fed the story by police, promised Rs. 1,000 and future employment if he admitted to the crime.

Though 1950s Ceylon was a society obsessed by class – a world where the word of a servant-boy would usually get little credence – Aluvihare was willing to take William's testimony as gospel.[158] His new story – that Satha coerced him into killing his wife in the couple's bedroom – was discredited by the forensics expert who conducted the post-mortem. Nonetheless, William was given a full pardon. He would become the prosecution's star witness.

When he got to the stand, his testimony was a mess, littered with contradictions and full of unexplainables.[159] At one point, he claimed he could not remember whether a detective had offered him a Rs. 1,000 bribe, but was certain that Sathasivam had given him Rs. 3. It was farcical – and Satha's defence wasn't solely reliant on holes in William's story.

A partner at the legal firm handling Mrs Sathasivam's divorce case said he received a call from her between 10:30 am and 12:00 pm on the day of her death.[160] The operator at 'Quickshaws' also said Mrs Sathasivam ordered a cab for her husband; the driver swore she was standing at the door when he picked Satha up at around 10:30 am. The local forensics expert put the time of death between 10:45 am and 11:30 am – world-renowned pathologist Sydney Smith agreed, but thought it could have been even closer to midday.[161] Both were firm that the crime must have occurred after Satha left the house.

The jury took just sixty-four minutes to return a verdict of 'Not guilty'.[162] Sathasivam was free – but twenty months behind bars had tarnished his reputation and robbed him of his last good years of cricket. The public, on the whole, still thought he was guilty; even today, Sri Lankans question Satha's innocence. Yet, the fact remains he probably should have never stood trial.

The thrust of the case was troubling: in his closing statement, Justice Gratien spoke of clues 'tucked away and withheld and not investigated', of policemen 'in a hurry ... on one day, or sleepy ... the next'.[163] He even had to confront accusations that 'the Police behaved in a most suspicious manner in their investigations'.[164] The force seem to have worked backwards from the position of Satha's guilt, making every effort to ignore evidence that could lead them down a different path. The likelihood is that we'll never know why – but there is reason to suspect the investigation was not just lazy, but Machiavellian. All the evidence points to Satha's innocence, but back-alley gossip goes a long way. It is sad that such a special cricketer should be blighted by such a stain.

Still, prison did little to dull his spirit. The summer of his release, he cracked 153 against the Indian Gymkhana in London – and was back at the Tamil Union too, giving opposition bowlers and captains fresh nightmares.[165] De Saram always had plans, whether it was gifting a few boundary balls to lull him into a comfort zone or inviting him to the SSC on the eve of a match for a whisky or seven.[166] Getting him drunk normally backfired – Satha could go all night and still bat beautifully, while more than a few fielders were left nursing sore heads.

Still, the tactic caught on. On the eve of a crunch match with the Tamil Union, the Colts ran drinking relays with Satha.[167] Next morning, their fearsome round-arm quick Tita Nathanielsz decided he'd fire some short stuff into the treacherous matting wicket. Satha flicked bouncer after bouncer off his nose. When he got a chance, he appealed to his friend: 'Tita look, we drank last night – don't do this to me. I can't see the ball.' But the barrage continued until Nathanielsz realised it was futile. With Satha hitting 6 after 6, he had no choice but to give up.

During another crunch game, when the Colts were dismissed mid-Saturday afternoon, Satha told Nathanielsz that he would not be batting that evening.[168] He had promised to meet Yvonne in Bandarawela, high in the up-country hills, a slow and snaking five-hour drive from Colombo. But when play resumed the following day, Satha was nowhere to be seen. The nightwatchman sent to bat in his place didn't hang around long – and the Tamil Union dressing room began to twitch over the whereabouts of their star batsman. Suddenly he was in the car park – drenched in sweat, into his pads in a flash and ready to bat. He had left Bandarawela at 5 am, raced to the Oval for bacon and eggs, a shower and a half-hour in the nets. He scored yet another sparkling century, taking 54 off Tita's firebolts.

Whether you take these accounts as gospel or reckon them tall tales, their enduring existence strikes on something. For all the great players that had come before him, Sathasivam was probably Sri Lanka's first homegrown cricketing hero. Crowds thronged to marvel at his exquisite batting, its theatre embellished by his princely appearance and apparent insouciance. Nor was it just reverent schoolboys or ardent fans who came to watch: women, often notably absent from Sri Lankan cricket grounds, flocked to the Oval when Satha's name was on the teamsheet.[169] Like Richards or Imran or Warne, his force of character allowed him to transcend cricket. He was that rare sportsman who becomes bigger than the game he plays.

Sathasivam took to work more seriously after jail, and when his insurance firm closed their Colombo office, moved to Singapore with his family.[170] He captained Singapore and then Malaya, and had a stint in London during the 1960s too. He would head to 'cricket weeks' all over England, scoring runs and selling insurance with equal success. His daughter remembers him nipping to the pub with Basil D'Oliveira. She paints a picture of a loving father who only wanted to talk about cricket – and was protective enough to ban his daughters from wearing lipstick. 'He knew what men were like,' she joked, before letting out a laugh flecked with warmth and sadness.

He was never short of drinking partners. When Gary Sobers passed through Colombo in 1961, he and Sathasivam went on a crawl from the Grand Oriental Hotel to the Colts.[171] Satha teased Sobers that he would flay him all over the park, at one point Sobers told the gathered crowd, 'My boss [Worrell] says that he is the greatest batsman he has seen.' In later years, Sargo Jayawickrema visited most evenings. The pair would sit in Satha's garden and drink arrack and thambili, reminiscing over times they'd shared inside the boundary rope. He went back and coached at Wesley, too – when he saw a shot he didn't like, he would take the bat and show how it should be played. Once, he lost himself in his art and carried on until sunset. Enchanted by the masterclass, none of his charges said a word.

On 9 July 1977, while having lunch at the Wadiya in Wellawatte, Sathasivam had a heart attack and died. Just 61, he'd shown few signs of illness. Days earlier, Channa Gunasekara saw him stroll into the Ceylonese Rugby & Football Club, buy a pack of cigarettes and depart with a grin and a wave. Those who were with him in hospital say he left the world with a smile too.

Satha's career started too late and ended too early – but it provided some magical moments. And for the lucky few who saw him on the field, no lurid gossip can outshine what burns bright in their mind's eye: when he came to the crease, when the bar emptied, seats filled and an entire ground held its breath.

THE EMPIRE STRIKES BACK

Another Commonwealth XI arrived early in 1951 – with Worrell smashing 285 on the first day at the Oval, Ceylon were up against it from the start. Having wilted in a similar position the year before, the island readied itself for another innings defeat. But the batsmen dug in, avoided the follow-on and somehow survived, 9 down at the end of the match.

Ceylon was now a regular stop for sides touring India, and in February 1952 a game was organised between the MCC and a Commonwealth XI captained by Derrick de Saram. This was a novel experience for the Colombo crowd: a chance to see some of their own line up alongside stars of the game like Keith Miller, Polly Umrigar and Fazal Mahmood. What's more, the match offered a real chance for a rare victory over the English.

With de Saram all the way down at number eight, the Commonwealth's batting had a fearsome look. They were already going strong when

C.I. Gunasekara strolled to the crease. Miller was well set on 30; batting in tandem, these two brutal hitters spurred each other on.[172] Gunasekara overtook Miller in the 90s, and went to his century with a steepling 6 over mid-off. Miller responded in kind: from that day forward, he referred to Gunasekara as 'the master batsman'.

Conroy Ievers Gunasekara had proved a true find for Ceylon. Though yet to fully show his talent as a fastish leg-spin bowler, through six first-class matches he averaged 47 with the bat, his runs coming at breakneck speed. Here was a player capable of dominating any attack, and changing the course of a match in a session. Perhaps Gunasekara took to international cricket so confidently because he had to wait for his opportunity.[173] Like Sathasivam, he was in his late twenties before Ceylon came calling – having made it through Law College and war, he likely possessed a composure lacking in many younger men.

But whereas Satha had always been a mercurial talent, Gunasekara seems to have been a genuine late bloomer. Despite hailing from Ceylon's most famous cricketing clan, he struggled to find a place in the Army side during the war. As late as 1946, he was languishing in the SSC 3rd XI.* In his early years, some dismissed him as a slogger. It shows how wrong people can be. Gunasekara blossomed into a truly world-class all-rounder. After seeing him up close in 1962, David Sheppard declared he would 'have surely played Test cricket' were he born in another country.[174]

Few cricketers are so fondly remembered. When I met Shanti Gunasekara – the wife of C.I.'s cousin Channa – she told me that soon after marrying, she began to learn all about cricket. Her tutor was the great Dr C.H. Gunasekara; the main exhibit, his nephew Conroy Ievers. 'My God, they used to come and watch from outside – and he'd hit the ball all over the place,' she remembered with glee. 'Bowlers just couldn't bowl to him. Actually he was the first master blaster, and I watched in amazement. I was learning the game too, so it was just magic. He said that even if he just had a stick from the coconut tree he could still bat.'

---

* In all likelihood, he would never have gotten a chance to compete at a higher level had the club not fielded two teams in 1947/48.

Once, I was sitting with some wise old sages at the NCC, when one asked who was the hardest hitter Sri Lanka had produced. Names like Duleep Mendis, Sanath Jayasuriya, Thisara Perera were raised and discarded; as Uncle Percy confidently cast his vote for Ievers Gunasekara, there was a murmur of approval from all. Stories are prone to exaggeration, but a man who used to play against Gunasekara claimed if you stood at mid-off, he'd sting your hands with a forward defence.

When it came time for the Commonwealth to bowl, Miller noticed Ben Navaratne standing close up to the stumps.[175] He suggested he move back, but Navaratne was adamant. 'I know where to stand.' Though a classy and experienced keeper, Navaratne had little practice dealing with bowlers of such pace. The first two balls sailed over his head to the boundary rope; the 20 byes he allowed were more than any English batsman could muster. On the lightning Oval track, they couldn't get to grips with Miller or Mahmood. The Commonwealth completed victory by an innings and 259; England had been consummately smashed in Ceylon.

The result augured well for Ceylon's own 'test' against the MCC, but hope turned to ash on the first morning – the hosts bulldozed for 58 by Ridgway and Statham. Their own bowlers couldn't make similar inroads, and the English never looked like having to bat again. Navaratne, bandaged up after being clattered by a bouncer in the first innings, battled for a brave unbeaten 34. But this was another disappointment, a reminder of the inconsistencies that plagued Ceylonese batting. With Sathasivam out of the picture, and de Saram and Jayawickrema either side of 40, others needed to step up and score runs on a regular basis.

Ultimately, the island needed more cricket. By now, the waning British presence had seen the Europeans–Ceylonese 'test' dropped; as a minnow on the outside of the ICC, the country was left to rely on the goodwill of cricket's big boys. The calendar swung wildly between famine and feast: in 1950, Ceylon had visits from the Commonwealth XI and the MCC, plus their own tour of Pakistan. But, between the end of February 1951 and the start of February 1953, the national side played just one game.

It was naive to expect Ceylon to compete on the international stage without regular cricket, so the inauguration of the Gopalan Trophy in

February 1953 was a real boon. For the next three decades, these matches against Madras/Tamil Nadu kept the island's cricket going. During the 1950s and '60s, they were a barometer of sorts; from 1971, when away Gopalan matches became mini-tours of South India, the Trophy gave the team real stability. 'The conditions were harsh,' David Heyn told me when we spoke about those trips. 'Matting wickets, terrible outfields: you had to adapt. It hardened us. And it built team spirit as well.' Of the twenty-three games played between 1953 and 1983, Ceylon/Sri Lanka won sixteen.[*]

Derrick de Saram led the inaugural party on a ten-day trip to Madras.[176] Remarkably, C.I. Gunasekara, Sathi Coomaraswamy, Lucien de Zoysa and Mahes Rodrigo couldn't tour because their companies wanted them in Colombo for the Mercantile final. There was less glamour in playing for Ceylon back then. Channa Gunasekara remembers sharing a room with the keepers, H.I.K. Fernando and Jayalingam. Jayalingam couldn't sleep with the fan on, so the players agreed to go without every other night. He certainly seems like the kind of eccentric character who could only exist in the amateur game. Gunasekara later wrote:

> I considered Jayalingam to be the best stumper in Ceylon for the first 30 minutes or so. Thereafter his concentration began to sag and he would start singing popular songs on the current hit parade, doing a few intricate dance steps behind the stumps and engaging the batsman in friendly conversation. Though he had a bad stammer he had a good voice and sang regularly over Radio Ceylon, strangely without the trace of a stammer. He also played the piano and drums but was blind as a bat, wearing thick rimmed glasses. Paradoxically, he had a quick eye and his 'takes' and stumpings on the leg side had to be seen to be believed. Then he would turn around and ask the stupefied batsman where he was going.[177]

During a warm-up match against Madras University, Jayalingam botched a run-out in slapstick fashion. With both batsmen stranded at the non-striker's end, he received the ball from fine leg and threw to the bowler.

---

[*]   Drawn games were decided on first innings.

Naturally, the reprieved Kripal Singh went on to score a century. Later, when de Saram asked him what had happened, he struggled to get his words out. 'Someone said throw to the bowler, so I threw to the bowler.' Unamused, de Saram invited him to spend the rest of the tour shopping at Moore Market. That was the end of his cricket for Ceylon.

★★★

1953 was a year of change. With Learie Constantine hired on a three-month contract, Ceylon were boosted by the arrival of a superstar coach. Constantine went along on the first Gopalan tour, and even turned out for Madras Cricket Club. He knew sterner tests lay ahead; a month after the team touched ground back in Colombo, Australia arrived for a whistlestop.

Since they docked late, at 9:30 am on the morning of the match, some feared the game might not go ahead at all.[178] But the Australians were at the crease by 11 am, bludgeoning their way to 209-8 in 39 overs. Ceylon responded superbly, with Channa Gunasekara ending the day 66*. He had to cop one on the head from Miller, but would have happily accepted the bump. His innings was a new Ceylonese record against Australia; as he walked back to the pavilion Miller chucked him one of the bails. And after the Ashes, Jack Fingleton wrote, 'while on tour in England, I never came across a better opening batsman than Gunasekara who was top class.'

There was much to be buoyed about. Constantine returned to England, so impressed with Ceylon that he offered to arrange a tour to cricket's heartland in the summer of 1954.[179] He would take care of accommodation; all the team had to cover was their flights. Yet remarkably, this golden offer came to be spurned. Some have laid blame at Derrick de Saram's door, claiming he told Constantine Ceylon weren't ready for the challenge of cricket in England. Others say the board decided that Ceylon must beat Pakistani Combined Services (PCS) in the four-day 'test' over New Year for the trip to be approved.

Though the touring Pakistanis were no straightforward proposition, Ceylon dominated the game's first two days. De Saram struck a splendid

148, C.I. Gunasekara bagged 8 for 69 – but the hosts could not maintain standards for four full days. Rolled for 142 second time around, PCS knocked off 208 for the loss of 6 wickets. Two were run-outs: Ceylon failed to put enough runs on the board, and equally should have made a better fist of defending what they had.

That said, the team's struggles in three- and four-day cricket are understandable. For the most part, they played over a day and a half. Longer games remained rare, frugally sprinkled across the calendar. What's more, cricket was still very much secondary to work, even for the island's best players. In other countries, amateur cricketers held jobs that were largely ceremonial, but in Ceylon you were expected to earn your keep.

When Bertie Wijesinha made his international debut in 1949, he was still a teacher at S. Thomas'.[180] 'I had to get permission from the warden to go for the match,' he told Alston Mahedevan. 'He stipulated that I could go, but that I had to teach at least two periods before. I did teach the two, and then I had to walk to the main road to catch a bus to Bambalapitiya, and then from Bambalapitiya I had to get another bus to Borella – and there was the skipper, waiting for me at the gate, wondering why I was late.'

Channa Gunasekara had to work after the first day's play against Pakistan Combined Services – and spent the night 'jumping over tea chests, taking count of gunny bags and accounting for unblended teas'.[181] Even when his cousin C.I. was captain of Ceylon, he faced barbs at work when he had to take time off for international cricket. These conditions simply weren't suitable for producing players who could take on the best in the world. There was no shortage of talent, but the island's cricketers lacked the proper infrastructure to harness their skills.

A tour to England offered an opportunity to change that. Constantine promised that Ceylon's style of play, combined with the curiosity factor, would draw big crowds. Perform well and there could be talk of Test status. Even if they were humiliated it would cost them nothing – they would simply continue to languish outside the ICC. Either way, it would have been an invaluable learning experience. Squandering such an opportunity was crazy; sadly, it wasn't the last time the cricket community bungled a proposed tour of England.

Though the authorities' failings have been drawn into focus in recent years, Sri Lanka's cricket administration has long been ridden with problems. Strangely, Vernon Prins was named captain for the Pakistanis' visit over New Year – while there was logic to the decision,* blooding a captain in such a high-stakes match seemed ill-advised. What's more, when Madras visited for the Gopalan Trophy a month later, de Saram was restored as captain. This sort of circuitous flip-flapping was nothing new – but was still destabilising. More than anything, it reflected a lack of foresight – and gave the sense yet again, that there was no clear plan.

With de Saram's international retirement in September 1954, the path was clear for Prins to reassume the captaincy. He led a hugely success-ful trip to Madras in October 1955, but Ceylon found themselves in a strange situation – in many ways in no-man's-land. They were by now, on the whole, too strong for state sides, but inevitably floundered against Test-playing opposition. Elevation to the ICC would have benefited the team no end. They might not have been competitive straight away, but they would have learned on the job.

At least they had the support of their neighbours. The Gopalan Trophy was cancelled in 1956; in place of Madras, the full Indian side travelled to Ceylon. It was not a happy fortnight.[182] Colombo's Novembers are often blighted by bad weather: after a patchy first day, the teams arrived back at the Oval to find rain lashing down on the wicket. The umpires declared the ground unfit for play; Prins and Polly Umrigar agreed, so the players headed home.

But the crowd, stirred by the prospect of a first Indian visit in a decade, stuck around. By afternoon, the clouds had cleared – and the ground bathed in brilliant sunshine. The people demanded play. The Indian team, gathered at their hotel, were easy to recall. But their hosts were now scattered across Colombo. Things got ugly fast. Stones were thrown, and the pavilion doors hastily locked. Board President S. Sara made his way into the stands to try to quell the crowds, but rumours swirled that

---

* De Saram was nearing 42; Prins – who had led NCC to domestic glory in 1953 – was twelve years his junior. This way the new captain would be able to learn the ropes with the wily old veteran standing beside him.

he told the angry mob that Prins had refused to play. Whatever went on, the blame landed squarely at the captain's door. He was booed by sections of the ground the following day: wounded by the whole incident and lacking the support of his board, he stepped down as captain and made himself unavailable for the following 'test'.

'Vernon was a lovely man,' Ranjit Fernando told me. 'For someone like him – a gentleman to the fingertips – it must have caused huge upset. And to be accused of irresponsibility, for such a responsible man.' All I've spoken to agree that Prins was a man of decorum: the type of cricketer who never challenged an umpire's decision and only wanted the best for those he played with. It was unfair and wrong that he had to shoulder the brunt of the crowd's anger.

Nor was that the end of the drama. Before the series began, the board flew leg-spinner Gamini Goonesena in from England to strengthen the side; now, he was parachuted into the captaincy.[183] None questioned Goonesena's ability, but he was just 24. When he had last played for Ceylon, he was little more than a boy. Some of the players were entirely unfamiliar to him; plus, in C.I. Gunasekara, Bertie Wijesinha and Sathi Coomaraswamy, there were three well-worn members of the side, each at least a decade Goonesena's senior, who had been entirely overlooked. It was the kind of decision bound to cause contention in an already unhappy camp. It showed a lack of respect, and a lack of faith in the players who had been toiling away at home

Yet, Goonesena was head and shoulders above his teammates in the 'test' – without his first-innings contributions with bat and ball, Ceylon would have been beaten inside the three days. But if local fans thought the performance signalled the start of a new era with Goonesena at the helm, they were sorely mistaken. He would play just once more for Ceylon. Nor was he alone in deciding to ply his trade overseas. In the post-war period, some of the island's best cricketers realised they could play more cricket at a better standard – and in some cases, be paid too – if they left the land of their fathers.

Laddie Outschoorn was first to go. Sent to Britain for rehabilitation after the Second World War, cricket quickly came back into his life.[184] By 1947, he had qualified for Worcestershire: when the Invincibles came to town the following year, he purposely dropped Bradman at slip so he could spend longer watching him bat.* Bradman went on to make 107 – much to the delight of the eccentric Outschoorn, if not the rest of his teammates. At least Laddie managed 54 of his own in the second innings.

Equally adept opening the batting or coming in first drop, Outschoorn was one of the more unorthodox players in the English game. At times he rocked back and cut full-length deliveries, at others he charged down the track and swatted balls away on the full.[185] His idiosyncrasies didn't stop him scoring runs: 1953 aside, he struck 1,000 in the Championship each year from 1948 to 1955. Only in the second half of the 1950s, as he approached and passed his 40th birthday, did his powers start to wane.

For over a decade, Outschoorn was an outstanding ambassador for the island's cricket, and a source of delight for those at home. Boys in Colombo and Kandy would rush downstairs on Sunday mornings and fumble through the sports pages, hoping to see a score against Outschoorn's name. But this local hero hardly played any cricket in Ceylon, and never turned out for the national side. Though misfortune brought him to Britain, he felt no compulsion to head home until his playing days were over. In many ways, it's little surprise.

Goonesena followed Outschoorn to England in 1950, to train as an RAF pilot at Cranwell in Lincolnshire.[186] Before long, he was on the radar of neighbouring county Nottinghamshire. Though he struggled in his first season, Goonesena quickly developed into a real handful – clearly benefitting from the presence of Bruce Dooland, the Australian leggie who made his Championship debut alongside him. As Goonesena recalled:

> I might get slammed by a batsman for a couple of fours and a six in one over – and feel a little dispirited! I'd glance across at Bruce and receive a wide grin. Then, before my next over, he'd stroll over to me

---

*   His claim that the drop was deliberate holds some credence, since there were few finer slip fielders in all of England. Only four men, all wicketkeepers, took more catches than him in the 1949 Championship season. No other (gloveless) fieldsman came close to his tally of 52.

and say, 'Let him take another four, Gami – but you'll get him with your next ball.' And very briefly he'd proceed to tell me how I should get him. Nearly always it worked.[187]

Under Dooland's watchful eye, Goonesena took real strides. Wickets came at 21.48 during his second season at Notts – and as his bowling average continued to tumble, he began proving himself a handy lower-order batsman. Meanwhile, he enrolled at Cambridge to study law, and was rushed into the University XI for the 1954 season. Straight away he showed his class, bagging 8 wickets, including that of Outschoorn, as Cambridge beat Worcestershire. The following year, he took 10 wickets and scored 118 against Warwickshire, and received a second invitation to turn out for the Gentlemen against the Players at Lord's. He responded with second-innings figures of 6 for 83, including a ripper that had Ken Barrington stumped for a duck.

A gentleman of the East, with friends in high places, Goonesena caught the imagination of the British public more than any Sri Lankan cricketer that came before him, and more than held his own when invited by E.W. Swanton to join a tour of the West Indies in 1956. In the sole 'test', he had Conrad Hunte, Allan Rae, Rohan Kanhai and Clyde Walcott in the first innings, while making 24 (run out) and 45. And 1957 would prove his crowning year. Named captain of Cambridge ahead of Ted Dexter, he led from the front – striking twin 50s against the West Indies, taking 12 against Gloucestershire, and dominating the university match with a monstrous 211 – backed up by 4 for 40 to ensure Oxford were beaten by an innings.* For the second time in three summers, Goonesena had done the 1,000-run, 100-wicket double in first-class cricket.

For much of the 1950s, England's spin-bowling berths were jealously guarded by Tony Lock and Jim Laker – but in 1959, the former was remodelling his action while the latter had retired. Their places went to John Mortimore and Tommy Greenhough; on paper at least, Goonesena

---

* With P.I. Pieris bowling first change, the Cambridge side in 1957 had a particularly Sri Lankan feel. Pieris claimed that, as a captain, Goonesena 'stood head and shoulders above his contemporaries in England at a time when there were captains in the counties such as Peter May, Colin Cowdrey and Cyril Washbrook to name a few'.

stacks up well against both. Indeed, he holds his own when placed alongside the great county leg-spinners of the day – Dooland, Doug Wright, Eric Hollies and Roly Jenkins – who all played Test cricket. Goonesena was unlucky not to do so.

Instead he moved to Canberra in 1960, and served as a more than capable understudy for Richie Benaud at New South Wales, taking wickets whenever he was called upon. In the autumn of his career, he would often turn out alongside the likes of Jim Laker, Fred Trueman and Colin Cowdrey for the International Cavaliers – and in 1967, was given the honour of leading the MCC against Ireland.

Goonesena and Outschoorn's success abroad was a reminder of the talent brewing in Ceylon. Yet clearly, local cricket was facing a conundrum. With the talent pool still tiny, the island couldn't afford to lose good cricketers. Gaining recognition from the ICC would always be tricky if Ceylon could not get its best eleven inside the boundary rope. Yet, without a fuller cricketing calendar, the island would struggle to hang onto its best and brightest. Ultimately, a shabby structure encouraged cricketers to abscond from home in search of greener pastures.

The extent of the problem was underlined when Stanley Jayasinghe – probably Ceylon's best batsman in the early 1950s – left for England in 1956. This was a different kind of loss; one felt more keenly because Jayasinghe had been a regular in the national side for the past seven years. Nor was he leaving with any assurance of glory. He had to climb the ladder from the bottom rung: only after helping Penzance to the Cornwall League title in the summer of 1956 was he rewarded with an invitation to the big time of club cricket: the Lancashire League.[188]

Jayasinghe was a hit, scoring over 4,000 runs in five seasons as Colne's pro. Bottom of the table when he joined, by 1959 Colne were league champions. Counties soon came calling. He began qualifying for Leicestershire in 1960; a year later, he smashed 88 for the Commonwealth against England – reaching his half-century in just twenty-seven minutes. Though not a hefty man, when the mood took him he would tear into attacks with reckless abandon.

Jayasinghe made his Championship debut in 1962: over four seasons, he racked up twenty-six 50s and three 100s in the competition.

From 1961, he was joined at the club by Clive Inman, the outstanding batsman when a 'Young Ceylon' side toured Malaya in 1957. Inman proved an even greater success than Jayasinghe. In nine seasons, he only failed to reach 1,000 runs once; for six years he was the county's leading scorer. He was among the ten leading run-scorers in the Championship in his debut year and again in 1968, yet arguably reached his zenith in 1971, his last year in county cricket, when he made 1,322 runs at 45.58.

What's more, he scored them with style. A swashbuckling left-hander, strong through the covers and sharp on the hook, he brought pleasure to all those who came to watch him bat. At Trent Bridge in 1965, Nottinghamshire brought on opening batsman Norman Hill to try to force a declaration.[189] Inman tucked into his lollipops with glee, cracking five 4s and five 6s in his 2 overs. In doing so, he reached 50 in eight minutes – a record for all first-class cricket, which will surely never be broken. His consistency established him as one of the elite batsmen in the English game: as Edward Davey mused in *Playfair Cricket Monthly*, 'The tragedy for Inman of course is that unless selected by England – unlikely, but in one of his best seasons, a choice nobody could cavil at – he is virtually "stateless" as far as Test match opportunities are concerned.'[190]

By the early sixties, Sri Lanka's 'statelessness' in terms of Test cricket was travesty as well as tragedy. They had the players – a pool that included C.I. Gunasekara, Michael Tissera, Abdul Lafir, H.I.K. Fernando, Darrell Lieversz, Neil Chanmugam, Abu Fuard and, of course, the men lost to English cricket. It was simply the platform that was lacking. As it was, Inman hardly played for Ceylon after becoming a force in county cricket. He did join the tour to Pakistan in 1966 but seemed disinterested, telling teammates he was only there because the series was 'unofficial', so would not jeopardise his chance of an England cap.

These four were Ceylon's most high-profile cricketing losses, but far from the only casualties of the local scene. Malcolm Francke emigrated to England to become an accountant in the early 1960s, only returning to serious cricket after a move to Australia a decade later.* Well into

---

* In November 1971, Francke played his first first-class game in thirteen and a half years against a World XI. He gave no sense of being overawed, picking up the wickets of Clive Lloyd, Rohan Kanhai and Sunil Gavaskar.

his thirties, he emerged as one of the leading spinners in the Sheffield Shield – perhaps only denied an Australia cap due to a lack of residential qualifications. Remarkably, Francke made a second comeback in the 1985/86 season, at the grand old age of 46. The Sheffield Shield hasn't seen another such senior player since.

There are others, too. Mano Ponniah left the island in 1966 to study architecture at Cambridge and played no more cricket for Ceylon. Dan Piachaud went to study at Oxford: he turned out for the university, Hampshire and the MCC, but played just one game for his country. Years later, Gehan Mendis emigrated to England in his youth and scored forty-one 100s for Sussex and Lancashire – but showed no inclination to play for Sri Lanka, even once they became a Test-playing nation.

This talent drain was saddening and destructive. Already battling the odds, Sri Lanka's challenge grew as they struggled to hang onto their best and brightest. But there is a flipside. Every time these cricketers took to the field in a foreign land, they provided a moving billboard for their faraway island – a reminder, not only that Sri Lanka existed, but that its cricketers played the game with charisma and class. This was especially true when Inman and Jayasinghe batted in tandem for Leicestershire – as happened so often between 1963 and 1965.* It was a powerful symbol. They might have left Ceylon behind, but they continued to represent their homeland.

These cricketing expats helped cement the island's status as a fledgling force in the game. When I spoke to former England batsman Chris Tavaré, he told me about his first taste of Sri Lankan cricket, meeting Gajan Pathmanathan at Oxford. As he delved into memories of Pathmanathan's batting, his eyes lit up.

'Gaj was very wristy,' he recalled. 'But he'd try and smack the ball regularly. Nice shots, not slogs – but in our first game he tried to take on John Snow and got caught mid-off. There's one innings I remember, it was just fantastic. In 1976, we went up to Barnsley to play Yorkshire in the B&H Cup. Gaj opened the batting; Chris Old bowled at him and he just took him apart. Old got angry and tried to bounce him out, and

---

* Coming in at four and five, the duo would often share the crease: in 1965, they combined to score nearly 30 per cent of the county's runs.

those disappeared too. In next to no time he'd made 50-odd and we won the game. It just made you realise – if there were those sort of players in Sri Lanka who could control themselves ...'

So, Sri Lanka's cricketing diaspora was not all bad. For decades the country's players had toiled away in relative obscurity, but by the second half of the twentieth century, any self-respecting cricket fan would have known that there was an island in the Indian Ocean serious about cricket. It was another step towards becoming a part of the furniture.

2

THE LONG ROAD AHEAD
(1956–1982)

BIG DECISIONS

As much as Ceylon was hit by cricketing departures in the post-war period, it continued to benefit from the occasional arrival. So it was in 1957, when John Arenhold – a South African Shell employee – ripped through Madras to carry the team to a comfortable Gopalan victory.[1] Though the Indian side claimed a maiden victory at Chepauk the following year, the team could take spirit from almost defending 110.

The island's cricket owed a great debt to Tamil Nadu: really it was the Gopalan games that stopped the scene from growing stagnant during the 1950s.* Yet sadly at home, Sinhalese-Tamil relations were in rapid decline. D.S. Senanayake's sudden death in 1952 cleared the path for Solomon Bandaranaike, whose seductive vision substituted Sinhalese for Ceylonese, gave Buddhism special status and exploited the belief that the majority community had been denied their rightful role in shaping Ceylon.

---

*   In the five years since the Gopalan Trophy got going in February 1953, Ceylon's only other cricket had been a whistlestop against the MCC, and India's two-test visit.

Clearly, Bandaranaike struck on something – he romped to power in 1956, on the back of a resounding majority. But the hasty introduction of the Sinhala Only Act* set the island on a collision course. Tamils employed in public service now had to learn Sinhala or surrender their roles; Ceylon, without major ethnic conflict since 1915, was blighted by horrific bouts of violence in 1956 and 1958.

The MCC stopped for a pair of whistlestops in October 1958 – but what little play the weather allowed was marred by hapless Ceylonese batting. At least the side's next outing was more triumphant. In March 1959, Ceylon tore into Madras' bowlers: there were runs for Prins, Lafir and Lasantha Rodrigo, but the highlight was C.I. Gunasekara's bruising 212, punctuated by thirty-two hits to the fence. Some 3,500 turned up to watch him reach 200, which he followed up with 29 overs of fast leg spin.[2] For a man approaching 39, it was a gruelling workload – but Gunasekara was no ordinary cricketer. Though the game ultimately ran out of time, Ceylon's 481 was good enough for a comfortable first-innings victory.

After failures against the MCC and Madras, some questioned whether it might have been 'too much too soon' for young Michael Tissera. The former S. Thomas' captain had been catapulted into the national side after a couple of months in club cricket, but struggled to make an impression in his first few outings. Batting at eight in 1960's Gopalan, he managed 4 and 20 as Ceylon were undone by the vicious spin of V.V. Kumar. The team would have to wait for a chance to make amends, with no cricket until a Pakistani Eaglets' visit nine months later. Sadly it was a damp affair, with only C.I. Gunasekara – captain now that Prins had retired – impressing with the bat. Tissera, promoted to four, returned 11 and 0. By now, the selectors might have been losing patience.

They deserve praise for not making a knee-jerk decision. In February 1961, six West Indian cricketers stopped in Ceylon on their way to England.[3] They were given an audience with the Prime Minister and invited to play a game of cricket. So, fresh off the back of the tied Test in Brisbane, Conrad Hunte, Chester Watson, Rohan Kanhai, Seymour

---

*   The act saw Sinhala replace English as Ceylon's official language. But, since it left little place for the Tamil language, it proved highly prejudicial.

Nurse, Garfield Sobers and Wes Hall teamed up with four local cricketers – and Mr Hewson, a fellow passenger on their ship – to form *The Daily Mirror XI*. They would take on Ceylon in a whistlestop: the presence of a sponsor gives a sense of the unprecedented level of interest in the match.

I first met Michael Tissera in 2018. We shared a S. Thomas' connection – I even briefly taught his grandson – and when I called he said he would be happy to chat, inviting me to his house in Nawala. Straight away, I was struck by his old-fashioned, understated magnetism. He was trim – his forearms the sole giveaway that he spent years smiting a cricket ball – and youthful for a man on the cusp of his ninth decade. He told me he kept in shape ballroom dancing. It seemed strange that he began playing international cricket sixty years ago.

Still, he could recall that game with the West Indians vividly. 'The atmosphere was fantastic,' he said. 'That was the first time I'd seen the Oval really overflowing; they were even sitting on the grass, everyone was packed in. Huge crowd.' They weren't disappointed. The visiting stars all made runs as *The Daily Mirror XI* smashed their way to 305-6; now the batsmen had to face up to Wes Hall and Chester Watson on the glinting Oval wicket.

'In those days it was just a patch of grass,' Tissera smilingly told me. 'You couldn't even see the clay. The bounce was very good, and it was true – but the ball moved around.' Nor were Ceylon's batsmen helped by those in charge, who decided to do away with sight screens to accommodate a bigger crowd. There were shudders and gulps when they noticed Wes Hall marking a spot by the boundary, ready to steam in. His bite matched his bark. In a fearsome spell, he had three of Ceylon's top four back in the pavilion for a combined total of 1. At this point Tissera came to the crease. 'It was daunting,' he remembered. 'We weren't used to that kind of pace. When you play these fellows who are so much faster, the first twenty minutes is almost luck whether you survive.'

He did more than just hang around. Tissera played his shots, and over the course of the afternoon, showed grit, guts and guile in abundance. No other batsman reached 20, but when the match came to a close he was unbeaten on 102, having made well over half of Ceylon's runs. Hall gave him nothing for free until the final ball of the day, when – seeing the youngster stranded on 98 – he served up a juicy full toss.

It was a monumental knock. The whistlestops had been going for close to eight decades, but never before had a local batsman reached three figures. 'That innings gave me a lot of confidence. Really, it gave me a lot of confidence,' Tissera explained. In fact, it marked a turning point in his career. Two and a half weeks later, he made 61 and 62 (run out) as Ceylon easily dispatched Madras at the Oval. Nor was he the only member of the side growing in confidence. Abdul Lafir made a gritty second-innings 121* – cementing his status as the most accomplished opening bat Ceylon had seen to date. Meanwhile Anura Polonowita, who took 4 for 16 in both innings, was increasingly proving a wily left-arm spinner.

When Australia came to Colombo for a whistlestop in April 1961, the Ceylonese impressed again. Richie Benaud was enamoured by Abu Fuard's classical action, Bob Simpson described the fielding as 'world class' – and all were struck by the islanders' fearless pursuit of a 289-run target.[4] Though they fell short, Gunasekara's brutal assault on Lindsay Kline carried the day.[5] As confidence swelled, Ceylon's cricketers were becoming increasingly less obliging hosts.

The team had to wait nearly ten months for their next assignment, but continued their impressive run when the Gopalan finally rolled around. Madras were dispatched by an innings; across the week-long trip, the top five all averaged north of 50. None impressed more than Tissera, who fell 8 short of another century in the Gopalan game. Since the century against the West Indians, his runs had come at 81.40. Prior to that, he'd averaged 12.43. There had been false starts before, but it felt like Ceylon were entering a brave new era.

So the MCC's arrival in February 1962 – for their first proper tour in twenty-eight years – brought whispers of optimism.[*] The warm-ups did nothing to dampen spirits, but the Oval wicket for the unofficial 'test' only favoured one team.[6] Ceylon reached 210 thanks to a dogged

---

[*] Without May, Cowdrey, Trueman and Statham, the English had struggled in India and lost a five-match series 2–0. Plus, Goonesena, Jayasinghe and Inman had been flown home to bolster the squad.

84 from Lafir, but Ted Dexter, Barry Knight and Alan Brown all whistled balls past the batsmen's ears. Polonowita was struck and took no further part; Tony Lock was called to bowl a single over in the first innings, and opted to send down seamers.

While Ceylon were used to such tracks, they lacked the bowlers to exploit them. Lukshman Gunatilleke and Jayasinghe were no more than military medium, and the rest of the attack made up of spinners. They did well to dismiss the MCC for 284, but were bundled out second time around and well beaten by 8 wickets. It was an opportunity lost.

While it may seem absurd to prepare a wicket that so clearly plays into your opponents' hands, there was a certain amount of deference in the decision. Ceylon were still feeding off scraps: grateful for these visits, they were eager to ensure foreign cricketers would *want* to come back. Nonetheless, preparing such 'sporting' pitches defied logic. The easiest way to unlock the door to the ICC's inner circle would be to claim a 'test' scalp. Ceylon had four quality spinners in their line-up: a drier, dustier wicket would surely have made life harder for England. Abu Fuard's off-spin caused plenty of problems when the MCC were back for a whistlestop in October; it is a shame it took Sri Lanka so long to commit to turning tracks.

Still the scene was moving forward. After 130 years of bigotry, the CCC finally opened doors to local cricketers.[7] And while 1963 was a fallow year, when Ceylon returned to the field in March 1964 the Colombo crowd was treated to a genuine novelty: a pair of proper opening bowlers. Darrell Lieversz discomfited batsmen with his hooping inswinger: rejecting short stuff for line and length, he cleverly used the crease and varied the lateness of his swing. Norton Fredrick, on the other hand, was pure pace: short and stocky, with a square-arm action that batsmen found difficult to pick up. These two were on opposite sides of the seam-bowling coin, but forged a menacing partnership.

They made an instant impression, picking up 13 wickets between them in 1964's Gopalan game. Second time around, Lieversz's 6 for 29 helped Ceylon overturn a 40-run first innings deficit. Yet despite bursting onto the scene with all the ferocity of a pitbull, Lieversz and Fredrick made little mark when Australia visited the following month. Instead it was the quartet of spinners who bundled Australia out for 249. In reply, the hosts reached 103-3: another impressive innings saw Michael Tissera end the day unbeaten on 51.

The match was Gunasekara's last as captain. By now he was 43: though clearly one of Ceylon's true greats, he was perhaps not a natural leader. Like Prins before him Gunasekara was an introvert. Teammates recall a shy, modest man, who led through actions rather than words. With the selectors deciding it was time for a change, two options presented themselves: H.I.K. Fernando, apart from Gunasekara the side's senior statesman; and Michael Tissera, the young batsman who'd so impressed over the past five years. A trial match was staged, where Tissera emerged as the clear choice. At just 25, he was handed the reins to Ceylon's cricket.

Tissera would not have to wait long for his first assignment. In August 1964 a strong Pakistan 'A' side arrived in Colombo.* Though they were clear favourites, the hosts were as strong as they had ever been – and in a warm-up, a young Board President's XI punished their guests. The seamers stole the show, blowing Pakistan away for 157 and 112. 'We noticed they didn't play the moving ball too well,' Tissera remembered. 'Sometimes when these fellows play on baked wickets, they come and see the grass and go mad.' From that moment on, he knew his team were in with a chance for the 'test'.

At last, the Oval's treacherous greentop would play into the hosts' hands. Though rolled in the first innings for 152, Tissera knew the situation was far from catastrophe. 'We had confidence going in,' he reflects. 'We worked on the basis that under most circumstances we could get 170 or 180 – and restrict Pakistan to less than that.'

Plus, Ceylon had a secret weapon up their sleeve. Darrell Lieversz had been rested during the warm-up, and the Pakistan top order couldn't cope with his late inswing.[8] First Faqir Aizazuddin was trapped in front; two balls later Mano Ponniah clung onto a blinder at short leg.

---

*   Some claim the 'A' was only added retrospectively, with the team assembled close to the full Test side. Hanif Mohammed was missing, but Abdul Kadir, Javed Burki, Shafqat Rana, Intikhab Alam, Asif Iqbal and Pervez Sajjad – all of whom would feature in Pakistan's next Test – were there. Imtiaz Ahmed, a forty-one-Test stalwart who had been a fixture of the national side for a decade, was leading the group. Farooq Hameed would soon earn a Test cap, Ghulam Ahmed would have one in time too. This was no thrown-together bunch of ragtag regional cricketers.

The Pakistanis were 0-2. And there was no let-up the following morning. Lieversz kept picking up wickets – Javed Burki, Ghulam Abbas and Imtiaz Ahmed took his tally to 5 for 40 – before Neil Chanmugam cleaned up the tail. The visitors were done for under 100.

Tissera's men added 137 to their first-innings score: in the context of the game, 190 looked an imposing target. But while Pakistan quickly slipped to 27-3, Asif Iqbal and Burki mounted solid resistance. Each run frayed Ceylonese nerves: by the time the pair had put on 75, there was sweat on the brows of the men in the field. Relief flooded across them when Buddy Reid took a sharp catch at short mid-wicket to break the partnership. Tissera's men were superb in the field throughout the 'test' – in the first innings, keeper H.I.K. Fernando had run back almost all the way to the boundary to cling onto a steepling catch.

It seems the cricket gods were on their side too. Once Iqbal was gone, a burst of rain added extra spice to the wicket. Lieversz, near unplayable in such conditions, soon had Imtiaz caught at leg slip. When he got Burki lbw for 62, Pakistan knew they were finished. They slumped to 149 all out. Ceylon had finally won an unofficial 'test'.

Imtiaz moaned about the unpredictability of Sri Lanka – the pitches, the weather and the umpires included. But no amount of sour grapes could sully the sweetness of Ceylon's victory. The players were finally beginning to realise that the chasm they assumed existed between themselves and Test cricketers was in fact little more than a crack.

They had shown the restraint and resolve which had often eluded Ceylon sides. 'It was a matter of playing two balls in an over, because the ball was flying all over the place.' Tissera reflects. 'We were prepared for that.' Pakistan seemingly weren't. Plus, as the captain puts it, 'Pieris and Lieversz could really move the ball – and they had control.' Clearly, Lieversz deserves special praise: through two-first class games for Ceylon, he had picked up 17 wickets at 7.71. No seamer had been so miserly since the days of Greswell and Tommy Kelaart.

'Neil Chanmugam gave me a souvenir stump – he knew that I had missed out on getting one,' Lieversz told me when we spoke about the game. 'But I don't remember any significant celebration after. If I remember correct, I went home to celebrate with my family and close friends.'

Greater challenges lay ahead, but Tissera had clearly shown that he was the right man to lead this team forward. It is no coincidence that Ceylon experienced an upturn so quickly after he took the helm – indeed, the same happened when Ranatunga and Jayawardene, took charge of Sri Lanka. Like those men, Tissera was innovative and forward thinking. He knew the direction in which his team needed to travel, and had a clear idea of how to get them there. Several who played under him have told me he immediately brought a sense of purpose and professionalism hitherto lacking. He was the leader this young group needed.

There was plenty to be buoyant about. Ceylon finally had an attack based around more than bits-and-pieces bowlers. They had a shrewd and inspiring captain – one who led with his bat as much as his brain. And on the horizon hung a wonderful opportunity: a five-week tour to India.

THE GRAND TOUR

Ceylon's cricketers knew nothing would come easy in India. 'We were still real amateurs,' Tissera reminded me the first time we met. 'We all had jobs – we were part time cricketers. We could only get to the nets at 4 in the afternoon, and by 6 pm it's dark. We had no coaches, no trainers. And India were a strong side.'

The Indians were especially strong in their own backyard: fresh off a drawn series against Australia, they had lost just two of twenty-one home Tests since the start of the 1960s. What's more, the visitors' schedule would be relentless: after flying to Madras in early December, it was trains the rest of the way – around 2,500 miles on the tracks in the space of five weeks. The trip from Bombay to Madras alone was three days. Unwilling to buy food on the platform, the team had to survive on a diet of fruit.

When they were on solid ground, there would be no luxury hotels where they could rest and recuperate. Often it was four to a room; in Hyderabad and Bombay players were billeted at the ground. Nor was the build-up to the tour ideal, with real question marks over who would be able to travel.* The team ended up boarding the plane without their captain – a major blow, since Tissera was expected to organise practices and act as chief selector, as well as lead.

Though Tissera joined the team ahead of the first 'test' in Bangalore, his arrival did little to lift fortunes. The 20,000 who turned up for the opening day had plenty to cheer about; by the time Pataudi declared, India had pounded their way to 508-4.[9] Ceylon quickly wilted in reply, crumbling to an innings defeat as new spin sensation B.S. Chandrasekhar claimed 10 wickets.

It was a sobering beating – and with the five days between 'tests' dominated by the colossal journey north, a shift in surroundings brought little change on the field. India racked up 505-6 in Hyderabad; Ceylon – widely expected to be the better fielding side going into the series – shelled six catches in a single day. Equally, presented with shorn, unhelpful wickets, the bowlers looked lost for ideas.

Ceylon battled, but could not avoid the follow-on; at 70-3 second time around, they were sliding towards inevitable defeat. But Tissera and Jayasinghe – clearly the team's two best batsmen – dug in until the end of the third day. Neither would yield, and on the final morning the pair made India's bowlers toil as they both reached centuries. They had put on 224 when Jayasinghe finally fell for 135. Sadly, the rest could not match their resolve. From 294-3, Ceylon slid to 378 all out. India chased down 154 in 31 overs; Tissera's men knew they had dropped another ball. Had they managed to bat half an hour longer, they likely would have forced a draw.

The schedule remained punishing – but at least there was no time to wallow. The second 'test' ran till late on the 22nd; come Christmas Eve, Tissera was tossing a coin in Pune, over 800 miles away. The team had a rest for Christmas itself, but in an unfortunate echo of the nativity, there

---

* Tissera worked as an executive at Brooke Bond: with a strike ongoing, it was all hands on deck. C.I. Gunasekara and P.I. Pieris struggled to get leave and couldn't make the tour; Lieversz's request for time off was initially refused, before eventually being granted. Neil Chanmugam had an exam and arrived late, Buddy Reid had one too and missed the trip altogether. Ceylon's foreign exchange issues meant that Clive Inman couldn't feature; though Jayasinghe was eventually able to travel by doubling up as a correspondent for *The Daily News*.

was no room in any of Maharashtra's inns. A warehouse at the ground was painted and filled with beds, but some of the squad complained about the toxic smell seeping from the walls. Eventually, they found a handful of rooms at a rest-house in town. Several players shifted, but found conditions there even worse. Tail between their legs, they had little choice but to stay.

Touring was taking its toll. Trevelyan Edward was down with a temperature, Jayasinghe had a groin strain, while manager Nihal Seneratne – the only non-playing member of the party – was struggling with an upset stomach.[10] Those who were healthy had to deal with the stresses that arise from producing sub-par performances on the big stage. One Indian newspaper criticised the bowling as 'well below Test standard'. Having been away nearly a month, the players could be forgiven if they were hankering for home.

Ceylon's hosts weren't the only ones chastising their performance. Over the course of the tour, Jayasinghe used his column in *The Daily News* as a platform to criticise almost every aspect of his teammates' performance. Poor shot selection, lazy running between the wickets, sloppy fielding, not walking when the ball had been nicked – next to nothing escaped his ire. He wrote freely in the confidence that his teammates were well removed from the Ceylonese press, but came unstuck when Norton Fredrick got a letter from home, including an extract from Jayasinghe's pen. It read:

> Bowlers have learnt their share of lessons. Frederick [*sic*] I am sure, was taught a lesson on when and where to use bumpers by Hanumant Singh. On this batsmen's paradise, Frederick unwisely resorted to bumpers much to Hanumant's relish and the scoreboard rose as rapidly as a meter in a Colombo taxi.

Clearly unamused, Ceylon's 'Fiery Fred' found Jayasinghe and asked him to explain himself, as he held him by the scruff of his neck. I doubt Jayasinghe set out to disparage; rather, this was an experienced professional speaking bluntly. Much of his criticism was well founded, and tempered by the acknowledgement that Ceylon's domestic structure only allowed it to produce 'gay amateur cricketer[s]'. Still, it

reflected the fact that the tour was not going to plan. The team themselves accepted as much, enforcing a Rs. 1 fine for any loose shot in
the nets. It might not sound like much, but players were earning just
Rs. 15 a day.*

The tour matches between the second and third 'tests' offered little
respite and even less reward; almost a month into the trip, heading home
winless looked a distinct possibility. At least Ceylon's lacklustre performances gave Pataudi the confidence to tinker. Having fielded a full side
for the first two 'tests', the Indian captain took the chance to try out five
youngsters. That said, he still had Abbas Ali Baig, Dilip Sardesai, Farokh
Engineer, Hanumant Singh and Srinivasaraghavan Venkataraghavan by
his side. Nothing would come easy. In fact, on the first day's play, nothing
came at all. Jayasinghe reported:

> The laundry man in Ahmedabad, who entered our room early on
> Saturday morning, proved himself an excellent Weather Prophet,
> when he said with assurance, but regret: 'Rain coming today, sir, no
> playing cricket.' That was long before the radio had given the official
> forecast of '72 hours of heavy cloud and intermittent rain'. It really
> poured all day.[11]

Rain lashed down for much of the second day too – though a plastic cover
was placed on the wicket, it offered little protection. But about half an
hour after tea, the Indian captain approached Tissera. 'Pataudi came up to
me and said, 'there are 25,000 people here, shall we play?' he recalled with
a smile. 'So I said, "OK". Mind you, there was sawdust right up from the
wickets three quarters of the way across the ground, and the outfield was
very soft.' For the third time in the series, India won the toss. Conditions
looked horrible; all were astounded when Pataudi opted to bat.

It seems he only made this decision because he was recovering from
a fever. His doctor had told him to rest – with just over an hour left in

---

* For some of the squad, the trip actually cost money. There were no sponsors so they
had to provide their own kit. Most only travelled with one bat, and there was a shared
'coffin' with pads and gloves. A number of the players, Tissera included, had to take their
annual holiday allowance in order to travel.

the day, he thought he wouldn't be called to the crease. It was a stroke of luck for Ceylon, but almost immediately disaster struck. The bespectacled Trevelyan Edward was smashed in the face at short leg and rushed to hospital.[12] That was the end of his tour – and sadly, his cricket for Ceylon. When it came to batting, the side would be down to ten men.

But unlike before, India found themselves in trouble. Rain had soaked into the wicket; bowling fast, Fredrick unseated the top three early. The following morning, Jayasinghe took centre stage. Well used to treacherous tracks after years spent in England, he ran through India – varying the pace of his off-cutters and making the most of a pockmarked surface. His 6 for 38 saw the hosts routed for 189.

Still, the pitch showed no signs of improving, and Ceylon were soon floundering at 25-5. They were steadied by 28 from Tissera; once he went, Polonowita and H.I.K. Fernando built a crucial partnership, steering Ceylon to 144-7 overnight. Back at the hotel, an inspired call from Ceylon's captain changed the course of the match. Early morning moisture would give his bowlers the best chance to run through India; though 45 behind, they would declare first thing.

He gave no inkling of his plan: when the team arrived at the ground, Fernando and Lieversz padded up for throw downs. 'If we had given them a clue and the wicket was dicey, they might have delayed the start,' Tissera told me with a wry smile. Patuadi was certainly shocked, and his men never got going. Fredrick had Sardesai and Hanumant in the space of three balls: India were 4-3 before they knew it. And 'Fiery Fred' kept steaming in. Jayasinghe reported:

> Ceylon owes much of her glory to 'Bloomfield Bomber' Norton Frederick. He wobbled the new cherry so disconcertingly that [he] left the Indian batsmen 'groping in the dark' … Frederick's initial opening spell extended over an hour and he fully deserved the great ovation he received from the 'Full House' at the end of it. From then on, there was no holding Ceylon back.[13]

There certainly wasn't. Jayasinghe caused problems too, before Polonowita's quickfire 3 for 7 brought India crashing to 66 all out. Ceylon needed 112 for victory. Abu Fuard opened gutsily in Edward's absence, but Ponniah – thrust into the role of the aggressor – got over-ambitious and was stumped. Still, by tea Fuard's 40 had guided Ceylon to 77-1. The game looked in the bag.

But there was time for another twist in the tale. Fuard went straight after the break, and Lasantha Rodrigo was quickly run out too. Jayasinghe was bowled for 19, before Chanmugam and Fernando came and went without troubling the scorers. Suddenly, Ceylon were 98-6. Tissera, stranded at the non-striker's end, was starting to sweat. 'It was nervy,' he reflects. 'We were six down, which really meant seven because Edward wasn't there. But it was great to see Polonowita come in because he'd scored runs the previous day. That gave me a bit of confidence.' It was all Ceylon needed to scrape over the line. Polonowita hung around, and the team edged closer to their target. Tissera struck a boundary to take them past India's score; Ceylon had won a 'test' overseas for the first time.

The team were euphoric. There was little scope for celebrating in Ahmedabad, but spirits were at an all-time high in the hotel that evening. Dhanasiri Weerasinghe even composed a 'Victory Calypso', which he, Ranjit Fernando, Sylvester Dias and Lareef Idroos performed when they got home.[14] Sirimavo Bandaranaike sent her congratulations, while board president Robert Senanayake basked in the glory of a 'remarkable victory … which will put Ceylon in the map of world cricket'. Having waded winless through international cricket for almost a century, Ceylon now had two 'test' scalps in the space of six months.

Their ultimate hope was quickly realised. At the post-match reception, the president of the Indian Board of Control promised to sponsor Ceylon's bid for associate ICC membership.[15] His proposal was seconded by Pakistan: having been marooned for so long, Ceylon finally had a raft to cling onto. But instead of coming home to a hero's welcome, they were greeted by a rigorous customs inspection in Colombo.*

Dressed in a cream shirt and grey slacks, Tissera looked wearied after six weeks' non-stop travel.[16] 'We gained tremendously from the tour,' he

---

* Imports were tightly regulated in those days: only once the proper tax was paid could they return home to their families. Abu Fuard had picked up all manner of things in India, and faced a particularly hefty bill.

told local media. 'Four-day cricket really toughened our chaps – but sad to say, the benefit will all be lost when we return to our one-and-a-half day games.' For all that had been achieved, Ceylon's cricketers had an arduous road ahead.

Still, Tissera's honest assessment could not hide the fact that this was by far and away the greatest moment in Sri Lanka's cricket history. Fifty-four years on from that fateful match in Ahmedabad, I put it to him that his declaration was a masterstroke. 'I don't know about that,' he modestly replied. 'There was only one day left, so we thought "what's the point in batting – let's declare and see where we go." We decided overnight, and had a chat with the others and they all agreed.' His reluctance to take credit for his own decision reveals plenty. It is easy to see why he was such a popular and successful leader.

Beyond simply being shrewd and egalitarian, Tissera possessed a fear-less streak which stood Sri Lanka in good stead. He could have easily declined Pataudi's offer of playing on the second day, safe in the knowl-edge that taking time out of the game would improve Ceylon's chances of a draw. In declaring, he risked humiliation and a mauling by the press at home. But as in so many of Sri Lanka's proudest cricketing moments, risk brought reward. With his bravery in 1965, Tissera unlocked some-thing. In many ways, he set a course for others to follow.

That said, I'm continually struck by how much the victory depended on fate. The result – and the whole history of cricket in Sri Lanka – could have been entirely different. So much of cricket depends on luck, and you can only take it when it comes your way. Over the next few years, Tissera and his team would learn there was plenty of rough to go along with the smooth.

THINGS FALL APART

As much as the India tour was a triumph, it could have ended very dif-ferently. Ceylon struggled all the way up to Ahmedabad. The bowlers learned how unforgiving lifeless pitches could be, as India's first two trips to the crease brought 1,113 runs and just 10 wickets. The batters didn't settle in often enough;* even the fielding was a let-down. Tissera's declaration drastically altered the way those back home viewed the trip.

Nor was all well away from the field. Ceylon cricket would self-destruct in 1968 – and it seems that the roots of conflict may have first taken hold in India.[17] With Sinhalese nationalism rising across society, some of the players began to grumble about a perceived bias towards Royalists and Thomians – as well as a general preference for cricketers from anglicised backgrounds. Apparently, Tissera's appointment caused resentment: with hierarchies deeply ingrained in Sri Lanka, his youth was problematic. What's more, yesterday's amateur cricketers – many of them strong-minded intellectuals – were in many ways harder to manage than modern professionals. Still, Tissera only had trouble with one.

When I spoke to players of the era, Abu Fuard's name sprang up time and again. Some insist he's been wrongly maligned – but I've heard him described as 'abrasive', 'dishonest' and 'difficult'; as 'a dictator', 'a bully' and worse. At one point on tour, he turned up an hour late for practice. Tissera was forced to tell him off; Fuard wrote back to the board that he resented being treated like a schoolboy. Nor did his performances in India give him licence to act like a prima donna. Unable to rip the ball as viciously as Chanmugam, he resorted to bowling well outside off stump and caused little threat: his 3 first-class wickets cost 110.66 apiece.

When the squad returned home in late January 1965, few sensed a storm was coming. The island's cricket was taking baby steps towards professionalism – as an age-old tradition embodying the spirit of amateurism was coming to an end. In October 1965, the MCC stopped en route to Australia for one last time. There would be no more whistlestops;** the days of weary cricketers stretching their sea-legs in Colombo were set to become a thing of the past.

The layover was long enough for the MCC to play two games on consecutive days: in a sign of burgeoning strength, Ceylon stayed

---

*   Across the eight Tests in India prior to the tour, the average first-innings score had been 312. Ceylon only reached 300 once, in their second-innings rearguard at Hyderabad.
**   In June 1967, Gamal Abdel Nassar responded to attacks on Egyptian airfields by closing the Suez Canal. It would not reopen until 1975; by 1969, Qantas had eleven flights a week which could cut the travel time between London and Sydney to thirty hours.

competitive despite fielding largely different sides. Norton Fredrick had the openers John Edrich and Boycott early in the first; only rain saved the English from real embarrassment in the second. They were done for 127, the Reid brothers unbeaten at close, Ceylon's score 77-1. It was a wonderful way to bid farewell to the whistlestops.

Sadly, Ceylon had to bid farewell to Darrell Lieversz too. In less than a year and a half, he'd torn through the island's cricket like a whirlwind, his 32 wickets coming at an average of just 18.65.* As Ceylon's most impactful seamer since Greswell, Lieversz surely would have accomplished a great deal had work not wrested the new ball out of his hand.

His departure at just 22 is a reminder of the sacrifices Ceylonese cricketers continually had to make. For most, playing was financially detrimental. For many it created complications at work. Above all, staying in control of the balancing act between life as an international cricketer and a professional career was sapping business. H.I.K. Fernando was a successful doctor, Dhanasiri Weerasinghe a policeman, Michael Tissera an executive for one of the island's biggest tea exporters. Ceylon's cricketers' lives were full to the brim with work and cricket. They had little time for anything else.

With Lieversz gone and Tissera missing, the team struggled badly in the 1966 Gopalan game. Venkat and V. V. Kumar dragged them into deep water, but despite conceding a 255-run first-innings lead, Ceylon staved off outright defeat thanks to an unbeaten century from H.I.K. Fernando. Back home four months later, they mauled a strong State Bank of India XI, P.I. Pieris claiming 6 for 30 to send the visitors toppling to 96 all out. Though this was encouraging, two such contrasting performances spoke of the instability that lurked at the heart of Ceylon cricket.

It was an issue the team had to quickly address. At the end of October 1966, Ceylon would head off for a first full tour of Pakistan, a golden opportunity to show what they could do. Win a match, and they could find themselves in exalted territory: the ICC would struggle to justify the continued exclusion of a side who had beaten two Test teams away from home in as many years.

---

* That, too, despite more than half his appearances coming on discouraging Indian wickets. At home, Lieversz's first-class bowling average plummets to 7.70.

But trouble began before the plane left Ratmalana. If there was already discontent over selection policy, it was ingrained by the Pakistan squad. With three fewer places up for grabs – and a deeper talent pool to draw upon* – Fuard, Dhanasiri Weerasinghe and Anura Polonowita were dropped.

Though Polonowita's exclusion was hard to justify, Fuard and Weerasinghe had done little to cling onto their spots. Still, it is easy to see the narrative that was weaved. Weerasinghe and Polonowita were Sinhala speakers from Ananda; though Fuard had gone to Wesley College, he positioned himself as a champion of the downtrodden. Their replacements came from different backgrounds: Tennekoon, Thomas and Chanmugam were Thomians, Crozier was from Royal, Heyn a light-skinned legacy whose father commanded the army. Fuard had been handily out-bowled by Chanmugam in India, while proving himself a poor tourist – prone to antagonising teammates and arguing with umpires. Still, he never let it be forgotten that his rival was Derrick de Saram's son-in-law.

Nonetheless, the tour got off to a decent start. Three drawn warm-ups brought runs for plenty of the batsmen; though the bowlers didn't always find wickets easy to come by, they were better equipped to deal with thankless conditions after the India trips. The board seemed to have learned from India too. Instead of endless train travel, they organised flights and air-conditioned coaches, giving players a better platform to perform on the field.

Things were looking up, but when it came to the 'tests', all went horribly wrong. In Lahore, the seamers toiled for 65 fruitless overs as Pakistan racked up 425. Ceylon's reply was feeble. Forced to follow on, they were 57-2 heading into the final day: in deep water, but still alive in the game.

Jayasinghe's presence offered hope: 11* overnight, he batted with poise on the final day to make 118. Others dug in too. Heyn hung around for over an hour to help Ceylon reach tea five down, but was

---

*   Over the past year, Anura Tennekoon – and David Heyn on the domestic scene – had emerged as players of real promise. Clive Inman was back to strengthen the batting too, while left-arm spinner Fitzroy Crozier was back in the mix after a stretch working in Jaffna.

adjudged lbw first ball after the break. 'We got a lot of bad decisions,' he told me. 'Saeed Ahmed was bowling around the wicket and hit me outside off stump. After that, H.I.K. was given out on a bump ball. It was a bit demoralising that we thought we could do something and then very quickly the game was gone.'

Fortunes improved little in Dacca. Pakistan mounted another mammoth score; at 75-2, Ceylon were going OK, but late in the day – with students lighting bonfires in the rafters around the ground – they lost 2 wickets and never recovered. The hosts won by an innings. A double century from Javed Burki saw Ceylon hammered again in the third 'test'; at least Tissera's battling 120* helped the visitors save a little face.

It had been an arduous month. As in India, the seamers didn't have the nous to trouble batsmen on pancake-flat wickets. 'They were pretty ruthless,' Anura Tennekoon recalled. 'Because they had lost against us in 1964, they were smarting and wanted to give it back. The conditions were tough – it was hot, the ground was hard and fast – but they had a far better side in terms of experience and skill.'

Though the team returned home winless, none could say the tour was time wasted. This was a young side, and every chance to play over four days against hardened Test cricketers was an invaluable lesson. 'We got a lot of experience,' says Heyn. 'I certainly did. In fact all of us got tremendous experience across those six matches – Lionel [Fernando], Anura [Tennekoon], myself. It set us up. And to play alongside a guy like Jayasinghe, you could bounce things off him. And you didn't even have to talk to him, sometimes you just watched. He never gave his wicket away.'

Still, learning was one thing – putting those lessons into practice was a different story. Ceylon had no time to waste. At last, they were on the ICC's radar. When the English stopped in 1965, Billy Griffith – the tour manager and MCC secretary – invited them to tour England in the summer of 1968.[18] This was music to Ceylonese ears. There could be no doubt about it: the prospect of Test cricket glimmered clearly on the horizon.

What's more, foreign visits now came thick and fast: less than two months after the team got home, they welcomed Garfield Sobers and the West Indies. In some ways, the game marked a turning point for Sri

Lankan cricket. Jayasinghe was suffering from a back injury and unable to play, but was none too pleased about the prospect of his teammates facing Hall and Griffith on a murderous Oval wicket. Ceylon had no curator then, and were clearly hamstrung by groundskeepers' desires (or orders) to prepare sporting wickets. Still scarred by the MCC's visit in 1962, Jayasinghe persuaded the board that Ceylon should deaden the pitch.[19]

Clearly, his time as a pro in England gave him a little more clout with the administration, and he played an important role in ensuring players were better treated. Yet, the sense remained that they very much came second. The board balked at the team's request for extra tickets for the West Indies match – only acquiescing once players threatened a boycott. Still, it was the men in suits who got the best seats; their wives who were invited to functions while players' partners were left at home. Although away teams were given lunch in their dressing room, local cricketers had to eat at a general table with representatives, invitees and all sorts of hangers-on. Once, they made their way in from the field to find a table full of people already tucking into their lunch. They were told to come back later. Ceylon's success was time and again jeopardised by individuals' incompetence, selfishness and greed.

The team benefited from the more placid pitch against the West Indies, with Hall largely ineffective once the ball lost its shine. Come the second morning, a breakneck 110-run last-wicket partnership between Chanmugam and P.I. Pieris had the West Indians pulling their hair out.[20] The tailenders cracked sixteen 4s and two 6s to lift Ceylon to 400, a milestone never before reached against Test opposition. It mattered little that their opponents smashed their way to 549-8 in reply. Batsmen could take confidence from scoring runs instead of being blown away.

Work meant Tissera missed the Gopalan Trophy in 1967, so P.I. Pieris stood in as captain. His appointment ahead of H.I.K. Fernando may have caused resentment – but on the field, Ceylon never stopped fighting. Scoring 279 in the final session looked an impossible task, but Heyn tore into Venkat and Kumar on his way to a quickfire unbeaten century. Ceylon fell short, but plundered 225 from 32 overs. And there was swagger in Heyn's innings – he was already proving the kind of cricketer who wouldn't back down from a battle. 'I just went for it,' he reflects today. 'Went and swung.' Performances like this would stand Ceylon in good stead.

But beyond cricket, the past few years had proven especially turbulent. Ethnic harmony increasingly looked impossible, while an economic downturn led to a foreign-exchange crisis.[21] Unemployment rose to critical levels; clearly, it wasn't an ideal time for the country's cricketers to be planning the most costly tour in the island's history.

There were other hurdles standing in the way of the trip. The AGM of 1968 saw Sam Abeysekera, Dhanasiri Weerasinghe and H.I.K. Fernando join Chandra Schaffter as national selectors.[22] Looks must have been exchanged, drinks spluttered out, canapés choked on – for this was a highly unusual selection. Fernando was still Ceylon's first choice wicket-keeper. Weerasinghe had played as recently as 1965 and remained active on the club scene. He pledged that moving forward, he would not be available for national selection.

All signs suggest that Abu Fuard was responsible for putting this committee in place. Disgruntled at his extended absence from the national side, and desperate to tour England, he decided to make a play.* There were votes up for grabs: while Fuard could not manipulate the bigger clubs, he managed to put pressure on many of the smaller clubs' representatives, using his sway to have men he could rely upon manoeuvred into positions of power.

The first sign of trouble came with the arrival of Joe Lister's International XI in March 1968. The new selectors decided that Tissera, already the most successful captain in the island's history, should be replaced by H.I.K. Fernando, one of their own.[23] Crozier, Chanmugam and Pieris, all stalwarts in recent times – not to mention English speakers from Royal or S. Thomas' – were nowhere to be seen. After a three-year absence, Fuard was restored to the side. These decisions stank.

'I was very very shocked,' Chandra Schaffter told me. 'So shocked that I didn't know what to do or say. I went ahead with the meeting only because I was too shocked to react at the time.' Still, he told his colleagues that if they pulled something like this again, it would be the end

---

* The election process saw clubs – both from the P. Sara and *The Daily News* tournament – pick the selectors.

of the road for him as a selector. Tissera bore the indignity more stoically. 'I just accepted it,' he says. 'I had no problem with it at all. We'd been taught that you play for the side. Whether you're captain or vice captain, it doesn't matter. It didn't bother me.'

It's hard to believe that Tissera wasn't hurt — he had every right to be. That the selectors could even think of unseating him beggars belief. Despite all the drama, Ceylon bowled brilliantly against Lister's men. Fuard more than justified his recall, claiming six of the top seven while conceding 31 from his 26 overs. But Ceylon slumped to 28-3 by the close, and overnight showers thwarted any chance of a fightback. Embarrassingly, they added just 14 to their overnight score. The pitch had broken down, and Derek Underwood was nigh impossible to get away. Tissera made a resolute 36 second time around — a knock he considers among his very best efforts — but the hosts were skittled for under 100 again. Having started so promisingly, the game ended in humiliation.

There were few rays of sunshine away from the field. With the foreign exchange crisis worsening, the government embarked on an austerity programme — and rejected the BCCC's request for Rs.126,000 (around £8,775) to support the England tour.[24] Suddenly, Ceylon's English summer seemed very far away. Meanwhile the tour became a political rallying point. *Atha*, The Communist Party's paper, decried 'No Foreign Exchange for Milk Foods, Coriander and Dhal, but Two Lakhs for Cricket!' Politician Festus Perera suggested the money might be better spent improving rural playgrounds. Cricket was held aloft as the enemy of egalitarianism, a greedy *sahib* stealing food from the plates of the starving poor.

The anonymous donation of thirteen return flights briefly breathed life back into the tour — but when the selectors met, H.I.K. Fernando was again proposed for the captaincy.[25] As promised, Schaffter stormed out; the remaining selectors picked the rest of the tourists in his absence. They had an even bigger trick up their sleeves: Dhanasiri Weerasinghe, the selector who declared himself 'unavailable', would also be part of the squad.*

---

* The full list chosen to travel was: H.I.K. Fernando (captain), M. Tissera (vice captain), S. Jayasinghe, D. Weerasinghe, A. Fuard, D.P. de Silva, A. Polonowita, T. Kehelgamuwa, D. Sahabandu, B. Reid, A. Tennekoon and R. Fernando.

Joining the group from Ceylon would be three English-based players: Gamini Goonesena, Mano Ponniah and Dan Piachaud. This was an issue in itself, since some thought the opportunity should have gone to those grinding it out at home. Others have griped that three more tickets could have been found, and that a bigger squad would have been more suitable for such a gruelling tour.* At least funding was going well in England.[26] A number of the tea firms offered money, and *The Sun* claimed that the Warwickshire County Supporters' Fund had pledged £1,500. But another setback came when Gamini Goonesena declared himself out. 'I would be condoning the actions of the Selectors if I accepted the invitation,' he bluntly wrote to the board.

There was more drama at home, too. It soon emerged that Schaffter's early exit rendered the selection meeting null and void, but attempts to repick the squad only resulted in Weerasinghe launching legal action against the BCCC.** Supposedly, the Sports Minister was loath to dictate terms to Weerasinghe – since he happened to be one of his bodyguards.

After much flip-flapping, on 30 April the board decided to cancel the tour. Fernando offered to renege on the captaincy if it would help get the team to England, but the damage had been done. The promised flights were withdrawn; Ceylon would be going nowhere in the summer of 1968. The whole thing had descended into a farce; no doubt, many in England were annoyed at the trouble the MCC's kind gesture had caused. Counties had set days aside for matches. Learie Constantine had worked tirelessly planning the logistics. The cancellation was a slap in the face.

Nor was it easy for those at home to bear. For months, the forty players in the pre-selection pool had met up at 6 am every morning at the SSC for physical training. Day after day, a board-employed Navy Commander ran them ragged. 'I used to take the first bus from my home in Colombo 13, that left at 5 am,' remembers Ranjit Fernando. 'I'd get

---

*   Matches were planned against twelve counties, Oxford and Cambridge, Scotland and Ireland and the MCC.
**   Sathi Coomaraswamy was added to the selection committee, but the selectors could not surmount their differences. Weerasinghe's lawyer sent a letter to the board stating, 'his client will resist all attempts by the Board from following an illegal course of action detrimental to the interests of the Board'.

off at St Bridget's and walk all the way here – a long walk. And the SSC didn't open until 7:30 am so we didn't have water – we'd drink off the tap. Maybe four of us had cars. Lionel Fernando used to come from Negombo, and he'd pick up Melvin de Mel in the courtyard in front of his house. The courtyard had no lights, so he'd come with a candle to the car. Those were the sort of troubles those guys went through.' Sadly all of it was for nothing.

One sweltering February afternoon, I sat in the pavilion at S. Thomas' and talked about the tour with Anura Tennekoon. He remembered Sylvester Dias joking at the time – 'The way we ran, we could have made it all the way to England.' The players needed humour to cope with their anguish: each and every one knew the value of the opportunity they had just thrown away. 'It would have been ground-breaking,' Schaffter insists today. 'The world would have got to see how good we were.' 'I think that took us back ten years,' Tissera reflects. 'We would have got Test status much earlier if it had gone ahead. We knew how damaging it was.' Even those not directly involved seem to harbour resentment. The late Tony Opatha, who burst onto the scene in the early 1970s, was visibly riled when we spoke about the incident. 'Those guys really messed the whole thing up for Sri Lanka,' he said with venom. 'All our careers could have been different.'

These statements aren't hyperbolic. Though the trip to England came with no promises, it was clearly a trial for Test cricket. The abandonment took a sledgehammer to the island's immediate hopes for full ICC status. As in 1954, Ceylon had nothing to lose and everything to gain. But, for the second time in fifteen years, they had thrown a golden opportunity onto the fire. One newspaperman wrote:

> Cricket, so far free and untainted by the squalid smear of politics, has now been smudged and a game universally revered as Emperor in the Kingdom of Sport has been dragged to the mud and mire of market square machinations.[27]

While it's easy to hold Fuard, Fernando and Weerasinghe up as villains, the issue is more complex. Some maintain there were longstanding injustices in Sri Lanka cricket; for his part, Weerasinghe remained remorseless until the day he died. 'For a number of years nobody from Galle, Panadura, Kurunegala, Kandy, Ananda College, Nalanda College or any other schools could play for Sri Lanka,' he told *The Daily News*.[28] 'Without any doubt the tour cancellation was the opening of doors for cricketers from other schools and clubs to gain selection to the national team.'

Yet the squad he helped pick does little to prove his point. Seven of fourteen were from Royal and S. Thomas', three from other anglicised Colombo schools. Jayasinghe, Weerasinghe and Polonowita were all from Ananda, but had featured heavily over the past decade. Only T.B. Kehelgamuwa, from Dharmaraja College in Kandy, was a 'new face', having debuted against Lister's team earlier in the year.

'They didn't even bring in one new player from the outstations,' Schaffter exclaimed when we met; certainly, Weerasinghe's suggestion that he oversaw some kind of revolution doesn't stack up. It seems more likely that these men sought to shroud a decision based on personal ambition with a more palatable cover. One ex-player is insistent Fuard only wanted to travel to England so he could gamble on horse-racing. But, as Schaffter put it to me, 'Fuard was clever, he was very clever. He appealed to something which he knew people would fall for.'

That statement is striking. Sally James, the wife of a British diplomat stationed in Ceylon at the time, perceived the issue as revolving around language. 'There has been a lot of politics coming into the selection,' she wrote.[29] 'It always does, and neither Ian Pieris nor Neil Chanmugam were chosen because of their English-speaking backgrounds and they both should have been.' That James – who moved in the upper echelons of society, and whose husband was close friends with Pieris – should see it so, reveals something striking. Many saw Fuard and the selectors' manoeuvring as a cricket equivalent of the political policies the Bandaranaikes had pursued over the past fifteen years. Amidst the 'Sinhalisation' of Ceylon, it was easy to hide behind the historic favouritism shown to English speakers.

Still, Fuard did not simply invent the issue. I once heard an anecdote about the 1958 Gopalan trip – that despite batting beautifully, Weerasinghe was not picked for the marquee match. When another batsman offered to sit out so that he could play, captain Vernon Prins produced a teamsheet written up by F.C. de Saram. 'There was a huge bias earlier,' one ex-player told me. 'This goes back historically, back to F.C. de Saram. That perception of bias was built into guys like Fuard. It was ingrained.' 'Abu felt that he was always victimised by the powers that be,' confirmed another interviewee. 'He had a perception that Neil [Chanmugam] was picked over him.'

Clearly, Fuard resented Chanmugam's ever-presence in the side. He had been left in the cold for close to two and a half years, and proved on his return against Joe Lister's XI that he could still produce at the top level. Yet none would claim Chanmugam benefited from nepotism. In the second half of the 1960s, four quality spinners – Chanmugam, Fuard, Crozier and Polonowita – were battling for two berths. The team didn't have room for them all. It was easy for Fuard to claim his exclusion was due to his rival being a Thomian – but he might have been better off considering his own shortcomings.

Of course, Ceylon cricket was not without prejudice. There was a heavy sprinkling of strange selections in the pre-Test era, several instances of players who seem to have been given short shrift. But there is another side to the coin. Up until the 1960s, only four Colombo schools – Royal, S. Thomas', St Benedict's and St Peter's – had turf wickets. They had the best coaches too. Equally, some reckon the discrimination had more to do with club allegiances than any sort of school discrimination. 'People try to blame the elite schools,' former SLC CEO Ajit Jayasekera told me. 'But irrespective of whether you played for St Anne's Kurunegala or S. Thomas' College, if you played for SSC, you had a chance.'

Regardless, you can see why Tissera's appointment as captain might have rankled. H.I.K. Fernando was the side's senior man, by 1964, a fixture in the team for more than a decade. When he was overlooked, there would have been plenty who claimed that young Michael Tissera was given the job by virtue of being a Thomian. Thirteen of the previous sixteen Ceylonese captains had passed through the corridors of Royal or S. Thomas'.* That clearly made it look as though attending one of the island's two top schools was an entry requirement for captaining the

---

* Apart from them there was Sathasivam, M.K. Albert – a stand-in on tour for one match – and Malcolm Spittel, who also only led the side for a single game.

national team. 'I suppose there was an unconscious bias that those guys could lead better,' one ex-player told me. 'Like the professionals and the amateurs – a classic case of us and them.'

In earlier times that was likely the case, but Tissera was awarded the job on merit. Age doesn't make a captain, and several cricketers I've spoken to have said Fernando was no natural leader. Tissera's captaincy, on the other hand, is unanimously praised. Nor was his appointment universally popular among the cricket establishment. As Chandra Schaffter pointed out, 'Tissera was in his early twenties when we deposed C.I. [Gunasekara] and made him captain. That in itself was a big step. C.I. was from the SSC – and you don't buck the SSC unless you need your head examined. But we did, and they were very angry. We did what we thought was best for Sri Lanka cricket. Nothing else. We may have been wrong – but we weren't interested in anything else.'

Tissera repaid the selectors' faith many times over. He deserved better treatment than he got. In fairness to H.I.K. Fernando, many have said he had no real designs on the captaincy, but was manipulated into sharing the opinion that the selectors had wronged him. Still, there was no need for such a bold power play. The tour's schedule was relentless, and there surely would have been opportunities for him to lead his country onto the field.

That said, Weerasinghe's self-inclusion was the final hammer blow, as one journalist put it, 'the last straw – the one that broke the camel's back'.[30] His justification that he was 'good enough' is irrelevant: the chairman of selectors picking himself, after promising he would not, seemed nefarious. His selection does not stack up either: Lionel Fernando and David Heyn were younger, and had both already made bigger scores for Ceylon. In picking himself, he denied these two a place: on a long tough tour, Heyn was probably worth a spot based on his fielding alone.

And if Weerasinghe truly believed he was good enough, would he not have picked himself for the match against Lister's XI? To the outsider, it looks like he tried to sneak through the back door. Over the years, there have been scathing suggestions that some players treated trips abroad as shopping holidays. Most had never left Asia; a chance to visit England seems to have enticed like forbidden fruit.

No matter how far you dig, it's impossible to find concrete answers. Were Royalists and Thomians still favoured by the selectors? Were Fuard and Weerasinghe acting out of selfishness? Perhaps the answer to both these questions is yes. Half a century on, disputes arising from 1968 still haven't been put to bed. What's clear is that the 1970s should have been a time to celebrate how far Ceylon had come. Instead, they were a hard slog; another decade-long struggle to receive the recognition the island's cricketers had so long craved.

Youth Revolutions

Getting over 1968 must have been tough. Ceylon's best cricketers should have been in England: instead, they were left to languish at home and ponder what had been lost – largely through no fault of their own. Cricket was the best medicine. But the visit of a State Bank of India XI turned out to be curse rather than cure.[31] The U–27s were blown out by an innings, before a full-strength team lost a low-scoring game. There was solace in dismissing a quality side for 145 and 152, but Ceylon's own batting looked brittle. Set 171 for victory, they slumped to 95 all out. No one reached 20; down to the man they were unable to cope with the brilliance of Bishan Bedi.

Better days were ahead. At the start of 1969, Ceylon welcomed the MCC, warming up for a three-Test tour of Pakistan with four matches on the island. The first two were a novelty for Colombo's crowds: for the first time, they would watch their team playing limited-overs cricket. Both games were scheduled for 50 overs, but in the first, Ceylon were miserly in the field – so much so that when lunch came at around the 40-over mark, the MCC realised they were well behind the game. Eager to save face, the English management had a quiet word with their hosts, asking for the game to be extended to 60 overs.[32] Remarkably, the Ceylonese board agreed without complaint – yet another example of the imparity that existed between Ceylon and the big cricket nations. 'Perceptions were different then,' Ranjit Fernando explained. 'We thought England were doing us a favour by coming and playing here. So when they made a request, we didn't challenge it. As a board, we were very subservient.'

Even with a leg-up, the MCC could only reach 236. Sri Lanka's early sunsets meant it would always be a struggle to complete 120 overs, but the hosts controlled the chase as long as it lasted. Fernando and Buddy Reid put on 121 for the first wicket; when the light fully faded, Ceylon were 2 runs short with 4 overs left to play. They won the game on better run rate. For the first time, they had beaten the MCC.

The next day, they entered the second one-dayer with an all-new playing eleven. The English looked off the pace again but were spared further indignity as Ceylon fell 19 runs short. The defeat mattered little; it was spiriting to see a pool of twenty-two players hold their own against the best from England. Clearly, the domestic scene prepared cricketers better for limited-overs matches than for three- or four-day 'tests'.

The last thing anyone wanted was more captaincy drama, but Ceylon weren't in the clear just yet. When Tissera was declared unfit on the morning of the 'test', H.I.K. Fernando was expected to take over.[33] But the selectors came into the changing room and announced that Buddy Reid would lead the side. It was a bombshell that shocked the group – Reid, padded up and practising a few shots, seemed as surprised as anyone.

Thankfully, a sublime innings from Anura Tennekoon overshadowed the controversy. For close to six hours, he handled John Snow, David Brown, Derek Underwood, Pat Pocock and Basil D'Oliveira with aplomb. Though he struck just five boundaries, he refused to be beaten; finally, on the second morning he ran himself out trying to protect the tail.

His 101 was the first century by a Ceylonese against the MCC. All were taken by his tenacity and technical correctness, his willingness to leave the ball and strength through the on side. This was the first concrete sign of what a special player Tennekoon would become. 'Michael [Tissera] missing that match was a huge blow to us, because he was really the rock of the batting at that time,' he told me. 'The batting revolved around him. So I took it upon myself to try and bat as long as possible. Bat and bat. It wasn't a bad effort, although it took a long time.'

Though Ceylon struggled to make inroads, and the game dawdled towards a draw, those who stuck around until the final afternoon were amply rewarded, as Buddy Reid and Ranjit Fernando racked up their second century stand of the series. It was a fine way to cap a month full of firsts, and just the tonic Ceylon needed to restore faith after the horrors of 1968.

That said, the selectors had more surprises up their sleeve. With Tissera finding it harder to get time off work, Dhanisiri Weerasinghe was recalled to captain the side's Gopalan tour in March 1969. Having sullied his reputation a year earlier, all was forgotten remarkably quickly. Indeed, there was surprisingly little resentment at Weerasinghe's presence. 'By that time he had earned his place,' reflects David Heyn. 'People let bygones be bygones.'

Weerasinghe repaid the selectors' forgiveness with his best knock for Ceylon, his 92 spearheading a first-innings victory. Though the team he took to India contained just one Royalist and one Thomian,* it remained tough to tell whether the 'revolution' he and Fuard promised was being acted out. Six months later, a 'test' side with five from Royal or S. Thomas' held their own against Australia. Chanmugam, restored after more than two years in the cold, led the attack with 8 for 90 across the match. Tissera and the Jaffanese C. Balakrishnan struck 50s. Ceylon were certainly growing.

And at the start of 1970, they had a surprise English visit – lifted by a magical moment in the very first over of the 'test'. Steaming in and shaping the ball away, T.B. Kehelgamuwa beat Boycott for pace and clipped the top of off stump.[34] The most dogged batsman in world cricket was back in the pavilion with 0 against his name.

Though just under 5ft 8in, the barrel-chested Kehelgamuwa was quick enough to blow batsmen away. Against the MCC he produced one of his finest spells. Graham Roope and Geoff Arnold were clean bowled too, as he finished with 4 for 19 from 13 overs. The MCC were

---

* That was a big shift from the Pakistan tour two and a half years earlier, when half the squad had been drawn from the two schools. What's more, it looked like the selectors were finally casting their net beyond the 'big' Colombo schools: the 1969 Gopalan side had Gnani Razick from Zahira, T.B. Kehelgamuwa from Dharmarajah in Kandy and C. Balakrishnan from St John's College, Jaffna.

steamrolled for 132.* Although Ceylon lost control of the 'test', they could take heart from the fact that they were showing flashes of real quality in more or less every game they played. They just needed to take the final step of putting it together with more consistency.

This was H.I.K. Fernando's final game for his country: a near-constant presence for the past seventeen years, despite his involvement in 1968, he was a great servant to the Ceylonese game. No doubt, he would have hoped to sign off with a score, but he was run out in single figures by David Heyn. Notwithstanding the indiscretion, Heyn was one of a number of young batsmen starting to score regular runs. Having made 92 in a thrilling Gopalan game at the Oval in March 1970, he had an outstanding tour of India the following January: 86 against Kerala, 104 against the Andhra Chief Minister's XI and 97 in the Gopalan itself – which Ceylon lost narrowly on first innings. Tennekoon scored 99 against Kerala, while Ranjit Fernando blasted 89 against a strong Tamil Nadu C.A. President's XI. Meanwhile, Kehelgamuwa continued to cause problems with his pace – picking up 17 wickets in three games, two of them wins.

Looking back on his career, Heyn told me he was much more comfortable batting away from home. 'I found it easier to focus,' he says. 'When we played in Colombo the circumstances weren't right. We travelled to games independently, we didn't stay together, there wasn't much chance to discuss tactics. We just turned up and played.' The numbers support his gut: he averaged 45.50 abroad against just 20.76 at home. I wonder how many others felt the same. When the team played in Colombo, their preparation lacked any sense of professionalism. Though they often had to do without coaches on tour, at least they could be fully immersed in cricket.

★★★

---

* Some were sceptical about Kehelgamuwa's action – not least Boycott. At a drinks party after the match, Ceylon's players tried to chat to the Yorkshire great. But still fuming over his dismissal, he was in no mood for pleasantries. 'He's chucking, man,' was as far as the conversation went.

The JVP insurrection in April 1971 was the latest in a long line of political crises to grip the island.[35] Colombo's curfew was kept in place for months, bad news for the country's cricketers. Pakistan cancelled their tour, and no other side dared visit in 1971.

Meanwhile, the government began to crack down on personal freedoms. Emergency powers were continually extended; the new constitution, drafted in May 1972, promised to give Buddhism 'the foremost place' in society – declaring it the state's duty to 'protect and foster the Buddha Sasana'. Ceylon was to become the Republic of Sri Lanka; by promoting a singular religious identity onto a patchwork nation, the government was playing with fire.

At least 1972 saw the return of cricket. In January, a polished Australia U-19 side arrived to take on Ceylon's schoolboys. This was a big step forward: the country's youngsters had impressed in India in 1969/70 – for the first time, the system was giving them opportunities to bridge the gap between schools and international cricket. They fared well in two three-day games against the Australians – almost winning the second behind a Bandula Warnapura century. He, Duleep Mendis and Roy Dias proved there was burgeoning batting talent on the island, while Ajit de Silva looked a classical left-arm spinner – with the flight, guile and turn to discomfit top-quality batters.

Still, they would have probably lost the four-day game were it not for the help of some famous faces.[36] The public clearly missed cricket during a dour 1971, and 8,000 turned up for each day's play at The Oval. By the third afternoon they saw their boys slipping towards defeat: well behind, and losing wickets faster than the match was running out of time. But Percy Abeysekera had a plan. Still only 35, he was not quite yet 'Uncle', but was showing the sort of steadfast commitment to Sri Lankan cricket that has marked him out as unique. When captain Asitha Jayaweera reached 50, Percy rushed onto the pitch to congratulate him. His intention was simple, if a little nefarious: take time out of the game; help the schoolboys salvage a draw. The crowds loved him for it, but the police were less impressed. Not for the last time, they dragged Percy away in cuffs.

But as they took him from the Oval, they were given a stern word from one who had experienced their hospitality at first hand. 'Don't lay a finger on him,' warned Mahadevan Sathasivam. Four hours later, Percy was released from Borella Police Station. Satha appreciated his well-timed act of patriotism, and paid the Rs.100 bail. He wasn't the only one: close to 1,000 turned up to cheer Percy out of lockup. The young Ceylonese had saved the match – and he had played as big a part as anyone.

The board understood that blooding the next generation was vital, and when Tamil Nadu arrived for the Gopalan Trophy in March 1972, a warm-up was scheduled against Ceylon's schoolboys. Though they couldn't overcome the wizardry of Venkat and V.V. Kumar, Warnapura made an assured 79: off the back of his performances against Australia, people were starting to talk. But another youngster had moved ahead of him in the pecking order.

After smashing a blistering 184 in the Royal–Thomian, Duleep Mendis was rushed into the national side for the Gopalan Trophy.[37] Though he top-scored with 52 – and added 34 second time around – there was little joy for Ceylon, their best batsmen struggling with Madras' spin twins as much as the schoolboys had done. Being beaten by an innings at home stung, and was well short of what was expected for a side with Test aspirations. At least they had a chance to bounce back quickly. Malaysia arrived in April 1972, and were mercilessly put to the sword. Warnapura made 294, mounting a mammoth 426-run partnership with Tennekoon as a young Board President's XI ran amok. Mendis cracked an unbeaten century too; all in all the home side racked up 736-4, good enough to win by an innings and 483.

And on 9 November 1972, the national side emerged from the Oval dressing room under their new name – Sri Lanka. Though Pakistan were on top for much of the three days, an unbeaten 64 from Mendis on the final afternoon staved off the prospect of defeat. Young Duleep was proving a very special player. The 986 runs he scored during the 1972/73 P. Sara Trophy set a new national record; yet his impact was more than mere runs. 'Duleep had no fear,' reflects Heyn. 'Or gave the impression he had no fear. That was his biggest strength. Plus, he had a very good eye – and he had his own technique.' To bowl at Mendis when he was in his pomp was to feel entirely helpless; to watch him wield his bat like a club and crash the ball to the fence was bewildering. No matter the state of the game, whenever you ran in at the diminutive Duleep, the pressure was on your shoulders.

But the arrival of a new star could not hide the inconsistencies in Sri Lanka's performances. Since the JVP-enforced hiatus, their batting seemed to have taken a backward step. Things got no easier when the MCC arrived in February, as Sri Lanka were bundled out for 86 on the first morning of the 'test'. At least D.S. de Silva's leg-spin caused problems, and the team battled 100 overs in the second innings to secure a draw. The one-day game offered consolation too, as an anchoring 61 from Tennekoon helped Sri Lanka gun down 158 with 11 balls to spare. For the second time in four years, they had turned over the English in a limited-overs match. Confidence was growing that Sri Lanka could compete in this new-fangled one-day cricket.

Though T.B. Kehelgamuwa and a one-handed Mevan Pieris mounted a 48-run last-wicket stand in the 1973 Gopalan Trophy, the Lankan charge was stopped 4 short of victory when Kehelgamuwa took a fresh-air swipe. Worryingly, the fixture they were used to dominating had now been lost for three years running. All in all, the tour was a disappointment. Pieris and Kehelgamuwa bowled with heart for much of the trip, but with Tissera and Tennekoon missing, the batting lacked gumption. In four matches, only Heyn made a century. Worse, Sri Lanka were routed for 119 in a 40-over match against Kerala Chief Minister's XI.

Nor could they blame alien conditions for their failures. Back home, they failed to reach 150 against the National Cricket Club of India in May 1973 – though they managed to stave off defeat, the inability to put first-innings runs on the board was proving costly. Time and again, Sri Lanka found themselves battling to get back into games. They simply couldn't win matches behind such low scores.

If there is a mitigating factor, it is that the side could rarely call on their strongest eleven during the era. Take Michael Tissera, Ceylon's beating heart throughout much of the 1960s. From the start of 1970 to the 1975 World Cup, he played just five of twenty-nine first-class matches. 'I just accepted it,' he reflects. 'Cricket wasn't my main job. I had a family – I had to earn a living and it was working in tea that allowed that, not cricket. My preference was work, although I loved cricket. There just comes a time.' Tennekoon was finding it harder to get time off too. Without these two linchpins, the side's batting struggles were somewhat inevitable.

The year ended with the arrival of a talented Pakistan U-25s team, whose seven-game unbeaten run left the island's cricketers to reflect on opportunities lost. A Board's President XI squandered a 135-run first innings lead; Ceylon's U-25s slipped from 230-2 to 333 all out, and crumbled in the second innings to leave the visitors a regulation chase. At least a talented batting core was emerging. In Tissera, Tennekoon, Mendis, Warnapura, Sunil Wettimuny, David Heyn and Ranjit Fernando, Sri Lanka had seven batsmen who had shown they could produce against quality opposition. What's more, of this group only Tissera was over 30. The future looked bright.

That said, the most significant developments of 1973 came away from the field. On 10 August, the new 'Sports Law' dictated that squads now had to pass across the Sports Minister's desk before being ratified.[38] While Minister Ratnayake clearly wanted to prevent a repeat of 1968, the Sports Law ingrained and intensified the scepticism that has surrounded selection. It created a situation where the ultimate arbiter of squads was someone with little cricket experience, who likely had more pressing concerns than the game's best interest. Still, it was not all bad. After decades of relying on the goodwill of benefactors, Sri Lanka could finally call on the government for financial aid.* This was vital: already an underdog on the international stage, the island desperately needed cash to improve its cricketing infrastructure.

But more than money was required for the island's cricket to flourish. Since Kalutara town were crowned inaugural champions of the Premier Trophy, a Colombo club had won the tournament every year. So the establishment of District Sports Committees was a real boost. It came off the back of the completion of the Welagedara Stadium in Kurunegala in 1972 – and a more general surge in interest in cricket in the provinces at the start of the 1970s.[39] Maybe, Sri Lanka could finally begin to draw on the potential lying dormant in its rurality. The team would have a much

---

*   Rs. 25,000 was set aside to lay practice pitches at the NCC in 1972, followed by a Rs. 30,000 grant two years later. Meanwhile, a National Sports Council, a National Sports Fund and District Sports Committees were finally established.

better chance of competing with international sides if they could call on players from outside Colombo.

The city's cricket scene was developing too. Bloomfield had traditionally been a poor club, but under the presidency of Shelley Wickramasinghe it began to take strides during the 1970s.[40] At the start of the decade they had no turf wicket, and no proper pavilion – just a small shed on wheels. But the club found new premises just behind Colombo's racecourse and managed to drum up cash for better facilities. Grass replaced matting, and bright young talents – especially from Ananda and Nalanda – began joining the club. Warnapura, Lalith Kaluperuma, Ajit de Silva and Anura Ranasinghe all made it their home; this was a group that could mount a serious challenge. Nomads and the CCC were becoming forces to be reckoned with too: the disruption of the Maitland Place duopoly was no bad thing. Meanwhile, mercantile cricket was becoming more competitive and prestigious – with Browns and Maharajas making real efforts to employ national players. These were all steps in the right direction

While the Sports Law had profound and long-lasting effects for Sri Lanka, it was another announcement in 1973 that caught cricketers' ears. The inaugural Cricket World Cup would be held in England during the summer of 1975. Eight teams would challenge for the trophy, among them Sri Lanka. This was exciting news, especially sweet for those who had meant to be heading to England five years earlier. It wasn't quite Test status, but it was a chance to travel to the home of cricket and take on the game's elite. In their own backyard, Sri Lanka had seemed naturals when it came to one-day cricket. Now they just had to show the rest of the world what they could do.

THE FIRST WORLD CUP

As 1974 arrived, so did the touring Indians. If they'd expected an easy ride, they were given a rude awakening. In the first 'test', Mevan Pieris had openers Gopal Bose and Sunil Gavaskar early, Ajit de Silva spun circles around the tail – and Sri Lanka built a big first-innings lead behind Tennekoon's courageous 131. Though India managed to stave off defeat, the islanders had once again gotten the better of a fully fledged Test nation.

But old frailties still showed themselves. In the second 'test', the hosts were bundled out for 121 and asked to follow-on. At 30-3 second time around, they were staring down the barrel of a hammering until Tennekoon produced another innings of real fortitude. His 169* lifted Sri Lanka to 290. 'When it came to the fourth morning, we still had a long way to go to avoid an innings defeat,' he explained. 'Mevan Pieris, he was a character, and he said "skipper, let's give these guys a good fight." Our cricket board obviously didn't have much faith in us, and had started removing the chairs so they didn't have to pay for them on the final day. That made us more determined, to prove a point that we could bat on. It was a fairly fast, bouncy track so wickets kept falling at the other end, but we got ahead by 70. To have batted three sessions and end up being not out, I was very very satisfied.'

Tennekoon's grit clearly inspired his bowlers. Pieris and Opatha had India reeling at 43-4: though they crossed the line without further losses, Sri Lanka had made it a contest. Where earlier sides might have rolled over, this team dug in and fought. No one epitomised the battling spirit more than the captain. In scoring hundreds in back-to-back 'tests', he'd established himself as the best batsman the island had seen since Sathasivam. What's more, he cemented his status as leader ahead of the 1975 World Cup.

When I first met Tennekoon, I was taken aback. He is shy and softly spoken, short and slight – with a gentility that makes it hard to imagine him holding strong against the bruising fast bowlers of the 1970s. Or leading a team that was not without egos. But I soon realised that he has a singular focus. He speaks slowly but each word is considered. He may not have been a born leader like Tissera, but he galvanised his men through force of action. Each time he went out to bat and produced another gritty gem, their respect for him grew. Put simply, he led from the front.

Down to a man, the players could take plenty of confidence from competing with India. Pieris, for one, knew he had the rub on one of cricket's best openers. 'Gavaskar shuffled across onto off stump before the ball was bowled, so that inswinger of mine gave him problems,' he proudly told me. Ceylon's cricketers were starting to realise they were good, and recognition was coming from abroad too. Tennekoon and Heyn were invited to turn out for the World XI against India in Bombay in 1974; later in the year, these two and Mendis featured for Hindustan Breweries in the Moin-ud-Dowlah tournament.

Sri Lanka had the feel of a side on the charge. Mendis smashed a century for a Sri Lanka Colts side against Tamil Nadu in mid-February – and followed up with 104 off 149 in the Gopalan. There were players waiting in the wings too: in a one-day Mercantile match the same month, Roy Dias cracked a remarkable 228.

So Tennekoon's men left for Pakistan in March full of confidence, and continued to build momentum in the run-up to the first 'test'. They opted to field in Lahore: with Pieris left out after some internal squabbles, Tony Opatha stood up and led the attack with 6 for 91. Heyn and Warnapura carried the team to a solid lead: Sri Lanka were in the hunt. But wickets dried up in the second innings, and Intikhab Alam showed no interest in a sporting declaration. At the post-match dinner, board president A.H. Kardar chastised him for batting on past 100 overs.[41] It might have been negative, but it was nonetheless a sign of respect for Sri Lanka's batsmen – in a sense, another small feather in their cap.

With Ajit and D.S. de Silva (no relation) finding turn and bounce in Karachi, Sri Lanka were ahead for most of the second 'test' too. But set 176 for victory, Tennekoon's men collapsed to 114-7 and fell 18 runs short. Still, Pakistan knew they'd been in a dogfight. On the final day, some of the batsmen noticed Asif Masood bowling from the popping crease;* Tennekoon made a point of marking the crease to show the umpires – but they simply told him 'no'.

'Certainly, to come so close and not get across the line was a huge disappointment,' he reflected. 'But that's the way the game goes. Sometimes you miss out on opportunities.' At least Sri Lanka had shown they were a long way from being a pushover. Each time they took to the field now, they fought for their lives. In Tennekoon's words: 'Every match we played against an international side mattered to us, because

---

* At this stage cricket still used the back-foot rule, so his front foot would have been at least a yard in front of the no-ball line.

our performances were taken into consideration to see if we were fit to play Test cricket. So we played with a lot of pressure at that time – we felt if we failed we were letting the country down.'

Impressed, Kardar promised to propose Sri Lanka for full ICC status.[42] The holy grail was getting closer; the team's growth amply reflected by the players' personal returns during the tour. Seven batsmen averaged north of 30, and even without Pieris the attack carried plenty of depth. 'It was a fantastic tour,' remembers Heyn. 'And we did well – we got runs. That game in Karachi, it was just one of those things where you succumb to pressure. But, we weren't disheartened.'

Sri Lanka now had a group of players it could really rely on. No doubt, playing regular cricket helped. In the first four months of 1974, there were thirteen first-class games, against just sixteen in the five-year stretch from the start of 1968 to the end of 1972. Still, chasms in the calendar remained a salient feature of Sri Lankan cricket – and the team now had to wait ten months before they would be together on the field again.

After such a long break, they faced the fearsome prospect of the West Indies. Jayasinghe was brought in to deaden the CCC pitch, but Sri Lanka couldn't take full advantage. Despite a dashing 55 from Heyn and 44 from the returning Tissera, they only reached 205. At one point, Heyn leaned back and carved an Andy Roberts bouncer over the slips for 4. Less than impressed, Roberts couldn't help offering up a polite invitation: 'Come try that in Antigua, man.'

Such a meagre total left Sri Lanka up against it. Viv Richards cracked 151 to sink them further, but Tennekoon's men batted out 77.3 overs to escape with a share of the spoils. Their rearguard shifted the series' momentum. On the first morning of the second 'test', Opatha took full advantage of a drying Oval wicket with the spell of a lifetime. He had Roy Fredricks bowled, Alvin Kallicharan and Richards caught behind and Lloyd lbw; when Kaluperama got David Murray, the West Indians were 40-5. The best team in the world were being humbled in Borella.

Indeed, while Opatha is best remembered for organising the rebel tour to South Africa, up to this stage he was the most polished quick Sri Lanka had produced. I was lucky enough to spend an evening with him about a year before he passed; hearing him talk about fast bowling was fascinating. Whereas many of Sri Lanka's quicks were known for their 'danger ball', Opatha had a more progressive approach. 'I always thought that you have to bowl depending on the wicket and adjust yourself. If it's gloomy and you're moving the ball you don't have to bowl too fast,' he explained. 'I varied my bowling – six balls, I'd send six different ways. I don't bowl pace all the time. I have a change of pace, a slower ball, an inswinger, an outswinger, an off-cutter, a bouncer. I got the batsman worrying, "What's this guy gonna bowl next?" I played with batsmen, and enjoyed my cricket very much.'

'When I bowl, I don't care if it's Gavaskar or Richards,' he continued. 'It's just another guy. If you get scared, you can't bowl. I don't care, I don't respect my opponents while I'm playing. They're lower than me – I always think I'm the best. I never, ever overestimate those guys. I can get him for 0 – I've done it. It's a mental sport, it's all between the ears. If you're scared, you can't perform. Look at Virat Kohli: everyone's scared to bowl at him. Why? Who is he? If I had a ball, I'd shell the bugger.'

Strikingly, Opatha was one of the first in Sri Lanka to truly forge a career out of cricket. For so long, playing the game had meant making a financial sacrifice – but times were slowly changing. 'I had a very hard start,' Opatha told me. 'Four boys. My father didn't have a big job or a big income, so life was getting very hard. I thought I'd give up studying and go into cricket 100 per cent. Leaving school, I was offered a job with a car straight away – I thought, "here you are, this is an opening". I got that break and I grabbed it.' For Tony, cricket offered hope; in time it would lead him to jobs in England, Ireland, Holland, South Africa and Bangladesh.

But back to the West Indies. D.S. quickly cleaned up the tail to send Lloyd's men plummeting to 119 before Tennekoon produced another masterclass: 101 runs flowed from his bat, the innings taking him past 1,000 runs in 'tests' (1011 at 42.13). In defying the amateurish nature of Sri Lankan cricket to score centuries against three Test nations in the space of a year, Tennekoon proved he was truly world-class. He'd come a long way from practising shots with a ruler in the corridors of S. Thomas' College.

Tennekoon wasn't the only Sri Lankan ready to stand up to the West Indian battery. At the time, Mevan Pieris was working in a factory that made foam rubber products. 'The Oval was a nightmare to play on – and that's the first time you faced bowlers of that speed on that kind of track,' he animatedly told me. But Pieris had a plan. He cut up small pieces of foam and glued them onto a vest, fashioning an impromptu chest guard. Yet he failed to account for the heat. 'By tea I was 20 odd not out – but that thing was a bloody burden. I removed it and threw it away. I thought that was a very foolish thing I made.'

Sri Lanka could not capitalise on a 186-run first-innings lead, but this was another moral victory. For the first two days, they had been well on top of the game: had it been scheduled for four instead of three, they surely would have been favourites to chase down 121. 'More than being able to bowl them out, it was making 300-plus that gave us confidence,' Pieris told me. 'There was a general feeling among international circles that Sri Lanka had matured.' There were personal glories too, not least D.S. de Silva's match bag of 10 for 146.* At 32, he was entering his leg-spinning prime. Across the last two series, he'd bagged 43 first-class wickets at 23.27.

Disappointingly, drastic improvements in the longer game came with a notable downturn in limited-overs cricket. Since beating the MCC in February 1972, Sri Lanka had lost six straight – including chastening defeats to the Sind President's XI and Rawalpindi. One-day cricket had always come more naturally to Lankan cricketers, so it was strange the team should be struggling with the format – especially given the personnel at their disposal. The team was bursting with talent, but would need to find form quickly. The 1975 World Cup was without doubt the biggest opportunity in Sri Lanka's cricket history, a tournament they could ill afford to end in failure.

After the false dawns of 1954 and 1968, this was Sri Lanka's chance to impress the game's governors up close. The spectre of Test cricket had hung over the island for three decades; now it was close enough to touch. The BCCSL understood the significance of the opportunity, so decided to send a pool of players on a two-week, pre-tournament camp to Nuwara Eliya.[43] It was a good decision: practice usually meant a rushed hour between the end of work and the fall of darkness – clearly inadequate preparation for a test as stern as a World Cup. What's more,

---

*   Hailing from Unawatuna near Galle, de Silva was first picked for Ceylon in 1966 as a batsman, but had worked tirelessly over the past decade to turn himself into a quality leg-spin bowler, with an excellent googly and plenty of well-disguised variations.

the hill country was as close as the team could get to mimicking English conditions. The cooler climate and cloud cover represented something close to acclimatisation.

Though a sponsor offered the team a 'luxury' coach to ferry them to the hills, the journey was less grand than it sounded. There was no air conditioning, and when the bus reached Kadugannawa, it broke down. The players had to get out and push; all in all, it turned into a ten-hour trip. Bertie Wijesinha took care of coaching, while air-force officer Raja Wickramasinghe was brought in as the team's temporary trainer. He took to running them into the ground with the grim sadism of a drill sergeant. Each morning, the players would meet at 6 am to circle the Nuwara Eliya racecourse. The cold air and altitude made it an unpleasant exercise, aggravated by the fact that the army camp where they stayed had no hot water. 'There was only one tap,' recalls Ranjit Fernando. 'All of us used to go there to bathe. It was severely cold.' A hot water line was finally installed when some of the players started getting sick.

Once they were through the ordeal of morning runs, the team could focus on cricket. But the Radella ground where they practised was far from the perfect test site. The wicket was slow and stolid, the boundaries tiny. Some of the lower-order batsmen spent days gleefully smashing 6s into the surrounding tea plantations, warning they were going to do the same to Lillee and Thomson. The reality would be quite different. Still, the trip was undoubtedly worthwhile. Players returned to Colombo fitter and better prepared for their English adventure. Plus, they bonded as a group: some took the chance to climb Pidurutalagala; all enjoyed a tour of the Lion brewery. And happily, the selection of the squad was without controversy.

Some had been to England before, but this was most of the team's first trip outside Asia. They stepped off the plane into a rainy summer's day. Some were surprised to see a white man behind the wheel of their coach, others taken aback by the sprawling scale of the city. For most, it was a culture shock: 'I wasn't used to it,' Tony Opatha told me, laughing. 'The way y'all were kissing on the road. It was funny.'

The team were less amused when they arrived at their digs. Sri Lanka's cricketers knew their board survived on a shoestring budget: none expected a red carpet rolled out, but they weren't fully prepared for the disaster that was the Ceylon Student Centre. 'It was like a beggars' colony,' remembers Mevan Pieris. 'A beggars' home. Not the right place for an international team at all.' In fact, the building was soon to be condemned. The rooms were like dungeons, blankets were threadbare. As in Nuwara Eliya, there was no hot water. Dennis Chanmugam was in the bathroom when part of the ceiling collapsed on his head. 'The facilities were terrible, but we couldn't complain,' reflects Tissera. 'We had no money, and we had an opportunity to play in a World Cup in England, so why grumble? In the end it was all good fun.'

Nor was it all bad. There was a TV in the lobby – a device not introduced to Sri Lanka until 1979. And the student centre served good rice and curry: important, since food had been a genuine concern for the board going into the tour. Unable to budget for meals, they arranged for the squad to attend endless functions where free fare would be provided. But this meant trekking to all corners of London, a distraction the players could ill afford. After being forced to sit in Battersea Park and watch two teams of Sri Lankan Londoners play a low-quality match, they decided enough was enough. They were happy to fend for themselves; the team had come to play cricket.

Things took a turn once tournament sponsors Prudential took over. The team were moved to the Kensington Close Hotel, 2 miles and a world away from the Ceylon Student Centre. Competition stepped up a notch, too.* Although Sri Lanka lost two practice matches against New Zealand in Eastbourne, there were positives to take from both. Ranjit Fernando made a classy, unbeaten 98 in the first; in the second, the team were going well until Anura Ranasinghe was bizarrely run out. Comfortably home in his crease, he jumped to avoid being struck by a throw and was given by the umpire. Sri Lankan fans, sitting in parked cars around the ground, began hooting their horns in derision. The noise rose into a cacophony: the game had to be stopped until silence was eventually restored.

---

*   During the first weeks of the tour, the board had arranged matches against Hampstead, the Indian Gymkhana, Finchley, St Ives & Ramsey and Berkshire – hardly ideal preparation for the rigours of a World Cup. The biggest challenge they faced was adjusting to the cold: 'at times it was unbearable,' Mendis recalled forty-five years later.

After meeting the Queen at Buckingham Palace and an official lunch at Lord's, the squad headed up to Manchester for their tournament opener against the West Indies. As Tennekoon remembers, 'It was green. Overcast. Gloomy. And fairly chilly. And we lost the toss.' Not what Sri Lanka had been hoping for. Lloyd opted to field: the conditions allowed Bernard Julien to do things with the ball the Lankan batsmen had rarely seen. 'He was moving it in the air and off the pitch,' says Tennekoon. 'We couldn't counter it.' Indeed. The team batted less than 38 of their allotted 60 overs; only a gutsy 21 from number ten D.S. de Silva lifted them to 86. No one else managed 15. The West Indies easily knocked off the runs, losing just Roy Fredericks in the process. It was a nightmare start.

Yet, you could hardly blame the Sri Lankan batsman. The ball might swing or seam a little at home, but it wouldn't hoop through the air and then jag off the pitch. Against a world-class West Indies attack, this was a baptism of fire. To add insult to injury, a busload of Sri Lankan fans had gotten delayed and arrived as the game was petering out. The crowd continued to swell, but there was no cricket to entertain them, so the teams agreed to play a 'fill-up' 20-over match. 'By playing that, we were totally demoralised,' Ranjit Fernando told me. 'Thoroughly dejected,' agreed Duleep Mendis. 'But Australia was another game and everyone was keen to play better.'

The team headed back to London with a fire in their belly. But they were dealt a blow on the eve of the second match. David Heyn – without doubt the side's best fielder – arrived back at the hotel fifteen minutes after curfew. He was promptly suspended, a loss Sri Lanka could ill afford. Even members of the squad readily admit that they were not the most athletic outfit. 'Bloody rotten fielders,' one bowler angrily remembered. 'Some of those guys were like ants.' Having played so little one-day cricket, they perhaps didn't fully appreciate the importance of being sharp in the field. The realisation that games could hinge on 30 runs saved or lost had to be learned the hard way.

At The Oval, Sri Lanka were made to toil as Australian glutted themselves on a shirtfront wicket. They raced to 182-0, and with the boundaries pushed back all the way to the fence, managed to run 4 on several occasions. Although Tennekoon's men pegged Australia back to 328-5, it could have been less. Tony Opatha was by far and away the most economical bowler on the day, but a mix-up meant he only got through 9 of his 12 overs. It sounds a rookie mistake, but sides were still learning the ropes of one-day cricket.

For the second time in the tournament, Lankan backs were to the wall. They would not die wondering. Ranjit Fernando cracked Dennis Lillee for three 4s in his first over, including a glorious cut over the waiting cordon. Though he and Warnapura went, Sunil Wettimuny and Duleep Mendis steadied the ship. After 31 overs, Sri Lanka were 150-2. The chase was on.

Ian Chappell later described the match as 'haunting'.[44] Since arriving in England, Australia had faced backlash from the press over their short-pitched bowling. Chappell saw the game against Sri Lanka as a perfect PR opportunity – and before the match, told his bowlers to pitch the ball up.[45] But, by this stage, he'd seen more than enough dashing drives for one day. He threw the ball to Jeff Thomson. Captain and bowler's minds were in perfect harmony. It was time to see how the Sri Lankans played off the back foot.

Thomson is probably the fastest and most fearsome bowler ever to hold a cricket ball. And in 1975, he was at his zenith. None of the batsmen who played in this game hesitate to describe him as the quickest they faced. All agree the challenge was compounded by his slingy, round-arm action. 'He came in like a javelin thrower, so you had no idea what to expect,' explains Tissera. 'Because of the action, you picked it late,' agrees Tennekoon. In those days, with no helmets or chest guards, that was a seriously daunting prospect. 'Truly, I never saw the ball,' Sunil Wettimuny told me. 'I only saw an arrow-like red line passing me.'

Standing at the non-striker's end, Duleep Mendis had a more visceral reaction. 'Watching Thommo's thunderbolts at 100+ mph was no joke. Marsh was collecting his deliveries over head high almost another 22 yards back.' Nonetheless, Mendis was fearless. When Thomson bowled short outside the off stump, he tried to take him on.

His bat only found fresh air. 'Duleep tried to hook Thomson,' Tennekoon told me, still a little disbelieving forty-five years later. 'That was not the wisest thing to do.' The next ball pitched in the same spot – Mendis repeated the stroke. But the ball cut back off the wicket and came crashing into his forehead. He crumpled in a heap. The crack, like a gunshot, was enough to make the crowd feel sick. Horrifically, the ball ran away towards the cover boundary. 'Black lips went chalk white and shuddering,' Wettimuny recalled. 'I truly thought he would die. It made me shiver and chilled my spine.'

There was no stretcher at the ground, so Mevan Pieris and Dennis Chanmugam rushed to the middle to carry Mendis away. 'His eyeballs were turning,' remembers Pieris. 'He was in a very bad way. But he had the strength to put his arm around me. I could feel him holding on.' 'I was fully unconscious,' confirms Mendis. 'I came back to my senses only when I was being carried off the field. When I woke up the next day, it was like I was carrying 100kgs on my head.'

Tennekoon took Mendis back to the dressing room, so it was a good ten minutes before he made his way to the crease. The crowd might have thought he wasn't coming at all. Some booed the bullying Thomson, but he was unperturbed. He forced Wettimuny to wear a couple in the ribs, then sent a vicious yorker hurtling into the big toe of Wettimuny's back foot. As the batsman hopped around in agony, Thomson threw his stumps down.[46] Though none of his teammates joined the appeal, Thomson's blood was boiling and he remained remorseless. The next ball cannoned into the identical spot. Wettimuny could take no more. He tried to hobble off the ground but knew he couldn't walk. He too had to be carried to the changing room.

The fallen pair were taken to St Thomas' Hospital. Wettimuny had a broken foot, a cracked rib and a badly bruised body; by some miracle, Mendis suffered no serious damage to brain or skull.

While Wettimuny was lain up, a policeman began asking questions.

'Who hit you?'

'Thomson,' he replied.

'Where?'

'At the Oval.'

'What were you doing?'

'Playing cricket.'

Still, the constable was unable to join the dots. He looked stern. 'Do you wish to press charges?'

With two of their batsmen banged up in hospital, Sri Lanka could have easily wilted. But Tennekoon and Tissera battled bravely, standing up to the attack to make 48 and 52 respectively. Though they fell 52 short of their target, the 276 Sri Lanka scored remained a World Cup record for a chasing side through to 1983. What's more, they had shown they possessed skill and spirit in abundance. After the match, the Australians invited them for a drink in their dressing room. 'I think they felt a little bad about sending two of our guys to hospital,' Tennekoon told me. But it was more than guilt. Down to a man, the Australians knew they had been given a hell of a game. This was a performance Sri Lanka could be proud of.

So it was disappointing that they limped out of the tournament against Pakistan. Zaheer Abbas played a gem of an innings; in reply, Sri Lanka never got going. In many ways, this was more disheartening than the West Indies defeat. The track was good for batting, the foes familiar, but on the day it just didn't happen. Having conceded 330, they were skittled for 138. Their tournament was over.

Although the team's results were mixed, there were mitigating factors. They had no knowledge of English conditions and little experience of limited-overs cricket. Most would agree that their group contained the tournament's three best sides* – plus, the lack of a support team was undoubtedly costly. Sri Lanka had no coach, physio or trainer. Had they been able to hire an English pro familiar with the format and conditions, it would have been a great help. But there was no money. The players had to figure things out for themselves.

One man they could count on was Dusty Miller, who many claim was the unsung hero of the trip. Before the tournament began, he took the team to Len Muncer's shop near Lord's and told them each to choose a bat. And crucially, he organised and paid for a post-World Cup tour, designed to prove Sri Lanka's status as the 'best of the rest', indisputably the next cab off the rank in terms of full Test status.

---

* Australia and West Indies were eventual finalists, while Pakistan were a whisker away from knocking out the champions.

First up was a game against East Africa at Taunton. Sri Lanka were 4 runs behind after the first innings, but got it right on second attempt – hurtling to 332-5 dec. after 68 overs. It always looked like too many. Opatha did damage up front, while Tissera's leg breaks cleaned up the tail. In the twilight of his career, he claimed his maiden first-class five-for, as Sri Lanka cruised home winners by 115.

It might seem strange today, but in 1975 Holland and Denmark were up in arms about Sri Lanka's inclusion at the World Cup.[47] Both thought they were better sides. To prove them wrong, Dusty decided Sri Lanka should take both on in their own backyards. First up was Holland in The Hague. D.S. bowled beautifully on the matting, his 8 wickets leaving Sri Lanka needing 116 in the game's final session. It looked unlikely, but Heyn – promoted to number three – smashed an unbeaten 73 to ensure the target was gunned down in 15.3 overs.

After a stopover in Hamburg, the team headed to Hernig to take on the Danish. It proved a more straightforward proposition, with Mendis smashing a century as Sri Lanka won inside two days. In typical Scandinavian style, a smorgasbord had been laid out for the post-match tea. But while the visitors gazed longingly at the table adorned with lager, sandwiches and sweets, Denmark's captain could be heard castigating his team in their dressing room. For fifteen, twenty, twenty-five minutes Sri Lanka waited. After half an hour, they had little choice but to leave. They returned to England. The spread remained untouched. Perhaps the lecture still rolls on.

Today these matches are a mere footnote to the team's World Cup exploits, but at the time they were vital. 'If we dropped a game against one of those sides it would not have looked good for us,' Tennekoon reflects. 'It was important to win them.' Having beaten East Africa, Holland and Denmark away from home, there could be little argument that Sri Lanka were the best side not to have a seat at the top table.

There was yet another heartening footnote to the team's English adventure. On the flight back to Colombo, nearly half the squad were missing. Six had won contracts to play league cricket. To their genuine surprise, they discovered that they could earn some money from the game they had given so much to. It was a ground-breaking moment – one that changed the lives of those who stayed and set a precedent for many at home. What's more, it reflected a changing conception of Sri Lankan cricketers in England. The likes of Goonesena, Jayasinghe and Inman were no longer seen as one-offs. It was finally clear that there was plenty of talent brewing in the island in the Indian Ocean.

CROSSING THE LINE

Seeing the island's cricketers stand up on the biggest stage brought joy to many at home. But even during the World Cup it was impossible to ignore the storm brewing in Sri Lanka. Twice during the tournament, Tamil demonstrators invaded the pitch, forcing stoppages in play.[48] A leaflet handed out during the Australia match aligned 'Sinhala Sri Lanka' with Apartheid South Africa, bemoaning the 'decimation of the Thamil [sic] national identity', and the 'denial' of the Tamil language.

These were valid concerns, yet the leaflet fell flat in its claim that 'The Sri Lanka Cricket Team was not picked on merit.' Today, it is what the players remember from the demonstrations. Most were bemused by it, not least because Dennis Chanmugam was part Tamil. Equally, their insistence that 'there was discrimination against prominent Thamil players of international standard' seems unfounded. The leaflet gives no examples: Dias is the only name that springs to mind, and no one suggests there was anything Machiavellian about his exclusion. Ultimately, the protestors' attempt to paint the Sri Lanka team as 'racist' missed the mark.

However, the fact that the situation in Sri Lanka had reached a stage where Tamils in England were protesting was worrying. Tensions were rising – and Sri Lanka's Tamils had every reason to be dissatisfied. Amidst a raft of prejudicial policies, many began to feel uneasy about their place in Sri Lankan society.

★★★

Sensing that Test status was now within reach, the board hurriedly arranged a three-'test' tour of India in October and November 1975. Though the series was lost 2-0, there were plenty of positives for Sri

Lanka to take home with them. A Gavaskar double-hundred meant they were always up against it in the first 'test', but the team stood up and fought, with Heyn a whisker away from becoming the first Sri Lankan to score twin centuries in an international. Having made 104 in the first innings, he was dismissed 16 runs short of three figures in the second.

He is still annoyed over how. With India's spin stocks full to the brim, the great Venkat couldn't find a place in the eleven. When he was brought on as a substitute, stood ready to pounce in the gully, Heyn complained to the captain: 'He's a specialist fielder, you can't have him there.' Venkat was moved to third slip; Heyn slashed the next ball straight into his hands. Any hope of saving the game went with his wicket; when I asked him what he remembered about those innings, he gave me a wry smile. 'Everything.'

In Ahmedabad, D.S. de Silva's second-innings 6 for 47 gave Sri Lanka a shot at victory. But while five of the top six made starts, none reached 40, and Tennekoon's men fell 65 short of a 250-run target. Still, they grew through the tour, claiming a solid first-innings lead in the final 'test'. When the game drew to a close, India were 87 runs short of parity with 4 wickets in hand. A fifth day would have been a terrific spectacle.

But winning wasn't everything, and Sri Lanka could count the tour as progress. Their growth was again on show when Pakistan arrived in January 1976. The team won both 40-over games behind impressive bowling, and held their nerve when it came to the first 'test'. The match belonged to Lalith Kaluperuma, who arrived at the crease as night-watchman on the first evening with Sri Lanka floundering at 19-4. He was on 0* overnight, but added 96 the following day to ensure his side went into the second innings ahead. 'When I was asked to go and bat on the first evening, I thought "what to do",' he recalls today, with a chuckle. 'I faced three balls and left all three – managed to survive. The next day, I found that after some time, I got a little bit of confidence. I was lucky also: I was hooking the ball and it was falling away from the fielder or going for four.'

A 113-run stand from Pakistan's openers looked to have brought them back into the game, but Kaluperuma had both caught in quick succession. He trapped Intikhab first up too, and Pakistan crashed to

202 all out. Still, the 188 Sri Lanka needed looked a long way off at 108-6. Once again, Kaluperuma came to the party. He cracked an unbeaten 50 – and the winning runs – to bring his country a famous victory. 'That was a gift from Roy [Dias],' he explains. 'I was 49*, one run to get, and Roy was at the other end. He played out a maiden. That was one of the best games I ever played.' Indeed, Kaluperuma was in dreamland. In thirty-nine previous first-class innings, he'd never reached 50; now his twin half-centuries brought Sri Lanka a win over a Pakistan side packed full of stars.

Though the visitors bounced back to win a low-scoring second 'test', they did not have it all their own way. Disappointingly, seven batsmen passed 20 in the second innings but none notched a half-century; a few more on the board might have really tested Pakistan, and set up an unprecedented 2-0 series victory.

The tour wasn't without incident.[49] During the first 'test', Pakistan's bowlers grew unhappy with the local umpires. 'They wouldn't give out on the front foot; they wouldn't give out on any foot,' Heyn remembers. 'OK, the ball was bouncing, but they weren't giving lbws. And Pakistan did not like it at all.' Frustrations were riding high, and when the umpires warned the visitors overs slow over rates, it was too much to bear. Seamer Sarfraz Nawaz lost his cool, and allegedly angry words were exchanged. Although no official complaint was submitted, the Pakistan High Commission reported the incident to the government at home. At first, they wanted all three fast bowlers sent home, but eventually settled on removing Sarfraz from the squad.

In the 1960s, '70s and '80s, it was rare for a series to pass between these two nations without issues over umpiring. The visitors' complaints were usually well founded; though feeling cheated away from home was an unpleasantness, it did little to sully the special relationship between Pakistan and Sri Lanka. Throughout the 1970s, A.H. Kardar was the island's greatest champion, relentlessly pushing for Sri Lanka to be handed full ICC status.[50] The subject dominated conversation at the 1974 and 1975 Asian Cricket Council meetings; at the ICC meeting in 1974, when England and Australia used their veto powers to deny Sri Lanka's promotion, Kardar banged his fists on the table in anger and flat out accused the country's representatives of racism.[51]

But he didn't know what David Heyn learned in early 1976. 'Dusty [Miller, SL's ICC rep] told me,' he explains. '*He knew*. No matter how well we did, foreign exchange would be the stumbling block. With India and Pakistan, it was reciprocal. We put them up here, they put us up there. But that wasn't enough for the others. They weren't prepared to come here to that sort of situation. They'd say, "You've got to pay our players". And we simply couldn't do that.'[52] This was a hammer blow. For decades, Sri Lanka's cricketers had worked tirelessly to reach a stage where they could no longer be denied. Now they had proven their merit. They were experienced, competitive – even aspects like attitude towards practice were professionalising. But none of it mattered. They were to be held back by economics.

For Heyn, it was the final nail in the coffin. 'When I was in India, the guy who I was supposed to be taking over from at work passed away,' he explains. 'And when I got back someone else had been appointed in my place – so I didn't have any job prospects.' With no hope of playing Test cricket either, he decided he could build a better life for his family in London. He was just 30, and still very much in his prime: coming off an excellent tour of India, he had long been one of Sri Lanka's more reliable batsmen. Tennekoon aside, no one had scored runs as consistently over the past decade. And Heyn had a certain style: there was flair in his batting and fire in his belly. He was another great loss. As much as anything, Sri Lanka's fans would miss his electric fielding. 'No one came as close to Jonty Rhodes as David,' Tony Opatha told me, eyes wide with admiration. 'He was brilliant. Really something special.'

On the field, all Sri Lanka could do was continue to perform. Kaluperuma took 10 for 79 as they won a low-scoring Gopalan Trophy in February 1976; though they had to wait till the following February for more cricket, they showed few signs of rust when the MCC arrived in 1977. Having lost the opening one-day match by 23 runs, they bounced back brilliantly in the second, dismissing the visitors for 123 and making it home with 3 wickets to spare.

In the 'test', Sri Lanka batted the entire fourth day to stave off defeat. Tennekoon and Warnapura took the sting out of the match with a partnership of 163, though they had to endure some toxic verbals from

Tony Grieg at silly mid-off.* 'You've got to be tough enough to take it,' Warnapura flatly told me. 'Mind you, our English wasn't good enough to give it back. And no point saying anything in Sinhala. We realised the main reason these guys were doing it was to put pressure on.'

Though tough to take, in a twisted sense, Grieg's sledging was a compliment. It showed that the English no longer saw Sri Lanka as a pushover. This is especially significant given the strength of this MCC side: indeed, the inconsistencies which had plagued Sri Lanka's batting for so long finally seemed to be fading. They had reached 150 in all twelve of their 'test' innings since the World Cup, only falling short of 200 four times. Their bowlers were beginning to ask more questions of opposing batsmen, too. This was real progress.

And when Bandula Warnapura led a young side to Chepauk for the Gopalan Trophy in April 1977, Madras' cricket fans were treated to an innings they would not forget in a hurry. Coming to the crease at 0-2, Duleep Mendis bludgeoned the ball to all corners, cracking 194 in 222 minutes – 106 in boundaries – to give his team an easy first-innings victory. When Mendis was in this sort of mood, his batting was exhilarating. Standing around 5ft 2in, the stumps seemed to extend almost up to his waist; but with square shoulders and hulking forearms, he had a presence – defiance even – at the crease. His stature only grew once he began to pull and cut, crashing balls to the boundary with thunderous force. It would not be the last that Madras crowds would see of the pocket-sized powerhouse.

But while Sri Lanka's cricketers went from strength to strength, the island itself was falling deeper into turmoil.[53] The founding of the Liberation Tigers of Tamil Eelam (LTTE) in 1976 reflected increased ethnic tension: cracks widening since 1956 were now chasms, and many Tamils saw a two-state Sri Lanka as the only solution. If Bandaranaike's

---

* Grieg seems to have been in foul mood throughout the 'test'. Uncle Percy was greatly cheered by Tennekoon's innings, and decided he would run a lap of the field for every run past 90 Sri Lanka's captain scored. 'Grieg was staring at me,' he recalls. 'He tried a bowler called Geoff Cope, the Yorkshire off-spinner. I said "Cope? There's no hope, until you call The Pope."' Grieg confronted Percy at the break and was greeted with another rhyme. 'He didn't get offended,' Percy explains. 'He said to the umpires "I wouldn't mind taking that guy to England to cheer outside".'

crushing defeat in the 1977 election was further proof of a country in political crisis,* J.R. Jayawardene's appointment did nothing to abate violence. Sri Lanka was hurtling towards disaster.

The new Prime Minister's economic liberalism did at least ease foreign exchange concerns – clearing the path for D.H. Robins' invitational side's visit in October 1977.[54] In a tour blighted by rain, Warnapura's unbeaten 100 at the Oval was undoubtedly the highlight. Indeed, Warnapura was increasingly proving himself a leader for this young Sri Lankan group. He cemented his status when the team toured Bangladesh in 1978, cracking 116, 167* and 105 as Sri Lanka won all three 'tests' by an innings. 'Before we went they thought they were better than us,' Warnapura told me with a grin. No matter who they were up against, the team had to prove their worth each and every time they stepped inside the boundary rope.

Still, there was plenty to be excited about. The team won a shortened one-day game against the West Indies in February 1979, and clung on to draw both three-day matches. The tour wasn't without its scrapes – both Warnapura and Sunil Wettimuny took nasty bangs to the head – but the players got along famously off the field. The West Indians were treated to plenty of Sri Lankan hospitality, and left having made some new friends.

What's more, with 1979 being a World Cup year, Sri Lanka had another chance to prove their worth on the biggest stage. They were in much better shape than first time around. Six of the 1975 squad were still in place; and in the interim, Tony Opatha, Bandula Warnapura and D.S. de Silva had become regulars in the Lancashire League. Much of the fear factor from four years earlier had been stripped away – plus, since 1975 Sri Lanka had won List A games against England, the West Indies and Pakistan.

But the process of choosing a squad exposed problems lurking within the Sports Law. Despite initially being picked, Ranjit Fernando was deselected, replaced by the uncapped and unheralded Sunil Jayasinghe. He was told by the ministry players over 35 would not travel – a statement quickly modified to include only batsmen when they realised that their star bowler, D.S. de Silva, was fast approaching 37. 'It was hard to

---

* For three elections running, the sitting party had seen its returns slashed to almost nothing; clearly, there were no straightforward answers to the problems Sri Lanka was facing.

take initially,' Fernando told me. 'Quite honestly, Russell [Hamer] and I were probably the two contenders for wicketkeeping. But, there were so many people involved in lobbying, that they were never able to get it right. The selectors themselves would have found it difficult.' Having been a stalwart of Sri Lanka sides for fifteen years, Fernando was tossed aside with rankling flippancy.

His exclusion was not the only strange decision. Anura Ranasinghe and Lalith Kaluperuma – veterans of the first tournament who had been crucial cogs in the side for the four years since – both missed the trip. 'I was very disappointed, it was a shock,' Kaluperuma reflects today. 'In the first World Cup, I played all three games – I'd had a good domestic season also. But I don't know what happened. I think it was a surprise to omit Anura too.' Strangely, both men were stalwarts of the same club. When I asked Kaluperuma if he thought there was an anti-Bloomfield feeling among selectors at the time, he kept his cards close to his chest: 'I don't know, there were some funny people at that time.'

Despite the presence of six veterans, it was hard to overlook the sense of greenness in the squad. Sudath Pasqual hadn't even entered his final year at Royal – prior to the tour he, Stanley de Silva, Ranjan Gunatilleke, Ranjan Madugalle and Sunil Jayasinghe had ten List A appearances between them. Four never played for Sri Lanka again. Their selection did not pass without comment. Russel Hamer unsuccessfully petitioned the Sports Ministry over the wicketkeeping issue – causing all sorts of problems for David Heyn in London, tasked with supplying jumpers for the squad. He had to guess who'd be on the plane, and claims to have got fifteen of sixteen right. Only Gunatilleke's didn't fit.

Still, preparation for the tournament would be much better than in 1975. Heyn worked with Sri Lanka's new ICC representative Arthur Pinto on the pre-tournament schedule: having been part of the under-cooked 1975 squad, he arranged a mixture of one-, two- and three-day games to help the players adjust to English conditions. What's more, the ICC Trophy* would give Sri Lanka plenty of limited-overs practice.

---

* The new tournament saw associate nations square off before the World Cup, with both finalists earning a place in the main draw.

By the time the tournament proper got going, they had played twelve matches on English soil.

But their escape from the Trophy was no foregone conclusion, with a government-enforced boycott of their match against Israel throwing their campaign into disarray.[55] The ICC's first reaction was to boot Tennekoon's team out of the tournament; thankfully, Pinto had a good relationship with D.B. Carr, and managed to get the MCC stalwart to fight Sri Lanka's corner.

Still, with their clash against Wales washed out, Sri Lanka only reached the semis thanks to a better run rate than the Welsh or Americans. After selection had thrown preparations into turmoil, political jockeying almost cost the side dear. It would have been unforgivable if the Israel fiasco had cost Sri Lanka a place in the main tournament. It might well have put a halt on their ambitions for full ICC status too.

Having hammered Denmark by 208 runs to reach the main draw, Sri Lanka's World Cup got off to a rotten start against New Zealand. A steepling collapse saw them tumble to 189; and their misery was compounded when Tennekoon felt a twinge in his calf after the match. Since Sri Lanka's budget did not stretch far enough for a physio to travel with the team, he would miss the rest of the tournament.[*56]

So Warnapura took over for the West Indies game, still carrying scars from their meeting earlier in the year. 'When I was walking in to toss, the West Indies players were looking and pointing at me, saying "That's the guy who got hit",' he told me, letting out a nervous giggle. 'Their twelfth man was Wayne Daniel. That's the kind of bowling attack they had. And no restrictions on bouncers, twelve overs per bowler and no helmets.' One or two were perhaps grateful when the match was abandoned without a ball being bowled.

It certainly wasn't a classic English summer.[57] The Lankans last clash against India was rain-ravaged and required a reserve day – yet remains a marquee moment in Sri Lankan history. Though Warnapura lost the

---

*   Prior to the squad's departure, their physio gave them a heat lamp to treat any injuries. Only later did Tennekoon realise this likely did more harm than good. Had he iced his calf in the first forty-eight hours, he might have been able to play again in the tournament. As it was, it took him the best part of a month to recover fully.

toss, the top three built a solid platform for the combustive Mendis, who launched three meaty 6s in his 57-ball 64. Pasqual's late cameo pushed the score up to 238-5; when Dias caught Gavaskar for 26, electricity surged through the Lankan side.

That said, Jayasinghe's sharp run-out of Gundappa Viswanath was the real turning point. From then on, wickets fell like clockwork. D.S. flummoxed the batsmen with his variations; Stanley de Silva tied them down with tight lines: in a flash India were 162-7. And the tail had no answer for Opatha. He bagged the last three to send India tumbling to 191. Sri Lanka had completed a famous victory. For the first time in a World Cup, an associate member had beaten a Test-playing side.

In doing so, Sri Lanka put the ICC on notice. The sole sadness was that Tennekoon, who had led the side ably for close to a decade, had to watch from the sidelines. Like Tissera before him, he had given so much to Sri Lankan cricket, and deserved to be a part of the victory. 'It was bad luck for me that I couldn't play,' he reflects. 'But the fact remains, being the captain I had to be in the dressing room and put on a smiley face and encourage the others. We really enjoyed that victory – there was a real sense of achievement for us. We felt we were now ready to get into the big league.'

As in 1975, Sri Lanka left the tournament with their heads held high. Getting a win under their belt was a huge step forward, and they were a mere whisker away from qualifying for the semis. Some have looked back at the squad and wondered if Sri Lanka might have done even better.

Still, they won the ICC Trophy final, and performed impressively through a string of three-day games. After beating Oxford by an innings, thanks to triumphant bowling from D.S., they drew seven on the bounce, leading five on first innings. There was pride to be taken from these performances. Early in the tour, Sri Lanka had been handily beaten by Notts; they showed a clear ability to adapt and learn on the job. Above all, 1979 proved that the flashes of promise four years earlier were no fluke. The side had blossomed into a giant-slayer – and a hardened unit who could hold their own against strong first-class sides in foreign conditions.

Though Test cricket beckoned, Sri Lanka would have to face up to the challenge without the leaders who had done so much for the country's cricket. Tennekoon's retirement marked the end of an era. Though nearly 33, many sensed he had more cricket left in him. As was often the case, there were other concerns. 'I wasn't progressing enough in my job because of the time I spent playing,' he explains. 'I had to take this tough decision – was I going to play cricket and be static in my job, or would I concentrate on work and go up the ladder. By that time I had a son, so I chose the latter. It was difficult. Michael [Tissera] had the same problem.'

Indeed, Tissera, Tennekoon and Heyn – the heart of Sri Lanka's middle order in the late 1960s and early 1970s – all found their careers truncated as a result of the amateurism of the Sri Lankan scene. Like so many before them, they sacrificed much for the sport they loved, and were happy to forego professional advancement in order to drive Sri Lanka towards international recognition.

But there came a time when the players had to put themselves first. For most, carrying on much past 30 was unsustainable. Responsibility kicked in: cricket could not provide for their families. This trend had remained a constant since the island's earliest days. From Christoffelsz to Lieversz, long is the list of names who have left the game before they should have. A new age was dawning; it was up to the next generation to see that decades of hard work and sacrifice would not be squandered.

★★★

Though Abu Fuard played his last representative match at the start of the 1970s, he was central to the transformation Sri Lankan cricket underwent during the decade. At the 1978 board elections Fuard managed to manoeuvre N.M. Perera[*] into the presidency.[58] A decade on from the coup of 1968, Sri Lankan cricket had a very different look about it.

Fuard was clearly at the heart of things: as one cricketer who played in this era put it, 'It wasn't a Board of Control – it was one man in control.'

---

[*] Perera was a staunch socialist and long-time leader of the LSSP. He beat out F.C. de Saram by fifty-three votes to eight, a landslide that would have been unimaginable fifteen years earlier.

Having been denied the opportunity to visit England in 1968 and 1975, he finally made it in 1979, as Assistant Manager to the World Cup squad.[59] But during the tour, he had a furious disagreement with Manager B.R. Heyn over the trip to Buckingham Palace. The ICC had allocated places for fifteen from each country, but Fuard was insistent that one of the players should be left behind so that he could go. The incident speaks to an increasingly imperious outlook; it gives a glimpse of a man with a clearly clouded perspective.

At home, many felt Fuard was picking the team. Soon after the World Cup, Ceylon Tobacco launched a tournament called Batsman of the Year.[60] In 1979, it was held at NCC, with Bloomfield's Anura Ranasinghe crowned champion. The club's fans went wild; for many, Ranasinghe's World Cup snub was still raw. This was vindication – but for some it was impossible to take the high road. They found a stray dog, stuck a large label with Fuard's name on it, and sent it running around the ground. Livid, Fuard instantly vowed that no one from Bloomfield would play for Sri Lanka again. In fact, he told new captain Bandula Warnapura that if he wanted to carry on playing for his country he should find a new club, an offer Warnapura flat-out refused.

I first met Warnapura at Bloomfield, on a sticky April afternoon. Sandwiched between the Royal College grounds and the Colombo Racecourse, the club is an everyman's haven in the heart of the establishment. I sat happily waiting for ten minutes or so, watching kids practise cover drives on the patchy outfield, feeling strangely at home in the pavilion. It's shabby in a charming Sri Lankan way: faded pictures of club legends hang from flaking walls; creaky fans spin languidly overhead; groups of men gather and chat on ageing wood and rattan chairs, all lined up in rows facing out onto the field.

As soon as Warnapura arrived, he owned the room. At once, I could see why he was earmarked as a leader. Assured and affable, he carried a certain charisma: the moustache from his playing days still rested proudly upon his top lip, and he had a habit of following his jokes with the phrase 'isn't it' – breaking into a boyish gapped-tooth smile that belied his years. When we spoke about the Batsman of the Year incident, he laughed. 'Abu was so friendly with me up until 1979. And then it changed completely.' As his mind flashed back to years gone by, he chuckled again, not without a certain sorrow. 'Abu Fuard. Good friend, bad enemy.' Though Warnapura had just become his country's captain, he knew the road ahead was rocky.

But Sri Lanka's cricketers faced a more pressing problem. The rest of 1979 and the whole of 1980 passed without any international cricket. As long as the island remained on the fringes of the ICC, these droughts would continue to trouble them. And the first major news of the new decade was saddening. On 12 April 1980, Stanley de Silva was killed in a motorcycle crash in Balapitiya.[61] Seven months shy of his 24th birthday, de Silva had a bright future ahead. It is a real tragedy that he only got the chance to play four first-class games and two ODIs.

There was eventually some cricket for Sri Lanka's youngsters, as Ravi Shastri led India's U-20s on a two-week post-Christmas trip[*] – and opportunities for the next generation kept coming. Sidath Wettimuny led the U-25s to a comfortable first-innings Gopalan Trophy win in January 1981, and the team stuck around in Madras to play in the Bengal Golden Jubilee Tournament and take on Tamil Nadu's full side in a 50-over match. These were the kind of experiences that would stand them in good stead.

And finally, after a near two-year hiatus, the national side were back together to face Australia at home in May 1981. The one-day games provided punters with plenty of entertainment.[**] In the first, 78 from Hemantha Devapriya lifted Sri Lanka to 218-4 after their 45 overs. Though Australia were in deep water when play ended, they claimed a dubious victory on 'countback', a system which took into account neither Sri Lanka's excellent end to their innings, nor Australia's lack of wickets in hand.

The hosts did not have to wait long to take their revenge. The following day, the recalled Kaluperuma claimed 4 for 35 as Australia crumbled to 188 – easily chased down thanks to Warnapura's classy 106. Indian writer N.S. Ramaswami claimed it was worth the trip from Madras to watch that innings alone. It set up a thrilling decider. Australia produced

---

[*]   The hosts were good enough to draw both 'tests', with Arjuna Ranatunga making an unbeaten century in the first and Rumesh Ratnayake picking up 8 wickets in the second. Clearly, there was plenty of talent in the corridors of Sri Lanka's schools.

[**]   For the first time, these matches were broadcast on television in Sri Lanka.

their best effort yet with the bat; Sri Lanka looked dead and buried at 102-5 until a 96-run partnership between Madugalle and Ranasinghe brought them charging back into the match. Though both fell in quick succession, and the tail couldn't quite get Sri Lanka across the line, it had been a wonderful week. Warnapura's men knew they were a whisker away from a 3-0 whitewash.

Such scintillating one-dayers were a mouth-watering aperitif for the 'test', the first between the two countries since 1969. Though Australia opted to bat at the P. Sara, they couldn't get to grips with Ajit or Kaluperuma. De Silva's drift, dip and rip made him a constant menace – across 27 overs he took 6 for 36, as the visitors staggered to 124.

The hosts built a 53-run lead – and would not let their guests off the hook, finishing them a second time for 178. For the first time, the Lankans had taken 20 wickets against Australia. What's more, they had finished them twice for under 200. Had the rain-interrupted match not run out of time, Warnapura's men would have needed 126 for victory.

Clearly, such consistent performances against strong opposition were another stepping stone for Sri Lanka. After all, the visitors' blushes were only spared by a dubious victory in the one-day series and by Father Time in the 'test'. Having given Australia a scare in 1975, Sri Lanka once again showed they were no pushovers. Their performances deserved to be acknowledged and rewarded; they were good enough to take on Test teams as equals.

Australia's manager Fred Bennett realised as much, and pledged support for the Lankan cause. This was vital: England and Australia had often used their veto powers to prevent Sri Lanka gaining ICC membership, so they needed the big boys on their side. Crucially, Bennett also used the tour as an opportunity to study the island's cricket infrastructure. He pointed out the system's inadequacies, suggesting how they might be fixed. This was just what Sri Lanka needed.

Even before Australia's tour, there was a sense that the tide was turning in Sri Lanka's favour. Bob Parish and Sam Loxton, two prominent members of the Australian administration, increasingly supported Sri Lanka's cause having seen the boost Dav Whatmore and Owen Mottau had given their club Prahran CC.[62] Gehan Mendis' performances for Sussex caught the eye of many in England. Meanwhile, in the West Indies, Allan

Rae had taken over presidency of the board from his former opening partner Jeff Stollmeyer. Whereas Stollmeyer had a traditional outlook – and had generally sided with England and Australia in debates – Rae had more of an island spirit, and pledged his support for Sri Lanka. This counted for a lot: as long-time board member Nuski Mohamed explains, 'He contributed a lot to the debate, and he got a respected hearing. It also mattered because the West Indies were the big power in cricket. So he was listened to – there's no question about that.'

Still, the most critical development came from within. At the BCCSL elections in June 1981, the prominent UNP politician Gamini Dissanayake was named as the board's new president.[*63]

Mohamed is clear about the value Dissanayake brought. 'We needed leadership of a different sort,' he explains. 'Someone outside cricket – and also with a bit of political clout. We found that without that, we would not be able to succeed fast enough. It needed to be a senior politician, a strong politician. And Gamini was a man with a huge vision.' Certainly, Dissanayake had foresight. It was Fuard who approached him to join the board;[**] despite holding little interest in cricket, he saw the benefits of accepting the role. In Colombo at least, cricket was becoming an everyman's game: shepherding Sri Lanka to Test status would boost his popularity no end.

His relentless drive, and the impact of his standing, were clear straight away. On 6 June 1981, work began on converting Asgiriya into a Test stadium; incredibly, it was open for business less than nine months later.[64] Clearly, the other ICC representatives saw a man with the vision and means to drive Sri Lankan cricket forward. Dissanayake was confident heading into the ICC meeting on 22 July 1981, and sealed the deal with a rousing speech. Sri Lanka's bid to become a Test-playing nation was unanimously approved.

---

[*] Dissanayake had garnered huge respect in the late 1970s for his management of the Mahaweli Development Programme, one of Sri Lanka's biggest ever infrastructural undertakings. With him at the helm, it had progressed with remarkable speed. As such, he had rightly earned a reputation as 'a doer': hard-working, intelligent and erudite, his appointment conferred real credibility onto Sri Lanka's cricket administration.

[**] The pair lived across the road from each other on 5th Lane in Kollupitiya, and were close friends.

As it happened, the national squad were just up the road in Sheffield, playing a tour match against Yorkshire. It had been a long day in the field, a struggle to take wickets and keep warm. But when they got the call, they knew that every last sacrifice had been worthwhile. Down to a man, they were ecstatic. Their dream – and the ultimate hope of every Sri Lanka cricketer for the past five decades – had been realised.

The powers-that-be must have had one eye on Sri Lanka's performances in England, and been impressed with what they saw. Apart from a poor showing against Sussex, the team went unbeaten, leading on first innings in seven of the drawn matches. An unwise declaration from the Test and County Cricket Board XI gave them a three-day victory, and they won limited-overs contests against Middlesex, Essex and twice against the Netherlands. Perhaps the most pleasing aspect of the trip was Sri Lanka's batting depth. Only Roy Dias completed a century, but batsmen made scores in the 90s on six separate occasions. Sidath Wettimuny emerged as an opener of real skill – a more than worthy successor to the brother eight years his senior, who had prematurely left the game to take up a career as a pilot.

On the bowling side of things, there were positives too. Kaluperuma, Ajit de Silva and D.S. de Silva were by now veterans and bowling like it. These three were canny spinners, who knew how to bowl in partnership. Ajit really ripped the ball, while Kaluperuma and D.S. troubled batsmen with their accuracy and variations. Though Asantha de Mel and Ravi Ratnayeke found scalps harder to come by, their pace and promise was clear for all to see.

Yet not everyone was supportive. On 14 June, Robin Marlar used his column in *The Sunday Times* as a vehicle to denigrate Sri Lanka:

> I write more in sadness than in anger about the Sri Lankan approach to this tour. It is designed to promote and to coincide with their application for full rather than associate membership of the ICC … Potentially, cricket is at least as strong in Zimbabwe or Bangladesh and neither is now a serious candidate for full membership nor should they be until their domestic competition is stuffed with players whose ability would be recognised anywhere as first class. The Sri Lankans should dedicate

this tour to good cricket and improve players rather than follow the pursuit of status still sadly a favourite pastime in the Orient.[65]

Beyond dripping with post-imperial condescension, the lines paint Marlar as poorly informed. Sri Lanka had travelled to Bangladesh in 1978 and won all three 'tests' by an innings. Still, the very fact that an influential cricket correspondent could hold such a view is revealing. It shows the mountain Sri Lanka were up against: liable to lazy barbs from journalists, likely to be derided despite their obvious promise.

Dissanayake returned home to a hero's welcome, swarmed by men and boys on the runway of Katunayake airport. Percy was there, of course, waving his flag. Interviewed shortly after, the board president showed a diplomacy that eluded Marlar. 'Sri Lanka does not consider this to be a privilege, but a burden and a challenge,' he explained. 'A challenge to raise the standard of cricket, to lay out an infrastructure and all other facilities necessary for Test Cricket.'[66] A mountain had been climbed, but Sri Lanka's work would not stop. At last, they were part of the club, but the promotion came with expectations. Soon, they would re-emerge as a Test-playing nation. When that time came, they would have to compete.

Colombo's cricket lovers try to catch a glimpse of the visiting Australians, March 1938.

The CCA squad pose ahead of their famous victory vs South India, February 1947. Standing L–R: Unknown Indian dressing room bearer, Robert de Kretser, Lucien de Zoysa, T.B. Werapitiya, Sathi Coomaraswamy, Bertie Wijesinha, M. Makkin Salih. Seated L–R: Unknown Indian liaison officer, Malcolm Spittel, F.C. de Saram, Russell Heyn, Sargo Jayawickrema, Mahadevan Sathasivam, Ben Navaratne. Seated on ground: Don Thomas (physio). (B.R. Heyn collection)

The CCA and South India squads in front of the Chepauk pavilion, February 1947. (B.R. Heyn collection)

Government Services squad, 1952. (B.R. Heyn collection)

Farooq Hamed steams in at the Colombo Oval, Ceylon vs Pakistan 'A', August 1964. (Buddy Reid collection)

Ceylon's 1971 Gopalan Trophy squad in Guntur, ready to take on the Andhra Chief Minister's XI. L–R: Russell Hamer, Joe Saverymuthupulle, T.B. Kehelgamuwa, Indian liaison officer, Anura Tennekoon, Daya Sahabandu, Mevan Pieris, board secretary, Ralston Burke, Sunil Wettimuny, Lionel Fernando, Ranjit Fernando, David Heyn, Lalith Kaluperuma. (David Heyn collection)

Sri Lanka squad in Peshawar, March 1974. (David Heyn collection)

David Heyn cuts at Salem, March 1969. (David Heyn collection)

On the road to Nuwara Eliya: Sri Lanka's cricketers prepare for the 1975 World Cup. Standing L–R: David Heyn, Roy Dias, Sarath Fernando, Neil Perera (assistant manager), Raja Wickramasinghe (fitness trainer), K.M.T. Perera (manager). Seated L–R: Duleep Mendis, Bandula Warnapura, Ajit de Silva, Anura Ranasinghe, Lalith Kaluperuma, Dennis Chanmugam, D.S. de Silva, Ranjit Fernando, Tony Opatha, Anura Tennekoon, Mevan Pieris. Missing: Sunil Wettimuny, Michael Tissera. (Anura Tennekoon collection)

Sri Lanka Board President's XI and Pakistani cricketers at Galle, January 1976. (David Heyn collection)

3

LEARNING ON THE JOB
(1982–1988)

THE FIRST TEST

Full ICC status secured, thoughts turned towards the first Test. Sri Lanka would host England on 17 February 1982; a century after Bligh and his men played cricket in Colombo as a favour, the countries' cricketers would step onto the field as equals. But there was work to be done.

The P. Sara was the sole ground capable of hosting, but even it lacked the proper facilities. Chandra Schaffter, tasked with preparing it for Test cricket, faced a daunting task – with just three months to build two new stands, renovate dressing rooms and ensure the ground would stand up to international scrutiny. With little financial aid or practical support, it was stressful work. 'I didn't have much help, but no one interfered,' he reflects with a smile. 'I had to find the builders. We had no money to do the building, so we borrowed. But I think we did quite well. Hatton National Bank sponsored the game, and they helped a great deal.'

The English arrived on 5 February, most longing for home after three attritional months in India.[1] Still, they were pleased to touch down in Sri Lanka. Whisked off to Kandy by VIP train, those who sat out the warm-up went shooting or drove to Nuwara Eliya for a round of golf.

At least the eleven who played saw they weren't in for a holiday, as Ranjan Madugalle cracked 142* for a Board President's XI.

The English were forced to watch some special innings during their stay. In the first ODI, Sri Lanka were floundering in their chase, until Ranasinghe almost single-handedly changed the game with a spirited half-century. In the second, Wettimuny's more sedate 86 carried the day, with England collapsing in a flurry of run-outs. The 20,000 at the SSC celebrated raucously, invading the pitch and lighting bonfires that burned late into the night.[2] The ODIs had been thrilling, but were no more than aperitif. Fletcher's team had come to play a Test.

For Sri Lanka, it should have been a time of unbridled celebration, but the players had been clashing with the BCCSL – as Warnapura puts it, 'because there were individuals thinking they owned the board of control' – so had to do without a coach. The seniors, used to being self-sufficient since their school days, were happy to take stewardship over the team, but still there were problems.

'In those days there were always camps,' Warnapura explains. 'You'd go for a selection meeting – and you're from Bloomfield, there's someone from SSC, someone from NCC – and you can clearly see that you've come with the idea of getting your two boys in. So you'd say, "you help me get my guys in and I'll help you get yours": it was a barter process. But if someone else comes with the idea of putting someone else in, then there's a clash. The chairman ultimately got his way. During my time, I put my foot down and said, "Look, this is the national team. You can't be having yours, you can't be having yours – we need to balance the side."'

In the end, Warnapura was happy with the team he got, a powerful blend of youth and experience.* And no amount of squabbling could dampen the thrill of Test cricket for the eleven who took the field. 'We were excited, very excited – but we felt we deserved to be there,' reflects Sidath Wettimuny. 'It was a huge moment,' agrees Warnapura. 'Going into toss – there was a gold coin made specially for that –

---

*   Six of his charges were senior to him, with D.S. de Silva nearing 40. At the other end of the spectrum, Ashantha de Mel and Ranjan Madugalle were both 22; 18-year-old Arjuna Ranatunga pipped Anura Ranasinghe for the final place in the side.

winning the toss, electing to bat and getting to face the first ball. The fear for me at that time was if I get out first ball, that would be a record, isn't it? That didn't happen, thank God. I didn't realise how important it was at that time.'

England felt the pitch had been over-watered on the eve of the Test – so were surprised when Warnapura elected to bat.[3] With the top four departing early, it looked a poor decision. But Madugalle and the teen-aged Ranatunga counterattacked with spirit; only late in the day, with the pitch starting to turn, did England wrest back control.

A total of 218 was short of what Sri Lanka hoped for, but they made an excellent start in the field. Ashantha de Mel surprised the English with his pace: he had Geoff Cook caught at gully, before welcoming Tavare to the crease with a sharp bouncer. Next ball, a perfect yorker splayed his stumps. He got Graham Gooch lbw in his next over; had D.S. de Silva hung onto a tough chance at short leg, England would have been four down at lunch and clinging on by their fingertips.

David Gower and Keith Fletcher rebuilt, but Sri Lanka came charging back into the game on the third morning. D.S. found Gower's outside edge, Kaluperuma took a glorious, parried catch to get rid of Allott; when Willis was run out with a sharp bit of work, the visitors had slumped to 223. Only 5 runs behind, with three frontline spinners and the benefit of bowling last – Sri Lanka were in the box seat.

And in stifling conditions, the Lankan top order ran the visitors red-faced and ragged. Warnapura held firm while Dias brush-stroked his way to a quickfire 77. Percy got inside the hoardings and hoisted his flag high. Watching from the stands, David Frith felt the Lankans had 'grown up in 48 hours'.[4] On the field, Tavaré thought the pair 'never looked like getting out'. But as shadows lengthened, both nicked off in quick suc-cession. Still, Sri Lanka finished the third day 147 ahead with 7 wickets in hand. Prior to the match, few had dared to dream. Now, there were murmurs all over the island.

What came next still haunts Sri Lanka. 'I still can't understand why it happened,' Warnapura told me with a look that straddled anguish and disbelief. In the tenth over of day four, John Emburey had Madugalle caught at short leg, setting in motion a stomach-churning downward spin. From 167-3, Sri Lanka fell to 175 all out. In the space of 69 balls, they lost 7 wickets for 8 runs – and threw away a Test in the process. England eased home with 7 wickets and a day to spare. It was a huge disappointment, doubly so since the Lankans would only be paid for four days' work, not five. Above all, it was a reminder of how quickly cricket can turn.

Clearly, inexperience played a part. Warnapura reckons his side lacked the stamina to compete over four or five days' tough cricket; Wettimuny felt Emburey and Fletcher quickly figured out that the Lankans had a block-or-bang mentality: their in–out fields – with men under the batsmen's nose or clinging to the boundary fence – strangled the home side, who had yet to learn the art of manipulating strike and scoring risk-free runs. Credit has to go to the bowler too: even Emburey admitted he'd rarely bowled so well.[5]

And, defeat aside, the performance was encouraging. 'We didn't want people to say we weren't good enough to play Test matches,' Warnapura reflects. 'We proved we were good enough.' Indeed, a smooth transition into Test match cricket was by no means guaranteed.* Sri Lanka's ability to compete straight away was a boost, and vindication for years of tireless campaigning. They held their heads high in defeat – and forced those like Marlar, who questioned their ability, to eat humble pie.

More disappointing than anything on the pitch were the empty seats that speckled the Oval throughout the match. With the cost of admission equal to the average clerk's weekly salary – and the novelty of a television broadcast beaming events into hotels and bars – many stayed away. At the start of day one, there were 10,000 in the ground, no more than half-capacity.[6] The Tamil Union had hoped that proceeds from the gate would cover their building costs, but realised they would have to find other ways of repaying their loans.

It was a worrying omen, and Sri Lanka have struggled ever since to fill seats for five-day contests. The country can get giddy for Test cricket in flashes: when Kusal Perera muscled Sri Lanka to an impossible victory in South Africa in January 2019, the streets came to a standstill, with men and women alike swarming on roadside televisions to catch a glimpse of

---

* When Bangladesh joined the club in 2000, they waited for five years and thirty-four Tests without a victory. They lost thirty-one of those, twenty by an innings.

his 6-hitting glory. Yet, all too often, the main Sri Lankan presence at Test matches are schoolboys being treated to a day out. It is a great shame cricket's purest format has, on the whole, failed to capture the imagination of the Lankan public in the same way as the shorter contests which Sri Lanka were weaned on.

★★★

While it would be simplistic to suggest full ICC status transformed the Sri Lankan game overnight, the benefits of regular scheduling were plain for all to see. Sri Lanka's second Test, away in Pakistan, got under-way less than a month after their first. Again, de Mel charged in with venom up front, swinging the new ball and bagging three early wickets. With Pakistan 126-6, and 240-8 at day's end, Sri Lanka often held the whip hand. But Warnapura's men suffered another dreadful fourth day. Wickets would not come; when Pakistan declared 4 down on the fifth morning, Sri Lanka were 353 behind. Winning was out of the question. Nor could the Test newbies hold out for a draw. After 47.1 overs Sri Lanka were finished.

They bounced back superbly in Faisalabad. Wettimuny dug in for 157; with 90s from Dias and Madugalle, Sri Lanka reached 454. Then the spinners took over: D.S.'s variations constantly caused problems, while Ajit kept the stranglehold tight. At 184 ahead starting their second innings, Sri Lanka might have added a breezy hundred and put Pakistan back in. But Mendis – standing in as captain for the injured Warnapura – erred on the side of caution. Sri Lanka batted into the fifth morning, and could only carve out 7 wickets. Despite scoring in excess of 3 runs per over, Pakistan were nowhere near reaching their target.

These were the kind of opportunities Sri Lanka could ill afford to let slip. Internal squabbles had seen a number of Pakistan's seniors dropped for the first two Tests, but the Lankan performance had put the PCB under pressure.[7] Imran, Majid Khan and Zaheer Abbas were brought back into the fray; having battled fiercely for much of the series, the islanders wilted in Lahore. A sparkling Dias century aside, Imran ran roughshod over the batsmen. Sri Lanka's second Test series ended with a crushing innings defeat.

All was not well. When the team got home, Warnapura complained to the Press Council about an article penned by Elmo Rodrigopulle.[*8] Nor was there much support coming from the board. Selection meetings had grown increasingly spiky in the past couple of years, and the one ahead of the India tour in September 1982 was true to form. 'They wanted to drop Duleep,' Warnapura told me. 'We came to the selection meeting and picked ten of the fourteen. Then they said, "OK Bandula, you've got your ten, now can we have our four?" I said, "What do you mean 'my ten', these are not my ten. This is the Sri Lanka squad. All fourteen. It's not my team or your team – it has to be *our* team."

'We got to twelve and Duleep still wasn't there. So I said, "Look – all the matches when we've done well so far for Sri Lanka, we've mainly done well because of Duleep. We have to accept that, and he has to be part of the fourteen." They agreed, although they stressed that if he didn't do well in the warm-up matches that I wouldn't pick him. "Fair enough. Not only him – if I don't do well in the warm-ups, I won't play."'

Having slid to defeat in a pair of ODIs, Sri Lanka went into the Test at Chepauk hoping for a change of fortune. That looked unlikely as they slumped to 11-2, but Dias and Mendis produced a dizzying partnership to dig the team out of a hole. Like ballroom dancers moving to an ever-quickening beat, they pushed each other on, combining for 153 before Dias' absorbing 60-run appearance came to an end. Duleep smashed a steepling straight 6 to bring up his 100; with 346 on the board, Sri Lanka had a solid footing in the game.[9]

But the bowlers struggled for breakthroughs. It was sapping work: 329-1 when Dilip Vengsarkar was run out, by the fourth morning India looked to have batted Warnapura's men out of the game. But once again, Sri Lanka's star pair were inspired. Dias' 97 off 108 was a study in elegance spiced with eighteen hits to the fence; Duleep meanwhile made another 105 – the first twin centuries in a Test by a Lankan. Their

---

[*]   Rodrigopulle seems to have taken aim at Warnapura – who was injured for part of the tour – without doing the proper research. An inquiry concluded that his article presented 'a distorted picture of the complainant's captaincy, lacked objectivity, and its language was closer to the level of vituperation than that of fair criticism'.

heroics breathed belief into the rest of the side; India were left needing 174 in just under a session.

They thought they could win, but de Mel – who bowled 14 overs unchanged – produced another spiteful new-ball spell. 'They were quite alarmed,' he told me happily. 'That was one spell I was quite pleased with, my first five-wicket haul.' At 7 wickets down and in deep water, India had to send in the one-handed Gavaskar in a bid to save the game. Sri Lanka could not quite cross the line, but had given India their money's worth for a full five days' cricket. Teams across the world were learning that Test cricket's new recruits were no pushovers.

Still, there was trouble ahead. At a post-Test function, Gavaskar pointed out that Mendis' hundreds were only possible thanks to Warnapura's firmness; a gesture that unsurprisingly riled the Lankan board. Straight away, Warnapura received a message warning him that he was going to be sent home. That did not happen, but as he puts it, 'It was hotting up, because I wasn't allowing them to dictate. I was fighting back.'

Clearly, dropping Mendis had been a horrible idea. His early Test returns had been meagre, and he had a habit of getting out in galling fashion – but he was a special player: ahead of his time, that rare gem who could take the game away from the opposition in a hurry. In many ways he was a talisman: there was island spirit in his care-free batting; and his cricket seemed to continually defy the odds. But authority in Sri Lanka comes with a certain impunity, and pointing out the errors of those in charge is a dangerous game. Warnapura was skating on thin ice.

Though Dias cracked his second ODI century of the trip in Bangalore,* no one else came to the party – and India easily chased down 233 to complete a 3-0 series win. Too often, Sri Lanka had failed to stop their hosts scoring freely, but it was hard to see the tour as anything other than a success. Seven months in, Warnapura's men could reflect on a smooth start to life in Test cricket.

But their performances masked a deepening crisis at home. Cricketers felt undervalued and underpaid; the board held them in an increasingly

---

* Dias was in inimitable form throughout the trip. After falling for 39 in the first ODI, he made scores of 89, 102, 60, 97 and 121.

tight stranglehold. The situation was delicate. In the end, it took just one meeting in Rotterdam to set Sri Lankan cricket ablaze.

THE REBEL TOUR

A storm was brewing. Even before the India tour, some of Sri Lanka's players felt their days were numbered. Warnapura feared for his future after butting heads with Fuard, and had been upset by rumours that Gehan Mendis would be parachuted in as national captain.[10] Still, few could have predicted that Sri Lanka had seen the last of five of their Test cricketers.

Meanwhile, South Africa's administrators were trying to drum up support for the pariah nation's re-entry into world cricket.[11] In Tony Opatha, they found an unlikely ally.* On 16 July 1982, Ali Bacher and Geoff Dakin flew to Rotterdam, where Opatha was working as a cricket pro. Despite clashing over payment,** the two sides quickly struck a deal. Opatha would arrange for a squad of Sri Lankans to tour South Africa.

For Bacher and Dakin, securing the Sri Lankans was a real coup, not because of their profile or ability, but due to their status as non-white cricketers. Unwittingly, Opatha had agreed for him and his countrymen to become global poster boys for a supposedly reforming sports system.[12] Their presence was a sham: a tacit endorsement of Apartheid and a boost for a country that had been hit hard by a sporting embargo. No doubt, Sri Lanka's tour made it easier for a team of West Indian cricketers to head to South Africa the following year.

---

*   Quite how the South Africans and Opatha first came into contact is a mystery. So much about the rebel tour remains obscure, since very few are willing to talk about it. When I met Opatha, he was reluctant to discuss the tour since he was working on his own book; other members of the squad shrank away or stopped answering their phones when I tried to dig deeper into the matter.

**   Remuneration is another area shrouded in mystery. Luke Alfred has claimed the South Africans scoffed at Opatha's request for $30,000 a man – but two ex-players told me they were offered greater sums to travel. Some have suggested the players received a flat $20,000 fee, but it was also rumoured that the less established members of the squad got a smaller share.

But many at home didn't see such complexities. They saw what was in front of them: the pittance they earned from cricket and limited post-retirement opportunities. They saw the chance to build a life out of a six-week tour. Some saw a board of control who had antagonised or mistreated them. Ultimately, Opatha found no shortage of players willing to join him. In September, lawyer Colin Rushmere made a clandestine trip to Colombo, contracts stashed deep in his briefcase. The plan went off without a hitch. A couple of days later, Rushmere was on his way back to Johannesburg, contracts signed.

It seems that alongside Opatha, Duleep Mendis and Roy Dias were key figures in organising the tour.[13] Warnapura told me as much: he claims that when he was first approached he said 'No', since he was captain of the national team. But the India tour was a turning point. As he put it, 'with the individual who was antagonising me in the board, I knew my days were numbered. So I said, "OK, I'll come".'

Other Sri Lanka regulars were recruited: Mahesh Goonetilleke – arguably Sri Lanka's best keeper since Ben Navaratne – has said it was a financial decision.[14] The same was likely true for Ajit de Silva. Kaluperuma was 33 and in the twilight of his career; Ranasinghe was just 26, but had received hugely irregular treatment from the selectors. When Warnapura asked why he was making the trip, he flatly replied, 'Who doesn't like to earn some extra cash?'

Dias and Mendis are conspicuously absent from the final list of travellers. Warnapura claims Mendis 'backed out' after his twin hundreds in India since his place in the side was assured. Rushmere remembers it coming down to a financial disagreement;* others have claimed that K.M.T. Perera kept players' passports under lock and key during the Zimbabwe tour, stopping Mendis, Dias and D.S. de Silva absconding across the border.

Yet, other rumours have continued to circulate. Warnapura later alleged that Mendis and Dias were given a talking-to by Gamini Dissanayake; promised a two-year stint as captain and deputy if they abstained from the trip. Another story has done the rounds claiming Mendis received

---

* Supposedly the pair were unable to make the entire tour due to commitments with the national team in Zimbabwe, but still demanded the full fee.

a call from his boss at Maharajas. The message was simple: 'Go and you won't have a job when you get back. Nor will you be able to find another one.'

The inference of these stories – that the BCCSL knew about the tour and made no attempt to stop it – is scandalous, especially since Dissanayake responded with shock and indignation when he 'discovered' Sri Lanka's cricketers had made the trip. Yet, Warnapura and Opatha have both implied he was fully aware of what was going on.* There is certainly a school of thought that the board wanted Warnapura out of the way. 'In a way, I think they wanted us to go,' he told me with sadness. 'It meant Duleep and Roy could be captain and vice captain without pressure.' In Warnapura's mind, he paid the ultimate price for his clashes with Fuard.

The defence most readily put forth for the rebels is that they were unaware of what they were getting into. In a sense, it is true as much as it isn't. Yes, very few of the squad had a proper understanding of what Apartheid entailed. Yet on the other hand, the equation was straightforward: 'South Africa is a racist state; by playing there you are endorsing their policies, perpetuating people's suffering.' The players knew what they were doing was wrong, and probably illegal. They had heard they might be arrested if the government unearthed their plans. Warnapura freely admits that he stopped Ranatunga travelling, since he knew the tour would result in a Test-match ban. While he felt like he had reached the end of the road, he realised Arjuna was too young and too talented to throw his career down the drain.

Still, few expected the board to come down as hard as they did. During a stopover in Hong Kong, the rebels learned that Dissanayake had handed them a blanket twenty-five-year ban on all cricket-related activities.[15] Since he was a high-ranking member of the UNP government, there would be no inquiry; no opportunity for the players to appeal the decision or state their side. He had the full support of the president. This was akin to trial by execution.

---

* In 1997, Warnapura told the *Indian Express*: 'Had he [Dissanayake] spoken to a few others and given some assurances like he gave Duleep and Roy, the tour never would have taken place.'

Some maintain that Dissanayake didn't know about the tour – and that he was furious players were willing to jeopardise their Test careers when he had worked tirelessly to attain full ICC status. His public statement certainly oozed vitriol: 'The lepers who are surreptitiously worming their way to South Africa must understand that they are not playing fair by the coloured world.'[16] No doubt this stung. So did the rumours that the rebels would be taxed 100 per cent on their earnings. The second leg of their journey was a jittery affair. Players squirmed in their seats, silently stewing over a single decision which might have left their lives in tatters.

They arrived in South Africa with clouded minds and heavy hearts. And when they took the field as the AROSA Sri Lankans,* they realised it would not be a straightforward six weeks. Despite having been excluded from international cricket for over a decade, the South African scene remained formidable. A year earlier, an English rebel side had been dominated; a weakened Sri Lanka unit with worries hanging over their heads were always likely to struggle. And struggle they did. Without Dias and Mendis, the batting lacked muscle. Warnapura performed well below his potential: 'We were all in fear,' he admits today. 'Everybody was worried about what was happening at home. And maybe we weren't serious about the whole thing. Plus they were good, and the wickets were fast and bouncy – phoooph.'

Yet it was impotent bowling that really hamstrung the rebels. Ajit de Silva had been expected to be their star man, but it soon became clear he was ill equipped to cope with the turmoil the tour was creating. Across six games he took 2 first-class wickets at 141, leaking close to 6 runs per over. Lawrence Seeff, who opened the batting for South Africa in the second 'test', told Luke Alfred 'Ajit couldn't land a ball – he just had a complete breakdown emotionally'. Kaluperuma agreed: 'Ajit was not in the mood,' he told me. 'He worried about what was happening here, he was panicking. It's hard to play cricket with that.'**

---

* Opatha chose to name the side after himself and his hosts: *The Anthony Ralph Opatha South African Sri Lankans*.
** When I spoke to de Silva about the tour, he told me he'd struggled to grip the ball in South Africa. Even in Sri Lanka, he had struggled with sweaty palms, sometimes losing control of his deliveries.

Even if de Silva had been on song, it likely would have made little difference. The pitches were unreceptive to spin; apart from 5-123 in the first 'test', Kaluperuma was a non-factor too. Opatha – at 35, well past his prime – took 14 first-class wickets at 37; no one else managed 10, or finished with an average under 45. Rather than making strides during the tour, the team sank deeper into despair with each drubbing. In their penultimate game against Transvaal, 122 and 200 played 362-1 dec. – effectively a 19-wicket defeat. South Africa's parting gift was to hammer 663-6 in 159.3 overs. The last four first-class games were all innings defeats. In fourteen attempts, the AROSA Sri Lankans did not come close to winning a match.

Nor could the players enjoy themselves away from the field. For Sri Lankan cricketers, touring was usually a celebratory experience. Travel was a rare privilege in those days, and many viewed the opportunity to visit another country as an achievement in itself. But in South Africa, the situation was different. As non-whites in an openly racist country, their status was precarious.

Warnapura told me the team 'didn't have any problems', but this seems to have been down to a lack of exposure more than anything else. They weren't quite kept under lock and key, but their schedule was tightly controlled. When they took trips out, they were chaperoned. On the whole, they were shown the side of South Africa that white authorities wanted them to see. But the injustices which they were prepared to overlook in travelling were harder to ignore up close. As Warnapura put it:

> There was oppression. There were people with placards. Not many people came to watch because they were against the tour. We were kept in such a way as to avoid us getting mixed up with people – shepherded from place to place. But you see it on the road. You see the buses – 'BLACKS ONLY'. We didn't know how serious it was. Only later on, we got to know exactly what was going on. That's why I regret going there now. I met people who protested against us when I started working for the Asian Cricket Council, and I heard how they felt about the whole thing. So [his voice cracks, and he takes a long pause], I mean that's how it went. There was Apartheid. But the

extremes they went to we didn't know. Clearly there was a division between whites and blacks. It was sad.

The rebel tour cast a stain across every player who travelled. All those I've spoken to are remorseful about the whole thing. Warnapura admitted it still saddened him, and accepted that the rebel tour is a major part of his legacy. When we spoke about those few weeks, sorrow cast a shadow over his face. But the rebels have to accept that their cash-grab to South Africa caused real damage. Their presence endorsed the SACU's recent attempts at multi-racial cricket, which most black South Africans despised as bogus. Worse still, their pitiful performances on the pitch must have only served to bolster the ugly sense of white superiority that disfigured South African society.

During the tour, most of the squad struggled to avoid speculating on the kind of reception they would receive when they got home; once they landed in Colombo, their worst fears were realised. 'We lived it,' Warnapura admits. Most of the squad bought cars and built houses – luxuries they couldn't have afforded before the trip – but found they were exactly what Dissanayake branded them: lepers. Their jobs had disappeared and no one would give them new ones. They were isolated from the cricket community too, banned from even practising in the nets. Although Opatha was the brains of the operation, as on-field captain Warnapura faced the worst backlash. Those who thought the twenty-five-year ban wasn't punishment enough worked hard to make his life difficult. He faced a struggle to even get electricity connected up at his house.

Still, Anura Ranasinghe was probably hardest hit. Depressed at being ostracised and unemployable, he turned to drink – and over the years fell deeper into the bottle.[17] In 1998, he finally looked to be getting his life back on track. Bloomfield took him on as coach of their U-23 and Division III sides, but one afternoon he went for a nap and never woke up. He was just 42 – the years in the wilderness had taken their toll. It is especially sad because Ranasinghe had the most to lose in travelling to South Africa. Had his career been better managed, he might not have felt the need to make the trip at all.

In 1991, President Premadasa decided that the rebels had been punished long enough, and lifted their ban.* He deserves praise for such clemency – surely it was better that these men could give something back to cricket, rather than wasting away, full of resentment. In the years since, many have contributed to the game. Warnapura became manager of the national side and worked as a match referee; Bernard Perera coached Sri Lanka's women; while Kaluperuma served as chairman of selectors. He insists that the tour forced the BCCSL to take players' concerns more seriously – an allegation which may well have truth in it. Still, it was an ugly chapter in Sri Lanka's history, especially sad since the whole scandal might have been avoided. 'If they'd gotten us all together, and asked "Why are you guys doing this?" I think most of the boys wouldn't have gone,' Kaluperuma reflects. 'Nobody spoke to us. But it was very unfortunate.'

ARJUNA ARRIVES

While the rebels were being hammered in South Africa, Sri Lanka's official side were slogging it out in Zimbabwe with little more success. The ODIs were split; though Roy Dias' classy batting ensured a share of the spoils in the first 'test', the bowlers toiled for wickets and couldn't stop Zimbabwe scoring freely. Things got worse come the second 'test', with Sri Lanka blown out in 29.1 overs. Captain Mendis' 11-ball stay included three boundaries, and in many ways epitomised the innings. There was little fight: rather than digging in, Sri Lanka tried to bang their way out of trouble. They slid to defeat by an innings and 40 runs.

This was a catastrophe. Zimbabwe were a better side than many realised, but a Test team losing to an associate never looks good. When that loss comes by an innings, it sets alarm bells ringing. Sri Lanka left Africa licking their wounds, well aware of tougher challenges ahead.

---

* Warnapura was given an extra year's ban for captaining the tour, though Opatha received no additional punishment for organising it. Most of the rebels were too old to play again, but Flavian Aponso did make it back onto the international scene, turning out for Holland during the 1996 World Cup at the grand old age of 43.

In February and March 1983, the team made their first tour to Australia and New Zealand.

Despite only facing state sides in Australia, Sri Lanka found it tough going. Mendis smashed 141 in the opening game against Victoria, but no other batsman got close to three figures. And while the visitors clung on to draw each of their two-innings games, at no stage did they dismiss a team. Had these matches been scheduled for four or five days, Sri Lanka would have been on the wrong side of results.

They crossed the Tasman Sea hoping for a change of fortunes, but luck wasn't on Sri Lanka's side in New Zealand. Mendis, Dias and de Mel – probably the side's three most important players – picked up injuries and missed both of the Tests.[18] D.S. took over as stopgap captain; with the middle order shot to pieces, he was promoted to bat at number six. Unsurprisingly, runs proved the team's biggest struggle. In the first Test, the new nucleus of seamers – Vinothen John, Rumesh Ratnayake and the mountainous Ravi Ratnayeke – bowled with spirit to dismiss New Zealand for 344. But the batting looked threadbare, and Sri Lanka were well beaten by an innings and 25.

There were improvements in Wellington. A solid partnership between Madugalle and de Silva carried Sri Lanka to 240, before spiky bowling earned John a maiden Test-match five-for. The slingy Rumesh Ratnayake showed his teeth too, surprising batsmen with his pace, and breaking John Wright's nose with a nasty bouncer.[19] Ironically, Wright stayed standing, while Rumesh – sickened by the sight of blood – collapsed and needed reviving with smelling salts.

Ahead at the halfway stage, Sri Lanka threw the match away with a horrible second-innings effort, collapsing for 93. Perhaps it is no surprise the batting misfired: this was Sri Lanka's first taste of green New Zealand wickets, and they badly missed the experience and class of Mendis, Dias and Warnapura. Some of the batsmen didn't look cut out for Test cricket: Mithra Wettimuny and Yohan Goonasekera never played another Test, and it wasn't long before Susil Fernando was discarded either.

The biggest boost was the emergence of John and Ratnayake. Sri Lanka had used Warnapura and Anura Ranasinghe as opening bowlers in the Tests against England and Pakistan; a pair of out-and-out seamers to support de Mel would help in the quest for 20 wickets. Still, there was much improving to do. Six weeks after flying home from New Zealand, Australia would land in Colombo. Having received a rough ride from state sides Down Under, taking on the full Test team was a daunting prospect – but the kind of challenge Sri Lanka had to face head on if they were to start making strides in international cricket.

★★★

Before the start of the Australia series, the Lankans were spirited by the arrival of Sir Garfield Sobers as coach. Superstar appointments were a rarity in the 1980s, and Sobers' appearance instantly lifted the squad. 'I think he just inspired you because of who he was,' Sidath Wettimuny told me. 'You wanted to try and do well to make sure he thought you were a decent player.'

Even before the team took to the pitch, Sobers was making his influence felt. When he visited Sri Lanka in 1981, he had stumbled on a cricketer who stuck in his mind. As he later recalled:

> I was immediately entranced by the young batsman Arjuna Ranatunga. What a beautiful little player he was – still a teenager but so accomplished. When you see a youngster of that age playing with correctness of technique, not afraid of anybody and not afraid to hit the ball, it is a great thrill whatever nationality he may be. His mannerisms and characteristics immediately attracted me.[20]

Despite Ranatunga's clear potential, he had been dropped after recording a pair in Zimbabwe. Still short of his 19th birthday, he should have been given a longer leash; but when Sobers arrived, he was told that Ranatunga was out – Fuard, now chairman of selectors, 'didn't rate him'. Though due to attend the selection meeting as a mere observer, Sobers couldn't hold his tongue:

> When Ranatunga's name came up, it was immediately dismissed, but before they could move onto the next player, I interrupted and said that this particular player must play in the next game. They were amazed at my intervention and the chairman told me that I had no say

in the selection. I responded to the effect that whether I had any say or not, if this cricketer wasn't in the side, I would be speaking to the president about it. I pulled rank and it worked.[21]

In the first ODI, young Ranatunga proved he could do more than bat. He got through 9 overs for 26, picking up Hookes and Yallop in quick succession to send Australia into a tailspin. Then in the second, he smashed 55* off 39 – ending the match with a towering 6 off Greg Chappell. The first glimpses of Ranatunga revealed a fearless, feisty cricketer.

With the other ODIs washed out, Sri Lanka claimed a 2-0 series victory. This was real progress, and panacea for the despair of the past twelve months. What's more, it was a timely reminder that on home soil – in limited-overs cricket at least – Sri Lanka were a match for anyone.

The Test at Asgiriya proved an altogether different story. Australia smashed their way to 514-4; when Sri Lanka fell to 9-3, they knew they were wading towards an innings defeat. But Mendis was defiant, pugnacious and dealing in boundaries.[22] Lillee was carved over the slips, then hooked dismissively for a one-bounce 4; for just a moment, bowler and captain must have travelled back to the near-trauma of 1975. Mendis eventually cracked one straight to cover: he was out for 74 off 92 – not a game-changing innings, but one that altered the tone of the match. Sri Lanka would not go down without a fight.

His belligerence was infectious: no doubt, when a captain swings like a wood-cutter, it gives the man at the other end a certain licence. Young Arjuna batted as if he didn't have a care in the world.[23] Where Mendis' knock was defined by brutality, there was beauty in Ranatunga's strokes: the high swing, the speed of the bat, the perfect arc it formed as he scythed the spinners over fielders' craning necks. Tired of being driven to the fence, they increasingly dropped short – Ranatunga was happy to tickle them fine or rock back and cut. Either way he found the boundary. But 10 short of his century, he tried to launch Bruce Yardley into Kandy Lake: the ball only spiralled straight up in the air. It was a shame that he missed his century – and a great mystery why he didn't score more in his career. But Sobers had proven his point. None could watch the teenager bat and not be enchanted.

Despite his efforts, Sri Lanka couldn't avoid the follow-on – when Ranatunga fell for 32 second time around, they were beaten by an innings and 38. But if ever a team could take heart from a drubbing, this was it. After an awful first two days, Sri Lanka made Australia battle for victory. Sobers was impressed. 'When I saw the quality of the players ... I couldn't understand what I was doing there,' he reflected. 'Their technique was so good it looked as though they had already enjoyed the best of coaching.'[24] The only issue he noticed was a hesitancy against pace. With cold-blooded quicks ten-a-penny in international cricket in the early 1980s – and a World Cup in England just a month away – Sobers knew he had to help Sri Lanka stand up to the fire.

He helped in other ways too. 'When Garry came along, there was a change in the culture of cricket administrators,' Ranjit Fernando told me. 'He never changed his ways: he liked to have his cigarette, he would have his drink with the boys. The players found that they were much more free with Garry. They could go and speak to him.' And when the team headed to England for the 1983 World Cup, they saw that simply being associated with Sobers affected how they were treated. 'Sri Lanka didn't have an identity,' de Mel told me. 'But being Sir Garfield Sobers, wherever we went, we got a lot of respect from everyone because of his name. He was more like a leader in the sense that he had a huge name; he was like a brand ambassador, a presence'.*

What's more, during the World Cup the squad saw that Sobers was a canny reader of wickets; an easy-going tourist with a remarkable cricket brain. He would bowl in the nets every day; when they travelled by coach, he'd spout stories the whole journey's length. 'We were relaxed. Enjoying ourselves,' Wettimuny explains. 'We had a great time.' Yet, the tournament didn't quite go to plan. The batsmen went into the World Cup in good form, but the side's balance meant that the three main seamers had little support. In their first two games against Pakistan and England, they conceded 338 and 333.

---

* On previous trips, the Sri Lankan dressing room had been short on visitors; but when they took on India in a warm-up in Slough, a number of former England captains gathered around Sobers. He made Sri Lanka feel like part of the furniture.

Having lost their first three, Sri Lanka knew their tournament was likely over. It is testament to their spirit that they only got stronger in the latter stages of the group. De Mel (5 for 39) and Ratnayake tore into Pakistan's top order in their second meeting; when they slipped to 43-5, Duleep's men had the game in the palm of their hands. But Imran scored 102* to rescue his team; once Wettimuny was out, the Lankans crumbled against Abdul Qadir. In a familiar story, they slipped from 162-2 to 171-7, and ultimately fell 12 short of their target. 'I blame myself,' Wettimuny mournfully told me. 'I threw my wicket away, and I felt really bad, because it was something we should have done – if nothing else for him [Sobers]. But, I guess that was lack of experience again; being raw in the game.'

The next match followed an eerily similar course. The quicks bullied New Zealand's top order; with de Mel claiming another 5, the Kiwis slipped to 116-9. Though a 65-run partnership made the chase a little trickier – and Sri Lanka nervously lost a flurry of wickets as they neared the line – Dias played a steadying innings to bring them a 3-wicket victory. Sadly, after growing in stature throughout the tournament, they were skittled for 136 by England in their final game, ending on something of a sour note.

The World Cup was probably an accurate representation of where Sri Lanka were at this stage. There were positives to take home, chief among them the efforts of Ashantha de Mel – who consistently caused problems with pace and movement, and should have been credited as the tournament's joint-leading wicket-taker.*[25] He embodied the potential of this side – who, on song, could cause any team trouble. But while Sri Lanka were capable of superb flashes of cricket, they struggled to put it together for longer periods. 'Winning is a habit,' de Mel reflected. 'And it's an art. Sometimes when you don't know how to win, even from a winning position you start losing.' 'We never lacked confidence,' Wettimuny added. 'Maybe sometimes we were

---

* Though officially credited with 17 wickets, de Mel later realised that he dismissed Geoff Howarth at Bristol, but that the scorer mistakenly awarded the wicket to Rumesh. So he should have finished on 18, level with Roger Binny as the tournament's leading wicket-taker. Since India won the tournament, Binny played two more matches than de Mel. de Mel's amended wicket tally improves his tournament average to 14.72, third behind Richard Hadlee (14 at 12.85) and Malcolm Marshall (12 at 14.58).

impetuous or didn't quite have that pro attitude. That took time to build.' Despite the knockbacks, Sri Lanka's cricketers were clearly maturing. But they returned home to a society tearing itself asunder; to an onslaught of carnage and brutality that disfigured the island forever.

★★★

Politically, Sri Lanka had been spiralling out of control for decades – but there can be no doubt the burning of Jaffna Library in June 1981 marked a new nadir for Tamil–Sinhalese relations.[26] The LTTE launched more brazen attacks on the government. When they bombed an army patrol in Jaffna, 8,000 turned up for the funeral at Colombo's Borella cemetery;[27] the crowd grew restive as they waited for bodies to arrive, and before long they were rampaging across the city.

Borella is a traditionally Tamil area, so the mob didn't have to travel far to start wreaking havoc. The P. Sara Oval – home of the Tamil Union, but also Sri Lankan cricket's spiritual home for the past forty years – was sacked. By the following morning, much of Colombo was burning. Though horror seemed to be subsiding towards the end of the week, rumours that the LTTE were preparing another attack on the city gave rise to another frenzy. The testimonies from 'Tiger Friday' are so dense, so brutal and barbaric that they almost blend into one incomprehensible nightmare. I found it hard to reconcile the fact that twelve innocent men were burned alive yards from my home; that, once the killing was done, perpetrators downed clubs and knives and just went back to normal; that even today, they might stand on the street, greyed and shrivelled, and smile at me when I pass.

All told, up to 3,000 Tamils were killed in the rampage, and 150,000 made homeless. For the next twenty-six years, Sri Lanka would be trapped in a conflict that crept into every aspect of life. Jaffna had never been a fertile breeding ground for national cricketers;* now

---

* C. Balakrishnan is the only Jaffna Tamil to turn out for Ceylon/Sri Lanka, in 1969. He emigrated to the USA soon after. While the dearth has often drawn accusations of prejudice, breaking into the national side was difficult for players from outside Colombo. Given that Jaffna is around 250 miles from the capital, the shortfall is understandable.

wartime isolation slowed its progress further. With the region under LTTE control, leaving was akin to emigration.[28] Andrew Fidel Fernando has told the heart-breaking story of M. Kandeepan, the Jaffna legend whose hopes of playing international cricket turned to dust amidst the hostilities. It's painful to think of all the dreams dashed by conflict. For many years, cricket in the north meant matting riddled with holes, bats on the brink of breaking, balls bent out of shape. Peace has renewed the possibility of progress, but the road ahead is long.

Even beyond Jaffna, over the past four decades Tamils have increasingly gone missing from the Sri Lankan game. A common explanation is that Tamil parents often encourage their kids to focus on studies with an eye towards emigration – but, the very urge to emigrate is grounded on a history hostile to Tamil advancement. While discrimination may not have been institutional, it seems naive to insist it never spilled over into cricket. SLC proudly carries the slogan 'One Team, One Nation', but the country's minorities have all too often been left out of the picture. Still today, the question remains: does this team truly represent all of Sri Lanka?

LORDS IN A FOREIGN LAND

After the horrors of 1983, it must have been hard for the island to turn back to cricket. At least Zimbabwe's visit in December proved the previous year's African misadventure was an aberration. A Board President's XI hung on for a draw, before a team of U-25s led by Madugalle gave a solid showing in the unofficial 'test'. De Mel and Rumesh Ratnayake were a handful, and Zimbabwe twice dismissed for under 230 – no mean feat since they could call on players the calibre of David Houghton and Graeme Hick.

But New Zealand's arrival three months later proved another showcase of Sri Lanka's inconsistency. With de Mel missing, Vinothen John spearheaded the attack: his 5 for 87 kept the hosts in the the first Test in Kandy, but an ugly last-day collapse consigned them to defeat. Back in Colombo, a Dias century gave Sri Lanka a chance to press for victory in the second Test – but New Zealand dropped anchor and easily batted out a draw. At least Martin Crowe's 157-ball 19* gave local batsmen a valuable lesson in crease occupation.

The wheels really fell off in the third Test: blown out for 142 on second attempt, Sri Lanka were crushed by an innings. With Richard Hadlee immense throughout, the hosts failed to reach 300 at any point in the series. Clearly, there was still work to be done against high-quality fast bowling. They did at least manage to strike victory in the second ODI behind an unbeaten Ranatunga 50. Young Arjuna, who took 3 wickets to finish the match, was a bright spark throughout – clearly a backs-to-the-wall sort of cricketer. At 20, he was already punching well above his weight.

Though Sri Lanka's form fluctuated wildly at the Rothmans Asia Cup, these sort of teething problems were to be expected. At least full ICC status was giving the team plenty of chances to grow – and the sort of opportunities the island's cricketers had always craved. In August 1984, Sri Lanka would walk out for a Test match at Lord's. Though most in England felt the result a foregone conclusion, for the visitors it was a different story. 'We all had this dream about going to Lord's,' opener Sidath Wettimuny explained. 'It's like Wimbledon. That pressure was there – but we were confident.'

The warm-ups gave little sense of a coming storm, but those watching closely noticed a dangerous batting unit, growing in confidence and developing depth. It wasn't all plain sailing, but the sun peeped through the clouds come Test day. And Sri Lanka were delighted to discover a pitch without pace or grass; some cynically thought the groundsman had been given orders to prolong the shellacking all of England fully expected.[29]

The captains looked a sight strolling out to the middle, the dashing Gower alongside the diminutive Duleep – never anyone's archetype of an athlete, and now with the distinct look of one who heartily enjoyed his rice and curry. Gower won the toss: Sri Lanka's second stroke of luck came when he decided to let the visitors have a bat. 'There was a lot of discussion in the dressing room over whether to put them in or not,' Chris Tavaré told me. Ultimately, the English felt bowling gave them the best chance to exploit any moisture in the pitch – there was movement first up, and Duleep's men quickly found themselves in a sticky spot.

But while wickets fell around him, Sidath Wettimuny was a picture of poise.[*30] The English bowlers kept tossing up wide; time and again, Wettimuny banished them to the fence with imperious square drives. Just before tea, he cut Ian Botham to reach three figures, modestly raising his bat to the balcony. The steely look in his eyes spoke of one who knew there was more batting to be done.

In Ranatunga, he found a willing partner. The youngster repeatedly sent England's seamers to the cover boundary; 226-3 at close, it had been Sri Lanka's best day of Test cricket yet. England must have thought the worst of their torment was over when Arjuna went 16 short of a maiden century the following morning. Little did they know it was just getting started.

Mendis' arrival brought a change of tack and a flurry of short balls. Paul Allott was dismissed with an insouciant look-away hook; soon after, Jonathan Agnew hammered to the fence. England stuck to their tactic, confident Mendis would miscue, but he kept swatting balls as if they were pesky Colombo flies. Meanwhile, Wettimuny passed 150; the whirlwind and the wall were exasperating England.

None committed to the bouncer as steadfastly as Botham.[31] In quick succession, three of his short balls disappeared into the stands; after the third, he could barely hide his disgust. When he was withdrawn, the Lankan fans chanted 'we want Botham'. English onlookers seemed to be enjoying Mendis' fireworks too; his century came off 112 balls. From the commentary box, Richie Benaud put it best: 'Mendis is very severe on anything that's short. For that matter, he's very severe on anything that's well up.' On a shortened second day, England took

---

*   Wettimuny told me a number of incidents calmed his nerves before the Test. First, he saw a John Snow column in one of the papers with the headline 'Watch out for Sid'. Then he got a postcard from a friend, reminding him 'This is just a game of cricket, go out there and relax'. And as he was taking guard, Tamil demonstrators rushed onto the ground and sat on the square. 'Besides having a brief moment of horror, it turned out to my advantage,' he reflected. 'For two or three minutes I went close to the slip cordon. They started talking to me about it, and those few minutes made me completely relaxed. I thought 'even if I get out they'll have to excuse me' – all the adrenaline just fizzled out. And for a few minutes we were one, the slips and I. I was very relaxed – so I'm eternally grateful for that. It certainly changed things for me.'

1 wicket and conceded 217. Down to a man, they looked like they didn't want to be there.

Their horror had to end sometime. With Sri Lanka pressing the accelerator, Wettimuny went for 190 on the third morning.* 'I was waiting for the double century,' remembers Uncle Percy. 'I wanted to jump over the barrier and run around the ground. But unfortunately – or fortunately for me – he got out.' Mendis followed soon after, but there was time for one last humiliation. 'I wanted to hit a ball into the pub,' Ashantha de Mel told me when we spoke. He heaved Pocock into the Tavern stand; according to Percy the ball hurtled into the bar, smashing beer bottles and sending crowds running. Sri Lanka finally declared their innings with 491 on the board.

For over two days, the crowd had been heartily entertained. Now, they were forced to endure an utterly charmless England innings.[32] For long stretches, the scoreboard stood still. Despite blue skies, England's dour batting kept crowds away on bank holiday Monday. A fourth-day wobble almost saw them surrender the match. Gower and Botham went in quick succession, before Lamb nicked one which seemed to be heading into Wettimuny's hands at slip. But Amal Silva dived across him and shelled the chance. Had it stuck, England would have been 6 down and struggling to avoid the follow-on. Instead, Lamb made a century – carrying his team to safety.

No doubt, the hosts felt the final day pointless – but it would not be entirely without pain. The Sri Lankan crowd made themselves heard in a near empty Lord's: clearly riled, Botham bowed to them when he had Madugalle trapped in front. But once again, Mendis provided glorious theatre. Though none of the bowlers were spared, Pocock was singled out for the worst punishment – slapped for 6s straight and over mid-wicket. Having reached 50 off 65 balls, Mendis added 44 off the next 31. A place in the history books beckoned,** but Duleep wanted to do it in style. With Botham bowling the gentlest off-spin, he tried

---

* He made his way back to the pavilion to a standing ovation – the 642 minutes he batted remains a Test-match record at Lord's. To have lasted near eleven hours with cramps was a remarkable achievement.

** At this stage, only George Headley had made twin centuries at Lord's.

to fetch a ball from well outside off and heave it over the mid-wicket fence. It found his top edge and looped straight up; as soft a Test dismissal as you'll ever see. Mendis grimaced as he trudged towards the pavilion, 94 to his name. His relentless aggression had kept the crowd enchanted, but a modicum of restraint would have seen him through to a famous century.

While his skipper bludgeoned and blasted, Amal Silva went about business more methodically, batting all day to reach three figures just after 5 pm. Sri Lanka had dominated the Test from start to finish. Though the English press, public and players were hugely disappointed, there was an acceptance that the Lankans' batting was sublime. 'Many followers of the game were of the opinion that the most agreeable cricket they watched in 1984 was the first two days of the Test,' wrote John Woodcock.[33] In the *Daily Telegraph*, Dickie Dodds was even more effusive:

> Philosophy without technique produces a barren result. But when they work together you get harmony: something that is a delight to the eye, satisfying to the mind, and an inspiration to the heart. This was Sri Lanka in the Test at Lord's ... Young minds were stirred to wonder 'so this is cricket' as they watched the Sri Lankans bat. Old minds were stirred to memories of days long ago ... Commentators were stirred to find some 'modern' explanation for the Sri Lankan magic ... But most found it inexplicable – like men who have long lived in a gloomy jungle and are suddenly confronted by light.[34]

Certainly, after their mighty achievement at Lord's, English perceptions of Sri Lankan cricket changed. Wettimuny was named one of *Wisden*'s Five Cricketers of the Year; Woodcock wrote that his innings had 'converted sceptics who had previously doubted Sri Lanka's right to Test status'.[35] But, more importantly, the performance instilled a self-belief in Sri Lanka. Having gotten the better of England, they could walk tall – and move forward in Test cricket safe in the knowledge that they could compete.

A TEST-MATCH TRIUMPH

Since gaining full ICC status, Test matches had been front and centre, but as 1985 rolled around, Sri Lanka's focus shifted back towards one-day cricket. The shorter format still offered their best chance of success, and there were opportunities on the horizon – the 1987 World Cup – but first, the World Championship of Cricket.

Prior to the tournament, the Australian Cricket Board invited Sri Lanka to take part in a Tri-series with the West Indies.[36] This was a big deal. It brought cash and cricket; what's more, it offered batsmen the experience of facing up to world-class fast bowlers on bouncy Australian tracks. Though Sri Lanka lost nine out of ten, striking a single victory on Australian soil was a cause for celebration.

Aravinda de Silva – at 19, taking his first steps in international cricket – later reflected that the team had 'no real game plan' when it came to one-dayers. Still, they were taking strides. De Silva was left shamefaced when he ran out the well-set Dias at the MCG, but fearlessly made up for the misstep. He charged paceman Geoff Lawson and cracked him over mid-on for 6, before ending the match with a top edge that went sailing into the stands. The baby of the side had carried Sri Lanka to their biggest win yet. As he later put it, 'The reason you play is for matches like that.'

But the Lankans were unused to such a relentless schedule: as they struggled with injuries and lost momentum, Australia and the West Indies seemed to find an extra gear. Duleep's men faded so badly that by the end of the series the hosts had stopped sledging them.[37] The four frontline seamers averaged north of 50; and with no clear heir to D.S. de Silva, a spin dearth was developing. Even when the batsmen stood up to an onslaught, Sri Lanka struggled to stay competitive.

Still, the tournament gave them vital exposure – simply seeing Australia and the West Indies up close for such an extended period was instructive. Sri Lanka were well behind the curve in terms of profession-alism: with no proper fitness programmes in place, players were left to their own means, and often did more harm than good.* As de Mel put it,

---

*   Aravinda ended the tour on crutches with a stress fracture of the shin – a result of endless laps, which he thought were improving his fitness.

'We didn't have physios massaging us so we didn't get stiffness. We didn't even know. We were in the dark ages.'

At least they were closing the gap. But when the World Championship of Cricket got underway, the narrative frustratingly switched. Now the quicks bowled with menace, but were let down by listless batting. New Zealand were held to 223; against West Indies, de Mel knocked out one of Richie Richardson's teeth, before a rearing Rumesh bouncer had Larry Gomes retired hurt. It was tough to watch, but having often felt the brunt of bullying fast bowlers, Sri Lanka were showing they could dish it out too.

By March, they were home licking their wounds – with little prospect of international cricket on the horizon. Thankfully, a month-long Indian visit was hastily arranged for August and September. Arriving late, India had little time to acclimatise – and Mendis' men had a trick up their sleeves. 'We made a bold decision that tour,' explained Sidath Wettimuny. 'Normally, when teams came to Sri Lanka we'd say "oh, we'll prepare a flat track because they've got quicks." But that tour, we took a very different approach. We said, "these guys are used to playing on the wickets we would play on – flat. We are going to give them green wickets".'*

Though Indian captain Kapil Dev won the toss and opted to bat in the first Test, Sri Lanka's plan paid dividends straight away. De Mel, Ratnayake and debutant Saliya Ahangama all nipped the ball off the seam; when Ravi Shastri was caught behind, India had slipped to 65-5. The hosts' reply was not without wobbles, but they were rescued by restrained maiden centuries from Madugalle and Ranatunga, and carried a hefty lead into the second innings.

From thereon out it was all Rumesh Ratnayake. With broad shoulders, a bushy head of curls and a Dennis Lillee headband, he looked every inch a fast bowler. He charged in with a glint in his eyes that

---

* Even before the Test series started, India were on the back foot. They gave up big first-innings deficits to Colts and Board President's XIs, as youngsters Sumithra Warnakulasuriya and Asanka Gurusinha cracked unbeaten centuries. India did scrape home with 2 wickets to spare in the first ODI, but given the fact they had recently been crowned winners of the World Championship of Cricket, the closeness of that game was yet another cause for concern.

seemed to warn batsmen of an oncoming storm; here, he bagged 3 big wickets, including Gavaskar with a slower ball – to leave India 4 down heading into the final day. A maiden Test victory beckoned, but rain and a Vengsarkar rearguard combined to frustrate Sri Lanka. Another chance had slipped through their fingers.

Still, they travelled across town to the P. Sara Oval in fine spirits – and with just a single rest day, carried all the momentum. Everything seemed to be going wrong for India. They dropped seven catches through day one; though Sri Lanka fell away to 385, de Mel and Ratnayake quickly reduced the visitors to 3-3. The game fully turned when Ranatunga had Gavaskar stumped on the third evening; the next morning India were finished for 244.

Quick runs allowed Mendis to declare on the fourth evening: though India held out till close, wickets fell like dominoes on the final day. Rumesh kept finding the outside edge – when he sent Shastri packing, the visitors were 98-7. Having been empty for four days, the P. Sara flooded with fans. 'Offices were deserted,' wrote Lucien Rajakarunanayake. 'The few who remained, holding the fort as it were, had ears glued to transistors. Soon even they were rushing to homes, clubs, hotels and other places of hospitality.'[38]

But Dev held firm. Those who switched on TVs expecting a flurry of wickets were aghast to see the island's bowlers dispatched to all parts of Borella. Dev's 50 was spiced with ten hits to the fence; though de Mel and Ahangama scored breakthroughs to leave India 9 wickets down, you started to wonder if their captain could save the match single-handedly. He had reached 78 when Rumesh bluffed him with a slower ball. It seemed to float back to the bowler in slow motion; he shifted direction, dragging his body back towards the stumps to take a brilliant one-handed return. He stayed kneeling on the pitch, overcome with emotion. Sri Lanka had their first Test-match victory.

It sparked pandemonium in the middle. Within seconds, the stumps were uprooted; the players, and Dev too, carried from the ground.[39] The home dressing room was full of love and laughter; former players flocked to share in the celebrations – and the baila was sung with spirit. J.R. Jayawardene even announced a national holiday to mark the occasion. Amidst the suffering of civil war, cricket was bringing joy to Sri Lanka.

If the team could cling on for a draw in Kandy, they would have a series victory too. Duleep's men almost floundered. Pounded for 325 in 84 overs in the second innings, they found themselves 3 down heading into the final day. It provided chaotic cricket: Dias and Mendis calmed nerves with a pair of classy hundreds – scoring so freely that by tea, a Lankan victory had re-emerged as a possibility.[40] But Dias' run-out sparked a flurry of wickets: 7 down, Sri Lanka were left with an hour and a half to survive. A couple of happy hooks from Aravinda had hearts in mouths – at the end of each over, de Mel reminded him he hadn't bowled his heart out just to squander the series at the last hour. The two clung on to carry Sri Lanka to safety; victory was theirs.

The impact of winning was plain for all to see. 'You always think you need to win a Test match, and then suddenly you win and it changes the mindset,' explained Wettimuny. 'After that we got better and better. Our cricketers got more confidence.' They had every reason to feel good about themselves. Whereas the 'test' triumph in Ahmedabad twenty years earlier owed plenty to luck and Tissera's tactical nous, this time around Sri Lanka were clearly the better side. They were only dismissed once for under 300 in the whole series; India failed to reach that mark five times. Mendis and Dias both averaged over 50, while five Sri Lankan batsmen scored 100s. This was real progress.

For Dev, it was an unhappy month. Annoyed by a number of decisions, he bitterly declared Sri Lanka would never win a Test away from home. According to Uncle Percy, he wasn't in the state of mind to succeed all tour long. 'He looked shy, timid, too gentlemanly,' he reflects. 'I thought, "I can tackle him with words". When he was going to bat, I said "I bet you'll get out third ball," and he did. He looked half dead when he was coming back. He went and sat down and he was always looking at me. He thought I was a charmer. During the interval, Dev came down the stairs but as soon as he saw me he turned back, like he'd seen a ghost. So I pretended to be a charmer, and the whole tour he failed.'

A BITTER RIVALRY

Sri Lanka had come a long way in three and a half years. The team were en route to shaking off minnow status – and away from the field, change was also afoot. In 1985 former Pakistan player Khan Mohammad arrived for a short stint as coach, while Abu Fuard was officially appointed manager on a three-year basis.[41] For those who felt Fuard already wielded too much power, this was a worry. As one player told me, 'Abu was a one-man show. He was manager, chief selector, everything. If he didn't want you, you were out.'

The opening of BCCSL headquarters was another step forward.[42] Previously, board officials had to do business from their personal offices: now, Sri Lankan cricket had a home. There were rumours that Dissanayake had planned to install the offices at the P. Sara, but that President Jayawardene insisted they be housed at the SSC. That meant building from scratch – and costs stretching to Rs. 8 million – but in the midst of civil war, he seemed determined to distance Sri Lankan cricket from the Tamil Union.*

Still, Sri Lanka's ability to keep cricket going in these troubled times was a bonus – one that owed much to the Colombo-centric nature of the game. Had first-class cricket been founded on a territorial system, the domestic game would have fallen into tatters. But the proximity of first division teams meant that club matches could carry on much as normal.** Safely sequestered in the south-western corner of the island, cricket seemed almost oblivious to the conflict raging to its north and east.

That said, it wasn't easy to encourage foreign sides to a war-torn country – so, an invitation to tour Pakistan in October 1985, fresh off the back of the India series, was welcome news. Sadly, it turned into a forgettable month. Though the seamers held their own – Ravi Ratnayeke took 8 for 83 in the second Test and de Mel 6 for 109 in the third –

---

* During the 1980s, improvements to the SSC, Asgiriya and the De Soysa Stadium in Moratuwa, plus the construction of a new ground in Khettarama, saw the P. Sara increasingly marginalised. After hosting the third Test against Pakistan in 1986, the ground was completely ignored for Sri Lanka's next eleven home Tests.
** In the 1984/85 season, the only teams in the Lakspray Trophy from outside Colombo were Kurunegala, Kandy and Galle.

the batsmen struggled. Imran's hooping inswingers carried the day at Sialkot; on a dusty Karachi track, Qadir and Tauseef Ahmed were too much to handle. Mendis' men were well beaten twice in three matches.

Undoubtedly, the biggest boost of the tour was the lyrical batting of young Aravinda, who stood head and shoulders above the rest. He celebrated turning 20 with a maiden century at Faisalabad – brought up with a smashed 6 off Imran – and followed up with a sublime second-innings hundred in Karachi.[43] Though no one else passed 25, Fuard still felt the need to discourage – contemptuously announcing '105 is not enough,' for the whole dressing room to hear.[44]

As had become common when these sides met, issues over umpiring dogged the series. Mendis felt his men were hard done by – and at Sialkot, play had to be paused three times as Javed Miandad and Ranatunga got into a bitter war of words.[45] The Lankans felt a certain condescension from Pakistan; for his part, Imran reckoned Sri Lanka 'had come to Pakistan with a completely misguided estimate of their abilities'.[46] This was not the end of it: things would come to an ugly head when Pakistan travelled to Lanka three and a half months later.

Though Zimbabwe and Bangladesh cancelled tours over safety concerns, the hole in the calendar was happily filled when a strong England B side agreed to a five-week visit.[47] Now with a clear eye on the future, Sri Lanka tried out a number of youngsters.* With Mendis and Dias fast approaching 34, the board's investment in youth was prescient. Of course, a steady cricket calendar made it easier to blood players: the Pakistan Tests got under way in Kandy in February 1986, with England B still in Galle playing their final four-day match.

Hostility sprung up between the teams before a ball was bowled. Sri Lanka remained furious about the umpiring in Pakistan; Imran claimed, 'Duleep … had given such a biased account of his team's tour that the entire country was up against us.'**[48] It didn't take long for the situation

---

* Twenty-five players under 23 got a chance during the series – the teenaged Asanka Gurusinha, Roshan Mahanama and Hashan Tillakaratne all impressed with centuries. Ranatunga led the side out for the inaugural match at Khettarama – the first in Asia under lights, watched by a crowd of 40,000.

** According to Imran, Pakistan's ambassador to Sri Lanka had warned the BCCP it might be unwise to send a team given the current climate.

to explode. According to Imran, umpire Felsinger rejected an appeal on the opening morning of the first Test, telling the players this was 'not Pakistan'; they should shut up and get on with the game. Their wrath grew when a number of appeals against Ranatunga were rejected; Arjuna, meanwhile, complained about persistent chatter from behind the stumps.[49] When one of the Pakistani players called Felsinger a cheat, he took the bails and led the batsmen from the field.

The visitors opted against the walk-off, preferring to sit on the grass as if they were off on a summer holiday. Felsinger demanded an apology from Imran, and eventually the match restarted. There was less drama on the pitch. With no answers for Tauseef Ahmed's flight and guile, Sri Lanka were skittled for 109 and 101 – blown out by an innings.

The discord reached new levels as the second Test turned into a nip-tuck affair. Debutant Kosala Kurupuarachchi sent Pakistan tumbling to 132; with tensions high, even Wettiumny's decision to walk drove the teams further apart.[*50] Later in the innings, when Imran tore into Ravi Ratnayeke with bouncers and barbs, a war of words allegedly broke out with Arjuna.[51] 'I'll knock your head off,' warned Imran. 'You've got the ball, I've got the bat – take me on,' replied Ranatunga. Arjuna always had a way of getting under opponents' skin; no doubt Imran stewed as his gutsy 73 helped Sri Lanka to a 141-run lead.

Things really boiled over during Pakistan's second innings. When Sri Lanka complained about a misshapen ball, the umpires agreed to replace it; since they only had new balls in reserve, they roughed up the replacement on the ground to simulate 16 overs' wear.[52] For the padded-up Miandad, this was too much to bear. Armed with a copy of *Wisden*, he stormed onto the pitch, proceeding to lecture the umpires on the laws of the game. For the second time in the series, there was a serious stoppage; Miandad eventually left the field to a chorus of boos.

By the third evening, Miandad had been left to play a lone hand. Ravi Ratnayeke and de Mel had reduced Pakistan from 131-4 to 145-8; when Ratnayeke had Miandad trapped in front, Sri Lanka knew victory was theirs. Only Javed refused to walk. Instead, he shook his head slowly at

---

* Pakistan were livid when they learned Wettimuny was berated by some in the Sri Lanka camp. 'I lost all respect for the Sri Lanka captain and players,' wrote Imran.

the umpire while pointing towards his bat.[53] There was a fiery exchange with the fielders; eventually, the umpires had to order Miandad from the crease.

The crowd, annoyed by the interruption, soundtracked Miandad's slow trudge to the pavilion with a chorus of jeers. A stone chucked in his direction proved the final straw. Miandad charged at the crowd; holding his bat violently aloft, he hurdled a fence and tried to find his attacker.[54] The police had to pull him out; though there's something undeniably comical about a man dressed in pads launching himself into a sea of bodies, this was an ugly scene.

When play resumed the next morning, Sri Lanka finished Pakistan with minimal fuss. They had claimed a second Test victory, this time by 8 wickets. Yet it had come under a cloud of controversy. Imran wanted the team to head straight home to Pakistan, but was persuaded to stay on by the country's President General Zia.[55] He felt that Sri Lanka had been fundamentally changed by the civil war. He wrote:

I had toured Sri Lanka in 1976 and found it a pleasant, friendly place in which to play cricket. In 1986 I thought I had come to a different country. The hostility was unrelenting and unanimous. Even the waiters in the hotel and the people in the streets were rude to us. It was as though the entire population was united in its determination to beat us at all costs, and be thoroughly unpleasant as well. Not a single voice was raised against the umpiring or the behaviour of the spectators ... we felt as though we were locked in a darkened room without a chink of light. The Sri Lankans were obviously anxious to prove that they had come of age as a Test-playing country, but this in itself cannot explain the degree of antagonism we encountered. I think the civil war in Sri Lanka was responsible for a heightened patriotic fervour, which, on the cricket field, was transmuted into a blind hatred of the opposition. The souring of a series due to an uncertain political situation or traditional enmity between two peoples was not new to me, but on this tour it was as bad as it could possibly have been.[56]

Maybe mob mentality had sunk in: certainly, it is hard to imagine a stone being thrown at a Sri Lankan ground ten years earlier. The acrimony was especially sad since, away from the field, the Sri Lankans and Pakistanis were friends.* You have to wonder how things descended so fast. Pakistan were probably right to feel aggrieved – across the series, the lbw count was 14 to 2. Nor was it an aberration: S.S. Perera wrote that during the England B trip, 'Manager Peter Lush stressed the need for good manners in the face of decisions which may not have been agreeable.'[57] Yet, the Sri Lankans felt it was nothing short of justice. 'I don't think Javed can complain about umpiring, because when we played in Pakistan the umpiring was a hundred times worse than in Sri Lanka,' de Mel told me. 'I remember I was given lbw when I was hit on my hip bone; it was about 12 inches above the wickets.'

Some reckon Sri Lankan umpires – green at the top level – may simply have made mistakes. Aravinda admitted the team would sometimes exploit their frailties by 'zealously appealing whenever the slightest chance presented itself'.[58] But five different men stood in the three-Test series. Were they all poor umpires? Or all rogue crusaders? Though noxious, suggestions that orders might have come from higher up are not entirely unfathomable. In wartime, it's easy to see how a win-at-all-costs mentality might have developed. If true, it did little to serve Sri Lanka – who, as a fledgling Test side, still had to fight to prove their legitimacy.

Amidst the controversy, it was easy to overlook the fact that the second Test was a turning point for the island's cricket. Amal Silva and Dias were missing, and holes in the batting order were eagerly filled by Roshan Mahanama and Asanka Gurusinha. With Arjuna and Aravinda ensconced in the team, Sri Lanka now boasted one of the youngest top fives in Test history. When Hashan Tillakaratne was promoted to the side a year later, the nucleus that would carry the team towards World Cup glory in 1996 was in place. What's more, the assembly of this group

---

* Rameez Raja had come through the age groups playing against Arjuna and Aravinda. Mohsin Khan was a close family friend of the Wettimunys. Imran too – Sunil Wettimuny wrote that on the 1976 tour they 'had the finest times together'. He also claimed Wasim Raja intentionally dropped him on 99 in a tour match so he could reach his century. David Heyn told me relations were so cordial between the teams that Sarfraz Nawaz struck up a friendship with his mother.

brought a family feel.* They had their fallouts during long and arduous international careers, but – at the start, at least – that familiarity took some of the fear factor out of Test cricket.

For Mahanama and Gurusinha, there was benefit to coming into a pressure situation. Being thrown in at the deep end made sure they were tough straight away: important, since over the next decade, belligerence and intensity would prove crucial ingredients in the Lankans' transformation. For Sri Lanka's fans, it was spiriting to see the youngsters stand up at the P. Sara. With the team in a sticky spot heading into the final day, Gurusinha and Ranatunga batted through all three sessions, both notching unbeaten centuries.

For Gurusinha, the innings capped a remarkable twelve months. Having made 100s against the last three touring sides, he now had a Test century too – and was, in many ways, proof that the system was working. The experience he got on the fringes of the side meant he came to international cricket undaunted and ready. Equally, Arjuna's second Test century was the crowning glory on a period of real success. During Sri Lanka's first four years of Test cricket, he was probably the island's outstanding batsman. For all Duleep and Dias' class and experience, they retired from Tests with averages of 31.64 and 36.71: scoring consistent runs, while learning the art of Test cricket and coping with gaps in the calendar, was tricky work. Ranatunga did so while little more than a boy.** From the start, it was clear he was a very special cricketer.

GOING BIG AND GOING HOME

With Sri Lanka set to host the Asia Cup for the first time at the end of the Pakistan series, it was lucky Imran's men were talked out of heading home early. India had already pulled out citing security fears; another withdrawal would have turned the tournament into a real damp squib.[59]

---

* Gurusinha and Mahanama had been best friends at Nalanda: they'd grown up riding bikes together and staying at each other's houses. As kids, Mahanama and Aravinda had spent many happy hours playing cricket in the backstreets of Ratmalana. Tillakaratne and Gurusinha had made centuries for the same team aged 10, and Hashan was a schoolmate of Aravinda's too. They all knew Arjuna growing up.

** He averaged 38.42 in his first forty Test innings.

As it was, even neutral umpires couldn't save Pakistan come finals day, as Aravinda and Arjuna notched 50s to bring Sri Lanka a shiny piece of silverware. Ever eager to piggyback on the cricketers' success, President Jayawardene declared another public holiday.

Yet a showpiece victory couldn't mask the fact that Sri Lanka had failed to fulfil their potential as a one-day side in the past few years. In April 1986, they lost to India in their only match at the Austral-Asia Cup. Back in Sharjah seven months later, they were beaten in three of three, including an embarrassing blowout against the West Indies. Since the last World Cup, Sri Lanka's average score when batting first was a shade over 180; and since the start of 1985, Duleep's men had won four out of twenty-eight. It was a worrying trend, especially with a World Cup in India and Pakistan on the horizon. An Asian tournament should have been a great opportunity to cause a stir, but the team's form meant no one could look forward to it with any real optimism.

A six-week visit to India over New Year 1987 turned into an unhappy month. Dias relinquished the vice captaincy to Ranatunga; Madugalle was overlooked for the Tests despite a century against Pakistan – yet Wettimuny's sudden retirement emerged as the biggest talking point of the trip. After batting ten hours for 227 in the tour opener, he and Ravi Ratnayeke put together a 159-run opening stand in the drawn first Test. But, when it came to the first ODI, Wettimuny was left out. 'In those days, there was a weird thing where you'd play a Test match and then have a couple of weeks of one-day cricket,' he told me. 'Before the tour we had our Browns Trophy limited-over games, and I was scoring rapidly. I showed the captain, "Look, I'm scoring fast" and I told the guys, "Don't leave me out if I'm scoring runs – I don't want to sit around for two weeks without playing".'

His omission was strange, especially since Ratnayeke opened and Guy de Alwis played pretty much as a specialist keeper. Ratnayeke had a poor time up the order in the one-dayers; he could have been better used as a finisher, while Gurusinha might have taken the gloves to make space for Wettimuny.* That line-up gave Sri Lanka's batting a more daunting

---

* This eventually happened in the last ODI. Despite being one of the first names on the team sheet in red-ball cricket, Wettimuny hadn't been picked for an ODI in twenty-two months prior to this final appearance.

look: though Wettimuny's ODI average was modest, facing the new ball was a tougher task in those days – and it seems unwise for a struggling side to leave out their in-form batsman. Wettimuny felt the role he was asked to play in Test cricket counted against him. 'Duleep used to always tell me, your job is to stick there,' he reflects. 'Not just Duleep, the whole team. They wanted one side to be held. If there was a really good quick bowler they said "You just keep him off".'

Yet, that ability to absorb pressure saw him increasingly pigeonholed as a Test-match specialist. The India snub was the final straw. When he was omitted, he decided his time was up. Still only 30, Wettimuny might have had a good few years ahead of him. Through the first years of Test status, he married rock-solid technique with an iron resolve, boasting the unique ability to make really big scores. Sri Lanka had no ready-made replacement; in the twelve Tests after Wettimuny's retirement, they tried nine different opening pairs. His departure was a blow which could have been avoided were he better managed.

Of course, the exclusion wasn't the only reason Wettimuny retired. 'Every day, we questioned whether cricket was the right path,' he told me. 'As one of the more senior players, I was paid Rs. 10,000 for a Test match. And that was it, nothing else. So, if you played three Test matches in a year, you got Rs. 30,000. You weren't paid for anything else; you couldn't survive. Thankfully our employers kept our jobs going, but then you're not working – you're stagnating. I think that was our biggest problem in the 1980s: not being able to relax and focus totally on what we had to do due to the lack of security. That's a factor people don't appreciate. And in my era, most of us retired by the time we were 30. 30 was over the hill: time to get a job, find a livelihood.'

It seems Abu Fuard's management was also preventing some of the players from fully enjoying their cricket. He took a schoolmasterly, dictatorial approach: even Aravinda, whose parents were close friends of Fuard, wrote that his manner 'could make you seriously question whether there was any point in trying to do your very best as a cricketer'.

Furious when Sri Lanka were blown out by an innings in Nagpur, Fuard ordered the team into their tracksuits back at the hotel, and told them to run laps around the garden. It was embarrassing, especially with the Indian team watching on in shock and amusement. Some of the players remember being spoken to in an abusive manner: from the outside, it looks like his management style would have been ugly in any context – and it certainly wasn't suited to international cricket.

Clearly, a change of the guard was coming. Over the past couple of years, Ashantha de Mel's knee had proven increasingly troublesome. 'I got this thing called runner's foot, where my kneecap rubbed on the bone,' he told me. 'So it swelled up after a while: it wasn't as if I couldn't run or bowl, but my quality came down because of the swelling.' The first Test against India was to be his last – at just 27, his body could no longer handle the rigours of five-day cricket.

It was especially sad since the injury could have been fixed with a simple surgery. But in the 1980s, Sri Lanka's cricketers had no medical support, and little understanding of how to maintain their fitness.* Nor was de Mel the only senior calling time on his career. Roy Dias' farewell Test would be Sri Lanka's next; Duleep would play just one more, the following year in England. This was a team in transition, losing four of its stalwarts in quick succession. That kind of shift is never easy – but it did put the onus on younger players to step up.

With the India tour over, there was little international cricket to look forward to: it seemed a blessing when New Zealand proposed a last-minute visit in April 1987. Yet, the tour did more harm than good, ushering in a five-year international drought in Sri Lanka. Young Aravinda was dropped for the first Test, amidst rumours that Fuard would no longer tolerate cavalier batting. He wanted players who could knuckle down.[60]

Given the diktat, wicketkeeper Brendon Kuruppu was a surprise selection** – but flash strokes were shelved, replaced by dogged crease occupation. For two days, Kuruppu refused to be shifted: after 777 minutes, he was Sri Lanka's first double centurion.*** Though Duleep

---

* 'If you weren't well, you had to go and get yourself sorted out and then come,' de Mel reflected. 'Once you're fit then they'll select you, but they're not going to help you get well.'

** Kuruppu had already played twenty-two ODIs, but was put down as a dasher, not suited to Test cricket.

*** The innings sent statisticians into a spin: it was the slowest Test double-century recorded, just the third by a debutant and the first by a debuting keeper.

promptly declared, Kuruppu's work was not done. He spent the next 163 overs gathering balls behind the stumps, becoming the second man in history to be padded up for a whole Test. It was a Herculean achievement, one which should have cemented his place in the side moving forward.

But circumstances would conspire against him. When New Zealand got back to their hotel at the end of the Test, they heard that a bomb had gone off at the Central Bus Stand in Pettah.[61] Their usual route would have taken them right past the site; they only drove a different way to drop Phil Horne at the physio. The Kiwis may well have escaped disaster by a whisker.

Trapped inside their hotel, they feared the worst. Dissanayake did what he could to convince them to stay, but minds were made up, and the New Zealanders headed home. Moving forward, no international side would visit Sri Lanka until 1992. This was a bitter blow for a fledgling cricketing nation. Since the team carried little commercial appeal, they were rarely offered extended tours abroad. Having worked so hard for full ICC status, Sri Lanka now found itself a leper. The country's cricketers were back in the wilderness. Five years before, the road ahead had looked clear; once more, it was as treacherous as ever.*

Nor did the spectre of a World Cup bring any relief. Though the personnel were largely familiar, the team lacked stability. In six matches, Dias (once) Ratnayeke (twice) and Gurusinha (three times) were all tried at number three. Aravinda spent most of the tournament languishing at seven; only Ranatunga, who cracked three 50s and finished the tournament with an average north of 80, did anything to enhance his reputation.

No other side was so poor in the field, and the bowlers had a torrid time too. Wickets and control proved equally elusive: in six matches, Ravi Ratnayeke took 10; the rest combined for 18. Clearly, the flat pitches did not play into the seamers' hands, especially since injuries had stolen away some of de Mel and Rumesh's pace.

For many, the overriding memory of the tournament was Viv Richards' merciless assault on the Lankan attack. When he came to

---

* From the start of 1984 to the middle of 1987, Sri Lanka played seventeen Tests. Over the next three and a half years, there were just five. At one stage, they went nearly sixteen months without a Test.

the crease, Ratnayeke was on a hat-trick, the bowlers full of hope. By the time he departed, despair was etched on all their faces.[62] De Mel was smashed for 97; demoralised, he turned to off-spin. Back-to-back Ratnayeke balls disappeared for steepling straight 6s; faced with such fearsome batting, Sri Lanka had no answers.

If losing six out of six was horribly disappointing, the manner of those defeats was more damaging still. Only twice did the team come close to being competitive.* Sri Lanka were no longer World Cup novices. This was their fourth tournament – for the first time in more familiar Asian conditions – yet it was probably their worst performance yet. They left for home disconsolate, forced to confront the reality that they were a long way off the world's best one-day sides.

For Mendis, it was the end of the road as captain. He had led the side with aplomb over the past five years, and been a wonderful servant to the country's cricket for well over a decade. Few batsmen in Sri Lanka's history have been able to frighten and frustrate bowlers quite like Duleep. Elemental not elegant, he showed little regard for the rulebook. Instead, he bludgeoned bowlers like he was born to do it; struck the ball like he was trying to break it apart. In his hands the bat became a club. Still, there was beauty in his brutality.

Unlike Duleep, Roy Dias never struck a ball in anger. He was a smooth-as-silk player, with shots that seemed to fall straight from the textbook. He departed the international scene with a typically unflappable 80 – all fans of Lankan cricket would miss his stylish caress.

Duleep and Dias were batting partners, brothers in arms, and the beating heart of a fledgling cricket nation. Their names will forever be linked, yet as cricketers they were at polar ends of the spectrum. Where Mendis hooked with relish, Dias resisted short balls with a sway. Duleep loved to smite the ball over the infield, while Roy preferred to pierce it with precision and timing. One's shots carried an air of improvisation; the other's were grace personified. If Mendis was a whirlwind, Dias was the cool sea breeze. A clear forerunner to Mahela Jayawardene, Aravinda described

---

* Perhaps the team were upset by a relentless travel schedule. Having run Pakistan close in their opener, they were ferried from Peshawar to Kanpur, back to Faisalabad and then to Pune. Each was a two-day journey.

Dias' batting as 'straight-lines and classicism'.[63] He played the game with an elegance not soon forgotten.

Clearly, Dias and Mendis' returns do not fully reflect their calibre, or their impact upon Sri Lankan cricket. Both were hamstrung by the fact Tests only arrived when they were 29 – nor were they helped by the sparsity of matches. But there are other factors too. Both Roy and Duleep had to play more shots to compensate for their teammates' shortcomings: As Aravinda wrote, 'defending solidly while all else was collapsing … would have been no use at all to the team'.[64]

Equally, de Silva felt that Dias carried the whole team's expectations on his shoulders; that if he failed to get to grips with a bowler, the rest were 'defeated' before they walked out to bat.[65] He and Mendis had to keep raising their game despite the pernicious effects of ageing* – in spite of all their achievements, they were victims of their era. Had either come around today, he surely would have developed into a global star.

At least their departure shunted responsibility onto the younger batsmen. Madugalle led the side to Australia for a Tri-series at the start of 1988. Though Sri Lanka won just one match against New Zealand, there were promising signs, not least a top six that included Mahanama, Gurusinha, de Silva, Ranatunga and Tillakaratne. 'We knew that if we could play together for a while that we'd become a better team,' Gurusinha told me. 'We were going to play a lot of cricket – I knew that if I could play ten years with the other guys, that would give us a lot of experience. We never thought about a World Cup one day, we just knew we'd be competitive.'

At first, they couldn't even manage that. All five fell for under 20 in the tournament opener, but Aravinda and Mahanama starred in victory over New Zealand – and each managed three 50s in eight innings. De Silva looked more at home batting in the heart of the middle order; in the final game of the tournament, he stood up to the Australian bowlers with a lone hand of 79. Champaka Ramanayake proved he could confine international batsmen with tight lines, Graeme Labrooy

---

* This too, while lacking the professional grounding modern cricketers benefit from. There was little emphasis on fitness during the 1980s, and at the end of a series it was straight back to the office.

showed flashes of promise, while Ravi Ratnayeke continued to thrive in his newfound role as pack leader. To only concede 250 once was a boon after the poor showings at the World Cup – though helpful pitches clearly played a part.

There were few improvements at 1988's Sharjah Cup. Sri Lanka should have beaten India in their opening match: at 151-2, they were cruising towards 219, but the final blast proved elusive. De Silva and Mahanama were bowled in quick succession, and the lower order crumbled – the last three run out as Sri Lanka fell 19 short. Clearly they were missing the steadying presence of Roy and Duleep. They got nowhere close to targets of 258 and 249 against New Zealand; with Arjuna and Aravinda misfiring, the team struggled to put runs on the board. Since the start of the World Cup, they had won one of seventeen; Sri Lankan cricket was falling into a slump.

The inability to host teams was taking its toll too, starving Sri Lanka of the Test matches their cricketers had so long craved. 'It was tough for us, because you want to play a lot of Test cricket to get that experience,' Gurusinha explained. 'To have to go overseas to get that made it very tough. After '87, they were few and far between.'

At least 1988's tour of England brought plenty of tough first-class cricket. Sri Lanka went unbeaten through nine games, with five of the batsmen racking up centuries – but all too often, the bowlers laboured for breakthroughs. Ahangama and Labrooy found swing and caused problems, but Ramanayake lacked threat with the red ball; Ravi had an off series, while the search for a spinner to succeed D.S. de Silva had borne little fruit.*

But Sri Lanka had glorious memories of Lord's. Though Allan Lamb was the sole survivor from England's 1984 contingent, the hosts had failed to win any of their past eighteen Tests, and knew they could ill afford to take anything for granted. Sadly, there would be no repeat of

---

* Throughout the 1980s, Sri Lanka were hamstrung by a lack of quality spin options. It put extra pressure on the seamers. As de Mel pointed out, 'once the ball got old, it was very difficult. With the heat and the flat pitches, you're struggling when you bowl 20 overs a day. If you don't have a quality spinner, you tend to get over-bowled and your effectiveness reduces. If you have a guy that can block up one end, it's a lot easier.'

previous heroics. On a cold, cloudy first morning, Sri Lanka slipped to 63-6; only a gutsy last-wicket partnership between Ratnayeke and Labrooy spared them utter humiliation. Still, with England piling up 429, they were playing for pride. To their credit, the batsmen made a much better fist of things second time around. Had Sri Lanka managed as many in their first innings, they would have been right in the game.

The sole ODI was lost, too, though there were glimmers of hope. Mendis' presence steadied the side, while Labrooy looked a real handful when the ball was swinging. It is easy to dismiss these fallow years as an abject failure for Sri Lanka, but the unique challenges this young group encountered were bound to toughen them up fast.

Playing exclusively against better sides in alien conditions forces you to improve. And one-off Tests leave no room for hiding: there is immense pressure every time you walk to the crease, a knowledge that a single-figure score cannot be swept under the rug. Though losing game after game was arduous, the amount of one-day cricket Sri Lanka's youngsters were playing would pay dividends – sooner than almost anyone realised. They weren't a bad side, but they hadn't quite become a good one yet. What they needed was a spark.

4

THE AGE OF ARJUNA
(1988–1999)

THE TURNAROUND

It was immediately obvious that Arjuna was a force of nature, leading
the side as he did with edge and a sharp wit. It was as if cricket had
crawled under his skin to become the essential part of his DNA. He
gave nothing and expected nothing back; he was deliberately confron-
tational and often pushed boundaries, but we had the utmost respect
for his devotion to the cause and a quite overwhelming determination
to carry it through. He batted with an old head on young shoulders
and bowled tidy medium-pacers with an attitude more Lillee than a
gentle loper.[1]

So wrote Mark Nicholas, captain of the England B side that toured
Sri Lanka in 1986 – Arjuna's first audition as Sri Lanka skipper. Not all
felt the same way. Mark Taylor described him as 'an abrasive customer
who deliberately gets up the opposition's nose'; to Warne he became
any number of unspeakable things.[2] Yet, perhaps the most revealing testimony comes from Ravi Ratnayeke, who felt compelled to describe him
in distinctly Australian terms. 'We had a reputation for being cricketers
who enjoyed the game and never grumbled,' he told Gideon Haigh.

'But we realised that, if we wanted to progress, we needed to beat people at their own game. Arjuna was the right person. He brought a bit of muscle, a bit more cunt into the side.'[3]

So crucial was Ranatunga's character in Sri Lanka's transformation that he was worth his place in the side as captain alone. Of course, he benefited from the emergence of world-class players, but it was he alone who uprooted Sri Lanka's psyche, who forced the team to believe they were winners not weaklings. If Murali had a lesser captain when he was accused of chucking in 1995, his career could easily have hit the rocks then and there.

The passing of the torch from Madugalle, a Royalist, to Ranatunga felt symbolic. Arjuna was from Ananda, his family part of the Sinhalese Buddhist elite that flourished during the second half of the twentieth century. He was not the first captain to hail from a Buddhist background, but his appointment seemed to reflect a final shaking off of the colonial shackles that had long restrained Sri Lanka.

After all, the island was arguably the last bastion of the 'gentleman's game'. More than anywhere else, Sri Lanka clung tightly to the Victorian ideal of cricket as moralistic. The English schools where the game was established were seen as fine formative places – institutions which understood that a noble spirit was as worthy as a sharp eye or supple wrists. These were valid principles, no doubt, but clearly at odds with the professional sporting world of the late twentieth century. The English had long since abandoned such pretensions, yet Sri Lanka was still in the business of building gentleman cricketers. It was holding them back.*

Ranatunga was cut from a different cloth. Conflict seemed to be hardwired into his psyche. Perhaps this was natural. As a child, his family home was razed to the ground by political rivals.[4] When he arrived at the SSC, certain seniors questioned whether a 'sarong Johnnie'** belonged at

---

* When Sri Lanka's assistant manager was asked about sledging during 1981's England tour, he cluelessly replied: 'Sludging? What is sludging?' Roshan Mahanama was shocked to be verbally targeted on an U-19s tour to Australia; equally, earlier Sri Lankan players have often spoken about silently absorbing barbs, some of them openly racist. In adhering to a code of conduct which the rest of the world had abandoned, Sri Lanka were allowing themselves to be bullied.

** A pejorative term, used by anglicised Sri Lankans.

the club.[5] And at 18 – when most Sri Lankans are still living at home under hawkish parental supervision – Arjuna was out on the road, finding his feet in Test cricket. He grew up fast and learned to be tough.

'He was one of those guys who was an irritant to opposition,' recalls Wettimuny. 'Pugnacious from the start. Even during my time, he had that cockiness which benefited the side.' Where Tennekoon had been a gentleman and Mendis utterly congenial, Arjuna brought a tough streak to Sri Lankan cricket. He cared little about friendship and would bow before no one. Victory was what mattered. He would rather win ugly than lose like a sport. That made him unpopular with many, yet his single-mindedness drove Sri Lankan cricket to dizzying heights.

Equally, his presence liberated cricket on the island. In the same way the elite schools aped their English counterparts, Sri Lankan coaching was often grounded on a rigid fixation on 'correctness'.[6] It was all high elbow and straight bat, albeit with a little extra wristiness. Invention was, if not totally denied, certainly discouraged.[*] Yet such a dogmatic approach defied Sri Lanka's madcap nature. In their fealty to all things English, had their own spirit not been overlooked? Under Arjuna, the team learnt to play the Sri Lankan way. Without his influence, would the country have so wholeheartedly embraced the magic of Murali, the invention of Dilshan, the mind-boggling Malinga?

★★★

Arjuna's tenure got going midway through the 1988 Asia Cup. The dawn of a brave new era was marked by freewheeling batting and an upturn of results. Having lost twenty-one of twenty-two leading into the tournament, Sri Lanka reeled off three in a row – a first away from home. The following March, they struck a maiden ODI victory over the West Indies. It was hard to argue with Indian writer R. Sriman's assessment in Perera's *The Janashakthi Book of Sri Lankan Cricket* that the Lankans had 'come of age in one-day cricket'.

---

[*]   I once heard a story about a high-profile coach sending a boy home from practice because he refused to abandon the sweep shot.

A new generation of batsmen were starting to prove themselves, but the same could not be said for the bowlers. In the lead-up to a Test series in Australia in December 1989, Sri Lanka conceded first-innings scores of 423-7, 506-6 and 472-8.[7] Amidst their inability to discomfit state sides, many in Australia questioned their right to be playing Test cricket.[8] So the team entered the series with much to prove. It was their first Test in sixteen months; Arjuna's first chance to lead the side in a five-day encounter.

It started out a tough slog, but Graeme Labrooy led a fightback on the second morning of the first Test – from 178-2 overnight, Australia fell to 367 all out. And Aravinda grabbed the game by the scruff of the neck on day three. A dropped chance seemed to sharpen his senses; from then on he batted judiciously.[9] Still, there were glorious strokes. Twice, he walked down the wicket and whipped the quicks through mid-on; when the ball was pitched short, he happily hooked to the fence. He had made 167 by the time he found the man at deep-backward square – had David Boon and Tom Moody not been dropped on the fourth evening, the Lankans might well have forced home their advantage.[10] Nonetheless, outscoring Australia was a feather in their cap. Organisers had been so confident of a drubbing that they hadn't even bothered to print tickets for day five.

Sri Lanka made an even better start in Hobart. Having been sidelined with injuries for over two years, Rumesh breathed life into the team – bagging 4 in 5 overs, and 6 in all, as the hosts were skittled for 224.[11] Nonetheless, it wasn't an entirely happy return, with Greg Campbell allegedly calling him a 'black cunt' after the pair collided.[12] Come series end, Ranatunga insisted his side would remain gentlemen despite 'racial comments' from the Australians.[13] Battle lines had been drawn.

Though their own reply fell flat, Sri Lanka knew they were well in the hunt when they pegged the hosts back to 10-2. But from thereon out, the game raced away from them. Australia piled on 503 for the loss of 3 further wickets, 2 of which fell to Aravinda's twirlers; Rumesh aside, the seamers had to take a long hard look at themselves.

But, despite staring down the barrel of a 522-run deficit, Ranatunga's men remained optimistic. Hopes of a dramatic victory went with Aravinda's dismissal – but the very fact Sri Lanka entertained thoughts of winning is revealing. Ravi Ratnayeke and Asoka de Silva dragged the game into its final session: Ratnayeke felt he should have saved it for

Sri Lanka, but withdrew into his shell and tickled one through to Ian Healy.[14] Though this was a gutting loss, lasting almost 142 overs in a fourth innings was another boost in a series full of positives. Chief among them was Aravinda, who averaged 104.66 and made at least 70 on each trip to the crease. Clearly, this docile destroyer was a cornerstone Sri Lanka could build a future around. Denigrated and dismissed before the series got going, over ten days the team produced performances that demanded respect.

★★★

But the island itself was falling deeper into despair. During the course of the 1980s, indiscriminate violence seeped under Sri Lanka's skin.[15] Furious over Indian occupation in the north, the JVP unleashed a merciless campaign of terror across the south of the island. Meanwhile, the reintroduction of Emergency Rule swelled security forces' already bloated powers. The horrific became mundane; though most of the JVP leaders had been captured or killed by the end of 1989, the human cost of conflict in the south had been appalling.

The situation in the north was equally hellish. Civilians were often caught in the crossfire between the LTTE and Indian Peace Keeping Force (IPKF); yet the Indians' expulsion only re-emboldened the LTTE. In June 1990, 600 police officers were executed in the east; two months later, the Tigers surrounded four mosques in Kattankudy and killed 147.[16] It is hard to fathom living through such trauma, waking each morning to wave after wave of fresh, indiscriminate violence. As Sri Lankans watched their island ruptured by factionalism and ravaged by war, most found very little to be proud of. In this context, cricket became increasingly important to the national psyche: Sri Lanka's fledgling team gave ordinary people something to get behind.

Surely, politicians' personal investments in cricket during the era reflect the game's newfound emotive force. J.R. Jayawardene was president of the SSC right up until his death in 1996, while Ranasinghe Premadasa's decision to build a stadium in Khettarama was at least partially motivated by a personal rivalry with Gamini Dissanayake. By placing the ground in the impoverished neighbourhood of his youth,

Premadasa reminded Sri Lanka that he was a man of the people, and helped spread the game to Colombo's working class. This was important: the SSC and P. Sara were colonial in character and essentially belonged to the elite – up until the 1980s, there was nowhere for the common man to watch cricket.

Nor was the stadium the only democratising measure of the era. In 1971, Premasara Epasinghe gave Sri Lanka its first Sinhala cricket commentary – by the 1980s, his voice could be heard in villages across the island.[17] TV broadcasts – beginning with Australia's visit in 1981 – brought more eyes to the game; and in 1987, Ranjit Fernando and W.A.N. Silva helped produce the first Sinhala training manual.

Cricket won many acolytes during the 1980s – the decade Sri Lanka became hellbent on transforming itself into a burial ground. Wouldn't you want to look away? A broadcast from Sydney or Sialkot offered a chance to forget for a few hours – to curse and clap and cheer, to enjoy the innocence and exhilaration of international sport. For once, to take pride in the exploits of your countrymen. During the island's darkest days, Arjuna's plucky team were a small but significant ray of hope. Their adventures abroad gave many at home something to feel good about.

And the team continued to grow. In April 1990, they beat India at the Austral-Asia Cup in Sharjah, Arjuna leading the chase with a truly special innings. Even when the asking rate shot up to 11, he kept his cool – ending 85* off 77.[18] This type of knock was undoubtedly becoming his speciality: time and again, with the equation laid out in front of him, he executed his plan with patience and precision. It's no wonder Sri Lanka showed a marked preference for chasing in the coming years.

The tournament marked time on Ravi Ratnayeke's career. Like Wettimuny, de Mel and Madugalle before him, he needed a more stable source of income, and bowed out of international cricket on his 30th birthday. It was another big loss – Ravi had been a near constant in the side for eight years, and during the second half of his twenties started to shoulder much more responsibility.

Giant by Sri Lankan standards, his ability to extract steepling bounce first caught the eyes of selectors – but hard work and a solid technique helped him transform into a genuine all-rounder. At the same time, he bore a greater burden with the ball: with Rumesh and de Mel crippled by injuries, he became Sri Lanka's strike bowler and pack leader – the 'go-to' guy for a series of captains. One of the first names on the team sheet during the mid-1980s, his contributions would be sorely missed.

Sri Lanka's sole Test of 1990, at Chandigarh in November, was a reminder of the insidious effects of the red-ball chasms the side faced. Though the bowlers could feel pleased in restricting India to 288, on a crumbling wicket Arjuna's men only managed 82. Numbers five to eleven made 3 runs between them; if not for Gurusinha's dogged 52*, Sri Lanka would have faced utter humiliation.

While the dearth of Test cricket saw their progress stall, Arjuna's men were clearly developing into a limited-overs force. In India, 104 from Aravinda saw them almost gun down 245 in 45 overs. Next up, Ranatunga cracked a blistering 58 off 27 – but Sri Lanka fell away when he was run out for the second game in succession. They finally got it right in the third ODI: Ramanayake's 3 for 15 helped them keep India to 136, chased down with minimal fuss.

And over New Year 1991, Arjuna's men reached the final of the Asia Cup again. They couldn't stop India chasing 204 at Eden Gardens, but simply taking part in a showpiece at the colossal stadium was valuable experience. Six of the side would be back five years later for a World Cup semi-final.

Clearly, the team was moving in the right direction – though moving between the wickets was proving more of a problem. Ranatunga was run out again in the Asia Cup final: as stomach swelled and youthful exuberance waned, he was rightly earning a reputation as one of the worst runners in cricket. Nor was he the only culprit.[19] Gurusinha – run out in the final too – was probably even worse than his captain: nearly 20 per cent of his ODI dismissals were a result of dodgy running. Aravinda – no saint himself – described the team as 'diabolical' between the wickets: he (twenty-seven times), Atapattu (thirty-seven times), Kaluwitharana (twenty-six), Jayasuriya (twenty-three) and Vaas (twenty-two) were prolific victims during their careers, while Arjuna and Aravinda were responsible for running out a partner forty and forty-two times respectively.[20] Try as they might, one of history's great one-day sides never quite mastered cricket's most basic discipline. Luckily, they had plenty of batters who could deal in boundaries.

PARADISE LOST

For all Ranatunga brought to Sri Lankan cricket, there were difficulties that had to be dealt with. The spikiness which so greatly benefited the side was sometimes misdirected; the single-mindedness which drove Sri Lanka forward often seemed a step or two from despotism. Having been handed the keys to the car at such a young age, Arjuna expected to proceed with total authority.

A three-Test tour to New Zealand in early 1991 offered a rare chance for Sri Lanka to build rhythm in the longest form. Martin Crowe predicted a clean sweep for his men, but soon discovered this side were a different proposition to the team who'd been bullied in 1983.[21] Rumesh and Labrooy bowled superbly on a bitterly windy opening day in Wellington to dismiss the hosts for 174; in reply, Aravinda cracked 267. As fearless on the hook as he'd been in Australia, there were plenty of dashing cuts and drives too. All in all, he had forty hits to the fence as Sri Lanka racked up 497.

With a mammoth lead and time in the game, they would have hoped they were on the brink of a first away Test victory. But the pitch had flattened out, and the Lankans were frustrated by a Crowe marathon. Of the frontline bowlers, only Ramanayake managed a wicket. Rumesh, Labrooy, Asoka de Silva and Warnaweera laboured 146 overs without reward – a worrying sign, no matter how flat the pitch.

The hosts took control in Hamilton too. Though Gurusinha knuckled down for a first-innings 119, the rest struggled: set 418 to win, Sri Lanka were expected to wilt. But 'Guru' carried on where he left off, stroking the ball around the wicket en route to 102. 'We played to win that game,' he told me: ending 74 short, with 4 wickets in hand, the team weren't far off. 'That showed us we were good. We maybe didn't have the skill to convert those positions into wins yet, but we were on the right track'.

The final Test belonged to Aravinda – innings of 96 and 123 further proof of his immense ability. Having been caught on the hook in Wellington, New Zealand thought they could bounce him out again. Instead, they were flayed mercilessly into the advertising boards. Nor was he the only Sri Lankan to deal in lusty blows: in the first innings,

217

Labrooy set a new Test record by reaching 50 in thirteen scoring strokes – amongst them nine 4s and a pair of 6s.

Always ahead of the game, Arjuna's men gave themselves just over a day to dismiss New Zealand, but fell well short. Labrooy aside, the attack looked ineffective; twice in three matches, Sri Lanka had got themselves into winning positions only for their bowlers to fail to see them over the line. They especially missed a potent spinner: Asoka de Silva, who took 4 wickets at 98.25 during the series, was cut adrift after the tour.

But the batting of de Silva and Gurusinha was clearly cause for celebration. De Silva's performances cemented his arrival as a world-class player.* For many, his gutsy hooking dredged memories of Duleep – and in a way, he was a natural successor to his former captain. Though more graceful than Mendis – and slightly taller at 5ft 3½in – he was equally unpredictable; blessed with the same ability to play shots that lumped pressure back onto bowlers. A man of moods, most in Sri Lanka agree he is the best the island has produced – a fact not fully reflected by the numbers. Especially in his early days, he was mercurial, guilty of throwing his wicket away and not always trying his hardest. It took time to refine his run-scoring method; at this stage, he had well earned the nickname 'Mad Max'.

Gurusinha was a different kettle of fish. He wasn't necessarily the most talented player in the side but he worked tirelessly, and refused to be beaten. A man for a crisis, none of his seven Test centuries came in a winning cause. Yet, he was quite possibly the most determined run scorer Sri Lanka produced until Sangakkara. 'I knew technically I was pretty good, but I think mentally I was one of the strongest guys,' he reflects today. 'I will not let anybody get me, I'll fight back. And when the chips were down, I always stood up.'

It wasn't just the two of them either – top to bottom, this looked like a line-up that could hold its own against hostile attacks. Rookie

---

* Through fifteen Tests – six of them at home – he had averaged 25.38; in his last six – away in Australia, India and New Zealand – his runs had come at 81.90. Equally, in the last couple of years he had emerged as the linchpin of Sri Lanka's ODI line-up. In the thirty-three matches since the start of the Asia Cup in October 1988, he had averaged 35.45.

opener Chandika Hathurusingha eased the pressure on the middle order in his first series as an international opener; with the weight of run scoring taken off his shoulders, Ranatunga made useful cameos throughout. Sanath Jayasuriya and Hashan Tillakaratne were finding their feet; Roshan Mahanama would come back and bolster the group. Disappointingly, they were well short of their best in the ODIs, with New Zealand winning all three at a canter.

Yet, the biggest upset of the tour sprung from the opening game, when Arjuna's brother Dammika broke his finger opening the batting. Though manager Stanley Jayasinghe wanted him sent home, Arjuna was insistent he should stay. Jayasinghe eventually got his way, but the incident put strain on an already fraught relationship.

Jayasinghe had, in fact, tried to resign before the tour, annoyed by the inclusion of Dammika Ranatunga and Asoka de Silva. He was persuaded by the Sports Minister to 'travel under protest' – but if he felt Dammika was on tour by virtue of being the captain's brother, his suspicions wouldn't have been eased by the way things played out. He complained in his tour report that Ranatunga's 'conduct on the field in relation to umpires was questionable and at times embarrassing', and accused Ranatunga and assistant manager Paranathala of haughty attitudes and double standards.

Clearly, it was not a happy camp. Hathursinghe, called up as Dammika's replacement, told me he 'felt the tension' when he arrived. 'I had a good relationship with Arjuna and his family at that time, because I played with Sanjeeva [Ranatunga] – we were at the same school, and I used to go to his house. I *know* them. But the moment I walked in, I felt the coldness. I was not expected; it was not a good feeling.' The disunity fed into the team's cricket too: with the second Test up for grabs going into the final session, Ranatunga and Jayasinghe disagreed over whether to push for the win or settle for a draw. 'I'm 80* for the first time and I'm not sure whether I should go for my hundred, or think about the team,' Hathursinghe reflected.

For Arjuna, ostracising the well-respected Jayasinghe was a dangerous game. 'To me, Stanley was a fantastic manager,' Gurusinha told Gideon Haigh. 'And that is where we fell out, Arjuna and I, because I supported Stanley. I don't know whether Arjuna was doing it because Dammika was his brother. But I thought that the decision was a matter for the manager not the captain.'[22]

Back in Colombo, an enquiry found Ranatunga guilty of misconduct and decided to relieve him of the captaincy.[23] It was not universally popular: posters sprung up around town asking 'Was his removal due to politics, religion?' Yet, the implication – that the UNP government wanted rid of him because his father was part of the political opposition – seems speculative. More likely, there were those in positions of power who took exception to his pugnacious approach.

Indeed, a local newspaper reported that there had been problems on the India tour too, and that 'a strong case had been building up against Ranatunga over a period of time which had nothing to do with his father's politics. The basic fault of Mr Ranatunga had been his lack of restraint in dealing with members of his team and Managers. His disrespectful and aggressive behaviour has not been a good influence on the team.' You might well disagree with that conclusion, but it was clear that the tide had turned against Arjuna. Aravinda would lead the side to England in 1991; Sri Lanka's 'captain cool' was left to watch at home on TV. Ranatunga had done so much to flood this side with belief over the past two and a half years; could they prosper in his absence?

★★★

Sri Lanka's outlook was changing. Team meetings were increasingly conducted in Sinhala rather than English; before away trips, the side now took part in a short Buddhist ceremony.[24] At last, the islanders seemed to be embracing their Sri Lankan-ness.* But touring without their spiritual leader Arjuna was bound to pose problems. De Silva has written about Ranatunga's 'eloquent body language'; for all Aravinda's gifts, it would be a stretch to say he was blessed with the same.[25] Docile and

---

*   That said, there have been accusations that the national side substituted a pan-national identity for a specifically Sinhalese one. Mike Marqusee noted that, following World Cup triumph in 1996, 'Ranatunga and his men toured the south and west of the country ... receiving benedictions from the *bhikkus* who had engineered the most violent anti-Tamil flare-ups in the recent past ... The players did not take the trophy to Jaffna or indeed anywhere in the war-torn north or east of the island.'

mild-mannered, he often took to the cricket field as though he had just woken from a nap. Arjuna would gladly bark at his men; it was tough to envisage Aravinda getting above a whisper. But he would have to find a way to inspire them.

The biggest boon of the trip was the emergence of Sanath Jayasuriya, who shone in the Test with a shot-filled 66. Though Sri Lanka were always a step behind, there were moments to savour. Rumesh bowled with spirit to get himself on the honours board, before Aravinda lit up a gloomy London evening, blasting his way to 42* off 30. With a back-lift skewed towards gully, he readied himself for cross-bat shots.[26] Anything marginally short was punished: a back-of-a-length Chris Lewis delivery – which looked like it would crash into off stump – effortlessly picked up and swatted over mid-wicket. On commentary, an entranced Benaud announced, 'There's no better hooker in the game.' Yet Aravinda went the following morning, without adding to his score. For the first half of his career, these sparkling cameos were a stick he was beaten with. He still needed to develop hunger for runs – but these little gems were rare treats, each one a confirmation of a unique if untamed talent.

Unable to take wickets or stem the flow of runs, Sri Lanka lost their grip on the game in the second innings. Though they battled bravely, surviving four sessions was too tall a task – ultimately, they fell 20 overs short. Still, they could take heart from the performance. The match hinged on swing moments; Clive Lloyd struck a chord when he told the team they reminded him of West Indies in 1975.[27] The talent was there in droves, but they needed to build physical and mental strength if they were to cross the line in Test cricket.

Jayasuriya's success on the tour underlined the fact that Sri Lanka was starting to churn out a production line of quality cricketers. He steadied chases against England Amateurs and England A with scores of 57* and 35; at Taunton, he and Aravinda plundered 83 off 8 overs to bring Sri Lanka their maiden first-class win in England. There were more substantive knocks too,* while 3 for 26 against Durham hinted at the potency of his seemingly innocuous left-arm spin. Plus, destructive impulses made

---

*   Jayasuriya made 94 against Yorkshire, 78 out of 154 against Worcestershire, and an unbeaten 100 against Sussex. His first-class runs came at 53.55.

Jayasuriya a nightmare to bowl at; and his dynamism in the field was another string to Sri Lanka's bow. Though his true talent was not clear until the second half of the 1990s, Jayasuriya gave a glimpse of his lofty potential on his first England tour.

For another future great, the trip was not such a happy one.[28] Muttiah Muralitharan had found prominence after breaking schoolboy records in 1990/91, but was not yet the bowler the world would come to know. As a young man, he bounced to the wicket in a wider arc; he already turned his off-break like a wrist-spinner, but had not learned to vary speed or flight, to use the crease or control the drift he imparted. The doosra would not appear for a decade. Murali's rare natural gifts meant he'd never had to think batsmen out. He just had to give the ball a rip.

But if he wanted to test the best on unhelpful tracks, he would have to hone his skills. 'It didn't go my way,' he remembers. 'I played two four-day games and couldn't get a wicket. I had a few thoughts, "Am I good enough to play at this level?"* It was a disappointing tour, but a learning one too. It's not that easy to get into the national side and play cricket for Sri Lanka.' Away from the field, it was equally tough for Murali. With the board still pretty much broke, he and Romesh Kaluwitharana found themselves waiting on the rest of the team – moving from one laundrette to the next, loaded down with bags full of whites.

Top to bottom, the team had room for growth. Far too often, county sides were allowed to rack up big-first innings scores; against Sussex, Sri Lanka won in spite of the bowlers, not because of them. Gurusinha and de Silva managed just one first-class 50 each; the Lankans missed Arjuna's batting and leadership. To be skittled for 181 and 154 against Worcestershire, and 97 and 134 against Nottinghamshire, wasn't good enough; almost a decade on from their inaugural Test, the team still looked green in English conditions.

Ranatunga returned to the ranks for a tour of Pakistan, but, still stripped of the captaincy, seemed short of the confidence so crucial to

---

* Others could see his potential – when manager Chandra Schaffter asked Basil D'Oliveira what he thought of his young spinner, the response was forthright. Worcestershire's spinners were turning the ball a couple of inches, Murali was ripping it a foot and a half. 'That was all I needed to hear,' Schaffter told me with a smile.

his game. He made a pair in the drawn first Test at Sialkot: though Wasim and Waqar's threat drew the Lankans' inefficacy into sharp focus, at least Jayasuriya impressed again with 77 and 35*. As in England, Sanath looked the team's best player. He struck a blistering 81 in Faisalabad; with Pramodya Wickramasinghe claiming five lbw victims, Sri Lanka carried a 19-run lead into the second innings. But again, Wasim and Waqar were too hot to handle. Sri Lanka's 165 was 50 too few, and Pakistan crossed the line with 3 wickets in hand. Bowling frailties had often held the team back in recent times, but on this tour the senior batsmen had to shoulder much of the blame.*

But with the 1992 World Cup around the corner, the five one-dayers mattered most. Sri Lanka hadn't played an ODI for over eleven months, and were comfortably handled by the soon-to-be world champions. Pakistan's bowlers were miserly where Sri Lanka's were expensive; Miandad, Inzamam-ul-Haq and Salim Maliq stood strong while the Lankan batsmen were all too often blown over. The 4-1 result felt a fair reflection of a lop-sided series.

World Cup preparations hit another roadblock when Rumesh was injured in a warm-up against Pakistan. Sri Lanka's build-up had been far from ideal, and when the tournament rolled around they were undone by a gruelling travel schedule. Their group games took them on a grand tour: from New Plymouth to Hamilton, across the Tasman sea to Mackay, back to New Zealand for a match in Wellington, before a final Australian leg that took in Adelaide, Ballarat and Berri. The day before the South Africa match, the team were stuck on a fifteen-hour coach journey.** 'The travel was bizarre,' Hathurusinghe told me. 'We were in and out of Australia and New Zealand, back and forth. I thought we were a pretty good team even at that time – the challenge was the condition of the pitches and the travel. Nowadays, I don't think any team would agree to that sort of arrangement.'

---

* After his scoreless return in Sialkot, Arjuna made 0 and 6 to finish the series with an average of 1.50. Aravinda frustrated by getting in and getting out – scores of 31, 19, 12 and 38 suggested mental rather than technical shortcomings. Gurusinha had a forgettable time too, with 73 runs at an average of 18.25.

** What's more, on three occasions Sri Lanka had matches sandwiched either side of travel days – a situation New Zealand, Pakistan and England didn't face at all. This was poor planning from the ICC, and didn't seem particularly fair.

Most of Sri Lanka grimaced as they awoke to news that their men had conceded 312 against Zimbabwe in their World Cup opener. 'I was so angry I didn't even come and talk to them,' team manager Ranjit Fernando told me. But the wicket was flat and the boundaries tiny – Samarasekera dealt in lusty blows, and after a mid-innings wobble, Ranatunga and Jayasuriya counterattacked brilliantly. Sanath imperiously slapped a pair of 6s over mid-wicket: though he went, Arjuna continued to push the ball into the gaps. He timed his assault perfectly. Sri Lanka still needed 15 off the last 2 overs, but Ranatunga brought them home with 4 balls to spare.

But they put themselves under pressure by scoring slowly against New Zealand, losing wickets by the bundle when they tried to pump on the gas. The running between the wickets was poor: Aravinda and Jaysuriya engineered their own demise, and Gurusinha almost did the same in comical fashion. 'I don't know what he was doing,' Henry Blofeld exclaimed on commentary. 'It was just as though he was going for a walk in the garden.' Perhaps Gurusinha wasn't entirely sure himself. After suffering an unhappy tournament, manager Fernando put a blunt question to him. 'What happened, man?' He was shocked when Gurusinha admitted he'd forgotten to bring his contact lenses, and had played the whole tournament without them.

Though a clash against India was washed out, Sri Lanka held their nerve to sneak past South Africa in Wellington. Jayasuriya took two miraculous catches at short extra cover: the second, a full-stretch one-handed Superman, had Jonty Rhodes walking back to the pavilion wearing a look of disbelief. Though restricting South Africa to 195 put the Lankans in the box seat, Allan Donald steamed in with menace – when he toppled Aravinda's off stump, they were 35-3 and in the mire.

But Mahanama reached his third consecutive 50, and Ranatunga played another brilliant finisher's innings, bulleting the ball to the square boundaries and unusually scurrying between the wickets. At times he gasped for air, but he dug in, carrying Sri Lanka to a monumental victory. For the second time in the tournament, Ranatunga had produced a match-winning innings; though Michael Bevan is credited as cricket's first 'finisher', surely it was Arjuna who pioneered the role.

Having looked in good form through their first few games, Sri Lanka's tournament fell away. But, winning two of seven was a reasonable effort; plus, Ranatunga was back and firing, the unpleasantness of the previous tour to New Zealand all but forgotten. This was crucial: Aravinda had done his best in the interim, but was not really cut out for the captaincy.[29] He lacked Arjuna's inspirational force, and the burden of leadership detracted from his magic-making with the bat.* By contrast, Ranatunga was born to lead. His work was just getting started.

THE GREAT HEIST

So, the team had their captain back – and after five years of famine, Test cricket returned to the island. For all of Sri Lanka, Australia's visit in August 1992 was a moment to savour. After half a decade wandering vagrant, Arjuna's boys were back home.

They marked their return in style, inserting Australia on an unusually green SSC pitch.[30] After lunch, Hathurusinghe got the ball wobbling all over the place and picked up four scalps in quick succession. 'It wasn't just the batsmen who were clueless,' he told Andrew Fidel Fernando. 'Even I was not sure which way the ball was moving.'***[31]

After Australia slipped from 84-1 to 124-7, Ian Healy helped them up to 256. But Sri Lanka were batting before close, and piled pressure onto Australia on the second day. Gurusinha dropped anchor for the best part of nine hours, while Arjuna tucked into Warne with relish. They put on 230 in partnership, before debuting keeper Romesh Kaluwitharana lashed a devil-may-care 132*. For the first time, three Sri Lankans had scored centuries in a Test innings; as a team, 500 was uncharted territory.

But Sri Lanka were sloppy in the field second time around. Kaluwitharana badly fluffed a chance to get rid of David Boon; maddeningly, the team sent down 34 no-balls.[32] Still, the game was in their hands heading into the final day. 'Overnight we all thought if we hadn't

---

*   During his spell in charge, Aravinda averaged 17.85 in ODIs and 26.66 in Tests.
**   Hathurusinghe remembers one of the selectors joking, 'What's wrong with the wicket? They can't even face Hatu!'

won by lunch, we'd definitely win by tea-time,' wrote Aravinda.[33] But Australia batted into the second session as the Lankans laboured for wickets: eventually, Arjuna's men were set 181 for a famous victory.

Expectant bodies flooded into the SSC. The ground was awash with celebration; people smiled easily in anticipation of a national holiday. At 79-2 heading into the final session, Sri Lanka had the game in their hands. But Aravinda wanted to finish it in a hurry. Two consecutive Craig McDermott deliveries were slapped over Allan Border's head to the mid-on fence: though the second was not as clean as the first, Australia's captain could not get quite underneath it.[34]

In typical 'Mad Max' style, Aravinda failed to heed the warning. He wanted three in three. Next ball, he ran down the wicket and tried to whip McDermott from outside off to the mid-on boundary. He miscued: as the ball swirled in the air, Border charged back to the rope and took a remarkable outstretched catch. Two balls later, Ranatunga spooned one straight to the Australian skipper at mid-off. Out of nowhere, Sri Lanka were 132-4.

Worse, with Jayasuriya and Tillakaratne missing, they had exposed their callow underbelly. Atapattu, cripplingly short of confidence after three successive Test-match ducks, was bowled for 1;* Kaluwitharana and Ramanayake came and went; at the non-striker's end, Gurusinha was stranded – forced to watch the most misery-inducing *perahera*.** With 7 wickets down, Sri Lanka needed 34 to win. He wanted to try to blast them over the line, but the message from the dressing room was clear – stay at the crease, stick to the plan.

At this stage, Border threw the ball to Shane Warne, who responded with a nerveless spell of pressure bowling that launched his career. His last 13 balls were dots, 3 of them wickets. Ian Healy thought he'd thrown the match away when he missed a chance to stump Gurusinha, but Madurasinghe lamely popped Warne to mid-off in the next over.[35] Agonisingly, Gurusinha was left unbeaten on 31. Sri Lanka had fallen 17 short of victory. Having been in command for four and a half days,

---

* Some have said this should have been awarded as a leg bye. If so, Atapattu's Test career would have started with six ducks spread over three and a half years.
** Parade.

they'd thrown the match away in the course of an hour. The thousands who had rushed to the ground to share in the joy now stuck around to boo their own men. Border declared it 'the greatest heist since the Great Train Robbery'.

'I don't know what happened,' Hathurusinghe reflects. 'We put blinkers on. Got panicked.' 'It was like someone had died,' Kaluwitharana told Andrew Fidel Fernando. 'We heard them yelling their victory song, and each time they yelled and shouted in enjoyment, it was like being stabbed with a knife in the chest over and over again.' 'That's the only game I've ever cried,' Gurusinha admitted. 'I'm not a person who cries. Even when we won the World Cup, a lot of guys were crying, but not me. But the SSC game I cried. We couldn't have lost. It dampened the joy [of making a century] no doubt. That was a sad day.'

The sadness was compounded by how much Sri Lanka had riding on the result.[36] Trapped in an endless civil war, the prospect of an unprecedented victory over Australia allowed people to escape the horror, just for a moment. When things came crashing down there was anger and disbelief. Aravinda received death threats; the manner of the collapse, tied to subsequent revelations,* saw scrutiny lumped onto the captain and his deputy.[37]

As much as their dismissals rankle, players shouldn't be pilloried on the basis of stupid shots alone. It's unthinkable that Sri Lanka's captain and vice captain would purposely wreck their team's greatest triumph for financial gain. Aravinda has said he went home and cried, but that the match proved a turning point – the moment he realised the hubris of youth was holding him back. 'This Test series was the first one that left me looking inside myself,' he wrote. 'Change had to come from within. Batting was no longer a matter of being seen to challenge each and every bowler, batting was now a matter of carrying the team to its goals.'[38]

The rest of the series was rain-scuppered and far less enthralling. Murali was unleashed at Khettarama: having seen him flummox Border

---

* It was alleged that, during the series, Mahanama, Gurusinha and Jayasuriya were approached at a Chinese restaurant, while Dean Jones was offered £50,000 in a biscuit tin in return for information. In 2001, Hashan Tillakaratne raised eyebrows by claiming match fixing had been common in Sri Lanka since 1992.

in a warm-up match,[*] Ranatunga put full faith in the 20-year-old off-spinner.[39] 'He argued with the selectors,' Murali told me. 'He came and told me before the Test, 'I had to fight a lot to get you in. Do your best.' The Kandy Man responded by unseating Tom Moody and Mark Waugh with successive deliveries; as he put it to me, it was 'a decent enough start'. Equally, 1-0 was a respectable enough series scoreline – but down to a man, the Lankans knew they'd squandered a chance to mark their homecoming with a historic victory.

At least the one-dayers brought plenty of positivity, with a pair of Aravinda specials helping Sri Lanka to a 2-0 lead. Increasingly, they were backing themselves to chase big scores: only when asked to post in the final ODI did they struggle. Still, a series victory was cause for celebration: despite their limitations, Arjuna's men were beginning to challenge cricket's elite on a regular basis. 'We were getting that confidence,' Gurusinha reflects. 'I think that came mainly from our fielding. We sat down and looked at how we could compete with the top teams. Our bowling wasn't top of the world – but we knew that if we fielded well, we could be very competitive.'

Ranjit Fernando told me that, having seen Sri Lanka field so poorly at the 1987 World Cup, he desperately wanted to help them improve. 'They were dreadful,' he told me. 'It was such an embarrassment to see the national team dropping these catches. I had a meeting with the young players, and said "Look, if you watched that, you would wonder why you are playing for Sri Lanka. Let's set a high goal, of at some stage being the best fielding side in the world."

'All we did was hit it hard, made it *hurt* – and took the fear out of them. We challenged them to go that extra yard or two to chase the ball. It was a simple exercise. I used to be working – I'd leave the office about 5 pm. By the time I came to the ground, they had finished batting practice. They used to wait for me, and as it went on I felt they wanted to do more and more. We'd go on for about an hour into the night. From nothing, the fielding improved to be absolutely world class. Then, when

---

[*]   When Border arrived at the crease, Mark Waugh told him that Murali was bowling off-breaks. But, having seen the spinner rotate his wrist, he confusedly wandered down the wicket to quiz Waugh further: 'You sure he's bowling off-spin, mate?'

Duleep gave up, he also took pains in trying to do the same thing. He'd just finished playing, so he was more vicious than me.'

'Ranjit and Duleep, they were like old-school training,' Hathurusinghe remembers. 'Volume, volume, volume. We were very keen to get our hands dirty, to dive in and do things after practice until we couldn't see the ball. The thing that stands out for me is that we were very competitive. We were athletic guys, and we were competing with each other.' Fernando often ended practices with a round of high catches – each member of the squad had to take a tough chance before they could head home. If there was a drop, it would be back to the beginning.

It sounds simple, but this sort of training acclimatised the team to fielding with the weight of teammates' expectations on their shoulders. It soon became second nature. 'From '91, we spent a lot of time and sharpened up,' Gurusinha adds. 'We were over 90 per cent – maybe over 95 per cent – in terms of success. It was very rare that we'd drop a catch. To win one-dayers you have to have a couple of run-outs and some blinders. We used to do that every game. That changed matches.'

SPINNING TO WIN

08:35 am, November 15th, 1992. Sri Lanka's Navy Commander Clancy Fernando is en route to the Naval Headquarters. Little does he know an LTTE suicide bomber is waiting for him, with a motorbike sagging under the weight of explosives. The bomber spots Fernando and presses the gas. The explosion is devastating.

Metres away, the New Zealand team are waking up to their first morning in Sri Lanka. The blast shakes their hotel. Ken Rutherford's breakfast ends up on the floor. Many feel as if they've been yanked back to the horror of 1987. Once more, minds turn towards family, safety and home.[40]

The New Zealanders put it to a vote. Five years prior it had been unanimous, but this time nine were willing to stay. Of course, the BCCSL were desperate to stave off another series cancellation, which would have been catastrophic for the island's cricket. Thankfully, NZC were keen for the tour to continue too; before long, board president Peter McDermott was on a flight to Colombo.

Having sought advice from the British and Australian High Commissioners, McDermott spoke to players individually. Some of the nine wantaway players were swayed; Justin Vaughan, Michael Owens, Grant Bradburn and John Wright were flown in as replacements. Crowe would take over as makeshift coach and the tour would proceed as planned. McDermott claims he was convinced of the team's safety having received a call from the LTTE. He told reporters, 'I was contacted by someone who represented himself as being a member of the Tamil Tigers … He said "I just want to assure you that your team are very, very safe. We are all cricket people – I intend to go to the first Test – and if we did anything to your team our funding would dry up immediately." He said "we don't attack visitors".'

The conversation is significant: though the Tigers did not support Sri Lanka, the admission 'we are all cricket people' was an endorsement of the game's sanctity. I've heard about a Sri Lankan priest who used to joke that the island had five main religions – Buddhism, Hinduism, Christianity, Islam and Cricket. There's truth in the humour: especially in wartime, the game held an almost sacred appeal. In Sri Lanka's consciousness, cricket was beginning to occupy increasingly rarefied space.

The first Test got going twelve days after the blast, and was headlined by Roshan Mahanama's 153, a maiden century long in the making. Though the game dragged towards a draw, New Zealand's struggles against spin compelled Arjuna to pick Murali at the SSC, unleashing the sort of three-pronged spin attack not seen since the 1970s. Mahanama struck another classy century: elegant and upright at the crease, he was a joy to watch in this sort of form.

By the second evening, Sri Lanka had spun a web around their visitors: 100-7 overnight, New Zealand were bundled out the next morning, adding just 2 to their total. Murali's dismissal of Martin Crowe for a duck, with a ripper that spun from outside off to clip leg stump, left all who saw it slack-jawed. Here was a sign of the greatness to come.

The young off-spinner kept turning the screw. He finished with 7 for the match, as Sri Lanka ticked their way across the line on the fourth afternoon. For the first time, Ranatunga's men had spun their way to a Test-match victory. They dominated the ODIs too: with Ranatunga using up to nine bowlers, the attack carried increasing flexibility.

While New Zealand's absentees made the task a little easier, going unbeaten through a Test and ODI series showed Sri Lanka were growing up fast. Tillakaratne and Mahanama were shouldering more responsibility. Ranatunga, de Silva and Gurusinha were entrenched in the middle order. Murali had made a splash in the Tests, and would soon be let loose in ODI cricket. Had New Zealand abandoned the tour, it would have paved the way for a spate of cancellations. Their decision to stay allowed future tours to proceed as planned. The fledgling Lankans needed cricket; had they been forced back into pariah status, would they have improved fast enough to challenge at the 1996 World Cup?

Three years out, the team were a long way from the finished article. Arjuna acknowledged as much after a pair of heavy losses to Pakistan in February 1993, telling Rupavahini TV, 'The burden has fallen too heavily on me and Aravinda de Silva and perhaps Roshan Mahanama to carry Sri Lanka forward.[41] Young players like Jayasuriya, Tillakaratne and Kalpage must take their responsibilities more seriously.'*

Since Sri Lanka have often done without a long-term coach, the captain has traditionally been at the heart of things. That suited Arjuna fine, but his dictatorial approach was not always popular. During 1993, factions seem to have emerged among the senior players. At one team meeting, Mahanama openly challenged Duleep Mendis for giving Arjuna and Aravinda an easy ride during fielding practices.[42]

It is unsurprising that Ranatunga rubbed some up the wrong way. Where Sri Lankans are generally conflict-averse people, Arjuna felt making an omelette meant breaking plenty of eggs. But he was a shrewd tactician, with a clear vision of how his team should move forward. After success against New Zealand, Ranatunga saw that Sri Lanka could spin teams out. When England arrived for a one-off Test in March 1993, he again opted for a single specialist seamer. Don Anurasiri was phased out

---

*   The fact Ranatunga made no mention of Gurusinha is striking; it seems their relationship hadn't fully recovered from the spat in New Zealand in 1990.

in favour of the fledgling, but short-lived, partnership between Murali and Jayananda Warnaweera.

The duo's differing styles made them a menacing pair. While Murali was already earning a reputation for his eye-bulging turn, Warnaweera was a throwback to the fast spinners of earlier eras. They combined to bowl 85.1 of 130.1 overs in England's first innings, taking 8 between them. And Sri Lanka's reply showcased the sort of consistency Ranatunga had been asking for. The top six all passed 40, with Tillakaratne – who shepherded the tail superbly en route to 93* – carrying Sri Lanka to 469.

Faced with a first-innings deficit, a fourth-day wicket and a spin-heavy attack, England crumbled. Their measly 228 left Sri Lanka needing just 140 to win. Arjuna gave a rousing team talk; though the top order wobbled, Jayasuriya strolled to the crease and smashed Phil Tufnell for a first-ball 6 to take his team home.[43] For the first time, Sri Lanka had seen off England in a Test.

The ODIs proved equally one-sided. In the second, with 12,000 crammed into the Moratuwa ground, England self-destructed against Sri Lanka's part-timers. Jayasuriya stole the day with 6 for 29; in *The Independent*, Glenn Moore uncharitably reflected that 'several batsmen were out heaving across the line to a series of bowlers who would only be seen in the County Championship when a declaration was being set up'.[44] Little did he know that Sri Lanka's odd-job twirlers would become crucial cogs in a World Cup winning machine.

Having comprehensively dispatched England, Sri Lanka faced a much tougher challenge when India arrived in July. The first Test was washed out, but thereafter the visiting batsmen proved their reputation as esteemed players of spin. Hundreds from Vinod Kambli, Navjot Sidhu and a young Sachin Tendulkar put the Lankans under pressure in the second Test; despite scores from Arjuna and Aravinda, they were blown out by 235 runs. Although the batsmen gave a better account of themselves at the P. Sara – and the recalled Murali posed plenty of questions – Sri Lanka could only claim a share of the spoils.

While the Tests had seen their fair share bickering and gamesmanship, the ODIs were blighted by umpiring too Machiavellian to be described as poor. Having collapsed in the first match, Sri Lanka were helped over the line in the second when umpire Ponnadurai triggered Kapil Dev.* The finale was overshadowed by an even more brazen decision. Roshan Mahanama had deftly controlled the Lankan chase, but the wheels came off when he had to retire with cramps. Left to the bowlers, things got nervy.

One short of parity, Javagal Srinath trapped Ramanayake in front of leg stump.[45] It looked a stone-dead lbw; as the batsman scrambled to complete a single, he frantically pointed to his bat. Only afterwards did he realise that the ball had ballooned up into gully's hands. The umpire was unmoved, but eventually realised he had to signal a leg bye or award India a wicket. It was farcical: the sort of flagrantly partisan umpiring which can sully a special performance. Still, fans joyously flooded onto the pitch as Ruwan Kalpage cracked the next ball to the fence. They had plenty to celebrate: at home, Sri Lanka had won four ODI series on the bounce.

And no sooner had India left than South Africa arrived for a three-Test tour, the two countries' maiden Test-meet. Their polar approaches brought forth enthralling cricket. While Donald and Brett Schultz steamed in to claim 9 first-innings wickets at Moratuwa, Murali danced and deceived, bagging 5 of his own to give Sri Lanka a first-innings lead. Second time around, Ranatunga made a virtuoso 131, declaring on the fourth evening with victory in his sights. Yet his bowlers could only manage five breakthroughs on the final day; for nearly five hours, Murali was frustrated by the front pad of Jonty Rhodes.[46] It was a wake-up call: his hooping off-break had carried him far, but he'd struggle against the best players with such a limited arsenal.**

A varied attack would come in time, but Ranatunga wanted results now. Furious over his spinners' inability to take second-innings wickets,

---

* Apparently, Dev had upset Ponnadurai prior to the series by sarcastically asking 'Are you still umpiring?' When he came to the crease at the SSC, India needed just 27 for victory. But second ball, Dev was rapped on the pads by Jayasuriya. Though it clearly pitched outside leg, Ponnadurai had no hesitation in raising his finger. India lost their last 4 wickets for 17, and the match by 8 runs.

** The most pressing need was for Murali to develop an arm ball. But his unique mechanics meant it was easier said than done. 'I wanted to learn to bowl straight,' he told me. 'But because I'm bowling with the wrist it doesn't happen. I'm a different spin bowler: I'm not a finger-spinner, I'm a wrist-spin off-spinner. So it's very difficult to bowl a straight ball.'

he blew up at the team when they got to the changing room. Piyal Wijetunge was showered with words probably too harsh for a debutant; he reacted badly and never played international cricket again. Once more, signs were springing up that sooner or later, Arjuna's spiky leadership style would see casualties mount up.

For Tillakaratne, who made 92 and 33* from number seven, the first clash against South Africa ended a period of remarkable productivity. But the brains trust felt he should be returning centuries: with Gurusinha absent, he was shunted up to three and responded with twin scores of 9. Spirited by their escape at Moratuwa, South Africa were rampant. Schultz cowed the batsmen with pace and bounce; though Murali bagged another 5 wickets – including a comic-book dismissal of Brian McMillan – Sri Lanka fell to an innings-and-208-run defeat. With the third Test washed out, it meant they surrendered the series too. While that was a setback, Murali's performances suggested Sri Lanka had unearthed a vital piece of the puzzle. His emergence profoundly changed the way the team went about their cricket.

By now, Murali had been unleashed in ODIs too – unsurprisingly proving an immediate threat. He bowled 3 overs in the abandoned first match, claiming a couple of scalps while conceding just 4 off the bat. Sanath grabbed 4 in the second, as Sri Lanka's part-timers bowled 27 overs between them. Although they lost the game thanks to pitiful batting, the abundance of bits-and-pieces bowlers was giving Sri Lanka flexibility, and allowing them to field seven specialist batters. They got it right in the final match of the series, toppling South Africa for 154 to escape with a share of the spoils.

1993 had been a breakout year. A flurry of ODI series wins went a long way to shifting the image of this team. They took major strides in Tests too: the young batting core continued to progress, and visiting sides knew they would now face a trial by spin in Sri Lanka. For non-Asian teams, that was a daunting prospect. Murali's breakthrough gave Arjuna a genuine strike bowler, who could bowl long spells and maintain stifling pressure. In both formats, Sri Lanka were finding ways to win. Crucially, their self-perception changed too. As Aravinda put it, 'We walked taller on the field, were more positive, Arjuna more authoritative. There were smiles on our faces where before there had been smudges of worry.'[47]

But the yo-yo ride was not over yet. All too often, Lankan progress has been derailed by sudden catastrophe, and so it proved in 1994. An awful tour of India in the New Year would eradicate any thoughts of thriving, and send the island's cricket back into survival mode.

THE SKANDAKUMAR REPORT

Though Sri Lanka's recent performances spoke of a fledgling unit brimming with potential, the reality was muddier. This was a team beset by rifts, skating on increasingly thin ice.[48] The embarrassment in India did not spring from nowhere; for some time now, trouble had been brewing.

The Skandakumar report – commissioned to investigate the embar-rassing tour – claimed the roots of the discord stretch back to mid-1993.[49] Duleep Mendis' appointment as manager had initially been a success, but by the time India toured Sri Lanka in July, 'a noticeable change' had occurred. The report claimed Mendis now largely dealt only with Arjuna and Aravinda, who had 'isolated themselves from a majority of the team'. Team meetings became increasingly brief; apparently 'senior players had no idea what the tactics were' during the India and South Africa series. Clearly there was a disconnect between the leaders and their men.

If factions had developed, it is understandable that Mendis sided with the captain and his deputy. Ranatunga played with him for a decade at the SSC, and it was Mendis who was captain when Arjuna and Aravinda came of age as international cricketers. They referred to him as 'Aiyya':* the trio shared a special bond which left little room for the rest of the team.

Yet, their exclusionary attitude wasn't the only problem. The report revealed that the board had been unhappy when players passed their share of sponsorship fees from Coca Cola onto Mendis – a move 'initi-ated' by Arjuna and Aravinda. Damningly, it claimed that 'players had

---

*   Big brother.

once pleaded with former cricket manager (Duleep Mendis), current captain and vice-captain, that "we can win without cheating"'.*

The accusation played no part in Mendis' sacking – but the decision to relieve him after the South African series wasn't properly explained to players, and Arjuna and Aravinda certainly weren't happy. It seems possible that disaffection manifested itself in poor ODI performances in the final months of 1993; at least by the end of the Hero Cup, Jayasuriya was opening the batting. Still, far too often only one batsman was standing up. Indian wickets should have been familiar by now, but there was still real disparity between Sri Lanka's form at home and away.

Bandula Warnapura was named as Mendis' replacement ahead of West Indies' arrival in Sri Lanka in December 1993. Unlike his predecessor, Warnapura had no real personal relationship with Ranatunga or de Silva – and their partnership got off to a rocky start when he told the team that he should be addressed as 'Bandula or Sir': aiyya was no longer appropriate.[50] Clearly, Warnapura would be adopting a more autocratic approach.

Though the sole West Indies Test at Moratuwa was rain-ruined, it was encouraging to see Sri Lanka dismiss a quality batting unit for 204. With Arjuna opening the bowling, the team fully committed to a spin-first approach, but struggled with the pace of Curtly Ambrose and Winston Benjamin. Weather spoiled the ODIs too, but the hosts won the only completed match thanks to a masterful 66* from the captain.

It had been a busy twelve months. Never before had Sri Lanka played eight Tests in a calendar year: alongside twenty-three ODIs, that amounted to a lot of cricket – especially for 'amateurs', still expected to pop into the office now and then. What the team really needed was rest – but the BCCSL seemed more concerned about boosting their coffers.

---

* When I spoke to Hathursinghe, he confirmed that the team weren't always happy with local umpiring. 'It's not that the standard of Sri Lankan umpiring was bad,' he explained. 'There was a lot of pressure on the umpires. I can remember once, the gentleman who was in charge got a few of the umpires into a room and said "You don't know what happens when these guys go out of the country. You have to think about your country." Things like that, I remember I stood up after they went and said "We don't need to do that kind of thing to win." I was really bombarded, "You haven't played elsewhere, shut up and wait."'

With scant regard for the team's preparation, the board accepted a last-minute offer to tour India at the start of 1994.[51]

While cash was a real concern for the administration, their oft-avaricious approach still rankles. When Gurusinha was forced to fly home early from the Hero Cup, he got a letter from the board, requesting the return of his $1,400 fee.[52] But he couldn't pay it all back at once; remarkably, the board refused his offer to reimburse the cash in instalments, preferring to suspend Gurusinha for the West Indies and India series.

That the board was willing to alienate a hugely important senior player over such a trivial financial issue doesn't sit well. It seems like they wanted to send a message. The decision becomes even more galling in light of the inexperience in the India squad.* The BCCSL were well aware of the challenge ahead, yet happily sent out a half-baked unit. They threw their men into the fire with little thought of the consequences.

Sri Lanka were under the pump as soon as the series started. Intent on stopping Murali from settling, Navjot Sidhu smashed eight 6s in his 124: staring down the barrel of 500, Arjuna's men wilted once a strong opening stand was broken. In sliding to an innings-and-119-run defeat, they knew they had let themselves down.

Meanwhile, Arjuna and Aravinda's relationship with Warnapura was rapidly deteriorating.[53] Aravinda claims the problems started when he refused to get the manager an ice cream.[54] He later wrote, 'I had no respect for the man for the way he pushed his weight around, abused his position of authority and bullied the youngsters.'[55] Ranatunga seemed to show little hesitation in badmouthing Warnapura to his teammates; when the duo skipped a training session in the lead-up to the second Test, the manager applauded the team's attitude in their absence. According to Aravinda:

---

*   Twelve of the sixteen were under 25, while seven were first-time tourists. According to Skandakumar, 'Anura Gunawardene was not included in the original national pool selected on 17 December and yet made the tour on his performance in a couple of hastily arranged trial games.' He, Ravi Pushpakumara and Chaminda Vaas had not played for Sri Lanka before: given that practices only began on 18 December – and were interrupted by the Christmas and New Year holidays – the board were asking a lot of them.

On the field we were batting without any appetite for a fight. All our fighting was being done off the field. Management was at the throats of the players, the dressing-room was seething with anxiety; everyone seemed to be defeated before we even went out to play. Everyone spoke in whispers and nobody cared to laugh out loud. Plus with such a strong security presence it was impossible to escape from the confines of the hotel, from the presence of chafing management.[56]

India won another toss at Bangalore, and were soon pounding their way towards 500 again. Skandakumar reckoned the umpiring 'led to an attitude where games appear to have been given up ... before the first ball was bowled'; but damningly countered that poor shots had been the cause of twice as many dismissals.[57] Failing to reach 250 in either innings, Sri Lanka slid to another innings defeat. Two shoddy performances did nothing to help a fractious atmosphere. Arjuna grew edgy that a plot was afoot to unseat him: though he finally won a toss at Ahmedabad, the team squandered their opportunity. Skittled for 119, they were blown out by an innings for the third match running.

This was a serious setback. On the field, Sri Lanka were humiliated from start to finish. Off it, morale was at rock bottom, and little could be done to turn it around. A cake was brought forth to celebrate Murali reaching 50 wickets in Tests, but when Aravinda smeared some on the team physio, the air grew fraught. Mortified, the physio announced that he wanted to go home; his reaction upset Aravinda, who blurted out that he wanted to leave too.

Perhaps the incident had been brewing. The Skandakumar Report claimed that de Silva's 'attempt to almost completely monopolise' the physio – and 'his attitude towards him' – 'hardly did his image as vice-captain any good on tour'.[58] At least he and Arjuna found some form during the ODIs, and Sri Lanka finally struck a victory in the rain-curtailed third match. Still, it had been a dreadful month.

The team were happy to head home – but doing so meant facing the music. Three consecutive innings defeats against anyone was bad news; given Indo-Lankan relations, the result swelled into a national embarrassment. Someone would have to pay. The Skandakumar Report accused Aravinda of moodiness and making disparaging remarks to his teammates. His inability to cooperate with Warnapura was said to show 'a lack of respect for decisions of the Board'.[59]

Yet the harshest words were saved for Ranatunga, said to be 'aloof and uncommunicative', as well as subject to tantrums.[60] The board gleefully commented on his 'bulky appearance', which it declared 'lends little evidence to any self-discipline'. Supposedly, his 'tendency to field in relatively insignificant positions' meant he was 'unable to raise the morale of his team when things went wrong'. The report reckoned fitness levels 'require urgent review', ultimately concluding 'a lack of commitment ... and an absence of national pride' had cost Sri Lanka.[*]

So Skandakumar and co. declared it 'essential that the Board specifies minimum standards for physical fitness to qualify for selection'.[61] It was a reasonable enough suggestion: as recently as 1987, Sri Lanka had been a shoddy fielding outfit – through hard work, they had sharpened considerably in a short space of time. Clearly, a more resolute attitude towards fitness would equally benefit the side. It may have only been a minor improvement – but small margins matter. Especially when you're being badly beaten, and your best players give the impression that they're more interested in takeaways than training.

Still, the Skandakumar Report caused real upset. Having handed the keys to Arjuna, the board was now telling him how to drive – or worse still, taking the wheel out of his hands altogether. It was the sort of provocation Sri Lanka's hot-blooded captain would not take lying down.

★★★

At first, it seemed there would be no crisis at all. Despite the report's criticisms, the squad named for the Sharjah tournament in April 1994 included Arjuna and Aravinda.[62] Even when the board asked players

---

[*]   To support his claims, Skandakumar quoted Don Smith, who left Sri Lanka with the sense that 'players must change their attitude to practising and training'. The board felt nothing had changed since. Supposedly files tracking the players' fitness – opened in the wake of Smith's stint as coach – had suspiciously disappeared.

to take a pre-tour fitness test, it seemed little more than a formality.* So when news broke that five players, Aravinda included,** had failed and were out of the tour, shockwaves spread across the island.

A few days later, Arjuna didn't turn up to practice.[63] He resigned as captain, and announced he would take no part in the Sharjah trip. Murali, Pramodya Wickramasinghe and Dulip Samaraweera joined the boycott after a meeting with Ranatunga. That three youngsters would make such a bold choice is revealing. In part, it shows the reverence Arjuna inspired as a leader, at least to some members of the squad. Yet it also reflects the fact that many felt the fitness tests were sloppy and unfair.

Aravinda later wrote that the board acted with 'cunning and deviousness'.[64] While it is perfectly plausible that he was no bleep test champion, Ravi Pushpakumara's exclusion raised more eyebrows. 'At that time, I was super fit,' he told me in disbelief. 'I was a young guy, I'd been at MRF [Pace Foundation]. They dropped me, failed me. I was crying. I was shocked.' At least for Pushpakumara, there was a happy twist of fate. 'I was so lucky,' he remembers. 'When I got up the next day, I had chicken pox. My father said 'You stay at home for fourteen days'. No telephone, nothing. Nobody contacted me. I didn't know what was going on in Colombo. They went to Sharjah and came back; I got better and was back in.'

Still, the fitness test created a rift in an already fractured squad. It was especially difficult for the younger players, many of whom felt forced to pick sides.[65] Mahanama refused to support Arjuna's stand because it was not 'a *team* decision'; he agreed to lead in Sharjah, but felt his career suffered as a result.[66] Discord spread well beyond the squad too, with a number of the selectors resigning. Mahanama received death threats, Gurusinha's house was stoned, and there were lively protests outside the board's headquarters. Sri Lankan cricket was facing its biggest split since 1968.

---

*   Instead of jumping through hoops, the players were asked to run laps to prove their endurance; to drop and catch a ruler to showcase their reflexes. Surprisingly, the squad weren't told passing was a prerequisite for making the Sharjah trip.

**   The others were Ravindra Pushpakumara, Don Anurasiri, Sanjeeva Ranatunga and Ajith Ekanayake.

Though a short-handed side struggled in Sharjah, the trip wasn't a total waste. Gurusinha stood up with a heroic century against New Zealand, while the discovery of a 20-year-old left armer who could swing the new ball was a real breakthrough. Moving forward, Chaminda Vaas would prove a vital piece of the puzzle, a bowler worth his weight in gold.

Arjuna was back at the helm – and the ousted lot back in – for a home series against Pakistan in August 1994. Still, Sri Lanka's rotten year continued. They surrendered the ODIs 4–1, and had now been on the wrong side of seventeen of their last twenty-one. Equally, the Tests reflected the gulf that separated the sides. Aravinda gave his doubters a pointed reminder with an elegant century at the P. Sara, but the rest struggled as Sri Lanka slipped to a heavy defeat. Inauspiciously, Murali returned match figures of 1 for 165 and was dropped.

Things got even worse at Asgiriya: Wasim and Waqar flattened the Lankans on the first morning, bowling 28.2 overs unchanged to set up a crushing innings defeat. There could be no denying the team was in a slump. They had lost four of their last five Tests by an innings, their worst run since promotion to full ICC status.

At least the Singer World Series brought a welcome reminder of what winning felt like. Sri Lanka rattled off three straight to qualify for the final; though rain scuppered the big day, this was just the sort of run Ranatunga's men needed. It had been a tumultuous year, but in a sense, Arjuna's authority had been reinforced by the fitness test scandal. He had taken a stand, made his point and emerged unscathed. Plus, he and Aravinda had again proven themselves invaluable to the Lankan cause. They would lead the team to Zimbabwe. The board was free to choose the coach and manager, but this was Arjuna's team, whether they liked it or not. 'Arjuna was the boss,' Pushpakumara told me unflinchingly. '*He is the boss.*' Now, it was up to him to pick up the pieces that had been scattered over the past nine months. The 1996 World Cup was less than a year and a half away.

DISTANT GLORIES

Sri Lanka had been on the road for twelve years as a Test side, but a maiden away victory still proved elusive. There had been chances – in England, Pakistan and New Zealand – but most felt the team would get no better opportunity than a three-Test series against Zimbabwe. Yet the clashes proved short on excitement, with Sri Lanka opting to play safety-first cricket. There was trouble in trouble in the second Test, but Ranatunga's little brother Sanjeeva notched his second century of the series to keep the teams tied at 0-0. With players mourning the untimely passing of Gamini Dissanayake, it was a particularly special escape.[67]

It was far from the only important innings of the series. In the opening game, Gurusinha had crawled to the third slowest 100 in Test history, compiled over eight hours and fifty-five minutes. 'A lot of people say, "You were playing Zimbabwe, what the hell was that?"' he volunteered when we met. 'But they were new to Test cricket and were bowling a foot and a half outside off stump with eight men on the off side. We just had to bat and bat until they bowled straighter.'

The happiest – and most significant – raise of a bat came in the third Test, when Hashan Tillakaratne finally scored his maiden Test century. He had proved he belonged well before this knock, but the sight of three figures against his name seemed to provide an extra surge of confidence.[*] That said, the biggest boon was Chaminda Vaas – who, fresh off a stint at the MRF Dennis Lillee Pace Foundation, consistently swung the ball and claimed 10 wickets at 23.50. And auspiciously, Pushpakumara – who built genuine pace during the six months he spent with Lillee – tore through Zimbabwe in the final Test; the emergence of two potent young seamers suggested Sri Lanka could call on a more balanced attack moving forward.

Vaas carried his form into the ODIs, picking up the big wickets of Alistair Campbell, David Houghton and Andy Flower in the first match to cut Zimbabwe down. You can almost imagine Arjuna smiling in the field, smug in the knowledge he had unearthed another gem. Mahanama

---

[*]   In the past twenty-five months, he had notched eight 80+ scores without crossing the line. After Zimbabwe, he produced centuries in the next four series.

notched back-to-back centuries; after dropping the second, Sri Lanka produced a complete performance in the third. Aravinda and Arjuna carried the team up to 296, before Vaas and Pushpakumara reduced Zimbabwe to 22-5.

It was a great way to end an important tour. Fans back home might have been disappointed that a Test victory didn't present itself, but for the players, it was a real period of growth.[68] They enjoyed themselves off from the field too, and as a unit began to rebuild bridges. For many, the tour was a chance to regain form and confidence. It was undoubtedly a turning point.

The Mandela Trophy offered further proof of the team's potential in ODI cricket. Though they only won two of five, they competed throughout – and looked a clear step ahead of New Zealand. Jayasuriya gave a tantalising taste of the future with two eye-catching innings against the Kiwis; Vaas had 8 wickets and was ever economical, while the spinners did an excellent job of keeping things tight. Most pleasing of all was the strength and depth Sri Lanka were showing. Five years earlier, the side seemed reliant on a small group of players; now, nearly everyone was chipping in.

So, the team set off for a five-week tour of New Zealand in February 1995 in good spirits. That said, after brittle batting on the opening day in Napier, it looked like their lean run in Tests would continue. But the Kiwis didn't count on Sri Lanka having bowlers who could exploit the conditions. The seamers caused problems from the very first over; in no time, the hosts were 6-3. They crumbled to 109.

The lead could have evaporated amidst a flurry of early Lankan wickets, but Aravinda and Tillakaratne built an important stand, before debuting wicketkeeper Chaminda Dunasinghe wrested back control with an assured 91. At 426 ahead, Sri Lanka knew they were on the brink of a historic triumph. The manner in which it came hinted at a glorious future. Murali found turn and bounce and ran amok; he and Vaas took 5 wickets each to secure victory by 241. After thirteen years' toil, Sri Lanka had won a Test away from home.

It's hard to describe how much the victory meant to the island's cricketers. Ever since Kapil Dev questioned their ability on the road, the lack of an away win had rested heavy on their heads. Suddenly, a weight was lifted. 'Unbelievable,' Pushpakumara told me. 'Nobody believed we could win outside the country, but 1995 – that was the turnaround in Sri Lanka cricket. My God, I still remember after the match, we were in the dressing room and the boys were overjoyed. It was like a dream. And I can see it: Arjuna and Aravinda were sitting on one side and Arjuna was crying. I can see the tears. I was so shocked to see that, so I went and asked "What happened, Aiyya?" And he said, "No, I'm so happy. I've sacrificed so much, for so long, to get a win out of the country. Nobody has achieved this."'

A pair of workmanlike centuries from Gurusinha and Tillakaratne helped Sri Lanka stave off defeat in Dunedin, ensuring it would be a series victory too. Pleasingly, young Chaminda Vaas was the star contributor, his 16 wickets coming at 11.06 apiece. The ODIs were less positive, but this tour nonetheless showed Sri Lanka had come of age. In the subsequent days, they made it to the final of the Asia Cup, but were easily handled by India. Sri Lanka were building, but were not quite there yet. Two more vital pieces were about to fall into place.

★★★

Sri Lanka couldn't have risen so fast without the foresight of Ana Punchihewa. Surely the most unsung of the World Cup heroes, Punchihewa took control of the BCCSL after Gamini Dissanayake's assassination in October 1994.[69] The following March, he was elected board president unopposed. Though he had none of the political clout of his predecessor, Punchihewa brought the kind of business acumen Sri Lanka sorely needed. Having served as the head of Coca-Cola on the island in the 1980s, he sought to revamp Sri Lankan cricket with the savvy of a seasoned industrialist.

Punchihewa put in place simple targets:* crucially, he had the capacity to think big. Aware of the danger of being leapfrogged by Bangladesh or Zimbabwe, he understood that developing the game meant stretching

---

* In the short term, the team should focus squarely on the World Cup – if not on winning the tournament, then progressing as far as possible. Longer term, Punchihewa hoped to turn Sri Lanka into the world's premier cricket nation by the year 2000.

into the outstations, shoring up the cricketing infrastructure and improving the standard of coaching. A new national coach* was a top priority – but there was a hitch: the board had just Rs. 300,000 (roughly £3,750) in its accounts.[70]

Still, Punchihewa cast the net wide. Allan Border, Bob Woolmer and Ian Botham were interested but unaffordable; meanwhile, the ACB suggested Dav Whatmore,** whose dual status as local and outsider made him an ideal candidate. Whatmore was Sri Lankan enough to understand the players and their culture, allowing him to dismantle barriers other coaches may have been oblivious to. Hierarchies broke down with Dav in charge of the side; as Pushpakumara told me, 'He took all the senior players around him, especially Arjuna and Aravinda. He created the environment, "OK junior guys, these are my seniors. Look how much they've sacrificed for Sri Lanka cricket. Follow them, listen to them." So then juniors and seniors talk, bond. When you walk into the middle, there is no barrier between juniors and seniors. Our communication was great at that time.'

Whatmore's Australian upbringing was an equally vital part of the recipe. He brought a sense of professionalism and toughness that, at this stage, no Sri Lankan coach could provide. Plus, he was enough of an outsider to avoid being dragged into labyrinthine board politics.

Though he came cheaper than Botham, Whatmore was still well out of Sri Lanka's price range. Remarkably, the ACB offered to double Sri Lanka's guarantee for their upcoming tour: the BCCSL should use the extra cash to bag Whatmore, and say no more on the matter.[71] The Australians were even prepared to send the money in advance, ahead of Sri Lanka's trip to Pakistan. Punchihewa had found his man.

---

*   Up till now, Sri Lanka had, on the whole, done without a full-time coach. Ranjit Fernando and Duleep Mendis helped the side on an ad hoc basis; foreign coaches like Frank Tyson, Don Smith and Khan Mohammed had worked with the team as short-term consultants.

**   A Sri Lankan of Burgher heritage, Whatmore had briefly trodden the corridors of Royal College before emigrating to Australia aged 8. He grew up to play for Victoria, with enough success to earn seven Test caps in 1979. More recently, he had been head coach at the Victorian Institute of Sport.

This very private act of generosity marked the pinnacle of the two countries' cricketing relations. Sri Lanka had benefited from much goodwill over the past century, but no single gesture had as grand an impact as the Australian gift of Whatmore. Sadly, within months, tensions had frayed sufficiently to leave these long-time friends locked in cricketing conflict. In the most straightforward version of the Lankan fairy tale, the Australians are the bad guys – the bullying foul-mouthed ogres standing in the way of our heroes' quest for glory. But the truth is more nuanced. The teams may have been embittered by unshakable animosity on the field, but beyond the boundary, Australia's help was a crucial ingredient in unlocking Lankan greatness.

★★★

Whatmore had little time with his men before they set off for Pakistan, but it was instantly clear that his arrival would bring a fresh approach. He saw Sri Lanka were soft and wasted no time implementing a programme that would turn them into fitter, tougher cricketers.[*72] And as a good talker, he struck a bond with the team straight away. Emphasising back-to-basics cricket – trusting yourself, playing your way – he quickly instilled a self-belief in the group which had often been lacking.

Still, his tenure got off to a rocky start. Sri Lanka were thrashed in a warm-up in Rawalpindi, then thrown into a cauldron at Peshawar. The contrast between their benign seamers and the Pakistani quicks was stark. Akram especially bowled fiercely, his speed and skill far too much for Sri Lanka's lower order. Arjuna's men were smashed by an innings. In the stands, fans threw oranges and firecrackers.

---

[*]	Gone were the gentle jogs and amateur attitude; in their place, tailored fitness regimes that would challenge the players. Skills training was reduced from five days a week to three – while gym sessions, speed and endurance training and new fielding drills were introduced. Net bowlers were brought in, with the attack's workload regulated, especially in the days leading up to matches. And for the first time, Sri Lanka started training in official kit. At long last, this team was starting to resemble a professional outfit.

Though it was a humbling defeat, the match was crucial in Sri Lanka's development. Whatmore assured his men the series was still alive, but they'd have to overcome their hesitancy against pace and bounce. As Pushpakumara put it, 'Davvy went really mad.' He took the team to the side nets and told the bowlers to get into the batters. It didn't matter if anyone got hit – he wanted to see them fend balls off their throat. They didn't like it, but it worked – Sri Lanka looked more comfortable against the quicks moving forward, though injuries to Wasim and Waqar no doubt helped their cause.

Meanwhile, Murali had been entranced watching debuting spinner Saqlain Mushtaq send down a hodgepodge of off-breaks and 'doosras'. Still struggling to incorporate variations into his own bowling, it was a lightbulb moment. 'He bowled brilliantly,' Murali told me. 'I was interested, I asked him after the match. We had a chat – and then I went back and I tried so many things. Shorter run-up, everything – and it took me about three or four years to bowl the doosra. In years to come, I saw how Saqlain did it, and my idea came. Someone can say bowl straight, but you have to know how to do it.'

The bounce back in Faisalabad underlined the team's burgeoning depth. Tillakaratne made a counterattacking century; Murali bagged 5 for 68, while Gurusinha and Aravinda scored crucial breakthroughs with the ball. Pakistan were set 251 for victory: when Vaas trapped Sohail with his fourth delivery, belief coursed through Lankan veins. Arjuna's men won by 43 to level the series. Having fumbled on the road for so long, Sri Lanka had two far-flung victories in the space of six months.

Still, they struggled on the opening day in Sialkot – needing Kumar Dharmasena's 62* to lift them out of the mire. Thankfully the hosts found the low, uneven pitch no easier to get to grips with, and Sri Lanka took control of a nip-tuck game in the third innings. A target of 357 looked imposing, and the match was up in a matter of minutes, as Vaas and Wickramasinghe reduced Pakistan to 15-5. Sri Lanka claimed victory by 144, becoming the first team to win a Test series in Pakistan since West Indies way back in 1981. What's more, this was only the third time in history a side had overturned a 1-0 deficit to win a three-match series.

Pakistan were hamstrung, but this was nonetheless a monumental victory – one that belonged to the whole team rather than just one or two players. In a low-scoring series, seven of thirteen Lankans made a score of 40 or more. Vaas and Murali led the way with the ball, but found plenty of support. Whatmore had made an immediate impact; Sri Lanka were suddenly in the habit of winning.

They repeated the trick in the ODIs, coming from behind to take the series 2-1 – and continued their charge a week later in Sharjah, qualifying for the final of the Champions Trophy at Pakistan's expense. On the big day, the Lankan expats in attendance had plenty to shout about. Jayasuriya smashed three 6s, one of them out of the ground, before Aravinda gallantly assaulted the West Indian attack. Seeing him run at fast bowlers was a rare thrill, and with Murali and Eric Upashantha brilliant, West Indies never got close to a target of 274. Sri Lanka had their hands on their second piece of silverware. With the World Cup just around the corner, things were starting to come together.

After much technical work with Whatmore, Mahanama looked increasingly assured, driving crisply as he returned scores of 101, 76, 45* and 66. His opening partner Jayasuriya was fearless and full of strokes – and he wasn't the only one.* Still, the most memorable innings of the tournament came from the usually more reserved Tillakaratne. Set 333 by the West Indies in a group game, Sri Lanka were dead and buried when he came to the crease at 103-5. But come the last over, Tillakaratne was unshifted – his team needing 5 runs from 4 balls with a single wicket in hand. Served up a leg-stump full toss, he tried to end the match with a single blow. 'It's going over the top,' cried Tony Grieg. In the excitement, the cameraman lost the ball, his lens zeroing in on the vacant square-leg boundary. Then came the horrible realisation: it had been caught, right on the fence. Had there been no man out it would have surely been 6; some still maintain the fielder's foot was brushing the rope.

Forget the result; this performance hinted at a newfound freedom – and Sri Lanka's oft-homesick cricketers were coming off the back of three hugely successful trips in a row. It was probably the shift in mindset that benefited them most. As Pushpakumara told me, 'The pattern of thinking changed for the entire dressing room. It was the habit of

---

* Aravinda scored at a strike rate of 107.33, while Kaluwitharana's blistering cameos gave an exciting glimpse of the future.

winning. The boys are saying "My God, we can beat this team." The mentality, the thinking pattern, changed on the Sharjah tour.' What's more, winning reinforced Arjuna's authority, and bound the team closer together. Having been at breaking point during 1994, the group had by now regained some of its family feel.

And while the bowling attack was not the world's most fearsome, Ranatunga was becoming a master at cycling his part-timers. He won a Man of the Match award against Pakistan in Sharjah in a game where he did not bat, for his bowling and captaincy. The Lankans were getting fitter too; even before his right-hand man arrived, Whatmore was whipping his charges into shape. Bellies were firming up; Sri Lanka were getting tougher.

They would need all their strength. The next few months were set to be a real emotional rollercoaster, the kind none of these men could ever have imagined.

INTERLUDE: HOW MAD MAX BECAME ARAVINDA THE GREAT

I cannot believe any player, anywhere, has been so popular. Ari was an inspiration to me and the whole side felt the same. When he packed his bags, he hugged each of us and I have never known a professional sports team so close to tears.

Graham Cowdrey[73]

Anyone who had watched Aravinda de Silva bat over the past decade would accept that genius is rarely straightforward. 'Mad Max' was a rare talent; but with the brilliance came baffling moments, a sense that his batting lacked brainpower and application. Perhaps understanding the man accounts for some of the idiosyncrasies. Aravinda was a thrill-seeker.[74] Cricket aside, his greatest passion was fast cars.* At school, his 6-hitting caused so much damage that he declared himself 'a punk with a cricket bat'.[75] For young de Silva, cricket was another adrenaline rush.

---

* In his early years, he would break in batting gloves on his motorbike, wheelie-ing his way down the Galle Road.

'The more reckless and insane my batting appeared, the more irresistible and exhilarating I found it,' he wrote.[76] Supposedly, for a long time, he only knew the hook shot.

In his early years, he misconstrued the game as a personal battle.[77] Aravinda wanted to take on the best bowlers and come out on top. Being treated as the 'baby' of the Sri Lankan side in his early years didn't help – batting in the lower order, he was allowed to swing freely with little responsibility. Nor did the paucity of Sri Lankan club cricket, which Aravinda never valued, since the runs came too easy.[78]

But by the early 1990s, Aravinda was starting to realise that his all-or-nothing attitude was not serving Sri Lanka. He could bat better than anyone on his day, but was hardly reliable. The wicket which sparked a collapse against Australia in 1992 was a case in point – but also one of the moments when he realised he needed to be 'less of a strokemaker and more of a batsman'.[79] Still, arguably the biggest leap in his development came three years later, 5,000 miles away.

With a break in the international schedule, Aravinda headed to England in April 1995 for a season with Kent. He had big shoes to fill: Carl Hooper – probably the county's best-ever overseas player – was away on international duty. As a like-for-like replacement, there was pressure on Aravinda's shoulders: he would have to embrace the cold and the county slog, and score regularly if his time at Kent was to be a success. Aware that the club had taken a punt on a Sri Lankan overseas player, he felt desperate to repay their faith.

In his first couple of weeks, some at the club wondered if they had made a mistake.[80] One of England's cricket papers questioned Aravinda's ability in a pre-season report – wrapped up in seven jumpers, he didn't exactly seem to be relishing the challenge. And his early returns were meagre – 2 and 13 against Northants, where one of the fielders politely asked if he was the worst overseas signing in history, 16 against Surrey, run out for 10 against Somerset.

But in his second Championship match, he cracked 117 against Sussex and never looked back. In four-day cricket, Kent were a poor side in 1995, finishing rock bottom of the table at a time when all eighteen counties competed in one division. Yet Aravinda was unfazed. He made another five Championship centuries, and ended as the league's third-highest run-scorer – with 1,688 at 59.32 – despite missing Kent's last two matches.

From mid-June, he really heated up. Perhaps he just needed the sun to warm his bones. In his last eight Championship games, he made 52 and 115 against Yorkshire, 225 (off 273) and 16 in Nottingham, 255 and 116 against Derbyshire, rare failures of 11 and 5 at New Road, 0 and 89 against Surrey, 42 and 0 against Somerset, 88 and 60 against Middlesex and 46 and 95 against Essex.[*] When the touring West Indians came to town, he blasted a century between lunch and tea.[81] Canterbury had rarely witnessed such artistry.

As impressive as Aravinda's first-class form was, it was in limited-overs cricket that he truly inspired his teammates. There were some lean patches in the early stages of the league, but Kent kept winning: in August, his back-to-back centuries helped them continue their charge. Ultimately, they were crowned champions – their first piece of silverware since 1978. Aravinda averaged a shade under 37.

If only he had had a little more support, he might have carried Kent to an unprecedented double. In years gone by, the Benson & Hedges final was the showpiece event of the English summer. In 1995, the sun was out and Lord's packed – Aravinda seized the moment, producing a transcendent innings that served as a wonderful advert for Sri Lankan cricket.[82] He came to the crease under pressure – Kent were 37-2, needing another 238 to win. These were the situations Aravinda had asked for when he arrived in England: while many minds in the Kent dressing room were increasingly frazzled, he was fully focused on the target in front of him.

His Picasso-esque batting left his teammates looking like crude painter–decorators. Early in the innings, two back-of-a-length balls were slapped into the Tavern stand. By now it seemed the most quintessential Sri Lankan shot. There were scything lofted drives both sides of the wicket; a late cut that looked as effortless as the flick of a brush. With wickets tumbling around him, and the run rate climbing exponentially,

---

[*] In the second half of the season alone, he scored well over 1,000 Championship runs, averaging more than 75.

Aravinda remained a picture of calm. He smoked one through the covers to reach 102 off 88; none of his teammates managed to pass 25.

De Silva was playing a different game. He never looked ungainly – or like he was trying to smash the ball – yet you felt as long as he stayed at the crease, the game was in his hands. But he could not farm enough of the strike, and, 62 runs short, he holed out to cow corner. Kent's hopes of lifting the trophy went out the window with his wicket; Aravinda glumly trudged to the pavilion, hardly noticing the entire ground had risen to its feet. Some claim they saw Umpire Shepherd clapping along. Though Kent lost by 35 runs, Aravinda was a clear choice as man of the match. Go and find footage of his innings online; I defy you to watch it and not feel joy course through your veins.

For Aravinda, the innings was an assertion of national identity as much as a form of personal expression. In his own words, 'I was able to … stamp myself in the English consciousness as "Aravinda de Silva the Sri Lankan batsman".'[83] He used the post-match ceremony to champion the island's cause too. 'Since 1984, Sri Lanka has always played a one-off Test against England after each West Indian tour, but in 1995 we were dropped,' he complained. 'It is disappointing because we won the last time we played England, we feel we deserve a three-Test series and given the opportunity, we would prove good value.'[84] Few in attendance could disagree; any that did would change their tune soon enough.

For all the international cricket Aravinda had played, this was still a special moment: a final at Lord's, with all of England watching. He was expected to perform and he delivered. In many ways, it was a perfect trial run for the World Cup final eight months later. Most agree the summer in England changed Aravinda as a batter, that the weight of expectation made him hungrier for runs.

He had shone in flashes for Sri Lanka since he was a boy, but returned from Kent a different player. Having made three ODI centuries in his long career so far, he cracked four in 1996 and another three in 1997. Though Jayasuriya was named Player of the Tournament at the World Cup, Aravinda played the crucial hand in both the semi and the final; had the decision been made after the tournament, he surely would have won the award.

De Silva became more consistent in Tests too – scoring seven 100s in as many months in 1997, against the eight he made in his first decade in the side. As he approached his 30th birthday, Mad Max was starting to mature. He would never let go of his spirit, but had learned to cast aside enough of the madness to become the batsman Sri Lanka dreamed about – a cricketer the island could rely on.

THE TOUGHEST TOUR

For Sri Lanka, there was one last test before the World Cup: a near three-month tour of Australia. Nothing would come easy, but the opportunity to test their mettle Down Under meant a lot. Still short-changed by the bigger nations, beyond Asia Sri Lanka had still only played three-Test series in Zimbabwe and New Zealand.

At the start of the tour, the team were boosted by the arrival of Alex Kontouris as physio.[85] During his first months in the role, he introduced regular fitness tests and brought in personal trainers and dieticians. His presence would do much to professionalise Sri Lankan cricket.

But his task was not straightforward. Prior to meeting up with the team in Cairns, he faxed Whatmore a list of things he'd need to work; though Dav said it should be no problem, the coffin he brought Kontouris was stuffed full of pamphlets and paperwork.[86] 'I removed all that and there was no medication,' he told Sa'adi Thawfeeq. Instantly, Kontouris understood 'there was no culture for sports medicine' in Sri Lanka.

Luckily, he was able to beg, borrow and cadge from local contacts, and his approach quickly began to yield fruit. Several Sri Lanka players say they would have missed much more cricket were it not for Kontouris: as Gurusinha put it, 'Alex joining us changed a lot, because little injuries could be treated on tour. And he was a guy who would never keep us

---

*   Kountoris' predecessor Dan Keisel was an accomplished and knowledgeable doctor, who had studied sports science at university, but much of his professional experience had come as a (non-sporting) physiotherapist and general practitioner. By contrast, Kontouris had carved out a career working specifically with athletes.

inside. He would just chase us out and say, 'Get out there and play.' That was Alex's attitude. We were tough cricketers.'

Yet, to dismiss Kountouris as a mere physio is to do him a disservice. Whatmore had started Sri Lanka's fitness revolution, but Kountouris – a tougher task-master working from a scientific starting point – took the team to new heights. Sidath Wettimuny describes his arrival as a 'turning point'. 'Hats off to Dav for bringing him. They changed the way we looked at the game. And our fitness levels went up 40 per cent – till then we were mucking around. It was amateurish. Kountouris changed that. He brought a completely different mindset – luckily we had some great players. That's when you saw the game changed. That took us onto the next level.'

Still, when Sri Lanka boarded the flight to Brisbane, they had no idea of the difference he would make. All they knew was that they would be thrown into a pressure cooker. 'I remember on the plane, the senior guys said "It's going to be really tough. You have to be really tough to beat Australia in Australia",' Pushpakumara recalled. 'We thought "What do you mean tough? I don't know – honestly, what do you mean? We have to sledge? We have to fight? What do you do?" "No, you need to be tough mentally."'

Strikingly, Pushpakumara sees this toughness as a natural consequence of the Sri Lankan experience. 'We *were* tough, mentally tough,' he contests. 'Our cricketers come from the villages. They were very tough. I used to go to practice without food – that's mentally tough. I'd walk six, seven kilometres to go to practice – that's mentally tough. I didn't have shoes for the whole year – that's mentally tough. It comes from our nature.' It is a valid point. When you have to prove yourself a survivor day after day, how can something as trivial as cricket lump pressure on your shoulders? Pushpakumara's 'just a game' mentality, seemingly shared by a number of his teammates, no doubt helped Sri Lanka deal with the trials they faced Down Under.

From the moment they arrived, it felt like all of Australia was intent on destabilising their progress. Sniffer dogs met them at the airport, putting noses out of joint, and the team were shunted from the warmth of Cairns to the colder Tasmania before being dumped into the cauldron-esque WACA for the opening Test.[87]

Nonetheless, Ranatunga remained upbeat.[88] 'We are a very young, positive side,' he told the press before the match. 'Our fielding has improved and we have three bowlers who can take wickets.' Strikingly, he made sure to remind the world of the significance of cricket in Sri Lanka. 'Our players are deeply committed for their country,' he said. 'Everyone at home is keen on cricket rather than the other problems we have. If we can do well here, there will be a lot of smiling faces back home – and that is important to us.'

Optimism quickly dissipated. Sri Lanka might have been encouraged by the algal virus which slowed the pitch, yet it quickly proved curse rather than blessing. A number of batters got in, but none stuck around; it was a long, hard slog in the field as the hosts pounded their way to 698-5. The game was up: though Tillakaratne's 119 helped restore a little dignity, by this stage it was hard to gloss an innings defeat.

Ultimately, the match was defined by an incident that had little to do with cricket. In the 17th over of Australia's innings, umpire Hayat examined the ball and said its seam had been tampered with.[89] There were three conversations between Ranatunga and the umpires, but the ball was not confiscated – as Sri Lanka requested and the rules dictate.

Though umpire Parker was initially unconvinced, a report was submitted to match referee Graham Dowling.* With little evidence and no thought of consulting the Sri Lankan management, Dowling issued an extraordinary press release, stating, 'The Sri Lankan captain, Arjuna Ranatunga, was notified that the condition of the ball had clearly been altered by a member or members of his team during the course of the 17th over.'[90] The Lankans had been branded cheats prior to any proper investigation. Worse, they were effectively gagged by the ICC laws, barred from making any statement to the press.[91]

The next morning, the 'tampering' Lankans' name was dragged through the mud in newspapers the world over. Though they had no real reason to manipulate the ball – and certainly no bowlers looking

---

* Another unusual issue was brought before Dowling during the Test, when the umpires alleged that the Singer logo on Sri Lanka's shirts was too large. Dowling checked the logos and confirmed there was no problem.

to exploit reverse swing – Sri Lanka held an emergency meeting at the close of play. 'I was thinking, what do I gain by tampering if I'm Murali?' Hathurusinghe reflected when we spoke on the issue. 'And I remember Slater hitting one shot down the ground into the concrete stand. I was actually thinking, what would I gain, bowling 110, 120 [kmph]?' All eleven steadfastly denied tampering with the ball. A bewildered Ranatunga was seen on the brink of tears.[92]

The allegations were baseless. When Pakistan had been accused of tampering in a tour match at the WACA earlier in the summer, it quickly became clear that an algal virus had created an unusually abrasive pitch. Equally, there had been consistent complaints about the quality of Kookaburra balls all season.[93] Considering the facts alone – an abrasive pitch, a potentially dodgy ball and a Lankan defence hampered by the umpires' refusal to isolate it – how could anyone accurately assess the cause of the damage, especially with Michael Slater smiting the ball into the stands?

Secure in their innocence, Sri Lanka went on the offensive. The BCCSL threatened the ICC with legal action – and when the second new ball showed similar signs of degeneration, the media began to change tack. Two weeks later, the team were cleared of any wrongdoing. An editorial in *The Age* bemoaned the fact the ICC report 'expressed "sincere regrets" to the Sri Lankans but did not include an apology. It should have. The best that can be said is that the ICC came to the right conclusion, if belatedly, and that the Sri Lankan players conducted themselves with dignity throughout the unfortunate episode. However, the original accusation has not been settled: 'suspicions will remain and nothing can be done to dispel them.'[94] Sri Lanka's tour got off to the worst possible start – with the humiliation of an innings defeat compounded by the indignity of being branded cheats. Some felt the whole incident had racial undertones; certainly, there was a sense that England or New Zealand might have been treated differently.

The tampering scandal was swallowed whole by the circus that engulfed the second Test. In so many ways, this tour revolved around Murali. It changed his life: during the early carefree days of the trip, he would slip out of the team hotel and explore Cairns unrecognised; by the end of the tour, he couldn't step into open air without flashbulbs bursting in his face.[95] The storm had been brewing.* 'Chucking' was becoming an increasingly contentious issue – strangely, often couched in moralistic terms.[96] For many, it was a scourge on cricket, a repugnant canker that must be removed. The chucker was a dirty cheat – even today, few acts on the cricket field are accompanied by such a grave sense of wrongdoing.**

Perhaps, chucking was transformed into a deplorable crime by the way it was framed. As Australian influence grew during the early 1990s, the country's administrators seemed to declare themselves moral guardians of the game. Just as it was their duty to rid the game of the Asians who would pick at a seam, Australian administrators felt obliged to crack down on the chuckers who threatened to bring cricket into disrepute. Suspicion surrounding Murali's action amped up after he took 7 wickets in a warm-up match against Queensland.[97] Now, not only was he a threat to the sanctity of the sport, but to the reputation of this Australian side. Moving forward, TV cameras zeroed in on his action in the nets. Whatmore was troubled, and told Arjuna as much. Together, they decided that Murali should sit out the three-day game in Tasmania.

Meanwhile, ICC match referee Raman Subba Row had been in touch with the BCCSL, imploring Sri Lanka to take their own look at Murali.[98] Whatmore knew he had to get ahead of the game, so bought a video-camera and began shooting his star spinner. Both he and Murali were convinced there was no problem, but realised that might not be immediately clear to outsiders.

After all, Murali's mechanics simply cannot be replicated – in a sense, it is as though his body was built to bowl off-spin. Were it not for several

---

*   Murali had no idea that his action had been reported twice by match referees; nor that umpires Hair, Plews and Dunne had expressed concerns to match referee Raman Subba Row during Sri Lanka's recent trip to Sharjah.

**   Yet, as Ian Peebles pointed out in his 1968 book, *Straight from the Shoulder: 'Throwing' – Its History and Cure*, 'Surely the essence of sharp practice of cheating is the covert and deliberate disregard or breaking of a rule or agreement. The suspect bowler subjects himself to the judgment of the umpires and up to eighty thousand people. He makes no attempt to conceal anything, in the confidence that, in his own judgment, he is no way infringing the letter or spirit of the law.'

physical abnormalities,* there is no way he would be able to impart such lavish turn. Yet, these elements equally combined to create the illusion that Murali was chucking. Those defending him were clear in their stance: yes, the arm was slightly bent at the point of release, but only because it *cannot* straighten. It would take Murali many years to prove he wasn't breaking the rules.

The whole squad woke up with butterflies on Boxing Day morning. This was the big time: 55,000 crammed into the MCG; Australians from Darwin to Devonport gathered around their TVs. Pre-1996, Sri Lanka often struggled to attract broadcasters for their Tests; the marquee sporting event of the Australian summer was a chance for them to prove their worth.

Arjuna opted to bowl, turning to his star spinner just before lunch. Murali thought nothing of the fact that Hair stood further back than usual; nor was he concerned when his second ball was flagged.[99] Only when his third delivery was called a no-ball too, did he sense something was wrong. He asked Hair if he was cutting the side-crease. The umpire's frank response chilled Murali to the core. 'No. It's your action. You're chucking.'

Arjuna arrived on the scene for a lengthy discussion. Though he encouraged Murali to keep bowling normally, it's hard to imagine how the spinner found the strength to carry on. 'It was so insulting,' Murali told me when we spoke on the matter. Hair called no-ball another five times in the 3-over spell. Had a crack burst from the ground and offered to swallow Murali whole, there's little doubt he would have willingly obliged.

Instead, he soldiered on. Ranatunga switched him to Steve Dunne's end;** mercifully, the umpire's arm remained by his side. But, by tea on the second day, Hair decided he'd had enough.[100] Unless Murali was removed, he would call 'no-ball' regardless of where he was stood.

---

*   Not only was he blessed with an extremely supple wrist, his right shoulder was flexible almost to the point of double jointedness. On top of this, he has a slight deformity which means he cannot fully straighten his right arm.

**   Though Dunne had previously expressed doubts over Murali 's action, he told Chandika Hathurusinghe, fielding at square leg, that he wouldn't call him during the Test. In his mind, doing so was tantamount to playing God.

His sudden disgust strikes as strange, given the fact that he had stood in four Sri Lanka ODIs in the past four months. For many, it is hard to escape the sense that the incident was timed to cause maximum humiliation. Even Steve Waugh admitted 'it was a bit unfair the way it unfolded'.[101] Murali had been crucified for the whole world to see.

His tour, and his whole career, lay in tatters. Privately, Murali planned for the worst-case scenario, hoping leg-spin could provide a lifeline to his international career. But the team stood firm behind him. 'Arjuna and Aravinda supported me a lot,' he remembers. 'They said, you're not doing anything wrong; we will challenge this.' Sri Lanka could have easily yielded and sent Murali home, but Ranatunga insisted they rally around him. 'If he had any other captain, I don't think he would have survived,' Pushpakumara opined. The incident was hugely destabilising, but it helped the Lankans develop a sort of siege mentality. As Gurusinha put it, 'We were together [before], but that brought us very, very close.'

The ICC were quick to stand behind Hair: the umpire had become judge, jury and executioner. Murali made it through a 10-over spell in an ODI in Hobart, but was called three times by Ross Emerson during his first over in the following match.[102] At least the team had a plan. Sensing Hair had been calling haphazardly,* Murali switched to leg breaks – widely considered impossible to chuck. Emerson fell headfirst into the trap, calling one a thrown no-ball.

With this one fell swoop, humiliation shifted from bowler to umpire's shoulders. Clearly, Emerson had no idea if Murali was bowling some balls and throwing others. His calls were coming at random. The incident lifted Murali from his pit of despair. His tour was over, but the injustice he had been subjected to was plain to see. A volley of boos rained down on Emerson, who needed a police escort to leave the field.[103] Standing in his first ODI, he had made himself look a fool – and exposed the sham that simmered beneath the surface of the scandal.

Even in 1995, there was the stench of something rotten. On 27 December, Robert Craddock reported that 'A series of secret

---

*   The most prominent theory was that Hair decided to call or not based on whether the ball turned to leg, since the top-spinner was seen as being Murali's most suspicious delivery.

conversations between leading umpires, high-ranking officials and disgruntled players preceded the stunning decision to call Sri Lankan spinner Muttiah Muralitharan.'[104] He went on to reveal that 'At least one high-ranking Australian official felt strongly Muralitharan be exposed as a "thrower" and had a lengthy bar-side conversation with a Test umpire three weeks ago forcibly expressing this point.' Clearly, such a discussion between a partisan national representative and a supposedly impartial employee of the ICC saw both men wading into murky water. It suggested collusion: something Steve Waugh hinted, when he later said, 'I think Darrell Hair, we all knew, was probably going to make that call.'[105]

Steve Dunne subsequently claimed the umpires' 'dressing room was never free of at least one member of the ACB'.[106] Graham Halbish damningly admitted to telling Hair 'that if he called [Murali] for throwing he would have the full backing of the ACB'.[107] Prior to the tour, Australia's coach Bob Simpson asked the official board photographer to take photos of Murali's action – even suggesting his preferred angles.[108] This was the antithesis of a fair and balanced trial.

Yet shockingly, as Michael Roberts points out, all involved felt they were 'serving the long-term interests of cricket'.[109] They seemingly forgot that targeting one of the opposition's stars so forcefully created a serious conflict of interests. Equally, they went about their business without a shred of care for the bowler. Murali was just 23 – a rising star from a fledgling cricket nation; the type of talent that should be nurtured and protected by those who want to see the game flourish. No one can criticise these men for suspecting Murali of throwing, but did his humiliation need to be played out in front of the biggest TV audience of the year?

While Sri Lanka continued to toil across the country, Murali was sent to Darryl Foster in Perth to prove his legitimacy.[110] This was an ideal solution: the UWA's department of human movement and exercise science offered facilities, and an air of impartiality, that Sri Lanka could not. Murali bowled under the gaze of high-speed cameras; the footage was enough to convince doctors that he did not extend his elbow while delivering the ball. Murali had been vindicated.

Though he was in the clear for now, his trials were far from over. For the next fifteen years, Murali laboured under a cloud of suspicion; wherever he went, he had to endure grudging handshakes and brush off unfounded allegations. It must have been tough to carry on. 'It made me a very strong-minded person,' he told me. 'I will never give up.'

That iron resolve is arguably Murali's greatest gift, instilled in him long before he donned a Sri Lanka shirt. Growing up Tamil in an increasingly riven Sri Lanka presented extraordinary challenges. When Murali was 5, his father's factory was razed in the 1977 pogrom. The family lost everything and had to rebuild from scratch. Though Murali's father needed eighteen stitches after being hacked in the back, he refused to up sticks and run. Muttiah Muralitharan might have easily turned his back on cricket after Australia. He spent much of his career with an albatross around his neck. It took remarkable fortitude to not only endure, but prosper.

★★★

Amidst the ugliness of the Murali incident, the cricket at the MCG faded into the background. For Sri Lanka, there was little to shout about. Conceding 500 left them up against it; though Gurusinha impressed with 143, he couldn't stop the Lankans sliding to a 10-wicket defeat.

The early signs from the ODI Tri-series were hardly more auspicious. Having lost their first three, Sri Lanka looked in disarray. Arjuna was struggling with injuries and Murali's series about to be over.[111] Mahanama had fallen out of form and taken a nasty rap on the knuckles. Amidst fears of him being cracked again by the hard new ball, Duleep Mendis – by now restored as team manager – had an idea.[112] Why not try Kaluwitharana at the top? 'It was like light coming into a dark room,' Whatmore told Chandresh Narayanan. 'I thought to myself, "Shit man, let's do it".'*

---

* While the plan instantly struck a chord, it wasn't exactly conventional thinking. At this stage, Kaluwitharana averaged 11.26 in ODI cricket, with a top score of 31. With Sri Lanka unsure whether they wanted a keeper who could bat, or a batsman who could keep, he had been shunted in and out of the side in the past few years. Despite a century on Test debut in 1992, he had played just three Tests leading into this series. Equally, between December 1990 and the 1995 Asia Cup, he played just eighteen of Sri Lanka's seventy-eight ODIs. 'Kalu' felt the constant pressure affected his keeping. But Whatmore's arrival changed things: the team put their faith in him, and he began to flourish.

Kalu's promotion reflected a dynamic new approach to one-day cricket. In 1995, conventional wisdom dictated that the first 10 overs were for 'platform-building'. But Sri Lanka now sent out two destructive batters who preferred to smash the ball to all corners. Ranatunga told Sanath and Kalu to play their natural game, safe in the knowledge that there was a wealth of class and experience behind them. Mahanama's last knock as opener had produced 10 runs from 41 balls; Kaluwitharana would operate at a very different tempo.

In his first innings at the top, he smashed twelve boundaries in a 75-ball 77 to lead Sri Lanka's chase of 214. Though run out 23 short of his century, he picked up the Man of the Match award – an honour he earned twice in the next three ODIs. His half-century against the West Indies was bejewelled with a monstrous 6 off Ambrose; next, he pummelled 74 off 68 against Australia at the MCG.[113] Sri Lanka qualified for the finals at West Indies' expense; in earlier times, they surely would have folded against Courtney Walsh, Ian Bishop and Ambrose, but this was a unit getting tough. Kaluwitharana was named man of the series; when he scored, Sri Lanka won. Plus, his fireworks flooded the team with confidence.

They were well on top of the first final until Warne got Aravinda to spark a bewildering collapse. In a matter of minutes, 107-2 became 132-8; though Arjuna mounted a dogged rearguard, he tried a big swing with the team needing 19 – but only found clean air.

Blighted by storms, the second final descended into a squally affair. Tension had bubbled throughout the summer: with clouds surrounding the SCG, storms erupted on the field. First, a visibly riled Glenn McGrath stood firm in the middle of the pitch, blocking Jayasuriya's path as the batter attempted to complete an easy single.[114] After the match, members of the team were distraught at the suggestion McGrath had called Jayasuriya a 'black monkey'.

Though Sri Lanka kept the accusation to themselves, it wasn't the first rumbling of racism on the tour. In 1997, Ranatunga released a statement claiming his team had been subject to 'racial abuse' throughout; several testimonies claim the word 'black' was frequently employed as an adjective by Australia's cricketers during the series.*[115]

---

*   Aravinda wrote, 'surely athletes … can channel their will to win in ways that don't refer to the colour of a man's skin.'

Arjuna spent much of the Tri-series on the sidelines, but there was rarely a moment's calm when he was in the middle. He and Healy were constantly at each other's throats: in the second final, Australia were incensed when Ranatunga called for a runner.* Though the umpires rejected the request, Healy would not miss a chance to rub salt into the wound. 'You don't get a runner for being a fat, overweight, unfit cunt,' he goaded Arjuna.[116]

Clearly, the Australians felt he was trying to gain unfair advantage. But, for David Fraser, 'there is something more fundamental at stake'.[117] He reckons Arjuna offended the Australians so deeply because he subverted 'the cult of virility'. 'He is unfit and proud of it. This is a fat, effeminate foreigner, walking, yes walking his singles ... He is un-Australian and that is his greatest sin.'

Fraser strikes on something. Is it possible that the Australian team's dislike of their opponents stemmed, at least in part, from a disgust over Sri Lanka's brazen unmanliness? More than any other nation in the world, the islanders flew in the face of Australian ideals of sporting masculinity. Their best batsman was 5ft 4in tall and waddled around the park with one leg shorter than the other. Their star bowler was a double-jointed freak who 'flouted' the rules. And their captain looked like the proud owner of an all-you-can-eat restaurant. Maybe the Australians were annoyed at being pushed so hard by what they saw as a ragtag bunch of cricketers.

Equally, they might have been annoyed by the support the Lankans got. Sri Lankan expats turned out in droves at Melbourne and Sydney, cheering with raucousness reserved for Asian cricket fans. What's more, *Wisden* reported that 'as the series wore on, the home team found themselves subject to increasing criticism from their own public'.[118] Australia loves an underdog, and many admired Ranatunga's stoicism when speaking to the media.[119] Fans could see the bullying for themselves; Arjuna knew he didn't need to ram it down their throats. Tony Grieg did his

---

*   Arjuna claimed he had pulled a hamstring; the Australians reckoned he was simply out of shape. Healy, who regularly referred to Arjuna as 'Porky', was especially outraged. 'I saw what the physio was doing on his leg, nothing,' he reflected. 'Then Sanath Jayasuriya was padded up, the fastest man in world cricket, to replace the slowest man. So I blew up. There was no way he was as injured as he was making out. He was nine not out or something, and he said it was cramp.'

part too: when he cooed about 'Little Kalu' and the 'plucky' Sri Lankans, he built the contest up as a David-and-Goliath-esque battle. It's hard to imagine many neutral observers rooting for Taylor's men.

Still, Sri Lanka's decision to snub outstretched Australian hands – having fallen 10 runs short of their target in the second final – allowed some elements of the media to recast Ranatunga's team as the bad guys.[120] It was a gesture many later regretted, but tensions were high. And rather than sour grapes, the snub seemed to reflect Sri Lanka's objection to Australian hospitality. Whatmore's attempt to shake Ian Healy's hand was met with angry words; none would describe Taylor's team as charming hosts.

Though the series was marred by bad blood and controversy, there were so many positives for Sri Lanka to take. They had refused to lie down, and had run Australia close in their own backyard – despite Ranatunga missing much of the series, and none of the leading batsmen finding their best form.* Meanwhile Vaas, still on the mend after a troubling back injury, had shown himself to be on a level with the world's leading pacemen.** Kaluwitharana had transformed overnight from a misfiring keeper into a destructive opener, and the confidence brought on by his batting had a marked effect on his glovework. Most of all, the MCG final, played out in front of more than 72,000, was a perfect test-run for the situations they'd encounter at the World Cup.

Despite the clear strides Arjuna's men had made, they were still no match for Australia in red-ball cricket. At no stage did they manage to bowl the hosts out – wickets were again hard to come by during the third Test in Adelaide. Sri Lanka fought, but could not stave off a 148-run defeat. Yet what endures from the match is Jayasuriya's blistering batting. Promoted to open for the first time in Tests, he scored 48 off 57 in the first innings, and a brilliant maiden century in the second. Jayasuriya and Kaluwitharana had given a warning sign of the sort of damage they might

---

* No one in the Sri Lanka side averaged more than 30. Tillakaratne led the way with 29.28, largely thanks to three unbeaten efforts.

** Only Walsh and Ambrose bettered his economy of 3.67 during the Tri-series, just Otis Gibson returned more wickets.

inflict, but still, no one really believed. These were flash-in-the-pan performances; ultimately, Sri Lanka were still destined for failure. Weren't they?

CHAMPIONS

So no one – well, almost no one – believed Sri Lanka had a shot.[121] In the weeks prior to the World Cup, Arjuna's men were occasionally mentioned as 'dark horses', but most agreed that Australia, India, South Africa, West Indies, England and Pakistan had a better chance of lifting the trophy. It's easy to see how the Lankans were dismissed. After 99 ODIs, Jayasuriya averaged 19.73, his strike rate a shade under 75. Nor were teams losing sleep over Kaluwitharana. The middle order was Sri Lanka's biggest strength, but only Ranatunga averaged over 35.

On paper, the bowling looked even less assured. Pack-leader Vaas had found wickets hard to come by in Asia. Murali and Dharmasena had often struggled for penetration and control; while neither Pushpakumara nor Wickramasinghe had proven consistently reliable with the new ball. The team's overall record wasn't particularly promising either: since the start of the decade, they had won forty-one and lost sixty-three – although thirty of those victories had come in Asia, site of the 1996 World Cup.

At least the squad were optimistic. 'We believed we would at least make the semi-finals,' Murali told me. 'We knew in our conditions we had good spinners, very experienced players, very good batsmen.' The batters' experience was certainly a boost,* and Sri Lanka had grown into an excellent chasing side. Much of that was down to Ranatunga, still the best finisher in cricket. Auspiciously, he had a habit of stepping up on the biggest stage too: through three World Cups, he averaged 42.43, jumping to 64.25 if you disregard the 1983 tournament he played as a teenager.

What's more, having led his men through triumph and tragedy, Arjuna could count on their unflinching support. And he put faith in his charges.

---

* Heading into the tournament, Ranatunga, de Silva, Gurusinha, Tillakaratne, Mahanama and Jayasuriya had played 839 ODIs between them. Equally, much of their experience had come in Asia, with all six in the top twenty run scorers on the continent since the start of the decade.

Many thought it unwise picking Murali,* but Ranatunga would not move forward without his star spinner. 'Arjuna took a bold risk,' Murali reflects. 'He supported me wholeheartedly – and this is Sri Lanka. At the time war was ongoing: I'm a Tamil and he's a Sinhalese Buddhist. But he never thought about race or anything; he thought, as a player, he's good for our country, I'm going to back him. It is something special he has done for the whole of Sri Lanka. When you take it into relations between Tamils and Sinhalese, there were so many problems. But he took the decision that we are *Sri Lankans*. We are not divided by religion or race.'

Clearly, Ranatunga's leadership stretched well beyond the boundary. 'For three years, I didn't see my house in the daylight,' Pushpakumara told me. '05:35 train to Colombo, and straight to the NCC – then, the 18:50 train back to Panadura. I was so lucky after that. Arjuna said to Aravinda, "Why don't you let him stay at your house. He's coming from too far – we need this boy firing. Why don't you keep him in Ratmalana?" Aravinda said "OK," so I went and stayed there for a year. My God, father was there, mother, sister – unbelievable. They gave me food, looked after me really well.'

Meanwhile, Ranatunga's parents made room for several other players from outside Colombo, making sure they had plenty of dhal, sambol, bread and rice to survive.[122] 'Look at [what he did for] Sanath,' Pushpakumara went on. 'He used to give Sanath his bed and sleep on the floor. No one's done that in world cricket, made that sacrifice.' Though Ranatunga insists he switched rooms because he couldn't bear Jayasuriya's snoring, Pushpakumara has a point. This Sri Lanka team had been through a lot – surely no other side had shared such highs and lows. Through it all, Arjuna was both leader and inspiration to his men. With several still struggling financially, he insisted Man of the Match awards were split between the whole team. 'That's how we became a family,' he told Rex Clementine. 'We made sure players knew playing for the country was more important [than money].'[123]

As the longest-surviving player at the World Cup, by this stage Ranatunga's approach to ODI cricket seemed almost algorithmic.

---

* Hair had cleared the path for other umpires to call the off-spinner. Should any challenge Murali at the World Cup, Sri Lanka would end up a man short.

Most saw Sri Lanka's shortfall of seamers as a weakness, but Arjuna understood the value of taking pace off the ball in the subcontinent. No other side committed so steadfastly to spin. And when it came to scoring runs, the batsmen had crystal clear instructions. Sanath and Kalu were told to go out and hit. It didn't matter if they lost their wickets: given Sri Lanka's depth, the team were better off being 80-2 than 30-0 after 10. Gurusinha was 'the rock', asked to bat as long as possible. The captain, Tillakaratne and Mahanama were effectively an insurance policy, experienced players who could provide a buffer for Aravinda – allowing him to go out and play his natural game without fear that losing his wicket would be death knell for Sri Lanka.

Ultimately, Ranatunga's plans were rooted in a desire to maximise the potential of his star player. 'We wanted to get the most out of Ari, so as batsmen we always tried to bat around him,' he told Rex Clementine. 'Even during the World Cup, I told everyone not to say anything to him on the field or back in his room. Just to keep him happy and give him whatever he wants. Don't restrict him in any way – because when he scores runs, we get what we want.'[124]

But all of Arjuna's planning could not prepare Sri Lanka for the disaster that struck on 31 January. The Central Bank bombing rocked Colombo to its very core. With 91 killed and over 1,400 injured, it was the most devastating strike of the civil war so far. Already nervous about heading to Sri Lanka, there was little chance Australia would make the trip in the wake of such horror.[125] Though they pressed World Cup organisers PILCOM to move the match to an Indian venue, they were prepared to forfeit the points. So were the West Indies.* The most eagerly anticipated matches in the island's history were cancelled in a flash.

It was a godsend that neither Kenya nor Zimbabwe tried to boycott their group games in Sri Lanka. Still, Punchihewa had to convince ICC delegates that the forfeited matches should be declared walkovers; to prove the island was safe, he, Jagmohan Dalmiya and Chef Arris Abassi struck on the idea of sending a combined India-Pakistan XI to play a match at Khettarama.[126]

---

* The tournament's format, whereby eight teams qualified from two groups of six, meant a single match could be forfeited with little risk of serious repercussions.

For the island's cricket fans, gutted by the withdrawal of Australia and the West Indies, the game was real consolation. Indian and Pakistani stars hadn't played in the same side since partition, but came together to show solidarity for their smaller neighbour. Rivalries were couched for the day; from start to finish, the visiting cricketers were cheered as if they were Sri Lanka's own.

Though Arjuna's men struggled to impose themselves against a star-studded attack, for once the cricket wasn't a contest. It was a show of solidarity, one that quite possibly stopped Sri Lanka's World Cup quest from sliding off the rails.

★★★

The sun bore down on the SSC on 21 February as Sri Lanka's World Cup got underway against Zimbabwe. From the off, it was clear this side meant business. Sharp in the field, they restricted Zimbabwe to 228; Gurusinha and Aravinda mounted a mammoth partnership, and even scurried through for singles. Though 'Guru' was run out when he tried to jog one struck straight to mid-off, Sri Lanka crossed the line with 13 overs to spare.

Next, they travelled into the lion's den for a daunting clash against India at the Feroz Shah in Delhi. It was tough work for the bowlers: Tendulkar carried India to 271-3; though behind at the halfway stage, a fearless opening stand got Sri Lanka back on track. Sanath and Kalu attacked from the very first ball. Prabhakar's second over was flayed for 22; 42-0 after 3, Sri Lanka were back in the hunt. When Jayasuriya went for 79 off 76, they were 137-3 after 20.2 overs. Ranatunga and Tillakaratne reminded the world of the class lurking deep in Sri Lanka's middle order; for just the fourth time in their history, Sri Lanka gunned down a target north of 250.

Such a confident chase got the world talking, and sent belief coursing through Lankan veins. It brought the team closer together, too. 'Suddenly, they looked like fourteen brothers,' Pushpakumara told me. 'After the match, I remember the dressing room. I have a brother and a sister, but my home doesn't have that feeling. That family feeling. Honestly.' The unity clearly lifted Sri Lanka's standards. At Asgiriya, Sanath and Kalu pounded Kenya's attack for 83 in the first 6.4 overs.

Though neither kicked on, Sri Lanka were just getting started. Gurusinha clubbed steepling straight 6s as he and Aravinda put on 184 in 182 balls; de Silva casually cracked a 92-ball century, then broke out with 45 off his next 23.* On other days, the rest wouldn't get a word in – it's testament to Sri Lanka's verve that almost everyone warrants a mention. Ranatunga romped to 50 off 29, finishing 75* from 40 as his men pillaged 67 from the final 4 overs. The total of 398 was a new ODI record; Kenya couldn't get close to such an imposing target. Murali was probably the pick of the bowlers, though Hashan Tillakaratne stole the show by closing the innings with an over of ambidextrous spin. You simply couldn't take your eyes off this team.

They went into their quarter-final against England as clear favourites. Jayasuriya did for Robin Smith with a direct hit; in every match, Sri Lanka were producing game-changing moments in the field. None of the English batsmen got going; though their bowlers mounted a fight-back, 235 looked a sub-par total on a true batting track.

So it proved: Kalu went early, but Jayasuriya raced to 50 from 32 balls. 'They don't like running too much, this lot,' Geoffrey Boycott quipped on commentary; the very next ball, Sanath launched a hulking 6 onto the stadium's roof.[127] By the time he was stumped, he had smashed 82 off 44. The game was all but done: it ended in the 41st over, with De Freitas bowling off breaks – an act that seemed to sum up the depth of England's despondency.

For Aravinda, it was the crucial moment: as he told Rex Clementine, 'I had a feeling that if we beat England, we would go on to win the World Cup.'[128] Spirits were high, but Sri Lanka knew a semi-final clash against India, at the 100,000-seat Eden Gardens, would test them to the core.

That said, the team managed stress superbly through the tournament. The family feel amidst the squad no doubt helped. There was no legion of backroom staff: the fourteen aside it was just Dav, Alex, Duleep and Sidath Wettimuny. Wettimuny bought Jayasuriya a Longines

---

*   Aravinda had recently switched to a heavier bat on slow pitches, claiming its 3lb-plus weight allowed him to punch with more force.

watch after challenging him to bat 15 overs against England;* on one flight, Gurusinha and Whatmore cheerfully chucked plastic forks at one another.[129] Clearly, the Lankans' breezy spirit played a role in their World Cup success.

What's more, in wholeheartedly embracing Sanath and Kalu's relentless assaults, Sri Lanka built an environment that left no space for fear of failure. Win or lose, they would go down swinging, playing their own way. They seem to have worked from the starting point that any tournament success was a bonus, a blessing – as Pushpakumara repeatedly put it, 'a dream'. Arjuna told the team before the semi that they had achieved their goal; now they could relax.

Still, I was shocked by Pushpakumara's memories of the team's torrid start against India. 'I was really enjoying it,' he told me. 'You know, eating some grapes. It was like I was sleeping and having a dream. Sanath got out, Kalu got out – I didn't know anything. I was just enjoying the company, watching the match.' Not all were as carefree as him, but there seems to have been just the right amount of cricketing nihilism around the squad to keep Sri Lanka going steady.

But let's rewind a little. Sri Lanka could have easily been cowed by the spectre of Eden Gardens – but the Australian adventure stood them in good stead. 'I could see the ground from my hotel room,' Kaluwitharana told Clementine. 'About four hours before the start of play, I saw about 100,000 people around the stadium. We were told the capacity crowd in the stadium for that game was 115,000 – and I thought there was a similar number outside who couldn't get in.'[130] For Aravinda, each and every one was a blessing. His teammates have often pegged him as the greatest pressure player in world cricket. Now – against India in a World Cup semi, in front of a huge and hostile crowd – was the chance for him to go out and prove it.

Throughout the tournament, both teams had shown a marked preference for chasing. But, arriving at Eden Gardens, Whatmore found a soft,

---

* Jayasuriya only lasted 13 overs, but hoped his fireworks would provide an asterisk. After a day of teasing Sanath that he had lost the bet, Wettimuny presented him with the watch.

crusty deck.* 'It won't last,' he told Arjuna, convinced the team should bat first.[131] Ranatunga was reluctant to shelve such a successful strategy; thankfully, the coin fell Azharuddin's way. He promptly asked Sri Lanka to bat.

It was a stroke of luck, but Kaluwitharana slashed the second ball of the innings to third man; two balls later, Jayasuriya produced a mirror image of the shot. 'Aravinda was looking very serious,' Pushpakumara remembers. 'I used to run in at every wicket, but when I started running, Arjuna said, 'He's got out in the first over, how can you run out?' Whatmore claims Sri Lanka were ready for such a situation, but going 1–2 in a semi-final was bound to test their bottle.

Their faith in the middle order was crucial. Had Sri Lanka gone into their shell, it could have been game over – instead, Aravinda turned the tide with his full repertoire of strokes. To see him tickle Anil Kumble through the vacant slip region calmed fraying nerves; before long, he was playing textbook on-the-up cover drives, fetching balls from outside off and slapping them to the leg-side fence.[132] Though Gurusinha lodged a rare failure, Aravinda kept backing himself. Sri Lanka only had 85 on the board when he was outfoxed by Kumble in the 16th – but cricket is so much about momentum, and in scoring 66 off 47, Aravinda changed the tone of the contest.

Still, it was time for Sri Lanka's much-vaunted insurance policy to start paying out. They delivered in spades: Mahanama moved elegantly to 58 before he had to be carried from the field with cramps; Arjuna played a series of impish, open-faced nudges through third man; while Tillakaratne manoeuvred the ball cleverly before being caught in the closing stages. A few lusty blows from Vaas lifted Sri Lanka to 251 after 50. It wasn't a huge total, but with the pitch starting to crumble, it kept them well in the match.

Still, India were in control as long as Tendulkar was at the crease: after 22.3 overs, he'd carried his team to 92–1. But Kaluwitharana engineered a remarkable stumping to turn the game on its head. Struck on the pads by Jayasuriya, Tendulkar briefly lost the ball and thought about a single;

---

*   No international cricket had been played at Eden Gardens since 1994, though the middle had been buried underneath stages for the tournament's opening ceremony.

Kalu gathered it down the leg side and whipped off the bails before he could make it back to his crease.

Now, with the pitch ripping and bouncing erratically, the Indian innings fell apart. Azharuddin chipped one back to Dharmasena. Jayasuriya bowled Sanjay Manjrekar around his legs. Out of nowhere, India were 101–4. Jayasuriya stuck to his canny leg-side line, and had Ajay Jadeja bowled around his legs too. When Dinesh Mongia skied the ball into his outstretched hands, India were 120–7 and the game as good as gone. Bottles rained down from the stands: Upul Chandana, on the field as twelfth man, begged to stand on the rope in place of Aravinda in case the star batsman should get struck and hurt.[133] He was hit soon after: with Indian fans burning their seats to embers, Clive Lloyd had little choice but to call off the match.[134] It wasn't quite how they dreamed it, but Sri Lanka were on their way to the World Cup final.

They flew straight from Calcutta to Lahore, arriving in time to see Australia sneak past the West Indies in Mohali. As if written in the stars, the ugly Australian series would have a coda, the Lankans a shot at redemption. Crucially, when Ajruna's men practised the following day, they noticed dew forming on the outfield by about 6:30 pm.[135] Later that evening, Ranatunga and Duleep snuck out of a function and headed back to the ground. 'It was so wet, we thought they'd watered it,' Arjuna told Rex Clementine. The pair decided on the spot that with an attack so reliant on spin, they would have to field first if they won the toss.

Sri Lanka's whole march to the final has the feel of a heist. Having been mauled in the quarter-finals, Mike Atherton failed to acknowledge Jayasuriya's blistering brilliance, instead reflecting on his own team's failure to put up 300 against what he saw as a substandard attack. In the semi, India were running smooth until they were completely undone by a crumbling pitch and Jayasuriya's crafty lines. Now, Arjuna foresaw the conditions and decided to buck the trend: no team had ever won a World Cup final chasing. I can't help but imagine him and Duleep, driving through the backstreets of Lahore like something out of a 1990s thriller movie, soundtracked with blueish trumpets or sparse, foreboding strings.

The team did their best to savour the moment. Nothing changed in terms of planning or preparation; Whatmore reminded his men that they'd done the hard work. Playing in a World Cup final was a privilege: they should go out and enjoy it. They had the Pakistani public behind them;* some have said the final felt like a home game, only without the nervous energy players often sense from the crowd. Sri Lankan Airlines chartered a jet to bring a few lucky fans to Lahore. Whatever happened, the team would be heading home as heroes.

A story Pushpakumara told me highlights the lack of worry in the camp. 'The evening before the match, there was a carpet shop downstairs in the hotel,' he explains. 'The Australia team were having a meeting. They were very serious, and we were relaxing. I went first, and asked the owner, "Can I have one carpet?" He said, "it's this much," so I said, "Why don't you come down in price?" My God, he came down more than 50 per cent. I bought the carpet.'

Pushpakumara's teammates were impressed with his purchase, and the next morning decided to check the shop out for themselves. 'I walked in to have breakfast and saw the Australian team there,' recalled Arjuna. 'They were all seated in one table. All wearing the same dress and there was pin-drop silence. They were focusing on the game at hand. I looked around and couldn't see any of our boys. I saw Duleep, the manager, walking in for breakfast and asked him where they were.'[136]

'Duleep told me that there was a carpet sale going on in the lobby and they were all there. I was angry. I told Duleep that this is such a big occasion and these guys don't care and rushed downstairs to tell them to get off. When I went down, I saw the entire team there. Aravinda was bargaining for carpets. Sanath was bargaining and everyone was bargaining. I just told myself, "Hang on, the big match pressure is getting to Australia. Our guys meanwhile are carefree. Isn't this the ideal way to go into the big final?" So I joined the boys, didn't tell them anything. Eventually, I also started bargaining.'

'We were all looking at carpets, everybody buying,' Pushpakumara gleefully reflects. 'And that shop owner was really happy. Some small

---

* The countries' longstanding cricketing comradeship had been reinforced by Sri Lanka's victory over India, avenging Pakistan's humbling defeat to their old foe. Locals stitched Pakistan and Sri Lanka flags together. Rameez Raja asked Ranatunga what kind of pitch he would prefer.

carpets he gave free! My God, so we were relaxing – and the Australia team put themselves under pressure. I can remember that team meeting in the morning. Arjuna said, "OK guys, we have nothing to lose. Maybe you were planning to get to the semis, now we're in the final. There's nothing to lose. You guys give it your best shot, and we will win this game." He was a great leader.'

What's more, Ranatunga had an uncanny ability to get under the Australians' skin. On the eve of the final, he dismissed Warne as 'an average spinner'.[137] Irritated, Warne strolled over to Ian Chappell and asked, 'What's the fat bastard said about me now?' Ranjit Fernando reckons it was another Ranatunga ploy: 'He had a method in it – he thrived on it. And people like Warne were overly anxious to get the better of him, which made them lesser players.' In making himself the heel, Ranatunga shifted pressure off his players' shoulders too. He painted a target on his back, and was more than happy for all of Australia to take aim.

Still, perhaps the ultimate cornerstone of great captaincy is self-belief. In the lead-up to the final, there was uncertainty in the camp. Dav and Aravinda thought Sri Lanka should bat first; so too Imran Khan, who offered his advice to the Sri Lankans.[138] 'I was confused after hearing that from a World Cup-winning captain,' Arjuna told Rex Clementine. 'Aravinda ran in and said "I told you so," but I told them we will stick to our decision.'

Nerves jangled all around Ranatunga. Gurusinha nearly bit a changing-room attendant's head off when he moved his bag before the final; once the game got going, Duleep warded off a dressing-room jinx by stringently keeping players in their seats.[*][139] But Arjuna was the picture of calm as he strolled to the middle. Smiling, sunglasses on, he looked ready for the beach, not a World Cup final. I don't think he ever doubted that the coin would land on his side. 'We're going to have a bowl,' he declared, cool as a Colombo sea breeze.

Vaas got Mark Waugh early, but as Taylor and Ricky Ponting found their groove, the game looked to be getting away from Sri Lanka.

---

* If anyone so much as squirmed, they got a tongue-lashing. 'When we were watching the final, I was shocked,' Pushpakumara recalls. 'Because I have to carry the water and go. But Duleep said, "Wait, wait. Don't get up. Everything's going alright".'

It turned when Jayasuriya took a swirling catch to dislodge Taylor; between overs 25 and 30, Australia managed just 16 runs. Still, at 150-2 with 20 overs in the bank, they were clearly in the driver's seat, well set for a final blast.

But, the spinners applied the stranglehold: in the 31st over, Ponting got himself in a muddle and was bowled by Aravinda. Warne – promoted to number five to try to get Australia moving again – charged Murali and was undone by a sharp leg-side stumping. Suddenly, the momentum was all with Sri Lanka. They kept their foot on the neck, fielding with asphyxiating fury. When Steve Waugh skied one off Dharmasena, Aravinda took a brilliant catch on the run. Australia were 170-5. In the space of 10 overs, they had added 36 while losing 4 wickets. The game had turned on its head.

Stuart Law and Bevan rebuilt, but with no easy runs on offer, had to try to engineer shots. Law was caught trying to carve Jayasuriya over the off side; first ball of the next over, Aravinda bowled Healy with a beautifully flighted off break. After 6.1 overs, he'd picked up 3 wickets for 24 runs. Murali got through his 10 overs for 31. All in all, the spinners bowled 37 overs and conceded just 163.* Sri Lanka could feel very happy with a 242-run target. Having built a superb platform, Australia left a lot of runs in the middle.

Still, most felt Taylor's men were ahead at the halfway stage.[140] Finals are nervy affairs; runs on the board valued currency. Jayasuriya could have been run out on the 8th ball of the innings; next up, he tried to sneak 2 to McGrath and was found just short. Soon after, a direct hit would have seen Gurusinha run out. Kaluwitharana miscued a pull straight to square leg. At 23-2, Australia's score looked a long way off.

This was cricket at its most fraught, but you would not have guessed it looking at Aravinda. He strolled to the crease like a man playing a leisurely Sunday match, racing off the mark with a glorious on-drive. There was a 'Mad Max' moment early on, as he charged down the wicket

---

* Their performance was vindication for Ranatunga. Overall, 95.1 of the 134.1 knockout overs Sri Lanka bowled were sent down by spinners. These brought wickets at 20.31 runs apiece, costing near exactly 4 runs an over. Given the length of Sri Lanka's batting line-up, those start to look like match-winning efforts.

after Gurusinha had cracked the ball straight to backward point. Had McGrath gathered cleanly, it might have been curtains for Sri Lanka. Instead, Aravinda went on batting like he didn't have a care in the world.

He struck the ball with such artistry that you forgot the hopes of a nation rested on his shoulders. Damien Fleming was pulled over mid-on and flicked through the leg side; when Warne was introduced, Aravinda rocked back and punched him through cover point. As Ranatunga predicted, dew was making life hard for the spinner. Gurusinha cracked a full toss to the straight boundary then charged Paul Reiffel, slapping the ball over mid-off. He had the look of a man growing in confidence. At 71-2 after 15, Sri Lanka were back in the hunt.

With Aravinda at the crease, they had control of the match. 'Big game player,' Pushpakumara reflects. 'And he proved it to the world. Remarkable. As long as he was in the middle, we knew we could easily win. He had shots all over the place.' Time and again, Aravinda coaxed the ball to the boundary rope. As in the B&H Final the year before, there was none of the crash, bang and wallop of a demolition job. Rather, this was a sculptor chipping away at his subject, each stroke a study in precision.

But when the drinks break came, pressure shifted onto Pushpakumara's shoulders. 'Two overs before the break, the boys told me lots of messages,' he explains. 'There were a lot of stories I had to go and tell these two guys. I said, "OK, no problem." When I walked down to the pavilion, Davvy [Whatmore] was there. He called me, and talked for about one and a half minutes. From his action and body language, I knew there was something, but to be honest, I didn't understand a single word of English at that time.

'But I said, "OK, OK, right, right, no problem." Then I ran into the middle. I said, "Well played, keep going," gave them the water and came back. Everybody said, "Pushy, you told them this?" "Pushy, you told them that?" "Yes, yes, absolutely." Davvy asked – he was a little doubtful, a bit suspicious. "Did you tell them what I said?" "Yes". "How could you tell them Pushy, you didn't understand." "Yes, I told them". "OK. we'll see. Go and sit."'

Maybe, in not worrying his teammates with needless instructions, Pushpakumara kept their minds clear and at ease. Soon after reaching 50,

Gurusinha launched one straight to Stuart Law on the square-leg fence. It was the most straightforward of catches; the crowd let out an audible gasp as the ball slipped through Law's fingers. 'That's gotta be the World Cup gone,' Tony Grieg suggested. 'These Sri Lankans have got to the Aussies?'[141] Dew clearly hindered Australia, but there can be no doubt nerves played a part too. Incredibly, the underdogs seem to have handled the pressure of the final far better than their seasoned opponents.

But Australia would not lie down. In the 31st over, Gurusinha tried to charge Reiffel again, but a clean-air swipe saw him bowled. Ranatunga arrived at the crease with Sri Lanka needing 94 off 119. It was no straightforward task, but Arjuna had made these kind of innings his specialty. He and Aravinda added 17 from the next 6 balls; on the stroke of 40 overs, the captain tickled Mark Waugh to the third-man fence. It was the first boundary in 8 overs; Sri Lanka needed 51 from the last 10.

Aravinda eased pressure in the 43rd with a pair of brush-stroked 4s off Reiffel – urging his captain at the over-break not to get overexcited at the sight of Warne. But Arjuna smelled blood. As soon as he got on strike, he slapped one straight back to the bowler. It came fast, and slipped through Warne's fingers, racing off to the boundary. Next up, a waist-high full toss sailed over the ropes for 6. Sri Lanka plundered 13 off the over, crushing Australian hopes in the process. They needed just 17 from the last 6 overs.

Aravinda went to three figures with a fine tickle in the 46th; when he stroked the ball to the cover boundary later in the over, Sri Lanka were level. 'They've come such a long way, in such a short period of time,' Tony Grieg cooed – with more than a trace of pride in his voice. Ensconced in the commentary box since the Australian tour – rarely trying to hide which team he supported – Grieg seemed as much a part of the triumph as anyone. As Kaluwitharana later put it, 'He was almost an ambassador.'[142]

Fittingly, it fell to Ranatunga to end the match – a final insouciant clip declaring it done. Players charged inside the boundary rope; Aravinda grinned ear to ear, running into Arjuna's embrace. Only the captain remained calm. As soon as the winning runs left his bat, he turned and took two stumps as souvenirs, soberly shaking Taylor's hand. Each of his players received a congratulatory hug; yet there was little more than a hint of a smile on Arjuna's face. This was a man vindicated, one who believed he was doing nothing more than his job. Or one who *knew*. At the post-match ceremony, he took the trophy like it belonged in his hands.

In the wake of such glorious triumph, Sri Lanka's dressing room grew packed full of revellers having the time of their lives. Sadly, the saltiness between the two teams held firm. Warne refused to sign a poster for Murali; the bats Ranatunga sent into the Australian dressing room came back without Warne or the Waugh brothers' signatures.[143] Still, nothing could dampen Lankan spirits. Back at the Pearl Continental Hotel, there was a party in Punchihewa's room; it was 3 am before the charter took off for Colombo – with a few extra passengers on board.[144]

'There was no room for us,' Gurusinha told me. 'Sanath and I were actually sat on the floor, there were no seats.' But this was no ordinary flight. As soon as the plane reached altitude, Captain Sunil Wettimuny[*] announced it was 'party time'.[145] Free drinks were served from the front and back; Aravinda and Mahanama's fathers led a raucous sing-song. 'My God, that whole flight was dancing,' Pushpakumara remembers. At one stage, Wettimuny had to ask passengers to sit down since there were too many standing at the front of the plane. He was so tired – having flown into Lahore that morning and spent all day glued to the game – that he made an automatic landing in Colombo. The team were met at the airport by thousands of screaming supporters. 'Even with security, we couldn't get through that,' Gurusinha reflects.

Though the players were exhausted, they were told to head straight to the president's house; by the time they had made it home, it was 4 or 5 pm. 'That's when it hit me – the tiredness,' Gurusinha says. 'I hadn't slept for two days. But we were on a real high from winning.' It took time for the triumph to sink in. For some it was weeks, others years – but the sense of disbelief was universal.

It is hard to imagine a single victory has ever been so profoundly felt by a nation. After all, Sri Lanka was a tiny island trapped in a desperate war. This month-long quest had provided the most glorious escapism, and flooded a country with pride. Cricket elevated Sri Lanka onto

---

[*] You have to wonder if he and Duleep shared a moment. When the duo were brutalised by Thomson twenty-one years earlier, could they ever imagined they would one day carry a World Cup back to Sri Lanka?

the international stage. What's more, they bested the rest not by aping England or Australia, but by playing their own way. Arjuna and his men were on top of the world.

MONEY AND POWER

The 1996 World Cup wasn't just a watershed moment for Sri Lanka, but a turning point for the game in general; another giant leap in cricket's journey from Victorian relic to modern money-spinner.[146] Amidst India's failure, Sri Lanka unexpectedly emerged as the biggest beneficiary of the World Cup – each and every aspect of their triumph ensuring their rebirth as the darlings of world cricket.

They were the ultimate underdogs: whipping boys from a poor island nation who, in an age of professionalism, still had to make ends meet by working part time. They had overcome high hurdles to get their hands on the trophy: civil war and cricketing chasms in their own country; hostile and unjust treatment abroad. Above all, they played scintillating cricket: fierce and fearless, electric in the field, unpredictable with the bat. Flouting convention and embracing their own style, it is little surprise that wherever Sri Lanka went, they left lovestruck fans in their wake.

The Singer Cup, which got underway two weeks after Sri Lanka lifted the World Cup, saw the three leading Asian sides head to Singapore for a week-long Tri-series. Pushpakumara reminded me that newfound success brought fresh pressures: 'As world champions, there was a lot of expectation. You can't just play ordinary cricket.'

There was little chance of that. The Padang Sports Club ground, in the heart of downtown Singapore, is small – with square boundaries stretching barely 60 yards. Nervous about damage to the surrounding buildings, tournament organisers took out a hefty insurance policy before the tournament began.[147]

Their worst fears were realised when Sanath Jayasuirya showed up on 2 April. He viciously assaulted an Akram-less Pakistan, striking a record eleven 6s en route to a 65-ball 134. His century came off 48 balls, making it comfortably the fastest in ODI history. Unimpressed with Saqlain's efforts, Pakistan's new skipper Aamer Sohail bravely decided to bring himself on to bowl some left-arm spin. His third over disappeared for 30, including four consecutive 6s. Sri Lanka raced to 349-9: their World Cup success was clearly no flash in the pan.

Despite a narrow loss to India, Arjuna's men qualified for the final, and restricted Pakistan to just 215. For the bowlers, it must have felt like Groundhog Day, as Sanath set upon them once more. The ball yo-yoed between middle and fence; his 50 came up with a heave over square leg – it had taken just 17 balls, another record for Jayasuriya to add to his bag.* He went on to make 76 off 28, before Sri Lanka collapsed to 172, handing Pakistan the trophy. If the rest were a step off the pace – still basking in the World Cup afterglow – Sanath was on fire. The week had been all about him. As Ian Chappell wrote:

> He made some good fast bowlers look distinctly apprehensive. Pakistan's Aaqib Javed only half-jokingly said he wouldn't turn up for the next tournament if Jayasuriya was playing ... Every time he batted people put down their drinks and jostled for a vantage point because they didn't want to miss a ball of this mastery. On the final night Jayasuriya walked through the Singapore Cricket Club bar and everyone rose to applaud him, including four ex-international captains and that is a memory that will stay with me to the end.[148]

It didn't matter if you were a seasoned cricketer or a child watching the game for the first time: when you saw Sanath tear into quicks from the off, you knew you were witnessing something special. Jayasuriya was a visionary, the free swings of his blade as revolutionary as the brushstrokes of Vermeer or Van Gough. He rejected the Victorian axiom of 'playing yourself in', bringing the freedom of the beach to international cricket. He changed the game in the process: would the cast of destructive international openers who emerged during the late 1990s have been trusted at the top were it not for the Sri Lankan prototype?

---

* Remarkably, when Kaluwitharana was bowled off the first ball of the 7th over, the scoreboard read 70-1; his contribution to the partnership was 0.

The Sri Lanka squad pose with their first major piece of silverware, the 1979 ICC Trophy. L–R: Ranjan Madugalle, Rohan Jayasekera, B.R. Heyn, Sunil Jayasinghe, Duleep Mendis, Ranjan Gunatillke, Sidath Wettimuny, D.L.S. de Silva, Anura Tennekoon, Ajit de Silva, Bandula Warnapura, Roger Wijesuriya, D.S. de Silva, Tony Opatha, Sudath Pasqual, Abu Fuard, Roy Dias, Sridharan Jeganathan. (B.R. Heyn collection)

Sri Lanka squad prepare for the 1975 World Cup, Indian Gymkhana club. Standing L–R: Bandula Warnapura, Anura Ranasinghe, Dennis Chanmugam, Tony Opatha, Ajit de Silva, Lalith Kaluperuma, Duleep Mendis. Seated L–R: D.S. de Silva, Mevan Pieris, Ranjit Fernando, Anura Tennekoon, K.M.T. Perera, Michael Tissera, David Heyn, Sunil Wettimuny. (David Heyn collection)

Roshan Mahanama, Aravinda de Silva and Arjuna Ranatunga relax on the boundary ahead of the World Cup final. (© Prasanna Hennayake)

Tossing up: Arjuna and Imran locked in debate in Lahore. (© Prasanna Hennayake)

The Sri Lanka squad pray together ahead of the World Cup final, Lahore, March 1996. (© Prasanna Hennayake)

Aravinda holds his bat aloft, the third man to score a century in a World Cup final. (© Prasanna Hennayake)

Champions: the 1996 squad celebrate with the World Cup trophy in their changing room. (© Prasanna Hennayake)

On top of the world: Arjuna and Sanath cradle their cups on the charter flight home. (© Prasanna Hennayake)

Openers reunited: Ranjit Fernando and Buddy Reid meet in Australia, 1999. (Buddy Reid collection)

Adil Rashid rips one at the NCC, October 2018. (© Ben Hildred)

Locals play softball cricket in Nuwara Eliya. (© Ben Hildred)

Sri Lanka take on Pakistan in Galle, June 2015. (© Ben Hildred)

The famous P. Sara scoreboard, June 2015. (© Ben Hildred)

S. Thomas' host Trinity College at their ground in Mt Lavinia, February 2019. (© Ben Hildred)

English fans sprawl on the grass at the SSC, November 2018. (© Ben Hildred)

Sanath's runs were worth their weight in gold. New-ball bowlers, so used to being the bully, now found themselves outgunned. That brought sleepless nights and an unfamiliar sense of demoralisation. It seeped through the whole opposition: teams could no longer feel confident setting Sri Lanka targets under 270. If Sanath stayed at the crease for 15 overs, the ball would be soft and the scorer well-worked – your grip on the game almost inevitably gone. His sudden emergence as superstar lifted Sri Lanka no end.

And each box-office innings brought confidence. During the first four months of 1996, Jayasuriya was named Player of the Tournament at the World Cup, and broke records for the fastest ODI 100 and 50 – achieving far more than he had in his first six years in the side. Out of nowhere, he announced himself as a world-beater – rarely has a cricketer enjoyed such a meteoric rise. Whatmore felt that in Singapore Jayasuriya 'transitioned from being a junior to one of the seniors'.[149]

Back home for the Singer World Series, he made mincemeat of India's 226-run target with an unbeaten 120. The *Indian Cricket Annual* and *Wisden* both named him in their list of cricketers of the year, the former describing his batting as 'a curious mix of science, magic and madness, based on quickness of hand and eye'.[150] After 1996, Jayasuriya became a near-mythical figure.[151] Stories spread about forearms impossibly strong from a childhood spent climbing coconut trees; about dynamite fielding honed by years sprinting across sand.

If Jayasuriya was Sri Lanka's Basquiat – brash and bold and brilliant – Aravinda was their Banksy: the kind of batsman who snuck up on you in the night; more sedate but no less striking. The rest of the Singer World Series was his and his alone: unbeaten throughout, he anchored chases against Australia and Zimbabwe to see Sri Lanka top the group. Another final against their not-so-old foes beckoned.

In a reduced contest, Arjuna's men tore into the Australian attack. The reply was limp: Vaas did damage up front, before a spin-quintet applied the stranglehold. Chandana's leg breaks were especially effective; with Australia falling 50 runs short, Sri Lanka had another trophy for the cabinet. Once again, they'd shown that – in Asian conditions at least – they were the best, and most exciting, team in world cricket. The confidence seeped into the Test side too – with the spinners coming to the fore as Zimbabwe were handled 2-0 in September 1996.

That said, the biggest shift in the post-World Cup landscape was money. Where Sri Lanka had once been a tricky sell to foreign broadcasters, they were now must-watch TV the whole world over. Life became easier for the players, and the equation changed for local businesses too.

Suddenly, sponsorships and endorsements allowed companies to siphon off their own piece of national pride. This influx of cash should have been a real boon, but investors weren't the only ones circling. The cricket board now became attractive prey for influential businessmen. Roles brought power and influence; the ability to award contracts and curry favour. Sri Lanka's administration had been riddled with problems for decades, but the lack of money in cricket ensured a certain dignity. Post-1996, things went downhill fast.

As Ranjan Mellawa reflected in his book *Winds Behind the Willows*, it was worrying to see board vice president Upali Dharmadasa snatch the World Cup off Ranatunga and lead the team through the lobby of the Pearl Continental Hotel in Lahore.[152] During the tournament, Dharmadasa told Punchihewa he would run against him in the upcoming board elections.[153] His plot was supported by fellow vice president Thilanga Sumathipala, and by Arjuna and Aravinda too.[154] On the night, Dharmadasa beat out Punchihewa sixty-three votes to fifty-eight. Two weeks after the World Cup, Punchihewa – whose steady hand helped Sri Lanka lift the trophy – was ousted. Most fans were still too ecstatic to notice, but this was very bad news.

Board elections are themselves problematic. Though Sri Lanka only had fourteen first-class teams in 1996, fifty-three controlling clubs and associations got two votes each.* Since lobbying is widespread – with voters promised cash, infrastructural investment or elevated status – clubs often find themselves in situations where their own interests don't necessarily align with what's best for the country's cricket.[155] The

---

* That includes twenty-five district associations, other associations like Mercantile Cricket, Schools Cricket and a number of defunct cricket clubs, which somehow managed to cling onto their voting rights. On top of that, fifteen affiliate clubs, whose status was tenuous at best, were given a single vote.

NCC had long maintained a tradition of splitting its votes, but in 1996, K.M. Nelson defied this mandate and voted twice for Dharmadasa.[156] He was punished by his club, but rewarded with a role on the board of selectors. 'What price gratitude,' asked Sa'adi Thawfeeq the following morning. 'The actions of the voting clubs have made Sri Lanka the laughing stock of the entire cricket world.'[157]

Problems sprang up straight away. Dharmadasa's decision to appoint Dammika Ranatunga as BCCSL CEO dangerously conflated the relationship between cricket's on-field and off-field leaders.[158] WorldTel was awarded broadcast rights under highly suspicious circumstances – and before long, issues spread beyond the boardroom.[159] In early October, news broke that Whatmore was stepping down as coach to take a role at Lancashire.[160] A brief statement claimed 'the reasons ... are personal and domestic', but Sa'adi Thawfeeq felt that there was 'more in it than meets the eye'.

Reports reckoned Whatmore had gotten fed up with the treatment he'd received from the board.[161] Equally, there were claims that Arjuna was annoyed at sharing the World Cup glory. *He* was the architect of Sri Lanka's triumph; in his mind, the foundations were in place long before Dav arrived. He was the boss and he didn't want anyone challenging his authority.*

Whatmore wasn't Sri Lanka's only casualty. There had been complications in Arjuna's relationship with Asanka Gurusinha over the years, scrapes and tears that never fully mended. Old wounds reopened as the team struggled in Sharjah: with Whatmore's departure looming, the team won just one of four. Though rumours that Mahanama wanted to head back to Colombo were false, he was clearly upset at repeatedly being

---

* Subsequent Ranatunga statements shed further light on the situation. In 2001 – once Dav was back, and Arjuna had retired – he claimed Jayasuriya and Whatmore were clashing. 'This happens when you give the coaches more power than the captain,' he railed. 'I also had the same problems, but I stood firm on my ground. He was not given as much importance as he is being given now. So the problem didn't take such a shape.' Six years later, when a Pakistani board official approached Ranatunga about appointing Whatmore as their head coach, Arjuna's message was clear: 'Avoid.'

'rested'.*[162] Gurusinha lost his spot halfway through the tournament too; the situation was bad enough that Ranatunga had to refute reports of ill feeling. 'Our team is like a family and one or two people are trying to destroy it,' he cryptically explained. Off the field, the presence of ten BBCSL officials raised eyebrows – the board were forced to clarify that five had travelled at their own expense.

So many pieces fell into place in the months leading up to the World Cup – it was disturbing to see the puzzle break apart at such a remarkable rate. Sa'adi Thawfeeq hit the nail on the head when he wrote, 'the Sri Lanka team of today is not the same which won the Wills World Cup ... it is not the same happy family it once was'.[163] It was about to get a whole lot unhappier. After their last match in Sharjah, Gurusinha gave an interview where he praised Whatmore for breathing life into the national setup.[164] It must have annoyed Arjuna no end – Gurusinha was censured by the board for giving an unauthorised interview, and fined 50 per cent of his match fees for the tournament.[165] He hit back, telling the board to waive the fine if they wanted him involved in the upcoming tour to New Zealand.

Meanwhile, issues were emerging over his future commitments.[166] Gurusinha had just signed a three-year contract to become North Melbourne's captain/coach – and had missed the first six matches of the season to be in Sharjah. Clearly, he had made a financial commitment to his new club, and was obliged to maximise his availability. But new rules meant Gurusinha would have to be back in Sri Lanka a month before the start of any future tours. He wanted to meet the team in New Zealand, but the board were unwilling to budge. Ultimately, the tour went ahead without him; his international career was over. A statement announcing his retirement noted he 'had fallen out with Sri Lankan captain Arjuna Ranatunga' and that 'the departure of Whatmore as coach of Sri Lanka occurred because Whatmore was being undermined by Ranatunga'.[167]

Gurusinha was likely not blameless through all this. One of the more combustible characters in the Sri Lankan side, he acknowledged his part in the process: 'Yes, I'd had disagreements and things like that. But at the

---

★   During the Singer World Series, he went out of his way to tell the media that he had been dropped.

end of the day, it was my decision. Nobody forced me out.' Still, it was a sorry way to treat one of the island's stalwarts.

After all, Gurusinha was arguably Sri Lanka's most reliable Test-match batsman for as long as he was in the team.* And he was a real fighter: the first Sri Lankan to score home and away centuries against Australia. Though no stylist, Arjuna reckoned him the hardest hitter of a cricket ball he ever saw. It is testament to Gurusinha's character that he shelved his smiting instincts for several years, happy to make himself the glue that bound a team of strokemakers together. His brooding intensity meant he was probably the closest to Ranatunga in terms of character; were he born in another age, he could have been a commanding national captain.

Above all, it seems a shame that the island's cricket should be scuppered by personality clashes. The BCCSL could easily have made allowances for Gurusinha. Truthfully, it made little difference whether he arrived with the team or travelled straight from Australia. But, with Dammika entrenched as CEO, it looked like little brother Arjuna was calling the shots. From the outside, it felt as though he was confusing personal wants with what was best for Sri Lanka. Those who dubbed Ranatunga 'Little Napoleon' could reflect on the aptness of the nickname, now that generals were being guillotined left, right and centre.

The brief tenure of Whatmore's successor, former Australian offspinner Bruce Yardley, did nothing to dispel the idea that Ranatunga ruled the roost. Yardley's first trip in charge saw Sri Lanka slide to a 2-0 defeat in New Zealand: having prioritised white-ball cricket for the past fifteen months, the team looked undercooked and off the pace. 1997 would prove a frustrating year in Tests. Despite fourteen Sri Lankan 100s – including seven from Aravinda's bat – the team failed to win a match, drawing nine and losing three. Often, it was a tale of opportunities lost. In April, de Silva made unbeaten twin centuries against Pakistan to give Sri Lanka a commanding lead heading into the last day at the SSC – but with Murali injured, the visitors easily survived.

---

*   After forty-one Tests, he walked away with an average of 38.92 and seven 100s to his name. Up to that stage, only Hashan Tillakaratne – who had made five 100s in thirty-eight Tests, at an average of 42.81 – had an arguably better record. Aravinda – so often spoken about as being head and shoulders above the rest – had so far scored eight 100s in fifty-five Tests, at an average of 35.46.

In the West Indies, Sri Lanka were twice ahead on first innings – but squandered strong positions, and ultimately lost the series 1-0.

Their year ended with five Tests, home and away, against India. In Sri Lanka, the contest between bat and ball was one-sided enough to almost render matches an exercise in futility. Still, the first Test lives long in the memory. India held the upper hand after batting deep into the second day – but over the next six sessions, Jayasuriya and Mahanama ground the visiting bowlers into the dust. The pair put on 283 on day three and 264 on day four. Though Sri Lanka were 50 ahead going into the final day, with Sanath 326*, Ranatunga showed no inclination to declare. Some 30,000 expectantly flooded through Khettarama's gates, but the festival atmosphere fell flat when Mahanama and Jaysuriya went in the space of three balls.[168] Their partnership had been worth 574. Though Sanath was ecstatic to have made 340, he knew he'd come agonisingly close to bettering Brian Lara's record score.

By the time they were done, Sri Lanka had piled on an impossible 952-6, a record score in Tests that looks unlikely to be broken. Of course, there were detractors: those who pointed out that records lose value amidst such fruitless cricket, that Arjuna might have declared once Sri Lanka were well ahead, or that such flat pitches do little to serve the sport. It's hard to rebut those opinions, but Sri Lanka's run-glut no doubt boosted spirits. Dharmadasa reckoned it meant a lot 'in the development of a real Test team'.[169]

For the two men at the heart of the feast, the bounty of runs meant very different things. Since the World Cup, Jayasuriya had been soaring. But while runs had flown from his bat in Tests throughout 1997, he'd largely batted with the hurry of a man late for dinner reservations. Now, he looked hungry only for runs. Sanath was into his 290s before he struck a 6; in batting more than thirteen hours, he had shown the world that he possessed patience to go along with the pyrotechnics. There could be no greater tribute than Tendulkar's: 'I have not seen Don Bradman bat, but I have seen Sanath Jayasuriya. I have not seen a better batsman in my cricketing career.'[170]

Mahanama's situation was more precarious. For over a decade, he had been a true servant to Sri Lankan cricket – but his relationship with Arjuna had often been fraught, and in recent years he'd been shunted up and down the batting order with increasing flippancy. Plus, since the World Cup, Atapattu, Mahela Jayawardene and Russel Arnold had increasingly challenged for spots in the side. Gurusinha had gone; many felt Mahanama might be next out the door. Before the Test, Aravinda approached him with a message: 'Rosh, make sure you get some runs in this game.'[171] With his back to the wall, he made 225 – underpinning his value to the team and proving he could dig in for long periods despite his problems with cramps.

Runs kept flowing through a rain-interrupted second Test. Aravinda struck twin centuries for the second time in the year, while Jayasuriya bludgeoned the ball to all corners en route to a blistering, near run-a-ball 199. At one stage, Ajay Jadeja pretended to perform black magic on the ground.[172] It was a joke with serious undertones – this India team had no idea how to get Sanath out.

With these two at the crease, bowlers' margins for error seemed so slight. Anything overpitched was pounced upon; equally, marginally short balls disappeared to the square boundaries. No one has ever scored more runs in a two-match series than Jayasuriya's 571.[173] Aravinda became the first and only batsman to notch three consecutive Test centuries twice in a year. Say what you like about flat pitches, but there was no denying these were two rare batsmen at the peak of their powers.

Sri Lanka knew things would be tougher when they travelled to India three months later. Six of their seven previous Tests there had resulted in innings blowouts – ultimately, they were happy to escape the series with a share of the spoils. There were positives too: Atapattu overcame the horror start to his Test career with 108 in Mohali and 98 in Mumbai. And while India were on top for most of the series, Sri Lanka showed heart, twice batting through the final day to cling onto draws. In the first Test, they slipped to 106-5, and needed a masterful Aravinda century to carry them to safety. During the nine-Test run from the start of the Pakistan series to the end of the year, he scored 1,188 runs at 108.

But while Sri Lanka often excelled with the bat during 1997, they were much more ordinary with the ball. Murali had emerged as the clear pack leader, but in 501 overs could only muster 40 wickets at 31.65. Vaas struggled with back injuries and found his scalps costing more than 40; though Dharmasena bowled nicely on occasion, his fast off-spin wasn't really suited to Test cricket. At times, Jayasuriya still looked the most potent bowler.

But work was underway. Bruce Yardley had first worked with Murali at a spin camp in 1991; now the two got down to serious business.[174] Having watched Murali bowl poorly in his first Test in charge, Yardley told it to him straight. If Murali wanted to be the best off-spinner in the world, he had to learn to mix it up. He would have to work *hard*.

Where others might have shied away, Murali embraced the challenge head on. 'We used to talk a lot,' Murali told me. 'I didn't use to like to bowl around the wicket; he made me do certain things. And he helped me a lot through that period – that's the period when I was learning. He was there to guide me.' Over the next fifteen months, Murali and Yardley spent hundreds of hours practising. Murali learnt to dip the ball through the air – making it much riskier for batsmen to use their feet against him – and began understanding how to control and impart drift. Yardley also opened his eyes to the importance of angles: by using the crease he could keep batsmen guessing.* Yardley's tenure was a seminal period of development for Murali's bowling; it is no coincidence that 1998 was his breakout year in Tests.

Though Yardley had great success developing Murali, he couldn't get Sri Lanka to take Test cricket more seriously. The board remained focused on ODIs: after all, they were the money-spinner, the people's choice and the team's strongest suit. Arjuna's men played twenty-eight in 1997, losing just seven – and rediscovered the swagger which had slipped away towards the end of 1996. Aravinda was transcendent as Sri Lanka claimed the Singer-Akai Cup in Sharjah; Jayasuriya stole the show as they romped to the Pepsi Independence Cup the following month.

After losing a one-off ODI against the West Indies, the Lankans went on a nine-match winning streak, only broken when they rested Murali, Jayasuriya and Vaas. First, they easily won the Asia Cup; though India were more competitive in a head-to-head series, the batsmen continued to dazzle, carrying Sri Lanka to 3-0 victory.

---

* With Murali becoming more comfortable from around the wicket, it became harder for left-handers to pad him away. Once he'd developed the doosra, it became a menacing angle to right-handers too.

Back in Lahore for the Wills Golden Jubilee, it looked for all money like Sri Lanka would claim another piece of silverware. If chasing the West Indies' 238-run target in 39.4 overs wasn't impressive enough, they went one better against Pakistan, gunning down 281 in 40 overs flat. Though they lost momentum, and the final, after resting their strike bowlers, in the past few months Arjuna's men had reaffirmed their status as ODI cricket's wonderboys. Journalists compared them to the Harlem Globetrotters; with Sanath and Aravinda brutalising bowlers, Sri Lanka were unstoppable.

Jayasuriya was unique: a world-class batsman with the spirit of a pinch hitter;* a nightmare for opposition bowlers, who knew that the longer he batted, the less chance they had. Across 1997, an average Jayasuriya innings yielded 50 off 44 balls. That gave the rest of his teammates 256 balls to play with: considering there would usually be at least 10 extras, they only needed to add 220 – striking at 85 – to lift the team to 280. Of course, the spectre of Aravinda made bowling at Sri Lanka an increasingly daunting prospect. You could get through Sanath, but you'd still have to deal with a genius who'd effortlessly piled up more runs at a better average.

While much of their success rested on Sanath and Aravinda's shoulders, Sri Lanka found real strength in depth too, with seven batsmen averaging over 34 in ODI cricket across the year. And, unlike in Tests, the bowling was well stocked and penetrative. Murali, Sajeewa de Silva, Jayasuriya and Vaas all took north of 30 wickets – of the regular bowlers, only Jayasuriya (5.03) went at more than 5 an over. So, on the whole, Sri Lanka were keeping sides under 250 – the sort of total you'd back them to better every day of the week. The sole caveat was that almost all of their ODIs in 1997 took place in Asia. Outside of their home continent, they lost two of three: clearly bosses of their own backyard, Sri Lanka still needed to prove they could do it on the road.

A Test-match triumph finally arrived with Zimbabwe in January 1998, ending a sixteen-month barren run. Though victory was expected, there

---

* His 1,178 ODI runs in 1997 – the third most of any player – came at a strike-rate of 113.59, a mark no other batsman got close to. Of those who scored more than 100 runs, only Shahid Afridi struck faster than a run a ball.

were encouraging signs: Atapattu continued his charge with a maiden double-hundred in Kandy, while Murali bagged his first ten-for in Tests. During the first innings, he bowled 18 maidens in 29 overs; across the match half his victims were clean bowled. His big spin had long seen him terrorise tailenders; now, improved flight and subtle variations made him a tall order for top-order batters.

Sri Lanka understood the trip to South Africa in March would pose far greater challenges. Despite surrendering the Tests 2-0, they could feel proud of the way they competed. With eight scalps in each match, Murali enjoyed his best series yet outside Asia; had any of the batsmen stood up and scored a century, the team might well have left with a share of the spoils.

The Tri-series that followed was far less spiriting. In six attempts, Sri Lanka could only notch two wins – failing to qualify for the final. In an embarrassing sequence, Pakistan easily chased 295 in Kimberley, then won the next game by 110 – skittling Ranatunga's men for 139. In the last match, they were torn apart by South Africa, done for 105 in 37 overs. Batting for the first time in a while on bouncier, bowler-friendly wickets, Jayasuriya averaged just 29.50, striking at a much more human 71.37.

Nor was all well behind the scenes. During the tour, Yardley went for dinner with some of the squad and shocked the table into silence when he announced he felt the time had come to move on from Arjuna and Aravinda.[175] In his mind, they were lazy in the field and averse to criticism, prone to being selfish and stubborn.[176] Ranatunga's spiky captaincy sometimes spilled over into nastiness: the team would be better off led by Tillakaratne, Mahanama or Jayasuriya. What's more, ousting Arjuna and Aravinda would give the team fresh impetus, opening up spaces for hungry young batsmen on the fringes of the side.

He would have a tough time convincing others to see it his way. The duo's achievements, culminating in the triumphant World Cup showing, had lifted them to exalted status in Sri Lanka. Notwithstanding those feats, they'd both been in terrific form with the bat. Arjuna had enjoyed an extended purple patch in ODI cricket, while Aravinda's form since the start of the World Cup put him on a very short list of the world's elite batsmen. To top it all off, they had the backing of the board.[*]

So Yardley got singular advice: tell the board at your own risk, because you'll likely be the one that ends up getting sacked. Yardley knew the landscape of Sri Lankan cricket well enough by now, but was determined to speak his mind. Once his manager's report arrived at the BCCSL, he was summoned before Sumathipala. The eye he had recently lost to a melanoma was given as the official reason, but there could be little doubt as to why Yardley was truly dismissed. The World Cup had given Arjuna all the authority he dreamed of. Sri Lankan cricket was his. It would take something dramatic to unseat him.

ONE LAST HURRAH

Roy Dias was soon installed as Yardley's replacement – though foreign coaches had done much to propel Sri Lanka forward since 1995, for now, a local was a better fit.[177] The board needed someone to support Arjuna. A brains trust comprising Dias, Mendis, Ranatunga and de Silva had a comfortingly familiar look.

Dias' first engagement was a home series against New Zealand in mid-1998, largely made memorable by the batting of young Mahela Jayawardene. Though Jayawardene had made an assured start as a Test cricketer, it was only in the second Test at Galle that he announced the extent of his lavish talent. Rarely has a wicket been as tricky to bat on as curator Jayananda Warnaweera's first effort – which no one bar Mahela got to grips with. With the ball turning sharply, the visitors simply couldn't find ways to score; Jayawardene, meanwhile, anchored Sri Lanka's effort with a delightfully fluid 167.

---

[*]   Sumathipala's relationship with Dharmadasa had quickly broken down, but the bond with Arjuna and Aravinda remained strong. In the lead-up to the 1998 elections, the duo supported Sumathipala's candidature. As luck would have it, he was elected to the presidency unopposed, since a new law – which stated that board office bearers should have played Division I cricket – wiped out his opponent, Ana Punchihewa.

'It was a massive, massive Test match for me,' he remembered when we spoke. 'My instinct was, whatever happens, I need to look positive to score runs. Anything loose, I was scoring runs; when I wasn't, I forced myself to score. I kept attacking them.' This was the exuberance of youth all right – unburdened by the fear which cowed other batsmen, Jayawardene went about his business without a shred of worry.

Like all the best players of spin, he was so quick to pick up lengths, equally happy to rock back and dispatch anything marginally short or get well forward and smother the turn. His stay was spiced with eighteen hits to the fence: young Mahela looked to have every shot in the book. When he was done, all in attendance knew they'd seen something very special. Not all runs are made equal, and Jayawardne's were worth so much to Sri Lanka. 'It was a brilliant feeling,' he told me. 'Because after that innings we won the Test. I just felt that I belonged here. You need that kind of innings early in your career: that was the innings that defined who I was as an international cricketer.'

Having gone 1-0 down in the series, Sri Lanka completed the turnaround at the SSC, with New Zealand again unable to ward off the spinners. Murali was developing into a more thoughtful and threatening bowler, and the team were unearthing new reserves of toughness. For the first time since 1995, they had won a Test against a side other than Zimbabwe.

Next up was a tour of England, Sri Lanka's first since 1991. Despite the strides the team had made since then – and the fact Sri Lanka had won the sides' last four encounters – the English still deemed them unworthy of more than a single Test. 'Always when you go to England, you get one Test match,' Murali grumbled when we spoke. 'We were not regarded.' Such snobbery stung. There was a feeling at home that cricket had lifted Sri Lanka out of mediocrity: as Shanaka Amarasinghe eloquently put it, 'Sri Lankans live vicariously through their cricketers … They give us a sense of identity, recognition and achievement in a land whose potential seems to be eroding.'[178] Arjuna's men arrived with their backs up and a point to prove – with plenty of affronted fans ready to cheer their cause.

Roshan Mahanama's exclusion caused furore at home, but at least the schedule was in Sri Lanka's favour. The team landed in London almost seven weeks before the Test kicked off, giving the batters plenty of time to acclimatise and find form. In the Emirates Triangular final, Murali had Atherton caught in the 26th over; as England tried to push on in the last 10, he bagged 3 big wickets to stop them dead. These sides had scarcely met in the past five years, but Murali's 5 wickets here – allied to 18 scalps in two first-class matches on tour – should have given England ample warning of the dangers he presented ahead of the Test. Yet, Murali felt he remained an unknown quantity. 'They knew about me for bad reasons,' he volunteered when we spoke. 'Not for my performances. Even though I was close to 200 wickets, nobody knew.'*

Arjuna smilingly accepted the trophy after the match, but admitted it would be 'a totally different ball game' when the teams got to the Oval. Yet, he was pleasantly surprised when he arrived in South London. The English wicket he expected – the sort of grassy seamer that haunted Sri Lankan dreams – was nowhere in sight. In fact, it was England's coach, David Lloyd, who was left scratching his head at the dry, dusty wicket.

Though the coin came down Ranatunga's way, England's bowlers breathed a sigh of relief when they heard they could put their feet up. It looked a poor decision at stumps, yet Arjuna's reasoning was entirely logical. For Sri Lanka to win, Murali would have to shoulder a heavy workload. Were they to bat first and make a big score, he might well have to enforce the follow-on.[179] This way, Murali was assured of a break.

Having struggled to impose himself on the opening day, Arjuna's secret weapon was more central come day two – regularly outfoxing England's lower order as he took 5 of the last 6 wickets. After batting nearly 160 overs, the hosts never expected to lose the match – but Jayasuriya and Aravinda built a game-changing partnership. Having endured a quiet tour,** Sanath broke loose, dominating bowlers from the

---

* Three years earlier, when Aravinda spent the season at Kent, Murali tagged along. Jack Birkenshaw found him some club cricket at Leicester Ivanhoe – yet despite already having 100 Test scalps in his bag, no one had heard of him. Indeed, they wanted Murali to turn out for the second XI, until they saw him bowl and realised what they were dealing with.

** Worried about swinging freely in English conditions, he had been striking a little tentatively – and done nothing to change the minds of those in the England camp who had dismissed him as a mere slogger.

get-go. Width was what he wanted: when he got it, the ball disappeared to the fence. There were scything cuts and cover drives he just leant on – by the time Aravinda had arrived, he had already passed 50. The pair made running in seem an unenviable task; increasingly, the bowlers looked at a loss over where to land the ball. The worst punishment was reserved for leg-spinner Ian Salisbury: it was hard to know whether to feel sorrier for him or Jon Crawley, ever in the firing line at short leg.

While Jayasuirya played with the fury of one scorned, Aravinda oozed the quiet confidence of a man with no more to prove. In earlier times, he might have tried to match Sanath stroke for stroke – now, he was happy to play the understudy, contributing 69 of the pair's first 200. Nonetheless, there was something about his stillness at the crease, the precision and economy of his movement, that made it clear that you were watching a master. Once, you would nervously wait for him to make a mistake; now he had the look of a player who would never get out.

When Jayasuriya finally fell, the pair had amassed 243 in 54.1 overs – Sanath sprinting to 213 in 278 balls.* Those in the stands who'd once dismissed his shot-making as savagery rose in awestruck applause – aware of their folly. Jayasuriya wasn't degrading Test cricket; he was just playing it in fast forward. In doing so, he changed the game's equation. Arjuna and Aravinda kept squeezing the gas, and Sri Lanka went level 50 overs ahead of schedule. All in all, they batted 10 balls less than England but scored 146 more. A result was back on the table.

In the lead-up to the Test, when asked if Murali would be able to spin the ball on English pitches, Sri Lanka's manager Ranjit Fernando assured the media 'He would turn it on the M4'.[180] Having bathed in the hot August sun for three days, the Oval wicket was certainly not a road. Introduced in the 9th over, Murali immediately made Mark Butcher sweat. Time and again, Butcher pressed forward – but found that balls pitching on leg stump were fizzing past his outside edge.

It was a slow and tormenting assassination – with fielders crowded around the bat, chirping in Sinhala, Mark Butcher looked as lost and

---

* Jayasuriya's five Test centuries to this stage included a triple-hundred, a double-hundred and a score of 199. Throughout his career, he was hard to remove once well set. Of the fourteen centuries he made in all, only four were scores of 130 or less.

confused as a tourist at a Colombo bus stop. Each miss heaped pressure onto his shoulders; eventually, he decided to dance down the track and hoist Murali over extra cover. Some of the fielders clapped his bravery; Arjuna let out a guffaw. He wasn't so lucky next time around. Butcher charged, but couldn't get to the pitch of a vicious dipper. The ball jagged past his outside edge; Kaluwitharana whipped off the bails. Second ball, Graeme Hick got stuck on the crease and was trapped dead in front. England went into the last day 2 down and still 90 behind. They knew they had their work cut out.

The Lankans celebrated wildly when Steve James gave Murali his third the next morning – popping one up to Mahela at silly mid-off. Still, it was Alec Stewart's wicket they really wanted; though there seemed a shred of misfortune in the way that it fell. With Aravinda off the field for treatment, Mark Ramprakash tried to steal a run to twelfth man Chandana at square leg. The single would have been on to anyone else in the field, but Chandana was razor sharp. On the run, he gathered cleanly, and produced a perfect quick-release throw, gunning down the one stump he had to aim at.

Though Chandana's work spoiled Murali's shot at a perfect 10, it was crucial to Sri Lanka getting over the line. Had Stewart held out for the whole session, England might have been able to swallow enough time to cling on for a draw. Instead, Murali had Crawley bowled through the gate on the brink of lunch. Sri Lanka went in knowing they'd done the hard work; England might well have prayed as they broke bread – by now, it was clear only a miracle could save them.

Ben Hollioake was lbw first ball after the break; though Murali couldn't complete his hat-trick, it wasn't long before he had more to add to his bag. Cork and Salisbury were outfoxed in the same over; Ramprakash and Darren Gough held out bravely to take the game into the last session, but it was only a matter of time. They fell in quick succession, the innings coming to a close when Gough was bowled around his legs with a perfect top-spinner. The doosra, essentially an extension of the delivery, was clearly on its way. For all Murali's achievements – 16 wickets in the Test and 9 in the second innings – there was plenty more to come.

As if the crowd hadn't been entertained enough through four and a half days, Jayasuriya tucked into the 36-run chase with relish. The uppercut he launched into the stands, with both feet off the ground, felt celebratory. Sri Lanka romped home without losing a wicket; it was without doubt their biggest Test win so far. 'Until then, we didn't have the ammunition to win Test matches overseas,' Hathursinghe told me. 'By winning in England, we opened a lot of people's eyes.'

Murali's exploits transformed him into a star. His match figures of 16-220 were the fifth best of all time. Clearly, he wasn't afraid to roll his sleeves up either: the 113.5 overs he sent down an unprecedented workload for a modern bowler.* In an age of increasing professionalism, Murali was a throwback, happy to bowl and bowl until wickets came. Pundits might talk about the supple wrist and rotating shoulder, yet Murali's success was equally founded on physical fitness, an iron will and a refusal to let the ball out of his hand.

Disappointingly, with the scalps came speculation – what you might call the post-Hair effect.**[181] Of course, a degree of scepticism was natural. No one had ever seen an off-spinner turn the ball like Murali, nor deliver it with that sort of action. Every time he produced a magic ball, the batter would ask himself 'how has he done that?' It mattered little that Murali's wickets were as much a result of an unwavering work ethic as his physical tools. The more success he found, the more suspicion surrounded him.

For all the furore, most truly impartial observers were satisfied. *Wisden* included him in their Five Cricketers of the Year for 1999; and Aravinda helped broker a deal with Lancashire, who benefited no end from his insatiable wicket-lust. Across six first-class matches in 1999, he took 66 at a shade under 12; Murali felt they had never come so easy.

While his emergence as a matchwinner in all conditions was the crucial turn in Sri Lanka's development as a Test team, they were growing from top to bottom. Young batsmen shone during the inaugural Asian

---

*   The 683 balls Murali bowled in the Test was the fourteenth most of all time, and the fifth most in the post-war era. The last man to deliver as many in a Test was Tony Lock in 1962; no one has come close to bowling as many since.

**   At the end of the fourth day, Lloyd admitted 'I have my own opinions which I will make known to the authorities.' He's been gracious enough to retrospectively admit that Murali was 'a genius', and that the Sri Lanka Test had put him in a sticky situation. Even so, Butcher told Andrew Fidel Fernando that there wasn't a 'single bloke' in the team who didn't have doubts over Murali's action.

Test Championships in 1999: though well outgunned in the final by a formidable, full-strength Pakistan side, Sri Lanka could see these performances as progress.

Clearly, World Cup success expedited the team's development in red-ball cricket. For so long, self-belief had been a high hurdle the Lankans struggled to overcome; now, they had it in droves. Being tagged 'world champions' helped cast aside feelings of inferiority; a process started by Arjuna and developed by Whatmore came to a rousing, unexpected crescendo on a rainy night in Lahore. Players got better overnight. Just look at Jayasuriya, whose immense potential – for so long only seen in dribs and drabs – flooded onto the field in the wake of World Cup glory. On the field at least, Sri Lanka had successfully used the tournament as a springboard. Still, the road ahead was far from clear.

LOST ONCE MORE

So often in Sri Lankan cricket, triumph and tragedy seem to go hand in hand. Victory at The Oval, which launched Murali as a star and suggested a new ceiling for the team in Tests, was no different. The next twelve months would prove very tough going. Soon enough, the World Cup would be starting all over again – bringing a whole new set of challenges.

In 1996, Sri Lanka had snuck up on the rest of the world like thieves in the night; now they were the team with a target on their back. They had managed to circumvent a shortage of seamers in Asia, but could they do the same at the start of the English summer? Would the batters be able to gorge themselves with such reckless abandon with the ball wobbling left and right? The 1999 tournament would reveal much about this Sri Lanka side. Unfortunately, it brought answers the island might not have been ready for.

A young squad led by Hashan Tillakaratne fared well at the Commonwealth Games in September 1998, but Sri Lanka's stock in one-day cricket devalued during the course of the year. Where they had probably been the world's best team through 1997, by the time the World Cup rolled around they were 9-1 outsiders. It was little surprise given their form in the lead-up to the tournament.

The slump seemed to start at the Wills International Cup in Bangladesh. Sri Lanka suffered a humbling defeat at the hands of South Africa; more worryingly, Murali tore ligaments in his shoulder and missed the Sharjah tournament the following month.[182] Without him, the team failed to beat India and Zimbabwe in four attempts. It felt like the hunger once driving Sri Lanka had been replaced with a sense of contentment. The main movers were still the stars of 1996: though Atapattu had managed to make himself a regular, hopes that Avishka Gunawardene could be 'the next Jayasuriya' fell flat. As Steven Lynch put it, this felt like a group 'growing old together'.*[183]

Sri Lanka's struggles were drawn into sharper focus by The Carlton and United Series in Australia. It was clear from the get-go that the new enemy would not be obliging hosts. The media zeroed in on Murali: where crowds had once shown the spinner sympathy, they now took relish in crying 'no-ball' as he danced to the wicket.[184] Some even shouted at him in the street – it seems strange that a bowler's action should incite such vitriol.

Cynically, the release of Darrell Hair's autobiography coincided with the tour; during their first Tri-series game, the team learned he had labelled Murali's action 'diabolical'.[185] Since Murali had been cleared by the ICC, Hair's stance struck as strange and pompous. In effect, he was claiming to know better than the doctors. Equally, his opinion raised serious questions over how he could serve as an 'independent adjudicator' when he'd predetermined Murali a cheat.

The ICC censured Hair for bringing the game into disrepute, but couldn't escape a portion of the blame. Despite the no-balling of Murali swelling into an ugly international scandal, there had been no change to the 'chucking laws'. In fact, the last amendment still allowed any umpire not 'entirely satisfied' with the 'absolute fairness' of a bowler's action to

---

* Despite the increasing sense of staleness, and Jayawardene's impeccable start to life in Test cricket, there seemed a reluctance to include the young prodigy in the one-day team. Meanwhile Vaas' progress had been stalled by injuries; though not yet 25, Pushpakumara seems to have already been sidelined. Suresh Perera had failed to live up to lofty hopes – plus unwanted scrutiny from the ICC saw Dharmasena excluded until the next millennium.

call 'no-ball'. Once upon a time, such legislation had been necessary; now it was plainly nonsensical.

Hearts shot into mouths when umpire Steve Davis called Murali in Sri Lanka's opening match. The spinner turned to the umpire fearfully, and got a warm smile in return. 'Murali, [you] overstepped, don't worry. I don't have a problem with your action.'[186] Sadly, others didn't feel the same. In a bizarre turn of events, match referee Peter Van der Merwe gave an interview on ABC Radio where he announced that 'some of the balls [Murali] bowls look a bit doubtful,' and that he would 'be sending a report to the ICC.*

Why Van der Merwe would shoot from the hip so audaciously is beyond explanation. His words intensified the media circus – and freed the arm of any umpire who might wish to call Murali. I can't help but feel that Sri Lanka's lack of sway, their enduring perception as an insignificant minnow, influenced Murali's treatment. Would Van der Merwe and Hair have acted so boldly if it was England's star spinner under the spotlight? More to the point, would the ICC have allowed an obsolete law to remain in place? It is pointless speculating, but you can understand those who feel that justice and equality are afterthoughts when it comes to the 'gentleman's game'.

There was little respite inside the boundary. Sri Lanka lost twice in a day to Australia 'A' in the lead-up to the Tri-series, and showed scant improvements once the tournament got going. They failed to defend totals big and small in their first three matches, and had now lost eight on the bounce. Steven Lynch felt they were lacking an 'enforcer' with the ball, noticing Ranatunga had ballooned since the English summer.[187] Clearly, Sri Lanka's hunger hadn't disappeared entirely.

---

* This clearly contravened the procedure Van der Merwe should have followed. If a match referee felt a bowler was delivering the ball illegally, he was supposed to liaise with the home board and discreetly obtain video footage from the official broadcaster. That footage should then be sent to the ICC's advisory panel, who would come to a decision themselves. The ICC explicitly stated that a player going through this process should remain anonymous, since revealing his identity 'may be prejudicial to his public image and to the assessment of him by umpires in subsequent matches'. Strangest of all, Van der Merwe never submitted a report.

Though Vaas finally came good in Hobart, it was one of those games where winning looked like hard work. Chances slipped through Lankan fingers; 163-2 heading into the last 10 overs, they lost a flurry of wickets to set up a nerve-shredding finish. Thankfully Arjuna, runner and all, kept his head. While it was a relief to break the duck, nerves jangled ahead of Adelaide. Strangely, it was the umpires who inspired trepidation: Emerson and McQuillan, the pair standing the last time Murali had been called, would be presiding over the contest.

Murali got through 9 balls before Emerson's awful cry came. 'No-ball.' It was happening all over again. The cricket world had been bemused when Hair and Emerson assaulted Murali three summers earlier, but by 1999 most had formed an opinion. On commentary, Ian Botham wasted no time lambasting the umpire.[188] 'If I was Arjuna, I'd be telling him "If he's throwing, why haven't you called him the over before? You're a club cricketer, you have no experience in this matter."'

Ranatunga's response was equally visceral. Though it cost him public support, in a sense, it was his piece de resistance. Rarely has he looked more imperious. Inside he must have been bubbling with fury, yet watching on, you had the sense he was in total control. He marched over to Emerson, gesticulating across the field; once the finger-jabbing started, the umpire backed away. For a moment, Emerson clapped back, but he was visibly wilting in the face of Arjuna's fury. 'You can't just do this,' he berated Emerson, before swaggering over to the English batsmen. 'I'm taking my boys off,' he told them, patting Hick on the shoulder apologetically.

'[BCCSL president, Thilanga] Sumathipala had been getting calls saying there was gossip going around the social circles of Australia,' explained Sri Lanka's manager Ranjit Fernando. 'Thilanga premeditates a lot of things – he doesn't leave things to chance. He called me, and said in the event of him being no-balled, try to make a bit of a scene.' The plan had always been for Ranatunga to lead his men to the boundary's edge, but in the midst of his fury, he almost marched them straight into the dressing room. Fernando and Saliya Ahangama had to keep them inside the ropes, otherwise the match would have been forfeited.

It ended up being paused for around twelve minutes: eventually, the team agreed to play 'under protest'. It was good to see Sri Lanka huddling around Murali, and the young off-spinner mustering a smile.

Botham complained that 'One man's moment of glory,' was ruining an international cricket match.

Emerson's antics had raised tempers, and the game descended into a squalid affair. When the umpire ignored Murali's request to stand closer to the stumps,* Ranatunga saw red once more. 'You are out of order,' he chided Emerson. There was another round of finger-wagging; eventually, Arjuna made a mark on the ground and told Emerson where to stand. The umpire refused, insisting he was in charge. 'I'm in charge of my team,' Ranatunga countered. He had grown used to being the boss, and was unwilling to budge. Not when Murali's career was on the line. Emerson, on the other hand, seemed upset by the whole affair – and he and McQuillan completely lost control of the game moving forward.**[189]

The fractious atmosphere wasn't helped by England's combative attitude. Stewart's men took exception to Ranatunga's bickering with the umpires; at one point, Stewart ranted, 'Your conduct today has been appalling for a country's captain.' You have to wonder if he'd feel the same in hindsight. Of course, the umpire is the arbiter of actions on a cricket field – but, is he beyond reproach, free to govern the game any way he likes? Would England have blindly accepted Emerson's decisions if their star bowler was suddenly called a chucker?

The acrimony grew as the game went down to the wire. In the final over, Mahanama tried to steal a single and clashed with Gough halfway down the pitch: England felt he had changed his running line, and were annoyed he was allowed to stay at the crease. If Gough's dummy head-butt was inflected with irony, Stewart's shoulder barge was a clear act of aggression. England's captain defended his men's behaviour at the post-match press conference, high-handedly claiming, 'The way Ranatunga went about things with the umpire after the no-ball call was out of order. Things got very tense after that.'[190]

While drama and discord overshadowed the contest, the two sides produced cricket that kept the crowd enthralled right to the last. Having

---

* As in 1996, Murali switched to leg-breaks. This time, Emerson resisted the bait.

** Jayasuriya was awarded 6 runs for a ball that clearly bounced inside the ropes; a Vince Wells beamer managed to slip through the net. At one stage, Gough bowled a 7-ball over. Most strikingly, Jayawardene should have been run out on 33 when he was well short of his crease, but Emerson refused to send the decision to the third umpire.

posted 302, England were well in control after an early double strike. It took a superb innings from young Mahela Jayawardene to drag Sri Lanka out of the mire. In making 120 off 111 with minimal fuss, he showed himself to have a wise head on young shoulders. Murali sliced the winning runs over cover with 2 balls to spare. Having been coasting for months, Sri Lanka produced their best cricket with backs to the wall.

Unsurprisingly, both umpires lodged complaints against Ranatunga – though it seemed more than a little unjust that he should be hauled into the Match Referee's office alone. At least his predicament deflected gawking eyes from Murali's elbow. And he had the support of his countrymen. The post-match press conference was an absolute scrum; now it was manager Fernando's turn to play his own trump card.

'Normally the captain goes to the press conference, but I told Arjuna "You're not going",' he recalls. 'There were at least 200 people, and I was the one being grilled. Then I decided, I'm not going to be calm and cool – I'm also going to take it strongly. I said things that would have annoyed them: "Look, our captain has behaved with complete decorum." That annoyed them more.' Fernando has a certain way with words, and pinched headlines with his incontrovertible assessment that the game had been spoiled by Emerson's decision to 'play God'.[191]

Fernando and Ranatunga are men born in different times, cut from different cloths. The affable Ranjit played in an age when MCC requests were accepted as orders; Arjuna, a street fighter from the start, thumbed his nose at colonial deference and single-handedly moulded Sri Lanka into a more combative outfit. I had to put it to Fernando – was he always happy with Arjuna's pugnacity? 'I had to be,' he replied. 'I had to be supportive of him at every turn. Maybe it was something you would not have condoned in a different situation, but in that situation, I had to be very, very much with him.'

Of course, the fact Ranatunga's brother Dammika was CEO of the BCCSL – and that new board president Sumathipala remained a strong ally – meant that the country's cricket authorities were squarely in camp Arjuna. Sumathipala was on a flight straight away; in the meantime, he instructed Fernando to hire the best lawyers in Australia. Before long, the manager's suite had been transformed into a war room: this had swelled into a national issue.

Ranatunga rocked up to his hearing, four days after the match, flanked by a pair of hard-hitting, Melbourne lawyers.[192] Blindsided, Van der Merwe rescheduled the hearing for Perth; the international media, baying for Arjuna's blood, lamented the intrusion of legal professionals into the game. Van der Merwe spoke despondently at the end of the five-hour hearing – strongarmed by threats of legal action against him and the ICC, he could only impose a suspended six-match ban, and fine Arjuna 75 per cent of his match fee.

On the whole, the media felt Ranatunga and the BCCSL had sinned irredeemably by challenging the authority of the umpire and match referee. Writing in *The Telegraph*, Paul Newman complained that Ranatunga's fine was 'just £60', ignoring that this said more about Sri Lanka's salaries than any failing on the part of the ICC.[193] Bizarrely, *The Independent*'s Stephen Brenkley included telling the umpire 'where he should stand' on Arjuna's rap sheet – seemingly forgetting that it was the bowler's prerogative to ask the umpire to move, and not unusual for a spinner to do so.[194] Equally, you have to wonder if he was aware of Van der Merwe's radio outburst when he claimed the match referee had shown 'dignity … in abundance'.[195]

Through all of this, there was very little talk of Emerson. Journalists gobbled up the bones they were given, without realising that the true meat of the matter lay somewhere else entirely. Some swam against the tide. David Hopps hit the nail on the head when he declared that 'to many' Ranatunga had the 'air of a man behaving badly because of his sense of the greater good'.[196] Henry Blofeld refreshingly assessed that it was 'impossible to believe [Emerson] did not make the journey from Perth to Adelaide with his mind made up that he was going to call Muralitharan, come what may'.[197]

Scrutiny fully shifted onto the umpire's shoulders on 26 January, when several newspapers reported that he had been given sick leave from his day job due to a 'stress-related illness'.[198] The ACB, supposedly unaware of Emerson's condition, stood him down for his upcoming engagements. He responded by bringing a defamation case against the board president. Increasingly viewed as a 'loose cannon' by Australian authorities, Emerson never umpired another international match.[199]

His actions speak of a muddled mind. Officiating international sport surely ranks as one of the more stress-inducing professions the whole world over. That Emerson wanted to continue umpiring, while claiming himself too stressed to 'work', beggars belief. Once relations had soured between Emerson and the ACB, he claimed they directed his no-balling of Murali.[200] For his part, he remains unrepentant. In 2016, he gave a frenzied interview to *The Australian*, claiming he was the victim of an internationalist ICC conspiracy.[*201]

The way Murali's third public hanging played out will inevitably splinter opinion, yet surely all can agree the whole thing was a stain on cricket. Given the turmoil, it was little surprise that Sri Lanka were well short of their best for the remainder of the tournament. Blown away by Gough and Mark Ealham in Perth, they then allowed Australia to plunder 310 in Melbourne. Jayasuriya had his forearm broken; Murali struggled with a groin strain, and ultimately had to head back to the UWA for a fresh round of testing. He passed with flying colours.[202]

Without the duo, Sri Lanka struggled through a Tri-series in India. Though most felt these matches had little bearing on the upcoming World Cup, it was impossible to ignore the fact the team had lost fifteen of their last twenty. Any lustre from 1996 had worn off; the fear this batting unit once inspired had dissipated. And the squad selected for England exacerbated Sri Lanka's shortcomings. With eleven of the fourteen from the last World Cup still in place, and the other changes like-for-like,[**] it felt as though the selectors paid no mind to conditions. Three frontline spinners seemed excessive, and only left room for three out-and-out

---

[*]   'Because the countries are divided, the ICC used to always vote 7-3 because India and Pakistan want to throw nuclear bombs on each other in real life but in cricket they'll vote together, Sri Lanka will vote with Pakistan and India, and Bangladesh they brought in – so that's four out of the 10 straight off,' he explained. 'South Africa and Zimbabwe are so racist they'll only vote for the black countries, the West Indies are probably the most racist side in the world, so they'll always vote with the black countries … Now the ICC has started [*sic*] clamping down on chucking, why? Murali's not playing any more – that's why. They needed Murali to play for Sri Lanka because he was what kept them competitive. Now that he's gone … they're a rabble again.'

[**]   Jayawardene replaced the retired Gurusinha; Ruwan Kalpage came in for the banned Dharmasena. Eric Upashantha was preferred to Pushpakumara, and Hathurusinghe was the extra man.

quicks. 'And one of them was kind of like a standby,' Jayawardene told me. 'Eric – I don't think they had plans of him playing any matches.'

'I don't think [the selectors] knew we were playing with a Dukes white ball,' Hathurusinghe scathingly added. Rumours swirled that Ranatunga and de Silva had stormed out of a selection meeting.[203] For Aravinda, who had seen first hand at Kent the damage seamers could cause during the early English summer, it must have been especially frustrating. While there might not have been a cast of swing kings lurking in the Sri Lankan clubs, any one of Nuwan Zoysa, Pushpakumara, Sajeewa de Silva, Suresh Perera and Ruchira Perera might well have been picked. Instead, all five were left at home.

The selectors' misstep was enforced by the warm-up games, where 23 of 28 wickets fell to pace. Yet, despite the warning signs, and the fact that Jayawardene centuries had carried Sri Lanka to their last two ODI victories, neither he nor Hathurusinghe were included at Lord's. 'I remember that first match at the World Cup,' Mahela told me. 'I knew I wasn't playing. We had the meeting before the match, the previous evening, and everyone spoke. I was the youngster in the team, all the other guys had experience playing before me. In that meeting, I put my hand up and said "I don't think we're playing the right combination." We were going to play just Pramo [Wickramasinghe] and Vaasy, two seamers. At Lord's, and the wicket had a green top. We had the forecast as well, so I knew it was going to be cloudy. I said "We've only got 20 overs of pace in those conditions. At least play Eric, or play Hathurusinghe as the all-rounder – or look at playing both of them."'

'This was after them naming the team, and I come and put this out. The selectors and management and Arjuna were there. Aravinda said "If this kid can know that this is not our best eleven, I don't know what else …" I think he was opposed to it as well. They adjourned the meeting, got up and left the room. I remember Murali and Vaasy and all looked at me and said "You can go and pack your bags and head home now." I was like, "Oh shit. What did I get myself into?"'

Though there were some eyebrows raised about a junior speaking so candidly, the management realised Mahela was right. Upashantha was included alongside Vaas and Wickramasinghe. Ultimately, the combination mattered little. Sri Lanka lost the toss and stuttered to 204 under heavy clouds; with the sun coming out after lunch, England cruised home with 8 wickets in hand. From the start, this World Cup had the feel of a tricky sophomore album.

Sri Lanka's lack of viable seam options wasn't their only shortcoming. The management group of Dias, Duleep, D.S. de Silva and Trevor Chappell seemed unable to work in harmony, and a number of players have cited a muddled approach. 'For me, it's too many cooks,' Hathurusinghe reflected. Strangely, Arjuna seemed unable to stitch the team together, and lacked his usual decisiveness. Hathurusinghe had been penned in to play the second match against South Africa, but D.S. encouraged a change of tack on the morning of the match. 'They said, "Oh, South Africa can't play leg spin,"' so Chandana was brought in. 'Yeah. Some think they know better than others because they've played in these conditions about 25 years ago,' Hathurusinghe glumly told me.

De Silva's hunch proved a horrible one. With the ball wobbling around, Vaas and Wickramasinghe reduced South Africa to 69-5, but lacking a third frontline seamer, couldn't strike the finishing blow. Mahela – only able to play with the help of a cortisone shot[*] – had to bowl his full 10 overs; though he kept things tight, he lacked the penetration of Hathurusinghe or Upashantha. With the help of a late Lance Klusener charge, South Africa dragged themselves up to 199.

It was more than they needed. Mahanama toughed it out in the middle for over two hours and Mahela showed flashes of class en route to 22, but no one else reached double figures. Sri Lanka were blown out for 110; South Africa's embarrassment of seam-bowling riches highlighted their own shortcomings. The Ceylon Electricity Board claimed national wattage exceeded 1,200 megawatts for the first time during the match: so, most of the island watched the ignominious defeat.[204] In clubs and bars across Colombo, punters moaned that their countrymen were still all at sea against quality fast bowling. Worse still, they were already all but out of the 1999 World Cup.

---

[*]   Jayawardene was not accustomed to – nor had he expected to carry – such a heavy workload with the ball. Delivering 10 overs a game, plus the rigorous spot bowling D.S. de Silva demanded in training, saw him quickly strain his side. Yet he had to soldier on.

Though the team managed to sneak past Zimbabwe at New Road, the trauma was not quite done. With India up next, for once a green wicket might have come in handy; instead, Sourav Ganguly and Rahul Dravid gleefully exploited Taunton's flat track and short boundaries. India's 373 was a daunting target; Sri Lanka fell 157 short. Though they passed 250 for the first time against Kenya, victory against a non-Test-playing minnow did nothing to lift spirits. The World Cup had been a chastening fall from grace.

Admittedly, conditions didn't make life easy for Asian batsmen, but the engine room badly misfired. With Jayasuriya averaging 16.40, and Aravinda 14.60, the two stars of the last tournament couldn't have been less of a factor. It is easy to single those two out since much was expected, but none covered themselves in glory. Vaas topped the batting averages; no one made more in a single innings than Kaluwitharana's 57. There were real issues, both in terms of approach and application.

Throughout, Sri Lanka were thwarted by uncharacteristic indecision. It started at the top: the brains trust simply could not decide whether to partner Jayasuriya with Mahanama or Kaluwitharana.* To be fair, neither managed a solid score opening – but the vacillating reflected that Sri Lanka remained stuck between two schools, unsure whether to stick to the all-guns-blazing approach of 1996, or to show the moving ball some respect. At the last World Cup, Arjuna made difficult decisions and backed himself to the hilt; here, his influence seemed to be acutely on the wane.

Above all, Ranatunga had built a reputation for being a canny crick-eter – but at his fifth World Cup, logic went out the window. Aravinda's concerns over the lack of seamers were ignored; and the dogmatic refusal to play Hathurusinghe, even as Mahela was bowled into the ground, seems stranger still. As Jayawardene put it to me: 'Dukes ball, early summer. Every other team had five, six fast bowlers plus their all-rounders. So we got that wrong completely.' What's more, Ranatunga

---

*   The former got the nod against England, with Kalu back to his old slot in the lower-middle order before they swapped places for the game against South Africa. They continued to yo-yo for the rest of the tournament; neither got the chance to open in consecutive matches.

– once so conscious of protecting his players – now seemed happy to hang them out to dry. 'The three fast bowlers were really pathetic,' he publicly announced after his men were hammered by India. Such barracking did little to lift a dejected unit.

Yet, perhaps the single most shocking fact is that the team's preparations echoed what D.S. de Silva and Duleep experienced in England twenty-four years earlier. Though the BCCSL decided to send the team two weeks ahead of schedule to acclimatise, the extra days were largely wasted. In true amateur style, Arjuna's men ended up playing joke games at village grounds around Leicester. 'This is the defending world champions, preparing for the next World Cup,' Jayawardene laughingly told me. 'I didn't see the focus. I didn't see the preparation going right.'

It's hard to escape the sense that Sri Lanka's performances stemmed in part from carelessness, the nonchalance that can come with being branded the best in the world. In the lead-up to 1996, the team had been hungry to prove themselves. Yet, they sunned too happily in the afterglow of that glory: failing to adapt, innovate or even blood new players. Jayawardene was the only real 'find' since the last World Cup. 'I think they expected the old game plan to work,' Hathurusinghe told me. '[They thought] '96 will work in those conditions.' But you cannot bat like that – and you can't dominate by spin, or choke by spin. That's what took us by surprise, and by that time, it was too late.'

Start to finish, everything went wrong. 'We were literally not prepared,' Mahela ruefully reflected. 'We did not have the ammunition to counter whatever the other teams had come up with. It was a huge eye-opener. No one was happy. There was a lot of criticism. I think having looked at it, even twenty years later, well-deserved criticism, because I don't think we were prepared for that World Cup.' One thing was certain: the golden generation was golden no more. As a new millennium loomed, Sri Lanka were hurtling headfirst into a new era.

5

THE NEW GREATS
(1999–2007)

A NEW DAWN

'It was the spring of hope, it was the winter of despair.'
Charles Dickens, *A Tale of Two Cities* (1859)

Over the past hundred years, the island's cricket had grown from a crawling infant to a multi-headed monster. The game meant so much to so many people. For most, it was a source of pride and a special sort of escapism; for some nostalgic souls, it was still didactic. But there were a few – the unscrupulous, well-placed opportunists – who saw that cricket was now as valuable as the graphite and gems lurking in Sri Lanka's soil. The 'gentleman's game' was a resource to exploit: an oil spring, a deep well brimming with potential. Money, power, influence: all could be had, but they would have to be fought for.

As chastening as Sri Lanka's World Cup failure was, the team's on-field blunders paled alongside the goings-on in the offices of the BCCSL. Board president Sumathipala's carrot-and-stick approach had already ruffled feathers; and if previous board elections had given a glimpse of a rotten underbelly, it was laid bare by the 1999 contest.[1] Sumathipala had expected to remain president unchallenged, but in the weeks prior to elections, Clifford Ratwatte emerged as a high-profile alternative,[*] backed by the Dharmadasas and Abu Fuard.[2]

The election itself was a sordid affair.[3] With some of Ratwatte's supporters barred from entering, arguments broke out at the front desk. Staff told the disgruntled delegates others had already entered under their names; the meeting got underway with many stranded in the lobby. Understandably, the mood was jittery.

When it was time to vote, the Ratwatte camp's objections were promptly dismissed. Abu Fuard got up and voiced his displeasure. Quite what happened next is unclear. Ranjan Mellawa writes, 'It was pandemonium outside. Some thugs jumped into the premises by scaling the locked gate. Weapons were brandished and one group started assaulting Prasanna Ranatunga, a supporter of the incumbent.'

Meanwhile, a number of witnesses claim Sumathipala rolled up his sleeves and flew at Fuard, kicking Abu on the thigh before being restrained by his own backers. The moment is rich with symbolism: for all Fuard's shadowy dealings in the past three decades, he was no match for the street-fighter Sumathipala. Ratwatte and his team promptly headed for the exit.

The elections continued, with Sumathipala re-elected president by seventy-nine votes to eleven.[4] Allegations swirled that the president's personal security force were involved in the attacks. No one came out of this smelling like roses; such anarchy stained the face of Sri Lankan cricket.

Though Sumathipala batted away reports of misconduct like a well-set slugger being served up pies,[**] Ratwatte appealed to the courts.[5] The board was suspended – and before the World Cup was out, replaced

---

[*]   Ratwatte is elder brother to then Prime Minister Sirimavo Bandaranaike, and uncle of President Chandrike Kumaratunga.

[**]   'I am very disturbed that people are trying to accuse me and my committee of conducting an illegal and unprecedented election,' he complained. 'I think Clifford Ratwatte should come out and say, "I am sorry that if not for my candidature this wouldn't have happened to Sri Lanka cricket."' 'If you're a bad loser things of this nature can happen,' he gloated, before adding that no one had laid a finger on Abu Fuard. 'He is a very old man and we are not in the league to kick people.'

by a government-appointed interim committee.*[6] Sri Lanka would need every ounce of their experience: as Trevor Chesterfield put it, 'In August 1999 ... The nation wore a bruised face: pride had been hurt and most were weeping.'[7]

Had Sumathipala not fallen from grace, there is a slim chance Ranatunga might have clung onto the captaincy. But Arjuna's bulwark was removed when he was most vulnerable – amidst bitter public outcry, the Sports Minister announced his sacking before the World Cup was over.

While it's unfair to lump all of the blame on Ranatunga's shoulders, his personal failings clearly contributed to the 1999 disaster. Discussing national selection in 1995, Sumathipala said that 'Arjuna was given the freedom to make his moves as he had a wealth of experience like no other player in the business': subsequently, World Cup glory expanded his scope.[8] Michael Roberts reckons that 'by the time the next World Cup came around in 1999, Arjuna Ranatunga was given the freedom to select the team with Duleep Mendis at his side ... Some of Ranatunga's acolytes benefited'.

In Sri Lanka, there were rumours that nine members of the squad delayed their return out of fear of the public's fury.[9] Meanwhile, Bruce Yardley threw fuel onto the fire by claiming Arjuna faked injuries, and that he and Aravinda treated their teammates like servants.[10] A humbled Ranatunga eventually gave a press conference, broadcast live on TV. Sri Lanka's lion was a hero no more. Hearts were broken, and someone would have to pay.

After consulting Arjuna, the selectors struck on Jayasuriya as the country's new captain.[11] It was a surprising choice: he'd had a poor World Cup and was junior to Mahanama and Tillakaratne; plus, he'd emerged from outside Colombo's vaunted school system. M.K. Albert aside, no captain had ever come from outside the capital. It is significant. While Colombo's cricket scene is compact and entwined, Matara felt a long way away.

★ Headed up by Hatton National Bank managing director Rienzie Wijetilleke, 'The Committee of Five' was rounded out with Michael Tissera, Ashantha de Mel, Sidath Wettimuny and Somasundaram Skandakumar.

Sanath had no bat till he was 18; when he first toured with Sri Lanka, he didn't know how to use a kettle.[12] As a kid, there were no private nets or one-on-one coaching; much of his cricketing education was played out on backstreets and beaches. He brought the spirit of the south to cricket; his very existence a beacon of hope to kids from the hinterland. The path might not be straightforward, but at least it was in place. This was a decision bigger than cricket, a symbolic flinging open of the doors.

It may well have emboldened the selectors, who continued to overhaul the team with ruthless efficiency. If Sanath had fears about leapfrogging seniors, they proved futile, since most were shown the nearest door.[13] Tillakaratne and Mahanama* were axed altogether, Arjuna and Aravinda removed from the ODI team. Chandra Schaffter replaced Mendis as manager, and Roy Dias went too – with new chairman of selectors Sidath Wettimuny travelling to Manchester to bring Dav Whatmore home.

Boldest of all was the appointment of 22-year-old Mahela Jayawardene as the team's new vice captain. Mahela impressed everyone – clearly, he was no ordinary cricketer. Some of that must stem from childhood, when his cricket-mad father would bring home historic videos for young Mahela to gorge on. When we spoke, he recalled their contents with remarkable ease: clips from the Bodyline series, innings from Viv and Barry Richards, spells from Wes Hall and Charlie Griffith, highlights of the famous tied Test. 'When you get a tape like that, you literally keep watching it over and over and over again,' he said, a glimmer of childhood wonder still in his voice.

★★★

A home triangular with India and Australia threatened to be a tricky start to the new era. There were fresh faces aplenty; straight away, Sanath stamped his authority by banning mobile phones at practice.[14] Despite losing three of four, Sri Lanka snuck into the final ahead of India on

---

*   For Mahanama, the humiliation was too much to bear. He felt mistreated throughout his career – in his last ten ODI innings he batted 1, 5, 7, 8 and 9. To top it off, his dismissal was a disgraceful one: having been the favourite to succeed Ranatunga, he was suddenly told his services were no longer required. He promptly retired.

marginally better net run rate. Few expected anything other than a drubbing come finals day. After all, Australia were world champions, riding an
eleven-game unbeaten streak.

At least the wicket favoured the hosts. Sanath called on 35 overs of
spin: with Sri Lanka razor-sharp in the field, Australia staggered to 202.
There was a sense of rejuvenation: Kaluwitharana wound back the
clock with a blistering, unbeaten 95, as the team crossed the line with
10.3 overs in hand. Jayasuriya ended the contest with a slapped 6 over
mid-wicket. Surely, there could be no more fitting way for the new king
to announce his reign.

The sense of a new team with a new ethos was fully forced home
in the lead-up to the Tests. New manager Chandra Schaffter was certainly not Mendis. None of the team would be calling him 'aiyya' or
expecting an arm around the shoulder; his would be the sterner, more
grandfatherly approach. Where in the past there had been a suspicion
that the rules did not always apply to Arjuna, he would have to obey
them like everyone else moving forward. Having travelled to Canada for
an exhibition match without seeking the proper board authorisation, he
was banned from practice and told he would have to explain himself to
Schaffter before he could rejoin the group.[15]

Keen to avoid facing Murali last, Waugh opted to bat in Kandy. But
in no time, Sri Lanka's left-arm pairing had Australia reeling at 16-4.
While Vaas swung the ball and looked near to his best, Nuwan Zoysa
bent his back and drew extra bounce. Australia could only reach 188; a
failure that looked increasingly costly after a blood-curdling clash in the
field the following day. Both Steve Waugh and Jason Gillespie had to be
helicoptered to Colombo; with the wicket taking turn and the visitors
down to nine players, 46 was a serious deficit.

So it proved; Murali and Vaas grabbed three each as Australia were finished for 140; Sri Lanka knocked off the runs with minimal fuss. At the
eleventh time of asking, they had won a Test against Australia. Given the
ghosts of 1992, the lingering scars of the World Cup and the reputation of Waugh's team, it was a huge moment – and an emphatic start to
Jayasuriya's tenure as captain.

Were it not for rain, they might well have taken a 2-0 lead at Galle.
Murali and the debuting Rangana Herath dragged Australia into deep

water; Sanath's men were 123 ahead, with 10 wickets in hand, when the game was washed out for good. Frustratingly, monsoon rains swallowed much of the third Test too – still, a 1-0 series win over the best side in world cricket was cause for celebration. Straight after the tour, Australia went on a sixteen-match winning run. Clearly, Sri Lanka had the tools to trouble anyone in their own backyard.

Sanath's first away trip in charge was less positive. Sri Lanka struggled in Sharjah; though they advanced to the final, their tournament ended with a pair of embarrassing blowouts by Pakistan. That said, given the team's shortcomings in seaming conditions, the year-ending trip to Zimbabwe was encouraging. Zoysa sowed the seeds of victory in Bulawayo with a special hat-trick; Wickramasinghe and Pushpakumara picked up five-fors, while Vaas topped the wickets tally. Young batsmen were standing up too: Atapattu batted ten and a half hours for 216* in the first Test, Arnold carried his bat in Harare, while the free-wheeling Tillakaratne Dilshan cracked 163* in his second Test out. Sri Lanka won the ODIs 3-1 too, with another Arnold century, vintage Kaluwitharana fireworks and a Murali spell that offered another suggestion he was taking big strides as a white-ball bowler.*

Wettimuny's youth revolution looked to be working – the six months since the World Cup spawning fresh faces and new ideas. That said, the first opponents of a new millennium gave a reminder of how quickly fortunes could turn: Pakistan, after one failed tour to Australia, were in freefall. Though new-again skipper Saeed Anwaar won the toss and chose to chase in all three ODIs, his men never got close to matching Sri Lanka's scores. Atapattu – fast emerging as the team's most reliable run maker – followed an unbeaten hundred with two half-centuries; Murali, Vaas and Zoysa all went at under 4 runs per over. And again, Sanath's men were electric in the field. A 3-0 sweep away from home was confirmation of their resurgence.

---

* The statistics point to a marked improvement in Murali's white-ball bowling around the turn of the century. From the start of his career to the completion of the 1999 World Cup, Murali took 157 wickets in 113 matches, with an average of 27.89 and economy of 4.21. Over the next two and a half years (up to the end of 2001) he took 110 wickets in sixty-eight matches, with an average of 19.78 and an economy of 3.43.

The one-sided ODIs gave way to a thrilling Test in Rawalpindi. Though Aravinda put Sri Lanka in the driving seat with his eighteenth Test century, Pakistan fought back, and set Sri Lanka 220 to win. By the time they had slipped to 177-8, with Arjuna retired hurt, defeat looked inevitable. Had Ranatunga sent Murali out, the Lankans surely would have succumbed. Instead, with the help of some painkillers, he added 21 one-handed runs, leading the team to the narrowest of victories. At 36, Arjuna was still ready to offer everything for the cause.

That nip-tuck victory swung the series in Sri Lanka's favour. Murali was the star in Peshawar; he took another 8 wickets in the bad-tempered third Test, but Inzamam's resistance brought Pakistan a consolation victory. Still, the team's successes across the trip exceeded their greatest hopes. They became the first to win consecutive series in Pakistan,* and announced themselves as a resurgent ODI force. What's more, Murali confirmed his status as the best off-spinner in world cricket. In taking 26 wickets, he became the second off-spinner to pass 250. By contrast, his old rival Saqlain managed 3 scalps at 50.66.

Unfortunately, ODI teams were realising they could bat out Murali's 10 overs, then make up for the missed runs against the rest of the attack. During the Asia Cup, he conceded 3.41 an over, but took just 2 wickets in four matches. In the group stage, Pakistan were happy to take 18 from his quota. At least it was an important reminder: the faster Murali improved, the more teams would focus on keeping him out. He, and Sri Lanka, would have to keep working hard.

By the time Pakistan arrived in Colombo in June 2000, the two teams must have been sick of the sight of each other. In the past nine months, they'd faced off in eight ODIs and three Tests – now, here they were prepping for another full-blooded series. There was drama in the build-up, as Jayawardene – suffering an extended lean run since the last World Cup** – was replaced as vice captain by the increasingly influential Atapattu.[16]

---

* Ignoring the one-off Test which was part of the Asian Test Championship a year earlier.
** Since being named vice captain, Jayawardene had averaged 31.26 in ten Tests and 16.73 in twenty-two ODIs. Across both formats, he made just four 50s in thirty-five innings.

Most reckon the responsibility came too soon for Mahela and affected his batting. 'I can see why [the selectors] did it, but that initial year or so, for me it was a big change,' he told me. 'I said to them, "I'm not ready", but they went ahead with it. Till today, I still believe that was the wrong decision. I was too young.' While they should be praised for thinking long term, the selectors might have taken Mahela's reluctance into account. Instead, they were forced into an embarrassing U-turn less than twelve months down the line.

The first Test was Sri Lanka's 100th, but celebrations quickly turned sour. Ranatunga looked every bit his age as he was run out plodding for an attempted single; from 176-3, Sanath's men fell away badly. Murali took 5 – by now an expectation as much as an achievement – but a flurry of Akram wickets sent the Lankans tumbling to 123 second time around. Pakistan's chase wasn't straightforward, but they got there 5 down thanks to some lusty blows from Younis.

At Galle, a Abdul Razzaq hat-trick sent Sri Lanka tumbling to 181, before Akram's rollicking 89-ball century knocked the stuffing out of the hosts. Those who stuck around till the fourth evening were treated to a little entertainment: Murali, faced with a nine-man slip cordon, shuffled around the crease like a crab and cracked four on-the-fly boundaries in his 10-ball stay.

But for the team, it was no consolation. They had lost for the first time at Galle, and for the first time since 1993 at the SSC. It dulled the glow of victory in Pakistan – the hard truth was that Sri Lanka needed to find more consistency. At least they managed to dominate what play rain allowed in Kandy. Jayasuriya and Atapattu's 335-run opening stand – coming on a traditionally seamer-friendly wicket, against a fabled attack – was a reaffirmation of the quality in the side. Atapattu, who ended 207* and scored 380 runs in the series, enhanced his claim as one of the finest opening batters in world cricket. Remarkably, he'd now converted three of his first four Test centuries into doubles.

Sri Lanka arguably had more depth in their ranks than ever before. Murali had become a genuine matchwinner, and for the first time in his career could call on the backing of a penetrative seam attack. The batting had a pleasing blend of youth and experience, with class from top to bottom. If Sanath's men could put the pieces together, they could achieve something special. None would have guessed an erudite young-ster from Kandy, lurking in the 'A' team, would prove a major catalyst towards achieving the consistency they craved. From next to nowhere, Kumar Sangakkara strolled onto the international scene. At that stage, no one had any inkling he would become the most ruthless and reliable run-maker Sri Lanka had ever seen.

A BEGINNING AND AN END

Kumar Sangakkara is the island's biggest star and the nation's greatest ambassador. But, as much as he is unique, his story is uniquely Sri Lankan. Perhaps no other cricket culture could have spawned a Sangakkara.

In typical Lankan fashion, the father-son relationship was crucial to his progress. Kshema Sangakkara sought to instil the value of hard work in his children.[17] He once chided his son, telling him if he'd had his sister's work ethic, he would have been 'better than Bradman'. The criticism gives an idea of the family's lofty standards – for few would ever accuse Sangakkara of idleness. His childhood was filled with hours of throw-downs in the garden, with home exams on hurriedly devoured books. There were other lessons too. In July 1983, when Sri Lanka turned in on itself, Sangakkara's parents bravely sheltered thirty-four Tamil friends in their home. Had they been discovered, there is every chance young Kumar would not have reached his 6th birthday.

Though he grew into a remarkably well-rounded young man, he left school to none of the fanfare that followed Mahela or Murali. Few foresaw mountains of runs in his future. In fact, when he headed to Colombo to study law, he seemed to have no real sporting ambitions. Even the way he joined NCC owed much to fate.[*18]

Had 'Sanga' made it around the corner to the CCC, there's no guar-antee he would have ended up the same cricketer. He benefited no end from the NCC's family feel, which landed him in the midst of Sri

---

★   Sangakkara was heading to the CCC when he saw Asoka de Silva beckoning him towards the NCC gates. 'Come and have a look around the club,' he encouraged Sangakkara, remembering him from a game he'd stood in at Trinity.

Lankan cricketing royalty. Even as a shy teenager, he was erudite: from his first days at the club, he showed a sponge-like keenness to soak up the knowledge of the seniors. With Rumesh Ratnayake as coach, and a host of Sri Lanka players in the side, there were plenty of brains to pick.*

At first, he impressed with his brain more than his bat. There was no half-century until fourteen months after his first outing; if expectations hung heavy on the shoulders of his friends, Sangakkara had his hands full simply clinging to their coat-tails.[19] 'I was the worst of the bunch in terms of ability and talent,' he reflected. 'I remember once I was sitting in the dressing room, and we were all talking with each other, saying what do we want to do with our future. And everyone said, "Yes. I want to play for Sri Lanka" … And then they asked me what I wanted to do, and I said "I'd probably like to play for Sri Lanka as well," and I remember, everybody laughed.'

This was not the false modesty of an overachiever. Pushpakumara gave me his first impressions in no uncertain terms. 'When he came to NCC, I was one of the senior players. He was an average cricketer. Look at his batting style: average. But a lot of hard work, and the NCC helped him to be the cricketer he is. Every day he was working in the nets, even when he was a young guy. But I never thought he'd end up being such a legend.' Truly, none could have mapped Sangakkara's career. He averaged 17.00 during his maiden season in first-class cricket; two decades later, in his final year at Surrey, runs came at 106.50. On the precipice of 40, Sangakkara was the best batsman in England by a country mile. He turned out to be anything but average.

Though big runs initially proved elusive, Sanga had the sense of a player with potential. Amidst the youth revolution, his keeping helped him win a place on the 'A' tour to South Africa in October 1999. He was a hit, with three 50s across the trip, including 89 in the last one-dayer. He shone too, when a strong Zimbabwe 'A' outfit visited Sri Lanka in

---

*   Aravinda encouraged a change of grip: suddenly he could drive the ball straight and control his clips to leg. 'Aravinda taught me to watch the ball,' he said when felicitated by the club in 2019. 'Hashan Tillakaratne taught me how to be tough in the middle of the field, how to play tough attritional cricket, how to bat long.'

the summer of 2000, reaching the 90s for the first time in red- and white-ball cricket.

Then, he hammered 156* off 140 in the penultimate match of the series, his sole maximum smashing the Moratuwa changing room's window. Moment's later, Whatmore poked his head around the door. 'Who hit that?' he asked. 'That was serendipitous,' Sangakkara told me. 'The ball hitting the dressing-room window made him actually watch a bit of my batting.'

So 'Sanga' got a chance to take the gloves for the Singer Triangular, where the team recovered from a disappointing Test series by winning five on the bounce without breaking a sweat. The new boy was at the heart of things, averaging 66.33 despite being run out twice. The spinners were dominant; given both Pakistan and South Africa were a whisker away from World Cup glory the previous year, this was another impressive performance. In ODI cricket at least, Sri Lanka had come a long way in the past twelve months.

But, to truly emerge as a powerhouse, the team had to overcome frailties in the Test-match arena. The South Africa series was a chance to recover from the sucker-punch of home defeat to Pakistan, but the team couldn't capitalise on their early advantage. Sanath's men were far too much to handle on a big turner at Galle: the skipper cracked 96 in the opening session, Mahela stroked a sublime 167, before Murali bagged 13 across 76 overs. 'I think he's twice the bowler he is [sic] two years ago,' Jacques Kallis opined. 'Because he's got that straight one with the same action that is very difficult to pick.'[20] The doosra was well on its way, the occasional loose balls of his early career all but eradicated. On a minefield like Galle, Murali was close to unplayable.

A maiden victory over South Africa, off the back of the same against Australia, spoke of a blossoming Sri Lanka – yet Sanath's men threw away the second Test, botching a 177-run chase in spectacular fashion. Neither Atapattu nor Jayasuriya troubled the scorers; Mahela and Sanga only managed 6 between them. Ranatunga's stroke-filled innings brought them back in the hunt, but Vaas needlessly ran himself out with Sri Lanka 8 short of victory. Adjudged caught behind the very next ball, Murali shot the umpire an incredulous stare. Sri Lanka had lost the Test, and squandered a great chance for an unassailable lead.

Spots of rain ruled out a result at the SSC – nonetheless, the Test felt a fitting farewell to Arjuna; in many ways a celebration of all that had become great about Sri Lankan cricket. Murali bagged 8 – and for the second time in the year, finished a three-match series with 26 wickets. Jayasuriya smashed 85 in the first innings; Jayawardene eased to a century in the second. Sangakkara batted at three for the first time in Tests; Aravinda was back too, brush-stroking his way to 41. Ranatunga's race had been run – perhaps *walked* would be more appropriate – but he could continue to bask in the brilliance he had helped build.

SSC stalwarts made a guard of honour for a smiling Arjuna on the first morning; come the final afternoon, there was rousing applause as he swaggered to the crease one last time.[21] His unbroken, hour-long stay was spiced with six boundaries and just four other scoring shots. This was no time to scamper singles.

Ranatunga hung around for Mahela to reach three figures, then went to Shaun Pollock to call time on the game. That was that: the great Arjuna grabbed a stump, shook some hands and strode from the middle, cool as you like. The papare played a little louder; rare was the eye that did not grow moist. Sri Lankan cricket was saying farewell to its favourite son. Tony Grieg, by this stage almost an adopted islander, lauded the man who 'put steel back into Sri Lankan cricket'.[22]

Rantunga's legacy will never be straightforward. Some who played under him remain resentful; others insist he did more for the island than anyone else. Once upon a time, he'd been belittled by Old-Ceylon snobs; post-1996, even the most pompous elitist accepted his role in putting Sri Lanka on the map. Ranatunga took Sri Lankan cricket by the scruff of the neck and dragged it upwards through sheer force of will. He eschewed the gentlemanly good nature of previous generations, replacing it with a pugnacity and will to win that flooded through his side. It was not always pretty or popular, but it was mighty effective. In my mind, no other man could have turned Sri Lanka from no-hopers to world champions so quickly. Has any one person ever done so much for a country's cricket?

He had more than his fair share of enemies – were he put in the stocks, Warne would be front of the queue, with the rest of Australia not far behind. But not all thought Arjuna's actions were hurtful to cricket. In the final year of his life, Martin Crowe penned a touching tribute to Ranatunga:

> He saw the Australians as an easy target. He saw how false they could be: loud, lippy banter masking their own fears, often turning into personal abuse when the pressure mounted. He believed the more they resorted to mental disintegration the more they exposed themselves … I loved him, full stop. Mostly I loved the way he stood up to the big boys, the bullies, and bulldozed them back in his unique inspiring way. He represented the underdog.[23]

Ranatunga became a symbol of Sri Lankan pride. He could be belligerent, but he had a congenial and charming streak too. It is sad that the mud thrown by Warne left such a mark. Perhaps the Australians disliked Arjuna's individualism: in an age when most teams wanted to copy their cricket, Ranatunga showed little respect, let alone deference. He stood his ground and refused to be cowed; in the most un-Sri Lankan manner, there was always a barb on the tip of his tongue.

One of the very few who seem to exist as leader first and cricketer second, he deserves his place in the pantheon of all-time great captains. Yet, it should not be forgotten that Arjuna was a graceful enough batter to dazzle Sobers, and a canny enough bowler to win games for Sri Lanka. No doubt, he should have scored more centuries – but if he sacrificed personal glories, it was in pursuit of a higher cause. Ranatunga embodies the lofty ideal that cricket transcends the contest between bat and ball. So much of what he accomplished was intangible; his career is a great reminder that smarts and spirit can prove as vital as skill.

Ranjit Fernando once told me Arjuna would take tins of food on tour, so he could eat with the youngsters – who were often left behind at the hotel when the seniors went out for dinner. 'I sometimes see wedding photos,' he went on. 'In all of them, Arjuna is there. He was a captain who really cared.' Of all the island's leaders, Arjuna sits at the head of the table – the father of modern Sri Lankan cricket. He oversaw a revolution; with patience and steady vision he forged a team that filled a downcast nation with pride.

FINDING A FORMULA

Though Jayasuriya had been in charge for well over a year, only now could he really start to emerge from Arjuna's sprawling shadow. It is tough to reign supreme when the former king remains in court; now the senior man as well as the skipper, Sanath could start to firmly imprint his own ethos on the side.

Despite a loss against Pakistan in the quarters of the ICC Knockout in Kenya, Sri Lanka's steady ODI run continued. They won five of five in Sharjah in October 2000, with Sanath producing one of his best innings yet in the final – a tale of two halves, where early restraint gave way to riotous hitting. So often, Jayasuriya saved his harshest punishment for India – now, that same brutality flooded his side. Vaas got the top four inside 10 overs, and Ganguly's men never found solid ground: 54 all out, their 245-run humiliation was the biggest defeat in ODI history.

But a year-ending trip to South Africa heightened the image of Jayasuriya's men as weary travellers, there for the taking in alien conditions. In six ODIs, Sri Lanka couldn't reach 250; when South Africa batted first, they posted 290 and 302. The Tests were no better. Rain, and the hosts' reluctance to enforce the follow-on, spared the Lankans at Kingsmead, but there would be no more let-offs.[24] They were humbled for 95 after winning the toss at Cape Town; when Sanath needed his seamers to stand up, they combined to take 2 for 294.

Though Nuwan Zoysa came good at Centurion, Sri Lanka were brushed aside for 119 and 252; for the second consecutive match, beaten inside three days. At least, amidst a tour full of negatives, the young batsmen gave a solid account of themselves. None performed better than Sangakkara: clearly at ease against pace, his growth was staggering. A couple of years ago, he was struggling to hold his own in club cricket; over the past six weeks, he'd outperformed Sri Lanka's best batsmen.

And a strong showing in New Zealand – where Sri Lanka won four ODIs on the bounce – eased fears about the team's form outside Asia. There was much to smile about. Jayasuriya's 83-ball 103 was a thrilling affair; the support Murali got from seamers and spinners alike augured well for the future. Though Sanath's tenure had thus far been blotched by inconsistency, the team was in much better shape than when he took over. His conciliatory approach seemed just the tonic: Jaysuriya was always smiling, and some of that feel-good spirit filtered down to the rest of the side.[25]

That said, there was ongoing resentment over high-handed treatment from the English, who had deigned to visit Sri Lanka just twice, for single Tests, in the past two decades. A three-Test series spoke of the team's rising status; and Sanath's men were desperate to prove their mettle when England arrived in February 2001. It turned into an acrimonious series, blighted by umpiring poor enough to push both teams over the edge.[26] Gough was reported for swearing at Moratuwa and argued with an umpire at Kurunegala; Ruchira Perera was strangely accused of racially abusing Craig White* in Matara. That was just the warm-ups. On the field at least, Anglo-Lankan relations hadn't stooped so low since the days of Jardine.

Still, the tour was a vital economic springboard for Sri Lanka. For two decades, the looming presence of civil conflict had kept tourists away. Cricket, cheap beer and beaches brought them back.** Those who came discovered unique charms: the seaside ground at Galle in the shadows of a Dutch Fort, the rumbling train ride up-country into the lush hills of Kandy; the discerning and utterly devoted Colombo cricket fraternity. For the first time in years, hotels were full; the chairman of the Ceylon Tourist Board claimed the country ran out of beer for two days.[27] Ever since, England have arrived in Sri Lanka with a travelling horde. Months ahead of visits, tuk-tuk drivers in Galle and Kandy joyously sound the words 'Barmy Army', their minds flashing forward to days when pockets are packed full of bills. For so many, for a hundred different reasons, it means so much when England play cricket in Sri Lanka.

Galle soon became a firm favourite with travelling fans: in 2001, 150 busloads headed down from Colombo – spending the first two days watching Atapattu bat their men into submission. With Sri Lanka

---

* Though Perera did angrily sledge White, reports of the incident unanimously ignored the fact that the supposed racial insult also happened to be the batsman's last name.

** At least 7,000 fans travelled for the series; there had been 8,049 British arrivals in the whole of 2000.

declaring at 470-5, and the pitch breaking up, England were left with a mountain to climb. They didn't help themselves by shrinking into their shell. Murali, short of full potency, got through 97 overs for 145 runs. The tourists had some success padding him away – after The Oval, 7 wickets seemed like a modest haul – but were strangled in the process. Jayasuriya bagged 8, as the visitors crumbled on the last afternoon.

While Sri Lanka fully deserved their innings victory, England felt they weren't helped by the umpiring. Their fans cited seven dodgy decisions: a pair of lbws – against Alec Stewart and Craig White – probably the worst of them.[28] Travelling fans booed the umpires at the end of day four; later in the evening, a group of beery vigilantes searched for them in a nearby hotel.[29]

Things fully boiled over on the final morning, when Mike Atherton was adjudged caught behind off Vaas. Sangakkara was convinced he had taken the ball cleanly; had it been sent upstairs, the third umpire would have overturned the decision. The English felt they had been cheated. A window in their dressing room ended up smashed. Charlie Austin felt 'it was a frightful experience and it finally broke England's resolve'.[30]

With tempers frayed, the teams headed up to Kandy for what *Wisden* described as a 'bruising, bar-room brawl of a Test': a bloody, back-and-forth battle where both took chunks out of the other but refused to stay down.[31] Worse-tempered and more lawless than Galle, marred by poor sportsmanship and shocking umpiring, it was above all a thrilling game of cricket. The first day was packed full of swings: England had four breakthroughs by noon; Jayawardene struck a smooth-as-silk century after lunch, before the second new ball brought the innings crashing in a heap.

There were poor decisions during Sri Lanka's innings, but it was only on the second and third days that chaos really took hold. Atherton survived a strong lbw shout, Nasser Hussain was caught twice at silly point on his way to a century and Hick dismissed three times en route to an 11-ball duck. Stewart survived an appeal for a catch that came off the face of his bat, and was then given caught off a ball he hadn't hit. Meanwhile, Sri Lanka were forced to sweat as the lower order carried England to 387. The game was teetering on a knife edge.

If losing Atapattu in the first over was a stab in the chest, the Lankans were dumbstruck by the manner of Jayasuriya's dismissal. On the 8th ball of the innings, he slashed a full, wide delivery into the ground. It ballooned to Graham Thorpe at gully, who wheeled away in wild celebration, albeit with a decidedly conflicted look on his face. The rest of the cordon joined the appeal; umpire B.C. Cooray raised his finger. Disconsolate, Jayasuriya flung his helmet across the boundary rope.

The slips knew it wasn't out. The force of their appeal was surely an acknowledgement of Cooray's fallibility. This was murky ground, unsporting at best, but England felt they had suffered the same at least three times over in Galle. Now, Sangakkara – fast replacing Arjuna as the least popular member of the Sri Lanka side* – strode to the middle with his team up against it. He promptly accused England of cheating: still smarting from his wrongful dismissal earlier in the series, Atherton grew red-faced and rageful. A prolonged, ugly exchange ensued. Atherton later admitted he 'lost it for four overs'.

Watching on, Vic Marks reckoned Atherton was taken aback by Sangakkara's eloquence; more upset than at any stage in his long Test career. No doubt, 'Sanga' was a rare breed: a powerful fusion of Old Ceylon and new Sri Lanka; more articulate and assured than the whole England team, with more than a flicker of Arjuna's national pride. He stood tall; though he had yet to lodge a first-class century, many could sense he was made of the right stuff for international cricket.

It helped that he backed up his words with his bat, producing the innings of his career as wickets tumbled around him. For the best part of two sessions, Atherton stewed as Sangakkara set upon the English bowlers. Only overeagerness cost him his century: 95* on the brink of lunch, he tried to launch Robert Croft into the stands and was stumped. For England, it was a cathartic wicket – and a vital one too. Another 20 or 30 may have changed the outcome of the match. On the ground where

---

* Nor was it just the players who seemed annoyed. In *The Telegraph*, Michael Henderson wrote: 'He ought to enter the annual Kandy bird-fanciers' fair as a budgerigar because, with all the fluting, piping, chirruping, billing and cooing that has gone on in this series, he would walk off with the rosette for "Best in Show".'

he had played his schoolboy cricket, Sri Lanka's precocious keeper showed he was still prone to moments of naivety.

Still, England's 160-run chase was bound to be nervy. Vaas had Atherton for the fourth time in as many innings;* with Marcus Trescothick unseated four balls later, Sri Lanka were on their way. But Thorpe wrested back momentum with 46 priceless counter-attacking runs – England wobbled again, but scraped across the line with 3 wickets in hand.

Few Tests offer so many twists and turns. For the neutral, anarchy became part of the spectacle – yet, regardless of your affiliation, the atrocious umpiring left a sour taste. The overriding image of the Test is of the large white banners which sprung up on the fourth day. 'B.C. [Cooray], your VISA is ready,' one joked. 'Call over at the British High Commission.'

'Some of the lads reckoned the umpires had made at least fifteen major errors,' Stewart reflected after the game. 'Even though the majority favoured us, it was a little disturbing.'[32] The officials needed a police escort to leave the ground. 'Bad Call' Cooray, as many Sri Lankans took to calling him, was stood down for the next Test and retired soon after.

With the umpiring much improved at the SSC, the bickering between two sides all but disappeared. Still it was a nervy decider, a must-win which Sri Lanka surrendered with some pitiful batting. In the first innings, they slipped from 205-3 to 241 all out – though Vaas brought them back into the match with his best spell in years, Sri Lanka threw it away by slumping to 81 on second attempt. Panic set in as the *perahera* began. Last man Murali forgot to take guard, and then was trapped lbw trying to reverse-sweep Ashley Giles third ball. No doubt the crumbling pitch made batting tough – but Sri Lanka beat themselves. As Nasser Hussain told Scott Oliver:

My whole mindset was that once they see that they can lose, that's when they start to do some silly things. They started to run down the pitch and play big shots, when before that, in Galle, they just milked us.

---

*   Atherton pointedly stuck around until the third umpire confirmed Sangakkara had cleanly taken the catch.

All right, the pitches had changed, but so had their mindset. That was just the fear of losing a series at home against England.[33]

Equally, Murali was less of a factor than anyone anticipated.* While an abductor injury stopped him properly ripping the ball, his returns diminished across the course of the series: by the time the teams reached the SSC, he looked the fifth most effective spinner on show.[34] England deserve credit. Having been humiliated when the sides last met, they were prepared to tough it out and blunt him as best they could. Up to this stage, no side visiting Sri Lanka had taken so few runs an over from the Kandy Man. By largely taking the bat out of the picture, England made his exaggerated turn work in their favour. They frustrated Murali, and as the wickets dried up his confidence started to ebb.

While hugely disappointing to see a lead slip through their fingers, Sri Lanka showed strength and depth which surprised many. In taking 16 wickets at 15.25, Vaas put a poor tour of South Africa behind him and proved that the injuries which had threatened to derail his career were a thing of the past. Though Dilhara Fernando and Nuwan Zoysa only shone in flashes, the runs that flowed from Sanga and Mahela's bats warmed Lankan hearts. Aravinda reminded the world he could still coolly tick his way to Test match hundreds, Jayasuriya made up for a lack of runs with 16 wickets, while Atapattu lodged a double-century for the fourth year running. He made scores at every trip to the crease during the ODIs too, as England were crushed in all three games.

But in the background, political wheels kept turning in their typically creaky manner. Despite a host of objections, Sumathipala was allowed to contest the BCCSL presidency in June 2000; with his rivals withdrawing in protest, he was anointed at a 'behind-closed-doors' ceremony at the Sports Ministry.**[35] Back in the hot seat, he wasted no time breaking ground on a new stadium in Dambulla.[36] Every ounce of his energy went into readying it in six months: remarkably, the ribbon was cut ahead of the first England ODI.

---

*   His 14 wickets came at a strike rate of 101.1, his worst in a series at home since his first against Australia.

**   The BCCSL headquarters were no longer considered a safe space for elections.

But controversy bubbled beneath the surface.[37] In November 2000, Sumathipala had suspended Dammika Ranatunga, claiming their relationship had become untenable.* Then, two days after Dambulla's inauguration, Prasanna Ranatunga announced he would not seek re-election as board vice president because of corruption within the BCCSL. The very next day, Sumathipala sacked Dammika over his refusal to cooperate with a 'financial' investigation.

Such unabashed finger pointing from within stung supporters of Sri Lankan cricket – and the Sports Minister wasted no time dissolving the board.[38] Apparently, the BCCSL refused to furnish proper accounts. Sa'adi Thawfeeq claimed deals were brokered in a 'hush-hush' manner; a board spokesperson said it was 'impossible' to estimate how much was in the accounts.[39] For the second time in three years, an interim committee was appointed. This was an utter shambles.

It is easy to dismiss these machinations as peripheral, but the administration's instability dripped down onto players, who were scuppered by the lack of stable support. With adversarial boards on a carousel, it became impossible to build for the future. 'There isn't enough time to get anything going,' Sidath Wettimuny complained when we first met. 'You start something and the next guy comes along and wipes it out. Solid example: in Khettarama, we started an indoor facility and a swimming pool. You would think it's the most obvious thing: our main stadium doesn't have an indoor facility. We started a six-lane indoor facility with a pool. Columns are up, you can see even now. The foundations are there, but the next guy came and because *we* did it, because it wasn't *his* idea ... sadly this is what has brought us down in Sri Lanka. We don't build on what the other guy has done well. We bring it down to bricks and start again.'

Given the unrest at home, Sri Lanka's ability to keep producing the goods was impressive. Though Pakistan were the pick of the sides at the ARY Gold Cup in Sharjah, Sanath's men snuck into the final and stole away the silverware. Helped by a series of blunders in the field, they posted 297 – more than enough, as Zoysa, Vaas and Dilhara tore

---

*   The enmity sprung from the handling of the broadcast rights deal; clearly, money was the root of the problems.

through Pakistan. The story was similar during the Coca-Cola Cup in Colombo: beaten twice by India in the group stage, the Lankans struck a resounding victory come finals day.

Still, there was no escaping the fact the team had failed to win a Test series in their past five attempts – the Indian series, which got underway in August 2001, took on greater resonance than usual. The visitors missed Tendulkar at Galle: Murali bagged 8 wickets, while Dilhara bowled fiercely to earn a maiden five-for. He had Ganguly caught behind off a vicious, steepling bouncer: rarely had Sri Lanka's fans seen one of their own bully an opponent in such rugged fashion. A maiden first-class century from Sangakkara, and a blistering eighth from Jayasuriya, all but secured a 10-wicket victory.

But Asgiriya had done Sri Lanka few favours in recent years – for the third series running, the team squandered a chance to take an unassailable lead. Well ahead going into the second innings, they were undone by a dizzying collapse; 52-1 became 140-7, and only rare swashbuckling heroics from Murali gave Sri Lanka hope. But what should have been a nervy chase proved entirely straightforward; India cruised home with 7 wickets to spare.

For Sanath's men, it must have felt like Groundhog Day. The prospect of another series slipping away had suddenly become very real. Thankfully, Murali came to the fore at the SSC with 8 first-day wickets, before the batsmen brutalised India. The unbroken 194-run stand between Tillakaratne and Thilan Samaraweera – the gutsy old-and-new lower-middle order pairing – sapped any fight out of Ganguly's men. Sanath declared at 610-6; sharp and committed in the field, the Lankans fully deserved their innings win. It sealed a first series victory over India since 1985; Sri Lanka looked to be getting things right.

Murali was at the heart of the victory: the stark contrast between him and Harbhajan Singh – whose four scalps cost 73 runs each – was a reminder of what a special spinner he had become. But he couldn't win matches alone: auspiciously, the batsmen were finding real consistency.* Only once were Sanath's men shot out for less than 250, an indignity

---

* Mahela, Sangakkara, Tillakaratne and Atapattu averaged north of 50 for the series, while Samaraweera's career got off to the best possible start.

India suffered four times. These sort of performances built confidence: the victory turned out to be a springboard for Sri Lanka's best-ever stretch in Test cricket.

Everything went right as Sanath's men rattled off eight in a row. Murali tormented batsmen mercilessly, while the batters gorged themselves with unprecedented gluttony. Meanwhile, a newfound mastery of reverse swing made Vaas a much more threatening bowler. Even Brian Lara in career-best form couldn't stop the train rolling.

Having brushed Bangladesh aside with humbling ease, Sri Lanka swaggered through three Tests with the West Indies, recording the first series sweep in their three-decade history. Tillakaratne continued to bask in the glory of his return with another unbeaten hundred at Galle; though 130 overs were lost to rain in Kandy, Murali and Vaas produced when it mattered to take the team across the line. In the first innings, Vaas ripped through the tail with a superb spell of swing bowling; in the second, with time running out, Murali switched ends and grabbed the final 4 wickets in 3 overs. Incredibly, he became the first man to record four consecutive 10-wicket hauls in Test cricket. Clearly, his life was made easier by a fit and firing Vaas, who stole the show at the SSC.

At the start of the year, Vic Marks derisively wrote that injuries had 'neutered' Vaas, 'so that his prime function ... seems to be to create some rough outside the right-hander's off stump'.[40] Since then, he had silenced the critics with 54 wickets at 19.90 apiece, while maintaining his typically stifling economy. Where others had been derailed by injuries, Vaas kept himself going through sheer hard work – it is testament to his spirit that he is perhaps the most enduring Asian seamer of all time. He spent countless hours in the nets and the gym, steadily strengthening his body and building variations to compensate for his lack of pace.[41]

Here Vaas took 7 wickets in each innings, twice bettering his career-best figures in the process. For the second time in the series, five of Sri Lanka's top seven passed 50, with Tillakaratne handling the bowlers for nine hours en route to an unbeaten double-hundred. The selectors could certainly feel good about endorsing his comeback: since the recall, Tillakaratne had averaged 146.50.

The demolition of Bangladesh and West Indies proved that this line-up could trample attacks. Sri Lanka scored in excess of 550 five times in 2001; though four of those came on an oft-flat SSC wicket, this unit was clearly firing. Atapattu and Jayasuriya, the rock and the ravager, went together like rice and curry. Marvan brought substance to Sri Lanka's innings – his patience and ability to play the percentages making him a perfect foil for Sanath, whose cuts and drives assaulted the senses like rich spicy gravy.

Though not the finished article yet, Sangakkara's comfort in the cauldron of Test cricket suggested he was set for a long career. Mahela had bounced back from a lean spell and averaged 67.86 over the past four series, Tillakaratne returned in the form of his life, while Samaraweera averaged a shade under 100 in his first five Tests. The ageing genius Aravinda, the determined Russel Arnold and the hugely promising Dilshan all hung around the fringes of the side too; this was the deepest and most daunting batting unit Sri Lanka had ever put forth.

They could also boast a more well-rounded and penetrative attack than at any time in the past. Over a decade of international cricket, Murali had laboured tirelessly and transformed himself into a world-beater: the dance to the crease and the big rip remained, but by now there were plenty of other tricks too. Vaas had become much more threatening, Dilhara bowled with as much pace and hostility as any Sri Lankan in memory, and when Zoysa got it right, his bounce and left-arm angle were a real handful. Since the dire showing at the 1999 World Cup, the team had been well and truly revitalised.

But as always, trouble was never far away. The commercialisation which had taken hold of cricket during the 1990s was now fully entrenched. The game had become big business – yet players were still largely treated as pawns. They had little control or authority, and were expected to yield before an openly exploitative board. Such subjugation would not last forever. Over the next twelve months, administrators' brazen attempts to control and exploit players would finally spark a backlash. The long undisturbed hierarchy was about to be rattled. At last, Sri Lanka's cricketers would stand up to the men who had so often failed to support them.

PLAYER POWER

The island's cricket had never been so stable. For all Arjuna's achievements, Sri Lanka in the 1990s were unreliable; by 2001, they had done much to iron out those kinks. As a Test outfit, their progress had been extraordinary; in white-ball cricket too, they became more consistent. Whatmore had greater authority than during his first stint as coach: he saw eye to eye with his captain, and had a team chock-full of match winners. Things were looking up.

Still, the Lankans weren't immune to the occasional wobble. Having looked the form side in Sharjah in November 2001, they fell away during the second half of the week, skittled in the showpiece for 78. Having won four finals on the bounce, Sri Lanka were undone by Akram, Younis and Akhtar.

Still, up to that match, Jayawardene scored at every trip to the crease, while Murali – whose 40 overs in Sharjah cost just 80 runs – took 7 wickets at 11.42 apiece. Nor were those performances aberrations. Sri Lanka easily handled the West Indies and Zimbabwe in the LG Abans Triangular in December 2001, with Murali and Mahela on song again. But no one hit a higher note than Chaminda Vaas: at the SSC, he took a wicket with his first ball, 2 in his 3rd over and a hat-trick in his 6th to send Zimbabwe tumbling to 38 all out. Vaas' 8 for 19 was a new ODI record; Sri Lanka knocked off the runs with 274 balls to spare. To see the team perform with such swagger meant a lot: for all Whatmore and Jayasuriya's emphasis on progress in the Test arena, another World Cup win was what the average man, woman and child craved most. South Africa 2003 loomed on the horizon.

Few fancied Zimbabwe's chances in a three-Test series, but the manner in which they were brushed aside spoke volumes about how far Sri Lanka had come. The top order built a superb foundation at the SSC, and the punishment kept coming. Sanath's men were 450-6 when Tillakaratne fell 4 short of his century: through Samaraweera and Vaas, they added another 136 in 31.1 overs.

As against India and the West Indies, Samaraweera's knock was the gut-punch that felled an already battered opponent. Indeed, his sudden, surprising emergence was crucial to Sri Lanka's success in 2001.* His runs knocked the stuffing out of teams, turning foreboding positions into formidable scores, keeping tired bodies in the field when minds were drifting towards the pavilion. There was no coming back for Zimbabwe. Murali took 8 wickets – at his most miserly in the second innings, he conceded 35 from 36 asphyxiating overs.

Though the first Test illustrated the gulf in class between the two sides, the series would not pass without incident. Instead of heading up to Kandy with the team, Jayasuriya stayed back in Colombo for a selection meeting that left him stewing.[42] Without consulting the team management, Sri Lanka's selectors decided to rest Atapattu and seamer Charitha Buddhika for the second Test.

This was very strange indeed. While Atapattu's omission left Sri Lanka short of a specialist opener, Buddhika was a 21-year-old, two-Test veteran. The prospect of a 'rest' was no doubt discouraging; in all likelihood, he had been licking his lips at the prospect of facing Zimbabwe at Asgiriya. Equally, the visitors' quicks had a much better chance of finding help in Kandy, where Sri Lanka had been undone in three of their past four. With the series still on the line, nothing could be taken for granted.

In earlier times, there might have been furrowed brows and shrugged shoulders, but the dynamic between the players and the board was shifting. Murali and Mahela announced they would not play unless the decision was reversed; with the selectors still unwilling to budge, Sanath phoned the Sports Minister to explain the situation. The minister sided with the team, sparking a flurry of resignations from selectors. Atapattu and Buddhika were back in.

It was a power move plucked straight from the Arjuna playbook. Murali realised he was undroppable, while Mahela was fast approaching the same. Selectors, chief executives, board presidents come and go, but there was no replacing the wide-eyed off-spinner or the baby-faced batsman. Their commitment to their teammates helped shift the

---

* Brought in primarily to provide off-spinning support for Murali, he had two 100s, two 50s, three not-outs and an average of 140.66 in his first six innings.

balance of power. Rarely had Sri Lanka's cricketers so boldly refused to fall into line.

Murali brushed aside the New Year's drama with a performance that was ground-breaking even by his own standards. By now the doosra was near-perfect: starting to jag like a leg-break, it opened up a whole new range of options. Right-handers found their outside edge under threat; for left-handers, kicking Murali away became increasingly fraught.[43] And by blinding batsmen to which way the ball was turning, the doosra imbued Murali's stock ball with extra menace. Keeping him out had been hard enough when you knew what was being sent down; now, uncertainty reigned, crippling batsmen.

He bowled 40 dizzying overs on the first day in Kandy, tying the batsmen in knots with trickery and turn. Hamilton Masakadza played around a doosra, Gavin Rennie was beaten by flight and spin, Stuart Carlisle and Craig Wishart caught on the crease and pinned lbw. By the time Murali splayed Grant Flower's stumps, he had 9 first-day wickets. One more would have given him the best figures in Test history – but it was not to be.

Late in the day, Murali showed he was every inch a team man, diving for a tough chance on the boundary that would have denied him a per-fect ten.[44] He shelled it, and dislocated his finger in the process. Still, the adrenaline of history-making numbed the pain – and no one could wrestle the ball from his hands come the second morning. First up, a bat-pad chance slipped through Russel Arnold's fingers; three balls later, umpire Venkat was unmoved by an lbw shout. Though Vaas bowled wide of the stumps from the other end, he could not deter Henry Olonga from a wild swipe. The ball flew into Sangakkara's hand; the umpire remorsefully raised his finger. For once, no one wanted the wicket to be given. Vaas and Arnold were especially upset, but Murali was phlegmatic. 9 for 51 was a return to be proud of.

He had bowled Sri Lanka into a commanding position, and they kept tight control with the sort of collective batting performance that was fast becoming commonplace, setting up an easy innings victory. Hampered by his injured finger, Murali was less effective than in the first innings – but nonetheless bagged 4, equalling Hadlee's record of ten Test-match ten-fors in the process. And he was still just getting started.

With 400 Test wickets in his sights, Sri Lanka expectantly waited. Five more at Galle should be a trivial matter. Schedules were cleared, fancy glassware fetched from cupboards, kids ensconced on the floor, their noses pressed against TVs. Jayasuriya's maiden Test five-for looked to have delayed celebrations; but on the third morning, Murali had Travis Friend and Henry Olonga bowled off consecutive deliveries, to get the party started. He had become the youngest man to reach 400. 'If I keep performing well, then I can continue for another five years and could get 600,' he told reporters.[45] If only he knew he was halfway to where he'd end up.

The spin twins bagged another 4 wickets each as Zimbabwe crumpled to 79 in the second innings. Sri Lanka romped to a lop-sided 3–0 victory; as much as the series belonged to Murali – whose 30 wickets cost little more than 9 runs apiece – nine batsmen averaged over 40. Sanath's team were showing they could call on plenty of depth.

Riding high, they headed to Lahore for the Asian Test Championship Final. Stepping back into the Gaddafi Stadium brought forth special memories: six years on from the island's greatest glory, Sri Lanka toppled Pakistan in style. If the match rarely felt like a contest, it was at least spiced by pockets of wonderful cricket. Sangakkara's 230 included thirty-three 4s and three 6s; with the pitch flattening out, Sri Lanka never allowed Pakistan to settle.*

It was just as well they scored quickly, since much of the fourth day was washed out with rain. The skies were calming by the afternoon, but with the hosts heading towards defeat, there was little urgency to get the game restarted. 'The Pakistanis were taking it easy. They had one man running around the field,' recalled team manager Chandra Schaffter. 'We had to mop it up so we could play.'

Down to a man, the team grabbed their towels and began drying the outfield. Whatmore, Kontouris and Schaffter were there helping too – this was a wonderful show of unity, and a poignant illustration of how serious Sri Lanka were about winning. Nothing could slow their charge on the final morning: 248–5 overnight, Pakistan were finished for 325. Sanath's men knocked off the runs inside 7 overs. The only pity was that

---

* Numbers three to six put on 385 runs at 4.26 an over.

fans at home couldn't watch: amidst a dearth of advertisers, the game wasn't televised in Sri Lanka. India's withdrawal had cost the Asian Test Championship dear.[46]

Still, for all the team had achieved in the past twelve months, this was perhaps their crowning glory. Pakistan were riding a six-match win streak of their own; yet Sri Lanka strolled into their backyard and dominated with both bat and ball. The seamers backed Murali up, while Sangakkara superbly anchored the innings. Still without a century in club cricket, he had made four 100-plus scores for his country in the past seven months. His desire to succeed was extraordinary, his progress relentless.

Sri Lanka headed to Sharjah in April, knowing they likely faced another straight shootout against Pakistan. So it proved – but having bowled superbly throughout the group, they leaked 295 come finals day. Still, the bowlers' shortcomings were overshadowed by a horrendous collapse: from 52-1, the team slid to 78 all out. It was a stinging defeat, but given Sri Lanka's recent form, they could reasonably dismiss it as a bad day at the office. Even the best batting units flounder occasionally – plus, Shoaib Akhtar was nudging 100mph, while Wasim and Waqar swung the ball at pace.

There would be more scrutiny on Sri Lanka's ability to cope with the moving ball before the summer was out. A three-Test tour to England was further affirmation of progress; finally the team were shaking off their second-class status. Deservedly too, since Lloyd's West Indies and Waugh's Australia were the only sides to better their nine-Test winning streak.

Nonetheless, England in early summer was a dangerous place for Sri Lankan cricketers to find themselves – and the warm-ups painted a worrying picture. The batting looked brittle; worse, with Murali laid up and Vaas struggling to swing the Dukes ball, Sri Lanka's attack looked threadbare.[47] Kent thrashed their way to 419-6 dec in 63.3 overs; Durham too, scored over 4 an over as they racked up 469. Even a British Universities side managed to remain fairly competitive over the course of three days.

But Lord's had historically been a happy hunting ground, and the players arrived in North London relishing the chance to strut their stuff at the home of cricket. Helped by a good batting wicket and clear skies overhead, Sri Lanka made the English toil in the field like farm-hands of old. Mahela elegantly stroked his way onto the honours board, while Atapattu fell 15 short of a double hundred.

But trouble was brewing. As soon as Ruchira Perera entered the attack, murmurs about his action echoed around the ground.[48] Eyebrows were raised in the commentary box, changing room and stands; and the scrutiny amped up once he dismissed Michael Vaughan and Thorpe with successive deliveries. Before the Test was out, frame-by-frame images of Perera's action had appeared on the BBC website; after the match, he was duly reported to the ICC.[49] Being strung up on the most public of stages was becoming a uniquely Sri Lankan torment.*

The Test turned on its head with Jayasuriya's decision to enforce the follow-on. It wasn't entirely illogical: England were 280 behind, and Sri Lanka had 17 overs on the third evening to make further inroads. But the wicket was placid and the seamers unused to such a heavy workload. Without Murali to bank on, the game slipped through Lankan fingers: Jayasuriya dropped Vaughan twice in the slips as England ticked their way to 529-5 dec. Rarely has an away draw felt so disheartening.

Worse, England's great escape shifted the series firmly in their favour. With more on offer for the seamers, Sri Lanka fell flat inside 53 overs at Edgbaston. Though Murali was back, bravely grimacing through 63 of his own,** Sri Lanka were shot out by an innings. Nor was their anguish confined to the field of play. Rumours swirled that a new panel of selectors had quickly fallen out with manager Chandra Schaffter.***[50] He was told during the third Test that his services would not be required after

---

*   The fact that Perera was never again the same bowler – and indeed, that so many have struggled to recover from ICC scrutiny – gives some idea of the extent of Murali's resolve and mental fortitude.

**   He picked up 5 wickets, including a dipping off-break that jagged from outside leg to clip Butcher's off bail.

*** First, they were annoyed by his decision to pick Sajeewa de Silva and Pasan Wanasinghe for a warm-up match against Glamorgan. Then, rumours swirled that new chairman of selectors Guy de Alwis was annoyed at being barred entry from the team dressing room during the second Test at Edgbaston. Schaffter denied the incident, while admitting he had a 'standing rule' that nobody should enter without permission.

the series – though Schaffter had no plans to seek a contract renewal, the announcement was purposely timed to look like a sacking.

Meanwhile, bowling coach Darryl Foster resigned in disgust when the board refused to refund him for a last-minute trip to see his ill grandson in Australia. As the team toughed it out at Old Trafford, news of the departures spread across Sri Lanka. 'To have it announced in Colombo during the course of a Test match was distracting – the players and management team have more important things to worry about than leaks from the board,' Foster disappointedly told the media.[51] He and Schaffter were both treated appallingly: the whole issue exposed an administration that was despotic, petty and reckless. It is easy to see how the players could have been upset by such goings on. Schaffter is like an uncle to Murali; Foster had helped him through the toughest parts of his career. Was it wise to alienate such men?

Instead of needless distractions, Sri Lanka needed all the help they could get. Everything was going wrong. In between the second and third Tests, £3,000 went missing from Aravinda's hotel room; back on the field at Old Trafford, Dilhara and Upashantha leaked runs like they were advertising t20 cricket.[52] England passed 500 again, and then unsettled Sanath's men with sustained hostility. It was discouraging to see the captain drop down to number six – Arnold batted brilliantly in his place, but Sri Lanka were twice undone by the second new ball. Rain gave them a chance to cling on for a draw, but they slipped from 263-4 to 308 all out on the final afternoon. England were left needing 50 from 6 overs.

With Dilhara's first over going for 16, there was suddenly only one result on the table. Jayasuirya sleepily failed to stem the singles, and England cruised to their target with an over to spare. After the Lankan's nine-match winning streak, this had been a sobering series. Whatmore's admission that his side didn't have 'what it takes to win abroad' must have really stung.[53]

Criticism had to start with the captain – who averaged 19.80, with a top score of 35. For one of the game's elite opening batsmen, that was not good enough. Nor was it a one-off. In his last nine Tests outside of Asia, he had averaged 16.47 and failed to lodge a 50. For all Jayasuriya's brilliance, it was becoming increasingly difficult to deny that he was neutered when taken out of his comfort zone. As a captain too, he was outmanoeuvred by Hussain. Stripped of his usual masterplan – bat big, and plug Murali into one end – he looked flat-footed and bereft of ideas.

It was a difficult series for Sangakkara too – there were legitimate concerns that, as keeper and top-order batsman, he was carrying an unsustainable load. That said, the bulk of the batting did OK: even with a mountain of runs behind him, Samaraweera could not find a place in the XI. Really, Sri Lanka lost because of their bowlers. Vaas' control and swing were touted as crucial ahead of the series, but he hit a dud note with the Dukes ball – managing 4 wickets at 108.50, and crawling to 200 in Tests in the process. The other seamers fared little better: only Ruchira Perera, withdrawn after the first Test, made any impression. And for once, Murali couldn't pick up their slack – hit with injuries, and faced with a trio of left-handers in top form, he had a forgettable series.

Nonetheless, from the outside at least, the decision to send Murali home for rest ahead of the NatWest Triangular struck as foolhardy.[54] By now, Sanath's men were desperate to gloss a torrid tour; a triangular with England and India offered a chance to change the narrative and build momentum ahead of the World Cup. Instead, Sri Lanka lost their first four games, and five of six in all. With no Murali, the opposition easily plundered runs.

It had been an ugly couple of months. On the field, Sri Lanka had looked one-dimensional; off it, administrators failed to properly support the team. A home series against Bangladesh should have been an ideal tonic – but would not pass without incident. In cricketing terms at least, normal service resumed at the P. Sara. A fit-again Murali bagged 10 wickets; Aravinda exited the Test arena with a whirlwind double-century, as Sri Lanka racked up 509 on the second day alone.

Yet, the selectors were determined that the series would not pass without disruption.[55] Their surprise move to rest Atapattu, Jayawardene, Sangakkara, Arnold, Murali, Vaas, Zoysa and Dilhara was always likely to cause controversy – though Jayasuriya implored the Sports Minister to revoke the selection, he refused, seemingly fearing another bout of resignations. It did more damage to a faltering relationship – effectively, the team and the selectors were at loggerheads.

The players had a right to be annoyed: given the discord that had characterised their recent relationship with the board, the omissions strike as a needlessly antagonistic power play. Perhaps the selectors were wary of a repeat of the 1999 World Cup, but this group was a long way from reaching the end of the line. They would have all wanted to play: with salaries still lagging behind those of western professionals, a Test-match fee was not happily surrendered. Equally, with first-class cricketers struggling to make ends meet, it was unsettling to see another man audition for your place.

As strange as the omissions were the players the selectors opted to retain. If anyone needed a rest, it was the old pros: Jayasuriya had just turned 33, Tillakaratne was 35; Aravinda – who was included in the original thirteen but did not play – closing in on 38. Surely, the most pressing concern facing Sri Lanka was Sanath's successor: this could have been a good opportunity for Mahela or Marvan to gain vital experience.*

The drama between the players and board was just getting started. Though the team easily outplayed Pakistan and South Africa during a triangular in Tangiers – and reached the final of the Champions Trophy without breaking a sweat – it was not a happy time.

Indeed, the Champions Trophy was blighted by news that the ICC had struck a deal signing away players' image rights during major tournaments.[56] This meant personal endorsements would have to be frozen** – while the tournament itself was ultimately unscuppered, the image rights issue loomed large ahead of the 2003 World Cup. Most boards circumvented it by promising players a percentage of their tournament

---

*   Equally, the promotions did little to serve the men they supposedly benefited. Michael Vandort made 61 and 140 but did not play another Test until 2006, Sujeewa de Silva bowled impressively second time around but next turned out in 2007. Naveed Nawaz' returns of 21 and 78* were insufficient to earn him another cap – he promptly exited the Test arena with a batting average of 99. The whole exercise was utterly futile. Sri Lanka won the Test comfortably, but dredged up much hostility in the process.

**   Players faced the prospect of being sued by their current sponsors, and would find it harder to attract future deals if major tournaments were to become blackout zones. Equally, putting sponsorships on hold for ninety days every time a global tournament rolled around could mean sacrificing fifteen months over the next five years.

fee* – the BCCSL took a slightly different approach.[57] They hoped to pay their cricketers nothing; when it became clear that would not fly, the board tried to strongarm players into accepting 2 per cent of the tournament revenue.

Such a brazenly exploitative offer plunged a failing relationship deeper into acrimony. The numbers are especially ugly: the BCCSL would receive a guaranteed $6.4 million for the tournament; players got $700 for an ODI, and had base contracts ranging from $5,000 to $20,000.[58] At least four had to halt personal endorsements; it seems they were expected to simply suffer in silence.

But the team held firm: as Murali put it to me, 'We made everyone one voice.' Though initially hoping for 25 per cent, they agreed to settle for 20 per cent on the advice of Graeme Labrooy, the Sri Lanka Cricketers' Association representative.[59] That was far more than the board was willing to give up. They stalled, hoping the players would get cold feet as the signing deadline neared. Instead, it was the board who acquiesced, offering a 5 per cent, and then 10 per cent share. When those offers were rebuffed, they resorted to increasingly nefarious tactics. Details were leaked to the media; board president Hemaka Amarasuriya bogusly claimed the players were 'trying to squeeze the board out of every cent'.[60]

His plan worked: 'Murali and I were the ones who were labelled by the media, by the public, as playing for money,' Jayawardene told me when we spoke about the issue. 'This was a benefit the players should receive – it's funny that everything gets shown in a different manner when people can control what comes out [to the media].'** 'We were not greedy with money at all,' Murali added, when we spoke on the issue. 'We fought for the right reasons; we never fought for any wrong reasons. It upset me a lot.'

---

* Cricket Australia, for example, guaranteed 25 per cent of revenues would be passed onto players.

** Amarasuriya even tried tugging at the heartstrings by suggesting that the players' demands would destabilise infrastructural plans – a claim that was manipulative, irrelevant and plainly false.

With the ICC applying pressure, the board eventually wilted. Two and a half weeks before the World Cup got under way, they agreed to guarantee the players 12 per cent of tournament revenues, and to allocate two percent of the money to Sri Lanka's domestic cricketers.[61] 'We fought for the whole team, for the whole of club cricket as well,' Murali proudly reflected. With names signed, Amarasuriya's tone softened – but his grandstanding had done real damage. The scandal tarnished the team's image so severely that Sports Minister Johnston Fernando had to entreat the public to 'forget the past'.[62] In the context of usual Asian cricket fandom, his 'appeal to the entire country to support our players to win the World Cup' sounded very strange indeed.

Clearly, a major confrontation between the board and players had been brewing for some time. Board officials and selectors came and went like horses on a carousel, but the administration's tendency to disregard the players' concerns and treat them like pawns in a moneyfied game of chess, remained ever-present. Enough was enough: over the past year, the team had hit back – and showed the board they were done with being pushed around. Yet the image rights scandal lumped extra pressure on their shoulders.

As 2003 rolled around, and ugly memories of 1999 re-emerged from the recesses, some on the streets continued to rail against their cricketers. There were those who saw this lot as useless money-grabbers, who couldn't hold a candle to Arjuna's champs. Once again, Sri Lanka's cricketers had to prove their worth – this time to their own countrymen.

ANOTHER VICIOUS CYCLE

Getting through the Champions Trophy undefeated was a boost – but the squad knew it would have little bearing on their success at the World Cup. To succeed in South Africa, Sri Lanka would have to make strides on pitches that favoured fast bowlers. At least they had an auspicious run into the tournament – Test and ODI series in the hosts' backyard, followed by a tough triangular in Australia, offered crucial chances to build momentum.

But the team were in turmoil before they got on the plane.[63] Unhappy with the sixteen-man squad, Jayasuriya appealed to the Sports

Minister. He refused to ratify it, but chairman of selectors Guy de Alwis dug his heels in, ranting wildly to the media. 'Next time we have a selection committee meeting I will be taking a video camera so that no one can say he was not properly consulted – Sanath Jayasuriya was at the meeting.'

This constant bickering was getting absurd. With each passing squad announcement, de Alwis looked more like a playground bully winding Jayasuriya up for kicks. No doubt, he felt he was serving his country – but surely the selectors are in place to aid the captain and coach. In continually going against the team management, de Alwis was making their lives a misery. His stubbornness was becoming a distraction and a spectacle; ultimately, it was damaging the team.*

Squabbling over, Sri Lanka could get down to business, but their trial run in South Africa got off to a torrid start. After a couple of warm-ups on easy batting tracks, they arrived at The Wanderers to find a glinting green wicket. Supposedly the heavy roller had broken down: if true, convenient, as this was the prototype pitch for breaking down Sri Lanka.[64]

Though Sanath was uncowed, his decision to bat was foolhardy. Nor did abandoning opening duties look good once Arnold nicked off for a 6-ball duck. No one lasted long, and the Lankan seamers posed none of the threat of their South African counterparts. Dilhara overstepped seventeen times; Perera was withdrawn for running on the pitch. Done for 130 second time around, Sri Lanka fell to an innings defeat inside three days.

They could ill afford a repeat at Centurion. Despite missing Jayasuriya, injured playing football on the eve of the match, Sri Lanka stood up and fought. Tillakaratne ground out a five-and-a-half-hour century; come the fourth evening, Sangakkara and Jayawardene were batting with spirit. But their decision to decline offers of bad light proved naive: Sanga was snared moments before the heavens opened; next morning, Mahela fell victim to a dreadful lbw decision.[65] The one-two punch staggered Sri

---

* Though Kaushalya Weeraratne was not added to the squad as Jayasuriya had asked, he and Whatmore were at least somewhat placated by the inclusion of Ruchira Perera as a seventeenth man.

Lanka. They could only set 121: though Dilhara produced a career-best spell, South Africa limped home with 3 wickets in hand.

It was disappointing not to take anything tangible from the series, but Sri Lanka could hold their heads high. Torn into in Johannesburg – verbally as much as physically – they stood up in Centurion, refusing to take a backwards step. Jehan Mubarak told me he was 'surprised' by what he saw in South Africa. 'It can get nasty,' he pointedly explained.

'I don't think I can really say it was racially motivated,' Sangakkara added. 'I'm not sure everyone knew how to do it and keep within the boundaries of decorum. It was a very brutal confrontation verbally, and quite brutal on the field. But I think by the end of it, we were in the ascendency in terms of understanding why the South African team did that and how to respond to it.'

Ahead of the Centurion Test, the usually mild-mannered Atapattu told his men to go back hard at South Africa. Arnold and Sangakkara buzzed around the batsman like flitting flies; Jayawardene's angry response when Pollock grabbed him on the fourth afternoon showed there was no love lost between the teams.[66] And on the last day, Sangakkara went out of his way to irritate every batter who walked to the wicket. Kallis had mistakenly compared himself to Bradman during the series, and arrived at the crease to Sanga's smug shout: 'Ah, here comes Sir Don, lads.' Ashwell Prince was quizzed on divisions that ran through the side, Mark Boucher's verbiage corrected, Pollock told to 'be gracious'. This sort of chirping will appeal to some and appal others – but supped full of abuse, Sri Lanka had to fight back.

'That stood us in good stead,' Sangakkara reflected. 'Following on from that series, I think we've done very well against South Africa. We were very strong and upright in terms of going toe-to-toe with them. If there were verbals, there were people who were quite comfortable taking that pressure, converting that pressure into an advantage. We learnt a lot about ourselves, but more importantly we learnt a lot about that South Africa team and how to play them.'

There was support from the media too. Journalists who might usually have spoken of sanctions talked up Sanga as a future captain; former South African all-rounder Pat Symcox felt 'Sri Lankan cricket took a huge step forward'.[67] None would accuse this side of shrinking from a challenge. If echoes of meek gentleman cricketers still clung in the minds of some, this combative new breed were doing all they could to eradicate them.

Sadly, pessimism over the side's prospects beyond Asia returned during a disappointing ODI series. Though abject failure in the first ODI wasn't entirely Sri Lanka's fault,* things went from bad to worse. Amidst four thrashings, a superb chase in Benoni did little to lift spirits. Dav and Sanath could console themselves they'd have Murali next time around, but the results nonetheless augured badly ahead of the World Cup.

Sri Lanka's form lumped extra pressure onto the VB triangular in Australia too – but things would get worse before they got better. Having been decimated by England in their first two games, a desperate reshuffle began. Rather than trusting their players, the team frantically sought answers not readily forthcoming. Heading into the Christmas break, they had lost three of three – and came nowhere near producing a competitive performance. Being blown out by Australia 'A' in 25 overs was another dent to the team's confidence; with the image-rights saga still rolling on, it was an unhappy time. Surely some were starting to yearn for the comforts of home.

Jayasuriya's struggles seemed central to Sri Lanka's rut. Whenever technical flaws against pace were exposed, he had a tendency to grow pensive; to shy away from the very thoughtlessness that made him such a destructive force. It did the team few favours. His game was at its best when he committed to batting's most basic principle: 'see ball, hit ball'. And when he was firing, Sri Lanka usually won.

With the team on the brink of disaster, Sanath threw off the shackles at the SCG. Riding his luck early, he freed his arms; by the time the spinners entered the attack, he had played himself back into form. Jayasuriya went back to basics and emphatically turned Sri Lanka's fortunes. Supported by the more workmanlike Atapattu, he carved Australia to ribbons. When the first wicket fell in the 34th over, Sri Lanka had 237 on the board. Those runs had come at close to 7 an over, 122 of them from the captain's bat.

---

* The Wanderers was still without a working roller, rendering the pitch a nightmare prospect first up.

Australia never got close to a 344-run target, as Sanath took centre stage with ball in hand too. Brimming with newfound confidence, he cracked 106 in his next outing as Sri Lanka cantered to 284.* Suddenly, they had a shot at making the finals. Still, cynics pointed out that the SCG wasn't a million miles from the SSC, and things fell apart in Brisbane. After a nightmare start, Sri Lanka recovered to reach 211 − enough to render the chase nervy, but not prevent the hosts from crossing the line.

Though the cricket was often enthralling, the match was ultimately overshadowed by a pair of ugly incidents. On the whole, Murali bore abuse from the Australian crowds stoically, but something soured inside him as beery Brisbane goons cheered when he was helped from the ground with a thigh injury. 'The crowd was so horrible,' he told journalists. 'I got injured and they were laughing and jeering. What they were saying didn't affect my performance but I didn't want to field on the boundary.'[68]

There was worse. After being run out in the 40th over of Australia's chase, Darren Lehmann made his way back to the changing room and shouted 'Cunts. Fucking black cunts,' loud enough for Sri Lanka's backroom staff to hear. It was upsetting that such vile outbursts were still a part of cricket − but the ease with which Sri Lanka brushed the insult off was equally troubling. Both Whatmore and manager Ajit Jayasekera appealed to Clive Lloyd for clemency; had casual racism around the cricket field been so normalised that it no longer had any impact?[69]

Though Murali missed the rest of the Tri-series, Sri Lanka might still have qualified for the finals. England's 279-run target looked in danger as long as Jayasuriya was at the crease − but having pounded 99 off 82 he collided with Sanga and was run out. Sri Lanka fell 19 short, and were blown away by Australia in their last match. Nonetheless, their January resurgence was cause for cautious optimism; crucially, their captain had rediscovered the explosive form that was Sri Lanka's ODI cornerstone.

---

*   Prior to 2003, Sri Lanka had only made 280-plus six times outside of Asia; now, they had such scores in consecutive matches. The correlation between Jayasuriya's personal form and the team's success was clear. When he spent time at the crease, he eased pressure on those around him. Only twice to date had Sri Lanka lost when Jayasuriya scored a century.

Given Murali's injury struggles over the past year, his fitness ahead of the World Cup was another boost. Sri Lanka's two most important pieces were in place – though rounding out the squad presented challenges. A motley crew of seamers had been tried and discarded during the four-year cycle;* the selectors ultimately decided that Buddhika, Pulasthi Gunaratne and Prabath Nissanka were the best accompaniments to Vaas and Dilhara. On the batting side, Mubarak and Gunawardene snuck in, so too the evergreen Tillakaratne and Aravinda.** Top to bottom the squad had a pleasing blend of youth and experience. It was vital each man was up for the challenge – South Africa was a tricky place to play cricket at the best of times, and the World Cup bound to be a pressure cooker. Over the next month, nothing would come easy.

Sri Lanka's march through the group was a study in chaos. Against Bangladesh, Vaas took a hat-trick with the first three balls of the match. Canada were finished for an all-time low 36. Yet, when it came to the Kenya clash, Sanath's men self-destructed against the leg spin of Collins Obuya. They fell 54 runs short of a 211-run target – on the field at least, this was the worst day in Sri Lanka's cricket history.

The failure threw the group wide open, essentially transforming the West Indies game into a knockout. Dilhara sent Ramnaresh Sarwan to hospital with a violent bouncer – but just when his team looked down and out, Sarwan returned to the crease and launched a withering assault. With West Indies needing 16 off 12, Murali magicked up a miserly 49th over. Sri Lanka's passage was assured, even if their group-stage drama was not quite done.***

---

* Bowling all-rounders like Suresh Perera, Kaushalya Weeraratne and Akalanka Ganegama had failed to deliver on their promise. Equally, Indika Gallage, Chamila Gamage and Hashantha Fernando had made little impression when given chances, while Nuwan Zoysa and Ruchira Perera's careers had stalled.

** Having been out of the side for close to eighteen months, Aravinda was brought back into the mix in August 2002 after shedding 12kg. Tillakaratne was restored thanks to a mountain of runs in domestic and Test cricket.

*** In their last group game, Sri Lanka should have been beaten by South Africa, but the hosts got themselves in a muddle with Duckworth-Lewis. Mark Boucher flat-batted the last ball of the match to gift the Lankans a tie.

The wheels fully came off in the Super Six. First, the Lankans were brutalised by Australia, with Brett Lee at his bullying best. At least fans could take solace from Aravinda's masterful 92 – and especially from the two late 6s he struck off the world's fastest bowler. Even as he neared his fifth decade, the sharp eye and supple wrists and sturdy forearms combined to create something magical. Still, his brilliance could not prevent Sri Lanka falling to a 96-run defeat.

The capitulation against India was even more disheartening, with another old story rearing its ugly head. Murali and Vaas combined to take 5 for 80; the rest managed 1 wicket and leaked more than 7 runs an over. Any hopes of a competitive chase evaporated as the team slipped to 15-4. Still licking their wounds after the run-in with Lee, Sri Lanka collapsed to 109.

The team were in disarray, but the unwieldy tournament structure meant they only needed to beat Zimbabwe to scrape through to the semis. It wasn't entirely straightforward, but Atapattu's second century of the tournament helped carry them home. If another clash against Australia seemed a dubious reward, the Port Elizabeth pitch at least promised something for the spinners. And Sri Lanka flew out of the gates: Adam Gilchrist shocked the world by walking, Vaas got Matthew Hayden and Ponting to miscue – but Sangakkara's missed stumping of Symonds proved costly.[70] He stayed till the end, dragging Australia up to 212 – once again, Lee was too hot to handle. He castled Atapattu with a ball clocked at 99.4mph; Tillakaratne and Gunawardene were undone by raw pace too. There was no coming back from 43-4.

It had been a strange sort of tournament. Given the team's showing in 1999, it seems cynical to view reaching the semis as anything other than an unqualified success. But Sri Lanka never really got going. They lost four – three of them by a distance, the other the humiliation in Kenya – and were only spared defeat against South Africa by a mathematical mistake. In truth, the nervy victory over West Indies was the sole performance the team could feel really proud of.

While Jayasuriya was at his brutal best in the early goings, he fell away sharply after being assaulted by Brett Lee. Atapattu notched two 100s but failed in Sri Lanka's four toughest matches. Mahela had a miserable time; when the going got tough, the ageing Aravinda still looked Sri

Lanka's best player. Nor was it a great trip for Sangakkara: the young keeper reached 20 on five occasions but never made it out of the 30s; far more costly were his lapses with the gloves. He should have had Ponting run out in the Super Six, and Andrew Symonds stumped in the semi – on both occasions his errors were punished, and may well have altered the matches' outcomes.

That in itself was a reminder that results can hang on single moments – that for all Sri Lanka's struggles, they were a whisker away from another showpiece. Still, there can be no doubt that the team's confidence waned during the course of the tournament; that when things went wrong, they quickly began to question their plans. The clearest example was the decision to tinker with the batting order at the crunch stage of the cup.* Such a scattergun approach to selection, at the business end of a World Cup no less, suggests frazzled minds beset by insecurity. Sri Lanka's troubles were rarely eased by the tendency to question themselves when things went awry.

While the batsmen misfired, the bowlers surpassed all expectations. First and foremost, it was a special tournament for Vaas, whose 23 wickets – at 14.39 apiece – represented a record World Cup haul. Whether the ball was fresh or old, he found troubling movement; so often forced to live in Murali's sprawling shadow, these performances were a reminder that he was a rare talent in his own right.

Murali's unique ability to strangle batsmen was crucial,** while Jayasuriya and Aravinda combined for 19 wickets, going at fewer than 5 an over. The only disappointment was the failure of the backup seamers: eight years since Arjuna and Dav crafted a plan to strangle sides with

---

* The pre-tournament decision that Tillakaratne should bat at number three made sense: he had the experience, tenacity and technique such a challenge required, and could act as a stable anchor for the team's strokemakers to bat around. His returns had been steady rather than spectacular, but it was nonetheless surprising that he was the man sacrificed when the batting struggled to click. The untested Jehan Mubarak replaced him for the crunch game against India. After failing to trouble the scorers, he was promptly restored to twelfth-man duties. For the Zimbabwe match, Avishka Gunawardene went first drop; he too was only given one opportunity in the role, and shifted down a spot against Australia to make room for Tillakaratne's return.

** No other spinner matched his tournament haul of 17: of all those who bowled at least 50 overs, only Ntini, Bichel and McGrath bettered his economy rate of 3.63.

a surfeit of spinners, Sri Lanka were still reliant on the same men to get through overs.

As with the last World Cup, the tournament's conclusion marked the end of an era. Alex Kontouris decided it was time to head back to Australia: he had served Sri Lanka for seven and a half years, and was ready for a fresh challenge.[71] Rarely has a member of Sri Lanka's back-room staff been held in such high esteem. No one has a bad word to say about Kontouris – the decision to name a new high-performance gym in his honour was the ultimate show of appreciation.

Sadly, Whatmore's departure was considerably less smooth. For some time, he had sought clarity over his contract renewal.[72] He was met only with silence, although the decision to appoint Duleep Mendis as 'special advisor' to the team in July 2002 implied Sri Lanka were planning for life without him. Less than two weeks after the World Cup exit, the BCCSL released a statement citing the need for 'fresh thinking'.[73] Dav's time was up. While the decision itself was legitimate enough, surely Whatmore had earned the right to be treated with more respect. Sri Lanka's most successful coach was tossed aside without warning or fanfare.

'Dav was a wonderful man,' Ajit Jayasekera told me wistfully. 'I think it was he and Alex who brought these players together. Alex was working all the time, Dav was coaching: they brought a new dimension to Sri Lankan cricket. They were two of the most important people in the World Cup win and beyond.' Certainly, Whatmore and Kontouris belong in rarefied air; few men have had such a tangible impact upon the island's cricket.

The ultra-critical might point out that Dav never managed to settle on a band of bowlers to back up Murali and Vaas, that seamers in particular were tried and tossed far too frequently. But this was hardly his fault alone – and above all, Whatmore left a much better side than he inherited, and changed the course of Sri Lankan cricket. In seven and a half years, the team had shaken off minnow status and emerged as a major force. That's not a bad legacy.

He and Kontouris were not the only legends saying farewell. Few men anywhere can lay claim to the kind of reverence Aravinda enjoys among his countrymen. For all the stacks of runs Sangakkara and Jayawardene subsequently scored, any Sri Lankan cricket fan over 30 will dogmatically insist de Silva is the greatest batsman the island has produced. 'I still believe my cricketer is number one, Aravinda,' Ravi Pushpakumara proudly told me. 'What Aravinda has achieved is remarkable. I saw Sachin Tendulkar, I saw Brian Lara. If Aravinda was born in India, different story.'

'Club matches were nothing to him,' Pushpakumara gushed. 'If he wanted to play hard he'd get 100, 150, then take 5 wickets. No problem. I used to come off a long run: he'd stand at first slip, right behind the wicketkeeper and just take a fish bun and eat it as I was running into bowl.' Undeniably, Aravinda was blessed with an almost mystical quality that resonated with the Sri Lankan psyche. His performances in the semi and final of the 1996 World Cup went a long way towards enshrining him, but he fully deserves such exalted status. Though he existed in an era of very great batsmen, I would argue that during the second half of the 1990s, he sat at the top of the tree with only Tendulkar beside him.[*]

Of course, statistics alone belie the unique brilliance of Aravinda's batting. No numbers could come close to the thrill of seeing him hook bullets off the bridge of his nose; few batsmen have the courage or craft to stroll down the wicket and slap the world's fastest bowlers into the stands. All of this he did with a style so laconic it might have well been called lazy.

Though by no means classical, he was elegant in his own way; that rare sportsman who seems to reach into the lofty world of art. Many have described his batting as lyrical; certainly, he was capable of inspiring the sort of unbridled joy only a genius can. And as is the way with the very greatest, he became emblematic of his country: you felt you saw something of Sri Lanka each time he pulled or drove or cut. In a real show of respect, he was immediately absorbed into the board of selectors.

There were fears that Aravinda's fence-jump might throw up conflicts of interest – de Alwis, for one, made it clear he was none too pleased with the expedited promotion.[74] The chairman of selectors had constantly bickered with the team management since his appointment;

---

[*] If we take the final three years of the decade (1 January 1997–31 December 1999), Tendulkar (2,735 runs at 68.37) and de Silva (2,195 runs at 66.51) were leaps and bounds ahead of their contemporaries in Tests. During the same period, Rahul Dravid scored 2,262 runs at 52.60; Steve Waugh 2,872 at 49.51; Ricky Ponting 1,762 at 47.62; Lara 2,299 at 46.91.

Sports Minister Fernando's refusal to ratify his squad for a post-World Cup tournament in Sharjah was the final straw.*'The Minister of Sports has interfered in everything from the time I took over and there is no way that I can continue in such circumstances,' he bitterly complained. Fernando promptly appointed Lalith Kaluperuma in his place.

Restored to his armchair, de Alwis might have felt red-faced as he watched Sangakkara compile two unbeaten centuries in the course of three days in Sharjah. The Kenya defeat was avenged – but Sri Lanka's week hit the skids as they were handily beaten by Pakistan and Zimbabwe. Despite a spate of shock retirements, the African nation sailed through to the finals at Sri Lanka's expense. This was disturbing. The team bubble had been burst: Kontouris was gone, Whatmore packing his bags – now Jayasuriya reiterated his desire to stand down.[75] Sri Lanka left Sharjah in turmoil: without captain, coach or any sense of clear direction.

It is little surprise that Jayasuriya had reached the end of his tether. In the past year, he had been savaged by the media over image rights and forced to go to war with a stubborn Chairman of Selectors. The board had ignored his opinion that Whatmore's contract should be renewed – his tenure showed that leading Sri Lanka now meant walking a tight-rope.[76] Future captains had to be prepared to fight battles on all fronts, to take flak from all corners. Ranatunga was a tricky act to follow; all in all, Sanath handled the task with aplomb. Under his leadership, the team took on a more egalitarian feel – and a more victorious one too. He led Sri Lanka to eighteen victories in thirty-eight Tests,** a major achieve-ment given the struggles to win consistently under Arjuna.

---

*   Fernando's objections – to the dropping of Sangakkara and resting of Murali – seem reasonable. Certainly, de Alwis' obsession with resting his best bowler was strange. Other unusual selections managed to slip through the net. Though Sri Lanka were entering a new cycle, and starting to look towards the next World Cup, Tillakaratne was retained and Kumar Dharmasena recalled. While Jayawardene probably needed a break after a rotten run, Russel Arnold was harshly excluded.

**   Under his tenure Sri Lanka won 47.36 per cent of their Tests. In numerical terms, that places Sanath's Sri Lanka a smidgen behind Lloyd's West Indies (48.64 per cent wins) but well ahead of Border (34.40 per cent) or Greg Chappell's (43.75 per cent) Australians, Ganguly (42.85 per cent) or Dhoni's (45.00 per cent) Indians, Hussain (37.77 per cent) or Cook's (40.67 per cent) England sides.

Still, Jayasuriya had enviable tools at his disposal – much-improved versions of Murali and Vaas, a deeper and more consistent batting line-up and better back-up bowlers. And despite the team's progress, Sri Lanka remained alarmingly two-faced: assured in Asia, unreliable elsewhere.* On a personal level, there was a strain of thought that Jayasuriya's lapses of confidence were too ready and manifest. On a number of occasions he lost faith in his technique and dropped himself down the order: during the England series in 2002, Ranatunga wrote 'the message it sends to the opposition is that the captain doesn't fancy it. And if he isn't up for the fight, what about his team?'[77]

Next in line and the outgoing captain's choice, Atapattu was the clear frontrunner to take over. But the selectors sprang a surprise: while Marvan would lead the ODI team, Hashan Tillakaratne was handed the reins in Tests. None could resent Tillakaratne's promotion, though given the culture of leadership in Sri Lanka, and the near uniformity of the Test and ODI XIs, split-captaincy seemed an unwieldy solution.

Above all, being passed over for the Test captaincy was a slap in the face for Atapattu. He had been Jayasuriya's right-hand man for the past three years, deputised ably whenever the captain was missing, and at 32 was amply ready to lead. None were overly satisfied with the selectors' claim that they did not want to lump pressure on him too soon.[78]

It did not help that at times, Atapattu and de Silva's relationship had been rocky. Whatever drove the decision, it was a misguided one – the kind of move bound to destabilise, cause bitterness, and saddle a team with awkwardness. The 2003 World Cup had gone far better than 1999, yet it was difficult to feel positive in the months following the tournament. Once more, a World Cup had drawn Sri Lanka into chaos; again, the team would have to start more or less from scratch.

AN AWKWARD ALLIANCE

Despite wanting rid of Whatmore, the BCCSL failed to line up a replacement – and with board elections scheduled for the first time since 2000,

---

* Outside of their home continent, Sri Lanka won one (against Zimbabwe), lost five and drew four under Jayasuriya.

few wanted to throw their name into the hat.[79] Bob Woolmer, Graham Ford, John Bracewell and Steve Rixon all declined the opportunity to coach Sri Lanka; for the time being at least, Mendis would continue to take charge of the side.

Tillakaratne's tenure, meanwhile, got off to a shaky start: with two Tests against New Zealand producing cricket as soporific as the Sri Lankan sun, his perception as a negative leader was quickly ingrained.[80] Ragged in the field at the P. Sara, Sri Lanka redeemed themselves with the bat. But while Tillakaratne led from the front with a dogged 144, he showed scant desire to push for a result. With Sir Lanka 91 behind heading into the final day, many felt a Tissera-esque declaration could be the match-winning ticket. Instead, Sri Lanka batted halfway to lunch, and the game lurched towards a lifeless draw.

There was scant more joy in Kandy. Rain delayed the start of play until the second afternoon; by the fourth day, both captains seemed to be looking towards the finish line. When Stephen Fleming tried to bore Tillakaratne out, Sri Lanka's captain responded by milking 27 between lunch and tea. His 93 brought the team close to parity, but almost ground the game to a halt in the process.

It briefly sparked into life in the final morning. Murali found support from the rest of the pack: from 92-1 overnight, the Kiwis slumped to 139-7. But Tillakaratne was strangely reluctant to turn the screw. With three men on the fence, New Zealand's eighth-wicket partnership stretched almost 30 overs. Sri Lanka still might have won – but shut up shop once Jayasuriya went early. 'They gave up after losing the first wicket and that was very surprising,' said a baffled Fleming. 'They had nothing to lose and I can't understand why they were not willing to push on further. We were certainly not going to bowl them out in 38 overs.'[81]

Tillakaratne countered that with Jayasuriya gone and Atapattu missing, it would have been risky to try to force a result. But cricket is rarely risk-free – surely, Sri Lanka might have indulged in a few more swings of the bat before counting themselves out. After all, drawing twice against New Zealand – dispatched on their last two visits – was a tepid start to a new era.

Fleming leant on defensive tactics too, and the P. Sara and Asgiriya are Sri Lanka's least partisan pitches – but Tillakaratne was clearly overly cautious. Tied to his age and increasingly cagey batting, he gave the impression of one who had seen too much; a man scarred, still conscious of Sri Lanka's once-minnow status.

Meanwhile, with the interim committee growing increasingly unpopular, and the BCCSL facing the prospect of financial ruin, board elections were universally cheered as a return to democracy.[82] In a contest for the ages, Arjuna would run against Sumathipala. Before long these allies-turned-enemies were at each other's throats.

Ranatunga's blunt denouncement of his opponent's corruption earned him little support; ultimately, Sumathipala's blowout victory confirmed he was unbeatable when it came to board elections.[*83] Shockingly, Arjuna couldn't even secure the support of his own club.[84] 'It's an eye-opener that I wanted the world and country to see,' he insisted. 'If there's corruption in an elite club like the SSC, what can you expect from small clubs?' He angrily declined Sumathipala's olive branch – stating he was 'honest', and couldn't 'work with people who are corrupt'.

In the build-up to the elections, Sumathipala had mercilessly criticised the interim committee over their inability to secure a new coach. Now, restored to his throne, he wasted little time in naming John Dyson as Whatmore's successor.[85] An excellent game-planner, with a masters in education, a major in computing and thirty Tests experience, Dyson brought the sort of fresh approach the board thanklessly claimed to be seeking.[86] There would be cultural barriers for Dyson to clamber over – at press conferences and team meetings, his jokes were often met with baffled silences – but this was a good fit for both parties: a young ambitious coach, paired with a side in transition, still searching for its identity.

So Sri Lanka's trip to the West Indies in June 2003 would be the last with Mendis at the helm. Twice during the ODIs, the team defied the odds to rescue lost causes. First, Vaas, Prabath Nissanka and Murali stopped the Windies getting close to a target of 201; then, Chandana launched a brutal assault as Sri Lanka gunned down 313. These were the sort of performances that breathe life into a tired side, that flood flagging minds with belief. In the context of a new era, it was just the springboard Sri Lanka had been craving.

---

* Three months after the election, the board opted for a name change. Moving forward, the BCCSL would be known as Sri Lanka Cricket (SLC).

Yet they struggled to carry momentum into the Tests. After a rain-blighted draw in St Lucia, the second Test at Sabina Park offered much more entertainment. Nissanka kept Sri Lanka in it with some hostile fast bowling – but the team twice fluffed their lines with the bat. Though Murali bowled his heart out all series, he lost the battle against Lara, whose 299 runs came at 144.50. After Fleming's marathon double-hundred in Colombo, it did little to allay the impression that left-handers played Murali best – even with the doosra in his arsenal.

For Tillakaratne, pressure was starting to mount. At least, the team had the best part of five months off before England's arrival at the end of 2003. Dyson and his team touched down in early September: while the new coach spoke of developing a winning attitude, his first months on the island were far from straightforward. The death of his father forced him back to Australia, then dengue fever had him stuck in bed.[87] Meanwhile, rumours swirled that some of the seniors were sceptical about his appointment.

So it was a relief that his tenure got off to a dream start. A rounded Sri Lankan attack tore Vaughan's men to shreds in the first ODI. After a sticky-fingered series against New Zealand, Mahela took a couple of sharp chances at slip, before Sanath and Kalu knocked off the runs with consummate ease. The sole sadness was the disappearance of Prabath Nissanka: still short of his 23rd birthday, he was struck down with a career-ending knee injury. Another promising prospect was snatched away from Sri Lanka – had Nissanka, Dilhara and Nuwan Zoysa been able to stay off the treatment table, the island's oft-toothless seam attack would have carried a good deal more snarl.

Still, Sri Lanka were licking their lips ahead of the Galle Test, fully expecting a sixth straight win at their south coast fortress. The English had their hands full simply surviving: Gareth Batty and Vaughan were caught out by the currents and almost drowned in the days leading up to the match – a foreshadow perhaps, of their great escape in the game's final session.[88] England were 7 wickets down at tea, but somehow clung on, their tail showing real desire and toughness. Sri Lanka were upset by their brazen slowness, and by umpire Venkat's refusal to award Murali an all-important lbw – but may well have rued their own decisions too.*[89]

Still, they travelled to Kandy with their tails up, knowing they had fallen a whisker short of victory. By the second morning, the lower order's dogged resistance was grating on England. Hussain decided to up the ante, welcoming Murali to the crease by calling him 'a fucking cheat and a fucking chucker'.[90] Murali promptly reported Hussain to the umpire, leading Graham Thorpe to crudely try to recast him as the villain.[91] 'It is like trying to get players sent off in football; waving your hands at the referee,' he complained to the media. 'You don't need to do it, that's not sportsmanship in my view.' *Sending off* was a strange analogy to plump for: had Thorpe forgotten England's last trip to Kandy – when his wild aeroplane celebration saw Jayasuriya wrongly dismissed?

His hollow words were jumped on by the English media; ultimately, the reluctance to damn Hussain's behaviour struck of partisanship. Nasser escaped censure, but might have reflected it was unwise to rile Murali. After being swatted for a couple of 4s and a 6, he did for Trescothick and Vaughan; next morning, he ended Thorpe's four-hour stay with a devilish, dipping doosra. For the second time in as many Tests, Sri Lanka carried a solid lead into the second innings.

But while Dilshan's freewheeling 100 allowed them to score at near 4 runs per over, Tillakaratne delayed his declaration till just before tea on day four. He couldn't rid himself of his natural caution: even after striking two breakthroughs before close, Tillakaratne stuck with five boundary riders on the final morning.[92] He loosened the noose around England's neck, but Sri Lanka's bowlers still should have won them the game. When Murali ended Vaughan's resistance after tea, the visitors were 7 wickets down. A thrilling climax beckoned, but Chris Read and Batty unfussily saw their team to safety.

★ While Murali bagged 11 scalps, the four bits-and-pieces spinners managed just 4 in 107 overs. Equally, as skies darkened on the fourth day, Sri Lanka could have looked to push the game forward – instead, in an unwanted echo of the New Zealand series, they gingerly added 127 in 52.5 overs.

While sharpened knives were squarely pointed at Tillakaratne, he wasn't the only member of the side beset by over-cautiousness. In 2016, Jayawardene told Guarav Kalra that he tried to encourage an earlier declaration.[93] 'Murali's got ears like elephants,' he said. 'He came rushing in and said, "I know what you are saying to Hashan. You want to declare now. You're not the one who is going to bowl. I'm the one who has to bowl. We need 350-375 runs because then the England batsmen know they can't score." I said, "275 is enough. They are still going to defend. They aren't going to play shots." He said, "Yeah, but you don't know that. If you declare now I am not going to bowl. You can bowl." And he walked off. So Hashan didn't declare … After the match, Murali was in a corner not saying much and Hashan was really upset that he didn't make the early declaration.'*

A score of 0-0 after two Tests was disheartening, but with just three rest days, England were tossed from the frying pan into the fire. By the first afternoon at the SSC, Vaughan's men were wilting under the sapping winter sun. Once more, Murali was their scourge; conceding 40 from as many overs, his bowling was as stifling as the sticky Colombo heat.

England's first-innings total of 265 looked short of the mark, especially at a ground that Sri Lanka's batsmen were starting to cherish as their own slice of heaven. It was especially special for Thilan Samaraweera – now, promoted to three, he struck 140, throwing off the shackles once he reached three figures. He wasn't the only one doling out punishment. Sanath smashed 85, Mahela made a buoyant 134 – and as Christmas closed in, Dilshan and Chandana produced a partnership full of festive spirit. England wore the look of men who'd rather be sat by the fire. By the time Sri Lanka declared, at 628-8, the game was up. The visitors crashed to 148; Sri Lanka were winners by an innings and 215.

With 26 wickets at 12.30 apiece, Murali was the biggest difference between the teams. When he wasn't taking wickets, he built pressure, tightening the vice which eventually broke England's batters.** In 2001,

---

* The anecdote highlights the fact that Murali was a defensive cricketer. He liked to daunt opponents with mountainous scores, to strangle them with dot after dot. Had he adopted a more attacking mindset, it might have gone some way towards counteracting Tillakaratne's cautiousness. As it was, the two were peas in a pod.

** Across 231.4 overs, he maintained an economy of 1.38.

he'd been hampered by injuries and well handled by Thorpe; two years on, England's best player looked as clueless as the rest. Dismissed five times by Murali, he ended the tour dancing drunkenly towards a doosra. The mystery ball was getting more potent by the day.

While many felt Tillakaratne's lack of adventure cost Sri Lanka a 3-0 scoreline, the Galle and Kandy pitches held up better than expected, and his men twice fell just short of taking 10 wickets. Had victory been completed in either Test, the spotlight might have shifted elsewhere. Instead, scrutiny and speculation dogged his captaincy into a new year and another mouth-watering series.

★★★

With a new captain and an ageing core, Australia arrived in February 2004 a little short of their usual swagger. Having failed to beat India at home in Steve Waugh's final series, some wondered whether they could handle the Kandy Man and his back-up band of run-hungry batsmen. Five ODIs offered an absorbing aperitif. Sri Lanka were short of white-ball cricket and it showed: though they won two matches by the skin of their teeth, they were outplayed in the pressure moments and lost 3-2. It was an ominous forebear for the Tests. Twice, the team were well placed in chases but fell away; equally, they took wickets to claw their way back into the third ODI, only for a nerveless partnership between Symonds and Clarke to see Australia home.

The lead-up to the Tests was overshadowed by talk of Murali and Warne's 'Great Race' – first to 500 wickets, and then past Walsh's 519.[94] The prospect of cricket's greatest spinners going head to head was titillating enough; the idea of them racing towards history sent the media into a frenzy. Never before have two such undisputed masters of their craft met on a cricket field. But for all their similarities, the pair seem diametrically opposed. Where Murali danced to the wicket, Warne swaggered; while Warne revelled in his celebrity, Murali shied away from the spotlight. Warne relished the mental contest, Murali only ever wanted

---

[*]   Though Warne (491) had been well ahead for most of his career, during his year on the sidelines Murali had taken 48 wickets, cutting the gap to 6.

to bowl. Pundits unanimously agreed these two noble tricksters were destined to dominate a hard-fought series.

Yet the outcome ultimately rested on Australia's grit, a never-say-die attitude that Sri Lanka struggled to match. Three first-innings leads were surrendered; from repeatedly strong positions, the hosts lost every Test. The opener at Galle was as heart-wrenching as they come. For the first two days, Sri Lanka were in total control. Eager to attack, Australia fell headfirst into Murali's web, before another striking Dilshan century left them 161 behind.

But the slowness of the pitch played into the visitors' hands second time around.[95] Hayden swept like a Colombo cleaner en route to a muscular century: when he was caught on the fourth morning, Sri Lanka might have felt they had wrested back control. But the pitch had flattened out, Chandana and Dharmasena were ineffective, and Tillakaratne got his tactics wrong. With Lehmann and Damien Martyn easily mounting a 206-run stand, Sri Lanka started the final day 349 behind. Winning was out of the question.

And it soon became clear a draw was well out of their reach. Warne took 3 wickets in 13 balls to send the hosts tumbling to 56-4; after lunch, he bagged Tillakaratne to move to 500. The Lankans were finished inside 46 overs. They had squandered a golden position, and lost by a whopping 197. Tillakaratne blamed the batsmen for making 'the pitch look difficult to bat on', but admitted Murali lacked support – surely, the selectors had to accept part of the blame. Playing Chandana and Dharmasena together simply wasn't working. Neither was offering penetration or control;* their inefficacy was lumping extra stress onto Murali's already strained shoulder.[96]

Both were dropped for the second Test in Kandy. After nearly two years out of the side, Zoysa returned with immediate impact – when Murali ended Hayden's resistance, Australia had stumbled to 86-7. The Kandy Man, meanwhile, had moved to 498. Busloads of schoolchildren were ferried to the ground; firecrackers fizzed when Murali did for

---

* In six Tests since the World Cup, Dharmasena had taken 11 wickets at 58.54. Chandana's three appearances had brought 4 wickets at 77.25.

Michael Kasprowicz with a classic off-break to reach 500. In front of his home crowd, Muttiah Mularitharan had entered a very special club.

Australia's 120 was their lowest ever score against Sri Lanka – but on a tricky wicket, the hosts couldn't force home their advantage. Warne was near his swaggering best;* at one stage 92-7, they needed Murali and Vaas to drag them past 200. Still, Australia's second innings carried an ugly sense of déjà vu. Gilchrist launched a withering assault; once he went, Martyn batted and batted. Again, Murali had to toil more than 50 overs for his 5 wickets. Worse, the Australians wouldn't let him settle, cowing him into bowling negative lines.

While Australia's target looked imposing, all was not lost. In January, Central Province had mounted a world-record 513-run chase at Asgiriya; now, Sri Lanka fancied their own slice of history.[97] Jayasuriya's blistering strokeplay kept them in the hunt. His 145-ball 131 was spiced with seventeen hits to the fence and two big 6s, each one lifting Lankan hopes. But when he was caught behind off Gillespie, Sri Lanka were 218-5 and a long way from home.

By close, they were 7 down and relying on their bowlers – who'd need to add another 51 to bring about victory. Not many slept well on the eve of the final day's play. Vaas was 30* overnight and knew the result likely lay in his hands. He and the rest of the tail stuck around to practise on the fourth evening – but old habits die hard, and in the third over he couldn't resist a slog-sweep.[98] Zoysa went without scoring, and Lokuarachchi in the next over. Sri Lanka had lost by 27. It was gutting to go 2-0 down in a series that had been so hard fought, but where Sri Lanka surrendered in Galle, they battled till the last in Kandy. Tillakaratne rued soft dismissals; certainly he, Atapattu and Sangakkara – all without a 50 so far – needed to stand up and contribute.

Desperate to make amends at the SSC, Sri Lanka found their luck had run dry. Five days cricket, in unbearable heat, produced a close encounter and an inevitable result. Ponting won a third consecutive toss; finally, his batsmen finally managed to take full advantage. Murali was hammered for 56 off his first 13 overs, and went wicketless right up until the

---

*   He claimed to have figured Dilshan out after the century at Galle, and dismissed him first ball – lbw to a slider for the second innings running.

69th. By that time, he and the other spinners were bowling at leg stump with a 2-7 field.

Whereas England had been bogged down by Murali – lumbering forward, pad first – Ponting's men were much more proactive. On the whole, they danced: the twinkle-toed Lehmann, who Paul Coupar likened to a 'flyweight boxer', did it best, but Hayden, Gilchrist and the captain all made real efforts to smother the spin and stifle Murali with attacking shots.[99] It lessened the effect of the doosra – and upset the off-spinner, who loved to build pressure by strangling batsmen.

Though Ponting and Lehmann went hard at Murali here, it was a failure to resort to negative tactics so early in the Test. Despite the 505 Test wickets in his back catalogue, was Murali still lacking that crucial dash of bravado? 'The wicket had enough to bowl attacking lines, but they did not back their bowlers enough,' Lehmann opined at the end of day one.[100] By this stage, Murali should have been demanding catchers on the edge of the strip. A defensive field, on the opening day of a home Test, was a grievous insult.

The overriding memory of the innings is Justin Langer's mischievous bail-flick* – seemingly a nefarious attempt to try to trick umpires into giving Tillakaratne out. Hauled in front of match referee Chris Broad, he claimed he had 'absolutely no idea the bail had fallen off'.[101] Broad's own interpretation stretched the bounds of incredulity: he seemed to congratulate Langer, stating 'Justin was disappointed that the charge was brought and explained his position in a very honest and succinct way,' before contradicting himself: 'He was, however, reminded that in future [sic] to steer clear of any instances such as this.'

If Langer had explained his position honestly – and the bail-flick was inadvertent – how could he then be expected to avoid similar incidents in the future? Above all, it is nigh on impossible to watch the footage and think his action was accidental. It felt as though Broad knew Langer's

---

*   With Tillakaratne batting with the right-handed Samaraweera, the field had to switch each time the batsmen crossed. As Langer passed the stumps at the striker's end, he flicked one of the bails off with his fingers; before the next ball was bowled, the Aussie fielders asked whether Tillakaratne had hit his own wicket. The umpires checked the incident with the third umpire, who noticed Tillakaratne was nowhere near his stumps, and spotted Langer dislodging the bail.

action was Machiavellian, but decided against causing a stir. Of course, cries of prejudice sprang up from the east – as well as the inescapable hypothetical: would an Asian cricketer have received such clemency?

At times, it felt like there was an Old Boy's club that certain countries' cricketers weren't allowed into. *The Island* certainly felt so, one of its writers claiming that 'the Aussies and the English could get away with anything'.[102] Though subsequent rumours that Broad had been out 'boozing' with Ponting's team proved baseless, their very existence reveals plenty about attitudes in Sri Lanka. The light-handed treatment Langer received was always likely to upset – especially in light of what happened after the Test.

Langer went on to produce his best knock of the tour: though the rest of the top six failed, Australia dragged themselves back from the depths for the third time in as many matches. They were 98-5 when Lehmann went, but the scoreboard had swung to 316-6 by the time the next stand was broken. Remarkably, the three biggest partnerships of the series* had come in each of Australia's second innings, when they were behind or battling to stay in the game. It is a tired cliché that this Australia vintage were so successful because of their toughness – but has there ever been a team that so resolutely refused to be beaten? During the Sri Lanka tour in 2004, Ponting's men were like a pack of street dogs defending their turf. They never backed down, never believed they would lose. That was the difference between the two sides.

The heartbreak of the past month was compounded as Sri Lanka fell 8 balls short of securing a draw. They had surrendered a nip-tuck series 3-0, and been whitewashed at home for the first time in their history. The trauma was just getting started. Stung by criticisms of his leadership, Tillakaratne stepped down after the Test.[103] 'We were just so soft,' he mournfully told the media. He spoke of a desire to concentrate on his batting, but this was the last time he would don the Sri Lankan cap.

It was a sorry way for a legend to depart. Tillakaratne had done a huge amount for the island's cricket. He was a backs-to-the-wall player – his

---

*   The 218 between Langer and Katich here, the 206 between Marytn and Lehmann in Galle and the 200 between Gilchrist and Martyn in Kandy.

spells at the crease defined by steel and grit as much as strokeplay. In the early days, he carved out a niche for himself as a specialist number seven; after 1999, when all had abandoned him, he refused to give up – and returned to enjoy the best phase of his career.* During this period, he was Sri Lanka's most reliable batter, a trend which only turned once the stresses and strains of captaincy started to wear him down. In hindsight, his appointment looks a misstep. It affected his batting – and probably disrupted Atapattu's game, too. Though not the type to complain, Marvan was clearly upset at being passed over. It seemed strange that one who had been groomed for so long would be nearing 34 by the time he assumed the role.

Tillakaratne's biggest failing was probably a fear of failure itself: forget the boldness of youth, his tenure was driven by the nagging prudence of middle age. In each series, there were moments when Sri Lanka could have pressed for the kill, but instead decided to erect an impregnable barricade. With a little more courage they might have beaten England 3-0, and perhaps even stolen the Australia series.

But, there is another side to the story. Tillakaratne's leadership was blighted by a bounty of near misses. England needed patches of rain to cling on in Galle; on the final day in Kandy, Sri Lanka were let down by the bowlers. Against Australia, games were swung by incidents out of his control – Mahela dropped Martyn three times at Asgiriya, and Sri Lanka still might have struck victory had Vaas had shown a little more self-control come the final day. In Colombo, Sangakkara should have run out Lehmann on 62; had Sanath and Mahela not been wrongly adjudged caught, Sri Lanka would have surely held on for a draw. Had Tillakaratne led Sri Lanka to a 3-0 rout of England and a 1-1 draw with Australia, would there still have been such consternation over his fondness for rope-riders? I reckon not.

His departure left a sombre air, but there was sadder news yet. After the Test, Chris Broad reported Murali's doosra to the ICC, a hammer blow

---

* From the time he made his comeback in 2001 up to the New Zealand series in April/May 2003, he scored 1,290 runs at 80.62, making five 100s – plus a 96, a 93 and an 87 – in the space of nineteen Tests.

that struck right to the heart of every Sri Lankan.[104] For the third time in his career, Murali would have to fight to clear his name. Allegations were never far from the surface,* but by now Murali would have hoped his days of biomechanical testing were behind him.

The smear was awfully timed. Over the past month, Murali and Warne had treated the world to a symphony of spin bowling. The two men battled like gladiators, deceived like conjurers, and for three games running bowled their hearts out. If Warne emerged a baby step ahead of his rival, he held all the advantages: a better captain, better batters and a more capable support attack. However you saw it, their duel had been utterly enthralling – Broad's censure of Murali blighted it. For many, the indictment rendered their rivalry null and void. How could there be any contest? One bowled, the other threw.

There was also the spectre of Walsh's record to consider. With Sri Lanka penned in to play a two-Test series in Zimbabwe, it seemed certain that Murali would cross the line first. Now, there were questions over whether he would play in that series at all. 'Many Sri Lankans will feel that this decision was timed to block Murali and allow the glory to go to Shane Warne, a white man,' wrote Coupar. 'There is genuine anger here.'[105]

While Broad could not control the timing of his objection, there are aspects of his decision that rankle. The match referee claimed to have seen one delivery he was particularly troubled by, but by this stage Murali had sent down thousands of doosras in Tests.** Nor did he consult the standing umpires; in fact, Steve Bucknor, who stood in the second and third Tests, openly challenged the decision.[106]

Even as Murali closed in on history, his trial continued. Sri Lanka had played some inspired cricket in recent months – after all, they stood toe to toe with one of the great Australian sides and barely flinched. Yet, the

---

*   During England's tour, the Barmy Army repurposed the traditional 'Row, row, row your boat' to torment Murali. 'Throw, throw, throw the ball / gently down the seam / Murali, Murali, Murali, Murali / chucks it like a dream / NO-BALL!'

**   Despite claims from much of the English press, the doosra was not new – it had certainly not been 'unveiled' for the first time during the recent England series.

perception that they continued to lurch from crisis to crisis remained. In January, board president Thilanga Sumathipala had been arrested for passport fraud allegedly committed around the 1999 World Cup.[107] After incurring huge losses in 2002, there were rumours that SLC was on the brink of financial despair. Now, a new captain had to be blooded, Murali had to prove himself again, and that old wrecking yard – Australia – hung on the horizon.

ABSOLUTION

With shade surrounding Murali's action, and the leading Zimbabwean cricketers on strike, Sri Lanka's African expedition lacked the celebratory appeal that many had expected.[108] Zimbabwe's backups were hopelessly outmatched. In both Tests, they slipped to new record defeats. It was hard to escape the futility of the contests.

Still, none of the players will forget the moment when Mahela snaffled a simple chance at silly point, to give Murali his 520th Test wicket. Fourteen years after his first Test, Murali stood alone atop the mountain – the most decorated bowler of them all.[*] It was a shame there wasn't more atmosphere – the game was over, and the 200-odd in attendance had little idea what the fuss was about. But, this was a special moment for Murali and Sri Lanka. For a brief second, problems were forgotten as eleven friends and brothers danced with unbridled joy.

★★★

Despite the record, it was not a happy time for Murali. Broad's denunciation of the doosra had thrown SLC into a tailspin – and another round of testing at the UWA brought both good and bad news. At

---

[*] Whereas Walsh's 519 had taken 132 Tests to amass, Murali passed the milestone in just 89.

14.2 degrees, the doosra exceeded the ICC's new flexion limits* – but the tests also showed that Murali's arm rotated at a similar speed to fast bowlers.[109] In Darryl Foster's opinion, the distinction between seamers and spinners was faulty; and the 10-degree limit needed urgent revision since so many bowlers were exceeding it.[110]

What's more, with remedial work Foster and Murali managed to reduce the average flexion of the doosra to 10.2 degrees.[111] It still contravened current laws, but the UWA suggested that 'Mr. Muralitharan be permitted to continue bowling his "doosra", at least until a valid database is collected on the various spin bowling disciplines'.[112] The doosra seemed unlikely to be banned, until the Sri Lankan board botched the situation horribly. A report that was meant to remain confidential found its way onto the papers' front pages: within hours, news that Murali's doosra exceeded flexion limits sprang up the whole world over.[113]

This was criminally incompetent: not only did it irk the ICC, it irrevocably harmed Murali's reputation, since the global media got the negative headline, with none of the nuance. The subtext, that the laws themselves were crooked, remained buried in the report. As Dr Bruce Elliot put it, 'By leaking little bits of information at different stages, it [SLC] has put a lot of pressure on the ICC, Murali and ourselves. The ICC has been pushed into a corner and forced to react without actually having studied the report. As a result, the public perception will be that we are accommodating Murali.'[114]

Having done so much to raze the reputation of their best-ever bowler, you might think those in SLC's offices would have learned to keep shtum. Instead, the board inexplicably told the ICC they had instructed Murali not to bowl the doosra.[115] This was tantamount to a denouncement: it freed the ICC's hand to censure Murali without threat of any real backlash. 'The report forwarded by Sri Lanka Cricket proves that the degree of straightening is well outside the ICC's specified levels

---

* Biomechanical evidence had disproved the idea that all bowlers employed a pencil-straight arm; so some straightening of the arm was now allowed. For spinners it was 5 degrees, medium pacers 7.5 and quicks 10 – though the exact science behind those distinctions was curiously unclear.

of tolerance,' read an official statement from ICC president Malcolm Speed. 'Sri Lanka Cricket has now advised the ICC that it has instructed Mr. Muralitharan not to bowl this delivery in international cricket. The ICC supports this action.'

SLC's non-backing of Murali was a failure of the highest order. Can you imagine CA telling the world that McGrath's bouncer was thrown? Or the BCCI issuing a press release stating Harbhajan chucked? It is little surprise the off-spinner felt he had to take matters into his own hands. Local cricket historian Mahinda Wijesinghe struck on the idea of him bowling in a brace; come summer 2004, the 'experiment' was presented on English TV.[116] With Murali's arm locked straight, he sent down off-spinners, top-spinners and doosras. Mark Nicholas repeatedly claimed he was 'getting the sense of an illusion'; while not necessarily proof, the footage put forth a powerful argument in Murali's favour. Not all were convinced* – but as Murali phlegmatically put it when we spoke, 'I can't satisfy everyone in this world.'

Indeed, his elbow-flex was swelling into an international issue. With Sri Lanka due to visit Australia in June, Prime Minister John Howard was asked whether he thought Muralitharan threw.[117] 'Yes,' he replied, nonplussed. 'They proved it in Perth too, with that thing.' Murali was disconsolate. Already reluctant to tour Australia, Howard's comments were the final straw. If the country's chief diplomat couldn't properly examine the facts, what sort of reception could Murali expect from beery Test-match crowds?

At least he was about to get another significant slice of scientific backing. A recent arm-flex study showed a number of fast bowlers were up around 15 degrees; of twenty-three spinners filmed, only Ramanresh Sarwan's leg-breaks showed no flex.[118] Clearly the flexion limit was far too low; an ICC committee decided it should be raised to 15 degrees for all bowlers.

For Murali, this was the ultimate vindication. Yet the acceptance he craved was not forthcoming. When he claimed to have seen reports

---

* Murali's exclusion from ODI and Test Teams of the Year at the inaugural ICC awards was clearly a judgement on his action rather than his efficacy. English broadcaster Michael Parkinson crudely dubbed him 'muchichuckalot,' a name that felt bigoted and cruel.

showing that Australia's leading quicks bowled with a flexion range of around 12 to 14 degrees, he was accused of mudslinging. Matthew Hayden's opinion – 'Sticks and stones kind of stuff from Murali in the papers is not going to get him any favours in world cricket' – was strikingly framed.[119] When the Australians called Murali they were safeguarding the game; when Murali pointed out the issue was more complex, he was holding out a begging bowl and asking for charity.

No matter what Murali tried, the issue would not go away. Once the quicker ball became a more prominent part of his arsenal, he pre-empted objections and volunteered for another round of tests.* Even after he retired, Bishan Bedi gleefully claimed that the off-spinner had 800 run-outs to his name.[120] Murali learned the hard way that he would never silence his critics – that he would forever have to justify his crooked arm and plasticine shoulder and helicopter wrist. Still, he had done all he could to show his method was fair; as he put it to me, 'All I have to see is whether I am doing the right thing.'

★★★

There was little sadness in Australia over Murali's absence for the upcoming series: the general opinion held that the cricket would be better off without the distraction of a freak. So it felt almost karmic that the Australian public had to suffer the sudden emergence of a bowler even stranger than Murali.

In Sri Lanka, two types of cricket stand in opposition. There is the game brought by the English: the cricket of colleges and clubs, played by a fortunate few with a shiny, red ball. Then, there is the cricket of the people: the celebrated softball, the lifeblood of towns and villages across Sri Lanka. This was the cricket of Rathgama, the sleepy seaside village where Lasith Malinga was born. Though his father worked at the spluttering Galle bus depot, right across the road from the Test ground,

---

★   One criticism of the 2004 tests had been that Murali's average speed of 46mph was slightly slower than he would usually bowl in a match situation. This time, he bowled the doosra (53.7mph) and the off break (59mph) much quicker; at 12.2 degrees and 12.9 degrees flex respectively, both deliveries fell well within the ICC tolerance levels.

that oval might as well have been a million miles away. For young Lasith, there were only two cricket grounds: the coconut grove and the beach.

From the time that he could totter, Malinga was full of spirit. He was smart, infuriating his parents with claims he didn't have to study because his memory was so strong.[121] His body was powerful too: almost every day, he would swim across Rathgama Lake, climbing palms to pick *thambili* from the trees. He built sturdy shoulders, the kind that should be used for bowling fast. That was all he wanted to do. Each afternoon he was at the beach, targeting batsmen's toes with a tennis ball.

In softball, the key is to bowl full and fast and straight. A high arm and a good length are as useful as a pair of snow-shoes; as soon as the ball sits up, it can be swatted away. Malinga's low-arm action made it easier to bowl yorkers and generate skiddy pace. With his house just 60 yards from the shore, he was rarely without a ball in his hand. There was no shortage of victims either – a stroll up the coast brought new batsmen to feast on, fresh lambs to the slaughter. 'I was getting famous,' he told Shariar Khan, 'but famous means a hundred people know me.'[122] On a beach in the southwest corner of Sri Lanka, 'Malinga the slinger' was born.

But there was no path for him to follow. At 12, he watched Arjuna lift the World Cup trophy – but felt 'what they did there and what I was doing didn't seem connected'. Though a number of players' soft-ball experience has benefited Sri Lanka on the international scene,* little effort has been made to scout softball players for red-ball cricket. Malinga got lucky. Former Sri Lanka seamer Champaka Ramanayake was running a talent trial for the Cricket Foundation in Galle; Malinga's first ball was so fast he didn't see it.[123] Straight away, he asked the young slinger if he'd like to join Galle CC.

Ramanayake took Malinga under his wing, spending hours watching him spot bowling in the nets. When it quickly became clear a higher

---

* Jayasuriya is the most obvious example, but a number of Colombo players have benefited from softball too. In the 1950s, David Heyn ignored his father's warnings to stay away from softball, and claims his innovative fielding skills were honed in the back-alleys of Wellawatte. More recently, Aravinda, Gurusinha and Mahanama have talked of their softball games together as crucial to their development.

action wasn't working, he happily accepted the original round-arm style. He embraced the yorker too, nailing a pair of boots to the crease to make sure his young charge kept honing his most potent weapon.[124]

It helped that Malinga picked up skills fast, and soaked up knowledge like a sponge. He effortlessly learnt the shadowy art of reverse swing, and his unique mechanics changed the very nature of swing bowling. Where most fast bowlers would release the ball with the seam just off vertical, the lowness of Malinga's arm made it much more horizontal. This allowed him to generate dip by literally swinging the ball vertically. In the early days, many a batsman's eyes lit up at what they thought was a juicy full toss; before they knew it, they were crying out in agony, struck down by a toe-crushing yorker.

By the time Malinga was 18, Ramanayake was ready to throw him into Galle's first XI. It was a striking endorsement, but a daunting challenge too. The CCC side was full of proper players; up until recently, Malinga had only bowled at boys on the beach. Yet he tore into the Colombo team, taking 4 for 40 in the first innings, and 4 for 37 second time around. Raw as he was, his pace and unorthodoxy made him a nightmarish proposition; in his first season of club cricket, he took 27 wickets at 18.29 – a better average than Dharmasena, Ruchira Perera or Rangana Herath.

It wasn't all smooth sailing. Ramanayake took him to national training as a net bowler in 2001, but he didn't last the session. 'This guy came and he leathered his stuff,' Ajit Jayasekera remembers. 'Sanath came and said to me, "Sir, this guy will kill someone – please take him out!" So I had to tell Champaka. He was very fast.' And wayward too. During another net session, he broke a batsman's finger with a high full toss. Few wanted to face him after that – although Aravinda willingly volunteered to stand in the way of his firebolts.[125] 'He's hard to pick up when you first face him,' he told Shahriar Khan. 'Back then he was more difficult because you just didn't know where the ball was going to go. I'm pretty sure neither did he.'

Not all were so accepting. Malinga took 3 wickets in 3 overs during his first trial in Colombo, but was sent packing nonetheless. Even with Ramanayake's support, there were sceptics – not only of his action, but his pedigree. Cricketers had emerged from the south before, but they had on the whole moved steadily through the schools system. A beach boy breaking into the national side meant wholeheartedly embracing the democratisation of Sri Lankan cricket. In a sense, it insulted the school system that island cricket was founded on. Malinga showed that you need no high-elbow coaching or moral instruction to succeed – just a tennis ball and a strip of sand. As Khan put it, for many, he was simply 'too out-station, too other-worldly'.

But the lion-hearted Malinga refused to give up. He moved to the Academy boarding house in Colombo, working tirelessly in the gym once Rumesh Ratnayake told him more muscle would mean fewer wides.* By late 2003, he had been drafted into the 'A' squad – though he did well enough, he was still considered too wayward for one-day cricket. It was a surprise when he was picked for Australia. But the selectors knew Sri Lanka needed firepower. 'We have heard a lot about him and he is easily the fastest bowler in Sri Lanka,' Ashantha de Mel told the media.[126] That was enough to get mouths watering.

With Vaas, Zoysa, Dilhara and Maharoof in the squad, Malinga might have thought the sum of his duties would be carrying drinks. But he sparkled in the warm-up, affronting batsmen whenever he was called to bowl. 'He's a pocket rocket,' Dyson told the press. 'If he continues this innings and then bowls again really well in the next innings, he could come into serious consideration for the Test.'[127]

Malinga did just that, picking up 2 quick wickets on the second morning to finish with 6 for 90 and earn himself a Test cap. It must have felt like heaven: just a few years had passed since he was bowling at boys in the village; now, he had a cherry in his hand and Vaas at the other end. So accustomed to the burning sun and pudding-sand wickets, Malinga got the chance to bowl on a drop-in pitch in the Australian midwinter.

The up-and-down wicket dominated discussions as long as the Test lasted. Dismissing Australia for 207 and 201 read well on paper, but Sri

---

* Malinga's near horizontal release point offered very little margin for error: slightly early and the ball would be overpitched and off towards fine leg; late and it would be short and wide. Bowling yorker after yorker with that action required real precision – only possible through years of practice.

Lanka were no match for McGrath and Kasprowicz. Still, Malinga's presence gave them something to smile about. There was an air of expectation when Atapattu threw him the new ball on the first morning. No Ronald McDonald locks yet, only a neat centre parting fit for the first day of school – but it was clear Malinga was different.[128] A shade under 5ft 7in, he ambled to the crease like one who knew the pain of running through sand. Releasing the ball almost directly in front of Billy Bowden's navel, he was instantly up around 87mph. His first was well down the leg side, but Hayden looked nervous. Before the over was out, he had to fend an in-swinging yorker off his toes. Right from the start, Malinga was must-watch TV.

In the early days, the bouncer was his most menacing weapon – his ability to make the old ball sing instantly set him apart. He was at Lehmann's throat first up; though the ball looped to gully, Malinga had overstepped. Still, he'd clearly upset the batsman. Even after scoring 57, Lehmann looked glued to the crease and was trapped in front. Three balls later Gilchrist was done for pace, unsure whether to hook or leave; the ball ballooned into Sangakkara's hands.

The wickets seemed to spur Malinga on for the second innings. He found Martyn's inside edge with a sharp bouncer and Lehmann's outside edge with a full slower ball. Warne's toe was crushed by a yorker; Kasprowicz skied a hook straight back into his hands. Malinga's 6–92 was an impressive first effort, an outing that implied a fast bowler with more than mere pace. He made up for his rawness by besieging batsmen with two types of delivery: full and at the toes, or short and at the throat. It was a relentless, intimidating assault that worked brilliantly on a two-paced, up-and-down pitch.

His heroics gave Sri Lanka a glimmer of hope. Though they had been blown away for 97 in the first innings, Australia's own failures left them needing just 312 for victory. It was implausible, but not totally out of the question if one of the top four got going. Instead Sanga ran himself out and Sanath fell to a tame lbw; when Mahela and Samaraweera's promising partnership ended, so too did Sri Lanka's resistance. They lost by 149; watching on, Christian Ryan felt that 'two powerful batting sides self-destructed'.[129]

Gilchrist was so impressed that he brought a stump for Malinga after the match – though McGrath preferred to deride, saying he would struggle on flat pitches.[130] The world would find out soon enough. Atapattu's decision to field in Cairns looked an error: though there was bounce, it was slow and true – by tea, Langer and Hayden had pounded their way to 223-0. But where Vaas and Zoysa were innocuous, Malinga at least caused problems with his pace. He had Ponting, Langer, Gillespie and Gilchrist caught flashing; still, Australia's aggression saw them pile up 517 in 124.2 overs.

The Lankan reply showed plenty of spirit. Relieved of the big gloves, Sanga cut and drove and pulled sweetly for 74; Atapattu toughed it out for 133* – 455 was a best-ever effort on Australian soil. But another bullying Hayden century batted them out of the game. Sri Lanka would have to survive 85 overs for a share of the spoils.[131] Against the odds, they dug in and ate up balls. Vaas and Zoysa batted 9.3 overs to guarantee the draw; an effort the team could feel proud of. The attack stood up in Murali's absence, Atapattu looked revitalised as captain, while Sangakkara continued his steepling ascent. As a Test side, Sri Lanka have arguably never looked better-rounded.

But given a punishing turnaround and the team's recent lack of ODI Cricket, the Asia Cup had the potential to turn into a banana skin. Instead, Atapattu's men shook off jetlag and flu to bowl the UAE out for 123 and easily marched to the final. Though they could only muster 228 against India, the Lankans channelled the spirit of Lahore, producing a suffocating performance in front of a rocking Khettarama crowd. Vaas and Zoysa were superb up front; by the time the spinners were introduced, India were chasing the game.[132] Jayasuriya, Dilshan and the increasingly potent Chandana offered the batsmen nothing and gave their captain so much room for manoeuvre. Outstanding in the field, Sri Lanka bowled 195 dot balls. This team was showing an increasingly tough streak.

With just two rest days before the start of the South Africa Tests, cricket flowed thick and fast. A magnificent Jayawardene double-hundred

---

*   Since assuming the captaincy, he had three centuries in four matches and an average north of 95; there could be no denying the role had lifted his performances.

gave Sri Lanka control in Galle, but they couldn't score the required breakthroughs come the final day. With Atapattu departing early, some thought the SSC might betray Sri Lanka too.[133] But Sangakkara came to the party, notching his second double-century in the space of three months. Though he felt the pitch was 'a batsman's dream', his experience resonated little with the visitors.[134] First time around, the spinners did the heavy lifting – with Sri Lanka putting quick runs on the board, South Africa were left facing a 492-run deficit.

The match gave home crowds their first look at Lasith Malinga – he dominated what little play rain allowed on day four, etching his name onto Lankan hearts with a spell of fearsome fast bowling. Herschelle Gibbs was caught at leg gully trying to evade a violent bouncer; Graeme Smith and Martin Van Jaarsveld were roughed up by short balls too. But, there's more than one way to skin a cat: the final day belonged entirely to Vaas, who bowled with unerring control and clever variation to take 6 for 29. This new-ball pair were undeniably intriguing: as Robert Craddock put it, there was Vaas 'who hardly cares about his pace'; and Malinga, 'who cares about nothing else'.[135] Their efforts helped Sri Lanka to a first series win over South Africa. Marvan's men were surging. The close-but-not-quite air of Tillakaratne's tenure had evaporated; in its place stood a team of winners.

The ODIs confirmed this was a group growing into itself, full to the brim with confidence. Kaushal Lokuarachchi cracked a 6 to bring Sri Lanka a narrow victory in the first match, and in the second Zoysa produced a spiteful new-ball spell to help his team defend a small total. From then on, it was one way traffic: with series victory assured, Sri Lanka were happy to rest Atapattu, Vaas, Zoysa and Herath – and still came out winners. Hammering their way to 308 in the final match, they secured the most emphatic of whitewashes.

Atapattu's men had now won sixteen of their last seventeen ODIs. Though the age-old caveat remained – world-beaters in Asia; weak, weary travellers – there was so much cause for optimism. Zoysa, Sri Lanka's best bowler at the Asia Cup, was outstanding again – mixing up pace and length to constantly keep the batsmen guessing. Having been wild during the early part of his career, he had become an increasingly canny operator, especially in Asian conditions.

Chandana too, long on the fringes of the side, was enjoying a late-career breakout: ripping his leg-breaks harder and offering fewer boundary balls, he had suddenly become a wicket-taking threat. Dilshan showed he could chip in with ball as well as bat, Herath did well when called upon, while Lokuarachchi made a superb comeback. The seam-bowling stocks were unusually full, with pack leader Vaas enjoying an extended purple patch.* Sri Lanka bowled so well as a unit that they hardly missed Murali – and that really is saying something.

The batting was buoyant too. Test-match double-hundreds underlined Sangakkara and Jayawardene's growing prominence;** with Atapattu surging and Jayasuriya ever-deadly, Sri Lanka's top order contained the highest class. As such, their blink-and-you'll-miss-it appearance at the Champions' Trophy was a let-down – though the team were probably victim of an ungodly English autumn as much as their own failings.

That said, with Murali still sidelined, Sri Lanka seemed to be sliding during the PAKTEL Cup in October – but they turned on the style come finals day, comfortably defending 287 as Jayasuriya and Chandana spun a web around Pakistan. Perhaps they were spurred on by criticism from back home. Two days before the final, the selectors announced the squad for the upcoming Tests.[136] Dilshan's name was nowhere to be found. The next day, the chairman of selectors branded the team management 'selfish' for not blooding juniors on tour.*** For Dyson, Atapattu and Dilshan, this was a real slap in the face. Dilshan had endured a lean run of late in Tests, but centuries against England and Australia – plus his brilliance in the

---

* In twenty-two ODIs since the World Cup, he'd taken 34 wickets at 17.38, with an economy of 3.24.

** Jayawardene now averaged 49.28 in Tests, and 53.41 since the start of 2003. Sangakkara's average now stood at 49.04 – rising to 72.33 when he played as a specialist batsman. He was a coming force in white-ball cricket too, notching nine 50-plus scores in seventeen innings since the start of the year.

*** 'It has come to the stage that the selection committee felt that we have to reduce some of the options in order to get the team management to play them,' chief selector Ashantha de Mel said. 'There is a limit to being selfish. There has to be a situation where Sri Lankan cricket has also got to be thought of.'

field and useful part-time spin – should have been enough to safeguard his spot.

There are plenty of flaws in the selectors' logic, but one particularly rankles. This Sri Lanka side was going from strength to strength, yet those well versed in the country's cricket knew they had a final hurdle to overcome: winning away from home. With more than two decades of Test cricket behind them, Sri Lanka had managed it just ten times – half of those against Pakistan. By now, Wasim and Waqar had their feet up enjoying retirement: this was a golden chance to snatch a series away from home. For the selectors to jeopardise it at the last hour, and then criticise the team for 'giving the same excuse that they are wanting to win' was baffling.

Equally, Dilshan had only played eleven Tests since being brought back from the cold.* If this was really 'resting' not 'dropping', shouldn't the ageing Jayasuriya, or better still Kaluwitharana, be the one to make way? There seems little sense in blooding a prospect, if doing so threatened another's career. Hindsight is a cruel beast, but it is worth noting that Dilshan ended up with thirty-nine international 100s; the selectors' picks, Thilana Kandamby and Ian Daniel, never even managed a Test.

It was just as well the selectors didn't rest Sanath, as he single-handedly changed the course of the Test in Faisalabad with a riotous second-innings assault.[137] At 9-3 in the opening stages, Sri Lanka did not have it all their own way. They would have lost had Akhtar not overstepped with Jayasuriya on 9 – Sanath punished the error, batting within himself as he built sturdy partnerships with Sangakkara and Jayawardene.

Then, as the innings' coals turned to embers, he went on the charge, putting on 101 at a run-a-ball with Dilhara, whose sole contribution was a single. Jayasuriya became the first man in the history of Test cricket to bring up his century and double-century with a 6; the 253 runs he scored were worth their weight in gold. By close on the fourth day, the game was in Sri Lanka's hands. Dilhara nipped the ball off the seam and single-handedly reduced Pakistan to 91-4; next morning, it was all Herath. Sri Lanka sealed victory by 201.

---

* Malinga aside, there was no one less experienced in Sri Lanka's first-choice XI.

With Akhtar and Mohammed Sami out of the second Test with injuries, a series sweep was on the cards.[138] But a cluster of brainless dismissals saw Sri Lanka slump to 208 and concede a monstrous first-innings lead. Still they battled: Jayasuriya fizzed and crackled on the third evening, and completed his fourteenth and final Test century the following morning. Sangakkara dug in to add a workmanlike 138 while Samaraweera and Vaas stoically ate up time.

Their efforts left the hosts needing 138 in two sessions, but still Sri Lanka believed. At 57-4, with Inzamam unlikely to bat, the game was back on. Had Sanga clung on to a Razzaq edge, the team might well have cracked Pakistan's callow lower order. Instead, Shoaib Malik repeatedly flayed Herath to the fence to carry his team home. It was frustrating that the two-Test series left no room for a decider. Still, Sri Lanka could feel happy with their progress in 2004. After the near-miss against Australia, they palpably grew in strength once Atapattu assumed the reins. But the island's is a cruel history, and none would ever describe it as a happy year. In the days after Christmas, Sri Lanka faced unimaginable horror.

TROUBLING TIMES

The team were in Auckland when they heard.[139] They had just been hammered by New Zealand, humbled for 141 in the first of a five-match series. As they moped in the changing room, Jayasuriya got the first snippet of news: there had been flooding back home. Initially, there was little cause for concern. Even as the scale became clearer, the question remained: how much harm could a wave really cause? Only once the players saw the unspeakable footage did they understand the truth.

The scale of suffering was difficult to fathom. Some 500,000 were made homeless overnight; though Colombo escaped the brunt of the tsunami, Sri Lanka's southern cricketers were badly affected.[140] Jayasuriya and Chandana's mothers narrowly escaped the water; one of Champaka Ramanyake's relatives was dragged 500m before clinging to a coconut palm.[141] Had Murali not slept through his alarm, he would likely have been swallowed by the wave en route to Seenigama. These were the lucky ones. Nuwan Zoysa's maternal aunt, and three of Dilhara's wife's relatives were lost in the tragedy.[142] Upul Tharanga's house was flattened, his cricket gear washed away. Galle cricket ground was wrecked, filled with floating debris: most eerily, the carcass of a bus from the station across the road.

Clearly, the team were in no state to think about cricket. Many grimly waited for news of friends and family not forthcoming; left to contemplate the misery and destruction at home, it was an awful time. But SLC mishandled the situation, rejecting the players' plea to return to Sri Lanka.[143] Frustratingly, it seems the board barely bothered to explore their options.* Sense was finally seen, and the players landed back in Colombo on New Year's Eve – still, it was unfortunate that their return required an ungainly public struggle.

No smiles could be seen through the last days of December, as a country renowned for its cheer stood together in mourning. There was shock and bewilderment: through Sri Lanka's cruel history, mother nature had been solace. For it to turn on the island so suddenly tried a resilient people to their core. Ordinary Sri Lankans began the healing process – searching for the missing; piling supplies into cars and making the long drive south. So steady was the outpouring of aid that the coastal road became gridlocked; some say it took ten hours to get from Colombo to Galle.

The unity Sri Lanka showed in the wake of the tsunami was inspiring. It was spiriting too, to know that cricket could be leveraged as a force for good. When Murali suggested to his manager that they should build 1,000 houses, he was told he'd have an easier time bagging 1,000 Test wickets.[144] But he sank his own cash in, agreed to appear in a cement adverts – and remarkably got it done. Even more vital was the aid he agreed to take north, where supplies were desperately

---

* An ICC spokesman explained that there had been no approach from SLC on the subject, and that the claim that Sri Lanka would be forced to foot financial penalties was plainly untrue.

short.*[145] Murali used his contacts to arrange trucks, which he insisted on accompanying himself. He got Ruchira Perera on board, filled the containers with food and headed up to Kilinochi. This was the first convoy to pass the curtain. In all likelihood, it saved 8,000 refugees from starvation.

While the wider cricket community offered much support, it was sad to see SLC miss the mark. In truth, it was unclear whether their new charity Cricket Aid represented a genuine attempt to help or an effort to repair Sumathipala's image.[146] Rather than digging into their own coffers, the board proposed fundraising ideas which ranged from distasteful – player-guided tours of the refugee camps – to deceitful: a globally broadcast charity tournament that never got off the ground. Money came in by the bucketload, but it was hard to escape the sense that the charity promised much more than it delivered. From mid-2005, it disappeared from the news altogether.

With so much relief work ongoing, did SLC – an organisation with a questionable financial history and limited charitable experience – really need to get involved in the nitty-gritty of disaster work? Didn't Cricket Aid simply erect another barrier between those providing charity and those it was meant to help? There were others better placed to handle donations. One such organisation was The Foundation of Goodness. Though Murali and Vaas were trustees, Sumathipala took exception to their involvement in charity work apart from Cricket Aid – even preventing Vaas from attending a fundraising dinner.[147]

The idea that SLC tried to block the players' own charitable efforts raises the question whether they really intended on serving humanity at all. Clearly, perception was prioritised over action – large sums were spent on PR and marketing – and the suspicion remains that money going in was not necessarily coming out. If that is true, it is inexcusable. After falling dormant, Cricket Aid was resurrected in 2016; by September 2019, it was suspended by the Committee on Public Enterprises (CoPE)

---

* Ordinary civilians were unable to pass through LTTE checkpoints, while companies were reluctant to send their trucks past what they feared was a point of no return.

on account of financial irregularities. Members of the CoPE went as far as to describe SLC as a 'den of thieves'.[148]

★★★

Sumathipala's resurrection had his enemies in a spin. His resilience was remarkable. Little more than a year earlier, he was dead and buried, accused of using board funds to help a mobster travel to England for the World Cup.[149] Now, he had the SLC and ICC presidencies in his sights. With no one willing to stand against him in a board election after Arjuna's embarrassment, the issue grew more pressing.

Meanwhile, both the Sri Lankan government and the ICC were keen to keep Sumathipala away from the ICC meeting in March 2005. Though ICC CEO Malcolm Speed asked Sumathipala not to attend the meeting – and Sports Minister Kumaratunga appointed Damian Fernando in his place – Sri Lankan cricket's kingpin dug his heels in.[150] He turned up at the meeting on 17 March; by lunchtime, a cable reached Delhi, announcing Sumathipala had been replaced as the board's representative.[151] Given his designs on the ICC presidency, the humiliation was tough to swallow. This was a very public sign that the government was ready to stand against Sumathipala.

His personal reputation was not the government's sole concern. An audit of the board's accounts for 2004 revealed losses of Rs. 321 million: two days before Sumathipala's planned re-election, Sports Minister Kumaratunga dissolved the board.[152] Although another interim committee was appointed, Sumathipala ignored the diktat – going ahead with the AGM as planned.

On his first morning back in the hot seat, he gave SLC staff a week's paid leave, claiming they were suffering 'mental trauma'.[153] The offices were locked, extra security guards posted at the gates. Kumaratunga and the interim committee were being frozen out. Ultimately, Sumathipala managed to destabilise the interim committee through sheer bloody-mindedness. For the whole of April 2005, a fog of confusion hung over Sri Lanka, with no clarity forthcoming over who was in charge of the island's cricket.

The players got stuck in the middle. In the days before they were due to head off to New Zealand, a practice had to be cancelled because no one was authorised to take balls out of a locked store cupboard. The team travelled without contracts too – once in New Zealand, they were cast adrift. 'There was a cricket board when we left Sri Lanka,' manager Brendon Kuruppu told the media. 'Now we have nobody to contact.'[154] Confused and uneasy about the prospect of picking sides, they met with Sumathipala and Sports Minister Kumaratunga when they got back. Ludicrously, the players faced the prospect of going through contract negotiations with two competing boards.

After five weeks of stalemate, the crisis came to an ugly and emphatic resolution.[155] Kumaratunga successfully issued a parliamentary gazette – allowing him to alter the Sports Law and cede control to an interim committee. Around lunchtime on 3 May, a group of machine-gun wielding Criminal Investigation Department (CID) officers stormed SLC headquarters. They informed employees that all board property would be handed over to the interim committee. For now at least, the crisis was over.

★★★

It was exasperating. Over the past months, Sri Lanka had endured unimaginable trauma, yet the bigwigs continued to bicker as if oblivious to the currents that swirled around them. Preparations for New Zealand were further jeopardised by a stubborn refusal to deal with John Dyson's contract.[156] It was the same old story: Dyson had been asking about his renewal since October 2004, and while no response was forthcoming, titbits were leaked to the press. In March, with Dyson's contract about to expire, Mohan de Silva told *The Island* 'in all probability he will be offered a fresh contract for up to a year … although no final decision has been made'.[157]

As well as destabilising the squad, this sort of behaviour sullied SLC's already muddy reputation. Whatmore's mistreatment had done much to scare off potential coaches; by giving Dyson the silent treatment, the board were hardly selling themselves to prospective employees. Highly regarded assistant Shane Duff left because the board failed to act on his renewal.[158] This was nothing new, but it was nonetheless disappointing. Above all, it was a show of disrespect – an inaction which seemed to disregard the team's clear progress over the past eighteen months.

Even as Dyson took the team to New Zealand, the silence wore on. 'My contract is now complete and I will return to Sydney,' he told *The Island* at the end of the tour. 'I don't know what is happening in Colombo and at the moment things are unresolved. From this stage on, I am free for negotiations.'[159] The battle for control of the administration did not help, but the whole issue should have been sorted out much sooner. To leave a valued employee in the lurch like this was indecent. It undermined the value of the coach, ignoring his influence upon the team. From the outside, it seems those who wielded power within the SLC saw their coaches as cogs, who could be retained or replaced on little more than a whim.

★★★

The resumption of the New Zealand tour in April 2005 felt like a vital step for all of Sri Lanka. For the team, it was especially poignant. Down to a man, they returned to the field changed – newly conscious of life's frailty, but also inspired by the fortitude of their countrymen. Representing Sri Lanka made these cricketers stand taller.

'It was devastating,' Mahela told me when we spoke on the tragedy. 'There were a lot of guys who we knew, who we played cricket with back home, who'd been affected. It was a bad situation – but we've come through a lot of tough times, a lot of bad things, and the people are resilient. They always find a way to their feet, and work their way back with a smile. I think that's what everyone knows about Sri Lanka. We're tough, on and off the field, but we still play the game with a smile. That's how we grew up, that's what our culture is all about.'

At Napier, Sri Lanka showed an iron resolve – through unshakeable belief and flashes of brilliant cricket, they kept themselves in a contest that could easily have escaped their grasp.[160] Bat dominated ball: heads might have dropped as New Zealand recovered from 294-6 to reach 561, but the Lankans weren't cowed by the mountain of runs in front of them.

Centuries from Atapattu and Jayawardene brought them close to parity, before Malinga gave Fleming and co. a real fright. He had Craig Cumming and Hamish Marshall lbw on the fourth evening, and nightwatchman Paul Wiseman for a duck the next morning. When he bowled James Franklin, New Zealand were 148-7 on the brink of lunch and in deep water. But their ailing captain resumed his innings and carried them to safety; with the last session lost to bad light, the game petered out in a draw.

Still, in taking 5 for 80 in the second innings – and 9 in the match overall – Malinga took another big stride. He brought bite to an attack that had often lacked penetration beyond Asia; his easy mastery of reverse swing, and ability to take the pitch out of the equation, meant he was the kind of bowler who could prosper where others struggled. New Zealand found his low-arm action so hard to pick up that they asked umpires to remove their ties, and then to change the colour of their trousers.

Given the guts on show in Napier, Sri Lanka's capitulation in the second Test was a real disappointment. They never recovered from being 5 wickets down inside 21 overs. Vaas was superb, but the backup bowlers offered little, and Atapattu's men fell 38 short of making New Zealand bat twice. With winter fast approaching, they seemed to long for the warmth of home.

★★★

For the interim committee, there was much to sort out. The cricket board's civil war had hampered attempts to find a new team sponsor: though seven companies were initially interested – and SLC hoped to start the bidding at $5 million – the board had to accept $2 million from sitting sponsor Dilmah.[161] Equally, the hunt for a new coach was put on pause – thankfully India's decision to pass over Tom Moody left SLC with an open goal.[162] The young Australian was signed up till the 2007 World Cup; over the course of the next two years, he would establish himself as one of the game's premier thinkers.

Intensity was central to Moody's success. The structure of Sri Lankan cricket had always placed the captain at the top of the tree. Often, coaches have seemed almost peripheral figures – there to support the team, but only as long as they stayed in line. The straight-talking Moody took a wrench to the pipework: he had a clear idea of how he wanted to move the side forward, and demanded total control. 'Tom is a very scary guy,' Mahela volunteered when we spoke. That fear factor helped, since few were willing to stand in his way.

Certainly, Moody was quite a shift from the unassuming, jocular Dyson. A tough taskmaster with a more hands-on approach, he demanded the highest standards from his men. Still, working in the subcontinent brought a new set of challenges. During his first months in charge, he held one-on-one meetings with the players – explaining their roles, and what was expected of them moving forward. Yet he failed to account for the language barrier: four months down the line, Jayawardene had to explain that the Sinhala-speaking Malinga hadn't understood a word.[163]

West Indies' arrival saw international cricket return to Lankan shores after almost a year's absence.[164] It was a funny sort of series: sponsorship disputes forced the visitors to field a callow squad, yet they surpassed expectations, giving Sri Lanka scares in both Tests before succumbing to defeats. Murali, restored to the side and re-energised after shoulder surgery, had the biggest impact – but Vaas was close to his best, Malinga ambled in with menace, and though Herath didn't quite get it right, Sri Lanka finally seemed to be assembling a band capable of backing up the virtuoso off-spinner.

The usually commanding batting was more of a concern – against a green attack, Sri Lanka twice failed to post first-innings scores of 250, and right up until Sanga's brilliant second-innings 157* in Kandy, only Samaraweera notched a half-century. While it might be exaggeration to claim they fully rediscovered their swagger during the Indian Oil triangular, Marvan's men held their nerve when it mattered to get hands on the trophy. For Moody, it was a decent start to life as coach.

And while Sri Lanka expected to beat Bangladesh in September, it was encouraging to see new men standing up with vital contributions. Farveez Maharoof continued to impress with tight lines, Dilhara reminded the world of his danger when fit – but it was new boy Upul Tharanga who had the biggest impact, following 104 for the President's XI with 60 and 105 in the first two ODIs. Still just 20, his coastal upbringing and clean striking saw some liken him to a young Jayasuriya. That in itself was cause for excitement.

The equally one-sided Tests were another show of Sri Lanka's depth. At Khettarama, Herath tantalised Bangladesh on the opening day, before Murali massacred them in the second innings, triumphantly mixing doosras and off-breaks.[165] A week later at the P. Sara, the swashbuckling Dilshan and steadier Samaraweera dug the side out of a sticky first-morning position and set the foundation for another innings win.[166] Dilhara hurt Bangladesh with 5 quick wickets: having worked hard with Moody behind the scenes, his hostility now seemed tied to greater control. For the first time in memory, Sri Lanka's attack looked stacked with wicket-taking options.

Since Moody arrived the team had won four of four Tests and seven of eight ODIs. That said, they had often proved nervous travellers, and a tour to India brought an abrupt end to the honeymoon period. Even before the team boarded their flight, a bonding trip to Bentota brought disaster, as Jayasuriya aggravated his dislocated shoulder banana boating.[167] That should have kept him out of the first ODIs, but he rushed back and struggled. Atapattu's men looked short of confidence with both bat and ball. After leaking 350 in the first ODI, they were blown away for 122 in the second. In a sense, it was even more demoralising to see Sanga bat beautifully to carry the team to 298 – only for Dhoni to brutalise the bowlers and make light work of a tough target.

With little idea how to stop the surging Indian machine, Sri Lanka fell into the old trap of questioning themselves and trying too much.[168] Strangely, Atapattu recast himself as a number five.* Four different opening pairs were trialled; though Sangakkara's batting atop the order was one of the sole bright spots, he was shifted to number three for the last two matches. Chandana, Mahela and Dilhsan all had a go at number four, but the chopping and changing had little effect. A brilliant partnership between Dilshan and Arnold took Sri Lanka home in Ahmedabad, but the batting rarely looked unbridled – India chased down 261, 196 and 245 with minimal fuss to complete a 6-1 drubbing.

---

*   Since properly establishing himself in the one-day side, Marvan Atapattu had played 222 times for Sri Lanka and only batted outside the top three on nineteen occasions (11 November 1996–2 September 2005).

It was news to no one that Sri Lanka were a different side away from home – but their attack's total lack of control was alarming. Only Murali went at less than 5 runs per over, and even his impact was limited. The quicks offered little and the spinners even less: legitimate fears surfaced that the new powerplay rules were bad news for Sri Lanka's strangle-first bowling attack. Atapattu's captaincy did not escape criticism either, with some feeling he lost confidence as the series wore on. There was plenty to sort out before the Tests got underway.

At least Sri Lanka would get a much-needed break, while India slugged out another ODI series with South Africa. But their preparation was thrown into turmoil by the decision to drop Jayasuriya. The selectors originally cited form as well as fitness, but changed their tune when they realised their decision's unpopularity.*[169] Whatever the reasons, it was a brave and untimely act. Jayasuriya had disappointed in the ODIs – and endured a lean run in Tests since Moody's arrival – but he cracked four centuries in 2004, averaging 56.50 and striking at 70.01. If there was a sense his powers were on the wane at 36, he remained a far better player than most.

Plus, he had been a menace and a scourge to India: even as he struggled in the ODIs, Dravid's men celebrated his wicket wildly. Neither Sangakkara nor Jayawardene had played a Test on Indian soil, nor did Sanath's replacements look particularly match-ready.** Was this really the time to be trialling life without Jayasuriya? Clearly the new president did not think so: after several complaints, Mahinda Rajapakse ordered a government inquiry into Sanath's sacking.[170]

---

* Chairman of selectors Kaluperuma initially told reporters, 'We decided to drop Sanath on the grounds of poor form and a lack of fitness, but the selectors subsequently issued a press release, claiming Sanath's injury "was not brought to the notice of the panel of selectors or SLC management at any stage ... the selectors therefore decided to keep him out of the Indian Test series so that he could obtain proper medical treatment and recover from the injury to be considered for the New Zealand tour."'

** Avishka Gunawardene had done little to live up to his one-time next-Jayasuriya billing – and with a middling average in first-class cricket, seemed unlikely to be the long-term answer Sri Lanka were seeking. Upul Tharanga had a better shot, but at 20 remained a raw talent.

There were other concerns about the makeup of the squad.[171] The presence of three openers meant Sri Lanka had no spare middle-order batsman – yet remarkably, the selectors decided to blood 18-year-old prodigy Chamara Kapugedara. With just one first-class match behind him, it was probably best for everyone that he got injured and had to miss the tour. His withdrawal gave the selectors a second chance to call on Jayasuriya, but they stubbornly refused, sending for Jehan Mubarak.[172]

They had one more rabbit to pull out of the hat: Jayawardene was to be sacked as vice captain, and replaced by Chaminda Vaas. Clearly a captain-in-waiting, what Mahela had done to deserve demotion was unclear. 'Different administrators, different selectors view things in a different way,' he told me. 'Vaasy was appointed vice-captain. I didn't have a problem with that. Yes, disappointed. But I said, "It's fine. It's a good time for me to concentrate on my game, to try and contribute and be the best I can be."'

Still, it was impossible to escape the strangeness of the decision. Surely the selectors had not decided that Vaas might be Sri Lanka's next captain. But if this was a reward for service, shouldn't Murali have taken a share of the vice captaincy? All signs suggest that Moody was not consulted, nor keen on the decision.

As has often been the case, the selectors seemed to be playing their own, inscrutable game, with little concern over how their toying might affect team dynamics. Atapattu rejected chairman of selectors Kaluperuma's claim that he and Moody had been consulted about Jayasuriya; there appeared a clear disconnect between the team management and the selectors.[173]

Rangana Herath, who had played eight of Sri Lanka's last nine Tests, was axed for the unproven Sajeewa Weerakoon, who had never played a first-class game outside Sri Lanka. Despite his experience and good form, Russel Arnold was entirely overlooked. Losing can be a dangerous tonic; often the blame game starts and divisions emerge where once there was unity. After being hammered in the ODIs, this Sri Lanka side needed stability. But in place of a steady hand, the selectors had a worrying bout of shakes.

Though the writing was on the wall for a disastrous tour, Sri Lanka struck the first blow. Cyclone Baaz rendered play in Chennai academic, but Atapattu's men were nonetheless impressive.[174] Vaas bowled

11 straight maidens and picked up 4 wickets; the team were dynamite in the field as India lurched to 167. And once they got the chance to bat, Jayawardene produced an imperious display. So spirits were high as the team headed to Delhi, for what turned into a topsy-turvy affair. Day one belonged to Tendulkar, but he was far from the only match-winner on show. Murali produced one of his career-best spells – and with Marvan and Mahela carrying the team to 175-2, Sri Lanka were well set to force home their advantage. That is, until they suffered their own dizzying collapse.

Having worked so hard to build a solid position, Sri Lanka threw the game away in what Moody described as 'thirty minutes of madness'.[175] The next day, makeshift opener Irfan Pathan made an infuriating 93 – with Sri Lanka 5 wickets down by close, the game was gone. Though Atapattu and Jayawardene completed twin 50s, it was no compensation for their failure to cash in during the first innings. The others offered next to nothing; Sri Lanka fell to a 188-run defeat.

Things would get worse before they got better. Despite limited opportunities, Avishka Gunawardene's leaden footwork suggested he was not cut out for Test cricket, so Moody and Atapattu took the tough choice to promote the 20-year-old Tharanga. Vaas and Dilhara came down with flu and had to be replaced by Malinga and Maharoof.[176] Given the duo's greenness, and Murali's struggles with a thigh strain, that in itself spelled trouble. Ideally, the brains trust might have fancied a change in the middle order too, but hands were tied. They would have to stick with what they had been given.

At least India were beset by problems of their own. Ganguly's dropping sparked riots in Kolkata, while Dravid's gastroenteritis meant Virender Sehwag had to take on the captaincy.[177] Nonetheless, you somehow knew they were going to win. Atapattu lost his third toss on the bounce, but at least Malinga brought impetus: in no time, the hosts had slipped to 97-5. But Sri Lanka could not finish the job. Laxman was reprieved after a bat-pad catch and notched a century; the breakthroughs dried up as India reached 398.

Dilshan's 65 gave the scorecard some credibility, but the visitors were humbled by Harbhajan. They showed heart, but were always cruising towards defeat, nearly twenty-four years after gaining Test status, Sri

Lanka were still without a win in India. The longer that passed, the more impressive Tissera's victory started to look.

Tellingly, though Sri Lanka had nine individual innings worth more than 40, only twice did batsmen make it out of the 60s. None reached the 90s – while it was a let-down that Sangakkara, Samaraweera and Mubarak failed to lodge a 50, it was equally disappointing to see Mahela register four half-centuries but make no more than 71. Far too often, hours of hard work were undone by momentary lapses.

The selectors had to accept their share of the blame too. Dropping Jayasuriya looked a poor decision – as Gunawardene quickly showed, not every broad-shouldered slugger could dominate Test attacks. Sanath might well have missed out, but hadn't he proven with a decade's worth of awe-inspiring innings that he warranted the risk? Equally, with Samaraweera repurposed as a specialist batsman* and Dilshan only offering an occasional option abroad, Sri Lanka were unusually constricted to a four-man attack. That made it harder to pick Malinga – who early in his career had a habit of losing his radar and leaking runs. In the end, the selectors opted for the slightly more reliable Dilhara, who managed 2 wickets in 56 overs. Jayasuriya's presence might have given Moody and Atapattu a freer hand to risk their genuine wicket-taker; perhaps Malinga was the man they needed on the first evening in Delhi.

As 2005 drew to a close, Sri Lanka's fans had so many causes for concern. Charlie Austin wrote, 'There is now a crisis of confidence in the selectors, from the players right down to the average cricket-lover in the street.'[178] Accountability was becoming a problem, so too the selectors' relationship with Atapattu and Moody. When Zoysa and Chandana were excluded from the one-day tour to New Zealand, many naturally wondered whether captain and coach had been consulted.

Equally, with selectors constantly jumping on and off the carousel, there was a damaging lack of long-term thinking. Malinga Bandara was picked for the India series, having played a single Test back in 1998. The man he replaced, Rangana Herath, was cast into the wilderness

---

*   From the time Moody arrived, to the end of Samaraweera's Test career in 2013, he bowled just 8 overs.

from March 2000 to August 2004, and then again from September 2005 to March 2008. The proud owner of 35 Test wickets aged 30, he went on to end his career with 433 scalps to his name.

This selection committee was not to blame, but it was nonetheless a systemic failure. Time and again talent was correctly identified, but discarded before it was given a chance to flourish, only to be recalled several years later. Given club cricket's inadequacies, it was especially important that players deemed good enough were given a proper trial. Yet all too often, they were tossed aside with rankling flippancy.* It seems there was no streamlined process, where the best talents were identified, groomed and eventually picked. The selectors all too often worked with a scattergun approach: players were selected on a hunch and dropped on a whim. Doubts are often raised about the amount of club cricket selectors actually watch. 'Who do they choose?' Mahinda Wijesinghe incredulously asked when we first met. 'They look at the scores and say, "Ah. I should pick him." But my wife can do that.'

Worryingly, the selectors' job was as hard as it had ever been. For the first time in 2005/06, the Premier Trophy was expanded to include twenty teams – all ensconced in Sri Lanka's south-west corner. Sinking standards stooped lower; the island's first-class game was now so far off Test cricket that it became largely inconsequential. The revived inter-provincial tournament, a potential panacea for the bloated club game, went missing – not to return until 2008/09. Meanwhile, the much-vaunted schools system seemed to be heading in the wrong direction,

---

* Consider the fast bowlers of the era. Indika Gallage played a single Test and three ODIs between 1999 and 2001; cast aside at 25, he moved to Melbourne to drive a fork-lift truck. Hasantha Fernando played two Tests and five ODIs in 2002 – he was brought back for two more one-dayers in February 2006, but that was the sum of his international career. Sujeewa de Silva played two Tests in 2002, and one more five years later. Chamila Gamage took a wicket with his first ball in Tests, but found his international career over within six months. Dinusha Fernando played three times against England and then never again, Darshana Gamage crammed in three ODIs in a month and then disappeared; Pradeep Jayaprakashadaran bowled 6 overs against India, taking Virender Sehwag's wicket, before being cast out.

the steady production line of Colombo cricketers grinding to a halt.*
The seeds of Sri Lanka's recent mediocrity were sown long ago, at a time
when they still held realistic hopes of beating the best in the world.

It augured badly for 2006 – a year crammed full of cricket. With tough
ODI series in New Zealand and Australia, a three-Test tour to England,
plus visits from Pakistan and South Africa, the road ahead looked rocky.
But Sri Lankan cricket's path has always been impossible to predict.
A year on from the tsunami, innumerable problems faced the side. Few
could have guessed a brave new era lay just around the corner.

PARTNERS IN MIND

The rescheduled New Zealand ODIs which sprawled across the first
days of 2006 got off to a horrible start.[179] Blown out for 164 in the series
opener, Sri Lanka were dragged deeper into the mire when Jayasuriya
suffered a bizarre injury. 'Sanath was reaching for his shampoo when he
slipped in the bath,' manager Tissera glumly explained – leaving us all
asking what hair had he planned on washing?[180]

Though Sri Lanka failed to win until the last ODI, they built momentum as the week wore on. Still, it was a disappointing trip: second in the
ODI rankings a couple of months earlier, the team had now slumped
to seventh. An unusually blunt Murali managed just 3 wickets; Mahela
endured a lean run and finished the series at number six. And despite
leading Sri Lanka in both average and strike rate, Atapattu continued to
languish at five.

With just four rest days before the start of the VB triangular series in
Australia, there was little respite. Nor much optimism: Sri Lanka could
expect pace and bounce and baying Australian crowds. South Africa's
game looked better suited to the conditions. In all likelihood, they
would be heading home before the finals.

---

*   The best talents to emerge in recent times – Malinga and Tharanga from the south,
Kulasekara from Gampaha, Kapugedara from Kandy – had all come from outside the
capital and broken through in spite rather than because of the system.

Their opening encounter suggested a team in trouble. Murali leaked 67 as Australia surged to 318; any hopes for the Lankan reply quickly vanished.[181] Tharanga and Mubarak fell early, while Michael Vandort scratched around for 35 overs, tottering to 48 off 117. Given the target and the batsmen in the pavilion, it was a puzzling approach. The game was gone by the time Mahela magicked up a 47-ball 50; shunted down to seven, Atapattu didn't arrive until the 36th over. Sri Lanka seemed to have lost sight of the maxim that your best batsmen should face as many balls as possible.

These sort of trepidant starts had often foreshadowed all-out freefall – so it was a surprise when Atapattu's men found form. First, the flourishing Bandara picked up 3 big wickets to stop South Africa in their tracks. Then, fresh off the plane, Jayasuriya made a carefree 114 to lift the team to 309. But they couldn't keep the winning run going. After falling 9 runs short of South Africa's 263, they slumped to three tame defeats – unable to defend meagre scores of 218, 233 and 221.

There were more pressing issues at hand. If Vaas had imagined the vice captaincy was a ceremonial role, he was sorely mistaken. At once, he found himself at the coalface,* his limited captaincy experience somewhat exposed. Moody developed doubts over his leadership, and there seem to have been rumblings of discontent within the squad. Most felt Mahela was better suited to leadership, and struggled to see the logic behind his demotion.

Things came to a head during the crunch stages of the VB series. With Atapattu out against Australia at Perth, Vaas struggled to plug holes in the field – Gilchrist and Simon Katich slammed 191 in 32.2 overs, as the hosts coasted home with 9 overs to spare. Sri Lanka could ill afford a repeat performance; despite their poor run of form, victory over South Africa would carry them through to the finals.

Atapattu finally returned to the top of the order – though his composed 80 lifted Sri Lanka to 257, his back flared up and he was unable

---

* With Atapattu increasingly struggling with back issues, Vaas was getting plenty of opportunities to deputise. In India, he had led the warm-up in Bangalore and had to stand in whenever Atapattu left the field during the Tests.

to take the field. And while Vaas managed two early breakthroughs, there was a sense the game was getting away from Sri Lanka. Moody had seen enough.

'The incident,' Mahela said sternly when I asked him about the game:

I remember we were going nowhere. One of the reserves came and said that Tom wanted me to come in for a chat. So I excused myself. I went in and saw Marvan and Tom. I still remember the conversation. They said:
'You need to take over'.
'What do you mean take over?'
'You have to take over on the field as the captain.'
'I can't do that, it's not possible. I can help Vaasy, I'll tell him what needs to be done, but I can't ...
'No, you're taking over.'
'It's not proper. It's not right for Vaasy, and it's not right for the game. Everyone will see that'
'Don't care. You just have to take over.'

Those were the exact words. And when Tom talks like that – he's a very scary guy. So I said 'Fine'; I knew the situation, that we needed to win to get into the finals. It was a very awkward moment when I went back onto the field to tell Vaasy. I think they would have sent a message to him, but I had to go and tell him 'I'm sorry, the guys want me to take over.'
I could see the obvious disappointment in Vaas, right? But I told him 'It's fine – you can still do the things and I'll help you,' which I was doing anyway. But they didn't want Vaasy to field in the ring because he was a slightly slower fielder. So, that was one of the decisions: 'You have to send him to wherever he fields as a fast bowler; fine-leg or third-man boundary'. And that's an awkward thing.[182]

It was beyond awkward. For Vaas, a veteran with twelve years' international experience and 348 ODI wickets, being sent to the long grass when he was supposed to be leading the side was humiliating. 'It was,' Mahela agreed. 'I can totally understand that he was pissed off. I was upset as well. I still remember when we finished the game, I walked up to Marvan and Tom and said "This is the last time that this is going to happen. If you put me in that situation again, I'm walking away from the team. I don't care whether I play for Sri Lanka again." For me, I can't do something like that to a teammate who I came up with. I was very blunt, and that was one time I actually raised my voice with Tom. "You make a decision beforehand – whatever you want to do – but I'll never ever do that again." Then we moved on.'

As uncomfortable as it was, the decision had to be made. It was vindicated, too: Sri Lanka tightened up, and won by 76 with Bandara bagging 4 wickets. The selectors had made plenty of missteps of late, but recalling the leg-spinner was inspired. Across the VB series, he took 14 wickets; finishing with an average and economy better than Murali.

For the past few months, the vice-captaincy affair had cast a cloud of awkwardness over the dressing room; now the team could move forward once more.[183] Vaas handled the decision with dignity: he could have dug his heels in, and sparked all-out war, but stepped aside – tacitly agreeing the captaincy was not for him. Equally, Mahela acted with a clarity of thought and maturity that would stand him in good stead. No bad blood lingered; when Jayawrdene took charge of the side, he made sure that seniors like Vaas felt properly valued.

Meanwhile, Sri Lanka had reached the finals of a series most had dismissed as hopeless. They were superb in the first at Adelaide, turning on the style in the field to comfortably defend 274. Dilshan's direct hit to get rid of Damien Martyn had the team hollering with joy; all in all, he was involved in four of five run-outs, and took an excellent catch.

It would have pleased Trevor Penney no end: since arriving with Moody, he'd been on a mission to overhaul Sri Lanka's fielding. 'One of the best fielding coaches we could ever have,' Jayawardene reflected. 'He was so instrumental in us improving our fielding. He was one of those guys who makes you do two or three different drills every day on direct hits. And he demanded a run-out from us every game. It was a must. It didn't matter if we'd won the match, if we missed a couple of direct hits he would be at us.'

Sadly, Sri Lanka could not force home their advantage. Symonds and Ponting tore into the bowlers at Sydney, taking 21 off Murali's last over to hand him the worst figures in ODI history.* At Brisbane, it was Gilchrist and Katich's turn to make mincemeat of the attack. But while silverware proved elusive, it had been a restorative trip. After the drubbing in India, few thought them capable of beating Australia away from home – but they managed it twice, besting South Africa along the way. The vice-captaincy affair had been happily settled, and the jumbling of the batting order looked a thing of the past. Sri Lanka did lack a little cutting edge with the ball, and would have been disappointed that only one of twenty half-centuries was converted to three figures, but this was clearly a unit pulling together again.

Their schedule remained relentless. With Atapattu's back showing few signs of improvement, and just five rest days before the start of another series in Bangladesh, the selectors decided to send a young group, under Jayawardene's leadership.[184] Three months after losing the vice captaincy, Mahela was handed the top job. Some questioned his mettle, but the cuddly demeanour belied a surprisingly steely core. Plus, Jayawardene was an excellent man-manager – an area where the naturally shy Atapattu possibly struggled – and a natural democratiser.

When he debuted in 1998, juniors were still expected to be seen and not heard. Mahela made sure youngsters had a voice in team discussions, and were awarded contracts fit for international sportsmen. Vitally, he *thought* about things. 'We put certain things in place,' he told me. Prior to his tenure, senior players were occasionally joined by spouses on tour, but for the youngsters it could be a long and lonely slog. 'I know our culture is different, but I said "let's not just stick to spouses, let's open it up to partners as well." It could be anybody: if someone wants to bring one of their brothers, or if a parent wants to come and stay, they can. It just created a better environment for the team.'

Jayawardene understood that little things could make a big difference: both on and off the field, he was one of cricket's great innovators. 'I was

---

*   Spared the indignity of three figures by a single run, Murali will have been happy that this was one record he didn't hang onto for long. Mick Lewis went for 113 a month later – and eleven more bowlers have since joined the hundred club. Though Martin Snedden was hammered for 105 by England in 1983, this is generally discounted since it was a 60-over match.

very positive, very attacking with my mindset,' he explained when we spoke about captaincy. 'I wouldn't let things drift, I always tried things, I tried to create opportunities and I wouldn't let situations go by. For me, there's no point in going back to my room and thinking "Maybe I should have done this or that"; if I had an idea, I just wanted to do it. Or if someone else comes up with a brilliant idea – or whatever idea – if there's nothing happening, I'll always try it and see if it works.'

His leadership energised the team. Clearly, he and Moody had a shared understanding which served Sri Lanka well. Like Mahela, the new coach pushed his players and demanded growth. Often, he would end sessions by putting specific scenarios to the squad, asking them to come back the next day and explain their responses. It helped build self-sufficiency and a better understanding amongst the group.*

'Big bird,' Mahela said with clear affection when I asked about Moody. 'I really enjoyed working with Tom. He's a hard taskmaster, but at the same time a brilliant man-manager. A very tough guy, but there's a real gentle side to him too. For me, he really helped me grow into that leadership role. He helped me flourish.' A number of close observers applauded the duo's handling of senior players, but more importantly, Moody's take-no-prisoners approach with the board made Jayawardene's life much easier.

'I found him really good with the administration, tackling the admin-istration,' he explained. 'He was a good barrier for me as captain. He took it on, not that the other coaches didn't – but Tom was full on. He was happy to have a fist fight if he had to.' Over the next eight years, Sri Lanka went from strength to strength, especially in white-ball cricket. So much of their growth was down to Moody and Mahela's dynamic part-nership. This unlikely pair could not have looked more different, but in thinking they were two peas in a pod. Their axis was the most important for Sri Lanka since the uneasy Whatmore-Ranatunga alliance.

---

* Conscious of his early experience with Malinga – and the increasing number of Sinhala-speaking players in the squad – he encouraged free speech in any language, using the players with better English as translators.

That said, it got off to a rocky start. Sri Lanka lost the second ODI in Bangladesh,* and did not have it all their own way in the Tests. Having only managed a slender first-innings lead in the opener, Mahela's men slipped to 43-4 in Bogra. They were rescued by Tharanga's pounding 165; his brisk second-innings 71* suggested a man quickly making himself at home in international cricket.

Though records seemed to tumble more or less whenever Murali stepped onto the field, the dizzying landmarks he scaled during the series served as a reminder of his distinction. In the first Test he became the first man to 1,000 international wickets.[185] If that wasn't enough, he bagged his 600th Test scalp during the second Test, while becoming the first bowler to take 50 against every Test side. As a side-note, he became the first to claim fifty five-fors in Tests. Cricketers come and go; greats from one era can quickly fade into obscurity in the next – but surely Murali's name will never be forgotten. You have to wonder whether cricket will ever witness another such enduring, voracious wicket-taker.

Having crammed so much cricket into the past few months, Sri Lanka looked a spent force by the time Pakistan arrived in mid-March. They fell to lop-sided defeats in the ODIs,** and the Tests were a letdown too. Sangakkara batted them into the driver's seat at the SSC, but the visitors survived an eventful last day, and then dominated at Kandy, as Mohammad Asif trampled the Lankans with some compelling seam bowling.[186] Despite his clear talent, it was disheartening to see a side with such batting depth skittled for 73.

The result lumped pressure onto Moody and Jayawardene, and Jayasuriya's first red-ball 'retirement' meant they would be heading to England with two rookie openers.***[187] The opposition were daunting; the conditions hostile – and after a couple of excruciating days at Lord's, Lankan obituaries were already being penned. Unlucky in the field, they only had themselves to blame for their dismal batting. Four of the top

---

*   Never before had they lost a match to their fledgling neighbours.
** At least Malinga showed the first real flashes of his white-ball potential, with his radar rapidly improving, he was fast becoming a more reliable white-ball bowler, finding a miserly spirit that complemented his growing bag of variations.
*** Atapattu missed the tour to have surgery on his back.

seven went for ducks; all in all, Sri Lanka looked wildly underseasoned and fell well short of the follow-on target.

It would have been no surprise if Mahela's men had lost heart and surrendered. Instead, they fought back with spirit. Jayawardene led from the front with a six-hour 119, but Tharanga, Sangakkara, Marahoof, Dilshan, Vaas and Kulasekara all notched crucial 50s.* The teams headed to Edgbaston 0-0, with Lankan spirits boosted by the great escape.

They were unsettled by a storm in the Indian Ocean. Following his surprise reappointment as chairman of selectors, Ashantha de Mel wasted little time rattling cages.[188] During his first days back, he fumed about Sanath's 'retirement' like a love-struck fan, while publicly taking aim at Moody. Such an outburst raised real questions; for those on the inside, the stench of political interference was impossible to escape. It looked as though the selectors had been appointed with a mandate to restore Jayasuriya.

Indeed, it seems Sanath's retirement had been a 'collective decision' which included captain and coach.**[189] Now, unbeknown to Moody and Mahela, he was added to the squad. 'Lord's was an amazing fightback from all the guys,' Jayawardene told me. 'We fought and we were so happy, and Tom gave a great speech in the dressing room. I can still remember it. We went back to the hotel and got off the bus – and then, as we were going into the lobby we saw Sanath there. Him congratulating the team. He came and said "Hello" to Tom and I, and said "Well done".'

'Tom and I looked at each other; we pulled Michael [Tissera, manager] aside and said "What's going on?" Michael said, "I didn't want to bring it to you guys, but this was happening in the last 24 hours." We had no idea until we saw him. So we've got an additional player now, and the team is coming off a brilliant Test-match save, batting for two days and our entire thing just collapsed. For me as a captain and for Tom, we were upset. We got together that night, and went out for dinner as a team. We

---

*   When Dilshan was caught on the final morning, Sri Lanka were 8 down and just 62 ahead. Had Vaas or Kulasekara fallen quickly, the game would have been up – instead they batted 45.3 overs to take the sting out of the English tail.
**   Outgoing chairman of selectors Kaluperuma told the media, 'We felt Sanath might not get picked for the ongoing tour of England and told him so. We wanted to make sure he remained injury-free for the World Cup so we asked him to concentrate on one-dayers only.'

didn't show that emotion, but it was a very awkward situation. Because now, there's an opener in the team who knows he might not be playing in the next Tests. It was tough.'

Mahela and Moody stuck to their guns. Sanath would not be parachuted in at Edgbaston. Vandort repaid the faith with an excellent 104, but Kevin Pietersen's ebullient 142 dragged the game out of Sri Lanka's reach. A 78-run target was never going to make England sweat, though Moody felt 50 more would have caused them problems. With Murali in the ranks, he might just have been right.

Though there wasn't a single survivor from 'The '98 Oval' brigade, most of England must have felt a sickening sense of déjà vu as Murali danced and deceived during the third Test. Trescothick and Geraint Jones were bowled by dizzying doosras, Alistair Cook trapped dead in front, Pietersen and Paul Collingwood snaffled at bat-pad. Just like before, Murali's shot at a perfect ten was only scuppered by an elegant run-out. Still he bagged 8, and 11 in all as Sri Lanka won by 134.

For the Kandy Man, this final Test tour of England felt rich with symbolism. It was impossible to ignore the presence of Darrell Hair at Trent Bridge – glum-faced in hat and tie, unable to 'call' Murali. Equally, Hussain's assessment on commentary – 'there is no shame in being bowled out by a genius' – was a long way from his earthy analysis a couple of years earlier.[190] For Murali, it must have felt like acceptance. It was no less than he deserved.

This was a marquee victory; excluding Zimbabwe, only Sri Lanka's third outside Asia – and their first in the post-Arjuna era. So often in recent times, they had failed to force home their advantage; here, we saw the other side of the coin. Though England were on top for large chunks of the series, Jayawardene's men never sank into their shells. 'It was the first time that this young group was playing in England, and we wanted to show something,' he explained. 'This is what Sri Lanka is going to be recognised for – playing Test matches away from home. You can't just come out and lose. We have to at least fight.'

Yet, impressive as the drawn Test series was, it was the 5-0 ODI drubbing that really got fans at home purring. Everything seemed to click. All five innings were anchored by centuries: Tharanga's 120 at Lord's showcased increasing maturity; after Jayasuriya's violent 122 in the second, there was reason to believe the rookie and the relic were the most menacing top-order pair in cricket. Equally, when on song, few could match Jayawardene's elegance: run out on course for a century at The Oval, he more than made up with 126* and 100 off 83 in his next two innings. There were cuts and clips and deft touches all around the wicket; admittedly, England struggled for control, but the Lankan top order was so quick to punish anything loose.

They saved their best for last, as Sanath and his student partner Tharanga unsparingly assaulted a sub-par attack. After posting 321, England must have felt assured of victory. But it was barely a contest: Jayasuriya slapped and jabbed in vintage fashion; Tharanga struck so cleanly through the covers. After 10 overs, they had put 133 on the board; when they raced past 200, the result looked a formality. The duo amassed 286 in 31.5 overs, smashing records and English pride in the process. It was the perfect end to a very happy summer. After being beaten down at Edgbaston, Sri Lanka reeled off seven wins on the bounce. For a side that had traditionally travelled poorly, this was a special turnaround.

'Everyone was on a different level compared to the England boys,' Jayawardene proudly reflected. Auspiciously, Tharanga continued his charge, while Malinga – by now mop-headed and swaggering like one who's torn up the rulebook – bagged 13 wickets at 17.53. Having worked hard on improving his radar, Mahela and Moody had seen enough to give him their full backing. He had now played the last eight ODIs; his ability to carve out wickets at any stage of the innings was a crucial ingredient in an increasingly potent recipe.

Yet the most glowing praise was reserved for Sri Lanka's stand-in captain. Jayawardene led the team with unpretentious diplomacy, marshalled his men astutely on the field, and ended the tour in brilliant form with the bat. Jonathan Agnew felt he had 'visibly blossomed', adding it might be a 'foolish move' to demote him when Atapattu returned.[191] It was hard to disagree. Sanath's late addition could have sent Sri Lanka spiralling into chaos, but Mahela and Moody refused to let it tear the team apart. It took strength and courage to back their young openers; yet they weren't too proud to accept that Sanath could play a role at Trent Bridge once a turning track presented itself.

For now at least, speculation surrounding Atapattu's future remained academic. He was still laid up when South Africa arrived in late July; in his absence, the public were treated to a sumptuous feast of cricket.[192] The first Test at the SSC felt like a passing of the torch. Jayawardene and Sangakkara were fast approaching 30; with Murali, Vaas, Jayasuriya and Atapattu entering the twilight of their careers, these two knew they would have to shoulder more responsibility moving forward. The future was in their hands – in mounting a record-shattering 624-run stand, they stormed the fortress of cricket's all-time greats, consolidating their status as Sri Lanka's backbone and beating heart.

That said, their partnership might have been over before it got started.[193] With Dale Steyn steaming in on the first evening, Sangakkara was given a pair of lives in the same over. Those missed opportunities seemed to spur him on: twenty-four hours later, the stand was unbroken, South Africa's quicks beaten down by more than the blistering sun. This was far more than crease occupation. Sanga and Mahela put on 357 on the second day, scoring at 4.5 runs per over without ever appearing to rush.

The pair peppered the fence frequently. Sangakkara hooked and drove with conviction; with Nicky Boje attacking the rough outside Jayawardene's leg stump, he impishly danced down the track time and again, easing the ball over the infield. The inside-out shots over cover were transcendent; for South Africa, the glimmers of hope few and far between. By the time the duo approached their double-centuries, captain Ashwell Prince had turned to Jacques Rudolph's leg spin. Sanga's was sealed with a smash down the ground; Mahela's with a heaved 6 over mid-wicket.

After ice baths, a Thai meal with their wives and an early night, the two great friends were back at the crease for the third day running. They kept going: 4 byes took them past Mahanama and Jayasuriya's international record; though Sangakkara fell 13 short of his triple, Jayawardene never looked like getting out. His innings was chanceless: when he reached 350, all in attendance felt Lara's 400 was well in his sights.

But 26 short, he was beaten by a nip-backer from Nel that kept wickedly low. 'I was lucky I got that delivery when I was on 374 and not when I was on 10 or 12,' he phlegmatically told Sa'adi Thawfeeq.[194] For twelve and a half hours, Jayawardene gave a consummate demonstration of how cricket should be played. Though he had a share of cricket's highest partnership, the fourth best score of all time and the highest by a right-hander, it was hard to escape the sense that the ultimate personal achievement might have been within his grasp.

The disappointment did not linger long. The duo batted briskly enough to leave their team over two days to press for victory: like a tireless interrogator, Murali leant on the batsmen for 61 overs, taking 6 to finish with 10 for the match. Clearly, Sanga and Mahela weren't the only ones willing to suffer for the cause.

After three rest days, the players were back on the field in Borella. If the SSC is Colombo's Eden – a batting paradise in the poshest part of town – then the P. Sara is a once-glorious public garden fallen by the wayside. It has soul and history and a little something for everyone; yet rarely has it produced such enthralling cricket as in the first days of August 2006.

The South African attack made to look listless at the SSC was full of life here. Only lower-order contributions saved Sri Lanka from an irredeemable position;* though Murali was superb – claiming four consecutive ten-fors for the second time in his career – Sri Lanka were left looking up at a 352-run target. They stayed in the game thanks to a new-found, unshakeable belief. Only five bigger chases had been mounted in the history of Tests, but on the third evening, Mahela insisted he was 'very happy' with the position. Previous Lankan sides might have wilted in the face of such a challenge, but Jayawardene forbade negativity from clouding his men. They would bat with belief and put pressure back on South Africa.

The unpleasantness of 2002 provided extra motivation. As Jayasuriya told Andrew Fidel Fernando, 'We wanted to dominate them and trample them without letting up. We remembered what had happened to us when we played in their country.' He set the tone with a combative run-a-ball 73. Pollock was slammed for a huge 6 and came back bowling off-cutters; Steyn, too, looked to be forcibly knocked off his length. Still, Tharanga made nothing and Sangakkara 39; soon after Mahela arrived at the crease, Sri Lanka were 121-3 and sliding towards defeat.

---

* Kapugedera, Prasanna Jayawardene, Maharoof and Vaas made 225 of Sri Lanka's 321.

The captain followed his predecessor's example. 'Anything loose I was hitting,' he told Fernando. By this stage, Boje carried the greatest threat, but Sri Lanka never let him settle. In a 29-ball innings, Dilshan struck four 4s off the spinner; his 7th over disappeared for 17, including a glorious inside-out Mahela 6. Still, the wickets kept falling. When Jayawardene reached three figures, Farveez Maharoof was at the other end. Sri Lanka still needed 57, with just 4 wickets in hand.

This was undoubtedly one of Jayawardene's crowning innings – a lyrical knock that seemed to defy the state of the pitch and strength of the opposition – but on 123, he went for one shot too many, and was caught at slip. Sanath's pained cry from the balcony was worth a thousand words: though just 11 more were needed, the door had been opened a crack. With Murali and Malinga padded up, one more wicket could send the game spiralling into chaos.

So it proved. Andrew Hall found reverse, Vaas chased a wide one – and at third slip, A.B. de Villiers pounced like a cat. Sri Lanka still needed 4 to win. Murali strode out ahead of Malinga, and brought a message for Maharoof: *take a risk and finish it now* – but he was on strike, with five balls to face. After three-fresh air swipes, Murali managed to squirt a 2 through the off side, but was bowled next ball. Now, the game was truly in the balance.

Nerves jangled all around the ground – yet the two men in the middle looked oblivious to the tension. Maharoof ticked a single to mid-off to tie the scores. First ball, Malinga played a classic on-drive – out of the rough, against the spin – to seal the series for Sri Lanka.

Sweeping South Africa was a big deal – plus, the manner of victory suggested a metamorphosis; a group developing a steadfast belief in their own ability. 'If you put your mind and belief in the group of players that we have got, then we can do a lot of things that people have not seen before,' Jayawardene gushed. After a monumental performance in England, the series undeniably confirmed his status as Sri Lanka's leader. At the ICC awards in November, he was chosen as captain of the ODI World XI, and named Captain of the Year.[195] 'It's a shock,' he said. 'I am still a stand-in captain. Hopefully Marvan will be back from injury soon and I will be glad to just be there alongside him on the field.' That statement revealed much about the man – since by now it was eminently clear to all but Jayawardene that Atapattu was Sri Lanka's captain in name alone.

While Mahela stressed that the award belonged to the team, his captaincy clearly unlocked something in his charges. No doubt he was a natural leader – blessed with keen cricketing instincts and excellent people skills. Yet, it also seems his faith in the team filtered down. 'When I was asked to captain, the group of players I had was fantastic,' he told me. 'You had some genuine match-winners in that group, and they were at their peak as well. When you have those kind of resources, it was about me using them and giving them confidence. They make the job much easier.' Equally, the extra responsibility encouraged Jayawardene to raise his game.* 'I guess I was probably more determined, more focused,' he told me. 'You have to walk the walk. You can't just demand guys to play a certain way if you're not contributing and you're not a part of that.'

The South Africa series marked a turning point for Sangakkara too. Despite an average of 70.66 when he forewent keeping duties, he had played just twelve Tests as a specialist batter over the past five and a half years. 'The balance of the side always came first,' he explained. 'There were of course times, even though my ego told me otherwise, where my batting was affected negatively. It took me quite a while to understand that.' Ahead of the South Africa series, the selectors finally accepted the need for someone else to carry the big gloves. Right on cue, Sanga responded with 287. 'I was quite adamant that I could keep doing the job,' he explained. 'But it was a great that decision was made for me, and it really translated hugely into me making big scores in Test cricket because physically and mentally I was less fatigued.'

But for Sangakkara, cricket seems an almost academic pursuit. Although relinquishing the gloves coincided with a remarkable run in Tests, he reckons his development owed a greater deal to a newfound maturity. 'The real progression to scoring consistently happened when I recognised myself emotionally,' he explained. 'What worked for me

---

* In his past five Tests, he had scored 740 runs at 82.22, including a game-saving century at Lord's and two match-winning knocks against South Africa. In ODI cricket too, back-to-back centuries came after a 113-innings barren spell.

and what didn't, what really motivated me, how to plan practice sessions accordingly. Once that was set, it was very easy for me to become more consistent. I think once your mindset shifts, you understand what technical changes you need to make. How to make them, when to make them, how to balance out risk and take calculated risks at times. There's definitely a connection between the two. I have a personal theory that people who understand their own makeup, their personal characteristics, their emotions, all of that quicker, transfer that into their run-scoring or wicket-taking abilities.'

With Sangakkara and Jayawardene scaling uncharted heights, the future of Sri Lankan cricket was in safe hands. Having fully earned their keep through the first eight months of 2006, it was a relief for the squad to find the back end of the year less congested. If their inability to reach the semis of the Champions Trophy was frustrating, at least Murali, Vaas, Malinga and Maharoof forged as menacing and miserly a quartet as Sri Lanka had seen. They rode as four horsemen – and impressed again in Christchurch in the last days of 2006, dragging the team back into a Test they looked to have surrendered in the first two sessions.

Ultimately, the nip-tuck match was overshadowed by the unsavoury ending to Sri Lanka's second innings. Though no one outside the top three reached double figures, Sangakkara struck the ball with remarkable authority. From 99-8, he shepherded the tail to 170, battering bowlers in the process. When he reached his century, Murali came running down the pitch to congratulate him;[196] although he was clearly not attempting a second run, Brendon McCullum whipped off the bails. Murali had been run out.

'The whole team is disappointed,' Jayawardene told reporters. 'We play in an age when we talk about the spirit of the game. Hopefully it won't happen again. It's not the way to play cricket.'[197] Ultimately, another 20 from Sangakkara's bat would probably have made scant difference, though New Zealand did make a meal of their 119-run chase. Still, the incident created ill feeling – and an unrepentant Fleming was unusually provocative in the lead-up to the second Test.[198] He seemed to mistake Jayawardene's men for pushovers; meek church mice who would be sent scurrying at the first hint of confrontation.

But fire roared in Lankan bellies. Sangakkara remained in excellent touch – his 156* at Wellington was spiced with pulls and cuts. You felt, had he not run out of partners, he would have continued to punish New Zealand a good while longer. From thereon out, it was beautiful destruction. Malinga (5 for 68) cowed the top order with a frightening display of fast bowling, before Murali flummoxed the tail with indiscernible variations.

Rarely has the yorker been used so effectively in Test cricket. Don Cameron accurately described Malinga's approach as 'nose-or-toes'; the New Zealanders looked woefully ill equipped to deal with either.[199] When he pitched short, they fended fearfully; when the ball was full, their feet seemed stuck in sand. Pinpoint yorkers repeatedly splayed the stumps; regularly above 90mph, Malinga was too fast, too unorthodox and too accurate to keep out.

While his raw talents meant there were few more destructive bowlers in world cricket, Malinga possessed far more than a powerful shoulder. In three years, he had transformed from spray-gun to sniper, largely thanks to unflagging toil behind the scenes.* He was blessed with a sharp cricket brain, and a steadfast belief some of his compatriots seemed to lack. Plus, he was managed adeptly. As Jayawardene told me, 'I've never asked Lasith to bowl line and length. I just asked him, "Are you going to get him out with a yorker, a bouncer? What's your option?" And he was always given the ball to take wickets; he was never asked to contain runs. I knew that if he takes wickets, we control the game.'

His exploits gave Sri Lanka a 138-run cushion, which grew into a gulf thanks to a breath-taking innings from Chamara Silva.** The wide, hunched-over stance carried echoes of his near namesake Aravinda; but where de Silva employed the low-impact swing of a woodcutter, this Silva had the flair and flourish of a nineteenth-century swordsman.

---

* According to Moody, he put on 22kg of muscle in the space of two years to ease the strain on his back. Given Malinga is 5ft 7in and weighed 52kg when he joined the national setup, the achievement was even more remarkable than it sounded
** Silva had played ten ODIs between 1999 and 2002, before falling by the wayside – yet after one look, Moody plucked him from the obscurity of Sebastianites CC straight into the cauldron of Test cricket.

Despite bagging a pair on debut in the first Test, his game was unclouded by fear – the cover boundary was bruised time and again, the fielders split or left crane-necked as the ball sailed over their heads. After reaching his century, he played a lofted on-drive that was pure P.A. de Silva; 152*, tied to an emphatic first-innings 61, earned him the man of the match award, and gave Sri Lanka a 503-run lead.

New Zealand had no chance of surviving two days of Murali. McCullum's humiliating first-innings dismissal must have felt like karma – and his teammates were equally gormless against the doosra. Murali could now push it through quicker and still find rip, making it much harder to read him off the pitch. Batsmen had no answers; Murali had now claimed a ten-for against every Test-playing nation. And for the first time in history, Sri Lanka had staved off series defeat on three consecutive away tours. As 2007 rolled around, it was clear that this was a team on the charge.

★★★

With the World Cup getting underway in March, focus shifted to white-ball cricket. There were promising signs from the drawn series in New Zealand: Sanath could still smash the ball to all parts, and the bowling was going from strength to strength. Vaas and Malinga caught fire in Auckland; at Christchurch, the attack even made a decent fist of defending 112. The squad looked settled, the only surprise Arnold's continued exclusion. Despite the unique package he offered, he continued to be given short shrift by the selectors, yo-yoed in and out of the side without reason or explanation.

He was back in for the four-ODI tour of India in February 2007 – auspiciously, Sri Lanka managed to stay competitive while resting Vaas and Murali. Sangakkara made his sixth ODI century in the win at Rajkot; Chamara Silva his first at Visakhapatnam. Arnold dug the side out of trouble in Goa, while Bandara and Dilhara Fernando showed they remained reliable backup options. Despite the 2-1 scoreline, there was much to feel good about.

The World Cup squad was uncontroversial, but concerns over Jayawardene's form leading into the tournament intensified when he missed out in the warm-ups. Sangakkara dissuaded him from dropping himself, but Moody was said to be considering a change.[200] He might have been forced to make it. Jayawardene edged his first ball of the tournament to slip – only for Dwayne Leverock to spill a straightforward chance. He went on to score 85, headlining Sri Lanka's 243-run win. With Bermuda seen off, the team were on their way.

While encouraging to see Mahela play himself into form, it was strange to see a healthy Atapattu watching on from the sidelines – hard to escape the sadness of such a steepling fall. In the space of months, Sri Lanka's erstwhile captain had been recast as drinks carrier. Many were surprised the team could afford to omit such a proven campaigner, but Moody felt the side was better balanced without him. Tharanga had cemented his place at the top of the order; Silva had thoroughly impressed over the past few months, while Dilshan and Arnold brought flexibility to a team that carried just four frontline bowlers.* For Atapattu it was tough to take. Unsurprisingly, it soured his relationship with Jayawardene, and sparked all-out war with the chairman of selectors. Still, it showed how serious Sri Lanka were. They had come to the Caribbean to win.

And they were finding momentum. Bangladesh and India were easily cast aside – while Australia were clear favourites, Sri Lanka announced themselves as the tournament's most watchable team. First came Malinga's defining moment. With 10 runs required, and Kallis and Pollock at the crease, South Africa were on the brink of victory. TVs had been turned off, minds on the field might have drifted towards dinner – but Mahela threw the ball to his young tearaway, with a word of encouragement. 'Machang. Give it everything you've got.'

Malinga proved the extraordinary value of believing. After 4 balls, South Africa needed 4 to win.[201] Still, he was unburdened by doubt. On the 5th ball of the over, Pollock played around a curving slower ball; first up, Hall could only fend a fast yorker straight to cover. A frugal Vaas over meant Malinga returned for the 47th with South Africa still needing

---

* Considering Atapattu's career strike-rate of 67.72, these three were probably all better suited to batting at the back end of the innings too. There was the option of slotting the former captain in at number three, but this would have meant shuffling Sangakkara and Jayawardene – the engine room of Sri Lanka's batting – down a slot.

3 runs. Kallis surely knew the plan, but only managed to get a feather-edge on the ball. All of a sudden South Africa were 207-8, with two scoreless tailenders at the crease.

Malinga had the fifth hat-trick in World Cup history, and he was not done yet. Ntini's middle stump was uprooted by a vicious in-swinging yorker – 'The Rathgama Express' had ODI cricket's first ever four-in-four. More to the point, he had gotten belief coursing through his countrymen's veins.

Down to their last pair, South Africa still needed 3 runs to win. Pressure mounted as they managed a solitary single from the next 11 balls; one more perfect yorker would have won Sri Lanka the game. But Robin Peterson managed to connect with the outside edge: it raced away to the third-man fence and brought South Africa the narrowest of victories. Still, Mahela's men had shown rare resilience. This team would fight to the bitter end.

Nor was Malinga the only one standing up at pressure moments. After shining against India, Dilhara demanded the last over against England, and outfoxed Ravi Bopara with a good-length last ball to bring Sri Lanka another nail-biting victory. With West Indies dispatched by a Jayasuriya special, they needed one more win to reach the semis. New Zealand were brushed aside with minimal fuss; chasing Ireland's score in 10 overs flat ensured Sri Lanka would avoid a final-four clash with Australia. They rested their star bowlers for the Super Eight matchup with Ponting's men, clearly hoping to spring a surprise assault come finals day. Still, it was worrying to see them shackled by Nathan Bracken, Shaun Tait and McGrath; regardless of the makeup of their attack, they would struggle to hold Australia to under 226.

With Sanath and Sanga undone early in the semi-final, New Zealand quickly had Sri Lanka on the back foot. But the under-fire Tharanga produced a run-a-ball 73, allowing Jayawardene to bed in at the non-striker's end. He played a perfect captain's innings: the giddying strokes in the last 10 overs stole the show, but were only made possible by patience and maturity, an unclouded mind and an ability to expertly read the game situation. Mahela scored 9 off his first 33; when Tharanga fell in the 26th over, Sri Lanka were 111-3 with plenty to do. But in the final 10, he went through the gears with ease and efficiency, scoring

69 off his last 35 to end unbeaten on 115. This was one-day batting at its best: there were powerful hits down the ground and full-blooded cuts square of the wicket, but deft nudges through third man and fine leg too – the ball snuck through gaps with sniper-esque precision. Sri Lanka plundered 66 off the last 5 overs alone.

New Zealand never looked like reaching 289. Murali found turn: when Jacob Oram and McCullum were scuppered by doosras off consecutive balls, the writing was on the wall. An 81-run victory set up a repeat of 1996; though second favourites, Sri Lanka entered the clash in high spirits. 'Personally, I was so happy about that hundred,' Jayawardene told me. 'It was probably one of the top five knocks of my career,' But cricket aside, this six-week Caribbean sojourn had proven a happy adventure for the Lankan squad. As Mahela explained:

Still today, I think that was one of the best tours I've been a part of. Not just because I was captain, but because of the entire environment that was created by Tom and his team. All the guys in that group, we were just unbelievably cohesive. It was a very long tournament, and it was something special. As soon as we went, we started playing beach volleyball. It was fun: that entire trip, apart from match days we had two hour volleyball sessions on the beach every day. Everyone would turn up, that was our team bonding. No one had to organise dinners, no activities, nothing. Just volleyball and a swim in the sea. That was it; that was our whole tournament.

It was a shame that the final descended into a shambles. With the Kensington Oval track offering pace and bounce, Sri Lanka were up against it from the start. Before Australia's innings got underway, rain rushed in, reducing the contest to 38 overs. And frustratingly, by the time the match got going, the cloud cover Sri Lanka hoped to exploit had blown away. Gilchrist struck the ball straight and true – and often into the stands – en route to a 104-ball 149. Dilhara, who spilled a sharp caught-and-bowled chance when he was on 31, was left to ponder what might have been.

Indeed, with Australia racking up 281 in 38 overs, the game was slipping through Sri Lanka's grasp at the halfway stage, though they clung on while Jayasuriya and Sangakkara stayed in the middle. Their partnership was worth 116 from 105 – but when both fell in quick succession, chaos swallowed the cricket whole.

With dark clouds lurking overhead, eyes drifted towards Duckworth Lewis. Sri Lanka were well behind the par score when forced off in the 25th over – with darkness closing in, many feared that the tournament would be decided by mathematics. The players got back on the field, but by the end of the 33rd, Mahela's men were stumbling around in the dark at 206-7. The game was done, and the Lankans accepted an offer of bad light. Australia huddled in triumph; they were champions once more.

Except they weren't – not yet anyway.[202] The umpires and match referee seemed to have totally lost their grasp of the rules. They insisted that the 3 remaining overs would have to be bowled, or the teams would have to finish the match the following morning. A next-day return would have been anticlimactic; sportingly, Mahela agreed to finish the final under the cloak of darkness. Stands for the post-match ceremony were wheeled on and back off again; officials had allowed the World Cup final to become an absolute farce. 'It was a complete disaster,' Mahela reflects. 'But, you know, I became a mature person after that. I had to make some decisions. I spoke to the team in the dressing room and said, "Guys, we've come a long way. Yes, it's a final, but it is what it is. We have to do the right thing by the game. Let's finish the game today. I spoke to Ricky and said it was fine."'

With the lack of light proving dangerous, Ponting agreed to stick to spinners, and the tournament ended with Symonds bowling to Vaas and Fernando and no one able to see the ball. While it was bitterly disappointing for a World Cup to end in such a fashion, Jayawardene was phlegmatic. 'There were a lot of flaws in that whole structure,' he reflects. 'Yes, Sri Lanka were on the receiving end, but it could have been Australia if we had won the toss.'

Though the final was blighted by several mishaps, Jayawardene's men were ultimately undone by a special Gilchrist innings. As Murali put it to me when we spoke, 'We were beaten by the better side'. Mahela's men had not quite managed a repeat of Lahore, but had come mighty close. After seven weeks in the Caribbean they could board the flight home with their heads held high, happy in the knowledge they had done their country proud.

ANOTHER MARCH TO GLORY (2007–2014)

A BRAND-NEW MYSTERY

For those watching back home in Colombo, the final was blighted by more than bad weather and strange umpiring. While most of the city fretted over run rates, two LTTE planes flew south and dropped bombs on fuel storage facilities.[1] Desperate to prevent further damage, the government knocked out the city's power. With TVs cut, and lives on the line, you might think the tension of a faraway chase would dissipate. But across Colombo, people sought laptops or phones or any way of keeping up with the score. Cricket means so much to Sri Lanka.

The end of another World Cup cycle meant it was all change for the island's cricket again. Moody would be heading home, but for once, the split seemed unembittered by acrimony.[2] And despite the brevity of his tenure, his influence was resounding. Quite simply, Moody rerouted Sri Lankan cricket.

His assistant Trevor Penney would be heading to Western Australia too – but since his contract had a little longer to run, he was persuaded to take charge for the home series against Bangladesh in June and July 2007. For the visitors, it must have been incredibly deflating.[3] Humbled for 89 on a featherbed SSC pitch, they were put to the sword by centuries from Vaas, Vandort and Mahela and Prasanna Jayawardene.

From then on, it was all Sangakkara. His unbeaten double at the P. Sara was far his most fluid effort, but showed he was developing a better understanding of how to score big runs. Shelving the pull shot, he said he was inspired by Vaas' patient accumulation at the SSC. As he told reporters, 'It's just a case of getting in and staying there'. Having played himself into form, Sanga batted with far more freedom in Kandy, racing to 222* from just 277 balls. He became the fifth man to score back-to-back doubles; despite putting on 422 runs since his last dismissal, he admitted he had 'a few things to iron out back in the nets'.[4]

Hearing Sangakkara speak was almost as impressive as watching him bat, so clear was his demand for greatness. It felt apt that he should stockpile so many runs during Penney's final series, since he has paid special tribute to the one-time assistant coach. 'Tom [Moody] was a great influence, and at times Trevor Penney even more so,' he told me. 'With my batting, I always credit Trevor Penney, and that little period of time he was there with us, for really having changed my mindset about batting, changing my shot repertoire and really improving my batting.'

Nor was he the only member of this team scaling extraordinary heights. At the P. Sara, Malinga and Murali tore through Bangladesh, sending them tumbling to a lowest-ever 62. Arriving home to Asgiriya 12 wickets short of 700, Murali got halfway there in the first innings, the last 4 coming in the space of 14 balls. Second time around, the top order couldn't keep him out. Habibul Bashar was bowled wading down the wicket; Mohammad Ashraful and Shahriar Nafees pinned back by quicker balls. When number eleven Syed Rasel lamely chipped to Maharoof at mid-on, Murali had 12 for the match and 700 in his career. Teammates thronged, the crowd rose to their feet in rippling applause, but there was a sense of inevitability about the whole thing. By this stage

in his career, Murali felled milestones as often as others took wickets.*
The only real question was where he would end up.

Trevor Bayliss was announced as the team's new coach in August: auspiciously, he told reporters that he had spoken to Moody about the side on several occasions.[5] It remained to be seen, however, if an unassuming man like Bayliss could prosper in Sri Lanka. Unlike Moody, he was happy to keep his nose out of selection. That might have worked fine in New South Wales, but in Sri Lanka, such a passive policy could prove very risky indeed.

His first challenge was a novel one – the inaugural World t20 in South Africa. Despite Sri Lanka's lack of experience in the shortest format and Murali's forced exclusion, Bayliss was optimistic. He felt the team was naturally suited to short-form cricket, but while they cruised through the group stage, Sri Lanka struggled in the Super Eight. Comfortably beaten by Pakistan, Mahela's men were on their way home after Australia blew them out for 101. It was disappointing, but they were clearly still learning. Despite the moisture in the Newlands wicket, they tried to tear into the bowlers from the off – and found out the hard way that clever accumulation can bring more runs than all-out attack.

A frenzied schedule** meant there was little time to for Bayliss to find his feet, and an ODI series against England quickly went awry. Sri Lanka's batsmen have rarely looked so fallible in their own backyard: before the tour, they had not lost an ODI against England at home since 1982; here, they showed few objections in surrendering to Collingwood's men thrice in a row.[6] Dilhara's (6 for 27) superb two-paced spell brought an unlikely victory in the final match, but did little to gloss a dreadfully disappointing performance. The team headed to Australia under pressure to compete.

---

*   Remarkably, across a marathon career he kept on improving. While it took him twenty-seven Tests to reach 100 wickets (average 31.49, SR 71.47), he moved from 600 to 700 in just twelve (average 21.33, SR 53.41). With each and every hundred, his average and strike rate sank a little lower.

**   Sri Lanka would host England for five ODIs before heading to Australia for two Tests; return home for three Tests with England and then yo-yo back to Australia for a Tri-series in the new year.

With Sri Lanka still getting short shrift when it came to away trips,* the tour had the potential to act as a stepping stone towards proper recognition. For Murali, 8 wickets shy of Warne's world-record haul, it was a golden opportunity. The last time he played a Test in Australia, he was a raw 23-year-old dismissed as a chucker; twelve years on, he had a chance to cement his status as cricket's greatest bowler.

But Sri Lanka's prospects of success were jeopardised by infighting. Atapattu resisted attempts to reintegrate him into the side, refusing to meet with the selectors.[7] Riled at his omission for the post-World Cup Pakistan series, he would only resume discussions if Ashantha de Mel was removed from the panel. 'The squads are picked by the chief selector and his committee on a subjective basis with which I do not agree,' he vented to Sa'adi Thawfeeq. 'I have no respect for them considering the distasteful manner in which they have treated me in the past eight months.'[8]

Despite the outburst, the Sports Minister was intent on Atapattu's inclusion – and with the selectors' blessing, persuaded him to join up with the squad.[9] Yet, Marvan could not let sleeping dogs lie. Following the third day's play in Brisbane, he launched another stinging attack. 'Sri Lanka cricket at this moment of time is not going in the direction it should be going, especially with a set of muppets headed by a joker. I don't give credit to the way they have handled things.'[10]

An enraged administration wanted him sent straight home; ultimately, Bayliss and Jayawardene battled to keep him with the squad. Politics could wait; there was cricket to be played, and it was not going well.[11] The team struggled for runs in the warm-ups, and lost Sangakkara to a torn hamstring in the lead-up to the first Test.

Nor did they help themselves when they arrived at the Gabba. A damp, dreary morning did much to upset the management's thinking: Malinga was passed over due to the promise of seam movement; when the coin landed on Mahela's side, he asked Australia to bat. Both looked

---

* Since the start of the last decade, Sri Lanka had played three Tests in 1995/96 plus the two shoehorned into the Australian winter in 2004. Yet, during that same period, England played twenty-five Tests on Australian soil, the West Indies eighteen, India, Pakistan and South Africa twelve and New Zealand eleven.

like missteps: the bowlers struggled to grip the ball, the batsmen shelled catches and only Murali posed the mildest of threats. When Ponting called his men in on the second evening, the match was essentially over. Sri Lanka were beaten by an innings and 40 – the sting taken out of their tails across five days of merciless cricket. Still, Jayawardene was unshaken. 'We need to believe that we can beat Australia,' he told reporters. 'I firmly believe that we've got the personnel to do that and we just need to back our ability.'[12]

Though Sanga was back for the second Test, the Hobart wicket looked as flat as the Great Ocean Road. Australia raced to 542-5; Sri Lanka's reply lacked the same authority. Jayawardene's 104 was full of impressive strokes, but he couldn't carry his men past the follow-on target. Ponting declined to enforce; still Sri Lanka still faced the mountainous task of surviving five sessions. Their prospects looked ominous, but 247-3 at the end of day four a draw, even the unlikeliest of victories, had become possible. 'If we can get to lunch without losing a wicket, depending on the amount of runs we get, it becomes a lot clearer,' Sangakkara cautiously said.[13]

Sri Lanka would not get through to lunch uninjured. At the start of play, they fearfully eyed the second new ball, but the lower middle-order were carved to ribbons with such ease that Ponting delayed taking it until the 89th over. By that stage Sri Lanka were 8 down and clinging on. Sanga's presence was their sole consolation. Fluid from the start – and especially harsh on an off-colour Stuart MacGill – he began to improvise wonderfully as he ran out of partners.[14]

Whenever the field was brought up, Sangakkara pierced it with ease or cleared it with confidence. There were glides through gaps in the cordon and cleared-front-leg swats over cover. It was the kind of innings that makes bowling seem a futile art and scoring runs as simple as getting out of bed. Feather touches raced to the boundary; in total control, Sangakkara seemed to read bowlers' minds. A Lee bouncer was anticipated, stepped inside and massaged to the fine-leg fence; on commentary, Benaud seemed dumbstruck by the batsman's grace.

Sanga batted well enough to fish hope from a pit of despair. In little more than 15 overs, he and Malinga had put on 74, lifting Sri Lanka to 364-8.* But he was early onto a Stuart Clark bouncer. The ball ballooned from his shoulder onto his helmet and into Ponting's hands; though it was nowhere near the bat, Rudi Koertzen raised his finger.

While Sri Lanka's chances of taking something from the game went with Sangakkara, his heroics inspired Malinga and Murali. This madcap pair – proud owners of two of the more homemade batting styles in international cricket – gleefully backed away and swatted 46 from 30 balls. Clark looked dazed and confused as Malinga, tufts of bleach-blond hair sprawling through cracks in his helmet, repeatedly mowed him over the boundary ropes. Sri Lanka were finished for 410 – at that stage, the tenth highest fourth-innings score of all time. At last they had found some fight. Australia knocked off the runs with little trouble, but Sanga's innings was so dominant that you had to ask: if Koertzen hadn't erred, how far could he have carried Sri Lanka?

Still, outstanding knocks from the team's two best players could not paper over a disappointing tour. The bowling was the biggest let-down, 11 wickets across two Tests a paltry return. Murali, who managed just 4 scalps – 2 of them on the first day of the series – had hoped the pace and bounce on offer would work in his favour, but on good first-day pitches ended up trying too much. Equally, the seamers had work to do. If Vaas could be excused, the rest were given a lesson in controlled hostility by Brett Lee. The batting looked brittle: a worrying burden was starting to fall on Sanga and Mahela. Jayawardene asked for patience – accepting that his team had entered 'a transitional period'.[15]

★★★

Unsurprisingly, Atapattu retired at the end of the series.[16] His upset over the way he'd been treated was understandable; ultimately, a bitter end should not cloud a glorious career. He showed guts to overcome a torrid start in Tests; for years the ying to Sanath's yang, he brought stability at the top during the first years of the noughties. Even in his final series,

---

* Though personal achievements pale in comparison to a maiden Test win on Australian soil, he was also on the precipice of history – 8 runs shy of becoming the first to notch doubles in three consecutive Tests.

after months on the sidelines, he showed more authority than most; though fast approaching 40, none would have complained if he chose to carry on a while longer. Indeed, with Jayasuriya soon to announce his second red-ball retirement – and Tharanga enduring a protracted slump – Sri Lanka were facing a sudden vacuum at the top.

At least three Tests against England brought a hearty dose of the feel-good factor back.[17] Though Hoggard ran through Mahela's men on the first morning at Asgiriya, England's grip on the game was undone by the Kandy Boys. First, Sanga struck 92 to stave off disaster; then Murali bagged 5 big wickets to surge past Warne and into the history books. Mobbed by his teammates, his toothy grin seemed to stretch from ear to ear. This was a moment the city would never forget.

Perhaps it inspired his teammates, as Sri Lanka came charging back into the game. Sanath rolled back the clock, smashing 24 off a James Anderson over, before Sangakkara's 152 put the hosts in the driving seat. Though England mounted stoic resistance, Murali took out Ian Bell and Matt Prior with the second new ball; and Sri Lanka claimed victory with twenty minutes to spare. After the match, Mahela applauded his team's character. In deep trouble in the first morning, they dug in and eventually triumphed.

The Test capped a remarkably fertile period for Sangakkara, who leap-frogged Ponting to top the ICC batting rankings.[*18] There is something about the thrust of his career that strikes as utterly un-Sri Lankan. In a sense, he was the antithesis of the greats who came before him. Murali, Jayasuriya, Aravinda, even Mahela – these men produced eye-bulging feats, but operated with a certain diffidence. There was charm in their unassuming nature: yet, I can't escape the sense that bashfulness held them back. Sangakkara was a different sort of character. In the beginning there was little extraordinary about his game, yet he carried himself with confidence. By 2007, the fresh-faced cockiness had transmuted into an

---

* Since giving up the gloves in mid 2006, Sangakkara had struck 1,529 runs in 14 innings, averaging 152.90. Four of his seven centuries were unbeaten, three were worth more than 200. Surprisingly, he also scored considerably faster than his contemporaries during 2007 – of the top 20 run makers, only Pietersen (60.95) and Ganguly (62.59) got anywhere near Sangakkara's strike rate of 64.49.

unshakeable self-belief. He chirped less on the field, but away from it spoke as if he had discovered a secret formula for batting.

Starting out with less talent than his contemporaries, he achieved more than any Sri Lankan bar Murali. The closest comparison I can find is Steve Smith – another workhorse who seems to operate on a higher mental plane. Perhaps the most prolific batsmen are made not born: Sangakkara's strokeplay might lack the aching beauty of Aravinda's, but at the very top determination trumps talent.

Though bad weather stopped Sri Lanka improving the scoreline, they emphatically enforced their superiority through the rest of the series. Mahela backed up 195 at the SSC with an assured double at Galle; together, he and Sanga formed an increasingly daunting bulwark. Still, the moment of the series came with Sri Lanka in the field, when Malinga zeroed in on Pietersen's throat with a blood-curdling bouncer.[19] It sent England tumbling towards 81 all out; Vaughan's men headed home aware that 1-0 was a very flattering scoreline.

Of course, nothing made the people of Sri Lanka happier than the rebirth of Galle International Stadium.[20] It is a rare treasure. My favourite days of cricket-watching have come at the ground; with the austere clocktower in its shadow, it is inarguably one of Sri Lanka's most iconic symbols. Its restoration was a beacon of hope and a marker of recovery. It was not perfect – the outfield had lumps, the pitch was far bouncier than its predecessor, the seating rickety – but Galle's return meant more than cricket. It was a show of Sri Lankan resilience; a reminder that, despite the difficulty of the past, a bright future beckoned.

★★★

Back in Australia at the start of 2008, Sri Lanka's efforts in the Commonwealth Bank Series confirmed their status as a team in transition. Less than a year on from the World Cup, they looked bereft of confidence. Tharanga's poor run continued and he found himself dropped – worryingly, Sangakkara and Jayawardene made 540 runs between them, while the rest mustered 554. Worst of all, Malinga's knee gave out – he'd be laid up for over a year, nevermore able to comfortably shoulder a Test-match workload.

There was disruption away from the field too. With Jayantha Dharmadasa stepping down at the end of 2007, Arjuna Ranatunga was announced as the country's new cricket chief.[21] Though the appointment was greeted with much optimism, Arjuna's relationship with the players quickly soured.[22] In March, he ordered them to sign plainly prejudicial new central contracts.* The team refused; with Arjuna resistant to amendments, they were left to survive on basic tour contracts for over four months.[23] Apparently, progress only began to be made once the team visited the president's house for tea. A deal was finally brokered in mid-July, with a much-needed pay rise for the juniors secured.[24]

But, the IPL was emerging as a far bigger bone of contention. Clearly, the new league had the potential to transform player earnings in a way internal contracts couldn't: with the board having signed a three-year No Objections Certificate, and eleven Lankans purchased in the inaugural draft, it looked set to be a great boon for the island's cricketers.[25] But Ranatunga immediately took exception to the IPL.**[26] While the team were away in the West Indies, he agreed for Sri Lanka to replace Australia on a tour of Pakistan, blatantly ignoring the players' commitments.[27] The BCCI were furious, and pressured the PCB to scrap the series. Still, Arjuna was just getting started.

Though the senior players had only accepted a contract freeze on the condition that future tours would not be scheduled during the IPL window, within weeks Arjuna verbally agreed for Sri Lanka to tour England in early summer 2009.[28] Understandably, the team felt let down; worse, the affair was dragged into the public realm – manipulated to

---

* At $15,000, the junior players' annual retainer was the lowest of any Test-playing nation. The players' match fees were also said to be lower than any of their contemporaries' but Arjuna was resistant to an increase – in fact, there were rumours he wanted to fine the team every time they lost a Test. He wanted players to cancel future media commitments, while his proposal regarding image rights revenues was a long way off ICC recommendations.

** Apparently, he had moral objections – likening t20 cricket to 'three-minute Maggi noodles' – as well as practical concerns. 'Why should a young player be bothered to play for his country if he can make so much money in just one or two months in the IPL?,' he publicly asked. Equally, Ranatunga seems to have taken an instant dislike to IPL chairman Lalit Modi.

present the players as prioritising cash over country. Yet, as Mahela put it, 'Before we put our names forward for the IPL, we got clearance from SLC. We were available. The new board that came in refused to let us go. But if we pulled out, there would be consequences for us personally, because we signed contracts with these franchises.'

What's more, while Arjuna ranted about the revenue that would be lost from cancelling the England tour, he intentionally ignored the repercussions of riling the BCCI. The Indian board confidentially offered SLC a 'financial package' to help surmount the impasse, but were shocked when details of the meeting appeared in the press.[29] Describing SLC as hostile, they announced that all future tours involving Sri Lanka would be put on hold.

Alienating India to such an extent was economic harakiri: ultimately, the government had to intervene and broker a cancellation with the ECB. By Christmas, Ranatunga had been sacked, publicly scolded for failing to cooperate with 'the company or the players'.[30] It was a sorry situation, which benefited no one.

Jayawardene had his name dragged through the mud, and the incident was clearly a catalyst for him resigning the captaincy. Yet Arjuna suffered too. The very qualities which had made him a superb captain hindered him when it came to running the board. In trying to operate with the same bullish single-mindedness, he alienated the players and tainted his own legacy – so much so, that he felt it necessary to launch a defamation case against Sports Minister Lokuge.[31] He said he wanted to clear his name, but the damage of the past year would not be easily undone.

★★★

Despite much turmoil beyond the boundary, inside the ropes 2008 turned into a surprisingly good year. Jayawardene's third Test hundred in as many innings powered his team to a maiden victory in the Caribbean; though they could not take the series – losing a nip-tuck Test in Port-of-Spain. Still there was much to smile about. The lower middle order batted with gumption; auspiciously Samaraweera, who had often scratched around on away tours, struck his first century outside Asia. The bowling did look a little short-handed with Maharoof, Malinga and

Dilhara missing, but Vaas was outstanding, and Sri Lanka on the brink of unearthing a new sensation.

The board asked Murali to sit out the ODIs so they could test some younger spinners – though rain scuppered two of the three contests, debutant Ajantha Mendis' 10-over spell in the first match was ample proof the selectors had struck gold.[32] Slow bowlers have long relied on trickery, but none in recent memory have carried as much mystery as Mendis.

Everything about him was unorthodox. The approach: the straight, seventeen-step run of a seamer. The grip: one corner of the ball glued to the tip of his thumb, the other pressed against index and middle finger. The action: where he momentarily drew the bowling hand to his mouth, as if whispering secrets into it. And of course, the deliveries themselves: fast, with little flight or dip, deviating inches rather than feet, more often than not pencil straight.

Yet above all, what fascinated the public – and reduced world-class batsmen to sweat-drenched wrecks – was the range of weapons at his disposal: with almost imperceptible changes, he sent down off-breaks and googlies, leg-breaks and flippers, plus the much-vaunted carrom ball.

Though Mendis did not invent the carrom, it was he who shoved it down the cricketing public's throat. It made batsmen sick to their stomachs, but we who didn't have to face it greedily gobbled up this exciting 'new' delivery. By mid-2008, the world was awash with talk of the finger-flicked carrom ball.[*] Breaking like a leg-spinner, it fast became the crowning jewel in Mendis' baffling arsenal. For a few months in 2008, he was nothing short of a phenomenon.

That first ODI earned him 3 scalps, rave reviews and a seat on the plane to Pakistan. June's Asia Cup was a crucial chance for the team to reverse their recent poor form in white-ball cricket:[**] though Mendis made little impression in the tournament opener, from thereon out he

---

[*] The name, supposedly coined by the Toronto-based Sri Lankan lawyer Mahendra Mapagunaratne, references the popular South Asian game, where discs are flicked across a board using the middle finger.
[**] Since the 2007 World Cup, Sri Lanka had won eight of twenty completed ODIs, three of them against Bangladesh.

was electric. The UAE looked like lost children, single-handedly reduced from 139-5 to 148 all out.[33] And Mendis wasn't a playground bully preying on the weak; against Pakistan, far better batsmen looked equally helpless. Meanwhile, his presence seemed to have revitalised Murali, who bowled superbly for his 5 in the second clash against Bangladesh.

Sri Lanka were starting to click. While Tharanga's disappearance was disheartening, Sangakkara was flourishing in his new opening role. He cracked three centuries in Sri Lanka's first four matches, culminating in a bruising 201-run partnership with Jayasuriya. For the first time in history, Sri Lanka recorded 300-plus scores in three consecutive games.

With the team guaranteed safe passage to the final, Jayawardene's decision to rest Mendis for the group clash against India was a masterstroke: a double win, that denied the Indians a look at the spinner while heightening his fear factor. After all, the perception of mystery was as potent as the mystery itself. Mendis appeared in international cricket like a magician from a puff of smoke. No doubt, there was sorcery in his bowling, but equally his image as sorcerer seems to have scrambled batsmen's brains.

When it came to finals day, India – so reverently spoken about as the world's best players of spin – emphatically flunked the 'Mendis Test'.[34] They had their moments: Sehwag looked like he could win the match on his own, but tried to charge Mendis as soon as he was introduced. The ball was short and wide, a quicker carrom. Sanga judged it, the batsman didn't. The bails were flicked off, India's danger man shifted.

Two balls later Yuvraj Singh was bamboozled by a straight skidder – the chasm between bat and pad as wide as the Palk Strait. Suresh Raina was outfoxed by a straight one too; Rohit Sharma misjudged a leg-break and was trapped in front. A googly grabbed Irfan Pathan's outside edge; next ball, a glorious carrom uprooted R.P Singh's off stump. India crashed to 173 all out. Mendis had unfurled his full repertoire, taking 6 for 18.

Dhoni looked dumbstruck.[35] 'It was like you were playing something else, and the ball was something else. I won't really blame the batsmen – we couldn't pick the deliveries,' he mumbled, confused. When quizzed about squad selection, he admitted 'the main reason to add one batsman was Menids ... we could have got 274 but for the Mendis factor'. On a July evening in Karachi, a legend was born. A 23-year-old spinner –

whose name meant nothing three months earlier – had reduced India's batsmen to clueless Sunday sloggers.

With 17 wickets at 8.52, Mendis was rightly named man of the tournament. A motorcade was arranged for his return home to Moratuwa – and friends and family would soon have more to celebrate.[36] Less than a fortnight on from the Asia Cup final, India arrived in Colombo for three Tests and five ODIs. The selectors decided it was high time to unleash Mendis in red-ball cricket.

It was a brave decision. With just nineteen first-class matches behind him, he had yet to truly develop a stock ball. What's more, as Jayawardene explained, he was still learning how to get batsmen out: 'When we first saw him in the nets, he wasn't accurate – we had to work with him for a little while to tell him what needed to be done. His cricket sense wasn't that good. Later on, it became better, but he didn't know how to attack batsmen.'

'So, Sanga and I would be stood at slip and keeper – and more often than not we had signals for him to bowl a particular ball. Because he has two or three different deliveries, and when we're setting a batsman up, he didn't understand that initially. So he'd always look up and say "OK, do I bowl a flicked one, do I bowl the leg cutter, do I bowl the googly?" We always had signals, so he felt comfortable doing that because he was in control. That's all he had to worry about. That's how we gradually built him up. Later on, once he understood, he knew exactly what needed to be done.'

The SSC opener was incredibly one-sided. Malinda Warnapura, Mahela Jayawardene, Samaraweera and Dilshan notched centuries; then, the master and the mystery bowled beautifully in tandem, humbling the world's most fearsome batting unit. Since none of Ganguly, Tendulkar, Dravid and Laxman had been at the Asia Cup, some thought Mendis might be in for a rude awakening. Instead, he and Murali bowled all bar 30 of Sri Lanka's 118 overs, taking 19 of 20 wickets in the process.*

Clearly, the confusion Mendis generated imbued Murali with extra threat. After a couple of early full tosses, the youngster hardly sent down

---

* This was the first time since 1969 that so many Indian wickets had fallen to spin. By comparison, Kumble and Harbhajan had combined figures of 2 for 270.

anything loose; with so much pitching on the stumps, batsmen had to focus hard and play almost everything. Few were brave enough to attempt attacking strokes – but the only reward for surviving the frazzling Mendis at one end was an over from the demon Murali at the other. It was too much to handle.

Jayawardene had no hesitation enforcing the follow-on; second time around, Mendis and Murali made even lighter work of India. For a team with 106 Test centuries between them, there was great shame in being skittled in 45 overs. Sri Lanka were winners by an innings and 239. This Indian batting unit had failed before, but rarely had they looked so all at sea against spin. Meanwhile, Mahela's men had not lost a home Test since April 2006. And in light of this performance, there was fresh hope that Mendis could ease the strain on Murali's shoulder – and allow him to hang on in Test cricket a little while longer.

Though most of the batsmen struggled to pick Mendis at Galle too, India came charging back into the series thanks to Sehwag's swashbuckling double-century. At least the result set up a thrilling decider at the P. Sara. Mendis bagged another 5 wickets on the opening day – the highlight a tormenting carrom ball that left Laxman floundering in no-man's-land – before a seven-hour Sangakkara marathon carried Sri Lanka to a 147-run advantage. It was too much to overcome. The hosts sailed home with 8 wickets in hand; their new spin sensation had carried them to a thrilling series victory.

Mendis was nothing short of a revelation. His wickets came at 18.38 – incredibly, Jayawardene called on him to bowl 14 more balls than Murali. Rarely had the Kandy Man been relegated to support act – yet he gladly accepted the role. Few expected Mendis' variations to bring such instant success in Test cricket, but he terrorised top-order batsmen and tailenders alike. Laxman was undone on five occasions, Dravid four – Kumble, Harbhajan and Zaheer Khan three times each. With Mendis and Murali bamboozling in tandem, it was so difficult for the lower order to put on runs. Across the series, India averaged 75 for their last 5 wickets.

But while Mendis stole the show in the most eye-catching fashion, Bayliss and Jayawardene got contributions from most of their men. Warnapura looked increasingly assured at the top, Samaraweera's superb run of form continued while Dilshan, dropped during 2007, rebounded with his first century in three years. After a lean run by his own lofty standards, Sangakkara produced a series-winning knock at the P. Sara, while the captain passed 50 three times in five innings. Dhammika Prasad showed steel to grab 3 big wickets on debut, Murali picked up 21 while happily playing second fiddle. Plus there were some very good cricketers on the outside of the team: Malinga, Maharoof and Dilhara, plus Tharanga and the Chamaras, Kapugedara and Silva. Rarely had Sri Lanka been able to call on such a strong pool of players.

Sadly, they could not press their advantage in the ODIs. Though Mendis shone again, three poor batting displays consigned Sri Lanka to overall defeat. And though the team rebounded during a tour of Zimbabwe, they thrice batted themselves into tight spots, and needed Murali and Mendis at their destructive best to secure a 5-0 sweep.

It felt like a tale of two teams was developing, with Sri Lanka flourishing in Tests but floundering in ODIs. So it continued during a tour to Bangladesh over New Year 2009. Though fast improving, the hosts were still no match for Sri Lanka with the red ball – the 2-0 victory was capped by an outstanding performance from Dilshan.[*]

Yet when it came to the ODI Tri-series, Sri Lanka batted with real timidity. Blown out for 147 by Bangladesh in Mirpur, they almost suffered a repeat in the final. Despite skittling the hosts for 152, it looked game over when Sri Lanka slumped to 6-5; even when Murali strode to the crease in the 44th, Sri Lanka were 114-8 and second favourites. But they had kept their last powerplay in the bank and the fly-swatting Murali took Rubel Hossain to the cleaners. He smashed 20 off the 46th – ending 33* off 16. For the first time in his life, he had won a match for his country with the bat.

You can bet your life he did not let his teammates forget it. While those who played with Murali are in harmony about his qualities, most agree he was a singularly irritating presence in the dressing room.[37] He would wind batsmen up before they went to the middle, or chide them once they returned with presentations on what they could have

---

[*]   Dilshan made 162 off 165 and 143 off 175 – joining Duleep Mendis, Gurusinha and Aravinda as the proud owner of twin centuries – before bringing the game to a close with a devastating spell of off-spin (4.2-1-10-4).

done better. Nor was it just with his Sri Lanka teammates: at Lancashire, when Andrew Flintoff suffered the latest in a line of soft dismissals, Murali approached with a wicked question: 'What happened? Another shit shot?'

Equally, on coach journeys he was always seated next to the masseur Lal Thamel, since none of his teammates could cope with the incessant chatter. He must have been insufferable on the way back to the team hotel, reliving his frenzied swipes with irrepressible gusto. No doubt there were groans and laughs aplenty; Sri Lanka could smile for now – but they knew they would have to be much better. If you exclude the thirteen victories over Bangladesh, Zimbabwe and the UAE, their record stood at 9-17 since the last World Cup.

They still posed unique threats. If Sri Lanka could get Malinga healthy, they had a three-pronged carnival attack, unlike any cricket had seen before. The three Ms' menace was tantalising enough, and each of these bowlers was totally original, using their right arm in ways other men could not fathom. Their success spoke of something deeper than cricket – of a resourcefulness, an enterprising originality which is keenly Sri Lankan.

RISING FROM THE ASHES

In the last days of his tenure, Ranatunga offered his team up to tour Pakistan in 2009.[38] It was a surprise: with the country's security situation worsening, most were running for the hills.* Arjuna was singing from a different hymn-sheet: conscious of the two countries' historic relationship, and Sri Lanka's own former status as cricketing outcast, he announced that the island had a duty 'to help Pakistan when it is needed most'.[39] Though the players had serious concerns, they agreed once the PCB promised 'head of state' security.

---

* Australia had cancelled a tour in March 2008, and supposedly refused another in early 2009; following the Mumbai terror attacks, the Indian government asked its cricketers to scrap their upcoming trip.

While Ranatunga's sacking briefly threw the trip into doubt, SLC's dwindling finances meant the team had to play all the cricket they could. So Mahela's men faced a dizzying, relentless schedule, starting with three ODIs in Pakistan. Those passed without incident; inside the rope, it was a breakout trip for Dilshan, finally starting to fulfil his long-latent potential. Despite his obvious promise, he had made just six international centuries during his first decade in international cricket. From the start of 2009, he made thirty-three – his averages leaping as a shift to the top saw him develop into a real focal point for this Sri Lanka side.

Jayawardene points to a conversation in 2007. 'We had an honest chat when he was left out of the team,' he recalled. 'He was the first to come and say, "I need to bat higher up the order." So I said, "Can you open the batting?"' Over the next year, Dilshan opened for Bloomfield in white-ball cricket – after his excellent showing during the Tests in Bangladesh, Bayliss and Mahela decided it was time to give him a go atop the Sri Lanka order. With 42 (off 33), 76 and 137*, he instantly made the opener's berth his own.

Though Dilshan was less effective as the team struggled against India, a workmanlike 97 in the last match ensured Sri Lanka staved off a 5-0 defeat. Still it was a disheartening ten days, with both bowling and batting a step behind Dhoni's men. The Indians had clearly done plenty of video analysis of Mendis too: he leaked 199 runs in 39 overs, claiming just 5 wickets in the process.

The biggest shock of all was Jayawardene's announcement that the Pakistan tour would be his last as captain.[40] 'It was way too much for me to manage my cricket being the captain,' he told me. 'Trying to make all those decisions off the field. It was way too much.' Over the past year, he had fought tooth and nail to secure better pay for the juniors, and seen his name tarnished over the IPL affair. Atapattu had stopped talking to him, his relationship with Jayasuriya had soured too. All of this took a toll; at 31, Jayawardene no longer needed the hassle.

It is a great shame that leading Sri Lanka had become such a thankless task – by now, it required such sacrifice that none wanted to stay more than a couple of years. Had Jayawardene come from any other country, he would have enjoyed a far longer run. But in Sri Lanka, it was untenable.

Though his captaincy deserved a fairy-tale ending, it came crashing to a close with the most harrowing of nightmares. The Pakistan series had been stifled by lifeless pitches:* after seven days' cricket, it was dragging towards a 0-0 draw. Nothing was out of the ordinary as the team left for the ground on the third morning of the Lahore Test. The players sat in their usual seats; one of the quicks grumbled about what hard work the tour had been.[41] 'Maybe something will happen and we can all go home,' he joked. Moments later, the team heard a loud crackle. Then the scream came from Dilshan at the front of the bus. 'Get down.'

Within seconds the bus was at a standstill, being torn into by a torrent of bullets.[42] Jayawardene was hit first; his sock filled with blood. Mendis was struck down with a shrapnel wound, Paul Farbrace saw a piece of metal lodge in his arm. Blood soaked through every inch of Tharanga Paranavitana's shirt; Samaraweera cried out as a bullet pierced his thigh. Sangakkara raised his head, and saw a bullet lodge in the spot where it had been a moment earlier. With the bus stationary, those inside were like fish in a barrel. Outside, twelve gunmen blocked the exit to Liberty Roundabout. They had shot down the police escort – uncowed by return fire, the assault wore on and on.

It is a miracle that none of the team were killed. Murali remembers the chaos around him unfolding in slow motion – blood gushing from Farbrace and Samaraweera's wounds, Prasanna Jayawardene immersed in prayer. After what felt like minutes, Dilshan stuck his head above the parapet and began shouting directions at the driver Mohammad Khalil. Crouched under the steering wheel, Khalil managed to get the bus moving, and with Dilshan's help, got off Liberty Roundabout. On flat tyres they hurtled the half-kilometre to the ground, crashing through the gates of the Gaddafi Stadium.

While the team feared the worst for Paranavitana, Samaraweera could not walk and had to be carried from the bus. Both were bundled into an ambulance and taken to the nearest hospital; in the changing room, the

---

* At Karachi, Jayawardene (240) and Samaraweera (231) put on 437 for the fourth wicket, only to be outdone by Younis Khan's 313. Samaraweera notched another double in Lahore; strangely unveiling his 'machine gun' celebration for the first time in international cricket.

rest could hear the relentless rattle of gunfire in the distance. They had been lucky. The 'head of state' security PCB chairman Ijaz Butt promised was sorely lacking. Police should have been stationed at the roundabout; since they weren't, the team's attackers faced no backlash until forces arrived from the ground. Khalil saw a man throw a grenade at the bus; though it rolled under the chassis, the pin hadn't been properly pulled.[43] Just as he got them moving, a rocket-propelled grenade flew past, smashing an electricity pylon.

Still, they were not in the clear. The team had to move, but Mahela refused to get back on the road. Instead a military helicopter was arranged to take them to the airport. After an emotional farewell with Khalil, the team boarded the chopper. For Murali and Vaas, a charter out of Lahore dug up incongruous memories. Back in March 1996, they'd fled the city in the small hours with cricket's most coveted trophy; thirteen years later, they were lucky to escape with their lives. There was cruel irony in the fact that the architect of that triumph's fingerprints were smeared across this tragedy.* Arjuna had to ask himself whether he properly considered the consequences before sending his team into such a volatile situation.

That said, any failure on SLC's part paled in comparison to the PCB's shocking negligence. Chris Broad told *The Independent* that the convoy were left as 'sitting ducks'; while all accepted the tragedy could have been much worse, six policemen and the umpires' driver lost their lives.[44] Their death was a sobering shock; as Farbrace later put it, 'It just shouldn't have happened, that people died trying to help us get to a match … That sadness I think will stay with me forever.'[45]

The horror would not easily subside. Still, it was a mercy that every member of the Sri Lanka squad would return to the cricket field, sooner rather than later. Sanga joked that Paranavitana must have endured the worst debut tour in history – he'd bagged a duck in his first innings, been run out in his second and then taken a bullet to the chest to top it all off. But he was incredibly lucky that the shrapnel

---

*   An agitated Chris Broad, who had probably endured the worst of the trauma, told the BBC that England's security expert Reg Dickason 'was amazed the Sri Lanka tour went ahead' since 'England clearly wouldn't have gone into the same situation'.

lodged in his sternum – an inch either side and he likely would have been killed.

Samaraweera had a real stroke of luck too.[46] With doctors reluctant to carry out a second, potentially career-threatening surgery, the president offered up the services of his personal Ayurvedic doctor, Eliyantha White.* The surgeons allowed him eighteen hours to work on Samaraweera's wound; remarkably, by the time they removed the bandage, it had begun to heal.

★★★

Sri Lanka's next assignment was the World t20 in early June.[47] Sangakkara was announced as the team's new captain: his and Mahela's shared understanding meant the philosophy would shift little moving forward. 'We've always had a very strong leadership group,' he told me. 'Whether you were the nominated captain or not, we were all pretty adamant that everyone should be part of that, buy into the fact that this is *our* strategy and everyone has equal and valuable input. I'd been a part of that leadership group for a few years, so taking the reins was not that overwhelming. I wasn't overawed by it.'

Though it was eerie getting back on the team bus for the first time, Sri Lanka refused to wallow. 'We didn't make a big deal about things,' Sangakkara explained. 'There was no song and dance about it. It was just about getting back to cricket, doing what we loved and what we did best. That's how we approached the t20 World Cup. There was no greater significance in terms of the fact that we had just gone through a horrific experience. It was just a World Cup. Fantastic. Let's go and have a great time playing it.'

Sri Lanka looked a potent force. Sanath, Dilshan, Sangakkara and Jayawardene formed an imposing top four; at the other end, the three Ms were finally ready to take the field in tandem. Youngsters Angelo

---

*   White had recently performed a wonder cure on Malinga, supposedly curing a long-term stress injury in five days with the help of a special herbal medicine.

Mathews and Isuru Udana* brought spark and balance; Mubarak and Silva were spare hitters who could blast the ball should the top order fail. As promised, this team played vibrant cricket from start to finish, easing past Australia and West Indies to top their group, before brushing Pakistan, Ireland and New Zealand aside to reach the semis.

In the process, they got the cricket world talking. At the top of the order, Dilshan was proving a spirited force.** Nor was it simply his returns that caught the eye. During the first match of the tournament, he unveiled 'the Dilscoop', an audacious stroke now eternally inscribed into cricket's folklore. Alongside skill and imagination, it demanded real courage – since it requires the player to get down on one knee and dip his head into the ball. Part knight of the realm, part crab – seeing it in action is utterly thrilling. In some quarters, it was nicknamed the starfish, as many reckoned you'd have to be brainless to play it. Regardless, once it worked against Shane Watson, Dilshan brought his shovel out time and again. Few have mastered the stroke with such dexterity; cricket's chaster fans will be pleased that its natural successor, Niroshan Dickwella's self-dubbed 'Dickscoop', never took flight.

As impressive as Dilshan was throughout the tournament, Sri Lanka were certainly not a one-man team. Jayasuriya, Sangakkara and Jayawardene notched 50s en route to the semis; whenever the batters failed, they were dug out of trouble by their bowlers. Malinga's ability to fire in yorkers on demand helped defend gettable targets, while Mendis and Murali were among the tournament's stingiest bowlers. Having beaten two of the final four already, Sri Lanka went into the semis as favourites.

Victory over West Indies ensured they'd be heading to Lord's for a final-day clash against Pakistan: if the Lankans could summon a repeat of

---

*   Udana's story is remarkable: hailing from a rural village in Sri Lanka's hinterland, he won a scholarship to Colombo's D.S. Senanayake College at 17, and was promoted straight from his school team to Sri Lanka's 'A' side. He was by far and away the best bowler during Sri Lanka's Inter-provincial t20 tournament in 2009, particularly impressing with his back-of-the-hand slower ball. So despite having played just seven domestic t20 matches, he found his way into Sri Lanka's XI.

**   He cracked 53 against Australia, 74 against West Indies, 46 against Pakistan and rebounded from a rare failure against Ireland with 48 against the Kiwis.

their earlier performance, the t20 World Cup would be theirs. But disaster struck early – Mohammad Amir strangled Dilshan with short stuff; fourth ball, his shovel scoop lobbed straight up to short fine leg. When the promoted Mubarak fell in the next over, Sri Lanka were in disarray. From 70-6 after 13, a captain's knock from Sanga, and late fireworks from Mathews, at least dragged them up to 138.

They would need early wickets – with none coming until the 8th over, Sanga's men were up against it. They battled, but as Mahela put it to me, Shahid Afridi was 'in a different mood'. He took 10 off the first 2 balls of Murali's 3rd; when the fresh-faced Udana returned for the 18th, Pakistan pillaged 19. That turned the match, and they crossed the line with 8 balls to spare. While disappointing to fall short in another final, this nonetheless felt a cathartic moment. To see the team huddled together brought shivers. Three and a half months on from unimaginable trauma, Sri Lanka's players stood tall on cricket's most famous field. 'You've got to be proud,' Sangakkara reflected. 'No matter how disappointed, proud of what they achieved.'[48]

Indeed, Sri Lanka's success in the tournament took many by surprise. 'We hadn't played good t20 cricket up till then,' Mahela told me. 'We found ourselves doing things we weren't before that tournament. Against the big hitters of world cricket, we found a different way of playing t20; we played the conditions better and got to the finals. Yes, disappointment was there that we couldn't win, but we understood we were doing good things. Our planning was good, our tactics were good, our players were learning; we're executing in big tournaments and we're doing it consistently.'

LONG GOODBYES

With a home series against Pakistan getting underway two weeks after the World t20 final, there was little chance to pause for reflection. Though clashes between the two nations flowed thick and fast, Sri Lanka had not beaten their near-neighbours in a Test since 2004. Through three days in Galle, that looked unlikely to change. Struggling to put runs on the board, Sanga's men set Pakistan 168 for victory.

At 71-2 overnight, it looked like game over – but Herath sparked a fourth-day collapse to send the visitors tumbling to 117 all out.[49] Sri Lanka had scored the unlikeliest of victories; incredibly, it was the first time they had beaten Pakistan at home since 1986. The win was all the more astounding given the greenness of this attack; not since the 1980s had the team beaten a major Test nation without Murali or Vaas.

Indeed, the two stalwarts' sudden departure greatly threatened the side. At 35, Vaas faced the awkward situation of no longer being an automatic pick, while Murali's body was increasingly struggling to deal with the strain of bowling over after over. So Sri Lanka entered this series with an attack boasting thirty-five caps between them. Herath had been plucked from playing league cricket in Staffordshire: when he left for England, he had written a letter to SLC imploring them not to forget about him.[50] With five-fors in the second and third Tests, he emphatically marked his return – claiming his 50th Test wicket a decade after his first.

Nor was he fighting a lone battle. Nuwan Kulasekara and Thilan Thushara formed a potent new-ball pairing – and set up victory at the P. Sara, tearing into Pakistan on the first morning. It was a much tougher series for Ajantha Mendis: less than a year into his Test career, the mystery had been debunked; clearly, he was not the Murali successor Sri Lanka had hoped for. It was he who made way for Vaas' farewell at the SSC – a forgettable affair, not helped by a listless wicket.

Really, the cricket played second fiddle to Vaas, who received a standing ovation at the end of the match. It had been an extraordinary career. 'Sri Lanka has made giant strides and is able to rub shoulders with the best,' he reflected. 'I am proud to have played my own little part in this process. I may not have been the most talented cricketer to play for Sri Lanka, but I've worked hard on my game and was able to produce good results. There is no substitute for hard work.'[51]

Indeed, through lateral movement, control and variation, Vaas managed to thrive on Sri Lanka's wickets, where so many fast bowlers have floundered. As a boy, he thought about entering the church; David Hopps reckoned he ended up 'the high priest of swing'.[52] That may have been hyperbolic, but he was certainly a zealot to the temple of skilful seam bowling. During his early years, he logged each international scalp in a battered old notebook. Plainly, Vaas loved bowling – unsurprising, since he so rarely delivered a bad ball.

While reductive to tag such a successful bowler as foil or sidekick, there can be no doubt Murali benefited immensely from Vaas' control. With no release to the pressure valve, batsmen stewed at the crease and eventually boiled over. 'I should say that most of Murali's success was due to me bowling at the other end and keeping things very tight,' he joked. His only regret, he said, was a lack of focus on his batting during the first part of his career. Vaas had been a wonderful servant to Sri Lankan cricket. We would no longer see him in whites, but he vowed to battle his way back into the ODI team.

Although Sri Lanka won the one-day series too, the manner in which they were blown out in the last two games was worrying. Still, their uncertainty in white-ball cricket was offset by an increasingly steady hand in Tests. Arriving in late August, New Zealand had no answers for Sri Lanka's batting consistency. Samaraweera and Jayawardene gorged themselves throughout, Sanga drew the curtain on the series with an authoritative hundred of his own, while Dilshan celebrated a move to the top with a 72-ball 92, and 131-ball 123*. Having searched far and wide for 'the next Jayasuriya', Sri Lanka realised he'd been lurking in the middle order all along.*

The 2-0 win lifted Sanga's men to second in the Test rankings. Though their white-ball form remained shaky, November's three-Test tour to India presented a golden opportunity. Given their current hot run, and Murali's imminent departure, Sri Lanka knew they would not get a better chance to strike victory on Indian soil. It wouldn't be easy. Only five of the squad had played a Test in India, and Dhoni's men were notoriously uncharitable hosts.

Meanwhile, assistant coach Farbrace's departure disrupted preparations – and the task facing the team grew taller when Thushara pulled up on the morning of the first Test.[53] If scorers the world over had been pleased to see the back of Warnakulasuriya Patabendige Ushantha Joseph Chaminda Vaas, they no doubt shuddered at the sound of Sri

---

* Indeed, Dilshan's sudden emergence as a world-class opener helped Sri Lanka cope with Jayasuriya's drop-off during the final years of the noughties.

Lanka's latest left-armer: Uda Walawwe Mahim Bandaralage Chanaka Asanka Welegedara.

Dhammika Prasad's extra pace earned him a last-minute nod too – this new-ball pair were undeniably green, but bowled with head and heart to reduce India to 36-4. Still, the batsmen kept coming. Though India recovered to reach 426, Sri Lanka's reply suggested a team in the hunt. Mahela effortlessly racked up 275; Dilshan struck his fifth Test century of the year – having never before passed 450 in India, they declared with 770 on the board.

But Sanga's men could only strike four breakthroughs in the game's last four and a half sessions. Herath was the pick of the bowlers: prepared to give the ball flight, he carried more threat and kept tighter control than Murali, whose worrying lack of success spoke of a bowler in decline. There were mitigating factors – the drowsy pitch, the SG ball – but this was the first time he had bowled more than 20 overs in a second innings without taking a wicket.[54] Perhaps age was finally catching up with him. Since the start of 2008, his average away from home had ballooned to 37.68.* At 37, Murali was well into the autumn of his career.

There would be no more opportunities for Sri Lanka. The decision to play three spinners at Kanpur backfired the moment Dhoni won the toss: by the time a breakthrough came, India had 233 on the board. Worse, the struggle for wickets was coupled with a total failure to slow the run rate; worryingly, Russel Arnold felt Murali was starting to show 'signs of self-doubt'.[55]

Starting 642 behind, Sri Lanka lost Dilshan first ball, and spent the next two days sliding towards defeat. The batsmen should have offered more resistance, but were facing a mighty task after leaking 417 on the first day. And the punishment wore on in Mumbai. Though Dilshan notched a century, and Mathews excruciatingly ran himself out one short, 393 was an undaunting total on such a placid pitch. Sehwag pounded 293 off

---

*　Drilling down into the numbers created an increasingly worrying picture. In the same timespan, Murali's average in the second innings swelled to 62.37. If we exclude Bangladesh, his average away from home rises to 60.55.

254 – again, the relentless rate of scoring sunk Sri Lanka, who slumped to another innings defeat.

It had been a gut-wrenching few weeks. India were a powerful unit and the conditions inhospitable – but Sri Lanka were a far better side than they showed. They fell short in every discipline – in a way, it felt like they never recovered from the first-day pounding in Kanpur. Arnold reckoned the team had 'great potential', but needed 'to work on being a bit stronger in the mind'. It was a familiar gripe; one that looked to have no foreseeable resolution.

Though they could only split the t20s and win one of four ODIs, Sri Lanka's efforts in the limited-overs series gave cause for optimism. Despite a spate of injuries to the bowlers, the batters stayed in step. At Rajkot, clean hitting from Dilshan (160 off 124) and Sanga (90 off 43) brought them within a whisker of chasing 415; next up, Dilshan cracked another breakneck century as Sri Lanka gunned down 302. Tharanga notched his first century since October 2006; if fair to wonder whether such pitches served cricket, it was encouraging to see the batsmen getting runs under their belt after a tough couple of years in ODI cricket.

Within a week, Sri Lanka and India were back on the field in Bangladesh. Though little surprise the two visiting teams reached the Tri-series' final, it was still a great start to 2010 for Sanga's men. Centuries from Dilshan, Samaraweera, Mahela and Tharanga spoke of an increasingly stable batting unit; Kulasekara and Welegedara came good in the final, and Sri Lanka left with their first piece of silverware since 2008's Asia Cup.

Next up was the World t20 in the Caribbean.[56] Just ten months on from the last tournament, Sri Lanka expected to compete again – but struggled to rediscover the form they showed in England. Dilshan was short of his best, Murali broke down during the very first match, while Malinga and Mendis failed to make any real impact.

Though Jayawardene started the tournament in sublime form, a heavy defeat to Australia set up an effective quarter-final against India. With 8 balls left, and 25 still needed, Sri Lanka looked to be on their way home. But Kapugedara and Mathews unleashed brutal destruction; 18 runs off the next 3 balls brought them right back into the contest. With 3 needed off the last, Kapugedara wandered down the wicket and slapped the ball into the stands. Sri Lanka were through to the semis.

Yet sadly, they were no match for England in St Lucia. There would be no red-letter day– but Sanga's men could take spirit from reaching the final four again. It was equally pleasing to see a young core emerging: Mathews, Thisara, Kapugedara and Chandimal all impressed; in years to come, these men would be the ones to carry the team forward.

That said, the tournament was another nail in the coffin of Jayasuriya's international career. Fast-approaching 41, he managed 15 runs in 6 innings. The eye was fading, and he could no longer be expected to throw himself around in the field. Though desperate to make the 2011 World Cup, Bayliss' public opinion – 'he is a spinning all-rounder now' – was surely a sign he was nearing the end of the road.[57]

★★★

The hearty helping of white-ball cricket continued: with a young Dilshan-led squad impressing in Zimbabwe, and Sri Lanka easily marching to the Asia Cup final, the team's ODI woes seemed to be well in the rearview mirror. Still, the most significant moment of the tournament came away from the field. Since taking over, Sangakkara had refused to pay lip-service to the seniors – and on the eve of the final, he sheepishly told Murali that he had not made the final eleven. Though a last-minute reshuffle saw the decision reversed, Murali was left mulling his future. After talking things over with his family and manager, he decided the upcoming Galle Test would be his last.[58]

With Murali on the doorstep of 800 Test wickets, all of Sri Lanka were keen for him to play the whole India series. 'Sanga and Aravinda said "play all three",' he told me. 'But I said "No. One Test match. If I'm good enough, I'll take the eight wickets and go out with a good send off." It's a number at the end of the day; why not have a challenge?'

He was nervous in the lead-up to the Test. Though desperate to go out with a roar, Murali had little rhythm early in the week. Only after endless hours in the nets did he start to find his groove. 'He's a unique person – he's so competitive,' Hathursinghe told me. 'When he fixes something in his sights, he goes and achieves it. He trains like nobody. His last Test match, he went through the same routine as he did in his first.'

On debut, he'd been driven to the ground by his uncle, worn his own whites and bowled in front of empty stands.[59] His last Test was a more celebratory affair – an enormous cardboard cut-out even prowled atop the ramparts.[60] Perhaps his teammates were inspired by the sight of Murali watching over them: Paranavitana and Sanga notched centuries, before a madcap partnership between Herath and Malinga broke India's spirit. The visitors gave Murali a guard of honour; if it was unkind of them to target him with bouncers, it at least gave the world one more glimpse of his trademark no-look smash.

Now, the real business began. Murali might have lost a little bite, but he emphatically showed he could still spin a web around batsmen. Tendulkar misjudged the bounce trying to sweep; Dhoni was bowled by a ripper that rolled back the clock. With Yuvraj, Abhimanyu Mithun and Ohja cleaned up too, the Kandy Man had his sixty-seventh 5-wicket haul.

But wickets were harder to come by second time around. All of Sri Lanka were happy to see Malinga back in whites, but many felt a career-best showing was mistimed. Every wicket he took was one less left out there for Murali – after 18 fruitless overs, he needed 3 of the remaining 6. Late in the day, Yuvraj took him to 798; still, Murali's last day of Test cricket was set to be a nervy affair.

Though Malinga struck first, Murali trapped Harbhajan to take his wicket tally to 799. But tension was getting the better of Sri Lanka. Malinga trapped Mithun with another reverse-swinging yorker – then refused to bowl, scared of scuppering Murali's special day. The second new ball brought Murali no success – when the next partnership was finally broken by a Mathews direct hit, India were 3 down. The Kandy Man was stranded on 799.

Twice against England, hopes of a perfect ten had been shattered by a run-out – now, conscious of spoiling Murali's special farewell, his teammates stopped attacking in the field. Welegedara bowled an over of nervously wide deliveries; only Murali seemed to have his eye on the victory. When the ball was struck in his direction, he shied at the stumps; with the clouds closing in, he told the team to forget about the landmark. 'If I end on 799, OK, no hard feelings,' he told me. Above all, Sri Lanka had a match to win.

For fifty-four agonising minutes, India's last pair survived. It felt like a lifetime to those at the ground, but finally the magic moment came. Murali flighted one outside off, it turned just enough to draw the outside edge. Once it stuck in Mahela's hands, Galle erupted. Murali managed a couple of leaping high fives before he was buried under a huddle; fireworks thundered off into the distance; the crowd seemed to roar louder than ever before. Murali left the Test arena on the shoulders of his teammates. He signed off a seventeen-and-a-half-year career with 800 wickets to his name.

Inauspiciously, with Murali gone, the series slipped through Sri Lanka's fingers. They failed to strike victory at the SSC despite typically gaudy scores from Sanga and Mahela; at the P. Sara, centuries from Sehwag and Laxman helped India complete the turnaround. After a great start to Sangakkara's tenure, back-to-back series against Dhoni's men stopped the Lankan train dead in its tracks. What's more, with Murali having shouldered so much of the wicket-taking burden, this team had to find new ways of winning Tests.

Though Sanga's men emerged victorious from the subsequent Tri-series, Suraj Randiv's intentional no-balling of Sehwag – which left the opener stranded on 99* – stole away most of the headlines.[61] It was petty, ugly cricket – a needless action that left Sri Lanka looking bitter and unsporting. Randiv was given a one-match ban; Dilshan, who seemingly spawned the idea, escaped with the loss of his match fee.* Sanga meanwhile was given a public dressing-down by the board, reminded that maintaining team discipline was his responsibility.

The ticking-off was especially galling in light of the recent Dilshan-led Zimbabwe tour, where SLC tried to cover up an incident involving the stand-in captain and local police.[62] Fragments slowly emerged, painting a sordid but shadowy picture; with the board refusing to look into the issue, many at home assumed the worst.

Indeed, while the opener was flourishing on the field, his conduct away from it was increasingly troubling. Amidst *The Sunday Times*' claim that bookies had been using Bollywood stars to lure cricketers, Dilshan's

---

*   SLC's punishments seemingly ignored the power dynamics that fed into the situation – Dilshan was an eleven-year vet, while Randiv had been in the side for just nine months.

relationship with little-known actress Nupur Mehta at the 2009 World t20 raised eyebrows.[63] She claimed they met by chance in the hotel lobby and that she ended up spending £800 on him. No charges were brought against Mehta or Dilshan, but it was hard to escape the sense her story didn't add up.

SLC's refusal to take action against Dilshan was drawn into sharper focus by shadow coach Hathurusinghe's unceremonious sacking.[64] He had initially been given permission to leave the Zimbabwe tour early for a coaching course in Australia, but D.S. de Silva subsequently asked Hathurusinghe to stay with the squad. When he ignored that instruction, he was let go.

Sanga penned a letter to SLC, begging them to reconsider, but they refused – instead leaking his letter to the press, rendering the fissure between captain and board increasingly clear.[65] Rumours swirled that the top brass felt threatened by Sanga's popularity; annoyed by his involvement in administrative affairs, there was talk the board wanted him gone before the 2011 World Cup. The petty decision to sack Hathurusinghe, while other more serious breaches were overlooked, must have riled Sangakkara no end.

Murali had considered retiring from all formats after Galle, but was persuaded to stay on for the World Cup, and joined up for the squad in October for one last tour of Australia. With Sri Lanka falling just short of a clean sweep, it was a joyous week. Mathews and Malinga rescued the side with a nerveless stand at the MCG; though Malinga went with scores level, Murali was on hand to finish the job. His career could have ended in Melbourne fifteen years earlier – instead he departed the ground on his own terms, flicking Shane Watson to the fine-leg boundary to secure a famous win.

There was much to feel good about. Mathews and Thisara, the two bulky Josephian all-rounders, were making a real impression; while Champaka Ramanayake's discoveries, Malinga and Nuwan Kulasekara, shared the new ball with menace and verve. Murali looked revitalised after a rest, the top four was packed with class and experience – and for the first time since 1996, Sri Lanka could look forward to playing a World Cup in home conditions.

But of three Lankan venues set to be used during the tournament, two were new, while Khettarama had undergone major redevelopments. Less than three months out, none were remotely closed to being finished. Realising Sri Lanka's home advantage was negated by unfamiliar new grounds, the board decided to host a West Indies Test at the half-finished Khettarama ground. Reporters complained of water leaks and shoddy internet; Andrew Fidel Fernando felt the stadium resembled a 'dystopian war-zone'.[66]

Though D.S. de Silva promised grounds would be ready and handed over to the ICC by 15 January – well past the original deadline – *The Sunday Leader* claimed they were denied entry to the P. Sara as late as 10 January.*[67] Frustratingly, the West Indies ODIs in the first days of February had to be played at the SSC, since ICC rules prevented official venues being used so close to the tournament.

It was shambolic, but Sri Lankan cricketers had grown used to blocking out distractions. They knew how to raise their game when it came to tournament cricket. Near misses had confirmed this team were a whisker away from the golden formula, and had left a profound hunger in their wake. In towns and villages across Sri Lanka, folks counted down the days until the 2011 World Cup.

THE END OF AN ERA

The island was full of hope in the days leading up to the World Cup. Hotels were full, the towns and cities buzzing – a decade and a half on from 1996, it was impossible to escape memories of Arjuna's team's triumph. But Sri Lanka's tournament got off to a rocky start.[68] Malinga strained his back on the eve of the opener; though Sanga's men cruised past Canada, they came unstuck against Pakistan when Dilshan, Mahela and Samaraweera fell in the space of 4 overs. It was a worrying hiccup, but at least the team had time to get things right.

---

* De Silva tried to rubbish those reports, asking the BBC, 'Have those newspapers ever said anything good?', but did admit that progress on the Hambantota ground had been slowed by heavy rains.

Malinga returned to claim a second World Cup hat-trick against Kenya, but the abandoned Australia clash meant through four games, Sri Lanka had built little momentum. That changed at Pallekele – the openers mounted a 282-run partnership, before Dilshan's 4 for 4 sent Zimbabwe's innings crashing to an early close. Sri Lanka were through to the last eight, but it wasn't all plain sailing. Murali hurt his groin scampering for a single in Sri Lanka's last group game – and in wrapping up New Zealand's innings 15 overs early, the team missed the worst of the Wankhede dew. It would come back to haunt them on finals day.

At least Murali was fit enough to get through his 10-over quota come the quarter-final against England. The Khettarama ground was built for days like this: though this concrete monstrosity lacks the charm of Galle or the Sara or even the SSC, it inspires a raucous joyfulness that feels utterly Sri Lankan. Outside, street-food carts sell *wade* by the bucket-load; the percussive sound of kotthu-chopping spills from cubby-hole cafes. The din of horns is inescapable, the hum of engines constant. At one corner of the ground sits a temple; on the other side a grass-green mosque. Both feel close enough to be pelted by a big-hitting batsman.

Inside it's a church of cricket hedonism: boundaries – and, if Sri Lanka are chasing, singles – draw wild cheers, arrack is swilled and spilled, pockets of papare begin playing from nowhere. For all the happy memories made at the ground, England 2011 ranks among the highest. No team had chased over 230 at Khettarama since 2004, but the pitch and lights were new, and the English total nowhere near competitive. After surviving a tricky opening spell, Dilshan and Tharanga thrashed the bowlers to all parts. The chase was so comfortable that Dilshan shepherded Tharanga to his century. Sri Lanka crossed the line with 10 wickets and 10.3 overs to spare.

They were back at Khettarama three days later for a repeat of the 2007 semi. Though Sri Lanka were superb in the field, restricting New Zealand to 217, Mathews' torn quadriceps was bad news – he would miss the final if Sri Lanka made it. That looked a formality heading into the last 20 overs, but Dilshan played a rash shot, Mahela missed a straight one, and Sanga holed out to send tension whispering through the ground. Nerves jangled when Mathews hobbled to the crease, but he showed the guts of a warrior and the heart of a lion, smashing Tim

Southee back over his head to seal victory. Sri Lanka were heading to another World Cup final.

While India had been favourites from the tournament's get-go, Sangakkara's men knew they were capable of springing an upset. Dilshan and Tharanga had been the tournament's most productive opening pair, the captain averaging 104.25 heading into the final, plus Malinga and Murali posed a unique threat. On the other hand, Mathews' injury left Sri Lanka with a real headache – since the balance he brought to the side could not be easily replicated.

Indeed, the brains trust were compelled to make four changes for the final. Thisara and Kulasekara came in to bolster the seam attack and lower-order batting; Chamara Silva's nervy semi-final innings saw him replaced by Kapugedara. And despite watching the semi from the stands, Randiv was parachuted in – his previous success against India enough to secure the second spinner's berth. It wasn't ideal: as Jayawardene told me, 'The balance was gone. We couldn't play the combination that we wanted to play, with a bit of pace. We had Dilhara in the squad just for that game, to play against India, but we couldn't play him because of the balance of the team.'*

After confusion in the middle culminated in a second toss, Sangakkara had no hesitation in electing to bat.[69] Sri Lanka did not want to be stuck chasing a tricky target under lights, especially without Mathews to bolster the lower-middle order. But Dilshan and Tharanga struggled to get going; by the 17th Sanga's men were 60-2. This was not the platform they had wanted: it was left to Sanga and Mahela to carry the team to a decent target. As they were starting to break loose, Sangakkara misjudged a cut off Yuvraj. At 122-3 after 28, the Lankans needed something special.

Jayawardene provided it. Though he had been short of runs since the tournament opener, he looked in rare form here – caressing the ball to the fine-leg and third-man boundaries. He moved from 50 to 100 in

---

*   At the time, and ever since, much has been of these changes – in some quarters, their very presence taken as proof that Sri Lanka threw the final. But the seamers' inclusion was totally logical given Mathews' injury, the middle order's frailty, and the Wankhede's promise of bounce. Kapugedara and Randiv were 50-50 picks; while assumed logic is that you should not change a winning team, Sangakkara and Bayliss had to select a side they felt could beat India.

just 35 balls, reaching his century with a trademark inside-out lofted slap over cover. With Kulasekara coming good, and Thisara plundering 16 off the last 4 balls, Sri Lanka surged to 274.

They carried momentum into the field, and Malinga tore into India up front. Sehwag was trapped by a skidder second ball; 6 overs later, Malinga found enough swing to draw Tendulkar's outside edge. Sri Lanka were right in the game. But India came charging back superbly. Steaming in from the boundary, Kulasekara couldn't cling on to a tough chance that would have sent Gautam Gambhir packing; though Dilshan claimed a sharp return to get rid of Kohli and breathe life into the game, India dominated the back half of the innings. Gambhir and Dhoni were commanding; and with the dew worsening by the minute, the bowlers couldn't grip the ball. 'It was unfortunate,' Murali told me. 'The dew hampered us a lot. I was pleading [before the toss]: the dew means the spinners, even Malinga, can't grip the ball. But Angelo's injury made them nervous to bat second.'

Clearly, Sri Lanka hadn't counted on the dew being such a factor. Jayawardene felt that once it came into play, the final was a 'no-contest' – neither Murali or Randiv had any impact; with the ball skidding off the bat, the Indians easily rotated strike. Though Thisara bowled Gambhir to give Sri Lanka a glimmer of hope, Dhoni ended it by slapping a straight 6 into the stands. India were World Champions once more. For Sri Lanka, it was the same old story: always the bridesmaid, never the bride.

'We were outplayed and we have to accept that,' Sangakkara said stoically after the match, though it was clear these near misses were getting harder to take.[70] 'It's very deflating,' he admitted to me nine years later. 'I always say it's better to lose long before the final, because at least you've seen that last hurdle is quite a way away. But when you're there, on the cusp, and it's the third defeat in a final, it does wear you down. The fact that you're a runner-up is neither here nor there. You're a champion if you win; if not, you've not done enough in that all-important match.'

Still, Sri Lanka could take some solace from their performance: as Jayawardene explained, 'Yes, you couldn't get out of bed for two or three days after the final. But still, you could come back and say we're doing a lot of things right. Let's keep pushing, keep pushing.' Perhaps Murali put it best: 'We weren't lucky enough. You need luck to win a final, no? In 1996, we had the luck on our side.'

While the allegations that sprang up at home were salt in the wound for the players, they ultimately reflected the Lankan public's inability to reconcile such defeats.[71] It was simpler to find a scapegoat than to accept second best. In 2007 it had been a squash ball; this time around suspicion was cast on their own players.

Of course, the end of a World Cup cycle meant another raft of resignations. Bayliss could head back to Australia with a proud legacy – but could not resist a parting swipe at the administration. 'Good teams like Australia usually have got strong or good management backing up the team,' he said. 'That's an area we can improve here.'[72] On hearing that Sangakkara and Jayawardene would be stepping down from their leadership roles, he said, 'It's a shame. They are the two best guys to take Sri Lanka forward. They probably had enough of putting up with distractions.'

For Sri Lanka, it was an utter waste that leaders of their calibre had such short tenures. Yet, the difficult truth was that the board did not want strong, assertive or opinionated leaders. They preferred men they could control. Sangakkara's offer – to stay on as Test captain for tough upcoming series against England and Australia – fell on deaf ears; nor did anyone ask him to reconsider his resignation.[73]

Clearly, Sri Lanka did not make proper use of their two best leaders since Ranatunga – and have dearly paid the price. In the decade since, the team has often lacked steady leadership; even in 2011, there was a worrying sense of an end of an era. Murali and Vaas were gone, Samaraweera and Dilshan almost 35, Mahela and Sanga about to turn 34. Even less senior members of the side – Herath, Chamara Silva, Prasanna Jayawardene – were past 30. Did Sri Lanka have the stocks in reserve to deal with so many departures?

Life without Murali was clearly not going to be easy. During his Test career, he bowled around a third of Sri Lanka's overs, taking 40 per cent of all wickets; in ODIs, he was a menacing, strangling presence too.[*]

---

[*]   If you consider strike rate (35.2) and economy (3.93) side by side, only two other bowlers from Murali's era match up: Glenn McGrath and Wasim Akram.

His departure left a huge hole in Sri Lanka's playing eleven – without him and Vaas, the attack suddenly had a very hollow look.

Equally, the team would miss Murali the man – a wonderful presence in the dressing room, full of warmth, humility and humour. Mindful of his own experiences, he probably did more than anyone to ease youngsters' passage into the national side. 'When I went on the England tour [in 1991] I was very, very disappointed,' he told me. 'I always told Sanath, "We should not be like that". We should help the youngsters and welcome them. They should be treated properly: their fear of the seniors, the fear of pressure, everything has to be taken out. We have to take them for dinner; we have to talk to them, then they'll feel part of the team. Alone we can't win; senior players only can't win. The younger players are the most important players in the team. If they're doing their job, we're OK.'

What's more, as a Tamil in a team of mostly Sinhalese men, Murali's career stood for more than cricket. Sangakkara told me he felt the team came to exist as a 'symbol, almost of what could be achieved without anyone concentrating on the issues that were tearing us apart'. Murali's enduring success spoke of the possibilities of reconciliation, hinting at the potential might of a united Sri Lanka.

The impact of losing him and Vaas was compounded by Malinga's retirement from Tests in April 2011.[74] It had been coming: since breaking down at the start of 2008, he had managed just two Test outings. Ultimately, it was irrational to expect a bowler with such an elastic action to last in red-ball cricket. Still, the decision to truncate his Test career dredged up much controversy – partially because he declared himself unavailable for the England Tests while healthily crushing toes in the IPL.* When SLC ordered him home for rehab, stating the situation was a 'bit awkward', Malinga announced his retirement from Tests.[75]

Really, this could have been sorted out privately. In making the issue public, SLC tarnished Malinga's name, ensuring his status as the poster-boy for cash-hungry Sri Lankan cricketers. No doubt there was a train of thought on the island that Malinga's decision was invalid because

---

*   This should not have come as a surprise; since his return from injury in 2009, he had regularly made himself available for ODIs while missing the corresponding Test series.

t20 was not 'proper cricket'. Equally, the board were clearly annoyed that the IPL was increasingly impinging upon the international calendar. Nonetheless, the way Malinga's retirement was portrayed was unfair and reductive.

★★★

The board had bigger problems. Though the World Cup had been expected to boost coffers, it had in fact left SLC in financial disarray.[76] Sports Minister Aluthgamage spoke of the cost of developing stadiums, but clearly money had been mishandled.*[77] It would be up to the team to drag the administration out of the mire. The selectors eventually settled on Dilshan as the new captain; Stuart Law would take charge of the side on an interim basis.[78] Once more, Sri Lanka had the feel of a team undergoing an evolution.

A new era got underway on a squally Cardiff afternoon in May.[79] Though a green five-man attack lacked bite, the game was dragging towards a draw until Sri Lanka threw it away in the last session, collapsing to 82 in front of a few dozen baffled punters. Lord's was a closer-run thing, but the team took another backward step at the Rose Bowl. With Dilshan injured, Sanga reluctantly agreed to lead; only his stoic six-and-a-half-hour 119 stopped Sri Lanka sliding to defeat.

Still, the team knew that were it not for rain, they would have surrendered the series 2-0. The bowlers only managed 30 wickets across the series: not since the days of Roy and Duleep and had Sri Lanka been so reliant on a couple of players. Life after Murali was starting to look very tough indeed – in eight Tests since he retired, Sri Lanka had failed to strike a single win.

Problems stretched beyond the boundary too. Tamil protests in England grew louder once Jayasuriya, now a sitting MP, was named in the white-ball squads.[80] By now unjustifiable from a cricketing perspective, his inclusion was unfair on the rest of the squad. John Stern reported

---

* While an SLC financial report revealed that Rs. 4.282 billion had been spent on the politically entangled Hambantota Stadium, a 2015 government valuation put its worth at Rs. 912 million.

that 'younger players, fearing their careers would be stifled, were said to be in tears'.[81] In truth, Sanath simply fancied a farewell tour: in what felt like his umpteenth retirement, he stated he would quit international cricket for good after the first ODI.

Still, as a member of a government under scrutiny over potential human-rights violations, his presence on the cricket field was increasingly untenable. Even for Jayasuriya's fans, it was a disheartening exit. I certainly found it upsetting. As a boy, few cricketing thrills matched a Jayasuriya innings; by 2011, you felt you were watching a different man – a bloated symbol of politics' cannibalisation of cricket; an embodiment of the abuses of power which blight Sri Lankan society.

If Sanath's presence twigged the wider world to the murky currents lurking under the surface of Sri Lankan cricket, Sangakkara's Spirit of Cricket Lecture emphatically forced the issue home.[82] His grievances will be familiar to readers of these pages, but in 2011 were quite a shock to the well-fed Lord's members.* His conclusion – 'unless the administration is capable of becoming more professional, forward-thinking and transparent, then we risk alienating the common man' – was prescient. If fans weren't disenchanted in 2011, they certainly are a decade later. At home, the administration quivered with fury. The Sports Minister quickly ordered a report, though ultimately realised there was little he could do now the cat was out of the bag.[83]

Though Sri Lanka were much more competitive through the ODIs, there would clearly be no quick fix for Dilshan's men. Predictably, Law's hopes of becoming full-time coach waned when he couldn't get answers from the board; by tour's end, he'd accepted a role with Bangladesh.[84] It had been a tricky few months for the Australian: ignored over the captaincy and turned into an unhappy bystander in the Jayasuriya affair, he realised the Sri Lanka job was about 'more than just cricket'.[85] Rumesh Ratnayake stepped into the hot seat for Australia's visit in August 2011, but the team had few answers for the pace battery of Lee, Doug Bollinger and Mitchell Johnson. At least Malinga extracted some revenge with

---

* He spoke of 'a mad power struggle that would leave Sri Lankan cricket with no consistent and clear administration'; of 'partisan cronies' and 'wanton waste of cricket board finances'.

a hat-trick in the final contest: if 3-2 wasn't out-and-out disaster, nor could it be considered a real success.

The Tests started more auspiciously – struggling with sickness, the Australians looked off-colour through the first day in Galle. But Sri Lanka never got to grips with the turning pitch; blown out for 105 in the first innings, they fell to a 125-run defeat. Though it was the bowling that was meant to suffer in Murali's absence, the batters struggled again at Pallekele – only a heavy dose of bad weather helped the Lankans escape with a draw.

And while Dilshan's men were much improved at the SSC, a bizarre fourth day left the public frustrated.[86] Having opened up a 112-run lead, stealing a share of the series was still possible – but Sri Lanka would have to push on. Quick runs or an early declaration seemed the only options, but Mathews, 86* overnight, took 49 balls to reach his maiden century. The match drifted away as Sri Lanka added 45 in 19 overs; they ended a fourth consecutive series on the wrong side of the result.

The Mathews affair was especially worrying because it was not an incident in isolation. Twice during 2011 – against England at the World Cup and again at Lord's in the summer – the team had prioritised personal landmarks over putting a game to bed.* Given it had been fourteen months since their last Test victory, Sri Lanka should have been doing everything they could to end their barren run. Dilshan said the team was 'still trying to find a bowler to win matches for us', but the side's mentality was an equally pressing concern.[87] With no long-term coach, and a captain learning his trade, Sri Lanka were lacking clear direction. Daniel Brettig felt 'Test cricket died a little' during Mathews innings; sadly, it was hard to disagree.[88]

Geoff Marsh was named coach ahead of the Pakistan series in the UAE, but his presence did little to ease the sense of a team in decline.[89] Sangakkara was superb, but Mahela averaged just 17,** while Dilshan

---

*   Those situations were somewhat different, since Sri Lanka were all but assured of victory – but they nonetheless spoke of a team placing too much value on personal achievements.

**   Jayawardene had now failed to lodge a 50 in Sri Lanka's past two away Test series.

spent much of the series at five in an attempt to lighten his load. Given the bowlers' inexperience, Sri Lanka needed more from their senior batters. They clung on to draw the first Test after stuttering to 197, but there was no overturning a sizable deficit in the second. Even when they built a solid platform in the third Test, Sri Lanka fell well short of taking 20 wickets. They had now played fourteen Tests without Murali and failed to notch a win.

The ODIs brought more disappointment. Though a Tharanga century and a searing Malinga new-ball spell carried Sri Lanka to victory in the second game, batting failures prevented them from winning any of the other four matches. In the third, they slipped from 111-1 to 236; and next up, tumbled from 155-3 to 174. The collapses were concerning, but it was equally worrying to hear Dilshan say Pakistan had 'more good players' than his own side. Losing his first six series on the trot can't have allowed him many easy nights. He accepted his team would have to improve fast before heading to South Africa.

When Sri Lanka were shot out twice at Centurion, you sensed it would be a very long trip.[90] At least there was some cheer in the lead-up to Christmas: with players unpaid by the board since the World Cup, the ICC sent Sri Lanka's tournament fee straight into their accounts.[*91] Perhaps it spurred them on: come Kingsmead, they produced their best performance of the post-Murali era. Samaraweera and Sanga scored centuries, Herath and Chanaka Welegedara bagged hauls – and Sri Lanka claimed an unlikely maiden victory on South African soil. 'We proved we are good,' Dilshan proudly stated after the match, fully aware that no one had given his team a hope.[92]

The wheels fell off at Newlands, but at least another gutsy Samaraweera century allowed Sri Lanka to stave off an innings defeat. Though these results were hard to reconcile, Dilshan seemed ecstatic. 'Before we came out here, everyone thought we couldn't win a Test outside Sri Lanka. After Murali, people said we couldn't take 20 wickets. Now everyone knows we can do both.'[93] Still, this side had a long way to go if they were to prove the Durban demolition was anything more than a happy accident.

---

*   It was less than half of what they were actually owed, but nonetheless a start.

As disheartening as their Test returns had been since Murali's retirement, the sudden slide in white-ball cricket was a greater concern. The team tumbled to a new nadir in Paarl: dismissed for an all-time low 43 in reply to South Africa's 301-8; victories in East London and Bloemfontein saw the hosts take an unassailable lead. For Sri Lanka, this was troubling: since falling a whisker short of World Cup glory, they had won six of nineteen ODIs, one against Scotland.

So Thisara's electric all-round performance at Kimberley was just the tonic to put smiles back on Lankan faces. And if there were fears this team was starting to look like the Sri Lanka of three decades before – capable of magical flashes amidst stretches of abject cricket – they were somewhat allayed by the final match. Dilshan's men controlled a 313-run chase as long as Sanga was at the crease. Still, when debuting number ten Sachithra Senanayake wandered to the wicket, they needed 5 runs from 3 balls. A first-ball block prompted fears that he might have misread the scoreboard – but next up, he launched a flat six into the stands. Despite losing both Test and ODI series, this was a spirited turnaround. In hostile conditions, Sri Lanka produced their best performance since the World Cup.

Still, the axe fell on captain and coach.[94] Having lost eight series in a row, Dilshan could have few complaints – though when he retired four years later, he implied that he had not always received the full support of his teammates.[*95] Whether true or not, it left the sense that Dilshan's tenure was blighted by mistrust; that the team had not necessarily been pulling in the same direction. Whatever the case, his tenure was ill fated; as knee-jerk decisions go, his removal was probably not the worst.

Marsh's sacking, after just four months as coach, was harder to justify. Ranatunga might have been playing politics when he claimed the board had 'no clue' about cricket, but he was right in stating the decision set 'a very bad precedent'.[96] 'Top coaches and physios will think twice before they accept a job from Sri Lanka in the future,' he warned – after a long

---

* 'Angelo Mathews had a calf injury for that year that stopped him from bowling,' he told Andrew Fidel Fernando. 'That must be because of my misfortune, because after I had stepped down we went to Australia after a week. In that week, Mathews started bowling. That must be because of Mahela's good fortune.'

history of mistreatment, it was a surprise Sri Lanka could attract anyone at all. Graham Ford was signed up; after some contemplation, Mahela agreed to step in as stopgap captain.[97]

If that felt like a backward step, it was an undeniably positive one. Jayawardene's first spell in charge gave the team a shot in the arm; Sri Lanka could desperately use the same to get through 2012. A Tri-series Down Under, and home series against England, would leave little room to hide. What's more, a World t20 on Lankan soil was a test and a burden. When it rolled around, the island's fans would expect their men to compete.

ANOTHER NEAR MISS

A trip to Australia looked an ominous start to Mahela's second spell in charge. Sri Lanka had often been written off ahead of these Tri-series – given their recent form, alongside India and Australia's strength, most felt they were there to make up the numbers. The early phases of the tournament suggested a side going nowhere fast: Jayawardene's men lost their first two, and conceded 23 in the last 2 overs of their third match to hand India an unlikely draw.[98]

Yet they turned on the style at the SCG; after cutting Australia down for 158, the team began to build momentum. Thisara bagged 4 to help keep India under 289; next up, Sri Lanka gunned down 280 to book their place in the finals. They played some enthralling cricket. Set 322 to win the first final, they looked dead and buried at 144-6, before Tharanga and Kulasekara almost pulled off the unlikeliest of rescues.

In the second final, Mahela produced a finger-wagging rebuke of Umpire Oxenford that would have made Arjuna proud – and seem-ingly restored his team's intensity in the process. Malinga and Kulasekara dragged Australia back with excellent death bowling, and Sri Lanka got off to a flyer. The captain's 76-ball 80 was a showcase of effortless artistry, but Dilshan stole most of the plaudits. He opened bowling and batting, got through 10 overs for 40 and notched his second century of the tour-nament. Had he not been struck in the face attempting a Dilscoop, he might well have felt this was the perfect night's work.

After keeping Australia to 231 in the third final, Sri Lanka were suddenly favourites to lift their first trophy on Australian soil. But they collapsed in the first 10 overs and fell 16 short. 'I am not disappointed because when we came to Australia we were not given any chance of getting anywhere, but we showed a lot of character,' Jaywardene said. 'In tough situations, we played some really good cricket. And it's not easy when you have a new captain, a new coach and a new way of thinking.'[99] Clearly, Sri Lanka deserved real credit for bouncing back so emphatically after the tumult of 2011; still, faltering in a straightforward but all-important chase must have stung a side far too accustomed to settling for second.

No one deserved higher praise than Dilshan. It must have been tough to return to the ranks after a cursed spell in charge, but the former captain was energised. Alongside being the tournament's leading run-scorer, his thrifty off-spin brought balance once Mathews and Thisara were struck down with injuries. That said, this was a real team effort: Chandimal, Jayawardene and Sangakkara also passed 400 runs, Malinga topped the wickets chart, while the attack seemed to possess a new-found balance.

After such a strong showing, Sri Lanka entered the Asia Cup as favourites, but the four-day turnaround proved too tall an order. The team never adjusted to conditions in Bangladesh: the bowling lacked bite and the batting lost its backbone. Once their 305-run chase against India collapsed, they tamely surrendered to Pakistan and Bangladesh. The graft in Australia had gone some way to repairing the team's reputation; now, much of that hard work was undone in a flash.

With Sri Lanka's form wildly fluctuating, few knew what to expect from two Tests against England: ultimately, a drawn series did little to shift the sense of a team in decline.[100] At Galle, Mahela walked to the wicket with Anderson on a hat-trick: though none of his team-mates managed more than 27, the captain's 180 lifted his men to 318. Meanwhile, England looked baffled by the turning ball; their frailties epitomised when Jonathan Trott stumbled down the wicket, missed a full toss and then ran headfirst into Prasanna Jayawardene. Herath took 6 in each innings, his flight and control too much to handle.

But Sri Lanka were a distant second at the P. Sara. Sanga's second golden duck of the series left Jayawardene again facing a hat-trick ball. He responded with another excellent century – but 275 was too few on a true batting wicket. Pietersen struck a ferocious 151; after Swann's double-strike on the fourth evening, there was no way back for Mahela's men. With Murali gone, they had to be near their best to win Test matches.

It was frustrating the series left no space for a decider, but with Pakistan arriving in June, fans could hardly feel short-changed. Thisara's impressive charge continued during the ODIs: he grabbed plaudits at Pallekele for 6 wickets and a 14-ball 24*; then produced a 41st over hat-trick at Khettarama to bring a first series victory since the World Cup. Clearly, he and Mathews would be crucial cogs for the team moving forward. Not only did they reduce the reliance on spin, they allowed Sri Lanka to field a far deeper batting line-up.

The ODI pitches had proven unusually seam friendly, and the teams had to check their eyes when they arrived at Galle and found smattering of grass on the pitch. There were rumblings that Sri Lanka were seeking new ways of taking wickets – yet they notched their third win of the post-Murali era by sticking to the tried-and-tested formula. No single bowler could replace the Kandy Man, but Herath and Randiv's shared 12-wicket haul was cause for celebration nonetheless.

Though the attack carried far less threat at the SSC, young Thisara – playing his final Test – turned on the style in Kandy. He found swing to dislodge four of the top five, before a lusty 75 helped his team to a solid first-innings lead. Sri Lanka couldn't finish the job, but happily exited the series 1-0 winners. It had been a long, tough road since Murali retired – but finally, they were rolling once more.

That said, hosting India for five ODIs and a one-off t20 did nothing to lift spirits. Very little went right. 300 was becoming the new normal, and the hosts were a step behind in the high-scoring games. The introduction of two new balls handicapped Malinga's search for reverse, while Sangakkara's broken finger was a real worry with the World t20 just over a month away.

Financial troubles had kept Sri Lanka's cricketers on the wheel since the last World Cup; though a break in the international calendar finally appeared, the inaugural Sri Lanka Premier League meant there was no rest for the island's cricketers. At least it gave players a chance to get into the rhythm of t20 cricket, and the selectors an opportunity to evaluate the island's stocks. 18-year-old Akila Dananjaya – still short of his first-class and List A debuts – was given a chance in the tournament after impressing as a net bowler. Baffling batsmen with Mendis-like variations, he was rewarded with a place in Sri Lanka's final fifteen.

Yet, it was probably an oversight not to include Hambantota in the SLPL schedule – since Sri Lanka would be stationed there for the group stage of the World t20. Home advantage saw plenty backing Jayawardene's men for the tournament: though undone by South Africa in a 7-over slog, they eased past Zimbabwe thanks to Mendis' eye-watering 6 for 8, to progress to a second group phase in Kandy.

Seemingly cruising towards New Zealand's 175-run target, Sri Lanka fell apart in the last 2 overs and found themselves facing a super over. Though Malinga had endured a quiet tournament so far, there was no one you would rather have bowl it. Defending 13, he produced four nerveless yorkers to leave New Zealand needing 8 from 2. But when he missed his length off the fifth, Martin Guptill launched the ball towards the long-off boundary. It swirled high in the evening sky; underneath it, Dilshan stood inches from the rope, on the edge of a proverbial cliff. Eyes fixed on the ball, he watched it right into his outstretched hands. Had he dropped it, it would have been 6 and the match; but Sri Lanka held their nerve.

It seemed a turning point for Jayawardene's men, who produced their best performance yet a couple of nights later against the West Indies. Backed by excellent captaincy and a slick performance in the field, the bowlers strangled Sammy's men, who could only manage 129. With Jayawardene and Sangakkara in the groove, Sri Lanka crossed the line with 9 wickets and 28 balls in hand.

There was confusion as Sanga walked out to toss in Mahela's place against England* – and some felt trouble was afoot when the dynamic duo went to consecutive Swann deliveries. But the less-heralded lower

---

* With Jayawardene facing a ban if Sri Lanka failed to adhere to the ICC's stringent over rates, the team cleverly switched captains.

middle order delivered, lifting Sri Lanka to 169 – and England's chase was cut down the moment Malinga entered the attack. Sri Lanka were heading to Khettarama for a semi-final clash with Pakistan, their conquerors three years earlier.

Having seen the crumbling wicket, Mahela had no hesitation in batting: his innings was a reminder that there were few better players of spin anywhere in the world. A score of 42 off 36 sounds unextraordinary in the context of t20 cricket, but the laps, reverses and sweeps were a delight to behold. With the ball bouncing unevenly and turning around corners, these runs were worth so much to Sri Lanka.

They dragged themselves up to 139 – better than it sounded, but by no means impregnable if Pakistan could adjust to the dusty wicket. The bowlers kept their heads, supported by chattering intensity in the field. Mathews engineered a double-strike in the 10th, but Hearth was the biggest difference-maker. A delightful off-break castled Shoaib Malik; 4 overs later, he did for Mohammad Hafeez and Afridi with consecutive balls to reduce Pakistan to 91-6. Sri Lanka would have a chance to seal the World t20 in front of a roaring Khettarama crowd.

Though seventeen months had passed since the World Cup final at the Wankhede, the scars of shattered hope were slow to heal. Now, expectation started to simmer again. Surely, Sri Lanka would not let their fans down. Last year, they had cruised to the final without really being challenged; through this tournament they had been tried and tested at every turn. And where India were favourites in 2011, this West Indies side was a less menacing proposition. Many felt if Sri Lanka could get rid of Chris Gayle early, the whole house could crumble.

It wasn't long before the Khettarama party got started.[101] Johnson Charles miscued to mid-off early; when Mendis tricked Gayle with a straight one, the Windies were 14-2 after 6 overs. They simply could not get going: at 38-2 after 11, they were meandering towards an undefendable score. But Marlon Samuels hung around and tore into an off-colour Malinga in the 13th, blasting three missed yorkers into the stands. Though wickets kept falling at the other end, Samuels kept going after Sri Lanka's spearhead. He carved a wide half-volley through third man, got enough bat on a bouncer to clear the ropes, and then sent a towering 108-metre hit into the second tier of the stadium. Suddenly, West Indies were 108-5 with 3 overs left. Against all odds, they ended on 139-6.

'That was a disaster,' Jayawardene told me. 'That's where we lost our way I think.' Usually, Malinga's yorkers were as reliable as the steady stream of tuk-tuks outside the ground; but come finals day, he fell a fraction short several times and was punished. Never before had he been struck for more than two 6s in a t20, here he conceded five – while leaking 53 in total.

In hindsight, Jayawardene also felt the brains trust erred by picking Dananjaya over Herath.*'In Kandy, [Herath] was taken down by some of the West Indies batsmen,' he remembers. 'But that wicket wasn't turning, whereas Khettarama was. We played Akila [Dananjaya] – obviously I was part of the decision-making process, and I was quite confident that Akila was a guy we should play because he had the variation. But with that batting line-up of West Indies all being right-handers apart from Gayle, a left-arm spinner taking the ball away from them on a spinning wicket would have been a game-changer once they were 5 or 6 down. But you can't think like that before the game. In my career, there are a few, but if there was one crucial decision that I didn't tactically plan well, it was not playing Rangana. Akila was bowling leg-spinners as well – and even though he went reasonably well, I think an experienced Rangana Herath in that situation would have been a key factor. But, we'll never know.'

Still, Sri Lanka should have made a better fist of their chase. Given the lack of experience in their middle order, there had been pressure on the top three throughout the tournament. When Dilshan's off stump was uprooted by Ravi Rampaul in the first over, a heavy burden fell on Jayawardene and Sangakkara's shoulders. They accumulated cautiously through the first 9 overs, but in the 10th, Sanga looked for a big shot and was caught at cow corner. At 51-2 off 10, they would need something special to carry them across the line.

---

*	The two had alternated throughout the tournament; although Herath had a superb showing in the semi, his struggles against the West Indies in the Super Eight clearly troubled the team management in the lead-up to the final.

Instead, Sri Lanka crumpled in a heap. Mathews tried to ramp Darren Sammy and was bowled; looking for the reverse slog, Mahela shanked Sunil Narine straight to point. Jeevan Mendis was run out trying to turn a fumble into 2, Thisara undone by a direct hit 4 balls later. In 3.1 crucial overs, they had lost 4 wickets and added 13. The game had gone. The West Indians were world champions: they whooped and hollered, danced to 'Gangnam Style' on the outfield as fireworks boomed. Their party would roll long into the night, but the rest of Sri Lanka had fallen silent.

'We had the West Indies absolutely on the ropes,' Sangakkara said ruefully when we spoke about the match. He mustered a laugh when I asked if the team considered themselves cursed, but admitted it was getting tough to take. 'I thought, "We've had the opportunities to win and we let them go." Because, at the end of the day, we had opportunities, from 2007 to 2009, 2011, 2012, they were all opportunities. We had missed catches, we had missed innings, we had various little opportunities that we could have taken that might have turned the matches in our favour. But we weren't good enough to do that on the day. So when it happened again in 2012, it was very very deflating. They were calling the South Africa team the chokers for losing in semi-finals, but we were the same in finals. It was very difficult.'

'I think that was the final that we felt just got away from us properly,' Jayawardene added. 'We just didn't turn up.' To miss out so narrowly stung incredibly deeply; worse, the players could see the pain etched on the faces of their countrymen. Malinga quietly went home and turned his phone off for days, well aware of the kind of outrage a 53-run outing would generate.[102] But Sri Lanka couldn't lick their wounds long. New Zealand were hanging around for five ODIs and a couple of Tests; straight after, Jayawardene's men would be heading to Australia.

NEW HOPES

There was a natural melancholy in the wake of the World t20, but Sri Lanka's run to the final reinforced the progress the team had made during 2012. Jayawardene's reinstatement as caretaker captain had been an instant success, but the team could ill afford to take their foot off the gas.

With five New Zealand ODIs blighted by rain, the highlight was probably Dilshan's 102* – incredibly, his thirteenth ODI century since the start of 2009.* Though injury kept him out of the first Test at Galle, Sri Lanka won easily thanks to a virtuoso performance by Herath, who stifled the batsmen with nagging accuracy. He mixed off-breaks with arm balls, imparted drift and dip, varied his pace and gave the ball flight – all in all, it was a classical display of spin bowling.

If Murali was the magician and Mendis the mystery, then Herath was Sri Lanka's master craftsman. There was nothing extraordinary about his bowling – and at 34 and 5ft 5in, with a pot belly and a trundler's action, he was one of the more unassuming figures in international cricket. Yet over the past two decades, he had dug into the spinner's toolbox and sharpened his weapons day after day. He might not get the ball to fizz and rip quite like Murali, yet he was nonetheless capable of working the best batsmen over. His success was an important lesson for Sri Lanka's next generation.

Herath's 6 second-innings wickets transformed a nip-tuck match into a 10-wicket thrashing. Remarkably, he had claimed 5-wicket hauls in three of Sri Lanka's four post-Murali wins.

'In terms of Sri Lankan bowlers I've seen, I would rate Rangana just after Murali, purely because of the way he controls an innings,' Jayawardene beamed.[103] Though Sri Lanka's not-so-new spin sensation was on song again at the P. Sara, he lacked support – and New Zealand built an imposing score. It might have been different had Mathews clung onto a tough chance from Ross Taylor; but with Dilshan, Sanga and Mahela falling early, Sri Lanka were facing an uphill struggle. They fell to a troubling 167-run defeat.**

---

*   During that period, Sangakkara and Jayawardene scored nine between them; as much as they were Sri Lanka's leaders, Dilshan's enduring excellence was a crucial factor in the team's sustained success.

**   New Zealand had not won any of their past seven Tests before arriving in Sri Lanka, nor would they strike victory in their next ten.

Clearly, Herath had to find partners to help in his lonely wicket hunt. Across the series, he took 20 while conceding 278 runs; the rest took 17 and leaked 658. Still, the bowlers couldn't shoulder all the blame. No batsman struck a century, a first in home series since 1999. Sangakkara, Jayawardene and Dilshan had been wonderfully consistent in recent years; now, Sri Lanka needed their runs more than ever.

The team must have been full of nerves as they boarded their flight to Australia – well aware of the risk of pinning their hopes on a left-arm spinner. Not since 1995/96 had the islanders been served up as the main course of an Australian summer; most expected a repeat of that 3-0 drubbing. By the end of day two in Hobart, Sri Lanka were clinging on.[104] They fought to take the game into the final session, but Siddle and Starc proved too much for the tail on a cracking pitch. Agonisingly, Mahela's men were 10 overs short of forcing a draw.

There was no respite beyond the boundary. In the lead-up to the second Test, Jayawardene was annoyed when a confidential letter he sent to SLC was leaked to the press.[*105] At the end of his tether, he penned a letter to the *Daily Mirror*, stating he had 'lost all confidence in dealing with SLC in the future'.[106] His disappointment was well founded. Clearly, the board's actions did not constitute supporting the team, who were about to head into the cauldron of the MCG. Of course, SLC would not let Jayawardene have the final word. They released a second statement, claiming he and manager Senanayake had breached their contracts by speaking directly to the press.[107] It did not take a moralist to see where the blame lay.

Though Mahela dismissed claims that the bickering was a distraction, the battle of Hobart seemed to have knocked the spirit out of Sri Lanka. There would be no fight come Boxing Day, just a steady stream of one-way punishment. Battered and bruised in the first innings, things got worse second time around. At 3-3, Sangakkara had his finger broken by Mitchell Johnson; with Prasanna Jayawardene and Welegedara already unable to bat, Sri Lanka's innings came to an end with the score at

---

[*]   He had written to the board to ask that players' fees from the World t20 be shared with the support team, ground staff and curators. The board dogmatically refused, stating they did not want to 'deviate from standard practice'.

103-7. They had lasted 24.2 overs, 2 balls fewer than in the catastrophe at Cardiff. Sri Lanka's second Test at the MCG felt only marginally less traumatic than their visit in 1995 – and that really is saying something.

Despite small improvements at the SCG, Sri Lanka twice failed to reach 300 and were well beaten inside four days. The 3-0 scoreline was distressing, but no worse than the team could expect. Bowling was clearly the biggest problem,* but the senior batters had their share of failures too. The islanders would have to do a lot better if they were to replicate erstwhile Test glories.

After a long, hard month, the white ball must have been a sight for sore eyes – and Sri Lanka reminded the world they could still produce rapturous cricket. Lahiru Thirimanne notched a superb maiden century at Adelaide; at the Gabba, a devastating spell of inswing from Kulasekara reduced the hosts to 30-6. Malinga joined the party to make it 41-9; seeing these two combine so emphatically felt special. During their rural youth – spent bowling tennis-ball grenades on makeshift pitches – the international arena must have felt a million miles away. Even when Ramanayake brought them together at Galle CC, could they have imagined terrorising Australian batsmen at the MCG? Twenty years earlier it might have been impossible – their very existence was proof that Sri Lankan cricket was decentralising.

Although Mahela's men couldn't chase 247 to seal the series, a 2-2 draw could clearly be counted as a success. The Lankans took the t20 series too, with Mathews leading for the first time. He praised Sri Lanka's electricity in the field, and there was fire in the Lankan bellies too. With Australia needing 4 from the final ball at the MCG, Glenn Maxwell's attempts to hurry the bowler drew two choice words from Jayawardene.[108] After a lengthy war council, Thisara trundled in and nailed a wide yorker to win the match.

Still, nothing sticks in the memory more than Dilshan, down on one knee, scooping the broad-shouldered Mitchell Starc into the stands for 6.

---

*   None of the seamers managed a bowling average less than 40 across the series, with only Welegedara slipping under the 50 mark. After the second Test, Ford publicly admitted he would not have minded the help of Lasith Malinga, plying his trade in the Big Bash with Melbourne Stars.

With the ball coming at him at 89.5 mph, it was a death-defying stroke which seemed to belong in the circus rather than the cricket ground. The Tests might have been sobering, but the shorter contests produced enough hedonism to send Sri Lanka home reasonably happy.

As expected, Mahela stepped down at the end of the series – the selectors decided to hand the keys to the car to Mathews (Tests and ODI) and Chandimal (t20).[109] Two young vibrant leaders was cause for cheer, but smiles were wiped away as soon as the squad returned to Sri Lanka. As in 2012, contract renewals brought disputes with the board.[110] With SLC's finances still in dire straits, those in charge decided the best path out of poverty involved penalising the players.*

Whereas previous contract negotiations had been allowed to roll on for months, the team were given less than a week to accept the forty-five-page-long English contracts.[111] When they refused to sign, SLC responded with a 'lock out' of its twenty-three leading players.[112] The whole affair was handled with a shocking lack of professionalism. Board officials spoke endlessly of a desire to make Sri Lanka the number one team in the world, but balked at the idea of treating its players like professional sportsmen. SLC's accounts had been slashed in highly irregular circumstances; now it wanted its breadwinners to foot the bill.

Putting a gun to the players' heads, and forcing them to sign blatantly unfavourable contracts was a stain on the administration. But SLC's media connections, and the modest working wage in Sri Lanka, allowed the board to paint the players as puffed-up prima donnas. On the whole, the public bought the Kool-Aid – much was made of an incident where Malinga told a reporter to mind his own business; the sticks which had been used to beat players whenever they stepped out of line were dusted off and sharpened.[113] Yet, a corrupt and crumbling administration was the real villain here. As Shanaka Amarasinghe vented:

---

* The board was no longer willing to pay the team 25 per cent of ICC tournament fees, nor were they willing to continue funding travel for the players' wives. Though SLC wanted 10 per cent of players' IPL salaries, payments from the board would be frozen while they were playing t20 tournaments. Equally, SLC would no longer recognise player agents, claiming their duty to maximise clients' earnings did not chime with 'the best interests of cricket'.

> The ICC Cricket World Cup 2011 secretariat was a den of thieves. The Hambantota and Pallakele stadium builds lined the pockets of everyone but the players, and are administrative disasters … The reason that players are being paid a high percentage of revenue is because the other revenue generating assets like tournaments, sponsorship rights and television deals are disposed of for a pittance via conflicts of interest and corruption.

The board executed the whole affair with timing that would have made Machiavelli proud. Mathews must have been aware that leading a boycott of the Bangladesh series would have made him public enemy number one. As a new captain, it was too grave a risk to take. Equally, SLC surely knew that Mahela was out of the country nursing a broken finger. I struggle to believe he would have accepted these contracts. But when new chairman of selectors Sanath Jayasuriya arranged a private meeting with the team, they caved and put pen to paper.*[114]

At least the resolution meant the public would not suffer. With Mahela injured and the selectors looking to blood young batsmen, Sri Lanka were served a featherbed pitch for the first Test against Bangladesh at Galle.[115] It helped a misfiring unit get some runs under their belt, but the biggest takeaway was the inefficacy of Sri Lanka's own attack. Where once fans had flocked to Galle to see Murali carve batsmen to ribbons, Sri Lanka's current bowlers were as blunt as a rusty spoon.

Playing his first Test in almost two years, Ajantha Mendis was all over the place – devoid of mystery, his bowling seemed little more than a flurry of half-volleys and full tosses. Shaminda Eranga struggled to maintain pace and control, while Kulasekara's lack of speed limited his effect once the ball lost its shine. Herath threatened the most, but could only return figures of 2 for 161. Despite missing Shakib al-Hasan and Tamim Iqbal, Bangladesh racked up 638. Never before had they scored so many in a Test, nor held on for a draw with Sri Lanka. The signs were undeniably ominous.

---

*   Remarkably, SLC rejected the players' suggestion that their ICC fee could be funnelled straight into cricket development.

The opening day at Khettarama brought happier narratives: a pitch offering help for spinners; a Herath five-for and a Bangladeshi innings that fell short of 90 overs. That said, at 69-4 Sri Lanka looked to be readying themselves for a dogfight – though they were rescued by a third consecutive century from Sangakkara and a second from Chandimal.

Faced with a 106-run deficit, and the wily old Herath on an increasingly powdery track, Bangladesh could not dig themselves out of trouble. Sri Lanka's left-arm star celebrated his 35th birthday with his first 7-wicket haul – in the process becoming the third Sri Lankan to 200 Test wickets. Still, the series was a wake-up call. Sri Lanka needed Herath just to sneak past lowly Bangladesh. But like Murali before him, he could not last forever. Life after Murali had been tricky enough, what on earth would life after Rangana look like?

Though there were positives to take from the ODIs, Bangladesh's victory stole away headlines, feeding into the sense of a fading Lankan machine. Meanwhile, Jayasuriya's decision to pick Ramith Rambukwella – the unheralded son of the Media Minister – in his first t20 squad spoke of increasingly brazen political intrusions into cricket.[116] The nexus of nepotism was almost comical: the Sports Minister picks his mate, the Postal Minister, to pick the side; he in turn, picks the Media Minister's son to play in it. Jayasuriya lamely tried to defend the decision, but the fact he felt he could reason away such an injurious move with a one-line denial was worrying in itself. Surely, the system that can no longer be bothered to hide its abuses of power is well past breaking point.

Things were not looking good – but Sri Lanka's fortunes have always been impossible to predict, and the team sprang a surprise during the Champions Trophy in June.[117] Sanga's unruffled run-a-ball 134* saw them power down England's 293, and they held off Australia to march to the semis. Sadly, a win over India proved a bridge too far. Some in the Sri Lankan side shuddered simply arriving at Cardiff's SWALEC ground; presented with a devilish pitch, they could only stumble to 181.

It was a similar story during the West Indies Tri-series that filled the first days of July. Though Sri Lanka struck a win over India in the group stages – with Tharanga hammering a breakneck 174* – they were undone, by the narrowest of margins, in the final. Herath's 4 wickets had sent India slumping to 167-8, but he couldn't dislodge Dhoni, who scratched around, bluntly refused singles and let the required run rate rocket to the point even his teammates lost faith.[118] Then, with 15 needed from 5, he blasted Eranga for 6-4-6, finishing the match with three cruel blows that crushed Lankan souls.

With South Africa landing in mid-July for five ODIs and three t20s, the glut of white-ball slogs continued. Sangakkara got the series off to a flying start with a career-best 169: at one stage 66 off 91, he blasted 103 off his next 46 balls to leave South Africa utterly disconsolate. Behind the stumps, the exasperation etched across A.B. de Villiers' face spoke volumes: once Sanga got going, everything seemed to be in his zone. At 35, he was playing the best one-day cricket of his life.

With the series still up for grabs after three games, he and Dilshan emphatically turned it in Sri Lanka's favour. Having swallowed plenty of criticism for being bowled swinging across the line, Dilshan ground out 115* in the fourth, adding 184 with Sanga as Sri Lanka cruised to victory. His 99 in the fifth ODI was equally uncharacteristic: short of frills, and overshadowed by Sangakkara's blistering 45-ball 75*. Despite resting Jayawardene, Malinga and Herath, Sri Lanka won by 128, to end the series with a commanding 4-1 advantage. It was spiriting to see Ajantha Mendis enjoy his best series in some time, but even as Sri Lanka celebrated – wasn't there something foreboding about leaning so heavily on two men fast approaching middle age? Dilshan and Sanga made 645 runs in the series; the rest could only manage 514.

The story was much the same during a rain-scuppered New Zealand series – while Sanga and Dilshan cracked 339 runs between them, the rest combined for 260. The spectre of their retirements loomed large, with few answers over how Sri Lanka would cope with their absence. Indeed, Malinga has described his age-group as a 'lost generation' – and it's striking how few cricketers born in the early or mid 1980s established themselves in national colours.[*119]

While the players have to take responsibility for not bedding themselves into the national side, the dearth also exposes a damaging lack of long-term thinking. Strikingly, Vandort, Tharanga, Warnapura and Paranavitana all notched at least two Test centuries, yet couldn't establish themselves as long-standing regulars. As Malinga put it, 'If we keep criticising everyone one by one, we will keep getting these new teams. We have to protect the players we have. The current thinking is always: "The player who is in the team is bad, but the one outside deserves a place." As a player who has played fourteen years international cricket, I think the people who are in the team are there because they are better than those outside.'

As it was, Sri Lanka's dads and lads headed off to the UAE in mid-December, for a six-week tour that saw its share of successes and failures. Kusal Perera's savage 89 helped them square the t20 series – and hang onto their number one ICC ranking – but Mathews' men could not build on their momentum during the one-dayers. Though they produced thrilling, against-the-odds chases to win the second and fifth ODIs, they were consigned to defeat by Hafeez centuries in the other three matches.

With Dilshan quitting the longest form so Sri Lanka could groom a young opener, they entered the Tests with a particularly callow line-up. But, having fallen well behind in the first Test, Mathews and Chandimal produced a backs-to-the-wall fourth-day partnership that felt like a passing of the baton to save the game for Sri Lanka.

The impact of the great escape was plain for all to see during the second Test. A green pitch compelled Mathews to bowl first, and Lakmal, Eranga and Pradeep responded with the sort of controlled performance

---

* It is especially strange when you consider that those born in this fallow period would have been teenagers in 1996, when Sri Lanka suddenly started to flourish on the international stage and an inflow of cash boosted the board's coffers. Malinga name-checked Chamara Silva, Thilina Kandamby, Jehan Mubarak, Malinga Bandara, Kaushal Lokuarachchi, Kaushalya Weeraratne, Tharanga Paranavitana and Malinda Warnapura – but I would also add Upul Tharanga, Michael Vandort, Chamara Kapugedara and Farveez Maharoof to the list.

most thought was beyond them. Time and again, the trio landed the ball in the right areas; staying patient, they reduced Pakistan from 78-1 to 129-7. Herath was on hand to finish the job; rarely in recent times had wickets been so evenly shared. Equally, it was a pleasant surprise to see the bowlers maintain such economy.

The positives kept coming. Kaushal Silva and Jayawardene batted with heart and soul on the second day; though the young opener fell 5 short of a maiden century, Mahela overcame considerable pain to make a long-awaited thirty-second. He carried his team to a 223-run lead; with Pradeep and Herath scoring early breakthroughs, the Test was in Sri Lanka's hands. Rain and resistance slowed their charge, but they completed a 9-wicket victory on the fifth afternoon. It was their first away from home since 2011; perhaps more significantly, the first in a long time to not have a spinner's fingerprints all over it.

It set the table for a rare away series win. Outside of Bangladesh and Zimbabwe, Sri Lanka had not won a series away since 2000: perhaps the spectre of that elusive achievement scuppered them. After three and a half days, a Pakistani victory seemed unthinkable. But in adding 214 in 101.4 overs on a true batting wicket, Mathews' men flat-batted them back into the game. It was dreary cricket which served no one; when the dawdling mercifully ended at lunch on day five, Sri Lanka were 302 ahead. Inexplicably, Mathews reckoned that his batsmen could have been 'a bit more cautious'.[120]

There was no benefit in Pakistan blocking out the last two sessions. Misbah-ul-Haq knew he had to attack Sri Lanka's bowlers; Mathews still might have won the match had he responded in kind. Instead, he was cowed by Pakistan's early intent – quickly resorting to the most negative tactics. Upon hearing Pakistan chased 302 inside 58 overs, you might imagine a whirr of blazing strokes: all switch-hits and ramps and dancing scythes down the ground.[121] Instead, they were allowed to tick their way to the target in singles.* Of the last 124 Pakistan scored, only

---

*   Mathews allowed 160 of them, against 146 dot balls. Never in recorded history had a Test side leaked so many singles in the first 80 overs. Azhar Ali eased to a 137-ball 103 despite managing six hits to the fence; Misbah managed a near run-a-ball 68* with just four boundaries.

24 came in boundaries. Though they needed 53 off the last 60, Sri Lanka persisted with seven, eight or nine men back on the fence.

This was a profound failure, made all the more hurtful since it seemed to stem squarely from a lack of ambition. Curiosity might have killed the cat, but Mathews ended up looking like the cautious kitten who starved to death. It was especially disappointing since the result turned the tour on its head, undoing much of the progress that the captain and his young charges had made in the past month. Up until the fourth evening, it had been a breakout tour for Mathews, yet he returned home with the vultures circling – derided as negative, nervous and naive. There were echoes of Sri Lanka's first awkward steps in Test cricket, when the team habitually squandered glorious opportunities.

Though Graham Ford had clearly stated his intention to leave when his contract expired in January 2014, Sri Lanka's search for a replacement yielded little fruit. By now, high-profile candidates were wary of the baggage that came with the post; ultimately Jayasuriya had to encourage Paul Farbrace – who had been coaching Yorkshire's 2nd XI – to take the role.[122]

Meanwhile, the team headed to Bangladesh for another potential banana-skin series. Auspiciously, the victory in Dhaka was a real team effort; though Sri Lanka could not achieve the same in Chittagong, Sangakkara showcased his class and concentration with a marathon performance. Most would have had their fill of batting after a ten-hour, first-innings 319, but Sanga looked fresh as a daisy come the second innings, cracking 105 off 144.

Clearly the team had a long way to go, but five Tests in quick succession had given cause for cautious optimism. Despite reaching an age where most batsmen are in steady decline, Jayawardene, and especially Sangakkara, remained at the peak of their powers. With Karunaratne, Silva, Vithanage, Chandimal and Mathews all showing promise, the batting looked in solid shape moving forward. Even more auspiciously, Eranga, Lakmal and Dilruwan Perera had enjoyed unexpected success, showing that the team did not have to place all its eggs in Herath's basket. Sri Lanka were starting to build again. Few could have predicted the emphatic success which lay just around the corner.

CHAMPIONS ONCE MORE

With Sri Lanka progressing through two t20s and three ODIs unbeaten, the team looked in good shape ahead of the Asia Cup and World t20 – and had gotten plenty of exposure to Bangladeshi conditions. Their Asia Cup run was bookended by strangely symmetrical performances against Pakistan.[123] Thirimanne notched centuries in both: in the tournament opener, 5 quick Malinga wickets cut Pakistan down in the last 10 overs; come finals day, he tore into Misbah's men with the new ball. Plenty of others stood up too: with Sanga, Mahela, Mathews and Kusal Perera all impressing with the bat, and a revitalised Mendis snapping at batsmen's heels, the team entered the World t20 full of confidence.

But, this was Sri Lanka – so, of course, it would not be smooth sailing. The days leading up to the tournament were blighted by the now seemingly annual contract disputes.[124] It felt like 2002 all over again: SLC were due to receive $8.9 million for the World t20, but balked at the idea of giving the players a 20 per cent share for use of their image rights. Though the team dropped to 12 per cent – the same proportion agreed upon in 2002 – the board felt this was still too steep a price to pay.

It was hard to escape the sense that SLC's approach had grown increasingly autocratic. Sixteen hours before the squad were set to leave for Dhaka, the board tried to pressure players into signing the contracts by threatening to send a second-string side. 'Even the night before we left for Dhaka, we were told that unless we signed we wouldn't go,' Sangakkara told me. 'But we actually told the board, "We're playing this World Cup for free. We don't want money for this World Cup – we don't even want our match fees." This is a World Cup, we're duty bound to play for our country. Yes, we have a written contract with the board, but we have an unwritten contract with the fans to play for the country – so we said, "We'll play for free."'

Still, that was not the end of the drama. Upon landing in Bangladesh, Sangakkara and Jayawardene had to attend an ICC press briefing. 'Someone popped the question, whether this will be your last t20 World Cup,' Mahela recalled. 'Sanga and I were 36, the next t20 World Cup was 2016. So pretty much everyone knew. It wasn't breaking news, it was a natural question. Kumar and I had decided it would be the last World Cup, but we didn't make an announcement. So we said "Yeah, it's most likely to be our last World Cup".'

But, when the ICC uploaded a picture of the duo to twitter, with the caption 'last world T20, let's make it count', SLC were furious. Jayasuriya was quoted in the *Daily Mirror* describing their actions as 'highly unethical'.[125] 'They should have the common decency to inform the selectors who could then prepare Sri Lanka for the next phase,' he vented. 'This shows they are ungrateful for what they got through playing for the country.'

It seemed like Jayasuriya and SLC were creating something out of nothing, with little thought of the team's preparations. Sanga and Mahela were put on a media ban for the rest of the tournament. 'We weren't allowed to speak,' Mahela laughingly told me. 'I don't think even when we won Man of the Match awards.' That looked a petty decision, and an unhelpful one too: for the past decade, the duo had handled the lion's share of Sri Lanka's media duties, leaving younger players free to focus on their game. The board decided it would be better for everyone if that situation was flipped on its head.

The tournament itself was stocked full of drama too. Having posted 165 in their opener, the attack showed control and courage to keep South Africa 5 short. Though all the Proteas' top four made at least 23, Sri Lanka took wickets at regular intervals to stay in the game. Still, with 2 overs left, South Africa were in the driver's seat – but Kulasekara produced a gem of a penultimate over, to leave Malinga defending 15 off the last. Some smart-Alecs at home might have branded it the battle of the chokers; South Africa handed Sri Lanka the match with a pair of disastrous run-outs.

After making light work of the Netherlands, Chandimal's men were in the box seat against England at the halfway stage too. Kulasekara struck twice in the first over to leave them floundering. But with dew forming across the Chittagong ground, Alex Hales produced a withering assault, condemning Sri Lanka to an effective quarter-final against New Zealand.

It was all change for that final group match. Chandimal was forced to sit out as penance for slow over rates; with dew around and little turn on offer, Mendis was replaced by the dependable Herath. The team management might have been regretting that switch after their own stuttering innings: with 119 on the board, Sri Lanka's only hope of survival was a flurry of wickets. This was an occasion for a magician, not a miser.

But Herath hadn't read the script. Brought on in the 3rd over, he promptly engineered a run out of Martin Guptill.[126] Next up came a glorious, five-ball interrogation of McCullum's technique: there were a couple of nervous defences, an arm ball went that went thudding into the pads; after four dots, Herath gave the batsman enough rope to hang himself. When he tossed the ball up, McCullum envisioned it sailing into the stands. But he failed to account for the dip and rip – wading down the track, he was beaten all ends up, bails broken in a flash by Sangakkara.

Next over, Ross Taylor got the same five-ball examination: flummoxed by the hodgepodge of off breaks and sliders, he played for turn that wasn't there and was trapped lbw. Herath stayed around the wicket to the left-handed Jimmy Neesham; next up, a flighted delivery broke back from middle – cannoning into the stumps. A run of thirteen Herath dots was snapped when Kane Williamson squirted a single into the leg side, but normal business resumed soon enough. His first to Luke Ronchi drifted a country mile: swerving from well outside off, it landed on middle and leg, ragged and crashed into the back pad. 29-5.

Brought back in the 15th, Herath saw Trent Boult coming down the track, fired in fast and short and wide, and took the outside edge. New Zealand had crumbled to 60 all out; Herath's figures were almost unfathomable. 3.3 overs, 2 maidens, 3 runs, 5 wickets. With the team readying themselves for the next flight home, he produced an astonishing spell of pressure bowling. It was particularly special because it seemed to fly in the face of t20 conventions. Herath was a throwback. He still worked in a bank, as if the professional era had unknowingly passed him by. On a warm March evening, he produced a Test-match spell for the t20 age, sending his team surging into the semi-finals. Though the match itself was no thriller for the ages, like all semi-finals, it was fraught with tension. Scores from Dilshan, Kusal Perera, Thirimanne and Mathews carried Sri Lanka to 160. In reply, West Indies were slow to get going: when Malinga got Gayle to chop on in the 5th over, you could almost hear the collective sigh of relief. By the time Sammy's men slipped to 34-3 in the 8th, you sensed Sri Lanka had one foot in the final.

Yet, as long as Marlon Samuels remained in the middle, nerves would not abate. In fact, his spectre held even after the teams left the ground for rain in the 14th over. Sri Lanka faced a nervy hour-long wait before the match was called off – but news eventually came through. With India seeing off South Africa in the other semi, the stage was set for a repeat of Mumbai 2011.

The prospect of Dhoni was as daunting as the spectre of Samuels – but after four failed finals, there was a sense of destiny in Dhaka. 'I told Sanga, "If we lose this, I don't care about the next World Cup, I'm just going to retire. I've had enough,"' Mahela remembers laughing. 'But, I think we were quietly confident: we had the resources, we had the talent and we played some really good cricket.' Malinga won the toss too, and Sri Lanka's fifth final got off to a dream start, with Mathews sneaking through Rahane's defences in the second over. That brought Kohli to the crease; after a slow start, he pulled Herath's first ball straight to Malinga. But it was struck hard, and would not stick in his hands: 'That brought back memories of 2011 and 2012, when we missed catches,' Sangakkara told me. Five balls later, Kohli wandered down the wicket and eased Herath over his head for 6. You sensed it would be a costly miss.

Indeed, though Sri Lanka applied the stranglehold, Kohli stuck around – and slowly started to accelerate. He reached his half-century off 43 balls, with 4 overs left he had moved to 70 off 50. At 111-2, India should have had 155 in their sights. But Sri Lanka were at their frugal best in the last 4 overs.[127] Senanayake kept the 17th to four singles; Malinga produced six perfect yorkers to keep the 18th to the same. Kulasekara mercifully ended Yuvraj's tortuous stay with the first ball of the 19th – though India managed 7 off the last, they had limped to 130, scoring 19 off their last 24. Yuvraj's pained 11 off 21 has borne the brunt of the criticism for India's shortfall, but in the final 4 overs, two batsmen as talented as Kohli and Dhoni could only manage a combined 11 off 15. Sri Lanka had summoned a masterclass of death bowling.

Remarkably, the innings unfolded just as Malinga planned it. According to Andrew Fidel Fernando, he tore up received white-ball wisdom, telling his bowlers not to worry about taking wickets. They simply had to squeeze the Indian batsmen; come the death overs, he and Kulasekara would fire in a volley of wide yorkers to a packed off-side field. Five years of IPL cricket fed into his algorithm; he knew the Indians would only reluctantly commit to the ramp or the paddle. His plan worked a charm; once the bowlers had executed, the trophy was in touching distance.

Of course, it would not be nerveless. Perera mistimed a swipe in the 2nd over; after a flurry of leg-side boundaries, Dilshan went for a big one and found Kohli's outstretched arms inches from the rope. But Sanga settled nerves with a pair of powerful slog sweeps; Mahela opened the face of his bat and played the most exquisite nudge down to third man. No one else in cricket could score quick runs with such delicacy; it seemed the gods were punishing him when he tried to smash the leather off Raina's next ball. Ravi Ashwin took an excellent diving catch; the game was in the balance once more.

Indeed, the usually dependable Sangakkara had endured a lean run of scores, and his new partner Thirimanne looked to have the weight of the world on his shoulders. A thick outside edge took his first ball to the boundary, but he could only manage 3 off the next 9. His 11th was nicked through to the keeper. After 13 overs, Sri Lanka were 78-4, still needing 53 from 42.

Sangakkara and Thisara handled the situation craftily, happily nudging singles off Raina's 14th, before deciding to get after Amit Mishra. Thisara got to the pitch of a loopy leg break and sent it sailing over long off, two balls later, Sanga paddled past the man at forty-five to the fine leg fence. They went one better off Mishra's next: Sangakkara struck a flashing lofted cover drive, Thisara the woodcutter sent Mishra over long on again. Now requiring 12 off 18, Sri Lanka knew the game was theirs. Sanga marched to 50 with a fine paddle-sweep, before Thisara finished the tournament with a vicious strike down the ground. He punched the air in furious celebration. This unlikely pairing – young and old; steel and silk – had carried Sri Lanka to a historic victory.

The rest charged in from the boundary rope, smiles wide. But Sangakkara broke out of a burial of hugs wearing a different look: part relief, part pride, part vindication. 'It was just an unbelievable feeling,'

Jayawardene remembers. 'The whole weight of not being able to cross that line had just come off our back. We were overwhelmingly happy, I can't even remember some of the stuff we did after the final in the dressing room. Guys were screaming, shouting. It was mayhem.'

There was a special sense of absolution in Dhaka that night. In 2007 and 2011 and again in 2012, they had been outdone by career-defining innings from genius batsmen, shrugged shoulders, and said 'There's little you can do when Gilchrist or Dhoni or Samuels are in the mood.' Yet, this time around, they had absorbed King Kohli's best shots, and come back firing with brilliant punches of their own. On the night, they were clever and courageous, creative and cold-blooded. An eighteen-year-long battle had at last been won.

Mahela fought back tears as he was hoisted onto his teammates' shoulders; Sangakkara spoke with the quiet passion of a statesman. 'It's wonderful that the side really meant it when they said they would like to win the tournament for myself and Mahela. But at the same time, we've got 20 million other people we've got to win it for as well. It's not about me or Mahela or any single person, it's about everyone who stands with you, or behind you. I'm thankful for all the Sri Lankan fans, because without them, to have won this tournament, it would have been impossible.'[128]

When the team returned home two days later, tens of thousands lined the streets from Katunayake to Galle Face. They danced and cried and cheered their heroes' achievements – more than that, they cheered for Sri Lanka. As much as man, woman and child had been inspired by what they watched, they also saw themselves in their cricketers. Dilshan's energy; Malinga's courage; Mahela's passion; Sanga's steel – all of them spoke of the Sri Lankan spirit.

Cricket could never cure all the ills the island has suffered, but on days like this it could bind people together; joyfully wash away worries, even just for a moment. There was pride and hope and love in the air that evening. An island danced. Eighteen years after Lahore, Sri Lanka were champions of the world once more.

EPILOGUE

2014 was no springboard. In the years since, Sri Lankan cricket has slumped to new depths. Sometimes I imagine an elephant – strong and proud and seemingly impervious – weighed down by a nation's baggage. As cases are slung onto its back, the noble beast trudges slower and slower. Yet still the cargo piles up, until one day the elephant collapses. There it lies deep in the jungle, unable to drag itself up, its very presence a sobering reminder of distant glories, long in the past.

Since triumph in Dhaka, Sri Lanka has won twenty-seven of ninety t20 internationals. Once the world's most consistent team in the shortest format, they have faced the indignity of having to qualify for the main draw of the last two World t20 tournaments. Nor is the shortest form an aberration. For so long king in their own conditions, Sri Lanka own a losing record at home in all forms over the past eight years. In 2017, the team dropped a home ODI series to lowly Zimbabwe. Once the prospect of being leapfrogged by Bangladesh only made the most neurotic Sri Lankan nervous; now there's a real threat of Afghanistan leaving the islanders in their rear-view mirror too. Having worked so hard to shake off minnow status, Sri Lanka once again finds itself regarded as a second-class cricket nation.

Perhaps this was always going to happen. Sanga and Mahela went. Dilshan and Herath too. When you lose such talents – off the back of saying goodbye to Atapattu, Jayasuriya, Murali, Vaas – there are bound to be tough times ahead. For two decades, the island team was propped up by extraordinary cricketers. Whenever one departed, a tailor-made replacement was ready to step into his spikes. By the time Aravinda raced off into the sun, Mahela was installed as the latest in a long line of Sri Lankan artists. The crippling loss of Jayasuriya was largely offset by Dilshan's extraordinary autumn bloom. Even the irreplaceable Murali's departure was felt less deeply thanks to the re-emergence of wily old Rangana Herath.

The fall could have come sooner. After all, Sri Lanka's greats showed an unnatural ability to endure. No one has scored as many international runs in their 30s as Sangakkara; in ODIs, he's outdone only by Dilshan and Jayasuriya. Murali and Herath have more Test wickets in their fourth decade than anyone else; Murali tops the tree in ODIs too. The distant scent of trouble might have twitched sharp nostrils from the turn of the century, but it was easy to ignore when Murali was bouncing to the crease or Sangakkara was caressing through the covers. Maybe, had their careers followed a more typical trajectory, something might have been done to stop the slide sooner.

No cricketer encapsulates enduring achievement quite like Sangakkara, whose relentless improvement seemed to defy reasonable logic. Without doubt a better player at 35 than 25, he is arguably the most reliable and consistent run-maker since Bradman. Yet was he not also the last in a long line of outstanding batsmen? Tennekoon, Mendis, Dias, de Silva, Jayasuria, Atapattu, Jayawardene, Dilshan, Sangakkara – for close to half a century, Sri Lanka was never without a world-class player at the heart of its line-up.

Has one emerged since? For all Angelo Mathews' lofty achievements – over 6,000 Test runs and an average of a shade under 45 – he retains the feel of a very good rather than great player. Chandimal and Karunaratne too. These three have been the island's most reliable run-makers during the tough transitional period, yet none has ever become a truly daunting presence. With all three now into their 30s, there are real concerns over who can carry the run-making burden – and assume the leadership mantle – after their retirement.

Over the past two decades, so many players have failed to deliver their full potential. Vandort, Mubarak, Tharanga, Kapugedera, Chamara Silva, Warnapura, Thirimanne, Vithanage, Kaushal Silva – and that's just the batsmen. Kusal Mendis seems further from fulfilling his potential than he was five years ago; at this stage, it seems unlikely that Kusal Perera will deliver anything more than flashes of brilliance. Or that Dickwella will ever score a Test century. It is fair to feel fearful about the prospects of the side once these men are its senior-most members.

The players must accept their share of the blame. It is a damning indictment of the current crop that effort and application are so often drawn into question. For all of Sanga, Mahela and Murali's blessings, there was an unshakable sense that they made the most of their talents through relentless hard work. Under their influence, players like Thisara and Thirimanne looked destined for greatness; in the wake of their departures, careers have hit the rocks. The side has lacked clear leadership. Rightly or wrongly, there has sometimes been the sense that the players simply don't care as much as they used to.

Yet Sri Lanka's failings are not truly the players' fault. By now, all would agree the first-class system is broken. A structure founded on clubs rather than territories has hindered cricket's spread beyond Colombo; there's no doubt that twenty-six first-class teams is far too many for a country of 22 million. The standard is poor, the chasm between club and Test cricket so vast that players arriving in international cricket are essentially learning on the job. During 2020, Ramesh Mendis cracked 300* off 270 balls in a first-class match for Moors to very little fanfare. When he came to Test cricket a year later, he looked to be playing a different game.

The standard is far from the only problem. Six of the fourteen clubs who played Tier A cricket during 2020 have no permanent home, meaning the same pitches are used over and over again – so of course they break down.

Meanwhile, most of the grounds used for internationals lie dormant. Spinners run amok while fast bowlers are a fleeting afterthought. Unsurprisingly, their progress tends to be slow and stuttering, while injuries are rife. In 2014, Shaminda Eranga told Andrew Fidel Fernando, 'You really have to push yourself to make something happen, and when you do that, you can get injured. It's easy to wonder if you wouldn't be better off doing something else.' Nor are they the only ones the system is hindering. Batsmen tend to be uneasy against pace, bounce or movement, and often seem to lack the application required for Test cricket. Spinners used to seeing the ball turn sideways can look short of craft on more even wickets. Those that succeed do so in spite of, rather than thanks to, Sri Lanka's domestic system.

But the clubs are the cornerstone of Sri Lankan cricket. Since they are also responsible for electing office-bearers, administrators have rarely shared the public's desire for systemic reform.

The provincial system touted as a potential panacea has been awkwardly embraced, appearing and disappearing without warning. Over the past few years it has taken the form of a whistlestop tournament played out over the course of a couple of weeks. It looks unlikely to ever serve as anything more than a complement to club cricket. The clubs are simply too ingrained and too powerful to replace so far down the line.

So how do you fix a system so clearly unfit for purpose? The best proposal I've heard was from a former administrator, who suggested drastically reducing the number of teams in the top tier.

Cutting the number to six would lift the standard: given cricket's popularity, a reformed structure should generate public interest and open up sponsorship, advertising and broadcast opportunities.

Those advances should allow top-tier cricketers to be better paid, bringing the domestic game closer to professionalism. The other twenty first-class clubs – probably split into two tiers – could serve as feeders to the Tier A teams, providing a better pathway for younger cricketers.

Sadly, club cricket's failures are but one symptom of a faulty administration. Disorganisation, a lack of professionalism, factionalism, political interference, financial opacity – all have hamstrung Sri Lanka time and again over the past two decades. The Sports Law was clearly well intentioned yet it contravenes ICC regulations and has consistently proven a curse since its introduction. Adding to the sense of farce is the fact that the current sports minister is the prime minister's son and the president's nephew. He and his brother owned the Carlton Sports Network, which won broadcasting rights for Sri Lanka matches in 2012 under questionable circumstances. Selectors come with political backing too; all too often there's a sense that they're serving neither the team nor the public.

Indeed, regardless of who has been in charge, perhaps the greatest failure of Sri Lanka's administration is a refusal to properly support its players. Rarely has there been a sense of harmony between team and board; rather, the social hierarchy so salient in Sri Lanakan society has disfigured the relationship. On the whole, the board's approach has been 'We know best' and 'What we say goes'. When players step out of line, SLC has been unafraid to weaponise the media against them. Sangakkara surmised the player–board relationship elegantly when we spoke:

> Whether it was for me or Mahela or a subsequent captain, the administration was always a challenge. It was not because they didn't love cricket, or the team itself. I think they absolutely loved cricket, and they loved the concept of the team – but that kind of love gave them a sense of entitlement, to determine everything that happened in the team. I think that was very, very unhealthy, so it was always a case of senior players who stood together to create a professional barrier between the administration and the team, to ensure the team had the freedom to play their cricket the way it should be played – without any outside interference, without any outside influence. To almost create a bubble, within which people can operate.
>
> To create that bubble, some people have to take a hit – and that would usually be the captain, vice captain and a few of the senior group, who will constantly withstand that pressure and isolate the younger players from it so they can be mentally quite free and relaxed. But it also takes a huge toll on you, because a lot of administrators tend to take things very personally, and it becomes quite acrimonious in terms of their political connections and how they use that to leverage, or negatively impact individual careers or individual players. You always have this balancing act: you have to anticipate, react and plan. You have to strategise, thinking quite a way ahead to ensure that the team remain safe and focused on doing the one thing we knew we could do, which was control our performance. That was why a lot of the captains had very short stints, because the pressure does get to you and you always tend to give up the reins before you are too bitter with the administrators, so that you stop enjoying playing.

Clearly, the way cricket is governed in Sri Lanka needs a serious overhaul. Just look at women's cricket: the administration has had little success in increasing engagement and has failed to build a consistently competitive side despite possessing a world-class batter in Chamari Atapattu. The only time women's cricket has made major headlines was in 2015, when it emerged that members of the national side were forced to perform sexual favours or face being dropped. Sadly, women's cricket in Sri Lanka reflects a wider gender inequality – a situation where women suffer from a shocking lack of autonomy.

Arguably, corruption is the biggest problem of all. For years now there has been the sense that a paper-thin facade could crack at any moment, revealing an underbelly more rotten than anyone had imagined. Most believe matches have been fixed, that money has improperly changed hands, that backhanders had become so common they're now delivered unashamedly from the front. Perhaps the truth will emerge in the coming years.

Perhaps that is what Sri Lanka needs more than anything.

Whatever happens, the island cannot rely on cricketers emerging from a puff of smoke and rescuing its national team. Without a more professional, transparent, forward-thinking administration, it is tough to envisage the island scrabbling out of the hole it has dug.

Still, sometimes I picture an elephant dragging itself from the jungle floor. Rising – proud, triumphant.

There will always be good days. There's too much talent for them to dry up completely. I once saw a 10-year-old bowling leg spin to right-handers and off spin to southpaws, with everything more or less pitching on the money. There aren't many kids in England or Australia who can do that. And the past five years – a period that no self-respecting Sri Lankan fan would celebrate – have seen the 3-0 demolition of Australia at home, the clean sweep in South Africa, triumph over champions England at the 2019 World Cup ... There will always be good days.

How many is hard to say. If the recent past is anything to go by, they will be few and far between. Perhaps they will be all the more thrilling thanks to their rarity: their sudden appearance a ray of sunshine bursting through a slate-grey sky. But there are glimmers of real hope. Jaffna-born Vijayakanth Viyaskanth's performances in the Lanka Premier League should inspire other northern cricketers, and at the delayed t20 World Cup, Sri Lanka seemed to fizz and crackle with an energy that had been missing for some time. There is an exciting young core to build around, and, for the first time in years, a proper Sri Lankan presence at the IPL. If the youngsters live up to their potential, they can go some way towards reversing Sri Lanka's recent slump.

Here's hoping they can manage it. Cricket is a fuller, more fun, more enchanting game when Sri Lanka are firing – and the island is a happier place too. After all, if there's one thing I've learnt through all this, it's that Sri Lanka needs cricket and cricket needs Sri Lanka.

I hope it always will.

NOTES

Prologue

1 www.youtube.com/watch?v=pCNHYBAiyiQ
2 Roberts, M., *Incursions & Excursions in and Around Sri Lankan Cricket*, p.113
3 See www.youtube.com/watch?v=pCNHYBAiyiQ
4 Roberts, *Incursions & Excursions*, p.113
5 Roberts, M., *Crosscurrents: Sri Lanka and Australia at Cricket*, pp.112–3
6 news.bbc.co.uk/onthisday/hi/dates/stories/january/31/
   newsid_4083000/4083095.stm
7 Roberts, *Crosscurrents*, p.134
8 Marqusee, M., *War Minus the Shooting*, p.38
9 Fernando, A.F., 'The Lion's Fairy Tale', www.thecricketmonthly.com/
   story/834255/the-lion-s-fairy-tale

1 Beginnings (1796–1956)

1 Perera, S.S., *The Janashakthi Book of Sri Lanka Cricket*, p.382
2 *Ibid.*, p.18
3 Wickramasinghe, N., *Sri Lanka in the Modern Age: A History*
4 De Silva, K.M., *A History of Sri Lanka*, p.303
5 Perera, *Janashakthi*, p.19
6 Wickramasinghe, *Sri Lanka in the Modern Age*, p.36
7 Perera, *Janashakthi*, p.21
8 Foenander, S.P., *Sixty Years of Ceylon Cricket*, p.2
9 Perera, *Janashakthi*, p.22

10 Wickramasinghe, *Sri Lanka in the Modern Age*, p.38
11 Perera, *Janashakthi*, p.34
12 *Ibid.*
13 www.sundaytimes.lk/170730/plus/tea-trails-to-the-past-252248.html
14 Perera, *Janashakthi*, p.26
15 *Ibid.*, p.29
16 Foenander, *Sixty Years of Ceylon Cricket*, p.25
17 Perera, *Janashakthi*, p.30
18 *Ibid.*, p.35
19 *Ibid.*, p.141
20 www.cricbuzz.com/cricket-series/2697/icc-cricket-world-cup-2019/teams/5/sri-lanka/squads
21 Roberts, *Incursions & Excursions*, pp.22–3
22 *Ibid.*, p.22
23 Perera, *Janashakthi*, pp.4–5
24 *Ibid.*, p.5
25 Royal College Union and S. Thomas' College Old Boys Association, *A History of 125 years of the Royal-S. Thomas' Cricket Match*, p.17
26 *Ibid.*, pp.296–8
27 Perera, *Janashakthi*, p.42
28 Wickramasinghe, *Sri Lanka in the Modern Age*, p.74
29 Roberts, M., 'Sri Lanka: The Power of Cricket and the Power in Cricket', *Cricket and National Identity in the Postcolonial Age: Following On*, ed. S. Wagg, p.138
30 *Young Ceylon*, ed. G.F. Nell, 1850–53
31 Perera, *Janashakthi*, pp.42–4
32 Wickramasinghe, *Sri Lanka in the Modern Age*, p.75
33 Perera, *Janashakthi*, p.46
34 Foenander, *Sixty Years of Ceylon Cricket*, pp.158–9
35 *Journal of the Dutch Burger Union*, Vol. 40, No. 3, 1950, pp.110–1
36 Perera, *Janashakthi*, p.46
37 *Ibid.*, pp.65–7
38 *Ibid.*, pp.69–70
39 Miller, K., *Gods or Flannelled Fools*, pp.146–7
40 Gunasekara, C., *Through the Covers*, p.200
41 Perera, *Janashakthi*, p.7
42 Foenander, *Sixty Years of Ceylon Cricket*, pp.3–4
43 *Ibid.*, p.173
44 Perera, *Janashakthi*, p.62
45 Foenander, *Sixty Years of Ceylon Cricket*, p.173
46 *Ibid.*, p.52
47 Perera, *Janashakthi*, pp.81–2
48 Foenander, *Sixty Years of Ceylon Cricket*, pp.186–7

49 Perera, *Janashakthi*, pp.68–9
50 *Ibid.*, pp.88–9
51 Wickramasinghe, *Sri Lanka in the Modern Age*, p.44
52 Foenander, *Sixty Years of Ceylon Cricket*, p.60
53 McGowan, W., *Only Man is Vile: The Tragedy of Sri Lanka*, p.138
54 Foenander, *Sixty Years of Ceylon Cricket*, p.145
55 Perera, *Janashakthi*, p.77
56 *Ibid.*, p.78
57 *Ibid.*, p.80
58 *Ibid.*, pp.78–9
59 Foenander, *Sixty Years of Ceylon Cricket*, p.52
60 *Ibid.*, p.55
61 Perera, *Janashakthi*, p.90
62 *Ibid.*, p.99
63 trove.nla.gov.au/newspaper/article/150670626
64 *Times of Ceylon*, 13 October 1909; roar.media/english/life/history/from-ivo-bligh-to- bradman-sri-lankas-first-international-cricket-half-century
65 Foenander, E.W., *Europeans vs Ceylonese Souvenir* (1911)
66 Perera, *Janashakthi*, pp.119–21
67 trove.nla.gov.au/newspaper/article/15475626
68 Perera, *Janashakthi*, pp.136–7
69 *Ibid.*, p.138
70 *Ibid.*, p.180
71 Wijesinha, B., *Love of a Lifetime*, p.23; Royal College Union and S. Thomas' College Old Boys Association, *History of 125 Years of the Royal-S. Thomas' Cricket Match*, p.121
72 Perera, *Janashakthi*, p.106; *Times of Ceylon*, 28 February and 1 March 1907
73 Foenander, *Sixty Years of Ceylon Cricket*, p.145
74 Perera, *Janashakthi*, pp.94–5
75 cricmash.com/cricket-during-wars/the-first-south-african-side-to-play-in-the-sub-continent- boer-prisoners-of-war-in-1901
76 Perera, *Janashakthi*, p.93
77 *Times of Ceylon*, 15 February 1906
78 *Times of Ceylon*, 8 March 1906
79 *Times of Ceylon*, quoting *Bombay Gazette*, 3 March 1906
80 *Times of Ceylon*, 28 February 1907 and 1 March 1907; Perera, *Janashakthi*, p.95
81 *Times of Ceylon*, 28 February 1907
82 Perera, *Janashakthi*, p.104
83 Foot, D., *Beyond Bat and Ball*, pp.114–5
84 *Ibid.*
85 *Ibid.*
86 Perera, *Janashakthi*, pp.79–80; Ryde CC Club Records

87 Gunasekara, C.H., 'My Cricket in England: Early Twentieth Century', in Roberts, M., *Essaying Cricket*, pp.263–7

88 Wijesinha, *Love of a Lifetime*, pp.31–9

89 Roberts, *Essaying Cricket*, p.267

90 Wickramasinghe, *Sri Lanka in the Modern Age*, pp.82–5

91 *Ibid.*, pp.126–7

92 Perera, *Janashakthi*, pp.118–9

93 *Ibid.*, p.136

94 *Ibid.*, pp.206–7

95 *Ibid.*, p.9

96 *Ibid.*, pp.152–3

97 Wijesinha, *Love of a Lifetime*, pp.32–3, 102

98 Bradman, D., *Don Bradman's Book*, p.113

99 Perera, *Janashakthi*, pp.163–4

100 *Ibid.*, p.165

101 *Ibid.*, p.171

102 Gunasekara, C., *The Willow Quartet*, pp.5, 17

103 Perera, *Janashakthi*, p.190

104 *Ibid.*, pp.160, 168–9

105 Ricketts, E.W.C., 'MCC Tour to India and Ceylon (1933–4): Report by Manager of the MCC team'

106 trove.nla.gov.au/newspaper/article/137260863

107 Douglas, C., *Douglas Jardine: Spartan Cricketer*, p.173; trove.nla.gov.au/newspaper/article/143590459

108 Douglas, *Douglas Jardine*, pp.173–4; trove.nla.gov.au/newspaper/article/137260863

109 trove.nla.gov.au/newspaper/article/137260863

110 www.theguardian.com/sport/blog/2012/mar/20/england-sri-lanka-douglas-jardine

111 trove.nla.gov.au/newspaper/article/92358768

112 trove.nla.gov.au/newspaper/article/137260863

113 Jardine, D., Personal Correspondence: 28 February and 9 March 1934

114 www.theguardian.com/sport/2007/nov/27/comment.sport

115 trove.nla.gov.au/newspaper/article/218834556

116 Gunasekara, *The Willow Quartet*, pp.23–4

117 lionsofsl.lk/SargoJayawickreme%20.html

118 Gunasekara, *The Willow Quartet*, pp.16, 34–5

119 Wijesinha, *Love of a Lifetime*, p.107

120 trove.nla.gov.au/newspaper/article/17068322

121 Gunasekara, *The Willow Quartet*, p.205

122 *Ibid.*, p.36

123 Perera, *Janashakthi*, p.178

124 *Ibid.*, pp.177–8
125 *Ibid.*, pp.123–4
126 *Ibid.*, p.191
127 *Ibid.*, p.164
128 Wijesinha, *Love of a Lifetime*, p.111
129 Fernando, R., *Sathasivam of Ceylon: A Battling Legend*
130 Fernando, R., *A Murder in Ceylon*, p.334
131 Roberts, *Essaying Cricket*, pp.173–6; Fernando, *Sathasivam of Ceylon*
132 Gunasekara, *The Willow Quartet*, p.59
133 *Ibid.*, pp.48–9
134 Perera, *Janashakthi*, p.228
135 Wijesinha, *Love of a Lifetime*, p.28
136 Gunasekara, *The Willow Quartet*, pp.50–1
137 *Ibid.*, pp.57–8
138 en.wikipedia.org/wiki/Singhalese_Sports_Club#Club_Presidents
139 Perera, *Janashakthi*, pp.12–4
140 Gunasekara, *The Willow Quartet*, p.69
141 www.thecricketmonthly.com/story/1164266/in-colombo--three-is-not-a-crowd
142 De Silva, *A History of Sri Lanka*, pp.554–69
143 Gunasekara, *The Willow Quartet*, pp.51–2
144 Perera, *Janashakthi*, pp.236–7
145 trove.nla.gov.au/newspaper/article/52631459
146 Jayaweera, N., 'Don Bradman and His Men in Ceylon', in Roberts, *Essaying Cricket*, pp.268–76
147 Perera, *Janashakthi*, pp.238–9
148 *Ibid.*, p.241
149 Perera, *Janashakthi*, pp.238–9
150 Wijesinha, *Love of a Lifetime*, p.108
151 Gunasekara, *The Willow Quartet*, p.52
152 *Ibid.*, p.56
153 Fernando, *Sathasivam of Ceylon*
154 Quoted in Perera, *Janashakthi*, p.253
155 Fernando, *A Murder in Ceylon*, pp.1–3
156 *Ibid.*, pp.4–17
157 Fernando, *A Murder in Ceylon*, pp.49–52
158 *Ibid.*, p.35
159 *Ibid.*, pp.86–111
160 *Ibid.*, pp.285–93
161 *Ibid.*, pp.162, 230–4
162 *Ibid.*, p.444
163 *Ibid.*, pp.354–5
164 *Ibid.*, p.347

165 Gunasekara, *The Willow Quartet*, pp.59–60

166 Wijesinha, *Love of a Lifetime*, p.109; Gunasekara, *Through the Covers*, p.85

167 Fernando, *Sathasivam of Ceylon*

168 Gunasekara, *The Willow Quartet*, pp.53–4

169 Wijesinha, *Love of a Lifetime*, p.111

170 Fernando, *Sathasivam of Ceylon*

171 Gunasekara, *The Willow Quartet*, pp.57–8

172 Wijesinha, *Love of a Lifetime*, pp.119–20

173 Gunasekara, *The Willow Quartet*, pp.64–5

174 Sheppard, D., *Parson's Pitch*, p.104

175 Wijesinha, *Love of a Lifetime*, p.134

176 Gunasekara, *Through the Covers*, pp.94–6

177 *Ibid.*, p.97

178 Gunasekara, *Through the Covers*, pp.101–3

179 Perera, *Janashakthi*, pp.262–3; Gunasekara, *The Willow Quartet*, pp.39–40

180 Mahedevan, A., *Sri Lanka's Journey to Test Status: Part I*

181 Gunasekara, *Through the Covers*, p.105

182 *Ibid.*, pp.122–4; Mahedevan, *Sri Lanka's Journey to Test Status: Part I*; Perera, *Janashakthi*, pp.267–8

183 Gunasekara, *Through the Covers*, p.123

184 Perera, *Janashakthi*, p.315

185 Chalke, S., *Runs in the Memory*, p.104

186 www.trentbridge.co.uk/trentbridge/history/players/gamini-goonesena.html

187 Goonesena, G., *Spin Bowling: The Young Cricketer Talks to Gamini Goonesena*, p.27

188 www.themorning.lk/nonagenarian-and-legend-that-is-stanley-jayasinghe/

189 archives.dailynews.lk/2013/03/05/spo06.asp

190 archives.sundayobserver.lk/2004/06/13/spo02.html

2 *The Long Road Ahead (1956–1982)*

1 Perera, *Janashakthi*, p.261

2 Gunasekara, *The Willow Quartet*, p.78

3 *Ibid.*, p.79

4 dailynews.lk/2017/02/09/features/107131/abu-fuard-irrepressible?page=5

5 Gunasekara, *The Willow Quartet*, p.80

6 Perera, *Janashakthi*, pp.296–7

7 *Ibid.*, p.297

8 Mahedevan, *Sri Lanka's Journey to Test Status: Part I*

9 Newspaper clipping, Ranjit Fernando's personal scrapbook

10 *Ibid.*

11 *Ibid.*

12 Mahedevan, *Sri Lanka's Journey to Test Status: Part I*
13 Newspaper clipping, Ranjit Fernando's personal scrapbook
14 *Ibid.*
15 Perera, *Janashakthi*, p.76
16 Newspaper clipping, Ranjit Fernando's personal scrapbook
17 Perera, *Janashakthi*, p.78
18 *Ibid.*, p.321
19 Gunasekara, *The Willow Quartet*, p.80
20 Perera, *Janashakthi*, pp.312–3
21 De Silva, *A History of Sri Lanka*, pp.649–51, 655–7
22 cricketique.live/2018/05/23/how-the-scheduled-tour-of-england-in-the-1960s-was-blown-apart-from-within/
23 Perera, *Janashakthi*, p.323
24 *Ibid.*, p.322
25 *Ibid.*, pp.323–4
26 *Ibid.*, pp.325–6
27 Quoted in *Ibid.*, p.324
28 www.dailynews.lk/2018/04/21/sports/148821/cricket-tour-never-took-place-changed-national-selection-policy
29 James, S., *Diplomatic Moves: Life in the Foreign Service*, p.52
30 Perera, *Janashakthi*, p.324
31 *Ibid.*, p.327
32 Mahedevan, A., *Sri Lanka's Journey to Test Status: Part II*
33 *Ibid.*
34 *Ibid.*
35 De Silva, *A History of Sri Lanka*, pp.662–73
36 Fernando, *Sathasivam of Ceylon*
37 Royal College Union and S. Thomas' College Old Boys Association, *History of 125 Years of the Royal-S. Thomas' Cricket Match*
38 www.commonlii.org/lk/legis/num_act/sl25o1973180/
39 Perera, *Janashakthi*, p.337
40 cricketique.live/2011/08/14/shelley-wickramasinghe-a-tribute-to-the-gom-of-bloomfield/
41 Perera, *Janashakthi*, p.346
42 *Ibid.*
43 Tennekoon, A., *Passionately Cricket*, p.76
44 Quoted in Wettimuny, S., *Cricket: The Noble Art*
45 Wettimuny, *Cricket: The Noble Art*, pp.40–5
46 www.espncricinfo.com/story/ashley-mallett-on-jeff-thomson-s-fearsome-spell-against-sri- lanka-at-the-1975-world-cup-826971
47 Tennekoon, *Passionately Cricket*, p.108
48 Roberts, *Incursions & Excursions*, pp.84–8

49 Perera, *Janashakthi*, p.362
50 Wettimuny, *Cricket: The Noble Art*, pp.9–13
51 counterpoint.lk/kardar-must-be-spinning-in-his-grave/
52 De Silva, *A History of Sri Lanka*, pp.664–6
53 *Ibid.*, pp.692–8
54 *Ibid.*, p.686
55 Perera, *Janashakthi*, p.373
56 Tennekoon, *Passionately Cricket*, p.109
57 *Ibid.*, p.111
58 Perera, *Janashakthi*, pp.369–70
59 *Ibid.*, p.373
60 Bandula Warnapura on *Legends with Rex*, www.youtube.com/watch?v=YPfnOZjfAzs&t=1173s
61 www.espncricinfo.com/wisdenalmanack/content/story/228576.html
62 Roberts, *Incursions & Excursions*, p.41
63 Perera, *Janashakthi*, p.394
64 *Ibid.*, pp.397–8
65 Quoted in *ibid.*, p.395
66 www.dailynews.lk/2020/10/24/features/232212/gamini-dissanayake-pio-neer-sri- lanka%E2%80%99s-test-status

3   Learning on the Job (1982–1988)

1 www.theguardian.com/sport/blog/2012/mar/20/england-sri-lanka-douglas-jardine
2 www.sundaytimes.lk/060806/sports/16.0.html
3 www.espncricinfo.com/story/rewind-sri-lanka-s-first-test-in-1982-558426
4 www.espncricinfo.com/story/sri-lanka-come-of-age-247624
5 Emburey, J., *Emburey*, p.81
6 www.sundaytimes.lk/060806/sports/16.0.html
7 Perera, *Janashakthi*, pp.412–3
8 *Ibid.*, p.413
9 www.cricketcountry.com/articles/duleep-mendis-smashes-identical-tons-in-sri-lanka-rsquo-s-first-test-against-india-31004
10 Bandula Warnapura on *Legends with Rex*, www.youtube.com/watch?v=YPfnOZjfAzs&t=1173s
11 Alfred, L., 'When Sri Lanka Went to Cuckoo Land', www.espncricinfo.com/story/luke-alfred-on-the-sri-lankan-rebel-tour-of-south-africa-in-1982-1079798
12 Lister, S., *Fire in Babylon*, p.177
13 counterpoint.lk/sri-lankas-rebel-tour-to-south-africa-in-1982/
14 www.espncricinfo.com/story/the-one-that-got-away-423563

15   roar.media/english/life/sports/cricket-in-cuckoo-land-the-rebel-tour-of-apartheid-south-africa

16   www.espncricinfo.com/story/luke-alfred-on-the-sri-lankan-rebel-tour-of-south-africa-in- 1982-1079798

17   www.espncricinfo.com/story/anura-ranasinghe-dies-in-his-sleep-76675

18   Perera, *Janashakthi*, p.424

19   www.espncricinfo.com/magazine/content/story/149094.html

20   Sobers, G., *My Autobiography*

21   *Ibid.*, p.223

21   www.youtube.com/watch?v=XHBH9a9pNv0

22   www.youtube.com/watch?v=mCJ1cRdOEMg

23   Sobers, *My Autobiography*

24   www.pressreader.com/sri-lanka/daily-mirror-sri-lanka/20200512/282063394146304

25   McGowan, *Only Man is Vile*, pp.179–81

26   *Ibid.*, pp.96–9

27   Fernando, A.F., 'The Lost Boys of Jaffna', www.thecricketmonthly.com/story/761915/the-lost-boys-of-jaffna

28   Williamson, M., 'Sri Lanka's Impressive Lord's Debut', www.espncricinfo.com/story/sri-lanka-s-impressive-lord-s-debut-517641

29   www.youtube.com/watch?v=dUJPgcEGEOs

30   Fernando, A.F., 'When Wettimuny Drove and Mendis Hooked', www.thecricketmonthly.com/story/752117/when-wettimuny-drove-and-mendis-hooked

31   www.espncricinfo.com/story/sri-lanka-s-impressive-lord-s-debut-517641

32   www.espncricinfo.com/wisdenalmanack/content/story/152302.html

33   Quoted in Perera, *Janashakthi*, pp.435–6

34   www.espncricinfo.com/wisdenalmanack/content/story/154461.html

35   De Silva, P.A., *Aravinda*, p.64

36   *Ibid.*, p.68

37   Quoted in Perera, *Janashakthi*, p.443

38   De Silva, P.A., *Aravinda*, p.79

39   *Ibid.*, p.81

40   Perera, *Janashakthi*, pp.439, 444

41   *Ibid.*, p.349

42   De Silva, *Aravinda*, p.88

43   *Ibid.*, p.92

44   www.thecricketmonthly.com/story/415544/scrappy-in-sri-lanka; De Silva, *Aravinda*, pp.90, 82

45   Khan, I., *All Round View*, p.72

46   Perera, *Janashakthi*, pp.454–5

47   Khan, *All Round View*, p.72

48 www.thecricketmonthly.com/story/415544/scrappy-in-sri-lanka
49 Khan, *All Round View*, p.72
50 De Silva, *Aravinda*, p.100
51 Mellawa, R., *Winds Behind the Willows*, p.42; De Silva, *Aravinda*, p.100
52 De Silva, *Aravinda*, p.101
53 Mellawa, *Winds Behind the Willows*, p.42
54 Khan, *All Round View*, p.74
55 Perera, *Janashakthi*, p.455
56 Khan, *All Round View* (Macmillan, 1989), p.74
56 De Silva, *Aravinda*, p.100
57 Perera, *Janashakthi*, p.464
58 De Silva, *Aravinda*, p.105
59 www.espncricinfo.com/story/saved-by-the-detour-424618
60 www.cricketcountry.com/articles/world-cup-countdown-1987-rampant-viv-richards-clobbers-181-against-sri-lanka-813626
61 De Silva, *Aravinda*, p.59
62 *Ibid.*, p.59
63 *Ibid.*, p.58

4 *The Age of Arjuna (1988–1999)*

1 Nicholas, M., 'Sri Lanka's Cricket Legacy is Glorious but What Does the Future Hold', www.espncricinfo.com/story/mark-nicholas-sri-lanka-s-cricket-legacy-is-glorious-but-what-does-the-future-hold-1162730
2 Haigh, G., *Game for Anything*, p.149
3 *Ibid.*, p.152
4 *Ibid.*, p.151
5 www.espncricinfo.com/story/kumar-sangakkara-s-mcc-spirit-of-cricket-lecture-522183
6 De Silva, *Aravinda*, pp.18–9
7 See Mahanama, R., *Retired Hurt*, p.46
8 De Silva, *Aravinda*, pp.134–5
9 *Ibid.*, p.136
10 *Ibid.*, p.136
11 *Ibid.*, p.137
12 Gemmel, J., *Cricket, Race and the 2007 World Cup*, p.xv
13 www.espncricinfo.com/wisdenalmanack/content/story/153160.html
14 www.themorning.lk/revisiting-ravi-ratnayeke-that-gritty-bearded-lanka-all-rounder-of-1980s/
15 Wickramasinghe, *Sri Lanka in the Modern Age*, pp.251–2
16 Subramanian, S., *This Divided Island*
17 Perera, *Janashakthi*, pp.194, 501–2
18 www.espncricinfo.com/wisdenalmanack/content/story/150812.html

19 www.espncricinfo.com/story/statistics-run-outs-in-odis-224487#thelist0
20 De Silva, *Aravinda*, p.130
21 www.espncricinfo.com/wisdenalmanack/content/story/153176.html
22 Haigh, *Game for Anything*, pp.153–4
23 Perera, *Janashakthi*, pp.498–9
24 Marqusee, *War Minus the Shooting*, p.287; www.deccanchronicle.com/sports/cricket/080519/monks-bless-sri-lanka-players-ahead-of-world-cup-see-pics.html
25 De Silva, *Aravinda*, pp.139–40
26 www.youtube.com/watch?v=ufYPRA0au9s
27 De Silva, *Aravinda*, p.73
28 Tufnell, P., *Tuffers' Hall of Fame*
29 De Silva, *Aravinda*, p.114
30 www.espncricinfo.com/wisdenalmanack/content/story/153615.html
31 www.thecricketmonthly.com/story/673807/-we-dominated-for-over-four-days-but-lost-in-half-a-session
32 *Ibid.*
33 De Silva, *Aravinda*, p.148
34 *Ibid.*, pp.149–50
35 www.thecricketmonthly.com/story/673807/-we-dominated-for-over-four-days-but-lost-in-half-a-session
36 De Silva, *Aravinda*, pp.152–3
37 www.espncricinfo.com/story/sri-lankan-players-approached-by-bookmakers-newspaper- 84648; archive.indianexpress.com/news/hashan-tillakaratne-says-matchfixing-rampant-in- sri-lankan-cricket/783403/
38 De Silva, *Aravinda*, p.154
39 www.thetimes.co.uk/article/spin-legends-who-failed-to-impress-on-debut-z7nz5pdtlk5
40 www.rnz.co.nz/national/programmes/eyewitness/audio/201857365/should-i-stay-or-should-i-go
41 Quoted in Perera, *Janashakthi*, p.528
42 Mahanama, *Retired Hurt*, p.57
43 www.independent.co.uk/sport/cricket-england-are-humiliated-by-historic-defeat-fletcher-bemoans-itinerary-as-sri-lanka-conquer-their-nerves-with-verve-to-secure-a-vivid-victory-1498669.html
44 www.independent.co.uk/sport/cricket-england-leave-in-more-shame-1498948.html
45 www.youtube.com/watch?v=kLQQ_doZpYU
46 De Silva, *Aravinda*, p.164; Mahanama, *Retired Hurt*, p.63
47 De Silva, *Aravinda*, p.163
48 Skandakumar, S., Tour Report (quoted in Perera, *Janashakthi*, p.534)
49 Quoted in Perera, *Janashakthi*, pp.533–40

50 Skandakumar, S., quoted in Perera, *Janashakthi*, p.534
51 Perera, *Janashakthi*, p.533
52 Haigh, *Game for Anything*, p.154
53 De Silva, *Aravinda*, p.166
54 *Ibid.*, p.168
55 *Ibid.*, p.166
56 *Ibid.*, p.165
57 Skandakumar, S., quoted in Perera, *Janashakthi*, p.534
58 Perera, *Janashakthi*, p.535
59 *Ibid.*, p.538
60 *Ibid.*, pp.535–8
61 *Ibid.*, pp.536–7
62 De Silva, *Aravinda*, pp.166–7
63 Mahanama, *Retired Hurt*, p.68
64 De Silva, *Aravinda*, p.166
65 Anonymous source
66 Mahanama, *Retired Hurt*, pp.67–9
67 Perera, *Janashakthi*, pp.542–3
68 De Silva, *Aravinda*, p.69
69 Marqusee, *War Minus the Shooting*, pp.181–7
70 cricketique.live/2011/01/31/1086/
71 www.thecricketmonthly.com/story/834255/the-lion-s-fairy-tale
72 Mahanama, *Retired Hurt*, p.76
73 www.espncricinfo.com/wisdenalmanack/content/story/154406.html
74 De Silva, *Aravinda*, p.33
75 *Ibid.*, p.29
76 *Ibid.*, p.25
77 *Ibid.*, pp.132–3
78 *Ibid.*, p.32
79 *Ibid.*, p.156
80 *Ibid.*, p.175
81 Perera, *Janashakthi*, p.565
82 www.youtube.com/watch?v=BXzktmwSngo&t=3s
83 De Silva, *Aravinda*, p.180
84 www.espncricinfo.com/wisdenalmanack/content/story/154406.html
85 Mahanama, *Retired Hurt*, p.76
86 archives.dailynews.lk/2003/05/17/spo05.html
87 www.dailymail.co.uk/sport/article-63844/Warne-Lara-squealer-ratty-Ranatunga-worst-lot.html
88 static.espncricinfo.com/db/ARCHIVE/1995-96/SL_IN_AUS/SL_AUS_T1_08-11DEC1995_DAILY_MR.html
89 Roberts, *Crosscurrents*, p.113

90 www.independent.co.uk/sport/tampering-sri-lanka-1525094.html

91 Roberts, *Crosscurrents*, p.114

92 *Ibid.*, p.114

93 Fraser, D., *Cricket and the Law*, p.242

94 Quoted in Roberts, *Crosscurrents*, pp.114–5

95 Anonymous source

96 Roberts, *Incursions & Excursions*, pp.44–5

97 *Ibid.*, p.112

98 De Silva, *Aravinda*, p.190

99 Roberts, *Crosscurrents*, p.116

100 Roberts, *Incursions & Excursions*, p.113

101 www.youtube.com/watch?v=Ivf1qI5ZalA

102 Roberts, *Crosscurrents*, p.119

103 www.espncricinfo.com/wisdenalmanack/content/story/892275.html

104 Quoted in Roberts, *Crosscurrents*, p.117

105 www.youtube.com/watch?v=Ivf1qI5ZalA

106 Quoted in Roberts, *Incursions & Excursions*, p.114

107 Halbish, G., *Run Out*; www.sundaytimes.lk/040530/sports/7.html

108 Roberts, *Incursions & Excursions*, p.112

109 *Ibid.*, p.114

110 *Ibid.*, pp.115–6

111 De Silva, *Aravinda*, p.193

112 Narayanan, C., *Sanath Jayasuriya: A Biography*, p.27

113 www.youtube.com/watch?v=GQxjqJckG-8

114 Mahanama, *Retired Hurt*, p.87

115 www.espn.co.uk/cricket/story/_/id/23271854/ranatunga-speaks-mark-taylor-19-feb-1997; De Silva, *Aravinda*, pp.197–9; Mahanama, *Retired Hurt*, p.87

116 www.cricketcountry.com/criclife/cricketainment/ian-healy-to-arjuna-ranatunga-you-dont- get-a-runner-for-being-overweight-unfit-fat-ct-498566

117 Fraser, *Cricket and the Law*, p.100

118 www.espncricinfo.com/wisdenalmanack/content/story/155289.html

119 De Silva, *Aravinda*, p.197

120 *Ibid.*, p.198

121 www.rediff.com/wc2007/2007/mar/13hadlee.htm

122 www.thecricketmonthly.com/story/834255/the-lion-s-fairy-tale

123 www.youtube.com/watch?v=PUl1qx_28fg

124 www.youtube.com/watch?v=g-6DSkkJ-QE

125 Marqusee, *War Minus the Shooting*, pp.32–3

126 www.pressreader.com/sri-lanka/sunday-times-sri-lanka/20171105/282364039947109

127 www.youtube.com/watch?v=VB9liDl2LJg

128 www.youtube.com/watch?v=StI-hTfjYew

129 www.youtube.com/watch?v=CinzBT78q9E

130 www.youtube.com/watch?v=X6iG1X8ZaRE&t=79s

131 www.youtube.com/watch?v=aTLRAsxokwY

132 www.youtube.com/watch?v=p7FzPAT8FPw

133 www.crictracker.com/march-13-1996-the-nuisance-at-the-eden-gardens/

134 Marqusee, *War Minus the Shooting*, p.259

135 www.youtube.com/watch?v=g-6DSkkJ-QE&t=1013s

136 www.cricbuzz.com/cricket-news/93355/fighting-for-muttiah-muralitharan-upul-chandanas- sacrifice-and-a-carpet-sale-before-a-world-cup-final-world-cup-1996-cricbuzzcom

137 www.thecricketmonthly.com/story/974779/the-genius-and-the-clown

138 www.youtube.com/watch?v=g-6DSkkJ-QE&t=1013s

139 www.thecricketmonthly.com/story/834255/the-lion-s-fairy-tale

140 Marqusee, *War Minus the Shooting*, p.11

141 www.youtube.com/watch?v=rl3L2SGgmNo

142 www.youtube.com/watch?v=X6iG1X8ZaRE&t=80s

143 Marqusee, *War Minus the Shooting*, p.281

144 Mellawa, *Winds Behind the Willows*, p.75

145 *Ibid.*, p.77

146 Marqusee, *War Minus the Shooting*

147 Narayanan, *Sanath Jayasuriya*, pp.37–8

148 www.espn.com.au/cricket/story/_/id/22870280/let-hear-veterans

149 Narayanan, *Sanath Jayasuriya*, p.38

150 www.espncricinfo.com/story/jayasuriya-honoured-by-wisden-and-indian-cricket-15-may-1997-73776

151 Narayanan, *Sanath Jayasuriya*, p.xvii

152 Mellawa, *Winds Behind the Willows*, p.75

153 www.espncricinfo.com/story/upali-dharmadasa-elected-to-top-cricket-post-01-apr-1996-72020

154 Mellawa, *Winds Behind the Willows*, p.109

155 *Ibid.*, pp.103–12

156 Mellawa, *Winds Behind the Willows*, p.104

157 www.espncricinfo.com/story/upali-dharmadasa-elected-to-top-cricket-post-01-apr-1996-72020

158 Mellawa, *Winds Behind the Willows*, p.109

159 *Ibid.*, pp.106–8; www.pressreader.com/sri-lanka/sunday-times-sri-lanka/20191027/282011854148230

160 www.espncricinfo.com/story/whatmore-sri-lanka-on-course-to-become-best-test-nation-11-oct-1996-72671

161 www.espn.com/cricket/story/_/id/22987910/dave-whatmore-steps-down; www.deccanchronicle.com/140410/sports-cricket/article/1996-sri-lankan-world-cup-winning-teams-support-staff-was-not-%E2%80%98well

162 www.espncricinfo.com/story/ranatunga-no-ill-feeling-among-the-players-on-tour-24-nov-1996-72607; Mahanama, *Retired Hurt*, p.105

163 www.espncricinfo.com/story/sri-lankan-cricket-strikes-discordant-note-9-dec-1996-72156

164 www.espn.co.uk/cricket/story/_/id/23271936/sri-lanka-chief-executive-asanka-gurusinha-12-feb-1997

165 www.espncricinfo.com/story/sri-lanka-chief-executive-on-asanka-gurusinha-12-feb-1997-73142

166 www.espncricinfo.com/story/sri-lanka-cricket-team-to-new-zealand-leaves-february-24-10-jan-1997-73400; Mahanama, *Retired Hurt*, pp.109–10

167 www.espncricinfo.com/story/asanka-gurusinha-retires-29-oct-1997-73984

168 www.cricketcountry.com/articles/india-vs-sri-lanka-1st-test-at-colombo-1997-heartbreaking-for-sanath-jayasuriya-backbreaking-for-indians-16745

169 www.independent.co.uk/sport/sri-lanka-s-952-hints-new-era-1244218.html

170 Quoted in Narayanan, *Sanath Jayasuriya*, p.73

171 Mahanama, *Retired Hurt*, p.115

172 Narayanan, *Sanath Jayasuriya*, p.77

173 stats.espncricinfo.com/ci/engine/stats/index.html?class=1;filter=advanced;orderby=runs;qualmax3=2;qualmin2=500;qualval2=runs;qualval3=matches;template=results;type=batting;view=series

174 www.cricbuzz.com/cricket-news/107313/yardley-was-the-first-to-tell-the-world-i-can-play-tests-muralitharan

175 *Ibid.*

176 www.tribuneindia.com/1999/99jul09/sports.htm#4

177 www.espncricinfo.com/story/sri-lanka-don-t-expect-results-overnight-says-dias-11-may-1998-76231

178 Amarasinghe, S., *The Nightwatchman*

179 www.thecricketmonthly.com/story/1087120/arjuna-versus

180 www.espncricinfo.com/story/janaka-malwatta-murali-magic-at-the-oval-704655

181 www.thecricketmonthly.com/story/1156553/-the-next-time-we-visited-england--they-were- giving-us-three-test-series

182 Engel, M. (ed.), *Wisden Cricketers' Almanack 1999*

183 www.theguardian.com/sport/1999/jan/19/cricket3

184 www.smh.com.au/sport/cricket/crowd-taunts-may-force-murali-to-chuck-it-in-20030117-gdg4dl.html; https://www.espncricinfo.com/story/the-british-sports-media-s-witch-hunt-against-sri-lanka-s-cricketers-8-february-1999-79556

185 news.bbc.co.uk/1/hi/sport/cricket/252663.stm

186 www.espn.com/cricket/story/_/id/23254671/council-clarifies-muralitharan-case-16-january-1999

187 www.theguardian.com/sport/1999/jan/19/cricket3

188 www.youtube.com/watch?v=4mcmxYIGKJY

189 www.espncricinfo.com/wisdenalmanack/content/story/151590.html

190 www.espncricinfo.com/story/the-ugly-face-of-cricket-24-janu-ary-1999-80351

191 www.espncricinfo.com/story/muralitharan-unfair-victim-of-an-umpire-on-a-crusade-25-january-1999-80361

192 www.espncricinfo.com/story/ranatunga-gets-suspended-sentence-fine-28-january-1999-80469

193 www.espncricinfo.com/story/icc-open-to-ridicule-after-ranatunga-escapes-ban-29-january-1999-80470

194 www.independent.co.uk/sport/cricket-stewart-called-to-ranatunga-hear-ing-1076794.html

195 archive.org/stream/Independent1999IrelandEnglish/Jan%2029%20 1999%2C%20Independent%2C%20%233832%2C%20Ireland%20 %28en%29_djvu.txt

196 www.theguardian.com/sport/1999/jan/28/cricket4

197 Quoted in Rae, S., *It's Not Cricket*

198 www.espncricinfo.com/story/throwing-umpire-on-sick-leave-80177

199 107.6.21.207/Publications/ATheoryOfCivilization/decline/emerson.htm

200 cricketique.live/2014/09/24/no-ball-acb-behind-emersons-no-balling-decisions-against-murali/

201 www.theaustralian.com.au/sport/cricket/emerson-reflects-on-muralidaran-and-noball-controversy/news-story/832afb95dff41c93b850a15dc9d34293

202 www.thecricketmonthly.com/story/1034337/when-murali-bared-his-soul

203 www.espncricinfo.com/print/story/82266

204 www.espncricinfo.com/wisdenalmanack/content/story/151486.html

5   *The New Greats (1999–2007)*

1   Mellawa, *Retired Hurt*, pp.109–11

2   www.espncricinfo.com/story/sri-lanka-bccsl-elections-17-march-1999-81883

3   Mellawa, *Winds Behind the Willows*, pp.112–4

4   www.espncricinfo.com/story/bccsl-election-mayhem-29-march-1999-81884

5   www.espncricinfo.com/story/bccsl-elections-sumathipala-alleges-sri-lanka-s-image-tarnished-31-march-1999-82272

6   www.espncricinfo.com/story/partners-in-the-progress-of-sri-lanka-cricket-16-june-1999-81377

7   Chesterfield, T., 'Cricket in Sri Lanka: In Need of a Messiah', in *Cricketing Cultures in Conflict: World Cup 2003*, eds Majumdar & Mangan

8   Roberts, M., 'Sri Lanka: The Power of Cricket and The Power in Cricket', in *Cricket and National Identity in the Postcolonial Age*, ed. Wagg, S.

9   Mellawa, *Winds Behind the Willows*, pp.116–7
10   www.tribuneindia.com/1999/99jul09/sports.htm#4
11   Mahanama, *Retired Hurt*, p.151
12   Narayanan, *Sanath Jayasuriya*, pp.4–10
13   *Ibid.*, pp.83–90
14   *Ibid.*, p.88
15   *Ibid.*, p.89
16   www.espncricinfo.com/story/jayawardene-being-groomed-as-long-term-sri-lankan-captain-131215
17   www.thecricketmonthly.com/story/902493/the-cult-of-sanga; www.espncricinfo.com/story/andrew-fidel-fernando-meets-kumar-sangakkara-s-father-kshema-701961
18   timesofindia.indiatimes.com/sports/new-zealand-in-india-2016/top-stories/how-lankas-club-of-gentlemen-cricketers-moulded-a-legend/articleshow/48533671.cms
19   www.youtube.com/watch?v=iAmef8PrUno
20   www.youtube.com/watch?v=anVfSbyDsOo
21   www.espncricinfo.com/wisdenalmanack/content/story/153919.html
22   www.nation.lk/online/on-this-day-10-august-109206.html
23   www.thecricketmonthly.com/story/865287/large-and-in-charge
24   www.espncricinfo.com/wisdenalmanack/content/story/154277.html
25   Narayanan, *Sanath Jaysuriya*, p.93
26   www.espncricinfo.com/wisdenalmanack/content/story/154217.html
27   www.sundaytimes.lk/031102/sports/8.htm
28   www.espncricinfo.com/wisdenalmanack/content/story/154219.html
29   www.espncricinfo.com/series/england-tour-of-sri-lanka-2000-01-61786/sri-lanka-vs-england-1st-test-63916/match-report
30   *Ibid.*
31   www.espncricinfo.com/wisdenalmanack/content/story/154221.html
32   www.espncricinfo.com/story/sri-lanka-v-england-2000-01-bc-cooray-s-umpiring-nightmare-521543
33   www.thecricketmonthly.com/story/1164159/thorpey-and-gilo-mug-sri-lanka
34   Anonymous source
35   www.espncricinfo.com/story/thilanga-sumathipala-dismisses-objections-to-his-nomination-for-forthcoming-the-bccsl-elections-89444
36   www.espncricinfo.com/story/the-dambulla-construction-race-commences-94729
37   news.bbc.co.uk/sport1/hi/cricket/1244314.stm
38   news.bbc.co.uk/sport1/hi/cricket/1249136.stm
39   www.rediff.com/cricket/2001/apr/05sri.htm
40   www.theguardian.com/sport/2001/jan/28/englandinsrilanka200102.cricket

41   www.espncricinfo.com/story/the-silent-achiever-229380

42   www.espncricinfo.com/wisdenalmanack/content/story/154963.html

43   Rajan, A., *Twirlymen*

44   www.espncricinfo.com/wisdenalmanack/content/story/154966.html

45   www.espncricinfo.com/story/muralitharan-believes-600-is-a-possibil-ity-115552

46   www.espn.co.uk/cricket/story/_/id/23177033/non-telecast-asian-test-championship-final

47   *Ibid.*

48   www.theguardian.com/sport/2002/may/21/cricket

49   news.bbc.co.uk/sport1/hi/photo_galleries/1998327.stm

50   news.bbc.co.uk/sport1/hi/cricket/england/2047066.stm

51   www.espncricinfo.com/story/foster-dismayed-by-bccsl-treatment-117877

52   www.espncricinfo.com/wisdenalmanack/content/story/154973.html

53   *Ibid.*

54   www.espncricinfo.com/story/muralitharan-out-of-natwest-series-117977

55   Narayanan, *Sanath Jayasuriya*, p.95; www.espncricinfo.com/wisdenalmanack/content/story/155109.html

56   www.campaignlive.co.uk/article/analysis-image-rights-pose-threat-tourna-ments/156640

57   www.rediff.com/wc2003/2003/jan/17lanka.htm

58   www.rediff.com/wc2003/2003/jan/21lanka.htm; www.espncricinfo.com/story/sri-lankan-players-provided-performance-based-incentives-127815

59   www.espncricinfo.com/story/world-cup-2003-player-contracts-127951

60   archives.dailynews.lk/2003/01/23/spo00.html

61   www.espncricinfo.com/story/sri-lankan-board-reaches-agreement-with-players-128064

62   timesofindia.indiatimes.com/cricket/lanka-offers-players-more-cash-for-world-cup-win/articleshow/35780913.cms

63   www.espncricinfo.com/story/sri-lanka-in-selection-chaos-over-south-africa-tour-squad-122060

64   www.espncricinfo.com/wisdenalmanack/content/story/155936.html

65   www.espncricinfo.com/wisdenalmanack/content/story/155935.html

66   www.youtube.com/watch?v=HQzOGx4QUcg; www.nationtoday.lk/sports/when- sanga-said-mark-boucher-dogs-dont-shout-they-bark-mister/

67   www.espn.co.uk/cricket/story/_/id/23173206/sri-lanka-test-cricket-takes-giant-leap

68   www.theguardian.com/sport/2003/jan/17/cricket.davidhopps

69   archives.dailynews.lk/2003/01/20/spo01.html

70   www.thecricketer.com/Topics/australia/world_cup_moments_no25_adam_gilchrist_walks_the_walk.html

71   archives.dailynews.lk/2003/05/17/spo05.html

72   www.espn.co.uk/cricket/story/_/id/23151981/whatmore-contract-not-renewed
73   news.bbc.co.uk/sport1/hi/cricket/2902195.stm
74   www.espncricinfo.com/story/sri-lanka-s-chairman-of-selectors-resigns-in-protest-123791
75   Naryanan, *Sanath Jayasuriya*, pp.104–5
76   *Ibid.*, p.104
77   news.bbc.co.uk/sport1/hi/cricket/england/2051534.stm
78   www.espncricinfo.com/story/atapattu-receives-captaincy-backing-from-de-silva-137718
79   www.espn.com/cricket/story/_/id/23150532/mendis-appointed-sri-lankan-coach-west-indies-tour
80   www.espncricinfo.com/wisdenalmanack/content/story/214568.html
81   www.espncricinfo.com/story/fleming-surprised-by-negative-attitude-131165
82   www.espncricinfo.com/story/pitched-battle-in-offing-in-bccsl-elections-129373
83   colombogazette.com/2017/08/24/defamation-case-filed-by-thilanga-against-arjuna-dismissed/
84   www.espncricinfo.com/story/ranatunga-rejects-pact-with-sumathipala-131497
85   www.espncricinfo.com/story/dyson-set-to-be-named-as-new-sri-lanka-coach-129418
86   www.theage.com.au/sport/cricket/dyson-takes-a-leap-into-the-testing-waters-of-sri-lankan-game-20030628-gdvya5.html
87   www.espncricinfo.com/print/story/132213
88   www.espncricinfo.com/wisdenalmanack/content/story/155895.html
89   www.espncricinfo.com/wisdenalmanack/content/story/155904.html
90   www.theguardian.com/sport/2003/dec/12/cricket.englandinsrilanka2003041
91   www.walesonline.co.uk/sport/cricket/thorpe-backs-hussain-after-murali-2457780
92   www.espncricinfo.com/wisdenalmanack/content/story/155905.html
93   www.thecricketmonthly.com/story/1039645/-i-felt-as-captain-i-had-certain-responsibilities-to-change-the-culture
94   www.theguardian.com/sport/2004/mar/08/cricket.davidhopps
95   www.espncricinfo.com/wisdenalmanack/content/story/237484.html
96   www.espncricinfo.com/story/i-totally-blame-the-batting-tillakaratne-139966
97   www.espncricinfo.com/story/central-province-complete-world-record-run-chase-137438
98   www.espncricinfo.com/wisdenalmanack/content/story/237487.html
99   www.espncricinfo.com/story/a-day-when-tillakaratne-just-couldn-t-make-up-his-mind-139931

100 www.espncricinfo.com/story/lehmann-i-was-a-little-bit-bored-at-times-140321

101 www.theage.com.au/sport/cricket/langer-cleared-as-lankans-post-lead-20040327-gdxkip.html

102 www.espncricinfo.com/story/the-murali-muddle-is-more-than-just-cricket-140460

103 www.espncricinfo.com/story/tillakaratne-steps-down-from-captaincy-140457

104 www.espncricinfo.com/story/chris-broad-sours-special-series-140493

105 www.espncricinfo.com/story/the-murali-muddle-is-more-than-just-cricket-140460

106 www.espncricinfo.com/story/chris-broad-sours-special-series-140493; www.espncricinfo.com/story/bucknor-murali-s-action-looks-terrible-134634

107 news.bbc.co.uk/sport1/hi/cricket/3444279.stm

108 www.espncricinfo.com/wisdenalmanack/content/story/238105.html

109 www.espncricinfo.com/story/murali-told-not-to-bowl-the-doosra-140848

110 www.espncricinfo.com/story/degrees-of-guilt-139581

111 www.thecricketmonthly.com/story/1034337/when-murali-bared-his-soul

112 www.rediff.com/cricket/2004/may/15murali.htm

113 www.theguardian.com/sport/2004/apr/19/cricket.davidhopps

114 www.espn.co.uk/cricket/story/_/id/23143174/elliott-critical-sri-lankan-board

115 www.espn.co.uk/cricket/story/_/id/23125613/murali-told-not-bowl-doosra

116 www.thecricketmonthly.com/story/1034337/when-murali-bared-his-soul

117 www.theage.com.au/sport/cricket/no-doubts-pm-says-muralis-a-chucker-20040515-gdxuq7.html

118 www.espncricinfo.com/story/icc-study-reveals-that-99-of-bowlers-throw-141558

119 www.rediff.com/cricket/2004/nov/16murali.htm

120 www.thehindu.com/sport/cricket/Muralirsquos-800-wickets-were-run-outs-Bedi/article15594104.ece

121 www.thecricketmonthly.com/story/1147532/the-last-battles-of-lasith-malinga

122 www.theguardian.com/sport/2007/nov/25/cricket.sport1

123 www.hindustantimes.com/india-vs-sri-lanka-2017/i-didn-t-see-first-ball-lasith-malinga-bowled-sri-lanka-pace-guru-ramanayake/story-mc2r4A4aFGmtMhRlt1M5VO.html

124 www.thecricketmonthly.com/story/1147532/the-last-battles-of-lasith-malinga

125 www.theguardian.com/sport/2007/nov/25/cricket.sport1

126 www.espncricinfo.com/story/murali-named-in-party-for-australian-tour-139263

127 www.rediff.com/cricket/2004/jun/24lanka.htm

128 www.youtube.com/watch?v=9qblGF2Hmk0

129 www.espncricinfo.com/story/kasprowicz-takes-seven-as-australia-romp-to-149-run-win-138310

130 www.theroar.com.au/2019/08/01/malinga-the-magnificent-a-memoir/; www.espncricinfo.com/wisdenalmanack/content/story/238023.html

131 www.espncricinfo.com/wisdenalmanack/content/story/238024.html

132 www.youtube.com/watch?v=hLbzALfZ2sc

133 www.espncricinfo.com/wisdenalmanack/content/story/238029.html

134 www.espncricinfo.com/story/sangakkara-it-s-a-batsman-s-dream-135103

135 www.espncricinfo.com/wisdenalmanack/content/story/238023.html

136 www.espncricinfo.com/print/story/142457

137 www.espncricinfo.com/wisdenalmanack/content/story/238060.html

138 www.espncricinfo.com/wisdenalmanack/content/story/238061.html

139 www.youtube.com/watch?v=KnpMxCXeKII

140 www.theguardian.com/world/2005/jun/19/tsunami2004.internationalaid-anddevelopment

141 Narayanan, *Sanath Jayasuriya*, p.110; www.independent.co.uk/sport/cricket/mothers-of-sri-lankan-pair-lucky-to-survive-tsunami-17353.html

142 www.espncricinfo.com/story/players-reveal-how-their-families-were-affected-144996

143 www.espncricinfo.com/story/callous-and-cruel-136279

144 www.theguardian.com/sport/2010/jul/17/muttiah-muralitharan-800-wickets-retirement?CMP=gu_com

145 www.espncricinfo.com/story/murali-leads-from-the-front-145035

146 www.espn.co.uk/cricket/story/_/id/23116341/slc-launches-rs-200m-cricket-aid-program

147 www.espn.com.au/cricket/story/_/id/23117010/officials-accused-bullying-sri-lanka-players

148 www.sundayobserver.lk/2019/09/08/news-features/glaring-financial-irregularities-surface

149 www.espncricinfo.com/story/sumathipala-s-day-of-reckoning-looms-137355

150 www.pressreader.com/sri-lanka/sunday-times-sri-lanka/20160424/282046211281381; africa.espn.com/cricket/story/_/id/23113130/sumathipala-not-sent-icc-meeting

151 www.sundaytimes.lk/050320/sports/1.html

152 archives.dailynews.lk/2005/03/28/spo02.htm; www.espn.com/cricket/story/_/id/23112277/sri-lankan-board-dissolved

153 www.espncricinfo.com/story/sumathipala-challenges-government-decision-146519

154 news.bbc.co.uk/sport1/hi/cricket/other_international/sri_lanka/4395267.stm

155 www.espncricinfo.com/print/story/208561

156 www.espn.com/cricket/story/_/id/23116239/slc-undecided-dyson-contract-extension

157 www.espncricinfo.com/story/sri-lanka-hint-at-persisting-with-dyson-145870

158 www.islandcricket.lk/sri_lanka_cricket_ne/greg-chappell-declines-sri-lanka-coaching-offer/

159 www.espncricinfo.com/print/story/144188; www.espncricinfo.com/print/story/144188

160 www.espncricinfo.com/wisdenalmanack/content/story/289013.html

161 www.espncricinfo.com/story/dilmah-sign-cut-price-sponsorship-217134

162 www.espn.co.uk/cricket/story/_/id/23097936/moody-named-sri-lanka-coach

163 wisden.com/stories/news-stories/when-young-malinga-helped-tom-moody-learn-important-coaching-lesson

164 www.espncricinfo.com/wisdenalmanack/content/story/289037.html

165 www.espncricinfo.com/wisdenalmanack/content/story/289824.html

166 www.espncricinfo.com/wisdenalmanack/content/story/289825.html

167 Narayanan, *Sanath Jayasuriya*, p.112

168 www.espncricinfo.com/wisdenalmanack/content/story/289057.html

169 www.espncricinfo.com/story/sri-lanka-facing-unknown-territory-225478; Narayanan, *Sanath Jayasuriya*, p.112

170 www.espncricinfo.com/story/sri-lankan-president-orders-inquiry-into-jayasuriya-s-axing-228292

171 www.espncricinfo.com/story/sri-lanka-facing-unknown-territory-225478

172 www.espncricinfo.com/story/sri-lanka-send-for-jehan-mubarak-227654

173 www.espncricinfo.com/story/a-chronicle-of-underachievement-230660

174 www.espncricinfo.com/wisdenalmanack/content/story/289065.html

175 www.espncricinfo.com/story/a-chronicle-of-underachievement-230660

176 news.bbc.co.uk/sport1/hi/cricket/4534336.stm

177 www.espncricinfo.com/wisdenalmanack/content/story/289070.html

178 www.espncricinfo.com/story/a-chronicle-of-underachievement-230660

179 www.espncricinfo.com/series/sri-lanka-tour-of-new-zealand-2005-06-226336

180 www.rediff.com/cricket/2006/jan/03jaya.htm

181 www.espncricinfo.com/wisdenalmanack/content/story/291228.html?matches=1

182 www.thecricketmonthly.com/story/785171/sri-lanka-s-heartbeat

183 www.sundaytimes.lk/051218/sports/1.html

184 www.espncricinfo.com/wisdenalmanack/content/story/289099.
html?matches=1
185 www.espncricinfo.com/story/murali-breaks-the-1000-wicket-bar-
rier-239296
186 www.espncricinfo.com/wisdenalmanack/content/story/291205.
html?matches=1
187 www.outlookindia.com/newswire/amp/emotional-jayasuriya-announces-
test-retirement/374321
188 Narayanan, *Sanath Jayasuriya*, pp.115–6
189 www.iol.co.za/capeargus/sport/jayasuriya-was-forced-to-quit-tests-557462
190 www.theguardian.com/sport/2006/jun/06/cricket.sport
191 news.bbc.co.uk/sport1/hi/cricket/england/5137184.stm
192 www.espncricinfo.com/wisdenalmanack/content/story/291119.html
193 www.espncricinfo.com/wisdenalmanack/content/story/291123.html
194 www.espncricinfo.com/story/i-am-happy-with-what-i-have-achieved-
jayawardene-254974
195 www.espncricinfo.com/story/jayawardene-named-captain-of-the-year-at-
icc-awards-2006-266786
196 www.youtube.com/watch?v=6zgvjC9WUCs
197 www.rediff.com/cricket/2006/dec/09murali.htm
198 www.espncricinfo.com/wisdenalmanack/content/story/291175.html
199 www.espncricinfo.com/wisdenalmanack/content/story/291158.html
200 www.espncricinfo.com/story/sl-s-brothers-in-arms-prepare-for-sunset-at-
home-810299
201 www.espncricinfo.com/series/icc-world-cup-2006-07-125929/south-africa-
vs-sri-lanka-26th-match-super-eights-247482/ball-by-ball-commentary
202 www.theguardian.com/sport/2007/apr/30/cricket.cricketworldcup20071

6 *Another March to Glory (2007–2014)*

1 www.reuters.com/article/uk-cricket-world-lanka-reaction-idUK-
COL13056420070429
2 www.espncricinfo.com/story/moody-quits-as-sri-lanka-coach-294056
3 www.espncricinfo.com/wisdenalmanack/content/story/395691.html
4 www.espncricinfo.com/print/story/301892
5 *Ibid.*
6 www.espncricinfo.com/wisdenalmanack/content/story/346999.html
7 www.reuters.com/article/idINIndia-29841320071003
8 www.espncricinfo.com/story/i-have-no-respect-for-the-selectors-ata-
pattu-314035
9 www.espncricinfo.com/story/atapattu-included-for-australia-tour-316001

10 www.espncricinfo.com/story/selectors-are-a-set-of-muppets-headed-by-a-joker-atapattu-319220

11 www.espncricinfo.com/wisdenalmanack/content/story/345708.html

12 www.espncricinfo.com/story/failing-to-walk-the-talk-319477

13 news.bbc.co.uk/sport1/hi/cricket/7101217.stm

14 www.youtube.com/watch?v=7aO3BLDDIFA

15 www.espncricinfo.com/print/story/321240

16 www.espncricinfo.com/story/atapattu-announces-his-retirement-321194

17 www.espncricinfo.com/wisdenalmanack/content/story/346999.html

18 www.espncricinfo.com/story/sangakkara-no-1-test-batsman-in-icc-rankings-324130

19 www.youtube.com/watch?v=A8ZHfelRjKQ

20 www.theguardian.com/sport/2007/dec/15/cricket.englandcricketseries1

21 www.espncricinfo.com/story/ranatunga-appointed-head-of-sri-lanka-cricket-328293

22 www.sundaytimes.lk/080316/Sports/sp206.html

23 www.sundaytimes.lk/080629/Sports/sp208.html

24 www.espncricinfo.com/story/sri-lanka-players-contracts-finalised-360684

25 www.bbc.com/sinhala/news/story/2008/09/printable/080912_cricket_england

26 twocircles.net/2008mar16/twenty20_three_minute_maggie_noodles_ipl_bad_cricket_ranatunga.html

27 www.espn.co.uk/cricket/story/_/id/22894493/ipl-shadow-sri-lanka-pakistan-tour

28 www.hindustantimes.com/cricket/ranatunga-tells-lankan-players-to-skip-ipl-for-england/story-yExrFF99yD3weTHWbYuuRP.html

29 www.reuters.com/article/cricket-india-lanka-idUKLQ1397920081026

30 www.espncricinfo.com/story/sri-lanka-s-interim-board-dissolved-ranatunga-sacked-384065

31 www.espncricinfo.com/story/ranatunga-sues-sports-minister-387663

32 www.espncricinfo.com/series/sri-lanka-tour-of-west-indies-2007-08-319119/west-indies-vs-sri-lanka-1st-odi-319134/match-preview

33 www.espncricinfo.com/wisdenalmanack/content/story/430815.html

34 www.youtube.com/watch?v=d580vNKY318

35 www.espncricinfo.com/story/we-never-had-a-reply-for-mendis-dhoni-360209

36 www.espncricinfo.com/story/the-boy-who-became-an-enigma-391369

37 www.espncricinfo.com/story/charlie-austin-on-muttiah-muralitharan-468412

38 www.espncricinfo.com/story/sri-lanka-s-pakistan-tour-cleared-384307

39 www.outlookindia.com/newswire/story/ranatunga-sacked-sl-unlikely-to-tour-pakistan/650153

40 www.espncricinfo.com/story/jayawardene-to-step-down-390368
41 www.youtube.com/watch?v=KnpMxCXeKII
42 www.bbc.co.uk/sport/cricket/50726039
43 www.theguardian.com/world/2009/mar/04/pakistan-cricket-terror
44 www.independent.co.uk/news/world/asia/chris-broad-there-were-no-security-forces-to-be-seen-they-had-clearly-left-us-there-to-be-sitting-ducks-1637708.html
45 www.bbc.co.uk/sport/cricket/50726039
46 www.espncricinfo.com/story/i-thought-my-career-was-over-samaraweera-395721
47 www.espncricinfo.com/wisdenalmanack/content/story/473208.html
48 www.espncricinfo.com/story/sangakkara-rises-above-the-sting-of-battle-410135
49 www.espncricinfo.com/series/pakistan-tour-of-sri-lanka-2009-403361/sri-lanka-vs-pakistan-1st-test-403367/full-scorecard
50 www.espncricinfo.com/story/scott-oliver-rangana-herath-s-cold-summer-at-staffs-913813
51 www.espncricinfo.com/story/proud-to-have-contributed-to-sri-lanka-s-growth-vaas-416270
52 www.theguardian.com/sport/2002/may/16/cricket.srilankainengland20021
53 www.espncricinfo.com/story/farbrace-quits-as-sri-lanka-assistant-coach-417092; www.espncricinfo.com/wisdenalmanack/content/story/473619.html
54 www.espncricinfo.com/story/is-murali-losing-his-touch-435989
55 www.espncricinfo.com/story/russel-arnold-murali-and-mendis-need-to-attack-437261
56 www.espncricinfo.com/wisdenalmanack/content/story/520740.html
57 www.thedailystar.net/news-detail-120486
58 www.theguardian.com/sport/2010/jul/06/muttiah-muralitharan-retire-test-cricket
59 *Ibid*.
60 wisden.com/comp/2314/india-in-sri-lanka-2010
61 timesofindia.indiatimes.com/sri-lanka-tri-series/top-stories/randiv-banned-for-one-match-dilshan-fined-for-no-ball-fiasco/articleshow/6331889.cms
62 www.islandcricket.lk/blog/dilshans-antics-in-zimbabwe-comes-to-light/; timesofindia.indiatimes.com/sports/new-zealand-in-india-2016/top-stories/dilshan-in-rape-scandal-too/articleshow/6533649.cms; www.islandcricket.lk/trevor_column/big-mouth-dilshan-escapes-lightly-over-no-ball-call-issue/
63 www.indiatoday.in/sports/cricket/story/match-fixing-nupur-mehta-2009-t20-world-cup-96598-2012-03-21
64 bleacherreport.com/articles/416472-sri-lanka-cricket-to-ban-shadow-coach-hathurusinghe-who-will-lose

65   www.cricketage.in/2017/09/13/chandika-hathurusinghe-the-coach-who-could-have-changed-sri-lanka-cricket-forever/

66   www.espn.com/cricket/story/_/id/22488897/sri-lanka-cricket-defends-choosing-premadasa

67   www.sundaytimes.lk/110130/Sports/sunday_Musings.html; news.bbc.co.uk/sport1/hi/cricket/other_international/sri_lanka/9377047.stm

68   www.espncricinfo.com/wisdenalmanack/content/story/565763.html

69   www.youtube.com/watch?v=lwagwGliPHI

70   en.espn.co.uk/cricket/sport/story/83219.html

71   www.hindustantimes.com/cricket/sri-lanka-police-calls-off-2011-wc-final-fixing-probe/story-oy78GLIeZeyJzmazQBh41N.html

72   www.espn.com/cricket/story/_/id/22452995/trevor-bayliss-calls-improvement-management

73   www.espncricinfo.com/story/sri-lanka-news-sangakkara-steps-down-as-odi-and-t20-captain-509607

74   www.bbc.co.uk/sport/cricket/13143641

75   www.thehindu.com/sport/cricket/SLC-asks-Malinga-to-return-from-IPL/article14691449.ece

76   www.bbc.co.uk/news/business-13666155

77   www.espn.co.uk/cricket/story/_/id/22451825/slc-debt-world-cup

78   www.theguardian.com/sport/2011/apr/07/stuart-law-cricket-sri-lanka

79   www.espncricinfo.com/wisdenalmanack/content/story/586881.html

80   www.theguardian.com/sport/2011/jun/21/the-spin-sanath-jayasuriya-england

81   www.espncricinfo.com/story/england-v-sri-lanka-in-england-wisden-almanack-review-586881

82   www.espncricinfo.com/story/kumar-sangakkara-s-mcc-spirit-of-cricket-lecture-522183

83   timesofindia.indiatimes.com/sports/new-zealand-in-india-2016/top-stories/lankan-sports-minister-wants-report-on-sangakkara-speech/articleshow/9125808.cms

84   www.espncricinfo.com/story/sri-lanka-news-stuart-law-to-take-over-as-bangladesh-coach-520898

85   www.theguardian.com/sport/2011/jun/21/the-spin-sanath-jayasuriya-england

86   wisden.com/comp/3435/australia-in-sri-lanka-2011

87   www.espncricinfo.com/story/dilshan-to-stay-at-no-5-533173

88   www.espncricinfo.com/story/sri-lanka-v-australia-3rd-test-a-hundred-that-mathews-might-grow-to-regret-532985

89   www.espncricinfo.com/wisdenalmanack/content/story/574159.html

90   wisden.com/comp/3637/sri-lanka-in-south-africa-2011-12

91   www.espncricinfo.com/story/sri-lanka-news-icc-pays-part-of-sri-lanka-players-dues-directly-546251

92   www.espncricinfo.com/story/south-africa-v-sri-lanka-2nd-test-durban-4th-day-a-win-to-savour-for-sri-lanka-547421

93   www.espncricinfo.com/story/south-africa-v-sri-lanka-3rd-test-durban-win-can-t-erase-sri-lanka-s-scars-548450

94   www.foxsports.com.au/cricket/geoff-marsh-sacked-as-coach-as-sri-lankan-cricket-shake-up-continues/news-story/f1617d2fe3c9d76d08057ca19ccb8264

95   www.espncricinfo.com/story/tillakaratne-dilshan-opens-up-on-lack-of-support-during-captaincy-tenure-1051459

96   www.skysports.com/cricket/news/12123/7457455

97   www.espncricinfo.com/story/sri-lanka-news-graham-ford-appointed-sri-lanka-coach-550933; www.theguardian.com/sport/2012/jan/23/mahela-jaywaradene-tillakaratne-dilshan-sri-lanka

98   www.espncricinfo.com/wisdenalmanack/content/story/694039.html

99   www.espncricinfo.com/print/story/556715

100 www.espncricinfo.com/wisdenalmanack/content/story/664871.html

101 www.espncricinfo.com/story/sri-lanka-v-west-indies-final-world-twenty20-samuels-best-malinga-s-worst-585974; www.espncricinfo.com/awards2012/content/story/604139.html

102 www.espncricinfo.com/awards2012/content/story/603047.html

103 www.espncricinfo.com/story/rangana-herath-is-sri-lanka-s-working-class-hero-592060

104 www.espncricinfo.com/wisdenalmanack/content/story/636135.html

105 www.deccanherald.com/content/300035/mahela-irked-over-mail-leak.html

106 www.dailymirror.lk/24432/i-have-lost-confidence-in-slc-says-mahela

107 www.dailymirror.lk/24465/mahela-charith-breach-contract-slc

108 www.espncricinfo.com/story/australia-and-sri-lanka-captains-play-down-ugly-finish-602549

109 www.espncricinfo.com/story/mahela-jayawardene-to-step-down-as-captain-after-tour-596903

110 www.espncricinfo.com/story/sri-lanka-contracts-dispute-threatens-bangla-desh-series-623221

111 www.eyesrilanka.com/2013/03/02/sri-lanka-cricket-team-in-contract-dispute/

112 www.espncricinfo.com/story/sri-lanka-cricket-locks-out-23-top-play-ers-623234

113 www.espncricinfo.com/story/lasith-malinga-censured-by-slc-624237

114 www.espncricinfo.com/story/sanath-jayasuriya-steps-in-to-help-settle-contracts-crisis-623329

115 www.espncricinfo.com/wisdenalmanack/content/story/964011.html

116 www.espncricinfo.com/story/sanath-jayasuriya-defends-selection-of-minis-ter-s-son-ramith-rambukwella-627269

117 www.espncricinfo.com/wisdenalmanack/content/story/780731.html

118 www.youtube.com/watch?v=lmEkjw_9mjc

119 www.espncricinfo.com/story/lasith-malinga-laments-lost-generation-after-another-sl-loss-to-india-1118999

120 www.espncricinfo.com/story/angelo-mathews-denies-sri-lanka-were-too-negative-711707

121 www.espncricinfo.com/story/pakistan-v-sri-lanka-stats-review-quick-chases-and-sri-lanka-s-third-test-woes-711631

122 www.batsman.com/pages/all/paul-fabrace-named-next-sl-head-coach_23879756-9930- 4127-8ecd-35ec4a9e3a81_N.aspx

123 www.espncricinfo.com/wisdenalmanack/content/story/887973.html

124 www.espncricinfo.com/story/the-sri-lanka-players-contracts-issue-739057

125 www.espncricinfo.com/story/i-feel-very-let-down-sanath-jayasuriya-729027

126 www.youtube.com/watch?v=PRUKaC2zuAs

127 www.thecricketmonthly.com/story/1147532/the-last-battles-of-lasith-malinga

128 www.espncricinfo.com/story/andrew-fidel-fernando-playing-for-the-peo-ple-735713

BIBLIOGRAPHY

Bradman, D., *Don Bradman's Book: The Story of my Cricketing Life to August 1930* (Hutchinson, 1938)

Chalke, S., *Runs in the Memory: County Cricket in the 1950s* (Fairfield Books, 2002)

De Silva, K.M., *A History of Sri Lanka* (Penguin Books, 2005)

De Silva, P.A., with Khan, S., *Aravinda: My Autobiography* (Mainstream Publishing, 1999)

Douglas, C., *Douglas Jardine: Spartan Cricketer* (Allen & Unwin, 1984)

Emburey, J., with Rogers, M., *Emburey* (Partridge Press, 1987)

Fernando, R., *A Murder in Ceylon: The Sathasivam Case* (Vijitha Yapa, 2006)

Fernando, R., *Sathasivam of Ceylon: The Batting Legend* (Vijitha Yapa, 2012)

Foenander, E.W., *Test Match Cricket in Ceylon: Europeans vs Ceylonese: An Illustrated Souvenir of the Fourteenth Struggle for Supremacy, 1911* (Industrial Home Press, 1911)

Foenander, S.P., *60 Years of Ceylon Cricket* (Ceylon Advertising & General Publicity, 1924)

Foot, D., *Beyond Bat & Ball: Eleven Intimate Portraits* (GB Publications, 1993)

Fraser, D., *Cricket and the Law: The Man in White is Always Right* (Routledge, 2003)

Gemmel, J. & Majumdar, B. (eds), *Cricket, Race and the 2007 World Cup* (Routledge, 2008)

Goonesena, G., *Spin Bowling: The Young Cricketer Talks to Gamini Goonesena* (Phoenix House, 1959)

Gunasekara, C., *Through the Covers* (self-published, 2012)

Gunasekara, C., *The Willow Quartette* (Sumathi, 2009)

Haigh, G., *Game for Anything: Writings on Cricket* (Gardners Books, 2005)

Halbish, G., *Run Out: My Dismissal and the Inside Story of Cricket* (Lothian Books, 2003)

James, S., *Diplomatic Moves: Life in the Foreign Service* (Radcliffe, 1995)

Khan, I., *All Round View* (Macmillan, 1989)

Lister, S., *Fire in Babylon: How the West Indies Cricket Team Brought a People to its Feet* (Yellow Jersey, 2016)

Mahanama, R., *Retired Hurt* (self-published, 2001)

Mahedevan, A., *Sri Lanka's Journey to Test Status, Parts I & II* (DVD)

Majumdar, B. & Mangan, J. (eds), *Cricketing Cultures in Conflict: World Cup 2003* (Routledge, 2004)

Marqusee, M., *War Minus the Shooting: A Journey Through South Asia During Cricket's World Cup* (Mandarin, new edition, 1997)

Mellawa, R., *Winds Behind the Willows: A Sri Lankan's Life in Love with Cricket* (self-published, 2017)

McGowan, W., *Only Man is Vile: The Tragedy of Sri Lanka* (Trans-Atlantic Publications, 1993)

Miller, K. & Whitington, R.S., *Gods or Flanelled Fools* (Macdonald, 1954)

Narayanan, C., *Sanath Jayasuriya: A Biography* (Rupa, 2019)

Nell, G.F. (ed), *Young Ceylon* periodical, 1850–53

Perera, S.S., *The Janashakthi Book of Cricket, 1832–1996* (Janashakthi Insurance, 1999)

Rae, S., *It's Not Cricket: Skulduggery, Sharp Practice and Downright Cheating in the Noble Game* (Gardners Books, 2002)

Roberts, M., *Crosscurrents: Sri Lanka and Australia at Cricket* (Walla Walla Press/ Mobitel, 1998)

Roberts, M., *Essaying Cricket: Sri Lanka and Beyond* (Vijitha Yapa, 2006)

Roberts, M., *Incursions & Excursions In and Around Sri Lankan Cricket* (Vijitha Yapa, 2011)

Royal College Union and S. Thomas' College Old Boys Association, *A History of 125 years of the Royal–S. Thomas' Cricket Match* (Royal College Union and S. Thomas' College Old Boys' Association, 2003)

Sheppard, D., *Parson's Pitch* (Hodder & Stoughton, 1969)

Sobers, G., *My Autobiography* (Headline, 2003)

Subramanian, S., *This Divided Island: Life, Death and the Sri Lankan War* (Thomas Dunne, 2015)

Tennekoon, A., *Passionately Cricket* (Stamford Lake, 2020)

Tufnell, P., *Tuffers' Hall of Fame*

Wagg, S. (ed.), *Cricket and National Identity in the Postcolonial Age: Following On* (Routledge, 2005)

Wettimuny, S., *Cricket: The Noble Art* (self-published, 1985)

Wickramasinghe, N., *Sri Lanka in the Modern Age: A History* (Oxford University Press, 2015)

Wijesinha, B., *Love of a Lifetime: Cricket from the Heart* (self-published, 2004)

Woodcock, J., Wright, G., Engel, M., de Lisle, T., Berry, S., Booth, L. (eds), *Wisden Almanack* (various) (John Wisden, 1985–2014)

ACKNOWLEDGEMENTS

I was shown so much help and kindness during the course of researching this book. I realise I can never repay it, but will endeavour to pass it on. It has meant the world to me.

I owe a great debt to so many. First and foremost to Peter Oborne, and to Father Marc Billimoria, Father Roshan Mendis and the staff and students of S. Thomas' College. To the writers who came before me – S.P. Foenander, S.S. Perera, Bertie Wijesinha, Channa Gunasekara, Rex Clementine, Shanaka Amarasinghe – and to those who were so generous with their time, contacts and wisdom: Michael Roberts, Andrew Fidel Fernando, Mahinda Wijesinghe, Ranjan Mellawa, Charlie Austin, Sa'adi Thawfeeq and Alston Mahadevan. To all the cricketers who agreed to help: Chandra Schaffter, the incomparable Ranjit Fernando, my dear friend David Heyn, Michael Tissera, Anura Tennekoon, Sunil Wettimuny, Sidath Wettimuny, Ajit de Silva, Mevan Pieris, Lalith Kaluperuma, Bandula Warnapura, Duleep Mendis, Ashantha de Mel, Darrell Lieversz, Mano Ponniah, Chandika Hathurusinghe, Asanka Gurusinha, Ravi Pushpakumara, the late Tony Opatha, Muttiah Muralitharan, Mahela Jayawardene and Kumar Sangakkara. To Lionel Gunasekara, Yajna Tyagarajah, Dijen de Saram, Shanti Gunasekara, the late Michael de Zoysa, Andrew Goodland. To Ajit Jayasekera, K. Mathivanan,

Nuski Mohamed, Kushil Gunasekara, Ashley de Silva, Daya Pandita Gunawardene, Channa Wijemanne, Roshan Abeysinghe, Wimal Perera, Dinesh Kumarasinghe, Eddie Appathurai, Oshanthaka Cabraal, Michelle Herft and Melinda Hettiarachi. To Jonathan Collet, Alby Shale, Oli Broom, Ben Cleary, Jerome Kerr-Jarrett and Dan Bell. To Tim Wigmore, Mihir Bose, Will Macpherson, Simon Barnes, Mike Selvey and Shehan Karunatilaka. To Ben Hildred, Benjamin Golby, Champaka Fernando, Jane Russell, Veeru Muruguppan, Chris Rowlands, Saskia Walker, Scott Hawkins, Matthew Aubrey, Kate Hamilton and Chris Jones. To Neil Robinson and his team at the Lord's Library, the staff at The British Library, the National Archives, Colombo and The National Library of Australia. To the good folks at Cricket Archive, Rob Moody, and all the other unsung heroes who upload archival footage to YouTube. To Mark Beynon, Chrissy McMorris and the wonderful team at The History Press. To Graham Banks, who so kindly persevered with early drafts that would have made most shudder. To each and every tuk-tuk driver who gave me their 2 cents on cricket; to all who I spoke to, and who made this journey so special. And above all to Sri Lanka, which crept under my skin, brought me so much joy – and will hold a special place in my heart for as long as I live.

INDEX

You may also enjoy ...

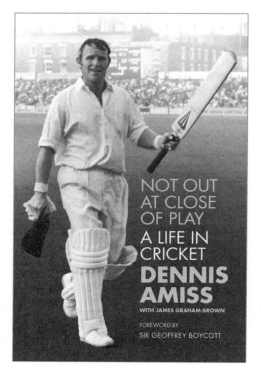

978 1 80399 005 7

'Dennis is a Warwickshire legend on and off the field. One of best batters of his generation, he set the standard for players to follow. He was a hero of mine growing up and now I have the pleasure of calling him my friend.' – Ian Bell MBE